DESIRE

The Politics of Sexuality

Edited by Ann Snitow,
Christine Stansell, and
Sharon Thompson

Published by VIRAGO PRESS Limited 1984
41 William IV Street, London WC2N 4DB

First published in the United States of America by Monthly Review
Press 1983 under the title *Powers of Desire: The Politics of Sexuality*

Acknowledgments

The editors and publisher would like to thank the following, who have kindly given permission to use copyrighted material: *Journal of Comparative Studies in Society and History* for "Sex and Society: A Research Note from Social History and Anthropology," copyright © 1981 by the Society for Comparative Study of Society and History; Adrienne Rich for "Compulsory Heterosexuality and Lesbian Existence," first published in *Signs: Journal of Women in Culture and Society* 5, no. 4 (1980), copyright © 1980 by Adrienne Rich; Irena Klepfisz for "they're always curious," first published in *Heresies* #3 (Fall 1977), copyright © 1977 by Irena Klepfisz; Ann Snitow for "Mass Market Romance," first published in *Radical History Review* 20 (Spring/Summer 1979), copyright © 1979 by Radical History Review; Myra Goldberg for "Issues and Answers," first published in *Feminist Studies* 6, no. 1 (Spring 1980), copyright © 1980 by Myra Goldberg; *Feminist Studies* for "Gender Systems, Ideology, and Sex Research," first published in *Feminist Studies* 6, no. 1 (Spring 1980), copyright © 1981 by Feminist Studies, Inc.; Amber Hollibaugh and Cherríe Moraga for "What We're Rollin Around in Bed With," first published in *Heresies #12*, copyright © 1981 by Amber Hollibaugh and Cherríe Moraga; *Poetry Northwest* for "Bestiary," first published in *Poetry Northwest* 21, no. 2 (Summer 1980), copyright © 1980 by *Poetry Northwest;* Alix Kates Shulman for "A Story of a Girl and Her Dog," first published in *13th Moon* (Winter 1975), copyright © 1975 by Alix Kates Shulman; the *Village Voice* and Ellen Willis for "Feminism, Moralism, and Pornography," first published in the *Village Voice*, October and November 1979, and "Abortion: Is a Woman a Person?" which first appeared in the *Village Voice*, March and April 1979, both copyright © 1979 by Ellen Willis; Joan Nestle for "My Mother Liked to Fuck," first published in *Womanews* 3, no. 1 (December and January 1981), copyright © 1981 by Joan Nestle; Judith Walkowitz for "Male Vice and Female Virtue," other versions of which appeared in *Signs* 6 (Autumn 1980) and *History Workshop* 13 (Spring 1982).

British Library Cataloguing in Publication Data
Desire: the politics of sexuality.
1. Sex
I. Snitow, Ann   II. Stansell, Christine
III. Thompson, Sharon
621'6   HQ21
ISBN 0-86068-526-8

1145184X

Contents

Acknowledgments

We want first to thank the present and former members of the committee that, with the publication of this book, has set the New Feminist Library going. Avanti!

Next we thank our authors. They have taught us much, clarified our course, been patient with us as we struggled to make a long and complicated book cohere.

Many others talked with us and shared their work with us. Here we can name only a few: Jan Clausen, Peggy Crull, Muriel Dimen, Mary Dunlap, Elizabeth Fisher, Daniel Goode, Meredith Gould, Liz Kennedy and the Lesbian Oral History Project (Buffalo), Jane Lazarre, Gayle Rubin, Lynda Schor, Nadine Taub, and the members of the Barnard Conference Study Group.

We are particularly grateful to those who read an early draft of the introduction, argued with us, agreed and disagreed with us, and gave us fresh insight and energy when we were most in need: Dorothy Allison, Harriet Cohen, Rhonda Copelon, John D'Emilio, Ellen DuBois, Kate Ellis, Amber Hollibaugh, Jonathan Katz, Barbara Kerr, Esther Newton, Gerry Pearlberg, Alix Kates Shulman, Laurie Stone, Paula Webster, Jeff Weinstein, Sean Wilentz, Ellen Willis, and Carole Vance.

Finally, we thank our willing designer, Cindy Carr, and our helpful editor at Monthly Review Press, Susan Lowes.

Preface
to the British Edition

Rosalind Coward

Since the earliest days of Hollywood, sexual fashions appear to have had a one way ticket across the Atlantic: if it happens in America, we are told, it's only a matter of time before it happens here. If the principal myth of Europe held by Americans is of ancient civilisation, Europe reciprocates with a myth of America's endless pursuit of novelty, especially sexual novelty. Europe dreams of America in a permanent state of sexual revolution, driven by a relentless commitment to sexual avant-guardism. And even though it's clear that the ideologies of sexual freedom have suffered setbacks and reports of political changes show us more and more evidence of sexual conservatism, Europeans merely readjust their myths. Today the myth is of urban America, barricaded against rural conservatism, bent on developing the ultimate type of sexual freedom – the consumer's paradise, where every brand of sex is on offer, each with its sub-cultural existence and its disciples.

These myths serve a function apart from the obvious one of a sort of sexual voyeurism. They provide the substance for fantasies about what might happen here and allow stances to be taken about these expectations: sexual conservatives, for example, use America to issue dire warnings about too much sex, too little morality – their deadliest weapon now being sexually transmitted diseases. All the myths share one feature: it's not just diseases that get caught, it's sex. Sex is seen as a sort of fashion, an activity which catches on unless carefully supervised. This sort of mythologising is profoundly unhelpful; it sets up sex as a sort of universal practice and ignores differences between cultures and differences between groups in the same culture. The idea of sex as a fashion becomes one of the major ways in which its social and political implications get hidden – the issues around sex get reduced to "too much" or "too perverse".

Given the simplifications which so readily settle in, it would be easy for *Desire: The Politics of Sexuality* to be received as another example of "what Americans are getting up to now" by providing incomprehensible vignettes of bizarre sexual activities. In fact, this collection is put together in order to highlight the political and theoretical issues behind different sexual practices. The articles are grouped around a series of issues, crucial for sexual politics, and the picture given by this collection is an interesting one for Britain. Feminists here also occasionally indulge in a myth of America as a source of contagious sexual fashions and this book will provide a chance to assess what exactly the similarities and differences are between sexual politics in the two countries.

It's clear, for example, that right wing politics towards the family are rather different in America, for in Britain the element of religious revival is almost entirely absent. Indeed in *The Subversive Family*, Ferdinand Mount, (an advisor to the Conservative Party) launches an attack on Christianity as hostile to the truly joyous commitments of earthly love and the human family. Such differences are salutary, emphasising the dangers of assuming that the appeal of conservatism is identical in two entirely different countries.

But the similarities with Britain are also illuminating: *Desire* represents a definite intervention in American feminism but some of the issues are very close to discussions here, and can be usefully appropriated for our own situation.* Put briefly, this intervention could be described as an attempt to re-locate feminist arguments about sex within, broadly speaking, two dominant kinds of theoretical explanation. One is the historical explanation; the other is the psychological or psychoanalytical. The historical approach is presented here to deliver a sense of how the meanings attached to sexual behaviour vary dramatically within different cultures and at different historical moments. There's a shift from seeing sex as either "repressed" or "liberated" and instead looking at the possibilities opened up for pleasure or control at different moments. This has implications, for example, for understanding homosexuality. Instead of seeing lesbianism or gayness as fixed, unchanging sexual practices which are especially subversive, they are seen as practices affected by the construction of the category of homosexuality itself. This construction is seen as creating possibilities for new pleasures but at the same time implying more constant scrutiny by the state and medical institutions. Heterosexuality is treated in the same way in the book's theoretical essays, as an institution changing over the course of history, the implications of which can be quite different not only for men and women but also for classes and races. There's also a move in the book

*In the British Collection, *Sex and Love: New Thoughts on Old Contradictions* edited by Sue Cartledge and Joanna Ryan, some similar issues are raised, ie, the historical

towards seeing sexual practices not in isolation but in the context of other social structures. This move is designed to allow us to *assess* sexual activity, not as being "progressive" or "not progressive" in and of itself but in relation to other historical forces – the intervention of the state, the power which men have over women, the divisions between races and classes.

The use of psychoanalytical perspectives extends this move. As well as examining changing historical meanings, there's a need to understand the meaning that sexual activity and desire have in the lives of individuals. Psychoanalytic theory is offered as a way of exploring how sexual identities are constructed, and how desire is structured.

This attempt to look simultaneously at the historical contexts of desire and the powerful hold which desire has is more than an academic exercise. It's aimed at countering what could be called "sexual reductionism" which is rampant in America and is characterised above all by a tone of moralism. This tone seems to have grown out of a particular interpretation of the feminist tenet, "the personal is political" which has been taken to imply that we can create in our personal (sexual) behaviour a prefigurative way of life, a feminist sexual behaviour. Although most women who call themselves feminists accept the notion of the personal as political, there's a lack of clarity as to what exactly this means. And many women are extremely unhappy with the way the slogan has been converted into a prescription about how to behave sexually. At issue here is the question of just how easy (and desirable) it is to prescribe a new form of sexual practice, purged of all the patterns of desire characteristic of oppressive heterosexual relations. After all, some women are asking, is sexual *desire* absolutely the same thing as sexual *relations*, and if it's not, aren't there ways of changing sexual relations without getting on to the quicksand of telling women what they should be feeling?

Two different interpretations of "the personal is political" are contending these questions. One is the prescriptive approach I've already mentioned; the other is represented by the essays in this collection. The prescriptive approach is based on an interpretation of the personal as political which, put crudely, runs thus; the relations between men and women are determined by the fact that men have social and economic power over women. This power is reflected in sexual relations themselves and is responsible for the fact that many people experience *desire* in terms of dominance or submission. Thus when these sadistic or masochistic desires are found, (be they in heterosexual or homosexual relations, images or real life, in fantasy or

changes in the meanings of sex and the power of fantasy.

actuality) they must be ruthlessly opposed because they help maintain the institution of male dominance. This analysis calls for remedies of personal salvation. Patterns of domination and submission can be broken by giving up sex with men. And if these patterns of desire crop up in your relations with women too, you'd better give up sex altogether or commit yourself to struggling on with women but rooting out or repressing any trace of these "heterosexist assumptions".

Against this sense of certainty many women have argued for a more nuanced understanding of power in personal relations, a more subtle investigation of the relationship between patterns of desire and fantasy and the social institutions of sexual relations. This is the position represented by *Desire*. Here we encounter a refusal to abandon questions of inequalities *other than* those between men and women, and there's a call to understand how sexual struggles might look very different when inflected through the divisions between races and classes. Secondly, "the personal is political" is taken more as a call for understanding the way our behaviour is related to external social circumstances rather than as a prescription for sexual conversion. This approach suggests that if domination and submission appear in relationships – whether in fantasy or in the real thing – our first duty is not to stamp it out but to understand what is at stake in such a structure, what pleasure it might be bringing and to ask whether this emotional dynamic will inevitably bring about our downfall as women. There's a strong political motivation in this approach; after all, unless we understand what we get out of such structures, how on earth can we ever understand why they achieve such widespread consent? These issues are a lot more raw and controversial than they might have appeared so far because underneath the reasonable justification for exploring the powers of desire lurks a question which is pretty well heretical to feminism. That question is whether sexual emotions and sexual fantasy are after all not so fatal? Is it really the case that if we submit to desires of domination and submission in bed we automatically invalidate the push to end men's domination?

This sort of questioning is actually fraught with dangers. It smacks of a sort of sexual laissez-faire, a tolerance to anything and everything which appears to render meaningless the claim that feminism reaches the parts other politics don't. And this in turn appears to invalidate one of feminism's principal claims – that attitudes, images and fantasies (proclaimed by liberalism to be the spontaneous product of the free individual) spring in fact from society's deeply held ideologies about women's inferiority.

When discussions touch on these issues, there's usually an audible hiss as the collective breath is drawn in and the implications chewed over. How can we possibly be saying that individual emotional dynamics are relatively autonomous from the actual power in sexual relations? What happens to feminism's insistence that what goes on in sexual exchanges is not free of the social structure but reflects the inequalities between men and women?

But however dangerous this ground, however shifting the sands, I, for one, find it interesting that feminism has chosen to travel along this path. And there's nothing to suggest that, in taking this route, either British or American feminists are thoughtlessly plunging on, giving credence to the dominant libertarian view of sex as the private affair of individuals. Even in those articles most explicit about the pleasure of power and submission, most apparently celebratory of the powers of desire, the question of the relationship between sexual acts and social structures is never far away. Here is no vicarious celebration of structures which have been so damaging for women, but an attempt to be more honest, to say, "If we want to bring sex into the political arena, let's at least be clear what we are talking about".

Given the careful context in which this honesty is being expressed, feminism stands to benefit from such explorations. One immediate gain is that this kind of talk successfully destroys the tone of sexual moralism with which feminism has recently come to be associated, a tone which isn't entirely the fault of feminism itself. In Britain the popular press has had a field day, promoting an image of feminists as either explicitly or implicitly criticising the sexual choices made by "ordinary" women. Given this conversion of feminists into every-woman's sexual bogey, a more tolerant, less prescriptive, perhaps even a more visibly confused feminism is no bad thing.

But there are also wider political benefits to be gained from such an exploration of sexual desire, sexual relations and social structures. This exploration also opens up the more general question of the relationship between personal experiences, personal behaviour and political movements – an issue which, in remaining repressed, regularly causes internal crises in these movements.

One of the great strengths of the initial moments of the modern women's movement was its revitalisation of the issue of personal behaviour. Feminism at that period, represented, to some extent, a stance against the usual left-wing approach to morality. On the one hand, feminism took a position against the idea that personal morality was irrelevant, against the idea that a man could claim to be sympathetic to women's rights but beat his wife. On the other hand, feminism also represented a radical break with the morality of abstinence, the morality which abstained from "capitalist pleasures" and saw political commitment as one grisly meeting after another. In the place of cynicism and hypocrisy, feminism appeared to offer a politics of political and personal integrity, together with an attention to pleasure and support, so blatantly neglected by other movements. In these respects, feminism appeared to be a very different kind of politics, already attentive to some of those areas whose neglect has been so crucial in the failure of some socialist regimes.

But as things have gone on, feminism has almost been hoist with its own petard. As so often happens when personal morality becomes an element in political discussion, there's room for abuse. Personal "morality" can quickly become a metaphor for something else – personal vendettas, political lines, ambitions. The British feminist movement has recently been rocked by arguments about the correct feminist sexual morality, and some women have staked their whole involvement with feminism on the question of sexual practice. It's hard to believe that such divisions have really been for the good of all women, or even for the good of the feminist movement.

Desire is a strategic contribution to these discussions. The book isn't a retreat from thinking about the relation between personal behaviour and political or social forces. Nor does it abandon the desire to change the relations between the sexes. But the essays do represent an attempt to unpick the tangle of certainties which has brought feminism almost to its knees. In the place of a drive for a feminist personal morality a question is asked: is personal morality *only* sexual morality? And in the place of prescriptions for a true feminist sexual morality, there's a push to debunk sex, to stress the waywardness of sexual desire, to investigate the resistances to change rather than offer easy agendas.

This knocking of simplistic assertions between political objectives and personal morality has other implications, a sort of political flip side. Another political scripture might take a knock if these kinds of ideas are seen through: there's an implicit challenge here to the idea that political authenticity, political progressiveness derives directly from a direct personal experience of oppression. There's an implicit "deconstruction" of the idea that there's a direct line of oppression which runs from the economy to the state, ending up in the bedroom with personal experience of sexual oppression, and then finding its way back as progressive politics. Feminist and socialist politics are pretty well synonymous with a struggle against oppression but the proposal of *direct* links between personal experiences of oppression and progressive politics has been very damaging politically. It's meant that discussions of politics often end up with attempts to win political arguments by simply proving you're more oppressed than anyone else. Thus within feminism, for example, an experience of being raped or battered within heterosexuality would give a truer political perspective than that generated by the oppression of the average marriage. A politics based exclusively on oppression has got a lot of trouble coming to it. At one moment all it can do is be guilty towards those who are the "most oppressed" (politics of solidarity); at the next moment, it has to try to keep together people by persuading them that there's an alliance between the various oppressions (a problem since the various oppressed groups don't necessarily recognise each other as having similar interests, and a problem because people who see themselves as "just ordinary" don't recognise themselves in the membership anymore).

It may seem far fetched to suggest a discussion of sexual pleasure contains these implications but it is clear that, certainly around the subject of sexual oppression, this collection is posing a large question mark. In asserting the pleasure of masochistic submission in, for example, lesbian relations, there's no denial of lesbian oppression or of women's subordination to men. However there is a challenge to the idea that it is the *experience* of oppression through sexual practice which underpins political involvement.

There's plenty in *Desire*, then, which could be heretical towards existing political faiths. And while the loss of belief can feel very unsettling, the outcome could be a thoroughly good thing. It may become possible to talk about feminism once again in terms of attitudes towards friends and work *as well* as sex, and to be able to evolve politics towards women and the family, *and* respond to pressing issues such as racism – all issues which have been swamped in the quest for purity of sexual position. It would be pleasingly ironic if, in pursuing an understanding of sex, it should free us from the tyranny of sex.

Introduction

Ann Snitow, Christine Stansell, and Sharon Thompson

Why write about sex?

Sex is everywhere. Why add to the tawdry glut?

What are the advantages and disadvantages—to individuals, to social groups—of elaborating and developing sex as a central form of expression, one that defines identity and is seen as a primary source of energy and pleasure?

In spite of its publicity, sex remains oddly taboo, particularly for women. The widespread exposure to sexual imagery and talk seems not to have made a dent in the embarrassment. The sexual shame that begins in childhood—and which the entire culture endlessly re-creates—keeps the sense of taboo alive even in a blitz of the sexually explicit. Perhaps taboo and shame are among the necessary products of capitalism; certainly shame, guilt, and trauma can short-circuit the radical traditions that have named sex as creative and life-affirming, so that even the most progressive works on sex are often stilted, cautious, or imbued with the melancholy of sex, its proverbial tristesse. But however much either the morally righteous or the politically earnest call sex trivial, a self-indulgent luxury, or one more consumer item in the capitalist marketplace, the commercialization of sex has failed to reduce it to a mere product. Perhaps, as novelist Jane Rule has observed, "A body we know is designed to die will never be a simple plaything."[1]

French philosopher and historian Michel Foucault gives a subtle rendering of the general argument that sex and capitalism have gone hand-in-hand too long for sex to be interpreted at face value as a radical force.[2] Foucault suggests that the public discussion of sex constitutes a chief way in which modern social institutions manipulate the consciousness and intimate experiences of great masses of people. Sex is supposedly secret and private, yet we do nothing but speak of it, he argues, and in speaking we unwittingly define and proscribe who may desire whom, when, and how. To advance the cause of sexual freedom, then, may paradoxically tighten the grip of the system.

Foucault's warning is on the mark: sex is, unquestionably, a public topic and a highly political one. But while Foucault raises important questions against which to test the current talk about sex, his analysis rests, as it must, on the obsessive male sexual discourse that runs through the centuries from St. Augustine to Philip Roth. Women's relationship to the sexual—like that of people of color and sexual minorities—has been very different. It has been tacit. To close a discussion that began for some only very recently is to leave those speakers once again beyond consideration, except insofar as those who previously monopolized the discourse deigned to describe them. Traditionally women, for example, have been "the sex"; we have represented the body and its mixed pleasures and pains for everyone. When feminists try to celebrate female sexuality, we find that men have been there first, rhapsodic and mythic about virgins, mothers, and whores. It is hard to throw off their obfuscating enthusiasm. As a result, while feminism has cast its own new, if variable, illumination on the subject of sex, the apprehension of sex as subject is still impeded by the density of former traditions. It is too soon, then, for silence.

Certainly, to skirt sexual issues now, given current political conditions, is to cede this crucial territory to those who have organized precisely toward the end of silencing feminism and the lesbian and gay movements. Beginning with the anti-abortion movement, the precipitant for much right-wing organizing in the last decade, sexuality has been at the heart of the New Right's domestic program, which seeks not only to eliminate women's access to abortion but—as the magna charta of domestic conservatism, the Family Protection Act, shows—to undermine sex education, contraceptive services, the rights of teenagers' sexual privacy and bodily control, the right of lesbians and gays to work in the public sector, and a wide range of feminist-inspired programs, from women's studies to battered women's shelters.

The Right offers this anti-sexual program in defense of monogamous, heterosexual, procreative, sanctified, legalized, natural sex at a time when it has never been more apparent that sexuality, like gender, changes. As we create masculinity and femininity, so we also make love. Sexuality is a construct.

It is common to resist this idea, to insist that sex is a natural force, yet the pieces collected in this volume, exploring the links between the organization of sexuality and of other social structures, discover meaningful and suggestive connections everywhere. Perhaps there is a reluctance to add sex to history because we treasure sex as a retreat from time. Certainly there are strong reasons to long for something spontaneous—either sacred, wordless, or romantic—a reliable private pleasure, a refuge from social exhaustion. But these feelings, too, are social and socially constructed. There is no escaping it: sex as refuge, or sex as sacrament, or sex as wild, natural, dark, and instinctual expression—all these are *ideas* about sex, and ideas about sex have never been more obvious than now, when sex is no longer coterminous with the family, or with procreation, or with sin. Indeed, historical changes that often seem to be trivializing sex are, at the same time, making of it a separate and newly meaningful category of experience.

In recent decades, Americans have experienced major shifts in what the culture expects from men, women, and sex. Transformations in work, family, gender—often in the course of one lifetime—foster rapidly changing sexual experiences. Marriage, childbearing, and childrearing are increasingly brief experiences for most Americans. The fertility rate has reached its lowest point in U.S. history. The stereotype of the nuclear family—man at work, woman at home caring fulltime for two or more children—is a reality for fewer and fewer people (14 percent at this writing). The average marriage lasts five years, and one of every three ends in divorce. Three-quarters of all married women have jobs; a single woman heads one in every seven households; lesbians are struggling for, and in many cases winning, custody of their children; and lesbian and gay cultures are sketching the bases for new social structures. One in five households contains only one person. As historian Ellen Ross notes, at the moment "there are more points in the life cycle when Americans are likely to be 'single' or courting actively," so that active sexual exploration, which used to be relatively circumscribed by the fear of pregnancy and re-strictive social conventions, is spilling out into all stages of people's lives.[3] Underlying many of these changes is cheap, accessible birth control, which places men and women in a historically unprecedented relationship to our bodies and to each other. Here lies the core of the "sexual revolution": those changes in ideology, culture, material condi-tions, and technology that have weakened and finally severed the link between reproduction and sexuality.

The New Right's attempt to regulate our sexual lives is thus a dra-matic countermove in a gradual long-term renegotiation of the mean-ing of femininity and masculinity. Can gender remain a primary organizing principle of social life? Historian Mary Hartman sees the breakdown of gender polarity as an ongoing process in Western society since the Middle Ages.[4] In our century this breakdown has ac-celerated, leading to swift changes that have sometimes left socialist and feminist theorists behind, but that are in many respects unnerv-ingly obvious to most Americans today.

When the new self-consciousness about gender impinges most di-rectly on sexuality, which Freud called the area of the most ragged and unfinished psychological development, the sense of change is particu-larly vivid, particularly unsettling.[5] Sex is elusive and draws on irrational layers of our personalities. Women have been particularly burned by the simplified freedoms, the cynical psychological shortcuts of the sexual revolution. We are suspicious of the sexual license of a self-proclaimed liberal culture insensitive to women's sexual vulnerability. Men, too, are uneasy. Men have been the first to benefit from a new era of sexual experimentation, but when women join them—when women, too, say "fuck"—*everyone* feels a tug on the deepest moorings of family, decency, and the eternal order of things. Certainly, in the context of recent political defeats, many feminists have become self-conscious and apprehensive about unladylike sexual desires and demands.

With good reason, the Left has traditionally been interested in what we think we can control: the subjective fantasy life of sex feels like a stumbling block to the organizer who has a distrust—sometimes an out-and-out doubt—of the powers of the unconscious. It now seems obvious to many activists, however, that any politics that ignores the complexities of motive, the interrelation of private and public experience, the unconscious attitudes we all have toward authority, is a hobbled, blinkered politics. We cannot afford simplicity if we are interested in understanding how change happens. Sex cannot be approached mechanistically. The current scholarship on sex makes it evident that change in sexuality, as in gender relations, is far harder to effect than present-day feminists initially recognized. Still, this difficulty cannot be evaded. As Jessica Benjamin argues in this volume, "A politics that tries to sanitize or rationalize the erotic, fantastic components of human life will not defeat domination, but only vacate the field."

The political struggle, then, is over who is going to make sex and in what form. The New Right has responded to the anxiety provoked by the acceleration of change with a politics of sex that is at once homophobic, ageist, sexist, and sexually repressive. It is attempting to reinstitute sexual constraints and gender divisions from which we have barely begun to break free. Our task is to imagine a sexual politics to counterpose to that of the Right. We know that we want the power to choose abortion and need public funding to make it possible for all the exercise that right. We want sexual information and opportunities for the young, the old, the handicapped, and all groups for whom sex has been taboo. We want civil rights for all sexual minorities. But what else? What aspects of sex can and should be publicly debated? What should political activism about sex look like? What erotic experiences will we encourage in our children? Do we favor the constraint of some kinds of sexual expression? Do we have any concept of a sexual "public good"? Or, if we advocate a more libertarian position (anything goes, as long as all parties consent), what are the limits of that consent? At what point does libertarianism shade into a laissez-faire position that posits, as it does in the realm of wage labor, a theoretical free choice with which abstractly equal individuals bargain and contract in the sexual marketplace? Do we gain more autonomy from saying "yes" or saying "no" in a grossly unequal world?

Although at first some of the terms of these debates may be unfamiliar (we hope this book will make them less so), for socialists and feminists all these issues do come together in a common concern: how best to integrate sexuality into the project of human liberation.

These questions take us far beyond our current capacity to speak definitively about sex, and they make it evident that, personal convictions notwithstanding, we are far from knowing what we need to create a political theory of sex. We are not the first to consider the problem. As in so many endeavors, once we pose a question, we discover a history of attempts to clarify and solve what seems initially to be a unique dilemma. Within both socialism and feminism, there are long traditions that have sought to elucidate the relationships between sexuality and broader movements for human freedom—traditions that are the point of departure for most of the pieces in this volume.

To fully understand the history of sexuality in the past two hundred years would require a thoroughgoing social analysis, a task far beyond the scope of our essay. Here we focus rather on the political and intellectual history of sex: the ways in which feminist and socialist women and men—mostly from the middle class—have sought to make sense of, and shape, their sexual lives. Like others of their time, these politicized people grappled with the great question of what role sexual expression should play in social life as it was progressively freed from its ages-old association with procreation. Their responses were not always linear: succeeding generations sometimes undermined, rather than advanced, the gains of their predecessors. Nor were they unified. Socialists and feminists disagreed within their own ranks and with each other about how sexuality should be directed within human relationships. Should sexual activity and desire be associated with the gender system, wherein one's sex determines one's erotic style? Or could sexuality be the basis for a new kind of community of freely associating individuals, limited by neither family ties nor gender, a paradigm of a more equitable and various future society?

Sex and Socialism

While later generations of Marxian scientific socialists saw sex as secondary, derivative of the real relationships of production, many of the earliest socialist theorists and movements took sexual matters very seriously. The French Charles Fourier (1772–1837), for instance, one of the earliest utopian socialists, saw passionate attraction as germinal to the egalitarian, extra-familial bonds he envisioned. It was Fourier, for instance, who first perceived the connection, popular with subsequent sex radicals, between sexual monogamy and the acquisitive mentality fostered by private property.

On a practical level, sexual politics also entered into early socialist and working-class agitation. In England during the 1830s and 1840s the Owenites, a mass movement of laboring people, preached a New Moral World that would overturn all oppressive relations, including those between the sexes. The Owenites also advocated extra-legal sexual unions. English artisan radicals disseminated birth control information as early as the 1820s; indeed, Jeffrey Weeks has argued that it was not the middle class but the radical artisans, those men and women most receptive to anti-capitalist propaganda, who first began to practice systematic contraception.[6]

Consideration of sexual politics waned, however, as questions of labor and property took precedence in the British and U.S. movements. Although there is evidence that Fourier's writings influenced the early work of Marx in the 1840s, in later work Marx paid little attention to sexual matters, generally dismissing them as part of a utopian socialism he rejected. Except for a handful of iconolasts like the U.S. socialist and sex radical Victoria Woodhull (1838–1927), the discourse on sex that did occur in the Left of the First and Second Internationals (1864–1914) usually hinged on vague predictions of an improved sexual morality under socialism—marital fidelity, the decline of the double standard, the abolition of prostitution.[7] Engels' *The Condition of the Working Class in England*, written in the 1840s, set the tone for these later discussions with its denunciations of the effects of capitalism on working-class morals. Bourgeois men, Engels complained, set their own women on a pedestal of chastity and preyed on working-class girls; they self-righteously condemned the immorality of their workers while perpetuating the poverty from which that immorality stemmed.[8]

Within the general Victorian discussion of sex, women, and the family, Marx and Engels advanced enlightened insights combined with conservative assumptions. Neither ever questioned the desirability of female chastity, marital fidelity, heterosexual romance, or the nuclear family—all cardinal bourgeois values. Yet both also inherited from the utopian socialists a belief in the beneficial power of mutual erotic attraction—"modern individual sex love"—an idea that constituted a break with the Victorian view of true love as an affinity between two disembodied souls.[9] Although they assumed that monogamy was inherent in sex love, Engels in later life edged toward a more searching position. His *Origins of the Family, Private Property, and the State*

(1884) presented monogamy as a historical construction, an evolution from an earlier system of sexual promiscuity but one which represented a world-historic setback for women, associated with the emergence of the double standard, private property, and class relations. Unlike earlier socialists, however, Engels did not extend his insights into a vision of a sexual order incompatible with the mores of his age. He criticized legally sanctioned monogamy as part and parcel of a system of private property, but he idealized the nuclear family and monogamy itself. The socialist future would bring an end to legal marriage, but monogamy, freed of the distortions of capitalism, would flourish on a higher plane. "Monogamy, instead of collapsing," he predicted, "at last becomes a reality" for men as well as women, a formulation which, whatever its enlightened intentions, still ironically paralleled the conservative goals of the contemporaneous bourgeois social purity movement.[10]

The mainstream Marxist movement in Europe and the United States took its cues in sexual matters from the least challenging views of its two leading theorists. The narrowness of sexual theory in Marxian thought, its implicit acceptance of Victorian norms, and its defensiveness in response to charges that socialists were free lovers all coalesced into a sexual conservatism in the British and U.S. movements that differed little from that of the respectable classes. A British socialist editor in 1893 spoke for many of his comrades when he rejected a request from a sex radical that he include more discussions of sex in his newspaper: "I am a radical but . . . the whole subject is nasty to me."[11]

Thus the advent of Marxian socialism represented something of a step backward in the development of a radical sexual politics. Still, a strain of sex radicalism persisted within the broader nineteenth-century movement: if official socialists were not sex radicals, the sex radicals were generally unofficial socialists. Like the Marxists, sex radicals assumed that changes in sexual behavior would accompany the creation of a better world. In the United States, John Humphrey Noyes, founder of the Oneida community (1848–1881), was the most notorious of a number of mid- and late-nineteenth-century utopians who organized their communities around reformed erotic behavior redirected outside the family. The Oneidans prohibited monogamy and taught male continence, a contraceptive technique whereby men experienced orgasm without ejaculating. Noyes personally supervised the Oneida system: he initiated female virgins and ensured, through community surveillance, that no two partners became unduly attached. The arrangements were authoritarian, strictly heterosexual, and hardly feminist. Yet Noyes did advance the thought and practice of sex radicalism. Oneida affirmed the value of sexual experience and of a variety of partners for both men and women; by associating birth control with pleasure and multiple contacts Noyes showed how sexual freedom could follow the separation of sex and conception.[12]

In the 1870s, the free lovers—a loosely knit network of free-thinking agnostics, communitarians, and advocates of birth control and divorce reform—began to develop the associations between sexual liberation, social freedom, and rationalism in a more democratic milieu. To its enemies, free love became a euphemism for promiscuity, but the earliest free lovers were actually quite wary of varied sexual relations; they preached instead the value of free monogamous unions, of affection bestowed and cultivated outside the strictures of the church.[13] In the next two decades, however, free lovers began to entertain thoughts of the creative value of multiple sexual relations. In the 1880s and 1890s, the advocacy of free love edged closer to socialist and labor radicalism, as German and Jewish immigrants imported Russian and Continental variants into the immigrant and Jewish labor movements. At this juncture, nineteenth-century free love reached its apotheosis in the figure of Russian-born anarchist Emma Goldman (1869–1940). The United States' most notorious sex radical to that date, Goldman linked the nineteenth-century traditions to the experience of a new generation of self-consciously modern young men and women in the prewar years. "Free love?" she rhetorically inquired in one of her more provocative formulations. "As if love is anything but free!"[14]

In the same period in Great Britain, the "new moralists" took free love one step further by questioning the exclusivity of heterosexuality itself. The socialist Edward Carpenter (1844–1928) posited the existence of an "intermediate sex"—homosexuals—who could mediate betwen the seemingly antithetical temperaments of men and women. More generally, he stressed the pleasures of sex, its ability to bind people together into broader communities of fellowship. In the context of a trans-Atlantic movement politically focused almost exclusively on trade unions and elections, Carpenter's ideas harkened back to the older utopian notions of socialism. Carpenter's *Love's Coming of Age*, published in the United States in 1911, crystallized the concerns of radicals with socialism, sex, feminism, and personal life. As Mari Jo Buhle writes, Carpenter pointed the way to an altogether new socialist vision of sex: "Socialists had always believed the Cooperative Commonwealth would enshrine love, but, fearful of erotic intensity, they envisioned the promised state as platonic and spiritual, as the realization of old aspirations rather than the efflorescence of new practices."[15] Carpenter shifted the focus from an abstract future to the transforming powers of sex in the present.

Goldman and Carpenter took sex radicalism out of its enclaves and brought it closer to mainstream sexual politics. Their ideas became popular at a time when changing sexual patterns and new sexual knowledge (the work of Freud and Havelock Ellis) made a young generation of U.S. leftists more receptive to previously heretical beliefs about the role of the erotic in human freedom. Throughout the middle class, a growing acceptance of contraception (within marriage) allowed men and particularly women to disassociate sexual pleasure from conception. At the same time, young single people began to move outside the strictures of their families and communities to experiment with sex outside of marriage. Although this may at first have been primarily a middle-class phenomenon—working-class women could not easily obtain contraception—young working-class women surely enjoyed their own erotic life, one that stopped short of intercourse. As the female labor force expanded, young single women flooded into the cities; changing demographic patterns meant that many of them lived on their own—alone or with other young women—rather than in family households, and thus, as Kathy Peiss shows in this volume, gained a certain freedom to come and go as they pleased. They experienced, if only for the short time before they married, unprecedented possibilities for sexual independence, played out in an emerging urban youth culture as well as, for some, a developing sexual underground of gay men and lesbians. The young socialists, feminists, and artists who constituted the bohemian circles of Greenwich Village in the first decades of the twentieth century, described by Ellen Kay Trimberger in this volume, tried to elaborate the most hopeful elements of this sexual revolution. For the new radicals (people like Crystal Eastman and her brother Max, Louise Bryant, John Reed, Mary Heaton Vorse, Floyd Dell) women were, theoretically, men's sexual equals—and, at times, their superiors—and women played a central role in their sexual avantgarde. "When the world began to change," remembered one radical, "the restlessness of woman was the main cause."[16]

Nevertheless, as Trimberger shows, the sexual equality of radical women in Greenwich Village was more imagined than real. Like other women of their time, marriage still represented their only real chance for security; in a highly discriminatory and sex-segregated labor market, whatever economic independence they possessed was precarious. Promiscuity and extra-marital sex posed many more risks for them than for their male lovers, who believed in women's sexual freedom in theory but in practice were often alarmed or alienated by it. In describing the complex situation of these new women, Linda Gordon has noted that "as with all women, their survival and success largely depended on pleasing men."[17] Still, they opened the way for a new understanding of women as sexual subjects in their own right, no longer simply recipients of male advances but beings with their own erotic needs, capable of making their own initiatives.

In the birth control movement of 1914–1917, many of the young radicals saw the chance to translate the sexual libertarianism of their generation into a class struggle. Birth control was illegal; although the affluent could acquire it from private doctors, the poor had virtually no access to any contraception except traditional modes like abortifacients and douches. The mass-based birth control movement initially consolidated around campaigns for sex education and contraceptive information which Emma Goldman and the young Margaret Sanger conducted within the socialist and labor movements. Birth control quickly came to command a wide following, including the new intellectuals of the Socialist Party (among them many Greenwich Villagers), women's locals within the party, and leaders of socialist workers, particularly from the Industrial Workers of the World (IWW—the Wobblies). The movement's intellectuals and propagandists were largely committed to a neo-Malthusian belief in family planning, the alleviation of the misery of unplanned pregnancies, as a means of working-class uplift. But another, more fully sexual, vision also ran through their work: the view that free sexual expression, especially that of women, was a basic human right, a legitimate goal of the class struggle.[18]

Old divisions on the sex question within the Left soon reappeared. The movement represented a practical politics of sex radicalism, and it antagonized many older and more orthodox socialists. Critics within the Socialist Party argued that the campaign was "a waste of time and energy," which distracted workers from the class struggle (defined narrowly as an economic and political one); under capitalism, such efforts were premature anyway, since the coming of the socialist state would automatically inaugurate an era of sexual enlightenment. Underlying such tactical admonitions, however, were more extreme patriarchal attitudes which official socialism had never fully challenged: as one male critic protested, sex education would only cause "FEAR and DISTRUST in the minds of hundreds of progressive wives and mothers," and so should be abandoned.[19]

In the short run, the prewar sex radicals made few gains. The birth control movement disintegrated under the pressure of internal conflicts and external political repression. It would only reemerge in the 1920s, under Margaret Sanger's direction, as a crusade of a professional medical elite. The insurgent, confrontational elements of sex radicalism waned, giving way to a new sexual order which, if liberalized in some respects, was also far more compatible with capitalism and the nuclear family than the radicals could have envisioned. The postwar flapper, younger sister of the revolutionary woman of the earlier milieu, was sexually active but seemingly apolitical; a new style of family life, the "New Deal" described by Barbara Epstein in this volume, theoretically incorporated her needs for emotional and sexual expression while a new mode of consumer capitalism declared its fashions, cosmetics, and household goods to be adequate expressions of her erotic identity. Sexual feminism, which earlier had posed some challenges to men's power to determine women's sexuality, declined in the 1920s. The new female sexual freedom became instead an imperative to say "yes" to male advances. In the similarly eroticized milieu of Weimar Germany in the same decade, analyzed by Atina Grossmann in this volume, liberal intentions and practices also converged with a renewed conservative and patriarchal agenda. In Germany, family and population policies repressed what freedoms the "New Woman" of the 1920s had managed to retain. In the United States, the consequences were less dramatic but nonetheless stultifying, as U.S. society in the next two decades moved toward what was, arguably, its nadir of sexual conservatism in the 1950s.

The official U.S. Left from 1930 to 1960 largely ignored or repudiated any association with sexual rebellion, even as the founding of the Mattachine Society (1950) and the Daughters of Bilitis (1955) indicated the first stirrings of the lesbian and gay movements. Whatever sexual mores operated within the Communist Party (fragments of evidence indicate that party members, especially the women, had a loose reputation), the organization formally focused almost exclusively on issues of public rather than private life: the threat of fascism, economic collapse, McCarthyism.[20] Moreover, the party's allegiance to the Soviet Union, with its sexually repressive policies, fostered a suspicion of any sexual questioning as a symptom of bourgeois degeneracy. Instead, the Communist Party often viewed sexual conservatism as a cultural bridge to the masses. Sex in capitalist society was just one more commodity, its proliferation a symptom of an ever expanding consumerism.

The generation of radicals that came of age in the 1960s tried to divest itself of the Old Left's sexual restraint. The New Left—especially its men—plunged into a second "sexual revolution," facilitated by cheap, accessible birth control. Student radicals identified sex as potentially revolutionary, a way to break out of the deadening psychological structures of U.S. middle-class life. Multiple and varied sexual relationships came to be associated with cultural liberation.

The contradictions and difficulties of this sexual politics became apparent quite early in the decade within the Civil Rights movement. When white students flocked South to work in the Student Non-Violent Coordinating Committee (SNCC) voter registration campaigns of Freedom Summer 1964, young whites and blacks began to view interracial affairs—especially those between white women and black men—as a powerful challenge to racist taboos. The resulting mixture of race, sex, and gender issues proved explosive. On the one hand, many activists found sexual affirmation as well as emotional support in these politicized relationships. As historian Sara Evans has written, "Where such needs came together with genuine mutual regard, there was a sense in which the 'beloved community' of black and white together took on a concrete reality in the intimacy of the bedroom."[21] On the other hand, many white women experienced themselves in these interactions as pawns in a fundamentally male game of assertiveness and rebellion. Their own guilt, moreover, made them extremely reluctant to say "no" to a black man lest their refusal expressed some hidden reserve of racism. Black women, for their part, soon became hostile to what seemed to be their relegation to the role of non-sexual Amazons while the white women monopolized the feminine quotient of the movement. "If white women had a problem," one black woman remembers, "it was not just a male/woman problem . . . it was also a black woman/white woman problem."[22] The tangled legacy of these years would endure, profoundly affecting the political development of all parties concerned, especially in regard to feminism.

The sexual conflicts of the Civil Rights movement were in many senses paradigmatic of the subsequent sexual history of the New Left. As in the 1920s, sexual revolution became a license for male promiscuity and female accessibility. It was at least partly the bitterness of radical women at sexual exploitation—exploitation which, practiced in the name of such high ideals, was all the more galling—that led to the acrimonious fragmentation of the New Left in 1969. The sexual revolution, radical women complained in retrospect, had been another male trick: the cool sex of the counterculture was a new version of men's old need to prove their property—now communal rather than private—in women. Marge Piercy's searing critique of the movement, "The Grand Coolie Damn," captured the substance of women's anger: "A man can bring a woman into an organization by sleeping with her and remove her by ceasing to do so. A man can purge a woman for no other reason than that he has tired of her, knocked her up, or is after someone else."[23] Ironically, by virtue of the very elevation of sexuality as a revolutionary force, it had become an even more powerful weapon of male dominance inside progressive movements.

Within the Left of the past ten years, perhaps the most common response to the experiences of the 1960s has been a revival of the more conservative strains of Marxist sexual politics. Organizations like the West Coast Friends of Families have attempted to capitalize on this retrenchment: while staying clear of what are now generally accepted elements of the sexual revolution like birth control and premarital sex, such socialists hold up the monogamous couple and the nuclear family as social forms worth preserving. They hearken back to an earlier Left politics in which gender differences were rarely acknowledged as central problems; they speak of "the family" without direct reference to the particular powerlessness of women and children within it. The non-feminist Left has been notably tepid on questions of reproductive rights. A notorious incident in 1979, when the leading socialist newspaper *In These Times* called for a dialogue with the anti-abortion movement, showed feminists how untouched much of the Left continues to be by the politics of female sexual autonomy.[24] Feminists and gay activists still encounter a blindness among socialists to the importance of sex radicalism, a sort of Puritanism empathic with the supposed sexual cautiousness of the U.S. working class and with the sexually conservative mores of socialist states like Cuba.

In contrast to the 1910s, however, the subversive potential of the sexual visions of the 1960s has remained alive, developed and sustained by mass popular movements. Lesbian and gay activists have challenged heterosexual norms and raised provocative and profound questions about the place of sex in everyday life. Feminists continue to reveal how much culturally accepted sexual patterns impoverish women's erotic and social lives. And the lesbian, gay, and feminist movements, in demonstrating the importance of sex as a major social construction, have called to account a Marxism that has viewed sexual politics as secondary, even a luxury for the self-indulgent. For those socialists willing to listen, both sex radicals and feminists offer a convincing case as to why the Left cannot afford to regard sexual politics as simply a diversion.

Sex and Feminism

Late-twentieth-century feminist discussions of sex have dealt, by and large, with incorporating some form of sexuality into women's lives. In contrast, nineteenth-century feminists shaped their sexual politics with a practical regard for the pressing difficulties for women which, in the absence of effective birth control, followed the inexorable link between heterosexuality and procreation. Obviously, these circumstances did not encourage a visionary politics of female sexuality. On the issue of marriage, for example, the subject of much Victorian sexual discussion, most feminists took a far more conservative position than contemporaneous sex radicals. While feminists were acutely aware of the legal and social inequalities of marriage, they also recognized that in a society that denied them the means to support themselves, most women had only two choices: marriage or prostitution—or, later, celibacy and career. For middle-class women this was no choice at all: feminist strategies focussed not on abolishing marriage—the goal of utopians and of free lovers—but on confining sex to marriage and on mitigating the deleterious consequences for women of sexual intercourse within marriage.[25]

Before the 1870s, the topic of female sexual experience was largely

taboo in public and private discussion. The early U.S. women's movement existed, for the most part, entirely apart from sex radical circles.[26]
Feminists in the 1830s and 1840s nevertheless did perceive a link
between male sexuality and female oppression, a connection which
they developed through an analysis of women's wrongs that turned on
the two metaphors of prostitution and female illness. Prostitution represented the victimization of female purity by male vice; analogously,
writers like Catharine Beecher associated female illness with the debilitating consequences of male lust and the pregnancies it engendered.[27] Today it is tempting to dismiss these analyses for their anti-
sexual character. It is important to recognize, however, that this discussion represented the first time in the nineteenth century that
women themselves raised the issue of sexuality: indeed, for perhaps
the first time in history, women were raising the issue of sexuality
toward political ends.

In the last decades of the nineteenth century, a new frankness entered feminist sexual discussion through two feminist-inspired campaigns, social purity, discussed at length in this volume by Judith
Walkowitz, and voluntary motherhood. The social purity movements
in England and the United States began as campaigns to abolish prostitution. Social purity, however, quickly reached beyond the feminist
intentions of many of its first adherents and became an attack on sexually active working-class youth, poor women, homosexuals, and female
boardinghouse keepers—those whose erotic activity outside of marriage placed them at odds with Victorian norms. If social purity af-
forded feminists the possibility of exercising some control over sexual
politics, the terms of discourse the feminists established ultimately
allowed men, not women, to dominate the movement. An abstract
image of woman as sexual victim, originated by feminists, became a
weapon with which the male ruling class on both sides of the Atlantic
strengthened its hegemony over women, sexual outlaws, and the poor
by establishing a state apparatus of protectionist sexual policies.[28]

The consequences of voluntary motherhood were more straightforwardly beneficial to women. Although advocates of voluntary motherhood, like most middle-class women of this period, were still opposed
to contraception, they nonetheless argued that women should be able
to choose when to become pregnant. In practice, this idea overturned
traditional assumptions about the husband's absolute right to his wife's
body and in its place substituted a female-determined calendar of sexual intercourse.[29] In the assertion that women had the right to refuse,
the movement's advocates developed what would later become an
axiom of radical and socialist-feminist thought. At the same time, the
campaign's sharpest break with the past was its acceptance of women as
sexual creatures. Female sexuality appeared in its arguments as a natu-

ral maternal instinct that sought expression in physical union with a beloved partner. If hesitant, this view of women still represented a significant departure from the official Victorian insistence on the asexuality of women.

In other respects, however, the proponents of voluntary motherhood mixed their radicalism with conventional ideas of women's nature. They assumed that men wanted sex more than women, that women would limit rather than multiply sexual contacts, and that female sexuality was more diffuse and soulful—less lustful—than men's. They held to the widespread assumption that mechanical contraceptive methods were only fit for prostitutes, and saw voluntary celibacy as a more amenable strategy for respectable women. To be sure, their resolve in the context of the late-nineteenth-century United States increased women's control over their bodies. In the twentieth century, however, to move beyond their legacy to create a theory of a fully physical female desire proved more problematic.

None of these feminist discussions of sex explicitly or implicitly touched upon lesbianism. The reasons for this exclusive focus on heterosexuality are not yet altogether clear; certainly there was a divergence between discourse and behavior, since, as a number of historians have shown, the cultural gap between men and women allowed, even encouraged, middle-class women to cultivate sensual and at times erotic relations with each other.[30] Rather, it was not the feminists but the first generation of medical sexologists that at the turn of the century opened up a public discussion of female homoerotic activity.[31]

The consequences of the new medical focus on same-sex relationships were damaging to all sorts of ties between women, sexual and otherwise. By broadening their definition of the pathological condition of female "inversion," the doctors contributed to the formation of the new heterosexual imperative. The limiting effects of the new heterosexuality, the keystone to the sexual revolution that began in places like Greenwich Village in the 1910s and continued into the 1920s, were not lost on an older generation of feminists. In 1930 Jane Addams associated the disintegration of the women's movement after the attainment of suffrage with the sexual revolution, the "breaking down of sex taboos" and the "establishment of new standards in marriage."[32] While young feminists like those of the Village heralded the struggle to break down the double standard, Victorian-bred women feared the adverse effects of promiscuity on their sex. Could men be held to their obligations, once conception was separated from sex and sanctions against extramarital sex disappeared? In a world where women held so little power, what power could a sexual revolution possibly offer them?

This was one of the chief questions that feminists in the mid-1960s took up again as the eroticization of daily life, which Addams had associated with the disintegration of feminism, became in turn a catalyst for its revival. Precious little feminism had illumined the intervening decades; the term "feminism" itself came to denote a deep illness contracted by "modern woman, the lost sex."[33] Nevertheless, the second wave of feminism in the 1960s coalesced around the conditions and contradictions of those seemingly vacant years: the slow but continuing progress of the birth control movement, the suburban and ex-urban ghettoization of middle-class women, the on-again/off-again employment market for women, and the evolution of sexual mores and communities. This evolution took place in relatively invisible lesbian and gay enclaves as well as among the visible majority, the actively heterosexual who felt themselves without immediate sexual community until the Kinsey report revealed that they were far from atypical, that the blank sexual affect of their neighbors and associates was, more often than not, a camouflage.[34]

The feminist relationship to these changes in sexual mores, accelerated in the 1960s by the new accessibility of cheap birth control, is central to our concerns here. Since the 1960s feminists have sought to maximize those changes that benefited women, but the attempt has been fraught with conflict. Feminists have not agreed on just what changes serve women's interests—or even, for that matter, on a definition of sex that is good for women. From 1968 on, this lack of agreement has divided the women's movement, often bitterly, as various factions have proposed solution after solution—some as global as the feminist revolution, others as seemingly trivial as the vibrator—each elevated into doctrine or vehemently rejected in a passionate and polarizing process. These were not the arcane debates of insular sects but the serious efforts of thousands of women living, for the moment, at the edge of the history of their gender, who were seeking to change their lives on every level through transformations in sexual consciousness and habit.

The development of modern feminist sexual thought has been a complex process, whose full history has yet to be told. Here we focus primarily on that part of the movement which, in the late 1960s, called itself "women's liberation," those feminists committed to militant direct action who saw themselves as in some sense insurgents, and as distinct from liberal feminism and its reformist goals. At first a common political temperament and style, if not an especially well worked-out ideology, unified women's liberation. In the intervening years, distinct and often opposed tendencies, no doubt latent from the beginning, emerged from these ranks: socialist-feminism, cultural feminism, separatism, radical feminism, lesbian-feminism. Two aspects of this sexual discourse of women's liberation are particularly relevant here:

the conflicting notions of sex as liberating or oppressive, and the collective public discussion, historically unprecedented, of lesbianism as an empowering female choice.

Women's liberation emerged from the experiences of a particular generation of women, those who came of sexual age between (roughly) 1960 and 1970 and were the first U.S. women to have ready access to birth control before marriage. The histories of some of these women bore out the fear of nineteenth-century feminists: the availability of birth control had shifted the sexual balance of power so that they had neither grounds to say no to men's pressing invitations nor to persuade men to commit themselves to the old terms of the sexual bargain, the exchange of sex for intimacy, fidelity, and economic support. Other women had few qualms about non-monogamy and greeted the possibilities of sexual liberation with enthusiasm, but they found that at least one aspect of the old bargain still prevailed: to take the sexual pleasure men offered still brought down the punitive force of the double standard. For the most part, men still retained the power to reject or validate women sexually, to determine the conditions of sexual relations.

The opening volleys in the women's liberation critique of sexual freedom came from women in the New Left and Civil Rights movements. Like abolitionist women, white New Left women, especially those who went south to work against racial discrimination, found that the acknowledgment of the oppression of others led to a recognition of their own sexual, social, and economic oppression. The analytic tools honed in the Left gave the recognition of exploitation and inequality in bed its political cast.[35] As Alix Kates Shulman has pointed out, "The most intimate aspects of male-female relations crystallized quite early in feminist analyses of sex, perceived squarely in its political dimension as an aspect of the power relations between the sexes."[36] Despite the complex experience of the Civil Rights movement, however, women's liberation was not equally insightful about sexual issues related to race and class rather than gender. The largely white, middle-class movement tended to pass over these differences in the name of the unity of all women struggling against oppression by all men.

A political analysis that began with such intense anger at sexual exploitation might well have taken a wholly anti-sexual direction at the outset. Yet while women's liberation began with a staunch critique of the oppressive aspects of women's sex lives, many feminists nonetheless sought a way to be sexually active outside the context of oppression. This goal eventually led to a number of highly serious and passionate sexual strategies—for example, living out the maxim that one's lovers should be one's friends and one's friends one's lovers—inconceivable a decade earlier.[37] The many sources of this affirmative sexual attitude included the accessibility of birth control, greater social permissiveness, and the experience of sex itself.

Certainly one theoretical influence was Simone de Beauvoir's *The Second Sex*. Originally published in 1953 but reissued in paperback in 1961, *The Second Sex* influenced countless women in the 1960s. - De Beauvoir insisted that sexual autonomy, although difficult and painful for women to achieve, was still a fundamental project for them; she saw the erotic as an intervention of human liberty, a perception that made it possible for her, well ahead of her time, to view lesbianism as a choice for freedom.[38] Radical feminists tended to echo de Beauvoir's belief in the erotic as a touchstone of life, implicitly repudiating the liberal views of Betty Friedan, the only other widely read theorist in the early and mid-1960s. In *The Feminine Mystique* (1963), Friedan assumed that women had more than enough sex, and she proposed to trade their purported erotic surplus for meaningful work. Underlying her willingness to make this bargain was a generally anti-sexual and homophobic attitude that led her to decry the specter of women's increasing sexual appetites, their "insatiable sexual desire" and unnatural capability for "multiple orgasms," as well as the homosexuality "spreading like a murky fog over the American scene."[39] Friedan's profound distrust of sexual liberation resonated throughout the liberal wing of the movement, resulting in later years in a serious blindness to the centrality of sexual issues to feminist progress.

De Beauvoir's affirmation of sexuality, rather than Friedan's caution, set the initial tone for women's liberation. The major political struggle of the late 1960s—the fight to eliminate laws restricting abortion—sprang from this affirmative attitude, the conviction that women had the right to be sexual without enduring the punitive consequences of pregnancy. Abortion was an immediate concern for millions of women, and this personal dimension dominated both discussion and political strategy. In consciousness-raising groups and speakouts, before the media and judicial authorities, women spoke openly about their illegal abortions. Although this confessional approach had its political limitations, it played a major role in opening up discussion of women's sexual experience. The courageous testimonies of hundreds of women, documented in books like *Abortion Rap*, revealed both the sexual repression that governed their experience and women's steadfast and ingenious refusal to knuckle under.[40] Before the late 1960s that refusal was, by and large, silent and individual. With the women's movement, women's rejection of biological determinism became public and collective. Three hundred women sued the State of New York in *Abramowicz* v. *Lefkowitz*, demanding the elimination of its highly restrictive abortion law.[41] The case precipitated repeal of the state's law, the first of the great abortion victories that were to follow.

In accord with a generally positive attitude toward sexuality, radical feminist discussions initially focused on improving heterosexual sex, an angle that fostered an interest in sexual technique. Thus in her loving but satirical novel about the early stages of the women's movement, *Burning Questions*, Alix Kates Shulman has one of her characters demand of her lovers cunnilingus and "three hours minimum" for sex.[42]

These concerns with both abortion and sexual technique assumed that female sexuality was heterosexual. The first shift away from this presumption came embedded in Anne Koedt's "The Myth of the Vaginal Orgasm" (1969). Like Mary Jane Sherfey's later *The Nature and Evolution of Female Sexual Response* (1973),[43] Koedt's article was a feminist rendition of the new findings of Masters and Johnson. But while Sherfey would focus chiefly and rather grandiloquently on the potential of the female multiple orgasm to destroy civilization, Koedt was impressed with the implications of the clitoral orgasm for female pleasure and heterosexual relations. Inferring from the sexologists' evidence on the clitoris that vaginal penetration was irrelevant to female pleasure, Koedt suggested that men might be "sexually expendable."

On its face, Koedt's essay was a rendering of often problematic sex research which, under less favorable historical circumstances, might have been coopted at once (like that of the Weimar sex reformers in the 1920s which Grossmann describes in this volume): redefinition of the location or intensity of the female orgasm by "experts" has little connection to women's ability to define and control sexual experiences for themselves. Perhaps we do not as yet have the distance to understand the extent to which such cooptation did occur, although this becomes an important question in light of current developments both within and outside the women's movement. Nevertheless, initially, in the context of a rising tide of women's activities, Koedt's work suggested possibilities for a female-controlled sexuality. Her ideas, however limited, helped women to decrease their dependence on men, increase their sexual autonomy, improve the odds that they would obtain pleasure from sex, and find through that pleasure not a new level of subjugation but an affirmation of identity and power.

With these gains, however, came losses, stemming from the movement's tendency to make law out of possibility. The ensuing discussion of masturbation and celibacy, which took its cues from many of the ideas implicit in Koedt's paper, is remarkable even today for its blunt disregard of the social conventions of sex, and its simultaneous unquestioning adherence to the new theories of the orgasm. Some of the contributors to this discussion—Betty Dodson, for example—celebrated eroticism of every sort;[44] others assumed that the orgasm was the sole interest of sensual life and that the self was world enough. Ti-Grace Atkinson and Dana Densmore, for example, did not appear to see the interest of a caress or an erotic connection of any kind—let alone of penetration. Indeed, after the salvos of Koedt and Atkinson, virtually no grounds remained for desiring sexual intercourse—other than, perhaps, that passivity had its delights, that a lover other than the self added an element of surprise, that a second body warmed the sheets. Certainly, it was very difficult for a feminist to admit that she found penetration pleasurable or orgasmic; later, in the face of lesbian-feminist ideology, it became almost impossible to explain theoretically, anatomically, or socially why any woman might want to go to bed with a man. [45]

The newly invented consciousness-raising process created the milieu for both discussing sexual experiences and spreading sexual admonitions. Insofar as sex was among the issues discussed, consciousness-raising groups broke the subject down into subcategories: for example, losing your virginity, being pretty, enjoying/not enjoying sex, asking for what you want. As anthropologist Gayle Rubin remarked recently, the objective of consciousness-raising—to shape women's discussions around the idea of oppression—structurally equated sexuality and subordination. [46] The general theme was "what men did to me around sex." In white middle-class women's groups, while sexual objectification and sexual wounds were typical themes, extreme instances of sexual coercion and violence were not, in this early period, substantive parts of the discussion. Rather, talk centered on the nuances of psychological oppression, which shaded and hampered in almost indiscernible ways the lives of the women involved, who experienced the men who were their fathers, lovers, and friends—liberal, white, educated, middle-class men, for the most part—not so much brutal as all-engulfing. If many of these women felt humiliated because they were sexually invisible, consciousness-raising became a platform in the midst of the sexual revolution from which they could insult men back. [47] Occasionally that anger boomeranged on other women: those, for instance, accused of "scabbing for the man"—sleeping with a man whom another woman had left because he would not reform his male chauvinist ways. [48] But for the most part, anger became in itself erotic, a bond among women, a step toward empowerment.

As women's liberation spread, consciousness-raising and other feminist public modes, such as the speakout, began to focus more on instances of real violence against women—for example, rape—instances that came to be metaphors for the sexual experiences of all women. In the few racially or ethnically integrated women's groups that existed, sexual issues, as they converged with those of rape and violence, created enormous internal group pressure. Jacquelyn Dowd Hall's paper in this volume gives historical perspective to the complex relationship between rape and lynching for blacks. Alice Walker's short

story, "Advancing Luna and Ida B. Wells," evokes some of these complexities, as well as the great personal anguish that the issue of rape
caused for black women.[49] The racism that tended to creep into feminist discussions of rape further complicated the issue for women of
color, as did, in integrated women's groups, the issue of white women
sleeping with black men.[50]

Two texts, Kate Millet's *Sexual Politics* and Shulamith Firestone's
The Dialectic of Sex, sum up much of the radical feminist theory and
practice of sex at the turn of the decade. Millet affirmed the progressive aspects of the sexual revolution: she saw women's sexual autonomy
as a prerequisite for sexual freedom itself. At the same time, she un-
compromisingly demonstrated how misogyny played itself out in sexual intercourse. Her approach—a close examination of male texts—
initiated a burst of criticism of male sexual culture.[51] Firestone's
Dialectic, a quirky blend of Marxism, Hinduism, and pop-psychology,
is less useful today, but it elaborated a key assertion of radical feminism: that sexuality is a primary structure of social life and that the
body itself is a material condition. Although Firestone advocated
artificial reproduction, her technological solution by no means revealed an anti-male or anti-sex bias. On the contrary, she reflected the
prevailing mood of the movement in her generally unquestioning acceptance of heterosexuality, and in her celebration of sexual freedom as
a potential wellspring of full-scale liberation.[52]

Lesbian-feminist ideology arose at the turn of the decade through a
complex series of erotic and political connections within the lesbian
community, the gay movement, and all sectors of the feminist movement.[53] In light of the subsequent rise of cultural feminism and separatism, which so promoted a desexualized image of lesbianism, it is easy
to forget that lesbian-feminism proceeded initially from the insistence
of women's liberation on women's right to be *sexual*, an insistence that
caused the feminist movement to take, until recently, a very different
political direction from that of the nineteenth century. Like early discussions of masturbation within women's liberation, the revelation that
lesbianism was a possible sexual alternative demonstrated that women
could take a sexual life for themselves, not only privately—as in auto-
eroticism—but together.

In retrospect, Koedt, Sherfey, and, more generally, radical feminist
consciousness-raising, seem to have laid the ideological basis for lesbian-feminism. There were, however, important distinctions: Koedt
did not follow up her remarks on the expendability of men with the
explicit suggestion that women replace them with female lovers, and
Sherfey did not follow out the logic of her romance of the multiple
orgasm with the conclusion that lesbianism was a workable solution for
women saddled with men's paltry sexual capacities. In consciousness-

raising groups the notion of sisterhood involved political and emotional support, not sex. The practice of banning men from some social and political contexts—women's groups, for instance—originally implied not an exclusively female erotic milieu but a context where women could discuss oppression without the presence of the oppressor. Some feminists also wanted to exclude men in order to exclude sex itself, which they dourly viewed as one source of the trouble between men and women.[54] Thus, although the ideological and social basis for a flourishing lesbian community existed quite early in the women's movement, lesbianism itself was, before the Stonewall Riots of 1969, buried in the general interest in, and assumption of, heterosexuality. Without understanding the heterosexism and homophobia of the movement, one can comprehend neither the reluctance of pre-feminist-movement lesbians to "come out" nor the bitter anger of lesbian chauvinism when lesbians did finally emerge as a public force.

Before 1969, most feminist lesbians belonged to NOW, which offered some program addressed to the economic discrimination that for lesbians, women living without male support, was a central problem. For the most part, these lesbians did not openly acknowledge their sexual identities. Despite the militance of individual women within the early gay movement, few lesbians within the ranks of liberal feminism or within pre-feminist lesbian social organizations, such as Daughters of Bilitis, were prepared to come out or struggle when the issue of homophobia first arose in a feminist context. In 1969, when Rita Mae Brown charged NOW with discrimination against its lesbian members, some lesbians within the organization tried to quash the issue.[55] When Ti-Grace Atkinson announced to the Daughters of Bilitis, to which she did not belong, that "Feminism is the theory; but lesbianism is the practice," DOB members cynically greeted her pronouncement as a straight woman's attempt to appropriate DOB as a power base.[56]

These women had reason to be cautious. The sexual repression of the war years and the 1950s had put a high price on even the suspicion of lesbian tendencies. Although there was certainly a public lesbian culture, most lesbians could—and did—pass. Indeed, passing was an accepted practice of DOB, whose members commonly used pseudonyms even with each other. And passing had an erotic underside. The habit of secrecy ran deep into the underground streams of lesbian sexual identity and arousal itself. Like so many aspects of the forbidden, the closet may have been itself eroticized, as was the act of breaking a taboo. Coming out as an individual and a community meant sacrificing some part of that eroticism, as well as risking open stigmatization.

But keeping the secret had a price as well. In a culture that increasingly identified sexuality with the self, to pretend that one did not live erotically—did not touch or care about another passionately, did not surrender or take or come—was to be nothing. Lesbians who passed as straight bore the humiliation of seeming to lack the rudiments of social and intimate life. Paradoxically, the more easily one passed, the lonelier one became. The cost of social safety was psychological danger—intense anonymity and alienation.[57] In the 1950s, Daughters of Bilitis had offered a meeting place outside the bars and a forum for exploring, however narrowly or prejudicially, what it was to be a lesbian. But in the late 1960s, as other stigmatized groups came forward, risking what little they had for what they wanted and gaining strength from the risk, this no longer seemed sufficient. The politics of blending in had become intolerable.

As a political identity began to surface, lesbians debated whether the gay or the feminist movement was the appropriate political alliance. There were two sources of hesitation about feminists. Liberal feminists, with whom lesbians first associated politically, tended to a moderated sexual style, which, in the middle-class manner, downplayed both sexual presence and traditional gender characteristics. This subdued approach was not congenial to those bar and street lesbians whose tradition of erotic rebellion involved, in contrast, flamboyantly elaborating the gender paradoxes of lesbian life. Liberal feminists, on the other hand, in the first line of defense against the incursion of lesbianism, dismissed such women as male-identified. To enter the feminist preserve, lesbians had to cast off, or pretend to cast off, sexual mores that, like passing, had profound erotic connections and meaning. Not every lesbian could, or would, do this.[58]

At the same time, many lesbians viewed the emergence of the "political lesbian" (a phrase coined to describe a woman who labeled herself a lesbian as a sign of her allegiance to the sisterhood and her refusal to "collaborate with the enemy") with grave reservations. As one self-described "old dyke" recalled:

> When the women's movement took hold, I thought it was just a bunch of privileged straight women who had nothing better to do. I never felt they could make any difference to my life. . . . As a dyke, I wanted to stay inconspicuous, so I couldn't get involved anyway. When the straight women became lesbians, I was sure it was for "political reasons." I was repelled by them. They could not possibly understand a "real lesbian" like me. They hadn't suffered like me. They had been accepted and acceptable all their lives. They didn't live a lie, with the fear and self-loathing I had. Their lesbianism must be a gimmick.[59]

Similarly, a correspondent in *The Ladder*, DOB's publication, disparaged lesbian-feminists as "lesbians who belong to the now generation and look just like any other hippie and who in fact rather seldom sleep with girls."[60] This contempt stemmed, in part, from a fear of betrayal, a fear that the alliance with feminism would lead to a political version of an old lesbian pulp plot: straight woman leads on lesbian only to leave her at the very moment that she lets down her defenses.[61]

But although lesbian-feminist chic did include the phenomenon of the "false lesbian," she who claimed a sexual stigma she did not earn with desire,[62] the suspicion that older lesbians felt toward those who came out in the feminist context did not sufficiently recognize the extent to which sexual identities are made, not born. Many a false—or political—lesbian became the genuine article, at least measured against a sexual criterion. But the lesbian who came out within women's liberation did relate to her sexuality very differently, in a highly politicized and conscious manner.

The first overt manifestations of a lesbian political presence within feminism followed Brown's accusation of homophobia in NOW. NOW proceeded to virtually purge its membership of lesbians between 1969 and 1971, and many turned to women's liberation, and particularly to radical feminist consciousness-raising groups.[63] These refugees from liberal feminism found radical feminists less homophobic but still disappointingly focused on heterosexual sex. For that reason, lesbians formed their own groups: at the height of this development in New York City, there were some eighteen lesbian consciousness-raising groups with up to twenty members in each. Through consciousness-raising, old and new lesbians quickly grasped the implicit lesbian conclusions of early radical feminist texts.[64]

"The Woman-Identified Woman," the first manifesto of lesbian-feminism, emerged from this germinative meeting of lesbians and radical feminists.[65] Presented at the Second Congress to Unite Women in 1970, the paper was part of a stunningly executed response to NOW that turned Friedan's put-down of the "lavender menace" on its head. Twenty women wearing "Lavender Menace" T-shirts took over the microphone, denounced the women's movement for homophobia, and called on sympathizers to join them.[66] The manifesto defined the essence of feminism in terms of a lesbian identity and argued that lesbianism was the "rage of all women condensed to the point of explosion."[67] The sources of lesbianism, then, were political not erotic and "The Woman-Identified Woman" and the Lavender Menace action sought to identify lesbians with all women by redefining lesbianism as the quintessential feminism. In the report of a participant in the conference, we can see the complicated response of one early feminist: Warned by an acquaintance that "there were going to be Lesbians there," she nonetheless went to the congress "with much curiosity. I had high hopes of seeing a Lesbian. And I did, I saw lots of Lesbians."[68] She was imaginatively enthralled with the lesbian militants:

Rita Mae Brown was the first up-front Lesbian I ever saw. . . . Small, beautiful, strong, wearing a "Super-Dyke" T-shirt which she had dyed lavender, incredibly articulate and funny as hell. She was a Lesbian I could identify with. When she asked for women in the audience to join their Lesbian sisters. . . . I jumped up, eager to be counted as a sister traveler.[69]

For straight women, lesbianism represented the magnetism of the forbidden and the dangerous, always powerful but especially so in the ferment of the 1960s. As this earnest young woman reported, a lesbian friend sitting near her would not join the swelling surge in support of Brown: "When I asked her why she said it was too dangerous." "That," she concluded, "made me want to be a Lesbian even more." (Later, denounced by a Gay Academic Union member as a false lesbian, she responded that "sleeping with men doesn't make me not a Lesbian.")[70]

In the fusion of lesbianism and feminism that "The Woman-Identified Woman" helped to bring about, there were a number of problems whose full import has become clear only recently. In pointing to anger rather than eros as the wellspring of lesbianism, the manifesto opened the way for the desexualization of lesbian identity.[71] While soft-pedalling differences was a general tendency of feminism in the late 1960s and early 1970s, it became especially characteristic of lesbian-feminist ideology; unsexing lesbianism was a way to stress the similarity between the lesbian and the straight feminist. Whether the topic was oppression, anger at men, or friendship between women, the manifesto asserted that the lesbian differed only in intensity, in degree, not in kind. While the pre-feminist-movement lesbian could not forget her differences from straight women, the feminist lesbian could scarcely perceive them. Ultimately, this homogenization suppressed but could no more eliminate the tensions of difference between lesbian and straight women than it could between white women and women of color.

In spite of its contradictions, in spite of its failure to grapple with the material bases of power, in spite of its double binds, double thoughts, and unsexed idealization of relationships between women, "The Woman-Identified Woman" was a brilliant strategic text. The success of the Lavender Menace can be attributed, in no small part, to the way the paper and the ensuing lesbian discourse turned so many of the concepts, dreams, and frustrations of the feminist movement and of feminist sexual negotiations with men to the service of its objective: checkmating homophobia in the women's movement. If new contradictions and confusions followed in its wake, this was partly because the strategy was so unexpectedly effective. At a time when the women's movement was rife with fears that lesbians were going to jump straight women and "have their way with them" as Judith Katz's spoof has it, how was the Lavender Menace to foresee that they could so completely unsex an identity that had been all sex just a short time before?[72] And although "The Woman-Identified Woman" did not end homophobia in the women's movement, it did reduce it to a whisper; moreover, it changed the balance of sexual power radically not only between straight women and lesbians but between straight feminists and straight men. Sexual pleasure no longer depended so entirely on being acceptable to men. Even women who had not the slightest inclination to cross the threshold of taboo reaped some benefits in their heterosexual negotiations from the general acknowledgment that lesbianism was now within the realm of the imaginable.

The rise of lesbian-feminist ideology divided some feminists from their closest friends and made allies and lovers of others; it enriched the movement with new possibilities but also confounded it with the complications of sex. Heterosexual women's reactions to the emergence of lesbian-feminism had a great deal to do with their feelings about sex itself: Was it the thick cream of life or did it curdle human relations? Was sex as much a source of oppression as gender? Without sex, could women preserve a collectivity free of betrayal, dominance, jealousy, mixed emotions? Would those women who spoke openly of their desire contaminate the rest? Did sex recharge the energies for work or drain them away?

For many lesbians of color, the imperatives of lesbian-feminism deepened the feminist bind. Coming out in the context of racial politics could be deeply isolating and painful. As black feminist critic Barbara Smith expressed it, "There's nothing to be compared with how you feel when you're cut cold by your own."[73] The issue of sleeping with whites further complicated these sexual politics. "The woman who takes a woman lover lives dangerously in patriarchy," wrote lesbian-feminist Cheryl Clarke, "and woe betide her even more if she chooses as her lover a woman who is not of her race."[74] With the crystallization of lesbian separatism, matters became triply confounded for lesbians of color, who were assailed as "male-identified" for not wholly abandoning their concern with racial politics. Feminist separatist declarations that getting rid of men would automatically abolish racism also maddened lesbians of color, who knew too well from the anguish of personal experience that men were not the only racists.[75] Finally, some lesbians of color were divided between the unisex style of lesbian-feminism and the bulldagger tradition, which in the black community invoked ostracism but was nevertheless a brave affirmation of sexual identity. To love a bulldagger, Pat Suncircle wrote in her moving story "Mariam," "is to be unable to lie."[76]

After the first shocks of lesbian-feminism had passed, a sexual consensus emerged within women's liberation. Lesbians and heterosexual feminists theoretically accepted each other's moderated, healthy sexual proclivities—although in somewhat the same spirit that St. Paul accepted the inevitability of marriage for those weak of flesh and soul. Among the liberals, even Betty Friedan briefly relented and declared that she saw the relevance of lesbianism to feminism.[77] *Our Bodies, Ourselves* (1971)—*OBOS*, for short—was one expression of this consensus. In comparison with the current exoticism in sexual discussions, *OBOS* seems a benignly reassuring sex manual. Still, it caused a stir when first published and is even today banned in some libraries. *OBOS* both elaborated the women's liberation interest in technique and knowledge as the keys to sexual happiness and unquestioningly affirmed sex as therapeutic. "Sexual feelings and responses" were seen as a "central expression of our emotional, spiritual, physical selves," and the collective authors were confident that we are born "loving our bodies," and that each of us has a "whole self" we carry into sexual relationships after preparing our sexuality through masturbation.[78] The book segregates lesbianism into a chapter prepared separately by a group of gay women but maintains a generally respectful, tolerant tone toward lesbian experience. But although *OBOS* summed up important advances in sexual knowledge and represented a remarkably comprehensive effort to think "new," it also—like the movement that produced it—rode the crest of a wave of optimism, a moment when feminism had not yet faced a critical confrontation with the knottier questions of erotic desire and pleasure.

In 1973, the struggle of women's liberation to achieve abortion on demand secured a major victory. The Supreme Court affirmed in *Roe* v. *Wade* that a woman's right to privacy extended in most circumstances to the right to abortion.[79] In breaking the silence about abortion, women had broken the back of the law as well. With this apparent triumph, and with the end of the war in Vietnam, the radicalism that had continually infused the women's movement with the energies of a more general cultural and political revolt began to decline. The palmy days of sisterhood were over. There followed a time of hibernation—of rethinking, integration, and solidification—as feminists dispersed into various sexual, social, and professional enclaves. But although the work of this period was perhaps less visible than the highly public activities of the late 1960s and early 1970s, it was nonetheless crucial. Institution building and intellectual ventures beyond feminism into other systems of thought were of particular importance. Socialist-feminism increasingly took root as a tendency that stressed the need to integrate an understanding of class and race into a more complex feminist analysis. Throughout the late 1970s and early 1980s, socialist-feminists took an active role in building coalitions and establishing and supporting political organizations that dealt with such issues as women's unions, the clerical worker's movement, and campaigns for affirmative action; and, although the thinking on sexuality *per se* was comparatively undeveloped in the 1970s, socialist-feminists did important work on contraception, abortion, sterilization, and reproductive hazards in the workplace. The feminism of women of color also began to emerge as a substantial political force in the women's movement, especially in regard to the issue of difference, a theme that became extremely important in the sexual debates of the 1980s.

The integration of feminism, Marxism, and psychoanalysis was, in terms of feminist sexual theory, an important legacy of these years. Juliet Mitchell's *Psychoanalysis and Feminism* (1974) sought to retake Freud for both the Marxist and feminist traditions, both of which had earlier repudiated him—Marxists because they disliked the ways in which neo-Freudianism in the United States substituted theories of individual pathology for analysis of social problems, and feminists because they objected to Freud's pervasive sexism. While feminists had also turned to Wilhelm Reich and Herbert Marcuse, Reich's homophobia and Marcuse's blandness about gender made these passionate reconstructions of the Freudian heritage likewise suspect. Mitchell's work circumvented Freud's equation of femininity with compensatory development, and retrieved his profoundly useful speculations about the psychological construction of gender.[80] Similarly, Dorothy Dinnerstein's *The Mermaid and the Minotaur* (1977) and Nancy Chodorow's *The Reproduction of Mothering* (1978)[82] mined Freud's analyses of childhood sexuality for elements of a theory of gender; both offered a feminist explanation of the commonly noted mental asymmetries between male and female sexual feelings and expectations. Gayle Rubin's extremely influential theoretical essay, "The Traffic in Women" (1975), also used the work of anthropologist Claude Lévi-Strauss and psychoanalyst Jacques Lacan to sketch out the structural elements of sexual inequality: Rubin showed, among other things, how cultural practices like the sexual double standard and the insistence on female chastity were not simply anachronisms of a sexist male mentality but essential to the functioning of whole social systems.[83]

In the late 1970s, the New Right's growing strength began to have an impact on the feminist politics of sex. The fulcrum of the New Right's anti-sexual offensive was, of course, the Right-to-Life movement. In 1977 the Hyde Amendment, the first of a series of legislative efforts to whittle away the right to abortion, cut off federal Medicaid funds for abortion. Among liberal feminists, ironically, the specter of the Right succeeded in reviving a conservative sexual analysis. Betty Friedan, for example, retracted her brief endorsement of lesbian-feminism and argued that by daring to talk about sex, feminists had unleashed a monster. Sexuality, she argued, was a "red herring" that could only distract and divide feminists. If only the radicals among them had been more mannerly, she implied, feminists might have persuaded solid, social conservatives that feminists meant no harm to children or family, that women's rights wouldn't infringe on theirs, that the ERA was A-OK.

For those whose feminism sprang from more radical perceptions, the New Right's direct hit on sexuality confirmed the analysis that sexual and reproductive issues were not marginal, not trivial, but central to women's liberation and to the project of human freedom. The blatantly divisive strategy of the attack—clearly intended to separate poor women from middle-class women, heterosexuals from lesbians— made the overwhelming need for unity apparent to many feminists. Moreover, the discriminatory nature of the Right's first major victory, the Hyde Amendment, forced feminists to confront directly race and class differences: although the government stopped funding abortions for poor women, it continued to fund 90 percent of sterilization under Medicaid.

In developing strategies to defend the right to abortion, activists drew heavily on socialist-feminist theory and scholarship. Linda Gordon's *Woman's Body, Woman's Right* (1976), a history of the birth control movement, became virtually a resource manual for the organizations that rapidly organized to fight for abortion. Gordon's book laid the groundwork for an analysis that made careful distinctions between involuntary and voluntary reproductive choices, especially between abortion and sterilization, and that placed abortion squarely in the context of women's liberation and sexual freedom. Similarly, Rosalind Petchesky's activism in the reproductive rights movement led her to a political, ethical, and philosophical exploration of the abortion issue which, in a sense, begins where Gordon leaves off. Her work grounds the struggle of the late 1970s and 1980s in the history of progressive ideas, and carefully sets forth and balances the tensions between socialism and feminism, and the public and the private, in regard to women's sexual and reproductive autonomy.[84] Both Gordon and Petchesky showed feminists how the battle for abortion was only one part of a much broader struggle for reproductive and sexual freedom, an invaluable political insight for the 1980s. This analysis has buttressed recent legal and political battles with the New Right.

But in responding to growing pressure from the Right, feminists also had to face conflicts on sexual issues within their own ranks. The conflicts—heated and acrimonious—derived not simply from disagreements over present tactics, but from long-standing ambiguities about sexuality, which the present political exigencies raised to the level of contradiction. The anti-pornography movement, for instance, emerged in the late 1970s as the most dramatic expression of cultural feminism, a tendency analyzed by Alice Echols in her critique in this volume. The anti-pornography campaign partly derived from feminist efforts against misogynist violence—rape crisis centers and battered women's shelters. However, anti-pornography organizing focused not on real instances of violence against women but on sexual images the campaign activists considered to evoke violence. Like other cultural feminists, they often implied that these images of female vulnerability were fixed, universal, natural. While the anti-pornography movement galvanized many women across the country, it also based its tactics and its message on a dichotomous view of erotic nature—male sexuality as violent and lustful, female sexuality as tender and gentle. Other feminists came to regard this constellation of views as reactionary, since it offers so few leverage points for action, so few imaginative entry points for visions of change.

Thus the sexual assumptions of the anti-pornography crusade and of cultural feminism have become, in turn, a springboard for a countervailing feminist politics that stresses sexual variety and pleasure. Especially important to this development have been the self-conscious lesbian "outlaws," those women who have rejected the role of desexualized lesbianism and replace the old downhome sisterly erotic style with a far more assertive and explicit erotic demeanor. As lesbians have reclaimed the rebellious traditions of their own history, they have also reconsidered their relationship to gay male culture, and thus to the world of male sexuality. Several lesbian groups, for instance, which support their members' experiments with formerly tabooed erotic forms, have challenged feminists' old notions about what kind of sex women like. The increased visibility of women of color in the feminist arena, especially evident in the founding of a number of new feminist small presses, also underlies this shift toward an interest in difference rather than an insistence on a homogenized unity—which was, after all, as often as not a dogmatic formulation of the sexual mores and preferences of white middle-class women.

These developments in the ranks of the women's liberation movement are only beginning to surface publicly. A recent special "Sex Issue" of the radical feminist *Heresies* magazine took up the gauntlet by purposefully treating only explicitly erotic experience and not reproduction, and by including writings from some of the most notorious feminist sexual heretics.[55] The now-controversial Barnard College conference on sexuality in the spring of 1982 continued the effort to develop a sexual politics that takes pleasure as well as danger into account. "Our theory, as it stands," declared conference organizer Carole Vance in her keynote address, "is based on limited facts marshalled by overdeveloped preconceptions. . . . Unarticulated, irrational reactions wreak havoc in our own movement and at the same time are cleverly used against us by the Right."[86] As she spoke, anti-pornography crusaders leafletted outside the hall. The conference's willingness to explore all varieties of women's erotic experience was, the protesters charged, but a manifestation of the organizers' internalization of "patriarchal messages and values."[87]

What contributions have feminist discussions and debates made to our understanding of sex? The most obvious point is the most important: while earlier sexual theorists included women at best as an afterthought (and often simply as a vehicle for male projections), feminists have insisted that sexuality cannot be comprehended without taking into account the experiences of women. As we have suggested, however, feminists have also encountered particular problems when thinking about sex. Even in the most sexually venturesome periods of recent years, dogmatism has marred most feminist analyses. In retrospect, it seems that the issues raised by the sexual revolution were so disturbing that we quickly grasped whatever idea was in the wind and made of it some basic principle of feminist eroticism. To be sure, not all grabbed for the same idea. Perhaps, rather, the movement's explorations involved a series of trials around the challenge: how far can you stretch your conceptions of gender and sex? At each new trial, some reached their limits and organized to enforce them on everyone else. Each time around, we have demonstrated a peculiar propensity to accept each other's dogmatism: did this come from our experience as daughters?[88] We easily submitted, and then took recourse, with neurotic repetitiveness, to sullen rebellion, doing what we wanted anyway or meeting fire with fire—organizing around our preference.

In part because of this dynamic, modern feminism has gone from extreme to extreme. Instead of adding each new possibility to the list of sexual gains, we have, rather, traded in the old for the new: the clitoris for the vagina, lesbianism for heterosexuality, sadomasochism for desexualized lesbianism. How much does this extremism reflect a habit with sexual language, as we take illuminating metaphors as literal and comprehensive descriptions: rape for sex with men, friendship for sex with women, vulnerability for victimhood? We oscillate between two perspectives: on the one hand, a self-righteous feminine censoriousness; on the other, a somewhat cavalier libertarianism, which deals but minimally with vulnerability. The puritanical among us have had as suspect a fascination with these extremes as the adventurous. How do we account for this fascination with the extreme: Is it an attraction to contained forms, an expression of the fear of not knowing any longer what it is to be female? Or do we continue to feel that being female is in itself to be extreme, an aberration of the human? Or, if these are but turns in a dialectic, where is the creative synthesis?

Surely not in a consensus that mutes difference, leaving it to fester in uneasy silence.

The problem lies not simply in these alternations between unsatisfactory positions, but in selecting the issues we choose to talk about and organize around. Too little attention goes to such questions as: Why are we thinking about this? And why now? The success of the anti-pornography campaign in galvanizing women raises important questions in this regard. Why, for example, has the struggle against sexual violence—which originally emphasized the politics of rape—taken so symbolic a turn? Does propaganda about women's fear and vulnerability encourage women to useful caution or make them more afraid to control their own lives? And, more generally, what is the psychological relationship between sexual taboo and arousal? Does sexual shame reduce, or enhance, erotic excitement? Does sexual excitement depend on creating and recreating taboo? Is there such a thing as a progressive taboo?

To these questions we must add others if we are to begin on the work of evolving a feminist sexual politics. What is the relationship between sexuality and gender? What is our stake in maintaining a still relatively rigid gender dichotomy in sexual temperament and behavior? What is the relationship between sexual fantasy and sexual acts? What is our rational control over fantasy and do we think there should be a sexual ethics that extends to fantasy? Is it inevitable that we sometimes see our lovers as objects, as things we wish to shape to our passion and will; or should all objectification be fought as dehumanizing, alienated, the opposite rather than an element of love? How malleable is sexual taste? In other words, how set are our individual scripts for sexual arousal?

It is crucial to remedy the lack of serious feminist study of the effects of class, race, and ethnicity on sexuality. A few pieces in this volume take up this task: Rennie Simson's exploration of the sexual identity of the Afro-American woman; Felicita Garcia's account, "I Just Came Out Pregnant"; Jacquelyn Hall's study of women, rape, and racial violence; Barbara Omolade's "Hearts of Darkness"; Amber Hollibaugh and Cherríe Moraga's conversation about butch-femme roles. Still, feminists are too ready to assume a homogeneity where, in fact, a much more complex and variegated history lies. As Sylvia Watts Vitale commented on black sexuality in the *Heresies* "Sex Issue," "There is a hell-of-a-lot of work to be done. . . ."[87] How do race, class, ethnicity, and religion change the perception and experience of sex? In general, what do we mean by "difference" when we talk about sex? For example, what of temperament? Early childhood experience? What kinds of sexual connections are set up among those who have different sexual and social histories? What sexual myths do different groups harbor about each other? What role does power and dominance play in sexual excitement? In what ways is sex managed differently in relationships with a relatively equal balance of power than in relationships between people who—for any number of reasons including race, class, or gender—are vastly unequal?

Perhaps the issues we have chosen to work on have disguised and deflected deeper concerns. Perhaps, for example, the debates about lesbianism and sadomasochism do not have to do with those issues very much at all, but rather with the more profound and general problem of erotic boundaries and our own stake in them. Some of us consider another's touch an act of territorial aggression; others have set the vagina apart. For still others, liberation involves the ability to open gates, to admit penetration, even to pierce the skin. Perhaps the avoidance of difference sprang not solely out of race, class, and heterosexist prejudice, but out of a deeply felt need for merging, for similarity—to no longer be different, be other, but to be we, us, of one prevailing mind.

Many other serious questions beg analysis. Every assumption about sex lies in uncharted terrain: Is there a basic energy source, a primary, early experience of pleasure necessarily connected to sex? Should we define heterosexuality as one sexual mode among many, or is it politically important to identify it as a primary institution of women's oppression? Is monogamy a possibility of sexual liberation or will it wither away, like the state?

Only in rare instances, and almost never in activist circumstances, has the women's movement broached questions of this nature. Rather, we have relied on far cruder models of sexuality than are adequately descriptive or exploratory: the drive model, the repressive model, the male lust model. We have had strategic reasons for simplification, for not questioning ourselves too closely, but now there are more compelling reasons to develop more complex explanations. Adding depth and dimension to the way we speak will go a long way toward moving us beyond the either/or and us/them polarizations that divide feminists from each other and from thousands of other women. Foregoing this complexity and talking about sexual experience as if it were wholly oppressive may make it possible to forge temporary bonds with sexually conservative, fundamentally anti-feminist women, but it will estrange us from women with whom we have much more in common, women who take their pleasure and make their own lives. We write off their pleasure and the pleasures of our own as "false consciousness" at the peril of feminism. We need to expose the hypocrisy of the Right, not invent our own version.

Those who created the modern women's movement could choose sex because it did not carry the same punitive consequences that it carried for previous generations of women, and we *have*, by and large, chosen sex. This is a victory, one both furthered and truncated by historical circumstance but one, certainly, that we grasped for ourselves, not out of false consciousness but out of desire and the impulse for freedom. This is not to imply that sexual violence does not continue to limit and shape our possibilities. But it is to affirm, at the same time, women's potential for autonomy and power. We need to do this at every level of feminism, in grassroots organizing as well as in intellectual work. We are on a long march. Linda Gordon has reminded us that the creation of sexual equality will require literally generations. Elevating one set of sexual practices over others—from whatever position on the feminist spectrum—as more correct, more fulfilling, or even more sexy only retards this process.

Sexual and reproductive politics require somewhat different strategies. At present reproductive politics necessitates constant and focused activism against the anti-abortion movement and the Right. In contrast, beyond the basic issues of civil rights, sexual politics requires feminists to bring our own understanding into consonance with women's contemporary experience. The metaphor of prostitution, as Ellen DuBois and Linda Gordon have pointed out, has held a deep significance for feminists since the nineteenth century; the metaphor of rape has profoundly shaped the twentieth-century understanding of sexual politics. These metaphors continue to illuminate a part of women's experience in this society, but only a part. Intercourse can be rape; it can also be profoundly pleasurable. Sexual experience with men or women can be abusive, objectifying, and degrading, but it can also be ecstatic, inspiring, illuminating. It can also be—and here the inadequacy of a polarized discourse becomes clear—a peculiar mixture of all these things: objectifying and pleasurable, degrading and inspiriting. We must bring together the complexities and contradictions: we must integrate what we know with what we do not want to know.

It is a custom among socialists and feminists to offer up some coherent program of change, or some vision of a sought-for future. We, the editors, are not prepared to do this. Our expectations, at present, are far smaller. Affirming women's sexual expression may be no more than a symbolic indication that we take seriously our daily pleasures. We don't think, as did the nineteenth-century sex radicals, that ending the obsessive and defensive focus on our sexual lives, endemic both to feminism and American culture, will usher in an era of freedom. We think it will help our movement and our condition slightly, free us a bit, make it somewhat easier for us to work together, to perceive our current material situation, to move the dialectic one square forward.

Sexuality is, at the moment, a comparatively open subject in a world dense with domination, despite the forces seeking to close the conversation down. It is an area for play, for experimentation, a place to test what the possibilities might be for an erotic life and a social world that would answer our desires as well as, centuries ago, the nuclear family and monogamy answered the requirements of the emergent bourgeoisie.

Pleasure, Roland Barthes has suggested, makes us "objective."[89] It allows us to lift our eyes for an instant to the horizon to see what might be coming in our direction. Desire is ever renewed—still, in sexual satisfaction, we find moments of rest and vision. This book, we hope, is a contribution toward hastening such moments our way.

Notes

1. Jane Rule, "Sexuality in Literature," in *Outlander: Short Stories and Essays* (Tallahassee, Fla.: Naiad Press Inc., 1981), p. 149.
2. Michel Foucault, *The History of Sexuality*. Vol. I: *An Introduction* (New York: Pantheon, 1978).
3. Ellen Ross, "'The Love Crisis': Couples Advice Books of the Late 1970s," *Signs* 6, no. 1 (Autumn 1980): 110. See also Rosalind Petchesky, "Antiabortion, Antifeminism, and the Rise of the New Right," *Feminist Studies* 7, no. 2 (Summer 1981): 206–46.
4. See Mary Hartman, *Sexual Crackup: A History of Gender Relations in Western Society Since the Late Middle Ages* (New York: Doubleday, forthcoming).
5. See Sigmund Freud, *Three Essays on the Theory of Sexuality*, passim, and particularly "The Transformation of Puberty" (1905; New York: Basic Books, 1962).
6. Jeffrey Weeks, *Sex, Politics, and Society: The Regulation of Sexuality Since 1800* (London and New York: Longmans, 1981), pp. 46, 168. On the Owenites, see also Barbara Taylor, *Eve and the New Jerusalem: Socialism and Feminism in the Nineteenth Century* (New York: Pantheon, 1983).
7. Weeks, *Sex, Politics, and Society*, pp. 168–71. See Woodhull's wonderful speech, "The Elixir of Life," reprinted in *Feminism: The Essential Historical Writings*, ed. Miriam Schneir (New York: Random House, 1972), pp. 152–54, in which she declares that "the problem of sexual love is the most important one that ever engaged the human mind" and denounces the debilitating effects of non-orgasmic sex on women.
8. Friedrich Engels, *The Condition of the Working-Class in England* (Moscow: Progress Publishers, 1973), pp. 186–87.
9. Weeks, *Sex, Politics, and Society*, pp. 168–69.
10. Engels, *The Origin of the Family, Private Property, and the State* (New York: International Publishers, 1970), p. 67.
11. Robert Blatchford to Edward Carpenter, quoted in Weeks, *Sex, Politics, and Society*, p. 171.
12. Linda Gordon, *Woman's Body, Woman's Right: Birth Control in America* (New York: Viking Press, 1977), pp. 84–89.
13. Ibid., pp. 95–96, 107–109, 122–25. Gordon stresses the conservative subtext of free love pronouncements; for the more radical elements, see Ellen Carol Dubois, "Free Love and Feminism in the Nineteenth Century," paper delivered in the Series in the History of Sexuality, State University of New York at Buffalo, March 1983.
14. Emma Goldman, *Anarchism and Other Essays* (1917; New York: Dover, 1969), p. 236. For the radical immigrants, see Mari Jo Buhle, *Women and American Socialism, 1870–1920* (Urbana: University of Illinois Press, 1982), pp. 261–62. For

Goldman's thought on free love, see the chapter on sexual liberationism in Alice Wexler's forthcoming biography of Goldman, to be published by Pantheon in 1984.

15. Buhle, *Women and American Socialism*, p. 61. See also Weeks, *Sex, Politics, and Society*, pp. 171–75.

16. Hutchins Hapgood, quoted in Gordon, *Woman's Body, Woman's Right*, p. 198. For the bohemians of Greenwich Village, see ibid., pp. 186–245, and Buhle, *Women and American Socialism*, pp. 257–68. For a closer look at one important woman in this milieu, see Blanche Wiesen Cook, ed., *Crystal Eastman: On Women and Revolution* (New York: Oxford University Press, 1978).

17. Gordon, *Woman's Body, Woman's Right*, p. 194.

18. Ibid., pp. 206–45; Buhle, *Women and American Socialism*, pp. 268–80.

19. Quoted in Buhle, *Women and American Socialism*, p. 273. On the opposition, see ibid., pp. 273–75, and Gordon, *Woman's Body, Woman's Right*, pp. 236–45.

20. On the ties of the early gay movement to the Left, see John D'Emilio, "Dreams Deferred: The Early American Homophile Movement," *The Body Politic*, issues 48–50 (November 1978–February 1979). We thank Evelyn Cohen for her comments about sexual mores within the Communist Party.

21. Sara Evans, *Personal Politics: The Roots of Women's Liberation in the Civil Rights Movement and the New Left* (New York: Random House, 1979), p. 79. For a general discussion of interracial sexual relations, see pp. 77–82.

22. Jean Wiley, quoted in ibid., p. 81.

23. Marge Piercy, "The Grand Coolie Damn," reprinted in *Sisterhood Is Powerful*, ed. Robin Morgan (New York: Vintage Books, 1970), pp. 421–38.

24. *In These Times*, 28 February–6 March 1979; see also responses in the issues for 18–25 April and 2–8 May.

25. Important exceptions to this general tendency were Victoria Woodhull and Elizabeth Cady Stanton. See Dubois' discussion of Stanton's sex radicalism in Ellen Dubois, ed., *Elizabeth Cady Stanton/Susan B. Anthony: Correspondence, Writings, Speeches* (New York: Schocken, 1981), pp. 94–97.

26. There were again exceptions, although they tended to work at the edges of the organized women's movement: Frances Wright and later Woodhull and Mary Gove Nichols.

27. Catharine Beecher, *Letters to the People on Health and Happiness* (New York: Harper & Bros., 1855). On the issue of prostitution in the antebellum period, see Carroll Smith-Rosenberg, "Beauty, the Beast, and the Militant Woman: A Case Study in Sex Roles and Social Stress in Jacksonian America," *American Quarterly* 23 (October 1971): 562–84.

28. Buhle, *Women and American Socialism*, pp. 249–57; Gordon, *Women's Body, Women's Right*, pp. 116–35.

29. Gordon, ibid., pp. 95–115.

30. Carroll Smith-Rosenberg, "The Female World of Love and Ritual," *Signs* 5, no. 1 (Autumn 1975): 1–29. For a persuasive argument about how, in the late nineteenth century, the discourse about New Women may have implicitly turned on issues of lesbianism, see Esther Newton and Carroll Smith-Rosenberg, "The Mythic Lesbian and the New Woman: Power, Sexuality, and Legitimacy," paper delivered at the Berkshire Conference of Women Historians, June 1981.

31. Lillian Faderman, *Surpassing the Love of Men* (New York: William Morrow, 1981).

32. Addams, quoted in Mary P. Ryan, *Womanhood in America*, 2nd ed. (New York: Franklin Watts, 1979), p. 152.

33. Marynia F. Farnham, M.D. and Ferdinand Lundberg, *Modern Woman: The Lost Sex* (New York: Harper Bros., 1947).

34. Lionel Trilling, "Kinsey Denied," in *The American Sexual Dilemma*, ed. William L. O'Neill (New York: Holt, Rinehart and Winston, 1972), pp. 71–82.

35. See, for example, Evans, *Personal Politics*.

36. Alix Kates Shulman, "Sex and Power: Sexual Bases of Radical Feminism," *Signs* 5, no. 4 (Summer 1980): 590.
37. Private conversation, Harriet Cohen, 1982.
38. Simone de Beauvoir, *The Second Sex* (New York: Alfred A. Knopf, 1953), pp. 175, 347–99.
39. Betty Friedan, *The Feminine Mystique* (New York: Dell Publishing, 1963), pp. 249, 256, 265.
40. Diane Schulder and Florynce Kennedy, *Abortion Rap* (New York: McGraw-Hill, 1971).
41. *Abramowicz* v. *Lefkowitz*, No. 69 Civ. 4469 (S.D.N.Y. 1969).
42. Alix Kates Shulman, *Burning Questions* (New York: Bantam Books, 1978), p. 356.
43. Anne Koedt, "The Myth of the Vaginal Orgasm," in *Notes from the Second Year: Women's Liberation* (New York: Radical Feminism, 1970), reprinted in *Voices from Women's Liberation*, ed. Leslie B. Tanner (New York: New American Library, 1970), pp. 157–65; Mary Jane Sherfey, M.D., *The Nature and Evolution of Female Sexuality* (New York, Vintage Books, 1973).
44. Betty Dodson, *Liberating Masturbation: A Meditation on Self Love* (New York: Bodysex Designs, 1974).
45. See, for example, Ti-Grace Atkinson, *Amazon Odyssey* (New York: Link Books, 1974) and Dana Densmore, "On Celibacy," *No More Fun and Games* (1969).
46. Gayle Rubin, "The Leather Menace: Comments on Politics and S/M," in *Coming to Power* (Berkeley, Calif.: Samois, 1981), pp. 214–16.
47. Private communication, Ann Snitow, 1982.
48. Private conversations, Harriet Cohen, 1982.
49. Alice Walker, "Advancing Luna and Ida B. Wells," in *Midnight Birds*, ed. Mary Helen Washington (Garden City, N.Y.: Doubleday/Anchor, 1980).
50. Private conversation, Susan Lowes, 1982.
51. Kate Millet, *Sexual Politics* (Garden City, N.Y.: Doubleday, 1970).
52. Shulamith Firestone, *The Dialectic of Sex: The Case for Feminist Revolution*, rev. ed. (New York: Bantam Books, 1970).
53. By lesbian-feminist ideology we mean that synthesis of feminist ideas with the lesbian sexual possibility that described lesbianism as a feminist political choice.
54. Private communication, Ann Snitow, 1982.
55. For more detailed histories of lesbianism in this period see, for example, Sidney Abbott and Barbara Love, *Sappho Was a Right-On Woman* (New York: Stein and Day, 1972), pp. 107–34; Toby Marotta, *The Politics of Homosexuality* (Boston: Houghton Mifflin, 1981), pp. 231–47; Del Martin and Phyllis Lyon, *Lesbian/Woman* (New York, Bantam Books, 1972), pp. 238–302.
56. Atkinson, as cited in Marotta, *Homosexuality*, p. 258.
57. The connection between secrecy and eroticism is elaborated in the works of Sigmund Freud, Robert Stoller, and Georges Bataille. In "I Have Four Coming Out Stories to Tell," Susan Madden suggests that there are "some advantages to this highly private mode of coming out. One has the time and the emotional space to allow love to grow in its own way. It can be its own justification" (*the coming out stories*, ed. Julia Penelope Stanley and Susan J. Wolfe [Watertown, Mass.: Persephone Press, 1980], and in *Nightwood* Djuna Barnes writes of Robin Vote, "Two spirits were working in her, love and anonymity." The points made here, however, are not made elsewhere in precisely this combination to our knowledge; they are drawn from "Cally," an unpublished ms. by Sharon Thompson. Post-feminist and lesbian liberation literature has naturally focused on the advantages of publicity rather than the hidden eroticism of the secret and taboo. It is only recently, in any case, that pre-feminist lesbians have begun to repossess the past and to integrate it with the present.
58. See, for example, Elly Bulkin, "An Old Dyke's Tale: An Interview with Doris

Lunden," *Conditions: six* (1980): 26–44; Joan Nestle, "Butch-Fem Relationships," *Heresies #12* 3, no. 4 (1981), "Sex Issue," pp. 21–24; Hollibaugh and Moraga in this volume; and Abbott and Love, *Sappho*, p. 176.

59. Pat Shea, "Bloodroot: Four Views of One Women's Business," *Heresies #7* 2, no. 3 (Spring 1979), 69.

60. "Readers Respond," *Ladder* 15 (October– November 1970).

61. With the increasing political and sexual conservatism of the 1980s, this fear has revived.

62. See, for example, Atkinson, *Amazon*, p. 132.

63. For the history of the NOW lesbian purge, see Abbott and Love, *Sappho*, pp. 107–34.

64. Private conversation, Esther Newton, 1982.

65. "The Woman-Identified Woman," in Radicalesbians, *Out of the Closet: Voices of Gay Liberation*, eds. Karla Jay and Allen Young (New York: Pyramid Books, 1972), pp. 172–177.

66. Marotta, *Homosexuality*, p. 114.

67. "The Woman-Identified Woman," *Closets*, p. 172.

68. Miriam G. Keiffer, "Coming In, or Will the Real Lesbian Please Stand Up?" in *coming out stories*, p. 208.

69. Ibid.

70. Keiffer, "Coming In," p. 210.

71. To be fair, the manifesto did not entirely beg the sexual question, but included a seductive though circuitous come-on to straight women in its claim that love was a power of positive thinking: that women who gave a primal commitment to other women, including sexual love, would lose "the sense of alienation" and "achieve maximum autonomy in human expression."

72. Judith Katz, "This Is About How Lesbians Capture Straight Women and Have Their Way With Them," in *coming out stories*, pp. 168–75.

73. Barbara Smith in "Across the Kitchen Table: A Sister-to-Sister Dialogue," by Barbara Smith and Beverly Smith, in *This Bridge Called My Back: Writings by Radical Women of Color*, ed. Cherríe Moraga and Gloria Anzaldúa (Watertown, Mass.: Persephone Press, 1981), p. 124.

74. Cheryl Clarke, "Lesbianism: An Act of Resistance," in ibid., p. 134.

75. Smith, "Across the Kitchen Table," pp. 120–23.

76. Pat Suncircle, "Mariam," in *Lesbian Fiction*, ed. Elly Bulkin (Watertown, Mass.: Persephone Press, 1981), p. 100.

77. Marotta, *Homosexuality*, p. 333.

78. The Boston Women's Health Book Collective, *Our Bodies, Ourselves*, 2nd ed., rev. (New York: Simon and Schuster, 1971), pp. 39, 40, 47.

79. *Roe v. Wade*, 410 U.S. 113 (1973).

80. Juliet Mitchell, *Psychoanalysis and Feminism* (New York: Random House, 1974).

81. Dorothy Dinnerstein, *The Mermaid and the Minotaur: Sexual Arrangements and Human Malaise* (New York: Harper and Row, 1977).

82. Nancy Chodorow, *The Reproduction of Mothering: Psychoanalysis and the Sociology of Gender* (Berkeley and Los Angeles: University of California Press, 1978).

83. Gayle Rubin, "The Traffic in Women: Notes on the 'Political Economy' of Sex" in *Toward an Anthropology of Women*, ed. Rayna R. Reiter (New York: Monthly Review Press, 1975), pp. 157–210.

84. See, for example, Rosalind Pollack Petchesky, "Reproductive Freedom: Beyond 'a Woman's Right to Choose,'" *Signs* 5, no. 4 (Summer 1980): 661–85.

85. *Heresies #12*, 3, no. 4 (1981), "Sex Issue."

86. Carole S. Vance, "Concept Paper: Toward a Politics of Sexuality," in Hannah Alderfer, Beth Jaker, Marybeth Nelson, *Diary of a Conference on Sexuality*, record of the

planning committee of the Conference, *The Scholar and the Feminist IX: Toward a Politics of Sexuality*, April 24, 1982, p. 40.

87. Sylvia Watts Vitale, "A Herstorical Look at Some Aspects of Black Sexuality," *Heresies #12* 3, no. 4 (1981), p. 65.

88. For related discussions of the mother-daughter dyad, see, for example, Paula Webster and Lucy Gilbert, *Bound by Love: The Sweet Trap of Daughterhood* (Boston: Beacon Press, 1982), and Helle Thorning, "The Mother-Daughter Relationship and Sexual Ambivalence," *Heresies #12* 3, no. 4 (1981): 3–6.

89. Roland Barthes, *The Pleasure of the Text* (New York: Hill and Wang, 1975), p. 32.

Section I
Current Controversies

The battles over abortion of the past several years have contributed greatly to our perception of sexuality as a political issue. Since the early struggles for legalization that culminated in feminist victory in 1973, the women's movement has seen abortion as an essential prerequisite, in a society that offers no entirely effective or safe form of contraception, for women's sexual autonomy.

While liberals have often viewed the abortion battle as one for civil rights, radical feminists like Ellen Willis and Deirdre English have insisted on its sexual dimension. The right-wing attack on abortion, they argue, is a key element in its offensive against all forms of sexuality outside the nuclear family and, more generally, against the liberation of women from the constraints of that family. This analysis has proved increasingly correct, as the New Right has declared its opposition to homosexuality and teenage sexuality and affirmed the "natural" fit between women's nature, homemaking, and motherhood.

In general, however, as Ellen Willis has shown elsewhere, the Right-to-Life movement seeks to enforce the idea that sex itself is bad and sinful, a human frailty that becomes permissible to indulge only when hedged in by law and custom. For the men and women of the New Right, sex is moral only when it is linked to reproduction or the possibility thereof; they therefore seek to reforge the connection between sex and procreation as best they can. If the illegalization of all contraception seems improbable in the late twentieth-century United States, it is nonetheless a goal for which the Right-to-Life movement strives. The denial of abortion, then, is ultimately not about preserving fetuses, but about handing women their just deserts: pregnancy is the punishment for sexually autonomous women.

If the fight for legal and accessible abortion has united feminists of different persuasions, then the anti-pornography campaign has revealed the extent of their differences. Members of groups like Women Against Pornography see their struggle as a powerful challenge to violence against women, a feminist offensive to "take back the night," to liberate social space from misogynist terror. Critics of the movement, like Ellen Willis, take it to task for its sensationalism, moralism, and emphasis on female sexual victimization. They challenge the veracity of its fundamental proposition that there is a demonstrable relationship between pornography and violence against women. Opponents are also troubled by the extent to which the aims of the anti-pornography crusade have converged with those of the Right. There is, they argue, a dangerous proximity between feminist concerns about obscenity and repressive legislation against sexually explicit literature and behavior, a possible convergence that, as Judith Walkowitz shows here, did historically occur in the feminist-inspired social purity movement at the turn of the century.

In the end, however, the pornography issue has stirred up so much controversy in feminist circles because the very intellectual foundations of the women's movement are at stake. Are men's and women's sexual natures quintessentially different? Those feminists generally associated with the anti-pornography campaign, Alice Echols argues, would logically answer in the affirmative, positing maleness and femaleness as essential psychic qualities based in biology. Conversely, critics of the anti-pornography movement are characterized not only by their sexual libertarianism but by a skeptical attitude to the question of sexual identity, arguing that differences between the sexes are not dichotomous and constant but arbitrary, relative, and subject to change. Is it only men who prefer and perpetuate pornography, who enjoy its imagery of subordination, domination, extreme sexual excitement, and promiscuity, or who are interested in sexual expression that includes aggression and penetration? Are such pleasures inherently violent and misogynist? Joan Nestle is among those who testify as to how very different female sexuality can be from the images of victimized womanhood that anti-porn activists present.

Despite our own strong disagreements with those whom Echols terms cultural feminists, we believe that the issues of sexual violence they have raised are crucial to consider. Walkowitz articulates the dilemma: How can we devise an effective strategy to combat sexual violence and humiliation in our society, where violent misogyny seems so deeply rooted and where the media continues to amplify the terror of male violence? This strategy, however, must stem from a more complex understanding of the symbiosis between pornography and the female outrage it engenders. If we cannot get beyond the dichotomies that pornography itself posits—women are brutalized, men are brutal—we can hardly find a third way to women's sexual freedom.

Male Vice and Female Virtue: Feminism and the Politics of Prostitution in Nineteenth-Century Britain

Judith R. Walkowitz

> *Phil Donahue:* You're not fearful of being looked down upon as a bunch of old-fashioned fuddy-duddies who don't understand our Constitution and the First Amendment?
>
> *Susan Brownmiller:* Well, we know we're not old-fashioned fuddy-duddies. We're radical feminists so I don't think they can accuse us of being old-fashioned; some people think we're too new fashioned.
>
> *Donahue:* But you understand—
>
> *Brownmiller:* —I think that words like purity, morality, and decency are very nice words. I wish that the women's movement would reclaim those words.[1]

Brownmiller's disclaimer aside, the radical feminist attack on commercial sex is old-fashioned; it has its roots in earlier feminist campaigns against male vice and the double standard. In this essay I will outline some of the historical precedents for the current feminist attack on commercial sex, as represented by the Women Against Pornography campaign.[2] Past generations of feminists attacked prostitution, pornograpy, white slavery, and homosexuality as manifestations of undifferentiated male lust. These campaigns were brilliant organizing drives that stimulated grass-roots organizations and mobilized women not previously brought into the political arena. The vitality of the woman's suffrage movement of the late nineteenth and early twentieth centuries cannot be understood without reference to the revivalistic quality of these anti-vice campaigns, which often ran parallel with the struggle for the vote. By demanding women's right to protect their own persons against male sexual abuse and ultimately extending their critique of sexual violence to the "private" sphere of the family, they achieved some permanent gains for women.

Nonetheless, judging by the goals stated by feminists themselves— to protect and empower women—these campaigns were often self- defeating. A libertarian defense of prostitutes found no place in the social purity struggle; all too often prostitutes were objects of purity attack. Feminists started a discourse on sex, mobilized an offensive against male vice, but they lost control of the movement as it diversified. In part this outcome was the result of certain contradic- tions in these feminists' attitudes; in part it reflected their impotence in their effort to reshape the world according to their own image.

In Great Britain explicitly feminist moral crusades against male vice began with a struggle against state regulation of prostitution.[3] Parlia- ment passed the first of three statutes providing for the sanitary inspec- tion of prostitutes in specific military depots in southern England and Ireland in 1864. Initially this first Contagious Diseases Act, as it was obliquely entitled, aroused little attention inside or outside of govern- mental circles. Public opposition to regulation did, however, surface in the 1870s, when a coalition of middle-class evangelicals, feminists, and radical workingmen challenged the acts as immoral and unconstitu- tional, and called for their repeal. The participation of middle-class women in these repeal efforts shocked many contemporary observers, who regarded this female rebellion as a disturbing sign of the times. The suffrage movement was in its infancy, and respectable commen- tators looked on with horror and fascination as middle-class ladies mounted public platforms across the country to denounce the acts as a "sacrifice of female liberties" to the "slavery of men's lust" and to describe in minute detail the "instrumental rape" of the internal exam.[4] One troubled member of Parliament was moved to remark to Josephine Butler, the feminist repeal leader, "We know how to man- age any other opposition in the House or in the country, but this is very awkward for us—this revolt of women. It is quite a new thing; what are we to do with such an opposition as this?"[5]

Under the leadership of Josephine Butler, the Ladies National Asso- ciation (LNA) was founded in late 1869 as a separatist feminist organi- zation. A "Ladies Manifesto" was issued, which denounced the acts as a blatant example of class and sex discrimination. The manifesto further argued that the acts not only deprived poor women of their constitu- tional rights and forced them to submit to a degrading internal exami- nation, but also officially sanctioned a double standard of sexual morality, which justified male sexual access to a class of "fallen" women yet penalized women for engaging in the same vice as men.[6]

The campaign drew thousands of women into the political arena for the first time, by encouraging them to challenge male centers of power—such as the police, Parliament, and the medical and military establishments—that were implicated in the administration of the acts. Rallying to the defense of members of their own sex, these women opposed the sexual and political prerogatives of men. They rejected the prevailing social view of "fallen women" as pollutants of men and depicted them instead as victims of male pollution, as women who had been invaded by men's bodies, men's laws, and by that "steel penis," the speculum.[7] This entailed a powerful identification with the fate of registered prostitutes.

Mid-Victorian feminists treated prostitution as the result of the artificial constraints placed on women's social and economic activity: inadequate wages and restrictions of women's industrial employment forced some women onto the streets, where they took up the "best paid industry"—prostitution.[8] They also saw prostitution as a paradigm for the female condition, a symbol of women's powerlessness and sexual victimization.[9] Feminists realized that the popular sentimentalization of "female influence" and motherhood only thinly masked an older contempt and distrust for women, as "The Sex," as sexual objects to be bought and sold by men.[10] The treatment of prostitutes under the acts epitomized this more pervasive and underlying misogyny. "Sirs," declared Butler, "you cannot hold us in honour so long as you drag our sisters in the mire. As you are unjust and cruel to them, you will become unjust and cruel to us."[11]

As "mothers" and "sisters," feminists asserted their right to defend prostitutes, thereby invoking two different kinds of authority relationships. A mother's right to defend "daughters" was only partially an extension and continuation of women's traditional role within the family. It was also a political device, aimed at subverting and superceding patriarchal authority: it gave mothers, not fathers, the right to control sexual access to the daughters, sanctioning an authority relationship between older middle-class women and young working-class women that was hierarchical and custodial as well as caring and protective. In other contexts, feminist repealers approached prostitutes on a more egalitarian basis, as sisters, albeit fallen ones, whose individual rights deserved to be respected and who, if they sold their bodies on the streets, had the right to do so unmolested by the police.[12]

This was the radical message of the repeal campaign. It was linked to an enlightened view of prostitution as an irregular and temporary livelihood for adult working-class women.[13] The regulation system, feminists argued, not prostitution per se doomed inscribed women to a life of sin by publicly stigmatizing them and preventing them from finding alternative respectable employment. "Among the poor," declared Josephine Butler, the "boundary lines between the virtuous and the vicious" were "gradually and imperceptibly shaded off" so that it was "impossible to affix a distinct name and infallibly assign" prostitutes to an outcast category.[14] In fact, the young women brought under the acts lived as part of a distinct female subgroup in common lodging houses, among a heterogeneous community of the casual laboring poor. They were both victims and survivors. They were "unskilled daughters of the unskilled classes,"[15] and their lives were a piece with the lives of the large body of laboring women who had to eke out a precarious living in the urban job market. For these women, sexual coercion was but one form of exploitation to which they were subjected. But prostitutes were not simply victims of male sexual abuse: they could act in their own defense, both individually and collectively. Prostitution itself often constituted a "refuge from uneasy circumstances"[16] for young women who had to live outside the family and who had to choose among a series of unpleasant alternatives.

Through their agitation, feminist repealers established a political arena that made it possible for prostitutes to resist, "to show the officers," in the words of one registered woman, "that we have some respect for our own person."[17] LNA leaders and their agents descended on subjected districts like Plymouth and Southampton, agitated among registered prostitutes, and tried to persuade them to resist the regulation system. Feminists knew they were dealing with an ambiguous social underground—with lodging-house keepers who made profits out of renting rooms to prostitutes and with "fallen" women who would "rise" again.

On the whole, the discussion of voluntary prostitution received far less publicity than exposés of innocent girls forced down into the ranks of prostitution by the "spy police."[18] Feminist leaders used sensational stories of false entrapment or instrumental rape to appeal to all supporters of repeal—to working-class radicals and middle-class evangelicals alike. These accounts depicted registered women as innocent victims of male lust and medical and police tyranny—appropriate objects of solicitude, even for middle-class moralists who chiefly condemned the acts for making "vice" safe.[19] Furthermore, feminist propaganda was still constrained by an extremely limited vocabulary—constructed around the theme of female victimization. Defenses of prostitutes as women who were not yet "dead to shame," who still had "womanly modesty," were common.[20] By mystifying prostitution and women's move into it, this propaganda imperfectly educated the LNA rank and file on the "politics of prostitution."

A politics of motherhood also structured the cross-class alliance between feminists and radical workingmen within the repeal camp. As mothers, LNA leaders called on the sons of the people to join with them in a servile rebellion against the evil fathers, clearly presuming that their working-class allies would follow their political lead. "Our working men . . . are not unwilling to follow the gentle guidance of a grave and educated lady" or to "devote the whole influence of their vote . . . when the right chord in their hearts and consciences is touched by a delicate hand."[21] Ironically, feminists encouraged workingmen to assume a custodial role toward "their" women and frequently reminded them of their patriarchal responsibilities as defenders of the family. One LNA poster, for instance, warned "Working Men!" to "Look to the protection of your wives and daughters. They are at the mercy of the police where these Acts are in force."[22]

Propaganda of this sort aroused popular indignation against regulation, but it also buttressed a patriarchal stance and a sexual hierarchy within the organized working class that feminists had vigorously challenged in other contexts. At the same time that Butler and her friends were trying to build bridges with the organized working class, they had to struggle with their new allies over proposals to restrict female employment. To feminists, a defense of free female labor and an attack on the slavery of prostitution were part of the same work, but working-class leaders saw it otherwise. They countered libertarian and feminist arguments against protective legislation with a defense of the "family wage" and with the view that prostitution resulted not from female unemployment but from the immiseration of the working-class family when adult male labor had to compete with the cheap labor of women and children.[23] Feminists knew they were treading on dangerous ground here. Despite her strong feelings against protective legislation, Butler hesitated to press the point at the annual meeting of the Trades Union Congress. "I think it might be wise for us not to raise the question of the restrictions on female labour in the Trades Congress, this year. . . . It is such a serious question for the future, that we must try to avoid that awful thing—a real breach between women and workingmen."[24]

LNA leaders did not entirely ignore their female constituency in the working class, but they tended to see working women principally as objects of concern rather than as active participants in the struggle. Although working-class women attended LNA lectures in great numbers and loudly voiced their indignation against "those blackguard Acts,"[25] they were not effectively organized into their own repeal associations.[26] In part this failure was due to the indifferent organizing efforts and elitism of the LNA, in part to the practical difficulty of organizing working-class women at that historical moment, given their economic dependence and exclusion from political culture.[27]

Although capable of enunciating a radical critique of prostitution, feminist repealers still felt ambivalent about prostitutes as women who manipulated their sexuality as a commodity. And although they had joined with radical workingmen in an attack against elite male privilege, this cross-class, cross-gender alliance was fraught with contradictions. By and large these anxieties and contradictions remained submerged during the libertarian struggle against state regulation, but they soon surfaced in the more repressive campaign against white slavery.

After the suspension of the acts in 1883, Butler and her circle turned their attention to the agitation against the foreign "traffic in women" and the entrapment of children into prostitution in London. When Parliament refused to pass a bill raising the age of consent and punishing traffickers in vice, Butler and Catherine Booth of the Salvation Army approached W. T. Stead of the *Pall Mall Gazette* for assistance. The result was the "Maiden Tribute of Modern Babylon," published in the summer of 1885.[28]

The "Maiden Tribute" was one of the most successful pieces of scandal journalism published in Britain in the nineteenth century. By using sexual scandal to sell newspapers to a middle-class and working-class readership, Stead ushered in a new era of tabloid sensationalism and cross-class prurience. New typographical and journalist techniques were introduced to sell an old story, the seduction of poor girls by vicious aristocrats, one of the most popular themes of nineteenth-century melodrama, street literature, and women's penny magazines. The "Maiden Tribute" resembled popular fiction and drama in that it contained a criticism of the vicious upper classes; but, as in the case of melodrama, this class criticism was immediately undercut by sentimental moralism, prurient details, and a focus on passive, innocent female victims and individual evil men that diverted attention away from the structural issues related to prostitution.[29]

In lurid detail, the "Maiden Tribute" documented the sale of "five pound" virgins to aristocratic old rakes, graphically describing the way the "daughters of the people" had been "snared, trapped and outraged either when under the influence of drugs or after a prolonged struggle in a locked room."[30] The series had an electrifying effect on public opinion: "By the third installment mobs were rioting at the *Pall Mall Gazette* offices, in an attempt to obtain copies of the paper."[31] An enormous public demonstration was held in Hyde Park (estimated at 250,000) to demand the passage of legislation raising the age of consent for girls from thirteen to sixteen. Reformers of all shades were represented on the dozen or so demonstration platforms. For one brief moment, feminists and personal-rights advocates joined with Anglican bishops and socialists to protest the aristocratic corruption of young innocents.[32]

Recent research delineates the vast discrepancy between lurid journalistic accounts and the reality of prostitution. Evidence of widespread entrapment of British girls in London and abroad is slim. During the 1870s and 1880s officials and reformers uncovered a light traffic in women between Britain and the continent. All but a few of the women enticed into licensed brothels in Antwerp and Brussels had been prostitutes in England. Misled by promises of a life of luxury and ease as part of a glamorous demimonde, they were shocked and horrified at the conditions enforced on them in licensed state brothels, a sharp contrast to what they had experienced in England.

In most cases, then, it was the conditions of commercial sex and not the fact that deeply upset the women.[33] Stead's discussion of child prostitution contained similar misrepresentations and distortions. There undoubtedly were some child prostitutes on the streets of London, Liverpool, and elsewhere; but most of these young girls were not victims of false entrapment, as the vignettes in the "Maiden Tribute" suggest; the girls were on the streets because their other choices were so limited. "Since sexuality in western cultures is so mystified," notes Gayle Rubin, "the wars over it are often fought at oblique angles, aimed at phony targets, conducted with misplaced passions, and are highly, intensely, symbolic."[34] The "Maiden Tribute" episode strikingly illustrates both this mystification and its political consequences. Shifting the cultural image of the prostitute to the innocent child victim encouraged new, more repressive, political initiatives over sex.

Why then did feminist reformers endorse this crusade? Why did they ally with repressive moralists and anti-suffragists who were as anxious to clear the streets of prostitutes as to protect young girls from evil procurers and vicious aristocrats? Like the image of the instrumental violation of registered women under the Contagious Diseases Acts, the story of aristocratic corruption of virgins "generated a sense of outrage with which a wide spectrum of public opinion found itself in sympathy."[35] Feminist repealers undoubtedly believed they could manipulate this popular anger for their own purposes, first to secure the full repeal of the acts (they were finally removed from the statute books in 1886) and then to launch a sustained assault on the double standard. They were also attracted to the radical message in Stead's exposé of aristocratic vice. The disreputable performance of M.P.s during the debates over the age of consent confirmed feminists' worst suspicions about "the vicious upper classes." During the debates, old rakes like Cavendish Bentinck treated prostitution as a necessary and inevitable evil, while others openly defended sexual access to working-class girls as a time-honored prerogative of gentlemen. One member of the House of Lords acknowledged that "very few of their Lordships . . . had not when young men, been guilty of immorality. He hoped they would pause before passing a clause within the range of which their sons might come."[36]

Feminists felt obliged to redress the sexual wrongs done to poor girls by men of a superior class, but they registered the same repugnance and ambivalence toward incorrigible girls as they had earlier toward unrepentant prostitutes. For them as well as for more repressive moralists, the desire to protect young working-class girls masked impulses to control their sexuality, which in turn reflected their desire to impose a social code that stressed female adolescent dependency. This code was more in keeping with middle-class notions of girlhood than with the lived reality of the exposed and unsupervised daughters of the laboring poor who were on the streets. Respectable working-class parents certainly shared many of the same sentiments toward female adolescents. Despite the fact that they often sent their own daughters out to work at thirteen, they nonetheless took pains to restrict their social independence and sexual knowledge and experience.[37]

A subtheme of this feminist discussion was that females of all classes were vulnerable to male sexual violence. "There was no place of absolute safety, neither in streets, nor parks, nor railways, nor in the houses, where the procuresses were often known to enter as charwomen, nor indeed in the very churches and chapels," one speaker announced at a meeting of middle-class women.[38] Although female victimization was a sincere concern of feminists, it also served diverse political interests. Whereas feminists identified the "outlawed political condition of women"[39] as the root cause of the crimes exposed in the "Maiden Tribute," anti-feminists used the occasion to activate men into a new crusade to protect rather than emancipate women—a crusade that was, at times, overtly misogynist. "Let us appeal to their manhood, to their chivalry, to their reverence for their own mothers and sisters—to protect the maidens of the land," declaimed one speaker, who rapidly acknowledged that the objects of such manly solicitude— "those poor, silly, weak children who know not the frightful ruin they are bringing on their lives"—were not worthy of the ideals they had inspired.[40]

What was the outcome of the "Maiden Tribute" affair? The public furor over the "Maiden Tribute" forced the passage of the Criminal Law Amendment Act of 1885, a particularly nasty and pernicious piece of omnibus legislation. The 1885 act raised the age of consent for girls from thirteen to sixteen, but it also gave police far greater summary jurisdiction over poor working-class women and children—a trend that Butler and her circle had always opposed. Finally, it contained a clause making indecent acts between consenting male adults a crime, thus forming the basis of legal prosecution of male homosexuals in Britain until 1967. An anti-aristocratic bias may have prompted the inclusion of this clause (reformers accepted its inclusion but did not themselves propose it), as homosexuality was associated with the corruption of working-class youth by the same upper-class profligates who, on other occasions, were thought to buy the services of young girls.[41]

Despite the public outcry against corrupt aristocrats and international traffickers, the clauses of the new bill were mainly enforced against working-class women, and regulated adult rather than youthful sexual behavior. Between 1890 and 1914, the systematic repression of lodging-house brothels was carried out in almost every major city in Great Britain. In many locales, legal repression dramatically affected the structure and organization of prostitution. Prostitutes were uprooted from their neighborhoods and forced to find lodgings in other areas of the city. Their activity became more covert and furtive. Cut off from any other sustaining relationship, they were forced to rely increasingly on pimps for emotional security as well as protection against legal authorities. Indeed, with the wide prevalence of pimps in the early twentieth century, prostitution shifted from a female- to a male-dominated trade. Further, there now existed a greater number of third parties with a strong interest in prolonging women's stay on the streets. In these and other respects, the 1885 act drove a wedge between prostitutes and the poor working-class community. It effectively destroyed the brothel as a family industry and a center of a specific female subculture, further undermined the social and economic autonomy of prostitutes; and increasingly rendered them social outcasts.[42]

But prostitutes were not the only objects of reformist attacks. In the wake of Stead's "shocking revelations," the National Vigilance Association (NVA) was formed. First organized to ensure the local enforcement of the Criminal Law Amendment Act, NVA soon turned its attention to burning obscene books, attacking music halls, theaters, and nude paintings. It condemned the works of Balzac, Zola, and Rabelais as obscene and successfully prosecuted their British distributors; it attacked birth control literature and advertisements for "female pills" (abortifacient drugs) on the same grounds. To these moral crusaders, "pornographic literature," thus broadly defined, was a vile expression of the same "undifferentiated male lust"[43] that ultimately led to homosexuality and prostitution. The fact that pornography was now available in cheap editions undoubtedly heightened middle-class concern over the emergence of a degenerate and unsupervised urban popular culture.[44]

While the social purity movement served middle-class interests, working-class support for social purity was far from ephemeral; neither before nor after the summer of 1885 was social purity an exclusively middle-class movement. Middle-class evangelicals may have predominated in the National Vigilance Association, but the values of social purity seem to have penetrated certain portions of the working class. By the mid-1880s, Ellice Hopkins, the female pioneer in social purity, had already organized hundreds of male chastity leagues and female rescue societies. Besides counseling working-class mothers on how to avoid incest in their homes, she regularly delivered speeches on purity before meetings of workingmen, and she and others success-fully recruited thousands of respectable workingmen throughout the nation into White Cross armies, which were dedicated to promoting the single standard of chastity and attacking public and private vice. The prescriptive literature distributed by social purity groups also seems to have influenced the childrearing practices of the time. Ed-wardian working-class parents were notable for their strict schedules, puritanical treatment of masturbation, and the severe restrictions they placed on their teenage daughters' social and sexual behavior. Al-though the late-Victorian and Edwardian years represented a "germi-nation" period for the formulation of a "new sexuality," the available facts about sexuality—the general decline in both venereal disease and prostitution, the high age of marriage and low illegitimacy rates, the apparently limited use of contraceptives among the working classes— all these seem to support the hypothesis that "sexual restraint" was indeed "spreading down through society."[45]

But sexual restraint could also serve women's interest. In a culture where women were often the victims of sexual coercion yet blamed for crimes committed against them,[46] and where it was difficult even to conceive of female sexual agency as long as women lacked agency in other vital areas, defenders of women's rights could and did regard the doctrine of female passionlessness and male sexual self-control as a significant advance over traditional assumptions of a dangerous and active female sexuality.[47] One obvious drawback of this sexual strategy was its effect on feminist views on birth control: social purity feminists opposed artificial contraception, precisely because they believed that the separation of reproduction and sexuality would render all women "prostitutes." On the other hand, desexualization resulted in some permanent gains for women: it made it possible for them to name incest and rape as crimes against their person (rather than crimes against the property of men). Most particularly, through the Incest Act of 1908, young women were for the first time offered legal recourse against sexual violence by male family members.[48] By insisting that women had the right to refuse the sexual demands of husbands, and by widely propagandizing this view in the early decades of the twentieth century, feminists within the social purity movement laid the founda-tion for a new egalitarian code of marital relations still to be fully realized in the contemporary era.[49] In feminist hands, desexualization could empower women to attack the customary prerogatives of men; it could also validate a new social role for women outside of the hetero-sexual family. The "New Women" of the late nineteenth century, as

Carroll Smith-Rosenberg and Esther Newton have noted, strove to achieve social autonomy, but at the cost of sexual identity, to legitimize their social and economic independence at the "price of donning the mask of Victorian [sexual] respectability."[50]

Since middle-class women elaborated these ideas, it is hard to know what working-class women thought of them. Laboring women participated in mothers' meetings, and they may have found the moral authority imparted to desexualized women attractive, as it reinforced the power of mothers and female collectivities.[51] In the dense urban neighborhoods of late-Victorian and Edwardian England, where female neighbors shared space and services, and where female relatives sustained the bonds of kinship, social and sexual norms were often articulated at "street level" through hierarchical female networks. The mothers of Plymouth, Lancaster, and Salford, for example, enforced incest taboos, socialized their daughters into a fatalistic and dependent femininity, and increasingly shunned "bad women" (often at the instigation of purity agencies).[52] On the whole, the activities of neighborhood matriarchs sustained social hierarchies and divisions, particularly along generational and sex lines.[53] Female sexual respectability in these neighborhoods was purchased at a high price, with little promise of social independence. The New Woman option was simply not available to working-class daughters: they could not aspire to a future outside of heterosexual domesticity—for working-class women, such a future could only forebode a life of hardship and hopelessness. As a result, the contradictory nature of the power imparted to women through "passionlessness" appears even more apparent for working-class women. To whatever degree such a doctrine mitigated the powerlessness of dependent wives, it left working-class women alienated from and ignorant of their own sexuality and bodies, and unable to control their reproduction—a disabling condition, to judge from the depressing letters collected by the Women's Cooperative Guild in their volume *Maternity*.[54]

Social purity presented workingmen with a different set of implications and opportunities; it could bolster their authority as responsible patriarchs if they were willing to submit themselves to a certain domestic ideology. In general, sexual respectability became the hallmark of the respectable workingman, anxious to distance himself from the "bestiality" of the casual laboring poor at a time when increased pressure was being placed on the respectable working class to break their ties with outcast groups. The social purity movement itself provided an avenue of social mobility for some men, like William Coote, a former compositor who became the national secretary of the National Vigilance Association. Changing employment patterns also seem to have reinforced patriarchal tendencies among skilled sectors of the working class by the end of the century, as the proportion of married women working outside the home declined and the family wage for male workers became an essential demand of trade unions. In this context, social purity—which called on men to protect and control their women—may have served as the ideological corollary of the family wage, morally legitimating the prerogatives of patriarchy inside as well as outside the family.[55]

What was the subsequent relationship between feminism and social purity? Although prominent feminists initially filled many of the committee positions of the National Vigilance Association, this connection was short-lived for Butler and her circle, who resigned when the prurient and repressive direction of NVA became apparent. Throughout the late 1880s and 1890s, Butlerites warned their workers to "beware" of the repressive methods of the social purity societies, which were "ready to accept and endorse any amount of coercive and degrading treatment of their fellow creatures in the fatuous belief that you can oblige human beings to be moral by force."[56] But their warnings were too late. The new social purity movement had passed them by, while absorbing a goodly number of the LNA rank and file.[57]

Moderate suffragists like Millicent Fawcett and Elizabeth Blackwell remained within the ranks of social purity, and feminist purity reformers, most notably Laura Ormiston Chant, were prominent in the attack on theaters and immoral public entertainments. Feminists still maintained a voice within social purity after 1885, but they were in constant danger of being engulfed by those whose positions were far removed from their own. To be sure, feminist repealers had earlier faced a similar dilemma, but the problem of social purity feminists was compounded by the fact that social purity was by no means an explicitly feminist or libertarian cause, and was not dominated by a forceful feminist leader like Josephine Butler. The reactionary implications of social purity, for feminists and prostitutes alike, are illuminated by the public controversy surrounding the Jack the Ripper murders.

In the autumn of 1888, the attention of the "classes" as well as the "masses" was riveted on a series of brutal murders of prostitutes residing in lodging houses in the Whitechapel area of East London.[58] Public response to the murders was widespread and diverse, but the people who mobilized over the murders were almost exclusively male. An army of West End men, fascinated by the murders and bent on hunting the Ripper, invaded the East End.[59] Meanwhile, a half-dozen male vigilance committees were set up in Whitechapel—by Toynbee Hall, by the Jewish community, by the radical and socialist workingmen's clubs.[60] These male patrols were organized to protect women, but they also constituted surveillance of the unrespectable poor, and of low-life women in particular. They were explicitly modeled on existing purity organizations already active in the area that had helped to close down two hundred brothels in the East End in the year before the Ripper murders.[61] As we have seen, the message of social purity to men was mixed: it demanded that men control their own sexuality, but it gave them power to control women's sexuality as well, since it called on them to protect their women and to repress brothels and streetwalkers.

These generalizations are borne out by the Ripper episode, when men ostensibly out to hunt the Ripper often harassed women on the streets; husbands threatened wives with "ripping" them up in their homes; and little boys in working-class Poplar and suburban Tunbridge Wells intimidated and tormented girls by playing at Jack the Ripper.[62] Female vulnerability extended well beyond the "danger zone" of Whitechapel: throughout London respectable women, afraid to venture out alone at night, were effectively placed under "house arrest" and made dependent on male protection. Despite the public outcry against the "male monster" who "stalks the streets of London"[63] in search of fallen women, public attention inevitably reverted to the degraded conditions of the Whitechapel victims themselves. "The degraded and depraved lives of the women," observed Canon Barnett of Toynbee Hall in the *Times,* were more "appalling than the actual murders."[64] Men like Barnett finally manipulated public opinion and consolidated it behind closing down lodging houses where the murdered victims once lived and replacing them with artisan dwellings. Through the surveillance of vigilance committees the murders helped to intensify repressive activities already underway in the Whitechapel area and to hasten the reorganization of prostitution in the East End.[65]

During the Ripper manhunt, feminists were unable to mobilize any counteroffensive against widespread male intimidation of women. Josephine Butler and others did express concern that the uproar over the murders would lead to the repression of brothels and to subsequent homelessness of women; but these were isolated interventions in an overwhelmingly male-dominated debate.

Although some feminists still maintained a national presence in the purity crusade, all in all, by the late 1880s feminists had lost considerable authority in the public discussion over sex to a coalition of male professional experts, conservative churchmen, and social purity advocates. On the other hand, social purity permanently left its imprint on the women's movement through the First World War. Both the sixteen-year campaign against state regulation and sexual scandals such as the "Maiden Tribute" ingrained the theme of the sexual wrongs perpetrated against women by men on later feminist consciousness. After the 1880s, the "women's revolt" became "a revolt that is Puritan and not Bohemian. It is an uprising against the tyranny of organized intemperance, impurity, mammonism, and selfish motives."[66] On the whole this attack on male dominance and male vice involved no positive assertion of female sexuality. Although a small minority of feminists like Olive Schreiner and Stella Browne were deeply interested in the question of female pleasure, they were far removed from the feminist mainstream, where the public discussion of sexuality and male dominance was still couched within the terms of a "separate-sphere" ideology, implying that women were moral, "spiritual" creatures who needed to be protected from animalistic "carnal" men, and demanding, in the words of Christabel Pankhurst, the Edwardian militant suffragist, "votes for women" and "chastity" for men.[67] Moreover, the obsession with male vice again sidetracked early-twentieth-century feminists into another crusade against white slavery (1912), while obscuring the economic basis of prostitution. It even prompted the most progressive women of the day to advocate raising the age of consent to twenty-one. Finally, it led to repressive public policies. Commenting on the enforcement of the White Slavery Act of 1912, Sylvia Pankhurst remarked, "It is a strange thing that the latest Criminal Amendment Act, which was passed ostensibly to protect women, is being used almost exclusively to punish women."[68] As late as 1914, first-wave feminists were rediscovering that the state "protection" of young women usually led to coercive and repressive measures against those same women.

These then are the early historical links between feminism and repressive crusades against prostitution, pornography, and homosexuality. Begun as a libertarian struggle against the state sanction of male vice, the repeal campaign helped to spawn a hydraheaded assault on nonmarital, nonreproductive sexuality. The struggle against state regulation evolved into a movement that used the instruments of the state for repressive purposes. It may be misleading to interpret the effects of these later crusades solely as "blind" repressive attacks on sexuality; in many ways they clarified and identified whole new areas of sexuality. According to Michel Foucault, this elaboration of new sexualities was a strategy for exercising power in society. By ferreting out new areas of illicit sexual activity and sometimes defining them into existence, a new "technology of power" was created that facilitated control over an ever-widening circle of human activity.[69] But power is not simply immanent in society; it is deployed by specific historical agents, who have access to varying sources and levels of power.[70] The reality of a hierarchy of power severely impeded feminists' efforts to use purity crusades to defend and empower women. Through rescue and preventive work, feminists and other women were certainly implicated in the regulation and control of sexuality. But there were others whose access to power was more direct. Rescue work, mothers' meetings, and moral suasion by no means carried the same authority as a morals police under the

Contagious Diseases Acts, male vigilance committees, or an emerging "science of sexuality" controlled by male professionals. The feminist challenge to male sexual prerogatives was a major historic development, one necessary precondition for the ideology of egalitarian heterosexual relations: but when feminists tried to use the powers of the state to protect women, particularly prostitutes who had been the original objects of their pity and concern, they usually came face to face with their own impotence.

What are the moral lessons to these moral crusades? If there is a moral lesson, it is that commercial sex as a locus of sexual violence against women is a hot and dangerous issue for feminists. In their defense of prostitutes and concern to protect women from male sexual aggression, feminists were limited by their own class bias and by their continued adherence to a separate-sphere ideology that stressed women's purity, moral supremacy, and domestic virtues. Moreover, they lacked the cultural and political power to reshape the world according to their own image. Although they tried to set the standards of sexual conduct, they did not control the instruments of state that ultimately enforced these norms. There were times, particularly during the anti-regulationist campaign, when feminists were able to dominate and structure the public discourse on sex and to arouse popular female anger at male sexual license. Yet this anger was easily subverted into repressive campaigns against male vice and sexual variation, controlled by men and conservative interests whose goals were antithetical to the values and ideals of feminism.

Yet this leaves us with a central dilemma: how to devise an effective strategy to combat sexual violence and humiliation in our society, where violent misogyny seems so deeply rooted and where the media continues to amplify the terror of male violence, as it did during the sexual scandals of the 1880s, convincing women that they are helpless victims. We must struggle to live our lives freely, without humiliation and violence. But we have to be aware of the painful contradictions of our sexual strategy, not only for the sex workers who still regard commercial sex as the "best paid industry" available to them, but also for ourselves as feminists. We must take care not to play into the hands of the New Right or the Moral Majority, who are only too delighted to cast women as victims requiring male protection and control, and who desire to turn feminist protest into a politics of repression.[71]

Notes

1. "Phil Donahue Show," July 18, 1979.
2. Writings supporting the Women Against Pornography position are included in *Take Back the Night: Women on Pornography*, ed. Laura Lederer (New York: William Morrow, 1980). Kathleen Barry identifies the British feminist mobilization against state regulation as the first wave of protest leading to the current campaign against

pornography and "sexual slavery." See Kathleen Barry, *Female Sexual Slavery* (Englewood Cliffs, N.J.: Prentice-Hall, 1979), chap. 2. Two useful critiques of Women Against Pornography include Ellen Willis, "Lust Horizons: Is the Women's Movement Pro-Sex?" *Village Voice*, 17 June 1981; Deirdre English, Amber Hollibaugh, and Gayle Rubin, "Talking Sex: A Conversation on Sexuality and Feminism," *Socialist Review* 4 (July-August 1981): 43–62.

3. Edward Bristow, *Vice and Vigilance: Purity Movements in Britain Since 1700* (Dublin, 1977); Deborah Gorham, "The 'Maiden Tribute of Modern Babylon' Reexamined: Child Prostitution and the Idea of Childhood in Late-Victorian England," *Victorian Studies* 21 (Spring 1978): 353–69; Paul McHugh, *Prostitution and Victorian Social Reform* (New York: St. Martin, 1980); Judith R. Walkowitz, *Prostitution and Victorian Society: Women, Class, and the State* (New York: Cambridge University Press, 1980); Jeffrey Weeks, *Sex, Politics, and Society* (London: Longmans, 1981), chap. 5.

4. Mrs. Kell of Southampton, quoted in Walkowitz, *Prostitution*, p. 170; *National League Journal* (London), 1 September 1879.

5. An M.P. to Josephine Butler, quoted in *Josephine Butler: An Autobiographical Memoir*, ed. George W. Johnson and Lucy Johnson (London, 1909), p. 90.

6. "Women's Protest," quoted in Josephine Butler, *Personal Reminiscences of a Great Crusade* (London, 1911), pp. 9, 10; Keith Thomas, "The Double Standard," *Journal of the History of Ideas* 20 (1959): 195–216.

7. Thanks to Martha Vicinus and Carroll Smith-Rosenberg for these perceptions.

8. Josephine Butler to Mary Priestman, 4 May 1874, no. 3327, Butler Collection, Fawcett Library, London.

9. Mary Hume Rothery, *A Letter Addressed to the Right Hon. W. E. Gladstone, M.P., and the Other Members of Her Majesty's Government and of Both Houses of Parliament, Touching the Contagious Diseases Acts of 1866 and 1869, and Their Proposed Extension to the Civil Population* (Manchester, 1870), p. 18. Sally Mitchell notes the changing definition and social identity of the "fallen woman" in women's fiction, from an object of charity in the 1840s and 1850s to a reader substitute in the 1860s. See "Sentiment and Suffering: Women's Recreational Reading in the 1860s," *Victorian Studies* 21 (1977): 29–45.

10. Nancy F. Cott, "Passionlessness: An Interpretation of Victorian Sexual Ideology, 1790–1850," *Signs* 4 (1978): 219–36; Thomas, "Double Standard," pp. 213, 214.

11. Josephine Butler, quoted in Bristow, *Vice and Vigilance*, p. 83.

12. *The Royal Commission as a Court of Justice. Being an Examination of the Declaration that "The Police Are Not Chargeable with Any Abuse of Their Authority"* (London, 1871).

13. Ibid; Judith R. Walkowitz, "The Making of an Outcast Group: Prostitutes and Working Women in Nineteenth-Century Plymouth and Southampton," in *A Widening Sphere: Changing Roles of Victorian Women*, ed. Martha Vicinus (Bloomington, Ill.: University of Illinois Press, 1977), pp. 72–93.

14. Butler, *Moral Reclaimability*.

15. Abraham Flexner, *Prostitution in Europe* (New York, 1914), p. 6.

16. *Downward Paths: An Inquiry into the Causes Which Contribute to the Making of the Prostitute*, with a foreword by A. Maude Royden (London, 1913), p. 48.

17. Registered prostitute to Josephine Butler, quoted in Walkowitz, *Prostitution*, p. 202.

18. Repealers referred to the plainclothes officers of the metropolitan police force, working under the Contagious Diseases Acts, as "spy police."

19. Josephine Butler, *Recollections of George Butler* (Bristol, 1893), pp. 272–77; Reverend Arthur, quoted in *Transactions of the National Association for the Promotion of Social Science* (London, 1869), pp. 448, 449.

20. Josephine Butler, quoted in Walkowitz, *Prostitution*, p. 186.

21. "Seventh Annual Report of the LNA, . . . 1876," *LNA Reports, 1870–1886,* Butler Collection, Fawcett Library, London (Hereafter cited as *LNA Reports*).

22. "Working Men!" LNA poster displayed during the Colchester by-election of 1870, H. J. Wilson Collection, Fawcett Library, London.

23. See the exchange between Robert Applegarth and Josephine Butler, *P.P.* 1871, Q. 13: 114–5. See also Applegarth's speech at "Great Mass Meeting in the Corn Exchange, Leeds," *Shield,* 21 October 1871.

24. Josephine Butler to Mary Priestman, 5 December 1876, Butler Collection.,

25. "Josephine Butler," *Woman's Dreadnought,* 24 October 1914.

26. York was a notable exception. "Twelfth Annual Report . . . of the LNA, 1881," *LNA Reports*.

27. For a fuller discussion, see Walkowitz, *Prostitution,* pp. 143–46.

28. "The Maiden Tribute of Modern Babylon," I, II, III, IV, *Pall Mall Gazette,* 6, 7, 8, 10 July 1885; Gorham "Maiden Tribute," and Bristow, *Vice and Vigilance,* are the best secondary discussions of the scandal.

29. On the New Journalism, see Raymond Williams, *The Long Revolution* (1961; Westport, Conn.: Greenwood Press, 1975), pp. 194–98; Alan J. Lee, *The Origins of the Popular Press, 1855–1914* (London: Rowman, 1976), chap. 4; J. O. Baylen, "The New Journalism in Late-Victorian Britain," *Australian Journal of Politics and History* 18 (1972): 367–85; H. W. Massingham, *The London Daily Press* (London, 1872), pp. 180–84. For popular literature, see Louis James, *Fiction for the Working Man, 1830–1850* (London, 1963), chaps. 2 and 6; Victor E. Neuburg, "The Literature of the Streets," in *The Victorian City: Image and Reality,* ed. H. O. Dyos and Michael Wolff (London: Routledge and Kegan Paul, 1963), pp. 191–210.

30. Gorham, "Maiden Tribute," p. 354.

31. Bristow, *Vice and Vigilance*.

32. For instance, George Bernard Shaw and Olive Schreiner, whose ideas of sexual hygiene and female sexual pleasure were at odds with evangelical moralists, were also drawn into the "Maiden Tribute" agitation. See Ruth First and Ann Scott, *Olive Schreiner* (New York: Schocken, 1980), pp. 155–56; Frederick Whyte, *The Life of W. T. Stead* (London, 1925), vol. 1, p. 175.

33. Gorham, "Maiden Tribute," pp. 376–78.

34. Gayle Rubin, unpublished essay (1981).

35. Gorham, "Maiden Tribute," p. 355.

36. Quoted in ibid., p. 366.

37. Ibid., pp. 372, 373; Walkowitz, *Prostitution,* p. 249. For reformers, "girlhood" was a stage in life marked by dependency but not any specific psychosexual development. Accordingly, debates over the age of consent rarely included reference to the actual sexual development of the girls they were seeking to protect. The age of consent was arbitrary; indeed, many reformers wanted to raise it to eighteen, some to twenty-one. Moreover, many of the same assumptions about protecting and controlling female adolescents ultimately led to the definition and incarceration of sexually active girls as "sex delinquents."

38. "The Crusade Against the Crimes of Modern Babylon," *Pall Mall Gazette,* 23 July 1885.

39. Mary Priestman to the editor, *Pall Mall Gazette,* 23 July 1885.

40. "A Crusade to Men," *Pall Mall Gazette,* 24 July 1885.

41. Jeffrey Weeks, *Coming Out: Homosexual Politics in Britain from the Nineteenth Century to the Present* (London: Quartet, 1977), pp. 18–20.

42. See Walkowitz, *Prostitution,* pp. 210–13.

43. Weeks, *Coming Out,* p. 18.

44. Bristow, *Vice and Vigilance,* p. 201. Similarly, purity reformers were concerned about the pernicious effect of music hall entertainment not only because they deemed many of the acts obscene, but because the acts encouraged workingmen to

emulate the parasitic, licentious life of the "swell." See Peter Bailey, *Leisure and Class in Victorian England: Rational Recreation and the Contest for Control, 1830–1885* (Toronto: University of Toronto Press, 1978), p. 47.

45. Bristow, *Vice and Vigilance*, pp. 103–6; Walkowitz, *Prostitution*, pp. 210–13, 253; Robert Roberts, *The Classic Slum: Slum Life in the First Quarter of the Century* (Bungay, 1971), p. 23, chap. 3; Paul Thompson, *The Edwardians* (Bloomington: Indiana University Press, 1975), chap. 5; Standish Meacham, *A Life Apart: The English Working Class, 1890–1914* (Cambridge, Mass.: Harvard University Press, 1977), pp. 64–67.

46. Susan Edwards, "Sex Crimes in the Nineteenth Century, *New Society* 49 (13 September 1979): 562–63; Anna Clark, "The Language of Rape and Seduction in the Nineteenth Century," unpublished paper, 1981; Jan Lambertz, "Male-Female Violence in late-Victorian and Edwardian England," B.A. diss., Harvard University, 1979. Linda Gordon, commentary on session on "Family Violence," Berkshire Conference on Women's History, Vassar College, May 1981.

47. I am following Nancy Cott's use of the concept of passionlessness to "convey the view that women lacked sexual aggressiveness, that their sexual appetites contributed a minor part . . . to their motivations, that lustfulness was simply uncharacteristic. The concept of passionlessness represented a cluster of ideas about the comparative weight of woman's carnal nature . . ." ("Passionlessness," p. 220).

48. Victor Bailey and Sheila Blackburn, "The Punishment of Incest Act 1908: A Case Study of Law Creation," *Criminal Law Review* (1979): 708–18; Sheila Jeffrys, "The Spinster and Her Enemies: Sexuality and the Last Wave of Feminism," *Scarlet Women* 13 (Pt. 2, July 1981): 23.

49. Ellen Holtzman, "The Pursuit of Married Love: Women's Attitudes toward Sexuality and Marriage in Great Britain, 1918–1939," *Journal of Social History* (XXX 1982); Angus McLaren, *Birth Control in Nineteenth-Century England* (New York: Holmes and Meier, 1978), pp. 198, 199. In the early twentieth century, British social purity groups distributed American purity literature defending women's control over conjugal relations. See, for example, Mary Wood-Allen, *Marriage, Its Duties and Privileges* (New York, 1901), and Sylvanus Stall, *What a Young Husband Should Know* (London, 1907).

50. Carroll Smith-Rosenberg and Esther Newton, "The Mythic Lesbian and the New Woman: Power, Sexuality and Legitimacy," paper presented at Berkshire Conference, May 1981. They argue that although physical and emotional love between "New Women" may have abounded, "loving women" was not described as sexual by the women themselves or by others—and that there was a price to pay for the absence of sexual self-definition. It was only after male sexologists like Havelock Ellis defined the category of the lesbian that women engaging in homoerotic relations were able to react to this negative definition and articulate their own sexual self-definition. For an analysis of homoerotic relations in the late nineteenth century see Martha Vicinus, "One Life to Stand Beside Me: Emotional Conflicts in First-Generation College Women in England," *Feminist Studies* 8, no. 3 (Fall 1982), 603–628.

51. Helen Meller, *Leisure and the Changing City, 1870–1914* (London: Routledge and Kegan Paul, 1976), pp. 133, 139, 174; Mrs. Layton, "Memories of Seventy Years," in *Life as We Have Known It*, ed. Margaret Llewellyn Davies (1931; London, 1975), p. 40.

52. Walkowitz, *Prostitution*, pp. 208–10, 244–45; "Emma Smith" (pseud.), *A Cornish Waif's Tale: An Autobiography* (New York, 1956), chap. 2; Elizabeth Roberts, "Learning and Living: Socialization Outside School," *Oral History* 3 (Autumn 1975): 20–23; Roberts, *Classic Slum*, pp. 22, 23.

53. Meacham, *A Life Apart*, pp. 64–67; Roberts, *Classic Slum*, p. 43.

54. Margaret Llewelyn Davies, *Maternity Letters from Working Women* (1915; London, 1978); "Transcription of Interview of Bertha with Marie Shardeloe and Frances Widdowson," South London Women's History Workshop, 1979.

55. Bristow, *Vice and Vigilance*, p. 118; Gareth Stedman Jones, "Working-Class Culture and Working-Class Politics in London, 1870–1900: Notes on the Remaking of a Working Class," *Journal of Social History* (Summer 1974): 474–79, 485–87; Walkowitz, *Prostitution*, pp. 201–13.

56. Josephine Butler, quoted in Jessie Higson, *The Story of a Beginning* (London, 1955), pp. 35, 36.

57. For recruitment of repealers into social purity, see Walkowitz, *Prostitution*, pp. 239–43; Bristow, *Vice and Vigilance*, pp. 98, 99.

58. Tom Cullen, *Autumn of Terror* (London, 1965); Dan Farson, *Jack the Ripper* (London, 1972); Alexander Kelly, *Jack the Ripper: A Bibliography and Review of the Literature* (London, 1973); Donald Rumbelow, *The Complete Jack the Ripper* (New York: New American Library, 1976); Jerry White, *Rothschild Buildings: Life in an East End Tenement Block 1887–1920* (London: Routledge and Kegan Paul, 1980); Chaim Bermant, *Point of Arrival* (London, 1975), pp. 112–18; Judith R. Walkowitz, "Jack the Ripper and the Myth of Male Violence," *Feminist Studies* 8, no. 3 (Fall 1982): 543–76.

59. *Echo*, 14 September 1888; *Times*, 12 November 1886.

60. *Daily Chronicle*, 15 September 1888; *Daily Telegraph*, 2 October 1888, 4 October 1888; *Daily News*, 9 October 1888.

61. Bristow, *Vice and Vigilance*, pp. 167–69; Henrietta Barnett, *Canon Barnett: His Life, Work and Friends by his Wife* (London, 1921), pp. 305–08. Purity leaders were not entirely pleased with the proliferation of vigilance groups outside their control. On Stead's response, see *Star* leader, 11 September 1888.

62. *Times*, 1 October 1888, 12 November 1888; Elwyn Jones, ed. *Ripper File* (London, 1975), pp. 147, 148; *Echo*, 3 October 1888; *Star*, 10 November 1888; Criminal Court London, vol. 109 (1888–1889): 76–77.

63. *East London Advertiser*, 24 September 1888; *Daily Chronicle*, 10 September 1888.

64. William Barnett to the editor, *Times*, 16 November 1888.

65. White, *Rothschild Buildings*, chap. 1; Walkowitz, *Prostitution*, pp. 210–13.

66. "The New Woman," *Woman's Signal*, 29 November 1894.

67. Christabel Pankhurst, *The Great Scourge and How to End It* (London, 1913).

68. "Protecting Women?" *Woman's Dreadnought*, 19 December 1914.

69. Michel Foucault, *The History of Sexuality*. Vol. 1: *An Introduction*, tr. Robert Hurley (New York: Pantheon, 1978).

70. Thanks to Jeffrey Weeks and Ellen DuBois for this perception.

71. Rosalind Petchesky, "Antiabortion, Antifeminism, and the Rise of the New Right," *Feminist Studies* 5 (1980): 206–46.

The New Feminism of Yin and Yang
Alice Echols

Introduction

> No politics remains innocent of that which it
> contests.
>
> —Elizabeth Fox-Genovese[1]

For any oppressed group it is tempting to seek solace in the reclamation and rehabilitation of that identity which the larger culture has
systematically denigrated. This approach becomes especially compelling when the possibilities for radical structural change seem remote,
and the only alternative seems to be the liberal solution of token representation and assimilation into an oppressive and inegalitarian system.
Unfortunately, as recent feminism has become synonymous with the
reclamation and establishment of a so-called female principle, it has
come to reflect and reproduce dominant cultural assumptions about
women.

This is particularly ironic since early radical feminists, rather than
accept such assumptions about women, had sought the abolition of
gender as a meaningful category: "We believe that the male world as it
now exists is based on the corrupt notion of 'maleness vs. femaleness,'
that the oppression of women is based on this very notion and its
attendant institutions."[2] "Masculinity" and "femininity" were thus
defined as socially constructed rather than biologically determined.
Today's radical feminists, however, are more likely to discuss gender
differences as though they reflect deep truths about the intractability of
maleness and femaleness. Some have argued, for example, that women
are more concerned with ecology and peace and less with sexuality
than men.[3] Women's traditional orientation away from what one feminist terms the "purely sexual" is interpreted as a virtue or an advantage
rather than an emblem of oppression.[4] This preoccupation with
defining the female sensibility not only leads these feminists to indulge
in dangerously erroneous generalizations about women, but to imply
that this identity is innate rather than socially constructed. At best,

there has been a curiously cavalier disregard for whether these differences are biological or cultural in origin. Thus Janice Raymond argues:
"Yet there are differences, and some feminists have come to realize
that those differences are important whether they spring from socialization, from biology, or from the total history of existing as a woman in
a patriarchal society." For Raymond the source of these differences is
irrelevant because as women "we know who *we* are."[5]

To be sure, since the beginning of the women's movement there
have been radical feminists for whom gender is an absolute rather than
a relative category. Valerie Solanas's 1967 *S.C.U.M. Manifesto* is the
earliest articulation of this view.[6] However, it has only been in the past
few years that this perspective has gained legitimacy and achieved
hegemony within the radical feminist movement. This view represents
such a fundamental departure from the early radical feminist vision
that it is important to differentiate the two. I will therefore refer to this
more recent strain of radical feminist as *cultural feminism* because it
equates women's liberation with the development and preservation of
a female counter-culture. The phrase *radical feminism* will be used to
describe the earlier antecedent of this movement.[7] Of course, to maintain that there exists a theoretical coherence to cultural feminism is not
to suggest that it is monolithic.

This essay is intended as a critical examination of cultural feminism.
This movement's belief in a male and a female sexual essence has
disturbing implications for future feminist practice and has already had
deleterious political consequences. After defining the basic characteristics of cultural feminism, I will examine one especially troubling
consequence of this movement, the feminist anti-pornography
crusade.

Defining Cultural Feminism

How does cultural feminism both derive and depart from radical
feminism? Compared with today's cultural feminists, radical feminists
of the late 1960s and early 1970s seem like raging materialists. Some
radical feminists, especially the original Redstockings, stressed the
material basis of patriarchy. For instance, they suggested that a
woman's decision to marry should be interpreted as a rational strategy
rather than confirmation of false consciousness. At the same time, most
radical feminists understood sexism as a primarily psychological dynamic that was manifested in material conditions. Cultural feminism
exaggerates this tendency and subordinates material reality to a supporting role. Andrea Dworkin, for instance, argues that "freedom for
women must begin in the repudiation of our masochism."[8] Thus the
goal of feminism becomes the development of an alternative conscious-

ness, or what Mary Daly terms the "spring into free space."[9] Unlike most radical feminists, cultural feminists assume that individual liberation can be achieved within a patriarchal context. This analysis has the disadvantage of denying agency to those who are "unliberated" or "male-identified" by cultural feminist standards. It can also encourage a dangerously elitist attitude among those who consider themselves "woman-identified." Daly's argument illustrates this problem:

> It is obvious to Hags that few gynecologists recommend to their heterosexual patients the most foolproof of solutions, namely Mister-ectomy. It is women who choose to be agents of be-ing who have pointed out that tried and true, and therefore, taboo, "method." The Spinsters who propose this way by our be-ing, living, speak-ing can do so with power precisely because we are not preoccupied with ways to get off the hook of the heterosexually defined contraceptive dilemma.[10]

In Daly's view heterosexual women are preconscious lesbians who simply need to "choose to be agents of be-ing."

By promoting an overdetermined psychological analysis of gender asymmetry, cultural feminists focus attention away from the structure of male supremacy onto male behavior. Thus Robin Morgan contends that "the Man's competitiveness and greed" are responsible for "sexism, racism . . . hunger, war and ecological disaster."[11] If the source of the world's many problems can be traced to the dominance of the male principle, its solution can be found in the reassertion of the female principle. To make this explanation work, cultural feminists reduce women and men to mere caricatures of themselves. Nowhere is this clearer than in their characterization of male sexuality as compulsive and violent and female sexuality as muted and ethereal. For instance, Kathleen Barry maintains that her mother correctly advised her to beware of the infamous "male sex drive":

> If I allowed a boy to kiss me and one thing led to another, then I would be getting him all excited and he wouldn't be able to control himself. His "thing" would get hard and then he couldn't be expected to stop. I would no longer be a nice girl.[12]

For Barry, as for her mother, it is women's responsibility to tame and restrain the irresponsible and irrepressible beast that is male sexuality.

Even more troubling than this attachment to traditional stereotypes of masculinity and femininity is the growing tendency among some cultural feminists to invoke biological explanations of gender differences. It is ironic to find cultural feminists advancing biological explanations of gender given the energy that radical feminists devoted to refuting biological justifications of gender hierarchy. Such arguments generally attribute patriarchy to the rapaciousness or barrenness of male biology. Thus Susan Brownmiller argues in *Against Our Will* that rape is a function of male biology. According to Brownmiller, male biology is destiny: "By anatomical fiat—the inescapable construction of their genital organs—the human male was a predator and the human female served as his natural prey."[13] For Daly, the "emptiness" of male biology explains male dominance. And, as though this proved her point, Daly cites arch-conservative George Gilder's view that "'while the female body is full of internal potentiality, the male is internally barren.'"[14]

While radical feminists viewed female biology as a liability and thus mirrored the culture's devaluation of the female body, cultural feminists have overreacted to this earlier position by arguing that female biology is in fact a powerful resource.[15] Cultural feminists distinguish between patriarchally conditioned femininity, which they characterize as passive and submissive, and female nature, which they define as nurturant, loving, open, and egalitarian. According to their logic, female passivity is but a conditioned response whereas male violence is a reflection of maleness.

Not all cultural feminists are enthusiastic supporters of biologically based explanations of gender. Both Florence Rush and Andrea Dworkin have expressed their skepticism about this approach. However, for others, like Morgan, the danger lies less in the concept itself than in the control of its application. Morgan warns us against embracing "biological-determination theories . . . until we have enough feminist scientists to right the current imbalance and bias and to create a genuinely value-free science."[16]

Radical feminism departed from both liberal and early socialist feminism by maintaining that individual men do oppress individual women. They argued that although men would benefit ultimately from the dismantling of male supremacy, they would resist changes that would diminish their power and privilege. However, most radical feminists were careful to identify the male role rather than maleness as the problem; men were the enemy only insofar as they identified with their role. As Anne Koedt contended, "Thus the biological male is the oppressor not by virtue of his male biology, but by virtue of his *rationalizing* his *supremacy* on the basis of that biological difference."[17] This distinction, so significant in its implications, has become buried with the rise of cultural feminism. By interpreting masculinity as immutable, the cultural feminist analysis assumes that men are the enemy by virtue of their maleness rather than the power a patriarchal system lends them.

Similarly, cultural feminists argue that the problem with the left is not the inadequacy of its analysis in explaining gender hierarchy, or its continued resistance to feminism, as radical feminists had maintained, but rather that its perspective is irrelevant to women.[18] For cultural feminists, the left, like pornography, is an intrusive and contaminating force that prevents us from fully "dispossessing ourselves" of our patriarchal past.[19] In fact, cultural feminism began to emerge as philosophically distinct from radical feminism in early 1975 with the establishment of the Circle of Support for Jane Alpert. Rather than deny the charge that Alpert had supplied the FBI with information about fellow members of the underground, the Circle rejoiced in her defection from the left and her conversion to feminism.[20]

But it was in the mid-1970s phenomenon of feminist capitalism that cultural feminism really took shape. These early cultural feminists treated capitalism as a relatively benign system that could be enlisted in the struggle to defeat patriarchy.[21] Some even embraced capitalism while repudiating democratic process and rationalized this position by invoking women's superiority and commonality of interests.[22] Those feminists who criticized their attempt to wed capitalism with feminism were characterized as "aping" the "correct-line politics" and "trashing" style of the male left.[23]

Cultural feminists vilify the left because its analysis so completely contravenes their belief system, especially their faith that truly radical change will be achieved only when the culture "returns" to female values and that race and class are merely ancillary to the gender hierarchy. In fact, cultural feminists treat race and class oppression like patriarchal fallout that will be swept away by a women's revolution.

Cultural feminists believe that the degree of dissidence within the women's movement demonstrates, not the diversity of the movement, but the extent to which patriarchy has defiled the mother-daughter bond and, by extension, all relationships between women.[24] They further make feminism synonymous with female bonding and contend that the rehabilitation of the mother-daughter relationship is central to feminism.[25] Their idealization of the mother-daughter relationship may explain why the cultural feminist analysis of incest blames the father while exonerating the mother:[26] if incest is explained as the confluence of male lust and female powerlessness, the cultural feminist fantasy of the idyllic mother-daughter bond can remain intact. For cultural feminists it is perhaps too threatening to acknowledge the extent to which women feel betrayed by one another.

Finally, cultural feminists are committed to preserving rather than annihilating gender distinctions. In *The Transsexual Empire*, Raymond argues that those women who support the integration of male-to-female lesbian transsexuals into lesbian communities "would have us believe that all boundaries are oppressive. Yet if feminists cannot agree on the boundaries of what constitutes femaleness, then what can we hope to agree on?"[27] In contrast with radical feminists, for whom women's oppression derived from the very construction of gender, cultural feminists argue that women's oppression stems from the repression of the female principle.

This difference is, of course, reflected in their respective visions. Radical feminists envisioned an androgynous society as their long-term goal. In the "Bitch Manifesto," Joreen described the rebellious woman, or the "Bitch":

> What is disturbing about a Bitch is that she is androgynous. She incorporates within herself qualities traditionally defined as "masculine" as well as "feminine." A Bitch is blunt, direct, arrogant, at times egoistic. She has no liking for the indirect, subtle, mysterious ways of the "eternal feminine." She disdains the vicarious life deemed natural to women because she wants to live a life of her own.[28]

This rather skewed idea of androgyny seems characteristic of those radical feminists who found "femininity" even less attractive than "masculinity." By contrast, cultural feminists explicitly reject androgyny as a masculinist concept and propose the reclamation of a female principle. Sally Gearhart suggests that

> in the spirituality arena of the women's movement there is the world's most radical political potential, for in its redemption of female values and female epistemology, woman-spirit returns to and begins again with the fundamental female nature of the race.[29]

Of course, many of the values commonly associated with the female or private sphere should be redefined as vital human values. However, cultural feminists encourage us to "maximize female identity" without questioning the extent to which that identity has been conditioned.[30] They correctly assume that mother-daughter conflict has implications for female bonding, but, by attributing this conflict to patriarchy, they encourage us to repress the ambivalence present in any relationship.

Given strong, countervailing theoretical tendencies, how did radical feminism devolve into cultural feminism? The debate around lesbianism and feminism was to a large extent responsible for promoting the assumptions that underlie cultural feminism. The struggle for lesbian visibility and recognition in the early 1970s was extremely important because it forced feminists to acknowledge that sexuality is socially constructed. But the homophobia, and to a lesser extent the anti-sex attitudes within certain elements of the movement, precluded lesbian feminists from promoting lesbianism as a sexual rather than a political choice. Many heterosexual feminists, reflecting larger cultural assumptions, defined and dismissed lesbianism as a solely sexual experience. For instance, Ti-Grace Atkinson cautioned:

> a case could be made that lesbianism, in fact *all* sex, is reactionary, and that feminism is revolutionary. . . . Because lesbianism involves role-playing and more important, because it is based on the

primary assumption of male oppression, that is, sex, lesbianism reinforces the sex class system.[31]

Given the context, it is understandable that many lesbian feminists found it easier to justify their sexuality on exclusively political grounds.

Lesbian recognition was achieved by locating the discussion within the already established framework of separatism.[32] Lesbian separatists such as the Washington D.C. Furies collective argued that heterosexual women were impeding the movement's progress. Rita Mae Brown opined:

> Straight women are confused by men, don't put women first. They betray lesbians and in its deepest form, they betray their own selves. You can't build a strong movement if your sisters are out there fucking with the oppressor.[33]

By defining lesbianism as a political choice, implying the immutability of gender differences, and promoting a sentimental view of female sexuality, lesbian feminists deprived heterosexual feminists of one of their favorite charges against lesbianism—that it was male-identified.[34] However, the assumption that relationships with men are inevitably debilitating while those with women are automatically liberating has had, as we shall see, serious consequences for lesbian sexuality. Furthermore, in establishing lesbianism as a true measure of commitment to feminism, lesbian separatists distorted the meaning of "the personal is political," giving it a prescriptive rather than a descriptive meaning. Of course, the tendency to judge a woman on the basis of her sexual preference, marital status, or hair length did not originate with lesbian separatism, but it was further legitimated by it.

Lesbian separatism's open hostility to heterosexual feminists guaranteed that it would remain a minority view. However, in its reincarnation as cultural feminism, lesbian separatism has been modified and refined in such a way as to make it more acceptable to a wider audience. Whereas lesbian separatists advocated separation from men, cultural feminists advocate separation from male values. And rather than promote lesbianism, cultural feminists encourage woman-bonding and thus avoid estranging heterosexual feminists.

With the rise of cultural feminism, relations between gay and heterosexual feminists have become more cordial. However, the very terms of this reconciliation have ensured that suspicion and acrimony would be preserved, though often below the surface. First, lesbian recognition has been achieved by further abstracting it from the realm of sexuality and cloaking it as female bonding. Lesbian acceptance is contingent upon the extent to which our relationships conform to feminist standards of egalitarianism. Second, heterosexual feminists are still made to feel as though they are the movement's backsliders by virtue of their proximity to contaminating maleness. Occasionally hostility surfaces as it did at the 1979 Women Against Pornography (WAP) conference when a lesbian separatist called Susan Brownmiller a "cocksucker." Brownmiller retaliated by pointing out that her critic "even dresses like a man."[35]

With the anti-pornography movement, cultural feminism has succeeded in mobilizing feminists regardless of sexual preference—not an inconsiderable task. Unfortunately, anti-pornography activists have united feminists by manipulating women's traditional sexual conservatism and appealing to widely held assumptions about male and female sexuality. In advocating a return to a female sexual standard, cultural feminists ignore the extent to which femaleness functions as the complement to maleness and therefore reflects dominant cultural assumptions—assumptions that encourage political expediency. By further treating femaleness as an unalloyed force for good, cultural feminists have tried to accommodate feminism with capitalism and sexual repression. As its brief history demonstrates, cultural feminism degenerates into the view, so eloquently articulated by cultural feminist entrepreneur Laura Brown, that "feminism is anything we say it is."[36]

Sexual Repression: The Case of Women Against Pornography

Take Back the Night, a recent cultural feminist anthology on pornography, opens with this excerpt of an 1853 letter from Elizabeth Cady Stanton to Susan B. Anthony:

> Man in his lust has regulated long enough this whole question of sexual intercourse. Now let the *mother of mankind, whose prerogative it is to set bounds to his indulgence,* rouse up and give this whole matter a thorough, fearless investigation.[37]

One fears this citation is more appropriate than its anthologizer intended. For despite the fact that the historical conditions confronting today's feminists differ significantly from those faced by nineteenth-century women, the current cultural feminist view of sexuality bears a striking similarity to that articulated by activists a century earlier. For the most part, nineteenth-century feminists, many of whom were active in the temperance movement, held conservative views on marriage, the family, and sexuality.

Radical feminists sometimes spoke of sexuality as incompatible with women's freedom, but they were far more likely to identify women's subjugation with the repression of female sexuality.[38] They understood that women's sexual inhibition was related to the lack of accessible and effective contraception, which rendered women sexually vulnerable.

They believed that women's attachment to traditional morality stemmed less from the immutability of female sexuality than from their economic dependence on men. This consciousness was reflected in the radical feminist struggle for abortion and safe, effective contraception. Radical feminists understood, as does the New Right, that the fight for reproductive rights is the struggle for women's sexual freedom and self-determination. As we shall see, cultural feminists, by contrast, argue that sexual freedom and feminism stand in mutual opposition.

The cultural feminist perspective on sexuality has emerged and crystallized only recently with the development of the feminist anti-pornography movement. Women Against Pornography maintains that pornography not only reflects our culture's misogyny, but causes violence against women as well.[39] The avowed purpose of the anti-pornography movement is to enlighten the public about the dangers of pornography. Many women involved in this struggle, including Susan Brownmiller, Andrea Dworkin, Diana Russell, and Kathleen Barry, further recommend some form of censorship to eliminate pornography. While the elimination of violence is crucial, there is reason to be dismayed by the movement's assumption, despite the dearth of solid, confirming evidence, that pornography is a causative factor. And there is reason to be alarmed by its casual attitude toward establishing causality. For instance, Kathleen Barry has cautioned us against getting "bogged down in academic research" and urged us to "rely more on our common sense, our own convictions, and 'what we see in front of us.'"[40]

Fantasy

What are the assumptions that underlie the cultural feminist understanding of sexuality and inform the anti-pornography movement? The argument that "pornography is the theory, rape the practice" represents cultural feminism's contribution to the domino theory of sexuality.[41] It identifies pornography as the scourge that leads inexorably to violence against women.

More recently, anti-pornography activists have extended their critique to encompass fantasy, which they suggest is dangerous because it entails the substitution of an illusion for the "social-sexual reality" of another person. If internalized, pornography compels women to accept dehumanization over personhood. In rejecting as so much "male-identified mind-body dualism" the notion that fantasy is the repository of our ambivalent and conflictual feelings, cultural feminists have developed a highly mechanistic and behavioristic analysis that conflates fantasy with reality and pornography with violence.[42] Such a view assumes that we can and should be held accountable for our fantasies and bedroom exploits. And if we fail to banish those dreaded fantasies, we can console ourselves with Julia Penelope's suggestion that fantasy may be another "phallocentric 'need' from which we are not yet free."[43]

However, cultural feminists' enthusiasm for correlating fantasy with reality wanes considerably when female fantasies are under discussion. Although some seem to attribute women's masochistic fantasies to their masochism, most argue either that they are a patriarchal invention or that they reveal women's powerlessness and socialization rather than their masochism.[44] Of course, men's sadistic fantasies are still seen as confirmation of their fundamentally murderous nature.

Male and Female Sexuality

Cultural feminists define male and female sexuality as though they were polar opposites. Male sexuality is driven, irresponsible, genitally oriented, and potentially lethal. Female sexuality is muted, diffuse, and interpersonally oriented. Men crave power and orgasm, while women seek reciprocity and intimacy. Robin Morgan claims:

> Every woman here knows in her gut the vast differences between her sexuality and that of any patriarchally trained male's—gay or straight . . . that the emphasis on genital sexuality, objectification, promiscuity, emotional noninvolvement, and coarse invulnerability was the *male style*, and that we, as women, placed greater trust in love, sensuality, humor, tenderness, commitment.[45]

Morgan assumes that somehow women's sexuality is not "patriarchally trained."

For cultural feminists, male sexuality is not only compulsive, but, as Dworkin has described it, "the stuff of murder, not love."[46] Thus, for men, sexuality and violence are inextricably linked and find their cultural expression in pornography. Cultural feminists are so convinced that male sexuality is, at its core, lethal that they reduce it to its most alienated and violent expressions. The actions of the Marquis de Sade or Son of Sam come to symbolize the murderousness of male sexuality, and sexual intercourse becomes a mere euphemism for rape.[47] Liberal and leftist men who oppose censorship are characterized as having a prurient interest in pornography, and men's growing interest in their partner's sexual satisfaction is said simply to demonstrate men's obsession with sexual performance. Everything, no matter how contradictory, confirms the premise that male sexuality is selfish, violent, and woman-hating.

By contrast, women's sexuality is assumed to be more spiritual than sexual, and considerably less central to their lives than is sexuality to men's. For instance, Adrienne Rich describes female sexuality as an "energy which is unconfined to any single part of the body or solely to the body itself."[48] And Ethel Person maintains that "many women have

the capacity to abstain from sex without negative psychological consequences." For Person, women's more highly developed "capacity for
abstinence, repression, or suppression [has] adaptive advantages" over
male hypersexuality.[49] Person fails to understand that women's apparent mental health in the face of anorgasmia or abstention testifies to
women's conditioning to subordinate and repress sexual drive. Unfortunately, sexual repression may very well become adaptive for women
once again if the Human Life Amendment and Family Protection Act
become law.[50] Cultural feminism in fact feeds what one feminist has
described as "our society's treasured illusion that male sexuality is like
a bludgeon or a speeding train," and its equally cherished corollary that
women seek affection rather than orgasm in their sexual encounters.[51]

Heterosexuality

It follows from this that cultural feminists would see heterosexuality
as a metaphor for male rapaciousness and female victimization. In
contrast with lesbian feminists, for whom heterosexuality generally
represented collaboration with the enemy, cultural feminists appear to
take a more sympathetic position toward heterosexual women. They
typically regard female heterosexuality as more apparent than real and
maintain that women are coerced into compliance with heterosexual
norms. Adrienne Rich, for instance, cites Barry's *Female Sexual Slavery* as evidence that "for women heterosexuality may not be a 'preference' at all but something that has to be imposed, managed, organized,
propagandized, and maintained by force."[52] Whether female heterosexuality is explained as the result of coercion, heterosexual privilege, or
what Rich terms women's "double-life," the assumption is that, for
women, heterosexuality is neither fully chosen nor pleasurable.[53]

Concomitantly, cultural feminists believe that any expression of tenderness and affection between women demonstrates the real
tenuousness of their heterosexuality. They define lesbianism as
identification and bonding with women, rather than as sexual attraction
to or involvement with women. Thus Rich urges us to view lesbianism
as a continuum because such a model can accommodate "many more
forms of primary intensity between and among women," including the
"intimate girl-friendships of eight- or nine-year olds."[54] Rich's expan-
sive definition of lesbianism completely disregards the attraction of
heterosexuality. Should not any affectional continuum embrace the full
range of erotic and sexual tendencies?

Transsexualism

Nowhere is the cultural feminist reduction of male behavior to
rapaciousness more inappropriate than when applied to male-to-female

transsexuals. The contradiction of transsexualism is that it both reinforces and undermines gender as a significant category. The way in which the medical profession has defined transsexualism has, of course, contributed to the former development. In *The Transsexual Empire,* Janice Raymond, without any apparent sense of contradiction, finds transsexualism dangerous because of both of its countervailing tendencies: it reinforces sex roles and it destroys the boundaries between maleness and femaleness. As the book degenerates into an attack on transsexuals for their "usurpation of female biology," it becomes clear that it is the latter she finds most disturbing.[55] For cultural feminists who lean toward biological determinism, transsexuals are indeed very troubling because, on one level, they do undermine the salience of gender and erase the boundaries between the genders.

Raymond argues that "all transsexuals rape women's bodies by reducing the real female form to an artifact, appropriating this body for themselves."[56] But her real contempt is reserved for those male-to-female lesbian-feminist transsexuals whose "whole presence," according to Daly, "becomes a 'member' invading women's presence and dividing us once more from each other."[57] Raymond maintains that those transsexuals who identify themselves as lesbian feminists simply seek to undo their surgery by pursuing relationships with women in order to become "the man within the woman, and more, within the women's community."[58] Although "he" can very often pass as female, Raymond contends that there are "subtle but perceptible differences" between the behavior of transsexual lesbians and real lesbians: "One specific example of this is the way a transsexual walked into a women's restaurant with his arms around two women, one on each side, with the possessive encompassing that is characteristically masculine."[59]

But, according to Raymond, the lesbian-feminist transsexual is especially dangerous because "he" can seduce us by appealing to our residual heterosexuality.[60] This analysis represents an extreme example of the cultural feminist tendency to impute the most sinister motives possible to all men regardless of the distortion required to do so. Once again, this view presupposes an innate and immutable maleness.

Gay Male Sexuality

For cultural feminists who define women's liberation in opposition to sexual liberation, the tendency of male gay activists to equate gay liberation with sexual freedom has simply confirmed their grim view of male sexuality. They contend that the centrality of public and anonymous sex to the gay male sexual landscape reflects men's sexual callousness. They maintain that the gay male sexual subculture of sadomasochism and cross-generational sex demonstrates male rapacity. Dworkin argues that the current popularity of s/m among gay men and the defense of cross-generational sex by some gay male activists are "testimony to the fixedness of the male compulsion to dominate and destroy that is the source of sexual pleasure for men."[61] Cultural feminists point to the purported absence of cross-generational sex among lesbians to prove that it is an exclusively male practice.[62] Robin Morgan contends that "boy-love is a euphemism for rape regardless of whether or not the victim seems to invite it."[63]

Cultural feminists' hostility toward the gay male sexual fringe reflects in part women's extensive experience with sexual abuse. However, their analysis ignores the realities of gay male life and denies participants' accounts. Many gay men, for instance, report that as boys they frequently engaged in sex with adult men. Moreover, they generally perceived themselves as the instigators of these encounters. Some gay men have suggested that relationships with older gay men offer boys the only real possibility for healthy acculturation into homosexuality. Accounts by s/m practitioners also suggest that the cultural feminist view of s/m bears little resemblance to its practice.[64]

Lesbian Sexuality

It is deeply ironic that some lesbians are in the forefront of a movement that has resurrected terms like "sexual deviance" and "perversion"—terms that one would have thought the feminist movement made anachronistic a decade ago. Lesbian cultural feminists would, however, explain, as does Adrienne Rich, that lesbianism is a "profoundly female experience" that needs to be dissociated from "male homosexual values and allegiances."[65] Their insistence that lesbianism is an issue of "radical female friendship" rather than sexual preference reflects an unwillingness to accept that within the larger culture lesbianism is viewed as a "perversion."[66] For instance, Sally Gearhart stresses the wholesomeness of lesbianism:

In being part of the word "gay" weary lesbians have spent untold hours explaining to Middle America that lesbians do not worry about venereal disease, do not have sex in public bathrooms . . . and do not want to go to the barricades fighting for the lowering of the age of consent.[67]

Even more, lesbian cultural feminists' hostility toward other sexual minorities reflects their fear that male sexuality, as it is symbolized to them in s/m, cross-generational sex, transsexualism, and pornography, will contaminate women's relationships and communities. Thus Rich suggests that pornography impairs the "potential of loving and being loved by women in mutuality and integrity."[68] And Gearhart complains: "I am frustrated and angry that . . . many gay men remain totally oblivious to the effect on women of their objectification of each other, their obsession with youth and beauty, their camped-up consumerism, and their demand for freer sexual expression."[69] Statements such as these betray an apprehension that women's sexuality may not be innately tender and nurturant and that lesbianism may not offer the uncomplicated refuge from what Rita Mae Brown in 1972 termed "the silly, stupid, harmful games that men and women play."[70]

The elusive quest for egalitarian relationships and politically correct sex has encouraged lesbian cultural feminists to deemphasize sex on ideological grounds. This flight from ambivalence inevitably leads to repression because sexuality is too conflict-laden to ever pass a political litmus test. Thus, lesbian cultural feminists have viciously attacked s/m lesbian feminists because they seem to undermine the formers' belief in an ideal lesbian sexuality.

The sexual repressiveness of the lesbian cultural feminists' orthodoxy has engendered the heterophobia that is, in turn, vented in the anti-pornography movement. Perhaps the movement's success in enlisting the support of certain sectors of the lesbian community reflects the extent to which the movement validates lesbianism through its demonization of maleness and heterosexuality. And the suggestion that lesbian transsexuals be excluded from women's communities lest they "seduce" us back into heterosexuality betrays the heterophobia of lesbian cultural feminists.

Sexual Permissiveness

For cultural feminists the proliferation of pornography, the apparent increase in rape and incest, and the growing assertiveness of the sexual fringe testify to the evils of sexual permissiveness. These feminists indict pornography for eroding the traditional boundary separating the virgin from the whore. Morgan argues that pornography has contributed to a "new 'all women are really whores' attitude, thus erasing the last vestige of (even corrupted) respect for women."[71]

However, the real culprit is the sexual revolution, more than its "propaganda" tool, pornography. While most feminists would agree that the ideology of the sexual revolution discriminated against women, cultural feminists go further and maintain that sexual liberation is only a "euphemism for sexual exploitation."[72] They argue that the sexual revolution has been an exclusively male revolution that allowed men to choose "swinging" over commitment, pornographic images over real people, and violence over love. Rich has even characterized the pill as a "mechanical and patriarchal device."[73] According to Barry, who here sounds disturbingly like Phyllis Schlafly, many women have rejected intimacy only to discover that "new problems arose as they escaped from male power into self-centeredness, and as they tried to depersonalize their sexual being."[74] Cultural feminists accuse rampant individualism of discouraging intimacy by encouraging us to become selfishly absorbed in meeting only our own needs.[75] They further suggest that sexual freedom is a conservative force lulling us into political apathy and inaction.[76] Barry even suggests that democracy, in breeding a "pluralistic notion of cultural diversity," in turn encourages a perilous tolerance toward "sexual perversion."[77]

This analysis fails to explain why the Reagan administration is more intent on ushering us back into the sexual repressiveness of the 1950s than in promoting sexual liberation. The equation of sexual freedom with irresponsibility, selfishness, and dehumanization has, in fact, already been used by the New Right in its struggle against feminism, abortion, and gay rights. The cultural feminist analysis further denies the extent to which the early women's movement was a rebellion against traditional sexual morality. By fingering individualism as the enemy, it further ignores the role that individualism played in the emergence of the women's movement. Individualism may be bourgeois, but it is precisely the breakdown of a familial orientation and the development of individualism that gave rise to the feminist movement.[78]

Respect and Repression

Because the sexual revolution is seen as enslaving women by promoting the male sexual values of promiscuity and rapacity, cultural feminists wish to establish a female standard of sexuality. They propose we embrace what they see as their mothers' sexual values. Thus Morgan argues that in repudiating sexual liberation, she is affirming her identification with her mother.[79] And Kathy Barry suggests: "In going into new sexual values we are really going back to the values women have always attached to sexuality, values that have been robbed from us, distorted and destroyed as we have been colonized through both sexual violence and so-called sexual liberation."[80]

The cultural feminist solution to male lasciviousness is the reestablishment of old-fashioned respect, which the sexual revolution has destroyed. This analysis confuses respect with equality and fails to recognize that respect is merely the flip side of violation. More importantly, this view suggests that sexual repression is a satisfactory solution to the real problem of violence against women. Diana Russell has admitted that censorship will not prevent a black market in pornography. However, she reasons that it is better "to have it underground than to see it flourish as an accepted part of our culture."[81]

Why does the leadership of the anti-pornography movement, while recognizing that it cannot eliminate pornography, continue to define it as *the* feminist issue? On one level the anti-pornography movement represents a highly pragmatic attempt to unify a movement that has been seriously divided by the issues of class, race, and sexual preference. The cultural feminists of WAP appeal to women's sense of sexual vulnerability and the resilience of gender stereotypes in their struggle to organize all women into a grand and virtuous sisterhood to combat male lasciviousness. Thus, when Judith Bat-Ada argues that to fight pornography "a coalition of all women needs to be established, regardless of race, color, creed, religion, or *political persuasion*," she abandons feminism for female moral outrage.[82] On a less obvious level, this movement's belief in men's utter depravity suggests that it is concerned with something more than the reformation of male sexuality. To a great extent, the movement's message is directed toward women rather than men. The movement attempts not only to control male sexuality, but to rationalize and control women's sexuality as well. It has become a vehicle to establish the proper parameters of lesbian sexuality so as to diminish the likelihood that lesbians will defect to "male-defined" sexuality, be that heterosexuality or s/m. More generally, the anti-pornography crusade functions as the feminist equivalent of the anti-abortion movement—reinforcing and validating women's traditional sexual conservatism and manipulating women's sense of themselves as the culture's victims and its moral guardians.[83]

Conclusion: The Retreat from Theory into Fantasy

By equating feminism with the so-called reassertion of a female identity and culture, cultural feminism seems to promise an immediate solution to women's powerlessness in the culture at large. Its growth is attributable to the frustrating fragmentation of the women's movement and the erosion of feminist gains in the recent past. Cultural feminism represents a retreat from the difficulties of political struggle into the self-validation that community-building offers. It further substitutes the fantasy of a united sisterhood for political theory.

Unfortunately, it seems that many feminists and leftists have abandoned transformative politics for the familiarity of sexual repression and the nuclear family respectively. For instance, Tom Hayden claims that liberalism failed because it "lost God, the flag, national defense, tax relief, personal safety and traditional family values to conservatives."[84] And Michael Lerner suggests that Americans could be sold on socialism were they to understand its salutory impact on family life.[85]

The years ahead promise to be turbulent. It would be most unfortunate if feminists respond to the likely inhospitality of the 1980s by further retreating into this fantasy of a morally pure sisterhood. Ultimately, cultural feminism offers us little more than the illusion of power and will fail us very badly in the difficult period ahead.

Notes

I want to thank the following individuals for reading and commenting on an earlier draft of this paper: Susan Contratto, Constance Samaras, Kathleen Stewart, Ellen Willis, Marilyn Young, and Patricia Yeghessian. Editing efforts by Sandra Silberstein, Ann Snitow, and Sharon Thompson have improved this essay appreciably.

1. Elizabeth Fox-Genovese, "The Personal Is Not Political Enough," *Marxist Perspectives* 2 (Summer 1979): 94.
2. Bonnie Kreps, "Radical Feminism 1," in *Radical Feminism*, ed. Anne Koedt, Ellen Levine, and Anita Rapone (New York: The New York Times Book Co., 1973), p. 239.
3. Adrienne Rich, Mary Daly, and Susan Griffin are the best known proponents of these views. However, the notion that women's more extensive experience with nurturance makes them natural pacifists is fairly widespread among feminists.
4. Julia Penelope, "And Now For the Hard Questions," *Sinister Wisdom* (Fall 1980): 103.
5. Janice Raymond, *The Transsexual Empire* (Boston: Beacon Press, 1979), p. 114.
6. Valerie Solanas, *S.C.U.M. Manifesto* (New York: Olympia Press, 1970).
7. The *reconstituted* Redstockings, a New York radical feminist group, termed this theoretical tendency "cultural feminism" in their 1975 publication *Feminist Revolution*. Although their critique identified some of the problems with cultural feminism, it was seriously marred by its paranoia and homophobia. More recently, Ellen Willis has critiqued cultural feminism especially as it informs the anti-pornography movement and eco-feminism. See her fine collection of essays, *Beginning to See the Light* (New York: Knopf, 1981) and her *Village Voice* articles. Major cultural feminist texts include: Adrienne Rich, *Of Woman Born* (New York: W. W. Norton, 1976); Mary Daly, *Gyn/Ecology* (Boston: Beacon Press, 1978); Janice Raymond, *The Transsexual Empire* (Boston: Beacon Press, 1979); Kathleen Barry, *Female Sexual Slavery* (Englewood Cliffs, N.J.: Prentice-Hall, 1979). The now defunct Los Angeles-based magazine *Chrysalis* has also served as a major outlet for cultural feminist work since its founding by Susan Rennie and Kirsten Grimstad in 1977. The best single radical feminist anthology is Koedt, Levine, and Rapone, *Radical Feminism*. Also see Shulamith Firestone, *The Dialectic of Sex* (New York: Morrow, 1970).
8. Andrea Dworkin, *Our Blood* (New York: Harper and Row, 1976), p. 111.
9. Daly, *Gyn/Ecology*, p. 12.
10. Ibid., p. 239.
11. Robin Morgan, *Going Too Far* (New York: Random House, 1978), p. 93.
12. Barry, *Female Sexual Slavery*, p. 218.
13. Susan Brownmiller, *Against Our Will* (New York: Simon and Schuster, 1975), p. 16.
14. Daly, *Gyn/Ecology*, p. 360. For an especially astute analysis of Gilder see Michael Walzer, "Gilderism," *The New York Review of Books*, 2 April 1981, p. 3.
15. Firestone's *The Dialectic of Sex* exemplifies the problem with the radical feminist view of female biology. For the cultural feminist view see Rich, *Of Woman Born*, p. 39.
16. Morgan, *Going Too Far*, p. 164.
17. Anne Koedt, "Lesbianism and Feminism," in Koedt, Levine, and Rapone, *Radical Feminism*, p. 249.

18. See Kathleen Barry, "Did I Ever Really Have a Chance? Patriarchal Judgment of Patricia Hearst," *Chrysalis* 1 (1977); Morgan, *Going Too Far*; Rich, *Of Woman Born*, p. 285; Jane Alpert's germinal "Mother-Right," *Ms.* (August 1973).

19. Barbara Deming, "To Fear Jane Alpert Is to Fear Ourselves," *Off Our Backs (OOB)* (May/June 1975).

20. Rennie and Grimstad of *Chrysalis* were instrumental in establishing the Circle of Support. It is worth noting that upon Alpert's surrender, her lawyer stressed her "renunciation of radical activities and her conversion to the feminist movement." This prompted *OOB* reporter Madeleine Janover to ask with great prescience, "What does this mean for radical feminism?" See *OOB* (December 1974): 5.

21. See Jennifer Woodul, "What's This About Feminist Businesses?" *OOB* (June 1976).

22. It was this view that informed the ill-fated and short-lived Feminist Economic Network (FEN) founded in Detroit in 1975 and dissolved less than one year later. FEN was the brainchild of the Oakland Feminist Women's Health Center, the Detroit Feminist Federal Credit Union, and Diana Press. For detailed accounts see Belita Crown and Cheryl Peck, "The Controversy at FEN," *Her-Self* (May 1976); Jackie St. Joan, in *Big Mama Rag (BMR)* 4, no. 1; Martha Shelley, "What Is FEN?" circulated by author; Janis Kelly et al. in *OOB* (March 1976). For an exoneration of FEN see Kathleen Barry et al., *OOB* (January 1977).

23. Barry et al., ibid.

24. See Rich, *Of Woman Born*; Pauline Bart, review of *The Reproduction of Mothering*, *OOB* (January 1981): 19.

25. See Daly, *Gyn/Ecology*, p. 39.

26. For the cultural feminist view, see Florence Rush, *The Best Kept Secret* (Englewood Cliffs, N.J.: Prentice-Hall, 1980); for a trenchant feminist counter-analysis, see Judith Herman and Lisa Hirschmann, "Father-Daughter Incest," in *Signs* 2, no. 4 (Summer 1977).

27. Raymond, *Transsexual Empire*, pp. 109–110.

28. In Koedt, Levine, and Rapone, *Radical Feminism*, p. 52.

29. Sally Gearhart, "The Spiritual Dimension: Death and Resurrection of a Hallelujah Dyke," in *Our Right To Love*, ed. Ginny Vida (Englewood Cliffs, N.J.: Prentice-Hall, 1978), p. 192. See also Daly, *Gyn/Ecology*, pp. xi, 387; Rich, *Of Woman Born*, pp. 76–77; Raymond, *Transsexual Empire*, pp. 154–64. Raymond argues, "Androgyny becomes a synonym for an easily accessible human liberation that turns out to be sexual liberation" (p. 162).

30. Ann Snitow, "The Front-Line: Notes on Sex in Novels by Women, 1969–1979," in *Women: Sex and Sexuality*, ed. Catharine Stimpson and Ethel Person (Chicago: The University of Chicago Press, 1980), p. 174.

31. Ti-Grace Atkinson, "Lesbianism and Feminism," *Amazon Odyssey* (New York: Links Books, 1974), p. 86.

32. The conviction that feminism is conditional on separation from men predated lesbian separatism. For instance, the radical feminist group The Feminists established a quota system to limit the number of members living with men.

33. Rita Mae Brown, "The Shape of Things to Come," in *Plain Brown Rapper* (Baltimore: Diana Press, 1976), p. 114.

34. See ibid.; Charlotte Bunch and Nancy Myron, eds. *Lesbianism and the Women's Movement* (Baltimore: Diana Press, 1975); Martha Shelley, "Notes of a Radical Lesbian," in *Sisterhood Is Powerful*, ed. Robin Morgan (New York: Random House, 1970), p. 309.

35. Susan Chute, "Backroom with the Feminist Heroes: Conference for Women Against Pornography," *Sinister Wisdom* (Fall 1980): 2.

36. Quoted in Cowan and Peck, "The Controversy at FEN," *Her-Self* (May 1976).

37. Laura Lederer, ed. *Take Back the Night* (New York: William Morrow, 1980), p. 21; emphasis added.

38. For the minority view, see Dana Densmore, "On Celibacy," in *Voices from Women's Liberation*, ed. Leslie Tanner (New York: New American Library, 1970), p. 264. For the majority view, see Anne Koedt, "The Myth of the Vaginal Orgasm," in Koedt, Levine, and Rapone, *Radical Feminism*, p. 199.

39. There are two major feminist anti-pornography organizations, Women Against Violence in Pornography and Media (WAVPM), established in the Bay Area in 1976, and Women Against Pornography (WAP), established in New York City in 1979. Though I refer only to WAP in this paper, the two groups share the same analysis.

40. Quoted in Deb Friedman, "Feminist Perspectives on Pornography," *OOB* (January 1979).

41. This slogan originated with Robin Morgan's 1974 article "Theory and Practice: Pornography and Rape," reprinted in Morgan, *Going Too Far*.

42. See Rich's critique of "male-identified" dualism in *Of Woman Born*, pp. 56–83; Susan Griffin, *Pornography and Silence* (New York: Harper and Row, 1981). For an insightful analysis of Griffin's indictment of dualism see Robert Christgau in the *Village Voice*, 15–21 July 1981.

43. Penelope, *Sinister Wisdom*, "And Now for the Hard Questions," p. 103.

44. See Diana Russell, "Pornography and Violence: What Does the New Research Say?" in Lederer, *Take Back the Night*, p. 231. In *Homosexuality in Perspective* (Boston: Little, Brown & Co. 1979), Masters and Johnson report that in their sample, heterosexual men's second most frequent fantasy was about forced sex and they fantasized being forced slightly more frequently than they did forcing another.

45. Morgan, *Going Too Far*, p. 181.

46. Andrea Dworkin, "Why So-Called Radical Men Love and Need Pornography," in Lederer, *Take Back the Night*, p. 152.

47. "Compulsory Heterosexuality and Lesbian Existence," in this volume. Rich praises Catharine MacKinnon, author of *Sexual Harassment of Working Women: A Case of Sex Discrimination* (New Haven, Conn.: Yale University Press, 1979), for criticizing Brownmiller's unexamined premise that "'rape is violence, intercourse is sexuality.'"

48. Ibid.

49. Ethel Person, "Sexuality as the Mainstay of Identity: Psychoanalytic Perspectives," in *Women: Sex and Sexuality*, pp. 50, 57.

50. See Larry Bush and Richard Goldstein, "The Anti-Gay Backlash," *Village Voice*, 8–14 April 1981; Deirdre English, "The War Against Choice," *Mother Jones* (February/March 1981).

51. Snitow, "The Front-Line," in *Women: Sex and Sexuality*, p. 165.

52. Rich, in this volume.

53. Ibid.

54. Ibid.

55. Raymond, *Transsexual Empire*, p. 31.

56. Ibid., p. 104.

57. Quoted in ibid.

58. Ibid.

59. Ibid., p. 102.

60. Ibid., p. 113.

61. Dworkin, "Pornography and Grief," in Lederer, *Take Back the Night*, p. 289.

62. For a view of cross-generational sex among lesbians see Beth Kelly, "On Woman/Girl Love—or, Lesbians Do 'Do It,'" *Gay Community News (GCN)*, 3 March 1979, p. 5.

63. Jill Clark, "Interview with Robin Morgan," *GCN*, 20 January 1979.

64. See Karla Jay and Allen Young, *The Gay Report* (New York: Summit Books, 1979); Nancy and Casey Adair, *Word Is Out* (San Francisco: New Glide, 1978), p. 68; Edmund White, "The Politics of Gay S/M," *New Times*, 8 January 1979; Pat Califia, "A Secret Side of Lesbian Sexuality," *The Advocate*, 27 December 1979.

65. Rich, in this volume.
66. Daly, *Gyn/Ecology*, p. 373.
67. Quoted in Richard Goldstein, "I Left My Scalp in San Francisco," *Village Voice*, 1 October 1979.
68. Rich in this volume.
69. Quoted in Goldstein, "I Left My Scalp."
70. Brown, *Plain Brown Rapper*, p. 112.
71. Morgan, "Theory and Practice," in *Going Too Far*, p. 168.
72. Rush, *Best Kept Secret*, p. 192.
73. Rich, *Of Woman Born*, p. 73.
74. Barry, *Female Sexual Slavery*, p. 228.
75. Ibid., pp. 223–26; Raymond, *Transsexual Empire*, p. 123.
76. Person, "Sexuality as the Mainstay of Identity," in *Women: Sex and Sexuality*, pp. 50–51; Irene Diamond, "Pornography and Repression," in Lederer, *Take Back the Night*, p. 202; Rush, *Best Kept Secret*, pp. 190–91.
77. Barry, *Female Sexual Slavery*, p. 211.
78. See Willis, *Beginning to See the Light*, for a good analysis of the relationship between feminism and individualism.
79. Morgan, *Going Too Far*, p. 16.
80. Barry, *Female Sexual Slavery*, p. 227.
81. Russell and Lederer, "Questions We Get Asked Most Often," in Lederer, *Take Back the Night*, p. 29.
82. Judith Bat-Ada, "Playboy Isn't Playing," in Lederer, *Take Back the Night*, p. 132; emphasis added.
83. See Deirdre English in this volume for an analysis of the anti-abortion movement.
84. Tom Hayden, "The Future Politics of Liberalism," *The Nation*, 21 February 1981, p. 209.
85. Michael Lerner, "Recapturing the Family Issue," *The Nation*, 2 February 1982. For a pithy response to Lerner, see Barbara Ehrenreich, "Family Feud on the Left," *The Nation*, 13 March 1982.

Feminism, Moralism, and Pornography
Ellen Willis

For women, life is an ongoing good cop–bad cop routine. The good cops are marriage, motherhood, and that courtly old gentleman, chivalry. Just cooperate, they say (crossing their fingers), and we'll go easy on you. You'll never have to earn a living or open a door. We'll even get you some romantic love. But you'd better not get stubborn, or you'll have to deal with our friend rape, and he's a real terror; we just can't control him.

Pornography often functions as a bad cop. If rape warns that without the protection of one man we are fair game for all, the hard-core pornographic image suggests that the alternative to being a wife is being a whore. As women become more "criminal," the cops call for nastier reinforcements; the proliferation of lurid, violent porn (symbolic rape) is a form of backlash. But one can be a solid citizen and still be shocked (naively or hypocritically) by police brutality. However widely condoned, rape is illegal. However loudly people proclaim that porn is as wholesome as granola, the essence of its appeal is that emotionally it remains taboo. It is from their very contempt for the rules that bad cops derive their power to terrorize (and the covert approbation of solid citizens who would love to break the rules themselves). The line between bad cop and outlaw is tenuous. Both rape and pornography reflect a male outlaw mentality that rejects the conventions of romance and insists, bluntly, that women are cunts. The crucial difference between the conservative's moral indignation at rape, or at *Hustler*, and the feminist's political outrage is the latter's understanding that the problem is not bad cops or outlaws but cops and the law.

Unfortunately, the current women's campaign against pornography seems determined to blur this difference. Feminist criticism of sexist and misogynist pornography is nothing new; porn is an obvious target insofar as it contributes to larger patterns of oppression—the reduction of the female body to a commodity (the paradigm being prostitution), the sexual intimidation that makes women regard the public streets as enemy territory (the paradigm being rape), sexist images, and propaganda in general. But what is happening now is different. By playing games with the English language, anti-porn activists are managing to rationalize as feminism a single-issue movement divorced from any larger political context and rooted in conservative moral assumptions that are all the more dangerous for being unacknowledged.

When I first heard there was a group called Women Against Pornography, I twitched. Could I define myself as Against Pornography? Not really. In itself, pornography—which, my dictionary and I agree, means any image or description intended or used to arouse sexual desire—does not strike me as the proper object of a political crusade. As the most cursory observation suggests, there are many varieties of porn, some pernicious, some more or less benign. About the only generalization one can make is that pornography is the return of the repressed, of feelings and fantasies driven underground by a culture that atomizes sexuality, defining love as a noble affair of the heart and mind, lust as a base animal urge centered in unmentionable organs. Prurience—the state of mind I associate with pornography—implies a sense of sex as forbidden, secretive pleasure, isolated from any emotional or social context. I imagine that in utopia, porn would wither away along with the state, heroin, and Coca-Cola. At present, however, the sexual impulses that pornography appeals to are part of virtually everyone's psychology. For obvious political and cultural reasons nearly all porn is sexist in that it is the product of a male imagination and aimed at a male market; women are less likely to be consciously interested in pornography, or to indulge that interest, or to find porn that turns them on. But anyone who thinks women are simply indifferent to pornography has never watched a bunch of adolescent girls pass around a trashy novel. Over the years I've enjoyed various pieces of pornography—some of them of the sleazy Forty-second Street paperback sort—and so have most women I know. Fantasy, after all, is more flexible than reality, and women have learned, as a matter of survival, to be adept at shaping male fantasies to their own purposes. If feminists define pornography, per se, as the enemy, the result will be to make a lot of women ashamed of their sexual feelings and afraid to be honest about them. And the last thing women need is more sexual shame, guilt, and hypocrisy—this time served up as feminism.

So why ignore qualitative distinctions and in effect condemn all pornography as equally bad? WAP organizers answer—or finesse—this question by redefining pornography. They maintain that pornography is not really about sex but about violence against women. Or, in a more colorful formulation, "Pornography is the theory, rape is the practice." Part of the argument is that pornography causes violence; much is made of the fact that Charles Manson and David Berkowitz had porn collections. This is the sort of inverted logic that presumes marijuana to be dangerous because most heroin addicts started with it. It is men's hostility toward women—combined with their power to express that hostility and for the most part get away with it—that causes sexual violence. Pornography that gives sadistic fantasies concrete shape—and, in today's atmosphere, social legitimacy—may well encourage suggestible men to act them out. But if *Hustler* were to vanish from the shelves tomorrow, I doubt that rape or wife-beating statistics would decline.

Even more problematic is the idea that pornography depicts violence rather than sex. Since porn is by definition overtly sexual, while most of it is not overtly violent, this equation requires some fancy explaining. The conference WAP held in September was in part devoted to this task. Robin Morgan and Gloria Steinem addressed it by attempting to distinguish pornography from erotica. According to this argument, erotica (whose etymological root is "eros," or sexual love) expresses an integrated sexuality based on mutual affection and desire between equals; pornography (which comes from another Greek root—"porne," meaning prostitute) reflects a dehumanized sexuality based on male domination and exploitation of women. The distinction sounds promising, but it doesn't hold up. The accepted meaning of erotica is literature or pictures with sexual themes; it may or may not serve the essentially utilitarian function of pornography. Because it is less specific, less suggestive of actual sexual activity, "erotica" is regularly used as a euphemism for "classy porn." Pornography expressed in literary language or expensive photography and consumed by the upper middle class is "erotica"; the cheap stuff, which can't pretend to any purpose but getting people off, is smut. The erotica-versus-porn approach evades the (embarrassing?) question of how porn is *used*. It endorses the portrayal of sex as we might like it to be and condemns the portrayal of sex as it too often is, whether in action or only in fantasy. But if pornography is to arouse, it must appeal to the feelings we have, not those that by some utopian standard we ought to have. Sex in this culture has been so deeply politicized that it is impossible to make clear-cut distinctions between "authentic" sexual impulses and those conditioned by patriarchy. Between, say, *Ulysses* at one end and *Snuff* at the other, erotica/pornography conveys all sorts of mixed messages that elicit complicated and private responses. In practice, attempts to sort out good erotica from bad porn inevitably come down to "What turns me on is erotic; what turns you on is pornographic."

It would be clearer and more logical simply to acknowledge that some sexual images are offensive and some are not. But logic and clarity are irrelevant—or rather, inimical—to the underlying aim of the anti-porners, which is to vent the emotions traditionally associated with the word "pornography." As I've suggested, there is a social and psychic link between pornography and rape. In terms of patriarchal morality both are expressions of male lust, which is presumed to be innately vicious, and offenses to the putative sexual innocence of "good" women. But feminists supposedly begin with different assumptions—that men's confusion of sexual desire with predatory aggression reflects a sexist system, not male biology; that there are no good (chaste) or bad (lustful) women, just women who are, like men, sexual beings. From this standpoint, to lump pornography with rape is dangerously simplistic. Rape is a violent physical assault. Pornography can be a psychic assault, both in its content and in its public intrusions on our attention, but for women as for men it can also be a source of erotic pleasure. A woman who is raped is a victim; a woman who enjoys pornography (even if that means enjoying a rape fantasy) is in a sense a rebel, insisting on an aspect of her sexuality that has been defined as a male preserve. Insofar as pornography glorifies male supremacy and sexual alienation, it is deeply reactionary. But in rejecting sexual repression and hypocrisy—which have inflicted even more damage on women than on men—it expresses a radical impulse.

That this impulse still needs defending, even among feminists, is evident from the sexual attitudes that have surfaced in the anti-porn movement. In the movement's rhetoric pornography is a code word for vicious male lust. To the objection that some women get off on porn, the standard reply is that this only shows how thoroughly women have been brainwashed by male values—though a WAP leaflet goes so far as to suggest that women who claim to like pornography are lying to avoid male opprobrium. (Note the good-girl-versus-bad-girl theme, reappearing as healthy-versus-sick, or honest-versus-devious; for "brainwashed" read "seduced.") And the view of sex that most often emerges from talk about "erotica" is as sentimental and euphemistic as the word itself: lovemaking should be beautiful, romantic, soft, nice, and devoid of messiness, vulgarity, impulses to power, or indeed aggression of any sort. Above all, the emphasis should be on *relationships*, not (yuck) *organs*. This goody-goody concept of eroticism is not feminist but feminine. It is precisely sex as an aggressive, unladylike activity, an expression of violent and unpretty emotion, an exercise of erotic power, and a specifically genital experience that has been taboo for women. Nor are we supposed to admit that we, too, have sadistic impulses, that our sexual fantasies may reflect forbidden urges to turn the tables and get revenge on men. (When a woman is aroused by a rape fantasy, is she perhaps identifying with the rapist as well as the victim?)

At the WAP conference lesbian separatists argued that pornography reflects patriarchal sexual relations; patriarchal sexual relations are based on male power backed by force; ergo, pornography is violent.

This dubious syllogism, which could as easily be applied to romantic novels, reduces the whole issue to hopeless mush. If all manifestations of patriarchal sexuality are violent, then opposition to violence cannot explain why pornography (rather than romantic novels) should be singled out as a target. Besides, such reductionism allows women no basis for distinguishing between consensual heterosexuality and rape. But this is precisely its point; as a number of women at the conference put it, "In a patriarchy, all sex with men is pornographic." Of course, to attack pornography, and at the same time equate it with heterosexual sex, is implicitly to condemn not only women who like pornography, but women who sleep with men. This is familiar ground. The argument that straight women collaborate with the enemy has often been, among other things, a relatively polite way of saying that they consort with the beast. At the conference I couldn't help feeling that proponents of the separatist line were talking like the modern equivalents of women who, in an era when straightforward prudery was socially acceptable, joined convents to escape men's rude sexual demands. It seemed to me that their revulsion against heterosexuality was serving as the thinnest of covers for disgust with sex itself. In any case, sanitized feminine sexuality, whether straight or gay, is as limited as the predatory masculine kind and as central to women's oppression; a major function of misogynist pornography is to scare us into embracing it. As a further incentive, the good cops stand ready to assure us that we are indeed morally superior to men, that in our sweetness and nonviolence (read passivity and powerlessness) is our strength.

Women are understandably tempted to believe this comforting myth. Self-righteousness has always been a feminine weapon, a permissible way to make men feel bad. Ironically, it is socially acceptable for women to display fierce aggression in their crusades against male vice, which serve as an outlet for female anger without threatening male power. The temperance movement, which made alcohol the symbol of male violence, did not improve the position of women; substituting porn for demon rum won't work either. One reason it won't is that it bolsters the good girl-bad girl split. Overtly or by implication it isolates women who like porn or "pornographic" sex or who work in the sex industry. WAP has refused to take a position on prostitution, yet its activities—particularly its support for cleaning up Times Square—will affect prostitutes' lives. Prostitution raises its own set of complicated questions. But it is clearly not in women's interest to pit "good" feminists against "bad" whores (or topless dancers, or models for skin magazines).

So far, the issue that has dominated public debate on the anti-porn campaign is its potential threat to free speech. Here too the movement's arguments have been full of contradictions. Susan Brownmiller and other WAP organizers claim not to advocate censorship and dismiss the civil liberties issue as a red herring dragged in by men who don't want to face the fact that pornography oppresses women. Yet at the same time, WAP endorses the Supreme Court's contention that obscenity is not protected speech, a doctrine I—and most civil libertarians—regard as a clear infringement of First Amendment rights. Brownmiller insists that the First Amendment was designed to protect political dissent, not expressions of woman-hating violence. But to make such a distinction is to defeat the amendment's purpose, since it implicitly cedes to the government the right to define "political." (Has there ever been a government willing to admit that its opponents are anything more than anti-social troublemakers?) Anyway, it makes no sense to oppose pornography on the grounds that it's sexist propaganda, then turn around and argue that it's not political. Nor will libertarians be reassured by WAP's statement that "We want to change the definition of obscenity so that it focuses on violence, not sex." Whatever their focus, obscenity laws deny the right of free expression to those who transgress official standards of propriety—and personally, I don't find WAP's standards significantly less oppressive than Warren Burger's. Not that it matters, since WAP's fantasies about influencing the definition of obscenity are appallingly naive. The basic purpose of obscenity laws is and always has been to reinforce cultural taboos on sexuality and suppress feminism, homosexuality, and other forms of sexual dissidence. No pornographer has ever been punished for being a woman-hater, but not too long ago information about female sexuality, contraception, and abortion was assumed to be obscene. In a male supremacist society the only obscenity law that will not be used against women is no law at all.

As an alternative to an outright ban on pornography, Brownmiller and others have advocated restricting its display. There is a plausible case to be made for the idea that anti-woman images displayed so prominently that they are impossible to avoid are coercive, a form of active harassment that oversteps the bounds of free speech. But aside from the evasion involved in simply equating pornography with misogyny or sexual sadism, there are no legal or logical grounds for treating sexist material any differently from (for example) racist or anti-Semitic propaganda; an equitable law would have to prohibit any kind of public defamation. And the very thought of such a sweeping law has to make anyone with an imagination nervous. Could Catholics claim they were being harassed by nasty depictions of the pope? Could Russian refugees argue that the display of Communist literature was a form of psychological torture? Would pro-abortion material be taken off the shelves on the grounds that it defamed the unborn? I'd rather not find out.

At the moment the First Amendment issue remains hypothetical;

the movement has concentrated on raising the issue of pornography through demonstrations and other public actions. This is certainly a legitimate strategy. Still, I find myself more and more disturbed by the tenor of antipornography actions and the sort of consciousness they promote; increasingly their focus has shifted from rational feminist criticism of specific targets to generalized, demagogic moral outrage. Picketing an anti-woman movie, defacing an exploitative billboard, or boycotting a record company to protest its misogynist album covers conveys one kind of message, mass marches Against Pornography quite another. Similarly, there is a difference between telling the neighborhood news dealer why it pisses us off to have *Penthouse* shoved in our faces and choosing as a prime target every right-thinking politician's symbol of big-city sin, Times Square.

In contrast to the abortion rights movement, which is struggling against a tidal wave of energy from the other direction, the anti-porn campaign is respectable. It gets approving press and cooperation from the New York City government, which has its own stake (promoting tourism, making the Clinton area safe for gentrification) in cleaning up Times Square. It has begun to attract women whose perspective on other matters is in no way feminist ("I'm anti-abortion," a participant in WAP's march on Times Square told a reporter, "but this is something I can get into"). Despite the insistence of WAP organizers that they support sexual freedom, their line appeals to the anti-sexual emotions that feed the backlash. Whether they know it or not, they are doing the good cops' dirty work.

My Mother Liked to Fuck
Joan Nestle

Dedicated to Amber, who speaks to the best parts of ourselves.

My mother, Regina, was not a matriarchal goddess or a spiritual advisor. She worshipped at no altars and many times scorned the label mother. She was a Jewish working-class widowed woman who from the age of fourteen worked as a bookkeeper in New York's garment district. My father died before I was born when my mother was twenty-nine and left her with two children to raise. My mother liked sex and let me know throughout the years both the punishments and rewards she earned because she dared to be clear about enjoying fucking.

Regina was in my mind that October afternoon I sat in the front row of 1199's auditorium to tape the panel discussion on pornography and eros. When my mother died, she left no money, no possessions, no property, no insurance policies. She left me only a sheaf of writings, scrawled letters and poems written on the back of yellow ledger sheets. I have written a longer piece about her and me, incorporating these letters, but for now I only want to talk about the courage of her sexual legacy and the sexual secrets I found in her writings and how she stood in my mind, the mind of her lesbian daughter who has loved women for over twenty years, the afternoon of the panel.

Like many working-class single parents, my mother used me as a confidante, a supporter, a witness. I had to grow up fast to learn how to duck the repossessors, the eviction notices, the subpoenas. I learned how to be quiet and good in the homes of others. We never had large apartments and my mother had many boyfriends so sex and her enjoyment of it were not secrets. I knew the phrase blowjob before I knew there was a right way to brush one's teeth. What I learned from her writings was how hard-bought this sexual freedom was.

At age thirteen my mother allowed herself to be picked up on a Coney Island beach and have sex with a good-looking Jewish boy who was in his twenties; three weeks later he invited her to his apartment where she was gang-raped by three of his friends. She became pregnant and had to have an abortion at age fourteen. The year was 1924. Her German father threatened to kill her and she left school in the ninth grade to go to work. When my mother writes of these experiences she tells of her sexual passions, of how she wanted sex.

89

> I remember as a little girl, the impatiency with my own youth.
> I recognized that I was someone, someone to be reckoned with. I
> SENSED THE SEXUAL ORDER OF LIFE. I felt its pull. I
> wanted to be quickly and passionately involved. God so young and
> yet so old. I recognized my youth only in the physical sense as
> when I exposed my own body to my own vision, saw the beautiful
> breasts, the flat stomach, the sturdy limbs, the eyes that hid
> sadness, needed love a hell of a lot of grit and already acknowledg-
> ing this to be one hell of a life. I was going to find the key. I knew
> the hunger but I did not know how to appease it.

She goes on to speak of her shock, pain, and hurt and later of her anger
at the rape but she ends the narrative with a sexual credo, that she
would not let this ugliness take away her right to sexual freedom, her
enjoyment of "the penis and the vagina" as she puts it.

Respectable ladies did not speak to my mother for most of her
widowed life. She picked up men at the race track, at OTB offices,
slept with them, had affairs with her bosses, and generally lived a
sexualized life. Several times she was beaten by the men she brought
home. In her fifties, she was beaten unconscious by a merchant seaman
when she refused to hand over her paycheck. My mother, in short, was
both a sexual victim and a sexual adventurer; her courage grew as the
voices of condemnation and threats of violence increased against her. I
watched it all and her belief in a woman's undeniable right to enjoy
sex, to actively seek it, became a part of me but I chose women. I
wanted to kill the men who beat her, who took her week's pay. I
wanted her not to need them and to come into my world of lesbian
friendship and passion, but she chose not to. We faced each other as
two women for whom sex was important and after initial skirmishes,
she accepted my world of adventure as I did hers.

The week before she died, she was sexually challenging her doctor in
the hospital, telling him he probably did it too quick for a woman like
her. He, red-faced and young, drew the curtain around her hurriedly.
At sixty-seven my mother still wanted sex and made jokes about what
she could do when she didn't have her teeth in. My mother was not a
goddess, not a matriarchal figure who looms up over my life big-bellied
with womyn rituals. She was a working woman who liked to fuck, who
believed she had the right to have a penis inside of her if she liked it
and who sought deeply for love but knew that was much harder to find.

As Andrea Dworkin's litany against the penis rang out that
afternoon, I saw my mother's small figure, with her ink-stained cal-
loused hands never without a cigarette held out towards me, and I saw
her face with a slight smile: "So nu, Joan, is this the world you wanted
for me, the world you wanted me to have, where I should feel shame
and guilt for what I like. I did for all the years of my life. I fought the

rapist and the batterer and I didn't give up my knowledge of what I liked. I looked at those dirty pictures and I saw lonely people. Sometimes I did those things they do in dirty pictures and wives would not speak to me. Their husbands fucked me first and then went home for shabbas. I made lots of mistakes but one thing I never did, I never allowed anyone to bully me out of my sexual needs. Just like you, Joan, when in the fifties I took you to doctors to see if you were a lesbian and they said you had too much hair on your face, you were a freak and they never stopped you either. They called you freak and me whore and maybe they always will but we fight them the best when we keep on doing what they say we should not want or need for the joy we find in doing it. I fucked because I liked it and Joan the ugly ones, the ones who beat me or fucked me too hard, they didn't run me out of town and neither can the women who don't walk my streets of loneliness and of need. Don't scream penis at me but help to change the world so no woman feels shame or fear because she likes to fuck."

Abortion:
Is a Woman a Person?
Ellen Willis

If propaganda is as central to politics as I think, the opponents of legal abortion have been winning a psychological victory as important as their tangible gains. Two years ago, abortion was almost always discussed in feminist terms—as a political issue affecting the condition of women. Since then, the grounds of the debate have shifted drastically; more and more, the Right-to-Life movement has succeeded in getting the public and the media to see abortion as an abstract moral issue having solely to do with the rights of fetuses. Though every poll shows that most Americans favor legal abortion, it is evident that many are confused and disarmed, if not convinced, by the anti-abortionists' absolutist fervor. No one likes to be accused of advocating murder. Yet the "pro-life" position is based on a crucial fallacy—that the question of fetal rights can be isolated from the question of women's rights.

Recently, Garry Wills wrote a piece suggesting that liberals who defended the snail-darter's right to life and opposed the killing in Vietnam should condemn abortion as murder. I found this notion breathtaking in its illogic. Environmentalists were protesting not the "murder" of individual snail-darters but the practice of wiping out entire species of organisms to gain a short-term economic benefit; most people who opposed our involvement in Vietnam did so because they believed the United States was waging an aggressive, unjust, and/or futile war. There was no inconsistency in holding such positions and defending abortion on the grounds that women's welfare should take precedence over fetal life. To claim that three very different issues, each with its own complicated social and political context, all came down to a simple matter of preserving life was to say that all killing was alike and equally indefensible regardless of circumstances. (Why, I wondered, had Wills left out the destruction of hapless bacteria by penicillin?) But aside from the general mushiness of the argument, I was struck by one peculiar fact: Wills had written an entire article about abortion without mentioning women, feminism, sex, or pregnancy.

Since the feminist argument for abortion rights still carries a good deal of moral and political weight, part of the anti-abortionists' strategy has been to make an end run around it. Although the mainstream of the Right-to-Life movement is openly opposed to women's liberation, it has chosen to make its stand on the abstract "pro-life" argument. That emphasis has been reinforced by the movement's tiny left wing, which opposes abortion on pacifist grounds and includes women who call themselves "feminists for life." A minority among pacifists as well as Right-to-Lifers, this group nevertheless serves the crucial function of making opposition to abortion respectable among liberals, leftists, and moderates disinclined to sympathize with a right-wing crusade. Unlike most Right-to-Lifers, who are vulnerable to charges that their reverence for life does not apply to convicted criminals or Vietnamese peasants, anti-abortion leftists are in a position to appeal to social conscience—to make analogies, however facile, between abortion and napalm. They disclaim any opposition to women's rights, insisting rather that the end cannot justify the means—murder is murder.

Well, isn't there a genuine moral issue here? If abortion *is* murder, how can a woman have the right to it? Feminists are often accused of evading this question, but in fact an evasion is built into the question itself. Most people understand "Is abortion murder?" to mean "Is the fetus a person?" But fetal personhood is ultimately as inarguable as the existence of God; either you believe in it or you don't. Putting the debate on this plane inevitably leads to the nonconclusion that it is a matter of one person's conscience against another's. From there, the discussion generally moves on to broader issues: whether laws defining the fetus as a person violate the separation of church and state; or conversely, whether people who believe an act is murder have not only the right but the obligation to prevent it. Unfortunately, amid all this lofty philosophizing, the concrete, human reality of the pregnant woman's dilemma gets lost, and with it an essential ingredient of the moral question.

Murder, as commonly defined, is killing that is unjustified, willful, and malicious. Most people would agree, for example, that killing in defense of one's life or safety is not murder. And most would accept a concept of self-defense that includes the right to fight a defensive war or revolution in behalf of one's independence or freedom from oppression. Even pacifists make moral distinctions between defensive violence, however deplorable, and murder; no thoughtful pacifist would equate Hitler's murder of the Jews with the Warsaw Ghetto rebels' killing of Nazi troops. The point is that it's impossible to judge whether an act is murder simply by looking at the act, without considering its context. Which is to say that it makes no sense to discuss whether abortion is murder without considering why women have abortions and what it means to force women to bear children they don't want.

We live in a society that defines childrearing as the mother's job; a society in which most women are denied access to work that pays enough to support a family, child-care facilities they can afford, or any relief from the constant, daily burdens of motherhood; a society that forces mothers into dependence on marriage or welfare and often into permanent poverty; a society that is actively hostile to women's ambitions for a better life. Under these conditions the unwillingly pregnant woman faces a terrifying loss of control over her fate. Even if she chooses to give up the baby, unwanted pregnancy is in itself a serious trauma. There is no way a pregnant woman can passively let the fetus live; she must create and nurture it with her own body, in a symbiosis that is often difficult, sometimes dangerous, always uniquely intimate. However gratifying pregnancy may be to a woman who desires it, for the unwilling it is literally an invasion—the closest analogy is to the difference between lovemaking and rape. Nor is there such a thing as foolproof contraception. Clearly, abortion is by normal standards an act of self-defense.

Whenever I make this case to a Right-to-Lifer, the exchange that follows is always substantially the same:

RTL: If a woman chooses to have sex, she should be willing to take the consequences. We must all be responsible for our actions.
EW: Men have sex, without having to "take the consequences."
RTL: You can't help that—it's biology.
EW: You don't think a woman has as much right as a man to enjoy sex? Without living in fear that one slip will transform her life?
RTL: She has no right to selfish pleasure at the expense of the unborn.

It would seem, then, that the nitty-gritty issue in the abortion debate is not life but sex. If the fetus is sacrosanct, it follows that women must be continually vulnerable to the invasion of their bodies and loss of their freedom and independence—unless they are willing to resort to the only perfectly reliable contraceptive, abstinence. This is precisely the "solution" Right-to-Lifers suggest, usually with a touch of glee; as Representative Elwood Rudd once put it, "If a woman has a right to control her own body, let her exercise control before she gets pregnant." A common ploy is to compare fucking to overeating or overdrinking, the idea being that pregnancy is a just punishment, like obesity or cirrhosis.

One hundred and fifty years after Freud it is depressing to have to insist that sex is not an unnecessary, morally dubious self-indulgence but a basic human need, no less for women than for men. Of course, for heterosexual women giving up sex also means doing without the love and companionship of a mate. (Presumably, married women who have had all the children they want are supposed to divorce their husbands or convince them that celibacy is the only moral alternative.) "Free-dom" bought at such a cost is hardly freedom at all and certainly not equality—no one tells men that if they aspire to some measure of control over their lives, they are welcome to neuter themselves and become social isolates. The don't-have-sex argument is really another version of the familiar anti-feminist dictum that autonomy and fe-maleness—that is, female sexuality—are incompatible; if you choose the first, you lose the second. But to pose this choice is not only inhumane; it is as deeply disingenuous as "Let them eat cake." No one, least of all the anti-abortion movement, expects or wants significant numbers of women to give up sex and marriage. Nor are most Right-to-Lifers willing to allow abortion for rape victims. When all the cant about "responsibility" is stripped away, what the Right-to-Life position comes down to is, if the effect of prohibiting abortion is to keep women slaves to their biology, so be it.

In their zeal to preserve fetal life at all costs, anti-abortionists are ready to grant fetuses more legal protection than people. If a man attacks me and I kill him, I can plead self-defense without having to prove that I was in danger of being killed rather than injured, raped, or kidnapped. But in the annual congressional battle over what if any exceptions to make to the Medicaid abortion ban, the House of Repre-sentatives has bitterly opposed the funding of abortions for any reason but to save the pregnant woman's life. Some Right-to-Lifers argue that even the danger of death does not justify abortion; others have sug-gested "safeguards" like requiring two or more doctors to certify that the woman's life is at least 50 percent threatened. Anti-abortionists are forever worrying that any exception to a total ban on abortion will be used as a "loophole": better that any number of women should ruin their health or even die than that one woman should get away with not having a child "merely" because she doesn't want one. Clearly this mentality does not reflect equal concern for all life. Rather, anti-abortionists value the lives of fetuses above the lives and welfare of women, because at bottom they do not concede women the right to an active human existence that transcends their reproductive function. Years ago, in an interview with Paul Krassner in *The Realist*, Ken Kesey declared himself against abortion. When Krassner asked if his objection applied to victims of rape, Kesey replied—I may not be remembering the exact words, but I will never forget the substance—"Just because another man planted the seed, that's no reason to destroy the crop."[1] To this day I have not heard a more eloquent or chilling metaphor for the essential premise of the Right-to-Life movement: that a woman's excuse for being is her womb. It is an outrageous irony that anti-abortionists are managing to pass off this profoundly immoral idea as a noble moral cause.

The conservatives who dominate the Right-to-Life movement have no real problem with the anti-feminism inherent in their stand; their evasion of the issue is a matter of public relations. But the politics of anti-abortion leftists are a study in self-contradiction: in attacking what they see as the violence of abortion, they condone and encourage violence against women. Forced childbearing does violence to a woman's body and spirit, and it contributes to other kinds of violence: deaths from illegal abortion; the systematic oppression of mothers and women in general; the poverty, neglect, and battering of unwanted children; sterilization abuse.

Radicals supposedly believe in attacking a problem at its roots. Yet surely it is obvious that restrictive laws do not keep women from seeking abortions; they just create an illicit, dangerous industry. The only way to drastically reduce the number of abortions is to invent safer, more reliable contraceptives, ensure universal access to all birth control methods, eliminate sexual ignorance and guilt, and change the social and economic conditions that make motherhood a trap. Anyone who is truly committed to fostering life should be fighting for women's liberation instead of harassing and disrupting abortion clinics (hardly a nonviolent tactic, since it threatens the safety of patients). The "feminists for life" do talk a lot about ending the oppression that drives so many women to abortion; in practice, however, they are devoting all their energy to increasing it.

Despite its numerical insignificance, the anti-abortion left epitomizes the hypocrisy of the Right-to-Life crusade. Its need to wrap misogyny in the rhetoric of social conscience and even feminism is actually a perverse tribute to the women's movement; it is no longer acceptable to declare openly that women deserve to suffer for the sin of Eve. I suppose that's progress—not that it's much comfort to women who need abortions and can't afford them.

Note

1. A reader later sent me a copy of the Kesey interview. The correct quotation is "You don't plow under the corn because the seed was planted with a neighbor's shovel."

The Fear That Feminism Will Free Men First
Deirdre English

For feminists, the most difficult aspect of the 1980s' backlash against women's abortion rights, and other emancipatory new rights and attitudes related to sex, is the fact that a large part of the anti-choice ("pro-life") movement is made up of women. What we have for the past ten years grown accustomed to calling the "women's movement" claimed to represent the collective good of all women: the opposition was expected to be male. But now we are faced with an opposing women's movement, and one that also claims to stand for the best interests of all women. It is as confusing, as frustrating, as if, at the height of the civil rights movement, a large percentage of blacks had suddenly organized to say: "Wait a minute. We don't want equal rights. We like things just the way they are."

The very existence of such a movement represents a deep crisis in the community of women, and a profound challenge to the analytical and synthetical powers of feminist theory. Before proceeding, an old feminist touchstone is a good reminder: though we may be in conflict with them, other women rarely prove to be our real enemies. Even in opposing the politics of the anti-feminist women, we must begin by recognizing and honoring her experiences, her prospects, her hopes and fears.

To do that, it is essential to separate the motivations of those men who organize against women's rights and the women who do so, even when they are found holding the same credo in the same organizations. For while men in the anti-abortion movement stand to increase the measure of male control over women, the women can gain nothing but greater sexual submission. Now that is a suspicious thing in itself, because any people asking only to give in to a more powerful group must be well convinced that their survival is at stake. After all, the anti-feminist woman is neither stupid nor incompetent, whatever she may wish her male leaders to believe. Legitimately enough, she has her own self-interest in mind, in a world in which she did not create the options.

The Other Woman

Clearly, the anti-choice activist is not primarily concerned with refusing an abortion for herself; that she has the power to do no matter
what the laws are. (By contrast, women in the pro-choice movement
are almost invariably women who feel, at some level, a personal need
for abortion rights.) But no one is taking away another person's right to
bear children, no feminist is circumscribing individual ethical or religious beliefs that would prohibit abortion. What is solely at question to
the anti-choice activist is the *other* woman's right to make this decision
herself; her objective is to refuse social legitimation for abortion decisions that are not her own.

The anti-abortionists are, as they have been accused, seeking to
impose their morality on society. But that is part of the very definition
of moralism: a *moralist* is "one concerned with regulating the morals of
others." The anti-abortion movement is a perfect example of a moralistic movement, and it demonstrates some interesting things about the
functions of moral systems.

In opposing the Right-to-Lifers, pro-choice advocates most frequently argue that a woman has an absolute right to control her own
body. The insistence on individual rights is at the foundation of the
feminist position. A woman's right to control her own body encompasses endless new meanings in feminism: from the right to refuse sex
(as in marital rape) to the right to a freely chosen sexuality; from the
right to be protected from sexual violence to the right to plan one's own
reproductivity. The complete realization of those rights alone would
mark a new era for women. For now, the recognition of woman's body
as the *terra firma* of female liberation must be counted as one of the
great political accomplishments of our day. But it is far from enough.

After all, this is a society: we are interdependent; individual actions
have repercussions. The struggle is not and can never be only over the
actual act of abortion. The struggle is necessarily over a larger sexual
morality—and moral systems do have a bearing on virtually
everybody's behavior. The anti-abortion people have tried to insist on
single-issue politics partly because it is much easier for them to attack
the keystone of abortion than to defend the system of morality that is
tied to compulsory motherhood. It falls to us to identify the moral
system they are upholding and, at the same time, to define our own.

The anti-feminist woman is right about one crucial thing: the other
woman's right to have an abortion does affect her. It does something
very simple and, to many women, very upsetting: it takes away their
ability *not* to choose. Where abortion is available, the birth of every
baby becomes a willed choice, a purposeful act. And that new factor
destroys the set of basic assumptions on which many traditional marriages have been based. It breaks the rules and wrecks the game.

The Sex Contract

Remember the rules of the old game? They began with this: men did not get to have sex with women (at least not women of their own class or higher) unless they married them. Then men were morally obligated to provide for the children they had helped to conceive. In other words, sex was supposed to incur a major responsibility for men—as it did for women. Only thirty years ago, the average marrying age in the United States was twenty for women and twenty-two for men, and hundreds of thousands of brides have been pregnant on their wedding day.

Men always complained about this sexual bargain. "Nature kidded us," said a young Irish Catholic father of two in a short story by Frank O'Connor. "We had our freedom and we didn't value it. Now our lives are run for us by women." But men's regrets, however deeply felt, were still the complaints of the relatively more powerful party. It was women who, for physical and financial reasons, really *needed* marriage.

In a society that effectively condoned widespread male sexual violence and severely restricted economic opportunities for women outside of marriage, the deck was heavily stacked. If men did not "value their freedom," women had little freedom to value. The one short-lived power women had was withholding sex; and even that was only good until marriage—possibly periodically thereafter, with the more tolerant husbands. But in general, women had to earn their keep not only with sex, but with submissiveness, and acceptance of the male not as an equal partner but as a superior. Seen in these terms, the marriage contract seems a little more like extortion under the threat of abandonment.

But to point this out is not the way to play the game. The essential thing about the system—like moral systems in general—is that everyone must play by the same rules. In the past, the community of women has often been hard on those who "give away" for free—or for money—what the rest trade for love and marriage. Then came birth control, the sexual revolution, and legalized abortion.

The Escape Clause

It was the availability of relatively reliable contraception that provided the first escape clause to the old marital Russian roulette, both for men and women. The "99 percent effective" pill sparked the sexual revolution in the 1960s and 1970s and permitted women for the first time in history to decisively separate intercourse from reproduction. (Only after that historic schism could the modern woman's new fascination with discovering her own sexuality begin to emerge.)

For the most part, women of all classes and religions enthusiastically welcomed the advent of reliable contraception. True, it did have the effect of releasing men from some responsibility for their sexual acts, but the gains for women seemed much greater. Sexual liberation and birth control brought women new-found sexual pleasure, began to erode the double standard, allowed women to plan their pregnancies—and therefore participate in the work world on new terms—and in general seemed to tend to equalize the sexes. Other things, unfortunately, did not change so fast. Especially not the economy.

Catch 22

Most women who want to have children still cannot make it, financially, without a man. In an era in which an increasingly larger number of people are spending significant parts of their lives outside of the marriage coupling, the socioeconomic differences between men and women become increasingly, painfully obvious. According to 1978 Bureau of Labor statistics, only some 7 percent of women make more than $15,000 per year, while more than 46 percent of men do. Marriage is still the major means of economic stability—even survival—for women.

In this sense, men have reaped more than their share of benefits from women's liberation. If women hold jobs, no matter how poorly paid, men may more easily renounce any responsibility for the economic support of women and children. Thus woman's meager new economic independence, and her greater sexual freedom outside the bounds of marriage, have allowed men to garner great new freedoms. Because there is no "trick of nature" to make the link between sex and fatherhood, and little social stigma on he who loves and leaves, a woman faces the abdication of any male responsibility for pregnancy—let alone for any ensuing children. If a woman gets pregnant, the man who twenty years ago might have married her may feel today that he is gallant if he splits the cost of an abortion. The man who might have remained in a dead-end marriage out of a sense of duty finds increasingly that he faces no great social disapproval if he walks out on his family, even while his kids are still in diapers.

Divorce leaves women putting a higher percentage of both their incomes and their time into child care. According to the U.S. Census, the number of one-parent families headed by divorced women jumped almost 200 percent in one decade—from 956,000 in 1970 to 2.7 million in 1981. During the same period, the number of single-parent families headed by men actually declined. (Nationally, there are more youthful products of divorce cared for by relatives other than a parent than by their fathers alone.)

It is also worth noting the difference in the economic impact of divorce on fathers versus mothers. Roughly 40 percent of absent fathers contribute *no* money for child support after divorce, and the other 60 percent average a contribution of less than $2,000 per year. A recent study of 3,000 divorces showed, shockingly, that men improved their standard of living an average of 42 percent in the first year following divorce, while women with children saw their living standard decline by 73 percent. Under these circumstances, the fear has risen that feminism will free men first—and might never get around to freeing women.

All this is not to imply that either men or women *should* stay in loveless, unhappy marriages out of some sense of duty. Rather, both sexes need the right to change their circumstances. So far, our progress, like all progress, has been ragged: men, more independent to begin with, have been able to profit from women's new independence sometimes more fully than women themselves.

It seems revealing that the anti-feminist backlash, as well as the anti-sexual-liberation backlash, took so long to develop the momentum that it has today. It is the period of unremitting economic decline that has brought it on, the nightfall of economic prospects for women. It is as though the country reserved judgment during ten or fifteen years of experimentation with sexual politics, as long as economic conditions permitted it. In a climate of affluence, women had more hope of successfully freeing themselves from male-dominant relationships. But today, a greater number of working women are perceiving that the feminist revolution may not rapidly succeed in actually equalizing the material opportunities of the sexes. When working-class men no longer hold their own against unemployment, union-management rollbacks, or even inflation, what hope is there for women to close the economic gap between the male and female worker?

Giving up marriage and children for an interesting career may be one thing (although this is an either/or choice that men rarely face), but it may not be a decent trade for a dead-end job in the pink-collar ghetto. If men can no longer support families on a single paycheck, most women certainly cannot. The media presents us with the image of successful management-level women, but in fact even these women are almost always contained in middle-management positions, at under $20,000 a year. For the less-than-fervent feminist who is not prepared to pay any price at all for independence, the future looks bleak.

Fear and Reaction

It begins to seem clearer that the anti-feminist woman, like other women, is grappling with the terms of her survival. She is responding to social circumstances—a worsening economy, a lack of support and commitment from men—that feminists did not create and from which feminists also suffer the consequences. The conditions she faces face all women.

The differences lie in our strategies for dealing with all this. The anti-feminist woman's strategy is defensive: reactionary in the sense of reacting to change, with the desire to return to the supposedly simple solutions of the past. Like other patriotic or fundamentalist solutions, like going to war or being "born again," the longed-for return to the old feminine style seems to promise an end to complexity, compromise, and ambivalence. For many of the advocates of the anti-choice movement, the ideal is ready-made and well polished. It is the American family of the 1950s: dad in the den with his pipe, mom in her sunny kitchen with cafe curtains, the girls dressed in pink and the boys in blue. It could be called nostalgic utopianism—the glorification of a lost past rather than an undiscovered future. What has not been accepted is that the road to that ideal is as impossible to find—and to many people, as little desired—as the road back to childhood.

To feminists, the only response to the dilemma of the present lies in pressing onward. We must continue to show how a complete feminist sexual and reproductive politics could lead to the transformation of all society, without curtailing the freedom of any individual. True reproductive freedom, for example, would inevitably require fair opportunities for financial equality, so that women could bear children without facing either dependency or impoverishment. There would be practical child-care support for working parents of both sexes and an equal affirmation by men of their responsibility for parenthood. Yet, the individual's right to choose whether to bear a child would remain at the heart of the feminist position.

Today, the individual decision to have an abortion remains a sobering one; it puts a woman face-to-face with her dreams and her prospects and with the frequently startling fact that she is choosing not to be a passive victim, but rather an active shaper of her existence. The difficulties she will encounter as she continues to try to create her own destiny will repeatedly call for that same strength of will. In demonstrating it, she is already helping to bring about a new order of sexual equality, a world more worthy of the next generation. Few who have clearly seen the vision of that new world will want to turn back.

Section II
The Capitalist Paradox: Expanding and Contracting Pleasures

In the past, studies of sexual variety have often been simply records of exotica. More recently, social scientists have begun to examine sexual variety with a difference: they now look at variety as evidence of the social malleability of sexuality, and turn their attention accordingly to how and why a culture determines what it considers to be sexual.

This study has gained impetus from the acceleration of change in sexual life in the West in the last two centuries, the period that encompasses the rise of industrial capitalism. The pieces in this section all record some aspect of the general truth that in our era, people can experience basic shifts in sexual mores within one lifetime. But all the writers here also note the paradox at the heart of these changes: while some opportunities for sexual diversity expand, other rich possibilities contract. Ellen Ross and Rayna Rapp describe how the movement from family-controlled sexual patterns to state-controlled ones has been a mixed blessing, creating new kinds of sexual autonomy and chances for personal adventure, as well as new impoverishments arising from the isolation of sex from other social ties. But Ross and Rapp also include in their wide store of examples instances of disturbing continuity: the Bastardy Clauses of 1834 made unwed mothers the sole support of their children, exonerating from responsibility an increasingly mobile male population, a situation that is still with us today in spite—or perhaps because—of easily available birth control.

Kathy Peiss offers another example of the difficulty in evaluating changes in her description of working girls at the turn of the century: while they developed an exciting social field for sexual adventure, their new freedom often exposed them to forms of sexual harassment that have since become all too familiar. Changing possibilities also involved new kinds of exploitations and oppression. Still, as John D'Emilio makes clear, capitalism has been a great wellspring for changes in all gender relations; even its contradictions are potentially inspiriting as they force us to reinvent "sexuality" in an increasingly self-conscious way.

Sex and Society:
A Research Note from Social History and Anthropology

Ellen Ross and Rayna Rapp

"The personal is political" was a central insight of the wave of feminism that gathered momentum in the 1960s. Within that phrase is condensed the understanding that the seemingly most intimate details of private existence are actually structured by larger social relations. Attention to the personal politics of intimate life soon focused on sexuality, and many canons of sexual meaning were challenged. The discovery of erotic art and symbols as male-centered, the redefinition of lesbian sexuality as positive and life-affirming, and the dismantling of the two-orgasm theory as a transparently male perception of the female body were among the products of this critique. Such reinterpretations suggest that social definitions of sex may change rapidly and in the process transform the very experience of sex itself.[1]

Sexuality's biological base is always experienced culturally, through a translation. The bare biological facts of sexuality do not speak for themselves; they must be expressed socially. Sex feels individual, or at least private, but those feelings always incorporate the roles, definitions, symbols, and meanings of the worlds in which they are constructed. "The mind can be said to be our most erogenous zone," as one commentator has phrased it,[2] and breakthroughs in sexual counseling have revealed that sexual dysfunction is best cured by teaching people to fantasize, a social response rather than a biological repair.[3] Conversely, without a social context to define them as legitimate, the sexual experiences of generations of American women were confused and distorted; properly brought-up Victorian women were taught that they need never be "bothered" by sexual passions, while their more "liberated" daughters learned that orgasms were their anatomical destiny.[4]

But if the biological facts do not speak for themselves, neither do the social ones. While it has become a standard tenet of sociology and social psychology that all human behavior, including sexual behavior, is shaped by social contexts, those contexts remain cloudy. The classics of the social science of sex divide either into mere catalogues of sexual variation (replete with initiation rites, puberty ceremonies, coital positions, *ad infinitum* among exotic peoples)[5] or vague assertions that sexual behavior is taught and learned in social groups.[6] As recent innovative essays by Michel Foucault and Jeffrey Weeks point out, scholars are just beginning to investigate the plasticity of sexuality in Western European history and its embeddedness in other social arenas.[7]

But *how* society specifically shapes sexuality still remains abstract. How are we to weigh and evaluate the claims of the different domains of society on the prescription and behavior surrounding sex? How, for example, do family contexts, religious ideologies, community norms, and political policies interact in the formation of sexual experience? Here we intend to bring the theories and methods of anthropology and social history to bear on the problem of structuring social contexts.

We realize that the most popular perspective on the social shaping of sexuality focuses on individuals in family contexts, almost to the detriment of larger social connections. This is most powerfully exemplified by psychoanalytic theory, which attempts to bridge the seeming gap between the social and biological worlds by describing human personality as a product of the experiences of love, hate, power, and conflict in families. Such experiences are presumed to leave important residues in the unconscious. Adult sexuality is thus a central aspect of personality, which takes form in earliest childhood. Experiences of dependency, merging, and separating, initially focused on the mothering figure, resonate deeply throughout adult sexual life.

Recent feminist revisions of psychoanalytic theory have focused on the social construction of motherhood under conditions of male dominance. They reveal the centrality of female parenting in the psychic structuring of gender identity. Scholars such as Gayle Rubin, Nancy Chorodow, Dorothy Dinnerstein, Juliet Mitchell, and Jane Flax have demonstrated how complex and deeply "unnatural" the social process of creating gendered and heterosexual beings is.[8] Such theories underline the tenacity with which sexuality is intertwined with unconscious relations of dominance not easily or automatically affected by social reform.

A focus on the psychoanalytic, however, holds the social world at bay, awarding it only minimal importance in the shaping of consciousness and sexuality. The examples cited below suggest that the social contexts in which sexual experience occurs are continually changing. While a truly social and historical theory of sexuality requires an explicit link between society and enduring psychic structure, such links are as yet far from clear.

The solution to the problem of connecting the individual unconscious and the wider society is not to read directly, as psychohistorians do, from a supposed universal psychosexual conflict between parents and children to general, society-wide antagonisms. Christopher Lasch, for example, posits a direct connection between the alleged decrease of paternal authority within families and the crisis of contemporary American capitalism.[9] In the hands of such scholars, the study of society becomes a mere meditation on psychosexual development and social history becomes superfluous.

The analysis of psychosexual development is a complement to the study of society, not its ahistorical replacement. Sexuality both generates wider social relations and is refracted through the prism of society. As such, sexual feelings and activities express all the contradictions of power relations—of gender, class, and race. We can never assume, for example, that the sexual experiences of black slave women and white plantation women—though sometimes involving the same class of men—were the same. To examine these sexual experiences we do not intend to focus on "disembodied" sex acts. Rather, we will sketch out the series of contexts that condition, constrain, and socially define these acts.

Attempting to describe the link between society and individual sexuality, we initially saw these contexts spiraling outward from the individual toward the larger world. Social relations that appear peripheral to individual sexual practices (labor migration, for example) may in fact influence them profoundly through intervening social forms (e.g., by limiting available sexual partners and influencing the age of marriage). Gayle Rubin suggests that intermeshed gears provide a better image; in the ratio of the gears would be found the narrower and broader determinants of sexual experience.[10] But we cannot measure such ratios, and this metaphor is too mechanical to describe relationships in constant flux. More satisfactory is Clifford Geertz's image of an onion, which he used in describing the permeation of culture in the human experience.[11] In sexuality as in culture, as we peel off each layer (economics, politics, families, etc.), we may think that we are approaching the kernel, but we eventually discover that the whole is the only "essence" there is. Sexuality cannot be abstracted from its surrounding social layers.

Whatever metaphor best represents the social embeddedness of sexuality, it must be able to contain at least the following contexts: (1) kinship and family systems, (2) sexual regulations and definitions of communities, and (3) national and world systems. We do not claim that any one of these contexts is causal, or that our list is complete. But we will claim that each and all of them simultaneously set up the external limits on sexual experience and give shape to individual and group behavior. As social contexts, they both mirror and are lived through the salient power divisions in any society: class, caste, race, gender, and heterosexual dominance. Such divisions are internalized at the most intimate level of sexual fantasies and feelings and become part of human personality itself. We will discuss each of the spiraling contexts to illustrate our conviction that sexuality is shaped by complex, changing social relations and thus has a history. Like all histories, it is capable of further transformation through the struggles of "sexual politics."

Family Forms and Kinship Systems

It is an axiom of cultural anthropology that family forms, embedded in kinship systems, vary cross-culturally and often over time within a single culture. Kinship systems encompass such basic relations as marriage patterns, the tracing of descent, and inheritance not only of specific offices or possessions, but of more abstract rights and obligations. All these aspects of kinship systems have a potential impact on sexuality: kin terminologies, inheritance practices, and marriage patterns are significant in sexual socialization.

Kinship terminologies, for example, may carry crucial information on degrees of incest, acceptable marriage partners, and even the "gray area" within which some kinsfolk may be available for sexual relations but not for marriage. The fourteen kin categories named in Dravidian terminologies (found in parts of South Asia, Australia, and the Pacific) orient children not only to naming their parents, or siblings, but to knowing their potential mothers- and fathers-in-law and their potential spouses as well.[12] In such kinship systems, major messages mapping permissible and outlawed sexual partners are transmitted in language itself. While most Western languages designate many fewer kin classifications than this, the power to name—and thus legitimate or abolish—a sexual relation within the family may occur locally and informally. In the villages of southeastern France, for example, many young brides are referred to as "little mother" from the day they enter the new husband's family. Such a kin term conveys not only the centrality of producing future heirs for the stem family, but the desexualization of the conjugal dyad as well.[13]

In delineating permissible or necessary marriage partners, kinship systems usually specify sexual objects as well. Among the Banaro of northern New Guinea, for instance: "When a woman is married, she is initiated into intercourse by the sib-friend [a member of the same sib or clan, a kin group organized by common descent] of her groom's father. After bearing a child by this man, she begins to have intercourse with her husband. She also has an institutionalized partnership with the sib-friend of her husband. A man's partners include his wife, the wife of his sib-friend, and the wife of his sib-friend's son.[14] In such a system, as Rubin points out, there are multiple triangulated heterosexual bonds set up in both the sib-friend and marriage systems. The point is not only that people are socially constructed as "heterosexual," but as specifically sib-friend and cross-cousin sexual as well. (A cross-cousin is a kinperson who is the child of the opposite-sexed sibling of the parent of the person to whom he/she is related. For example, my mother's brother's children are my cross-cousins—cross-sex of the connecting parental generations—while my mother's sister's children are my parallel cousins.) Sexual socialization is no less specific to each culture than is socialization to ritual, dress, or cuisine.

Permissible objects of sexual passion may be redefined as official definitions of family boundaries change. In an extremely thoughtful comparison of Catholic and Protestant family strategies and affective relations in early modern France, Natalie Davis points out that "Back in the thirteenth century, people remembered the days when one could not marry within the seventh degree, that is, any of the descendants of one's great-great-great-great-great grandparents. Then, at the Lateran Council of 1215, it became and remained within the fourth degree: one was forbidden to marry any one of the descendants of one's sixteen great-great grandparents."[15] The contraction of the field in which incestuous unions were defined affected what were natural or permissible sexual experiences among kinfolk, godparents, and their offspring. Medieval and Renaissance theologians debated the relative merits of directing passion inside and outside of nuclear families: the sixteenth-century Jesuit Emond Auger reasoned that "'Our carnal desires' are by nature strongest toward those closest to us and would be boundless if we married them."[16] Such theological speculation parallels modern anthropology's romance with the relation between incest prohibitions and the creation of marriage alliances.[17]

Incest prohibitions are not the only boundaries to sex and marriage that family systems set up. As many demographic and family historians remind us, European marriage patterns from at least as far back as the seventeenth century through the nineteenth century were based on a late age of marriage and a high proportion of persons who remained permanently celibate, that is, unmarried.[18] Such people might be domestic servants, prostitutes, or members of religious orders or armies, but often their celibacy was generated by the inheritance system into which they were born. Examining family practices among the late seventeenth- and eighteenth-century squirearchy of England, a group that favored impartibility (the practice of inheritance by a single person, by custom often the eldest male child, which ensures that estates remain undivided), Lawrence Stone found a celibacy rate of about 25 percent among daughters and younger sons, a rate more than twice as high as that of the sixteenth century. These low rates of nuptiality he attributes to primogeniture.[19] It is not only the sexual experiences of the young that are structured by inheritance systems, but also those of adults, especially widows. For though the English countryside in many regions had a substantial "female presence" of inheriting daughters or widows, their remarriage was always problematic for the children of the first marriage.[20] In the Cumbrian parish of Kirkby Lonsdale, a widow lost her "freebench"—her common law right to a portion of her husband's estate during her lifetime—if she either remarried or had sexual intercourse.[21] In such an example, the property and sexual relations of widows become fused.

The sexual life of celibates was probably quite different from that of the married population. As eighteenth-century observers noted, "The unmarried Ladies and Gentlemen . . . of moderate fortunes . . . are unable to support the Expence of Family . . . they therefore acquiesce in Celibacy; Each Sex compensating itself, as it can, by other Diversions."[22] Such diversions might include "a variety of alternatives [which] are and probably were available, notably, lonely or mutual masturbation, oral or anal sex, homosexuality, bestiality, adultery with married women whose offspring are attributed to their husbands and resort to prostitutes."[23] While this list was compiled by Stone in discussing alternatives to heterosexual premarital intercourse, it would equally apply to permanent celibates. As Jack Goody points out, even when more than one son married, the opportunities for love and romance might vary with inheritance practice. In traditional France, a common cultural perception was that first sons married as their families dictated, while second sons married "for love."[24]

While we have discussed inheritance as if it were generated out of family relations, it is important to note that inheritance patterns actually integrate family members (and their sexuality) into national and even international movements in law and in class formation. As E. P. Thompson notes, the "grid of inheritance" in any locality reflects the efforts of geographically wider social classes to secure the property, offices and training of their offspring in a world that is continuously changing.[25] Inheritance laws legislated by a central state implicate family formation and sexual patterns at the local level. What appear as local patterns organized around kinship are often products of much wider social relations.

Communities as Loci of Social Relations

Families and kin groups cannot organize sexuality for themselves; the partners and patterns they require are usually rooted in wider communities, where lively traditions of sexual prescription—courting behavior, ritual prohibitions, and sexual socialization—are played out. The varied use of charivari rituals illustrates how local sexual norms are intricately intertwined with other values. These were rituals that occurred in France and England dating from the seventeenth century or earlier, in which neighbors serenaded offenders of moral values—

especially values in the sexual/domestic realm—with "rough music" (banging, whistling, etc.), sometimes parading an effigy of 'the offender. Charivaris were directed not only against henpecked husbands, adulterers, notorious seducers, and homosexuals, but also against merchants who cheated customers, talebearers, habitual drunks, strikebreakers, those who worked during festival times, and magistrates issuing unpopular decisions.[26] The "Rebecca Riots" in southern Wales in the 1840s used the charivari form in both the "public" and "private" domains: against newly built toll roads and farm dispossessions, but also against the Bastardy Clauses of the 1834 Poor Law.[27]

But the community practices surrounding sexuality represent more than local traditions, for communities are also termini of worldwide economic, social, political, and cultural systems. They simultaneously exhibit patterns that are regionally rooted and also reflect the larger world. The introduction of rural industry into some English and Welsh farming communities in the early modern period, for example, changed courtship and marriage to reflect the new value that children's, and especially daughters', labor represented to the family economy as a whole. Earlier patterns in which parents arranged children's marriages through precontracts or spousals gave way in many areas to more clandestine courtship arranged by the young people themselves. Night-courting—peer-group-supervised heterosexual pairing, common in nineteenth-century northern Europe—was one such method. The use of intermediaries in bargaining between parents and children suggests the tensions involved in young peoples' marital decisions. Bridal pregnancy may have been a trump card in children's hands as they asserted autonomy from the family economy via their own sexuality.[28]

Many of the aspects of community sociability—peer groups, the transmission of sexual knowledge, ritual boundaries to permissible or impermissible sexual relations, the involvement of Church regulations on sex—that we discuss in this section reflect both the autonomy of community groups and the presence of a larger social world. Peer groups exhibit this ambiguity especially clearly, for while at the village level it may appear that the young men, for example, have complete control over the regulation of courtship, the ages at which the young may marry or the degree to which bastards may be supported are established by social forces, or laws, originating outside of local communities.

Peer groups are found in many cultures and they serve a variety of functions. Perhaps most important, they organize intergenerational relationships outside the family itself. Links between generations are especially significant in systems that depend on family economies,

where relations of production cannot be separated from those of kinship, marriage, and reproduction. In such systems, peer regulation of
sex and marriage is crucial to the politics and economics of both family
and community life. Peer groups are often age-based, but because they
encompass cultural experience beyond simple shared chronology, they
are not reducible to demographic age-cohorts. In the French language,
generational age and marriage status are conflated: *vieille fille/vieux
garçon* translates as spinster/bachelor, but its literal meaning is aged
girl/aged boy. In traditional Irish villages, unmarried men are boys, no
matter what their chronological age.[29]

Given a marriage pattern in town and country in which there is a
long period between the age of sexual maturity and the age of marriage, highly ritualized management of celibacy and courtship was
common in early modern Europe. In describing the history of youth
groups in eighteenth-century England and Germany, John Gillis
notes:

> Horizontal bonding of young single persons was a feature not only
> of the schools and universities, but also of many of the professions,
> the army, the bureaucracy, and the clergy as well. The clergy was
> the only one in which celibacy was an essential aspect of the
> brotherhood; but as a requirement of apprenticeship and as a kind
> of extended rite of passage, it was a feature of all trades and
> professions. In the crafts, journeymen's associations upheld the
> ideal of continence and the delay of marriage, relying on an elabo-
> rate imagery and ritual of "brotherhood" to solidify the social and
> moral bonds within their group . . . [for example] perhaps a pri-
> mary function of the *Wanderjahr* was to take young men out of the
> marriage market during those years when such a step would have
> had disastrous results for the entire community, and thus prolong
> the state of semidependence until a place for them opened up in
> the normal course of the generational cycle.[30]

As the massive process of proletarianization and urbanization broke
down the productive and reproductive patterns of traditional Europe,
"traditions of youth were redrawn along class lines."[31] Working-class
youth, by the later nineteenth century, were more economically and
sexually autonomous at younger ages than were middle-class young-
sters. Their peer groups were often labeled "promiscuous" and "delin-
quent" by middle-class observers, whose own children were
sequestered in single-sexed schools, universities, social clubs, and fra-
ternal orders. "Adolescence" was increasingly used to describe the
period of prolonged professional training to which middle-class offspring were subjected, during which time they were considered to be
asexual.[32]

For Western Europe, evidence of ritualized structuring of courting dates back a considerable time. In French peasant villages from medieval almost through modern times, groups of unmarried men, the "abbeyes" Natalie Davis describes, restricted the pool of marriageable young people and maintained village endogamy—marriage within a specified social group in a community—by fighting or fining strangers who came to court local girls.[33] Adolescent peer groups in traditional European villages might even more directly supervise sexual activity. Recently, historians have drawn attention to "night-courting" in northern France, the Vendée, Alsace, Germany, Switzerland, and Scandinavia.[34] In night-courting as practiced in many parts of Scandinavia, young unmarried men gathered at a central place on Saturday nights and set off on a round of visits to the houses of the village's unmarried women, hoping to leave one of their number with each woman. Couples spent the rest of the night in the women's beds, and courted according to detailed rules that outlined what clothing needed to be left on, what body parts might touch, and so on. At the end of the night, the group of men reformed, and public mockery was the fate of couples found violating these rules.[35] "Accidents are rare," according to a 1795 report on the practice in Neuchâtel.[36] Church spokesmen, especially in Catholic regions, attacked these practices as immoral from as early as the seventeenth century. But they survived in some places to the end of the nineteenth century, only to be deplored as primitive and immoral by middle-class lay observers. Yet the loss of such peer regulation, either through its actual suppression or through the breakup of communities, seems to be one of the cluster of forces that led to increased illegitimacy rates.[37]

Sexuality is a notorious source of tension between adolescent peer groups and adults. The teenage girls studied by Molly Dougherty in a rural black town in the southern United States play their peers against their adult kinswomen as they enter into heterosexual relationships. Attitudes toward sexual experimentation and courting are relaxed and positive among peers; adult women may castigate the teenagers for early pregnancy, but they also supervise the transition to the elevated status motherhood provides for the young girls. Teenage sex and its consequences are negotiated between the peer and parenting generations, allowing young women to test bonds in both directions as they court.[38]

Peer groups formed in adolescence may have an impact on the affective and sexual lives of their members throughout adulthood. Among the best-studied adult peers are the all-female networks that nineteenth-century middle-class American women formed. Girlhood friendships, often begun at boarding schools, deepened as the women began to share a common domestic fate and religious culture in which they were defined as the more sensitive and spiritual of the sexes.

These homoerotic friendships were nurtured in the informal but enduring bonds between women whose context is erased if sexuality is investigated only within the heterosexual marital dyad.[39]

Communities are the loci not only of the regulation of sexual partners and practices, but for the transmission of sexual knowledge as well. Indeed, before the proliferation of "how-to" books, communities were the only source of knowledge about sex and reproduction. Formulas for contraceptive substances and abortifacients, and access to midwives or abortionists, were in the hands of village women in traditional Europe, as were concepts of when it was acceptable to use them.[40] Urban females' networks also were sources of information, and pre-World War I British evidence suggests that abortion was more common in urban areas at least in part because such information networks could operate there.[41] In Sheffield in the 1890s, for instance, lead contamination of the water supply suggested to some women that a lead powder commonly used around the house might also bring miscarriages. From there the word spread to Leicester, Nottingham, Birmingham, and other towns, all by word of mouth.[42]

Loss of contact through migration could mean the absence of vital knowledge about sexuality and procreation. The early twentieth-century letters collected by the Women's Cooperative Guild on maternity in Britain eloquently speak of such losses. Many women knew close to nothing about sex or reproduction, even at their first pregnancy.[43] The especially high rates of illegitimacy and infanticide among French and English nineteenth-century servants suggests not only their isolation from country or town working-class communities, but their ignorance about contraception, abortifacients, and abortionists.[44]

Some contemporary non-Western cultures have well-organized procedures for the transmission of sexual knowledge. Verrier Elwin investigated child and adolescent dormitories among the Muria of Bastar, a central Indian tribe, where children from the age of six or seven spend increasing amounts of time living with their peers. Young members are taught by slightly older ones, and a range of sexual skills is transmitted, including techniques of massage, foreplay, and mutual satisfaction. Young girls are taught to think of their bodies as "ripening fruit"; they are taught, too, that "when the clitoris sees the penis coming, she smiles." Intense dyads are broken up by enforcement of shifting partners; it is only among the older adolescents that "serious" courting leading to marriage is permitted.[45]

The amount of autonomy from wider institutions that community practices express varies widely. Charivaris, night-courting, and gossip enforcing sexual norms seem to genuinely express at least a part of community opinion. Priests and parsons, while important members of the community and influenced by its values, are also representatives of powerful national or international organizations. Their presence has of course tremendous power to shape sexual attitudes and experiences, but that molding has not always represented official theological positions. Although canon law, judicial procedure, and confessional practice all condemned "sins against nature," by medieval times contraception was viewed as more heinous when practiced inside of marriage than when used in illicit sex. In the hierarchy of sins, an adulterous union that was sterile was less sinful in the clergy's eyes than one that produced offspring. In examining community confessional records, Jean-Louis Flandrin suggests that the "Malthusian revolution" spread, in sixteenth- and seventeenth-century village France, via illicit relationships. But by the latter half of the eighteenth century, husbands and wives had created a cultural innovation: they had moved contraception out of the adulterous affair and into the marriage bed. Thus the Church's teachings distinguishing levels of sin prepared the way for marital experimentation.[46] Flandrin also thinks that the eighteenth-century clergy's increasing emphasis on duty and obligation to offspring encouraged family limitation as well. It made responsibilities to the already born more salient, allowing parents to consider contraception "for the sake of" their children.[47] Thus, official Church discourse on sexual practices was transformed as it was appropriated at the community level.

Sex and "World Systems"

Large-scale social institutions and forces may appear distant and abstract, but they actually influence the intimate experiences people have, defining the circumstances under which shifting sexual mores are played out. The Roman Catholic Church, for example, is organized to operate simultaneously at the international, national, local, and intimate levels. Other institutions may exhibit a sexual regulatory aspect, as national laws frequently do. The discussion that follows focuses first on the power of such large-scale institutions to shape sexuality. It then suggests an examination of less formalized, but perhaps more pervasive forces—economic or demographic change, shifting town/country relations—that affect sexual transformations.

All of the world's major religions serve as arbiters of moral systems, an important aspect of which is usually sexuality, as amply demonstrated in the history of Roman Catholicism. Even before the Protestant Reformation, Catholic doctrine had begun to tighten the connections between sexuality, marriage, and procreation. It increasingly campaigned against all nonmarital and nonprocreative forms of sexuality. The Church's definition of marriage, for example, became more rigorous, sharply differentiating the married from the unmarried and making the difference between licit and illicit sex more important. Medieval practice came close to assuming that couples who had intercourse were indeed married, for at that point the promise to marry carried more weight than any public ceremony that might take place, and it was widely believed that cohabitation was what made marriage official. Gradually, witnesses to the marriage were required; then a priest's presence, to administer a sacrament previously offered by the couple themselves; and finally the betrothal promise lost its binding character.[48]

The same rigidifying of Church definitions occurred on the subject of concubinage, the open acknowledgment of illicit sexual relations and paternity, with support for mother and child. The Counter-Reformation campaign against clerical concubinage was accompanied by an effective one against lay concubinage as well. By the mid-seventeenth century, it was successful and the practice was rare in France; only kings and the greatest lords openly acknowledged their bastards. The campaign against concubinage may account for the steady decline in illegitimacy figures in seventeenth-century France and in England. But it meant particular victimization for unmarried mothers, now stigmatized and far more likely to flee their communities. The abolition of concubinage also spelled disaster for the children, as bastards in disproportionate numbers ended up as foundlings and almost certainly faced early death.[49]

Legal systems provide a material background against which sexual relations are played out, whether they affect sexuality directly (e.g., legitimacy clauses, the outlawing of abortion, and sex codes defining prostitution) or at a distance (e.g., welfare and the responsibilities of fathers). Laws defining paternity, for example, are important in setting up the context in which sexuality occurs. Their effect does not necessarily result from forcing fathers to support their illegitimate children. Few women in England, either before or after the 1834 Bastardy Clauses undermined putative fathers' legal obligations, seem to have applied for child support, and we know too well how few divorced fathers in contemporary America pay child support consistently over the years. Rather, as such laws become known, they help to establish an atmosphere that changes the sexual balance of power. The commissioners investigating the causes of the "Rebecca Riots" in 1844 were convinced that this is what had happened in southern Wales. Traditional marriage and courtship patterns in England had condoned premarital pregnancies, and eighteenth-century legislation made it relatively easy for mothers of bastards to collect regular support payments. The Bastardy Clauses to the 1834 Poor Law Amendment Act assigned financial responsibility solely to the mothers (or their parishes).[50] Now, courting men seemed to feel a new license to avoid marriage. "It is a bad time for the girls, Sir," a woman reported to a Haverfordwest Poor Law Guardian who testified before the Commission. "The boys have their own way."[51] The Bastardy Clauses were probably among the factors that influenced a shift in popular sexual culture: an earlier tradition of lively female sexual assertiveness as traced in folk ballads and tales gave way to a more prudish, cautious image of womanhood by the 1860s. Such a transformation appears quite rational in light of the shifting legal environment.[52] What Flandrin calls the "legal disarming of women vis-à-vis their seducers" took place earlier and more thoroughly in France. In the seventeenth century it was legally possible for a seducer, unless he married the woman, to be charged with rape if the woman was under twenty-five. As the penalty for rape was death, many seducers charged in court no doubt preferred marriage. The Civil Code of 1804, however, forbade searching for putative fathers and made unmarried women solely responsible for their children.[53]

Throughout Europe and in America, the mid- to late-nineteenth century witnessed a hardening of legal definitions of sexual outcasts, as sexual behavior came under increasing state and cultural surveillance. It is from this period that many of the sex and vice codes still prevalent in Western societies can be dated. In England, a series of Contagious Disease Acts passed from 1864 on to control venereal disease in the army and navy by registering prostitutes had the effect of stigmatizing the women and isolating them from the working-class neighborhoods in which they lived and worked. Although a campaign to repeal the acts was ultimately successful, its social purity orientation led to still further sexually restrictive legislation. The Criminal Law Amendment Act, an omnibus crime bill passed in 1885, raised the age of consent for girls from thirteen to sixteen in response to a movement to "save" working-class girls from the perceived evils of "white slavery" and aristocratic male lust. The newly increased powers of the police were turned not on the wealthy buyers of sex, but on its poorer sellers. Lodging-house keepers were commonly prosecuted as brothel keepers, and prostitutes were often uprooted and cast out from their neighborhoods. Forced to find new lodging in areas of cities more specialized in vice, they became increasingly dependent on male pimps once community support, or at least toleration, of their occupation was shattered by legal prosecution.[54]

In the Labouchere Amendment to the same 1885 act, all forms of sexual activity between men (with consent, in private as well as in public) were subject to prosecution. This represents a dramatic extension of the definition of male homosexuality (and its condemnation) beyond the "abominations of buggery" clauses promulgated under Henry VIII and remaining in force in the centuries that followed.[55] The

Labouchère Amendment was followed in 1898 by the Vagrancy Act, which turned police attention to homosexual solicitation. Anti-homosexual legislation was passed in an atmosphere of a purity campaign that viewed homosexuality as a vice of the rich visited on the poor. But the effects of the legislation were turned against working-class homosexuals, who were most likely to be tried, while wealthier men were often able to buy their way out of public notice and prosecution. As Jeffrey Weeks points out, the sex codes and their effects must be viewed in relation to evolving notions of respectability in both working-class and lower-middle-class culture. One aspect of that respectability was sexual; another was the growing belief in the purity and innocence of childhood. Both converged in support for the sex codes, which raised the age of consent and identified and outlawed a range of male homosexual activities.[56] It is within this cultural milieu that sexually specialized neighborhoods, cultures, and commodities were probably given impetus to evolve.[57]

Less obvious to the eye than Church policies or legal systems, but still more central in structuring sexual experience, are social and economic forces that, for example, determine the availability of resources for marriage, or the possibility of finding in expanding urban areas a setting for homosexual contacts. To analyze for Western society this widest level of determinants of sexuality would be tantamount to writing the first volume of a sexual *Capital*. Here we want merely to suggest that the intimate experience of sexuality is intertwined with the most global of social forces. The complex of transformations that accompanied the development of industrial capitalism in Western Europe—including increased wage-labor dependency and massive urban migration—generated statistical clues to changing sexual patterns.

The availability of wage labor in general made it possible for larger proportions of people to marry (especially by the nineteenth century) and for marriage to take place at earlier ages as couples could support themselves without waiting for sizable dowries or inheritances. For the eighteenth- and early nineteenth-century Leicestershire village of Shepshed, for example, knitters working for wages in domestic industry had different demographic patterns from those of artisans or the farming population. The knitters' wage dependency allowed them earlier marriage and encouraged more children, who were also employable.[58] In nineteenth-century industrial cities, too, waged workers tended to marry at greater rates than did the populations of towns with large artisanal or commercial sectors.[59]

Migration from country to city left profound, though complex, demographic traces, creating new situations in which migrants experienced courtship, sex, marriage, and childbearing. Different kinds of towns—commercial, industrial, or mining, as Louise Tilly and Joan

Scott have shown—provided migrants with different demographic and economic situations. In textile cities like Preston or Mulhouse, where the demand for both female and child labor was high, women outnumbered men and marriages were late. Where the labor force was chiefly male and jobs for women few, as in mining and metalworking centers like Carmaux and Anzin, women were scarce and marriage ages tended to be lower.[60]

While urban life seemed to promote illegitimacy in France, massive proletarianization in the English countryside is linked to higher rates of illegitimacy there.[61] Rising rates of illegitimacy may appear to be a new development, but recent work suggests that behind the figures lie traditional courtship and sexual patterns, reproduced under new and difficult circumstances. Young women, away from their families and communities to work as servants or in manufacturing jobs, courted and had sexual relations with traditional expectations that marriage would take place should a pregnancy result. But in the new situations of commercial and industrial towns, employment for many men was too unstable to permit marriage, and community pressure on them to support their bastards was weak.[62] Under new conditions of urbanization, old sexual patterns led to new social consequences.

From as early as the twelfth century, towns had provided foci for the formation of male homosexual subcultures. There is evidence of distinct homosexual communities in Italian towns in the fourteenth century, French from the fifteenth, and British by the seventeenth. In the relative anonymity of eighteenth-century London, a network of cafes, bars, meeting places, and brothels thrived, serving a wide clientele that represented most of the city's major occupations.[63] As the labeling of homosexuals as deviants became sharper toward the end of the nineteenth century, this subculture tightened, subdivided, and generated a political arm, which was predominantly upper and upper middle class.[64] The lesser visibility of lesbian subgroups in history probably reflects not only the lower level of legal persecution to which they were apparently subjected, but, more important, lesbians (like heterosexual women) have had far less independence than men and fewer resources on which to base their subcultures.[65]

Behind the dramatic economic and demographic changes of the era of industrialization in Europe lie cultural and ideological changes far harder to penetrate. The transformation of social relations of labor provides a general context for shifting symbolic relations, including the symbolism of sex and gender.

Domestic service, for example, was the most common waged occupation for women in England and France well into the twentieth century. It carried with it a specific demographic pattern, conditions of labor, and conditions of culture as well. Stringent codes of class and gender marked the relation between master and servant as one of personal dominance and subordination. Female servants lived as dependents, tied to their masters' households. One aspect of their subordination was expressed in exaggerated codes of meekness and cleanliness. Another was asexuality, transgression of which could lead to serious consequences, such as being "'placed' in institutional substitutes for homes: Homes for Orphans, Charity Homes, Homes for Fallen Women."[66] "No followers" rules imposed secrecy on courting and sexual behavior.

In an analysis of illegitimacy among London domestics in the nineteenth century, John Gillis traces the subtle and contradictory circumstances that led some upper servants to unwed pregnancy and abandonment of children. "Better" servants and their suitors, usually skilled or semiskilled workers, shared their masters' sense of respectability. They aimed to acquire some economic security as a basis for marriage. The men were quite geographically mobile, unlike the women, who were tied to bourgeois households. A too-early pregnancy might lead men to abandon women who lacked the savings and employment skills on which to found a new household.[67]

The strange romance of two Victorians illustrates the complicated intersection between erotic experience and wider social forces, such as the institutionalized patterns of dominance and subordination that prevailed between servant-keeping bourgeois families and their female servants.[68] Hannah Cullwick was a twenty-one-year-old kitchen servant when she met twenty-five-year-old Arthur J. Munby in London in 1854. Munby was in London studying to become a barrister, but his real passion was the working woman—pit brow women, crossings-sweepers, milk carriers, farm laborers, and lower servants all fascinated him.

By the time they met, both Hannah and Arthur had already focused their sexual and romantic fantasies not only on the opposite sex, but also on the opposite class. Munby's passion for working women was paralleled by Hannah's decision that any sweetheart she was to have "shall be someone much above me; and I will be his slave."[69]

Class polarities structured their relationship. Munby's sensual appreciation of Hannah Cullwick focused on her large size (which he exaggerated), sturdiness, large red hands and arms, and the frequently dirty face and arms her work produced. Munby loved to watch Cullwick scrubbing her master's front steps, and he found it natural that she should wash his feet and polish his boots. Hannah in turn cherished her servitude and passed up many chances for high-paying and comfortable upper servants' jobs because she could not give up her "lowliness."

A troubled secret marriage took place in 1872. It was followed by a few years of domestic life, Hannah posing as her husband's servant and both partners enjoying the game while Munby continued his regular round of bachelor activities. Marriage exacerbated their class differences. Their erotic life remained frustrating: rare kissing, cuddling, and Munby's sitting on his wife's large lap seem to have comprised the more directly "sexual" parts of their relationship.

As Lenore Davidoff suggests in her sensitive study of this relationship, the contradictions in Munby's emotional life may well be traced to the common upper-middle-class practice of hiring country women as the nearly full-time caretakers of children. His erotic biography comes into classic Freudian focus when we learn that another woman named Hannah served as a nurse in the Munby household throughout his childhood.[70] Hannah Cullwick's fixation on gentlemen and her association between romantic love and servitude are less classically oedipal: their analysis opens up the connection between patriarchy and class oppression.

Conclusion

We have argued that understanding sexuality requires critical attention to the idea that sex is a lived and changing relationship and not an "essence" whose content is fixed. Sex cannot be studied as a series of "acts"; nor should the sexual component in all social relations be ignored.

It is no accident, however, that contemporary culture tempts us to reify sex as a thing-in-itself. The modern perception of sex is an ideological reflection of real changes that have occurred in the contexts of daily life within which sexuality is embedded. The separation, with industrial capitalism, of family life from work, of consumption from production, of leisure from labor, of personal life from political life, has completely reorganized the context in which we experience sexuality. These polarities are grossly distorted and miscast as antinomies in modern ideological formulations, but their seeming separation creates an ideological space called "personal life," one defining characteristic of which is sexual identity.[71] Modern consciousness permits, as earlier systems of thought did not, the positing of "sex" for perhaps the first time as having an "independent" existence. While we have discussed family and kinship systems, communities, and large-scale institutional and informal forces as though they were separate contexts for shaping sexuality, they are, of course, interdependent. The power of each in relation to all others to provide the meaning and control of sexuality shifts with historical time. Recently, for example, a common American complaint is that families are losing control over their children's sexual education and behavior, challenged by public schools, the mass media, and state policies (which grant sex education and abortions to teen-agers, even without parental consent). The power of families and com-munities to determine sexual experience has indeed sharply diminished in the past two centuries, allegedly allowing for individual sexual "liberation."

Although the movement toward self-conscious sexuality has been hailed by modernists as liberatory, it is important to remember that sexuality in contemporary times is not simply released or free-floating. It continues to be socially structured, but we would argue that the dominant power to define and regulate sexuality has been shifting toward the group of what we have labeled large-scale social and eco-nomic forces, the most salient of which is perhaps the state. States now organize many of the reproductive relations that were once embedded in smaller scale contexts. Sexuality thus enters the "social contract," connecting the individual citizen and the state. In the process, an ideological space is created that allows us to "see" sex as a defining characteristic of the individual person, "released" from the traditional restraints of family and community. The rise of the two great ethnosci-ences of sexual and personal liberation—sexology and psychoanalysis—have accompanied this transformation, attempting to explain and justify it.[72]

But the ideology of sexual freedom and the right to individual self-expression have come increasingly into conflict with both state hegemony and the residual powers of more traditional contexts such as family and community control. Today, abortion, sterilization abuse, sex education, homosexual rights, and welfare and family policies are explosive political issues in the United States and much of Western Europe. For as states claim a greater and greater interest in the struc-turing of sexuality, sexual struggles increasingly become part of public, consciously defined politics. All the salient power divisions in any society—class, race, gender, and heterosexual dominance—structure the consciousness, demands, and resources different groups bring to these, as to any other, political issues. Politicians attentive to the sex-ualization of policy and the politicization of sexuality now know what scholars ignore at their peril: such issues have never been simply "private" or "personal," but are eminently part of the public domain.

Notes

This paper was originally written for an innovative conference, "Writing the History of Sexuality and Power," New York University, March 1978. Many friends read and criticized earlier drafts of this paper. We especially want to thank Shirley Lindenbaum, Harriet Rosenberg, Gayle Rubin, Sara Ruddick, Judith Walkowitz, and Eric Wolf.

1. The definition of what constitutes sexuality is currently under debate. Some analysts stress the biological basis of the experience, focusing on organic and neurological

response; others, more committed to a psychoanalytic perspective, stress the role of fantasy—originating in childhood—in eliciting these responses. As the recent work of Michel Foucault suggests, however, both positions presuppose that "sex" as a category of human experience can be isolated and is uniform throughout history. (*The History of Sexuality*, vol. 1: *An Introduction*, tr. Robert Hurley [New York: Pantheon, 1978]).

2. John Gagnon and Bruce Henderson, "The Social Psychology of Sexual Development," in *Family in Transition*, ed. Arlene S. Skolnick and Jerome H. Skolnick, 2d ed. (Boston and Toronto: Little, Brown, 1977), pp. 116–22, 118.

3. The classic works are William H. Masters and Virginia E. Johnson, *Human Sexual Response* (Boston: Little, Brown, 1966); and idem, *Human Sexual Inadequacy* (Boston: Little, Brown and Company, 1970).

4. A summary of this transformation is found in Michael Gordon, "From an Unfortunate Necessity to a Cult of Mutual Orgasm: Sex in American Marital Education Literature, 1830–1940," in *Studies in the Sociology of Sex*, ed. James Henslin (New York: Appleton Century Crofts, 1971), pp. 53–77

5. For example, Havelock Ellis, *Studies in the Psychology of Sex*, 2 vols. (New York: Random House, 1937–1942); Fernando Henriques, *Love in Action: The Sociology of Sex* (New York: Dutton, 1960).

6. James M. Henslin, "The Sociological Point of View," in *Studies in the Sociology of Sex*, pp. 1–6; Gagnon and Henderson, "The Social Psychology of Sexual Development"; Clellan S. Ford and Frank A. Beach, *Patterns of Sexual Behavior* (New York: Harper and Row, 1972), chap. 13.

7. Foucault, *History of Sexuality*; Jeffrey Weeks, "Movements of Affirmation: Sexual Meanings and Homosexual Identities," *Radical History Review* 20 (Spring/Summer 1979): 164–80; Robert Padgug, "Sexual Matters: On Conceptualizing Sexuality in History," ibid., pp. 3–24.

8. Nancy Chodorow, *The Reproduction of Mothering* (Berkeley and Los Angeles: University of California Press, 1978); Dorothy Dinnerstein, *The Mermaid and the Minotaur: Sexual Arrangements and Human Malaise* (New York: Harper and Row, 1976); Jane Flax, "The Conflict between Nurturance and Autonomy in Mother-Daughter Relationships and Within Feminism," *Feminist Studies* 4, no. 2 (June 1978): 171–89; Juliet Mitchell, *Psychoanalysis and Feminism* (New York: Pantheon, 1974); Gayle Rubin, "The Traffic in Women: Notes on the 'Political Economy' of Sex," in *Toward an Anthropology of Women*, ed. Rayna R. Reiter (New York: Monthly Review Press, 1975).

9. Christopher Lasch, *Haven in a Heartless World* (New York: Basic Books, 1977).

10. Personal communication, June 1979.

11. Clifford Geertz, "The Impact of the Concept of Culture on the Concept of Man," in *New Views of the Nature of Man*, ed. J. Platt (Chicago: University of Chicago Press, 1966), pp. 93–118; reprinted in Clifford Geertz, *The Interpretation of Cultures* (New York: Basic Books, 1973).

12. Roger M. Keesing, *Kin Groups and Social Structure* (New York: Holt, Rinehart and Winston, 1975), chap. 7.

13. Rayna Rapp, unpublished field notes, Provence (France), 1969, 1970, 1971–1972.

14. Richard Thurnwald, "Banaro Society," *Memoirs of the American Anthropological Association* 3, no. 4 (1916): 251–391; summarized and cited in Rubin, "The Traffic in Women," p. 166.

15. Natalie Zemon Davis, "Ghosts, Kin and Progeny: Some Features of Family Life in Early Modern France," *Daedalus* 106, no. 2 (Spring 1977): 87–114, 101. See also Jean-Louis Flandrin, *Families in Former Times: Kinship, Household and Sexuality*, tr. Richard Southern (Cambridge: Cambridge University Press, 1979), pp. 19–23.

16. Davis, "Ghosts," pp. 102–03.

17. Classic essays on incest prohibitions are found in Nelson Graburn, ed., *Readings in*

Kinship and Social Structure (New York: Harper and Row, 1971), chap. 14; Robin Fox, *Kinship and Marriage* (Harmondsworth, England: Penguin Books, 1967), chap. 2. Lévi-Strauss's most famous work, *Elementary Structures of Kinship*, tr. James H. Bell, John R. von Sturmer, and Rodney Needham (Boston: Beacon Press, 1969), is founded on this question.

18. Louise Tilly and Joan Scott, *Women, Work and Family* (New York: Holt, Rinehart and Winston, 1978), p. 26; Lutz K. Berkner, "Recent Research on the History of the Family in Western Europe," *Journal of Marriage and the Family* 35 (August 1973): 395–405; Lawrence Stone, *The Family, Sex and Marriage in England, 1500–1800* (New York: Harper and Row, 1977), chap. 2.

19. Stone, *Family, Sex and Marriage*, pp. 44, 46–48.

20. E. P. Thompson, "The Grid of Inheritance: A Comment," in *Family and Inheritance*, ed. Jack Goody, Joan Thirsk, and E. P. Thompson (Cambridge: Cambridge University Press, 1976), p. 349.

21. Alan Macfarlane, *The Origins of English Individualism* (Oxford: Basil Blackwell, 1978), p. 82.

22. Corbyn Morris, "Observations on the Past Growth and Present State of the City of London" (1751), cited in J. Hajnal, "European Marriage Patterns in Perspective," in *Population in History*, ed. D. V. Glass and D. E. C. Eversley (Chicago: Aldine, 1965), pp. 101–43.

23. Stone, *Family, Sex and Marriage*, pp. 615–16.

24. Jack Goody, *Production and Reproduction: A Comparative Study of the Domestic Domain* (Cambridge: Cambridge University Press), p. 63.

25. Thompson, "Grid of Inheritance," p. 360.

26. E. P. Thompson, "'Rough Music': Le charivari anglais," *Annales E.S.C.* 27 (March–April 1972): 285–312, 293, 305.

27. U. R. Q. Henriques, "Bastardy and the New Poor Law," *Past and Present* 37 (July 1967): 103–29, 118.

28. Interesting speculations on generational power relations in handicraft families appear in Hans Medick, "The Proto-Industrial Family Economy," *Social History* 1, no. 3 (October 1976): 291–315; and John Gillis, "Resort to Common-Law Marriage in England and Wales, 1700–1850," unpublished manuscript.

29. Rayna Rapp, unpublished field notes; Conrad Arensberg and Solon T. Kimball, *Family and Community in Ireland*, 2d ed. (Cambridge, Mass.: Harvard University Press, 1968), p. 55.

30. John R. Gillis, *Youth and History: Tradition and Change in European Age Relations, 1770–Present* (New York and London: Academic Press, 1974), pp. 22–23.

31. Ibid., p. 38.

32. Ibid., chaps. 2, 3, and 4.

33. Natalie Zemon Davis, "The Reasons of Misrule," in *Society and Culture in Early Modern France* (Stanford, Calif.: Stanford University Press, 1975), pp. 97–123, 104–05; Flandrin, *Families in Former Times*, pp. 34–35.

34. Pierre Caspard, "Conceptions pré-nuptiales et développement du capitalisme dans la Principauté de Neuchâtel (1678–1820)," *Annales E.S.C. 29*, no. 4 (July–August 1974): 989–1008, 993–96; Edward Shorter, *The Making of the Modern Family* (New York: Basic Books, 1975), pp. 102–05; Michael Drake, *Population and Society in Norway, 1735–1865* (Cambridge: Cambridge University Press, 1969), pp. 138–45.

35. Shorter, *Making of the Modern Family*, pp. 102–03. The sources on which his account is based are listed in notes 53–59, p. 298.

36. Caspard, "Conceptions pré-nuptiales," p. 995.

37. Jean-Louis Flandrin, "Repression and Change in the Sexual Life of Young People in Medieval and Early Modern Times," *Journal of Family History* 2, no. 3 (September 1977): 196–210, 200–03, 205.

38. Molly Dougherty, *Becoming a Woman in Rural Black Culture* (New York: Holt, Rinehart and Winston, 1978), part 3, pp. 71–107.

39. Carroll Smith-Rosenberg, "The Female World of Love and Ritual: Relations Between Women in Nineteenth-Century America," *Signs* 1, no. 2 (Autumn 1975): 1–29. See also Nancy Cott, *The Bonds of Womanhood* (New Haven: Yale University Press, 1977).

40. Jacques Gélis, "Sages-femmes et accoucheurs: l'obstétrique populaire aux XVIIe et XVIIIe siècles," *Annales E.S.C.* 32 (September–October 1977): 927–57; Mireille Laget, "La naissance aux siècles classiques. Pratique des accouchements et attitudes collectives en France XVIIe et XVIIIe siècles," ibid., pp. 958–92.

41. Patricia Knight, "Women and Abortion in Victorian and Edwardian England," *History Workshop* 4 (Autumn 1977): 57–69, 58–59.

42. Angus McLaren, *Birth Control in Nineteenth-Century England* (London: Croom Helm, 1978), p. 242; Knight, "Women and Abortion," p. 60.

43. See Margaret L. Davies, ed., *Maternity, Letters from Working Women*, reprint ed. (New York and London: W. W. Norton, 1978), p. 56.

44. John R. Gillis, "Servants, Sexual Relations, and the Risks of Illegitimacy in London 1801–1900," *Feminist Studies* 5, no. 1 (Spring 1979): 142–73; Theresa M. McBride, *The Domestic Revolution* (New York: Holmes and Meier, 1976), chap. 6.

45. Verrier Elwin, *Kingdom of the Young* (Oxford: Oxford University Press, 1947).

46. Jean-Louis Flandrin, "Contraception, Marriage and Sexual Relations in the Christian West," in *Biology of Man in History*, ed. Robert Forster and Orest Ranum, tr. Elborg Forster and Patricia M. Ranum (Baltimore and London: John Hopkins University Press, 1975), pp. 23–47.

47. Flandrin, *Families in Former Times*, pp. 211–12.

48. Sir Frederick Pollock and Frederick William Maitland, *The History of English Law Before the Time of Edward I*, 2 vols., 2d ed. reissue (Cambridge: Cambridge University Press, 1968): 2, chap. 6; Willystine Goodsell, *A History of Marriage and the Family*, rev. ed. (New York: The Macmillan Company, 1934); O. R. McGregor, *Divorce in England. A Centenary Study* (London: Heinemann, 1957).

49. Flandrin, *Families in Former Times*, pp. 180–84.

50. Henriques, "Bastardy and the New Poor Law," pp. 118–19.

51. Quoted in ibid., p. 119.

52. Gillis, "Servants, Sexual Relations and the Risks of Illegitimacy."

53. Flandrin, "Repression and Change," p. 204.

54. Judith R. Walkowitz and Daniel J. Walkowitz, "'We Are Not Beasts of the Field': Prostitution and the Poor in Plymouth and Southampton Under the Contagious Diseases Acts," *Feminist Studies* 1, nos. 3–4 (Winter–Spring 1973): 73–106; Judith Walkowitz, "The Making of an Outcast Group," in *A Widening Sphere*, ed. Martha Vicinus (Bloomington: Indiana University Press, 1977): 72–93, 85–87; and Judith Walkowitz *Prostitution and Victorian Society: Women, Class and the State* (Cambridge: Cambridge University Press, 1980).

55. Guido Ruggiero, "Sexual Criminality in the Early Renaissance: Venice 1338–1358," *Journal of Social History* 8 (Summer 1975): 18–37; Randolph Trumbach, "London's Sodomites: Homosexual Behavior and Western Culture in the Eighteenth Century," *Journal of Social History* 11 (Fall 1977): 1–33; Jeffrey Weeks, *Coming Out: Homosexual Politics in Britain from the Nineteenth Century to the Present* (London and New York: Quartet Books, 1977), pp. 1–44; Louis Crompton, review of *Coming Out* by Weeks; *Socialism and the New Life* by Jeffrey Weeks and Sheila Rowbotham; and *Homosexuality and Literature* by Jeffrey Meyers, in *Victorian Studies* 22, no. 2 (Winter 1979): 211–13.

56. Weeks, *Coming Out*, pp. 19–20.

57. This view is implicit in Weeks' *Coming Out*.

58. David Levine, *Family Formation in an Age of Nascent Capitalism* (New York: Academic Press, 1977).

59. Tilly and Scott, *Women, Work and Family*, pp. 93–96. See also Lynn H. Lees,

Exiles of Erin: Irish Migration in Victorian London (Manchester: Manchester University Press, 1979) for a discussion of changes in ages of marriage of rural Irish who migrated to London at the time of the famine; and Louise A. Tilly, "The Family Wage Economy of a French Textile City: Roubaix, 1872–1906," *Journal of Family History* 4, no. 4 (Winter 1979): 381–94.

60. Tilly and Scott, *Women, Work and Family*, p. 96.

61. Edward Shorter, "Illegitimacy, Sexual Revolution and Social Change in Modern Europe," *Journal of Interdisciplinary History* 1 (Autumn 1971): 231–72.

62. Shorter's "Female Emancipation, Birth Control and Fertility in European History" (*American Historical Review* 78, no. 3 [June 1973]: 605–40), opened a debate on the sources of Europe's high birth and illegitimacy rates in the era of early industrialization. On illegitimacy, the weight of scholarship supports the view that the urban migration of young women made them especially vulnerable to illegitimate pregnancies. See Louise A. Tilly, Joan W. Scott, and Miriam Cohen, "Women's Work and European Fertility Patterns," *Journal of Interdisciplinary History* 6, no. 3 (Winter 1976): 447–76; and Cissie Fairchilds, "Female Sexual Attitudes and the Rise of Illegitimacy: A Case Study," *Journal of Interdisciplinary History* 8, no. 4 (Spring 1978): 627–67.

63. Trumbach, "London's Sodomites"; Weeks, *Coming Out*, pp. 35–42; Mary Mackintosh, "The Homosexual Role," in *Family in Transition*, ed. Arlene S. Skolnick and Jerome H. Skolnick (Boston: Little, Brown and Company, 1971), pp. 231–42, 236–38.

64. Weeks, *Coming Out*, part 4.

65. Ibid., p. 89.

66. Leonore Davidoff, "Mastered for Life: Servant and Wife in Victorian and Edwardian England," *Journal of Social History* 8 (Summer 1974): 404–28, 413–14.

67. Gillis, "Servants, Sexual Relations, and the Risks of Illegitimacy," p. 167.

68. The discussion that follows is based on Derek Hudson, *Munby, Man of Two Worlds: The Life and Diaries of Arthur J. Munby, 1828–1910* (Boston: Gambit, Inc., 1972); and on Leonore Davidoff's interpretative study, "Class and Gender in Victorian England: The Diaries of Arthur J. Munby and Hannah Cullwick," *Feminist Studies* 5, no. 1 (Spring 1979): 87–142.

69. Hudson, *Munby*, p. 69.

70. Davidoff, "Class and Gender," pp. 87–100.

71. Although they have very different theoretical perspectives, both Eli Zaretsky and Christopher Lasch believe that sexual identity takes shape in "personal" space. Eli Zaretsky, "Capitalism, the Family, and Personal Life, Part I," *Socialist Revolution* 3, nos. 1–2 (January–April 1973): 69–126; and Christopher Lasch, "The Family as a Haven in a Heartless World," *Salmagundi* 34 (Fall 1976): 42–55; and idem, "The Waning of Private Life," *Salmagundi* 36 (Winter 1977): 3–15.

72. The labeling of sexology and psychoanalysis as "ethnoscience," suggesting a folk system of understanding that is quite logical, but based on "wrong" assumptions linked to turn-of-the-century social perceptions, is Gayle Rubin's. Seeing the context in which these models of personal relationships developed as a part of changes in wider social power arrangements is the contribution of Foucault and of Donzelot. See Michel Foucault, *The History of Sexuality*, and Jacques Donzelot, *The Policing of Families*, tr. Robert Hurley (New York: Pantheon Books, 1979).

"Charity Girls" and City Pleasures: Historical Notes on Working-Class Sexuality, 1880–1920

Kathy Peiss

Uncovering the history of working-class sexuality has been a particularly intractable task for recent scholars. Diaries, letters, and memoirs, while a rich source for studies of bourgeois sexuality, offer few glimpses into working-class intimate life. We have had to turn to middle-class commentary and observations of working people, but these accounts often seem hopelessly moralistic and biased. The difficulty with such sources is not simply a question of tone or selectivity, but involves the very categories of analysis they employ. Reformers, social workers, and journalists viewed working-class women's sexuality through middle-class lenses, invoking sexual standards that set "respectability" against "promiscuity." When applied to unmarried women, these categories were constructed foremost around the biological fact of premarital virginity, and secondarily by such cultural indicators as manners, language, dress, and public interaction. Chastity was the measure of young women's respectability, and those who engaged in premarital intercourse, or, more importantly, dressed and acted as though they had, were classed as promiscuous women or prostitutes. Thus labor investigations of the late nineteenth century not only surveyed women's wages and working conditions, but delved into the issue of their sexual virtue, hoping to resolve scientifically the question of working women's respectability.[1]

Nevertheless, some middle-class observers in city missions and settlements recognized that their standards did not always reflect those of working-class youth. As one University Settlement worker argued, "Many of the liberties which are taken by tenement boys and girls with one another, and which seem quite improper to the 'up-towner,' are, in fact, practically harmless."[2] Working women's public behavior often seemed to fall between the traditional middle-class poles: they were not truly promiscuous in their actions, but neither were they models of decorum. A boarding-house matron, for example, puzzled over the behavior of Mary, a "good girl": "The other night she flirted with a man across the street," she explained. "It is true she dropped him when he offered to take her into a saloon. But she does go to picture shows and dance halls with 'pick up' men and boys."[3] Similarly, a city missionary noted that tenement dwellers followed different rules of etiquette, with the observation: "Young women sometimes allow young men to address them and caress them in a manner which would offend well-bred people, and yet those girls would indignantly resent any liberties which they consider dishonoring."[4] These examples suggest that we must reach beyond the dichotomized analysis of many middle-class observers and draw out the cultural categories created and acted on by working women themselves. How was sexuality "handled" culturally? What manners, etiquette, and sexual style met with general approval? What constituted sexual respectability? Does the polarized framework of the middle class reflect the realities of working-class culture?

Embedded within the reports and surveys lie small pieces of information that illuminate the social and cultural construction of sexuality among a number of working-class women. My discussion focuses on one set of young, white working women in New York City in the years 1880 to 1920. Most of these women were single wage earners who toiled in the city's factories, shops, and department stores, while devoting their evenings to the lively entertainment of the streets, public dance halls, and other popular amusements. Born or educated in the United States, many adopted a cultural style meant to distance themselves from their immigrant roots and familial traditions. Such women dressed in the latest finery, negotiated city life with ease, and sought intrigue and adventure with male companions. For this group of working women, sexuality became a central dimension of their emergent culture, a dimension that is revealed in their daily life of work and leisure.[5]

These New York working women frequented amusements in which familiarity and intermingling among strangers, not decorum, defined normal public behavior between the sexes. At movies and cheap theaters, crowds mingled during intermissions, shared picnic lunches, and commented volubly on performances. Strangers at Coney Island's amusement parks often involved each other in practical jokes and humorous escapades, while dance halls permitted close interaction between unfamiliar men and women. At one respectable Turnverein ball, for example, a vice investigator described closely the chaotic activity in the barroom between dances:

> Most of the younger couples were hugging and kissing, there was a general mingling of men and women at the different tables, almost everyone seemed to know one another and spoke to each other across the tables and joined couples at different tables, they

were all singing and carrying on, they kept running around the room and acted like a mob of lunatics let lo[o]se.[6]

As this observer suggests, an important aspect of social familiarity was the ease of sexual expression in language and behavior. Dances were advertised, for example, through the distribution of "pluggers," small printed cards announcing the particulars of the ball, along with snatches of popular songs or verse; the lyrics and pictures, noted one offended reformer, were often "so suggestive that they are absolutely indecent."[7]

The heightened sexual awareness permeating many popular amusements may also be seen in working-class dancing styles. While waltzes and two-steps were common, working women's repertoire included "pivoting" and "tough dances." While pivoting was a wild, spinning dance that promoted a charged atmosphere of physical excitement, tough dances ranged from a slow shimmy, or shaking of the hips and shoulders, to boisterous animal imitations. Such tough dances as the grizzly bear, Charlie Chaplin wiggle, and the dip emphasized bodily contact and the suggestion of sexual intercourse. As one dance investigator commented, "What particularly distinguishes this dance is the motion of the pelvic portions of the body."[8] In contrast, middle-class pleasure-goers accepted the animal dances only after the blatant sexuality had been tamed into refined movement. While cabaret owners enforced strict rules to discourage contact between strangers, managers of working-class dance halls usually winked at spieling, tough dancing, and unrestrained behavior.[9]

Other forms of recreation frequented by working-class youth incorporated a free and easy sexuality into their attractions. Many social clubs and amusement societies permitted flirting, touching, and kissing games at their meetings. One East Side youth reported that "they have kissing all through pleasure time, and use slang language, while in some they don't behave nice between [sic] young ladies."[10] Music halls and cheap vaudeville regularly worked sexual themes and suggestive humor into comedy routines and songs. At a Yiddish music hall popular with both men and women, one reformer found that "the songs are suggestive of everything but what is proper, the choruses are full of double meanings, and the jokes have broad and unmistakable hints of things indecent."[11] Similarly, Coney Island's Steeplechase amusement park, favored by working-class excursionists, carefully marketed sexual titillation and romance in attractions that threw patrons into each other, sent skirts flying, and evoked instant intimacy among strangers.[12]

In attending dance halls, social club entertainments, and amusement resorts, young women took part in a cultural milieu that expressed and affirmed heterosocial interactions. As reformer Belle Israels observed, "No amusement is complete in which 'he' is not a factor."[13] A common custom involved "picking up" unknown men or women in amusement resorts or on the streets, an accepted means of gaining companionship for an evening's entertainment. Indeed, some amusement societies existed for this very purpose. One vice investigator, in his search for "loose" women, was advised by a waiter to "go first on a Sunday night to 'Hans'l & Gret'l Amusement Society' at the Lyceum 86th Str & III Ave, there the girls come and men pick them up."[14] The waiter carefully stressed that these were respectable working women, not prostitutes. Nor was the pickup purely a male prerogative. "With the men they 'pick up,'" writer Hutchins Hapgood observed of East Side shop girls, "they will go to the theater, to late suppers, will be as jolly as they like."[15]

The heterosocial orientation of these amusements made popularity a goal to be pursued through dancing ability, willingness to drink, and eye-catching finery. Women who would not drink at balls and social entertainments were often ostracized by men, while cocktails and ingenious mixtures replaced the five-cent beer and helped to make drinking an acceptable female activity. Many women used clothing as a means of drawing attention to themselves, wearing high-heeled shoes, fancy dresses, costume jewelry, elaborate pompadours, and cosmetics. As one working woman sharply explained, "If you want to get any notion took of you, you gotta have some style about you."[16] The clothing that such women wore no longer served as an emblem of respectability. "The way women dress today they all look like prostitutes," reported one rueful waiter to a dance hall investigator, "and the waiter can some times get in bad by going over and trying to put some one next to them, they may be respectable women and would jump on the waiter."[17]

Underlying the relaxed sexual style and heterosocial interaction was the custom of "treating." Men often treated their female companions to drinks and refreshments, theater tickets, and other incidentals. Women might pay a dance hall's entrance fee or carfare out to an amusement park, but they relied on men's treats to see them through the evening's entertainment. Such treats were highly prized by young working women; as Belle Israels remarked, the announcement that "he treated" was "the acme of achievement in retailing experiences with the other sex."[18]

Treating was not a one-way proposition, however, but entailed an exchange relationship. Financially unable to reciprocate in kind, women offered sexual favors of varying degrees, ranging from flirtatious companionship to sexual intercourse, in exchange for men's treats. "Pleasures don't cost girls so much as they do young men," asserted one saleswoman. "If they are agreeable they are invited out a good deal, and they are not allowed to pay anything." Reformer Lillian Betts concurred, observing that the working woman held herself responsible for failing to wangle men's invitations and believed that "it is not only her misfortune, but her fault; she should be more attractive."[19] Gaining men's treats placed a high premium on allure and personality, and sometimes involved aggressive and frank "overtures to men whom they desire to attract," often with implicit sexual proposals. One investigator, commenting on women's dependency on men in their leisure time, aptly observed that "those who are unattractive, and those who have puritanic notions, fare but ill in the matter of enjoyments. On the other hand those who do become popular have to compromise with the best conventional usage."[20]

Many of the sexual patterns acceptable in the world of leisure activity were mirrored in the workplace. Sexual harassment by employers, foremen, and fellow workers was a widespread practice in this period, and its form often paralleled the relationship of treating, particularly in service and sales jobs. Department store managers, for example, advised employees to round out their meager salaries by finding a "gentleman friend" to purchase clothing and pleasures. An angry saleswoman testified, for example, that "one of the employers has told me, on a $6.50 wage, he don't care where I get my clothes from as long as I have them, to be dressed to suit him."[21] Waitresses knew that accepting the advances of male customers often brought good tips, and some used their opportunities to enter an active social life with men. "Most of the girls quite frankly admit making 'dates' with strange men," one investigator found. "These 'dates' are made with no thought on the part of the girl beyond getting the good time which she cannot afford herself."[22]

In factories where men and women worked together, the sexual style that we have seen on the dance floor was often reproduced on the shop floor. Many factories lacked privacy in dressing facilities, and workers tolerated a degree of familiarity and roughhousing between men and women. One cigar maker observed that his workplace socialized the young into sexual behavior unrestrained by parental and community control. Another decried the tendency of young boys "of thirteen or fourteen casting an eye upon a 'mash.'" Even worse, he testified, were the

> many men who are respected—when I say respected and respectable, I mean who walk the streets and are respected as working men, and who would not under any circumstances offer the slightest insult or disrespectful remark or glance to a female in the streets, but who, in the shops, will whoop and give expressions to

"cat calls" and a peculiar noise made with their lips, which is supposed to be an endearing salutation.[23]

In sexually segregated workplaces, sexual knowledge was probably transmitted among working women. A YWCA report in 1913 luridly asserted that "no girl is more 'knowing' than the wage-earner, for the 'older hands' initiate her early through the unwholesome story or innuendo."[24] Evidence from factories, department stores, laundries, and restaurants substantiates the sexual consciousness of female workers. Women brought to the workplace tales of their evening adventures and gossip about dates and eligible men, recounting to their co-workers the triumphs of the latest ball or outing. Women's socialization into a new shop might involve a ritualist exchange about "gentlemen friends." In one laundry, for example, an investigator repeatedly heard this conversation:

> "Say, you got a feller?"
> "Sure. Ain't you got one?"
> "Sure."[25]

Through the use of slang and "vulgar" language, heterosexual romance was expressed in a sexually explicit context. Among waitresses, for example, frank discussion of lovers and husbands during breaks was an integral part of the work day. One investigator found that "there was never any open violation of the proprieties but always the suggestive talk and behavior." Laundries, too, witnessed "a great deal of swearing among the women." A 1914 study of department store clerks found a similar style and content in everyday conversation:

> While it is true that the general attitude toward men and sex relations was normal, all the investigators admitted a freedom of speech frequently verging upon the vulgar, but since there was very little evidence of any actual immorality, this can probably be likened to the same spirit which prompts the telling of risqué stories in other circles.[26]

In their workplaces and leisure activities, many working women discovered a milieu that tolerated, and at times encouraged, physical and verbal familiarity between men and women, and stressed the exchange of sexual favors for social and economic advantages. Such women probably received conflicting messages about the virtues of virginity, and necessarily mediated the parental, religious, and educational injunctions concerning chastity, and the "lessons" of urban life and labor. The choice made by some women to engage in a relaxed sexual style needs to be understood in terms of the larger relations of class and gender that structured their sexual culture.

Most single working-class women were wage-earners for a few years before marriage, contributing to the household income or supporting themselves. Sexual segmentation of the labor market placed women in semi-skilled, seasonal employment with high rates of turnover. Few women earned a "living wage," estimated to be $9.00 or $10.00 a week in 1910, and the wage differential between men and women was vast. Those who lived alone in furnished rooms or boarding houses consumed their earnings in rent, meals, and clothing. Many self-supporting women were forced to sacrifice an essential item in their weekly budgets, particularly food, in order to pay for amusements. Under such circumstances, treating became a viable option. "If my boy friend didn't take me out," asked one working woman, "how could I ever go out?"[27] While many women accepted treats from "steadies," others had no qualms about receiving them from acquaintances or men they picked up at amusement places. As one investigator concluded, "The acceptance on the part of the girl of almost any invitation needs little explanation when one realizes that she often goes pleasureless unless she does accept 'free treats.'"[28] Financial resources were little better for the vast majority of women living with families and relatives. Most of them contributed all of their earnings to the family, receiving only small amounts of spending money, usually 25¢ to 50¢ a week, in return. This sum covered the costs of simple entertainments, but could not purchase higher priced amusements.[29]

Moreover, the social and physical space of the tenement home and boarding house contributed to freer social and sexual practices. Working women living alone ran the gauntlet between landladies' suspicious stares and the knowing glances of male boarders. One furnished-room dweller attested to the pressure placed on young, single women: "Time and again when a male lodger meets a girl on the landing, his salutation usually ends with something like this: 'Won't you step into my place and have a glass of beer with me?'"[30]

The tenement home, too, presented a problem to parents who wished to maintain control over their daughters' sexuality. Typical tenement apartments offered limited opportunities for family activities or chaperoned socializing. Courtship proved difficult in homes where families and boarders crowded into a few small rooms, and the "parlor" served as kitchen, dining room, and bedroom. Instead, many working-class daughters socialized on streetcorners, rendezvoused in cafes, and courted on trolley cars. As one settlement worker observed, "Boys and girls and young men and women of respectable families are almost obliged to carry on many of their friendships, and perhaps their love-making, on tenement stoops or on street corners."[31] Another reformer found that girls whose parents forebade men's visits to the home managed to escape into the streets and dance halls to meet them. Such young women demanded greater independence in the realm of "personal life" in exchange for their financial contribution to the family. For some, this new freedom spilled over into their sexual practices.[32]

The extent of the sexual culture described here is particularly difficult to establish, since the evidence is too meager to permit conclusions about specific groups of working women, their beliefs about sexuality, and their behavior. Scattered evidence does suggest a range of possible responses, the parameters within which most women would choose to act and define their behavior as socially acceptable. Within this range, there existed a subculture of working women who fully bought into the system of treating and sexual exchange, by trading sexual favors of varying degrees for gifts, treats, and a good time. These women were known in underworld slang as "charity girls," a term that differentiated them from prostitutes because they did not accept money in their sexual encounters with men. As vice reformer George Kneeland found, they "offer themselves to strangers, not for money, but for presents, attention, and pleasure, and most important, a yielding to sex desire."[33] Only a thin line divided these women and "occasional prostitutes," women who slipped in and out of prostitution when unemployed or in need of extra income. Such behavior did not result in the stigma of the "fallen woman." Many working women apparently acted like Dottie: "When she needed a pair of shoes she had found it easy to 'earn' them in the way that other girls did." Dottie, the investigator reported, was now known as a respectable married woman.[34]

Such women were frequent patrons of the city's dance halls. Vice investigators note a preponderant number of women at dances who clearly were not prostitutes, but were "game" and "lively"; these charity girls often comprised half or more of the dancers in a hall. One dance hall investigator distinguished them with the observation, "Some of the women . . . are out for the coin, but there is a lot that come in here that are charity."[35] One waiter at La Kuenstler Klause, a restaurant with music and dancing, noted that "girls could be gotten here, but they don't go with men for money, only for good time." The investigator continued in his report, "Most of the girls are working girls, not prostitutes, they smoke cigarettes, drink liquers and dance dis.[orderly] dances, stay out late and stay with any man, that pick them up first."[36] Meeting two women at a bar, another investigator remarked, "They are both supposed to be working girls but go out for a good time and go the limit."[37]

Some women obviously relished the game of extracting treats from men. One vice investigator offered to take a Kitty Graham, who apparently worked both as a department store clerk and occasional prostitute, to the Central Opera House at 3 A.M.; he noted that "she was willing to go if I'd take a taxi; I finally coaxed her to come with me in a street car."[38] Similarly, Frances Donovan observed waitresses "talking about their engagements which they had for the evening or for the night and quite frankly saying what they expected to get from this or that fellow in the line of money, amusement, or clothes."[39] Working women's manipulation of treating is also suggested by this unguarded conversation overheard by a journalist at Coney Island:

"What sort of a time did you have?"
"Great. He blew in $5 on the blow-out."
"You beat me again. My chump only spent $2.50."[40]

These women had clearly accepted the full implications of the system of treating and the sexual culture surrounding it.

While this evidence points to the existence of charity girls—working women defined as respectable, but who engaged in sexual activity—it tells us little about their numbers, social background, working lives, or relationships to family and community. The vice reports indicate that they were generally young women, many of whom lived at home with their families. One man in a dance hall remarked, for example, that "he sometimes takes them to the hotels, but sometimes the girls won't go to [a] hotel to stay for the night, they are afraid of their mothers, so he gets away with it in the hallway."[41] While community sanctions may have prevented such activity within the neighborhood, the growth of large public dance halls, cabarets, and metropolitan amusement resorts provided an anonymous space in which the subculture of treating could flourish.

The charity girl's activities form only one response in a wide spectrum of social and sexual behavior. Many young women defined themselves sharply against the freer sexuality of their pleasure-seeking sisters, associating "respectability" firmly with premarital chastity and circumspect behavior. One working woman carefully explained her adherence to propriety: "I never go out in the evenings except to my relatives because if I did, I should lose my reputation and that is all I have left." Similarly, shop girls guarded against sexual advances from co-workers and male customers by spurning the temptations of popular amusements. "I keep myself to myself," said one saleswoman. "I don't make friends in the stores very easily because you can't be sure what any one is like."[42] Settlement workers also noted that women who freely attended "dubious resorts" or bore illegitimate children were often stigmatized by neighbors and workmates. Lillian Betts, for example, cites the case of working women who refused to labor until their employer dismissed a co-worker who had born a baby out of wedlock. To Betts, however, their adherence to the standard of virginity seemed instrumental, and not a reflection of moral absolutism: "The hardness with which even the suggestion of looseness is treated in any group of working girls is simply an expression of self-preservation."[43]

Other observers noted an ambivalence in the attitudes of young working women toward sexual relations. Social workers reported that the critical stance toward premarital pregnancy was "not always unmixed with a certain degree of admiration for the success with the other sex which the difficulty implies." According to this study, many women increasingly found premarital intercourse acceptable in particular situations: " 'A girl can have many friends,' explained one of them, 'but when she gets a "steady," there's only one way to have him and to keep him; I mean to keep him long.' "[44] Such women shared with charity girls the assumption that respectability was not predicated solely on chastity.

Perhaps few women were charity girls or occasional prostitutes, but many more must have been conscious of the need to negotiate sexual encounters in the workplace or in their leisure time. Women would have had to weigh their desire for social participation against traditional sanctions regarding sexual behavior, and charity girls offered to some a model for resolving this conflict. This process is exemplified in Clara Laughlin's report of an attractive but "proper" working woman who could not understand why men friends dropped her after a few dates. Finally she receives the worldly advice of a co-worker that social participation involves an exchange relationship: "Don't yeh know there ain't no feller goin' t'spend coin on yeh fer nothin'? Yeh gotta be a good Indian, Kid—we all gotta!"[45]

For others, charity girls represented a yardstick against which they might measure their own ideas of respectability. The nuances of that measurement were expressed, for example, in a dialogue between a vice investigator and the hat girl at Semprini's dance hall. Answering his proposal for a date, the investigator noted, she "said she'd be glad to go out with me but told me there was nothing doing [i.e., sexually]. Said she didn't like to see a man spend money on her and then get disappointed." Commenting on the charity girls that frequented the dance hall, she remarked that "these women get her sick, she can't see why a woman should lay down for a man the first time they take her out. She said it wouldn't be so bad if they went out with the men 3 or 4 times and then went to bed with them but not the first time."[46]

For this hat girl and other young working women, respectability was not defined by the strict measurement of chastity employed by many middle-class observers and reformers. Instead, they adopted a more instrumental and flexible approach to sexual behavior. Premarital sex *could* be labeled respectable in particular social contexts. Thus charity girls distinguished their sexual activity from prostitution, a less acceptable practice, because they did not receive money from men. Other women, who might view charity girls as promiscuous, were untroubled by premarital intimacy with a steady boyfriend.

This fluid definition of sexual respectability was embedded within the social relation of class and gender, as experienced by women in their daily round of work, leisure, and family life. Women's wage labor and the demands of the working-class household offered daughters few resources for entertainment. At the same time, new commercial amusements offered a tempting world of pleasure and companionship beyond parental control. Within this context, some young women sought to exchange sexual goods for access to that world and its seeming independence, choosing not to defer sexual relations until marriage. Their notions of legitimate premarital behavior contrast markedly with the dominant middle-class view, which placed female sexuality within a dichotomous and rigid framework. Whether a hazard at work, fun and adventure at night, or an opportunity to be exploited, sexual expression and intimacy comprised an integral part of these working women's lives.

Notes

1. See, for example, Carroll D. Wright, *The Working Girls of Boston* (1889; New York: Arno Press, 1969).

2. "Influences in Street Life," University Settlement Society *Report* (1900), p. 30.

3. Marie S. Orenstein, "How the Working Girl of New York Lives," New York State, Factory Investigating Commission, *Fourth Report Transmitted to Legislature*, February 15, 1915, Senate Doc. 43, vol. 4, app. 2 (Albany: J. B. Lyon Co., 1915), p. 1697.

4. William T. Elsing, "Life in New York Tenement-Houses as Seen by a City Missionary," *Scribner's* 11 (June 1892): 716.

5. For a more detailed discussion of these women, and further documentation of their social relations and leisure activities, see my dissertation, "Cheap Amusements: Gender Relations and the Use of Leisure Time in New York City, 1880 to 1920," Ph.D. diss., Brown University, 1982.

6. Investigator's Report, Remey's, 917 Eighth Ave., February 11, 1917, Committee of Fourteen Papers, New York Public Library Manuscript Division, New York.

7. George Kneeland, *Commercialized Prostitution in New York City* (New York: The Century Co., 1913), p. 68; Louise de Koven Bowen, "Dance Halls," *Survey* 26 (3 July 1911): 384.

8. Committee on Amusements and Vacation Resources of Working Girls, two-page circular, in Box 28, "Parks and Playgrounds Correspondence," Lillian Wald Collection, Rare Book and Manuscripts Library, Columbia University, New York.

9. See, for example, Investigator's Report, Princess Cafe, 1206 Broadway, January 1, 1917; and Excelsior Cafe, 306 Eighth Ave., December 21, 1916, Committee of Fourteen Papers. For an excellent discussion of middle- and upper-class leisure activities, see Lewis A. Erenberg, *Steppin' Out: New York Nightlife and the Transformation of American Culture, 1890–1930* (Westport, Conn.: Greenwood Press, 1981).

10. "Social Life in the Streets," University Settlement Society *Report* (1899), p. 32.

11. Paul Klapper, "The Yiddish Music Hall," *University Settlement Studies* 2, no. 4 (1905): 22.

12. For a description of Coney Island amusements, see Edo McCullough, *Good Old Coney Island; A Sentimental Journey into the Past* (New York: Charles Scribner's Sons, 1957), pp. 309–13; and Oliver Pilot and Jo Ransom, *Sodom by the Sea: An Affectionate History of Coney Island* (Garden City, N.J.: Doubleday, 1941).

13. Belle Lindner Israels, "The Way of the Girl," *Survey* 22 (3 July 1909): 486.

14. Investigator's Report, La Kuenstler Klause, 1490 Third Ave., January 19, 1917, Committee of Fourteen Papers.

15. Hutchins Hapgood, *Types from City Streets* (New York: Funk and Wagnalls, 1910), p. 131.

16. Clara Laughlin, *The Work-A-Day Girl: A Study of Some Present Conditions* (1913; New York: Arno Press, 1974), pp. 47, 145. On working women's clothing, see Helen Campbell, *Prisoners of Poverty: Women Wage-Earners, Their Trades and Their Lives* (1887; Westport, Conn.: Greenwood Press, 1970), p. 175; "What It Means to Be a Department Store Girl as Told by the Girl Herself," *Ladies Home Journal* 30 (June 1913): 8; "A Salesgirl's Story," *Independent* 54 (July 1902): 1821. Drinking is discussed in Kneeland, *Commercialized Prostitution*, p. 70; and Belle Israels, "Diverting a Pastime," *Leslie's Weekly* 113 (27 July 1911): 100.

17. Investigator's Report, Weimann's, 1422 St. Nicholas Ave., February 11, 1917, Committee of Fourteen Papers.

18. Israels, "Way of the Girl," p. 489; Ruth True, *The Neglected Girl* (New York: Russell Sage Foundation, 1914), p. 59.

19. "A Salesgirl's Story," p. 1821; Lillian Betts, *Leaven in a Great City* (New York: Dodd, Mead, 1902), pp. 251–52.

20. New York State, Factory Investigating Commission, *Fourth Report*, vol. 4, pp. 1585–86; Robert Woods and Albert Kennedy, *Young Working-Girls: A Summary of Evidence from Two Thousand Social Workers* (Boston: Houghton Mifflin, 1913), p. 105.

21. New York State, Factory Investigating Commission, *Fourth Report*, vol. 5, p. 2809; see also Sue Ainslie Clark and Edith Wyatt, *Making Both Ends Meet: The Income and Outlay of New York Working Girls* (New York: Macmillan, 1911), p. 28. For an excellent analysis of sexual harassment, see Mary Bularzik, *Sexual Harassment at the Workplace: Historical Notes* (Somerville, Mass.: New England Free Press, 1978).

22. Consumers' League of New York, *Behind the Scenes in a Restaurant: A Study of 1017 Women Restaurant Employees* (n.p., n.n.p., 1916), p. 24; Frances Donovan, *The Woman Who Waits* (1920; New York: Arno Press, 1974), p. 42.

23. New York Bureau of Labor Statistics, *Second Annual Report* (1884), pp. 153, 158; *Third Annual Report* (1885), pp. 150–51.

24. Report of Commission on Social Morality from the Christian Standpoint, Made to the 4th Biennial Convention of the Young Women's Christian Associations of the U.S.A., 1913, Records File Collection, Archives of the National Board of the YWCA of the United States of America, New York, N.Y.

25. Clark and Wyatt, *Making Both Ends Meet*, pp. 187–88; see also Dorothy Richardson, *The Long Day*, in *Women at Work*, ed. William L. O'Neill (New York: Quadrangle, 1972); Amy E. Tanner, "Glimpses at the Mind of a Waitress," *American Journal of Sociology* 13 (July 1907): 52.

26. Committee of Fourteen in New York City, *Annual Report for 1914*, p. 40; Clark and Wyatt, *Making Both Ends Meet*, p. 188; Donovan, *The Woman Who Waits*, pp. 26, 80–81.

27. Esther Packard, "Living on Six Dollars a Week," New York State, Factory Investigating Commission, *Fourth Report*, vol. 4, pp. 1677–78. For a discussion of women's wages in New York, see ibid., vol. 1, p. 35; and vol. 4, pp. 1081, 1509. For

an overview of working conditions, see Barbara Wertheimer, *We Were There: The Story of Working Women in America* (New York: Pantheon Books, 1977), pp. 209–48.

28. Packard, "Living on Six Dollars a Week," p. 1685.
29. New York State, Factory Investigating Commission, *Fourth Report,* vol. 4, pp. 1512–13, 1581–83; True, *Neglected Girl,* p. 59.
30. Marie Orenstein, "How the Working Girl of New York Lives," p. 1702. See also Esther Packard, *A Study of Living Conditions of Self-Supporting Women in New York City* (New York: Metropolitan Board of the YWCA, 1915).
31. "Influences in Street Life," p. 30; see also Samuel Chotzinoff, *A Lost Paradise* (New York: Knopf, 1955), p. 81.
32. On the rejection of parental controls by young women, see Leslie Woodcock Tentler, *Wage-Earning Women: Industrial Work and Family Life in the United States, 1900–1930* (New York: Oxford University Press, 1979), pp. 110–13. For contemporary accounts, see True, *Neglected Girl,* pp. 54–55, 62–63, 162–63; Lillian Betts, "Tenement House Life and Recreation," *Outlook* (11 February 1899): 365.
33. "Memoranda on Vice Problem: IV. Statement of George J. Kneeland," New York State, Factory Investigating Commission, *Fourth Report,* v.1, p. 403. See also Committee of Fourteen, *Annual Report* (1917), p. 15, and *Annual Report* (1918), p. 32; Woods and Kennedy, *Young Working-Girls,* p. 85.
34. Donovan, *The Woman Who Waits,* p. 71; on occasional prostitution, see U.S. Senate, *Report on the Condition of Women and Child Wage-Earners in the United States,* U.S. Sen. Doc. 645, 61st Cong., 2nd Sess. (Washington, D.C.: GPO), vol. 15, p. 83; Laughlin, *The Work-A-Day Girl,* pp. 51–52.
35. Investigator's Report, 2150 Eighth Ave., January 12, 1917, Committee of Fourteen Papers.
36. Investigator's Report, La Kuenstler Klause, 1490 Third Ave., January 19, 1917, Committee of Fourteen Papers.
37. Investigator's Report, Bobby More's, 252 W. 31 Street, February 3, 1917, Committee of Fourteen Papers.
38. Investigator's Report, Remey's, 917 Eighth Ave., December 23, 1916, Committee of Fourteen Papers.
39. Donovan, *The Woman Who Waits,* p. 55.
40. Edwin Slosson, "The Amusement Business," *Independent* 57 (21 July 1904): 139.
41. Investigator's Report, Clare Hotel and Palm Gardens/McNamara's, 2150 Eighth Ave., January 12, 1917, Committee of Fourteen Papers.
42. Marie Orenstein, "How the Working Girl of New York Lives," p. 1703; Clark and Wyatt, *Making Both Ends Meet,* pp. 28–29.
43. Betts, *Leaven in a Great City,* pp. 81, 219.
44. Woods and Kennedy, *Young Working-Girls,* pp. 87, 85.
45. Laughlin, *The Work-A-Day Girl,* p. 50.
46. Investigator's Report, Semprini's, 145 W. 50 Street, October 5, 1918, Committee of Fourteen Papers.

Capitalism and Gay Identity
John D'Emilio

For gay men and lesbians, the 1970s were years of significant achievement. Gay liberation and women's liberation changed the sexual landscape of the nation. Hundreds of thousands of gay women and men came out and openly affirmed same-sex eroticism. We won repeal of sodomy laws in half the states, a partial lifting of the exclusion of lesbians and gay men from federal employment, civil rights protection in a few dozen cities, the inclusion of gay rights in the platform of the Democratic Party, and the elimination of homosexuality from the psychiatric profession's list of mental illnesses. The gay male subculture expanded and became increasingly visible in large cities, and lesbian feminists pioneered in building alternative institutions and an alternative culture that attempted to embody a liberatory vision of the future.

In the 1980s, however, with the resurgence of an active right wing, gay men and lesbians face the future warily. Our victories appear tenuous and fragile; the relative freedom of the past few years seems too recent to be permanent. In some parts of the lesbian and gay male community, a feeling of doom is growing: analogies with McCarthy's America, when "sexual perverts" were a special target of the Right, and with Nazi Germany, where gays were shipped to concentration camps, surface with increasing frequency. Everywhere there is the sense that new strategies are in order if we want to preserve our gains and move ahead.

I believe that a new, more accurate theory of gay history must be part of this political enterprise. When the gay liberation movement began at the end of the 1960s, gay men and lesbians had no history that we could use to fashion our goals and strategy. In the ensuing years, in building a movement without a knowledge of our history, we instead invented a mythology. This mythical history drew on personal experience, which we read backward in time. For instance, most lesbians and gay men in the 1960s first discovered their homosexual desires in isolation, unaware of others, and without resources for naming and understanding what they felt. From this experience, we constructed a myth of silence, invisibility, and isolation as the essential characteristics of gay life in the past as well as the present. Moreover, because we faced so many oppressive laws, public policies, and cultural beliefs, we projected this into an image of the abysmal past: until gay liberation, lesbians and gay men were always the victims of systematic, undifferentiated, terrible oppression.

These myths have limited our political perspective. They have contributed, for instance, to an overreliance on a strategy of coming out—if every gay man and lesbian in America came out, gay oppression would end—and have allowed us to ignore the institutionalized ways in which homophobia and heterosexism are reproduced. They have encouraged, at times, an incapacitating despair, especially at moments like the present: How can we unravel a gay oppression so pervasive and unchanging?

There is another historical myth that enjoys nearly universal acceptance in the gay movement, the myth of the "eternal homosexual." The argument runs something like this: gay men and lesbians always were and always will be. We are everywhere; not just now, but throughout history, in all societies and all periods. This myth served a positive political function in the first years of gay liberation. In the early 1970s, when we battled an ideology that either denied our existence or defined us as psychopathic individuals or freaks of nature, it was empowering to assert that "we are everywhere." But in recent years it has confined us as surely as the most homophobic medical theories, and locked our movement in place.

Here I wish to challenge this myth. I want to argue that gay men and lesbians have *not* always existed. Instead, they are a product of history, and have come into existence in a specific historical era. Their emergence is associated with the relations of capitalism; it has been the historical development of capitalism—more specifically, its free labor system—that has allowed large numbers of men and women in the late twentieth century to call themselves gay, to see themselves as part of a community of similar men and women, and to organize politically on the basis of that identity.[1] Finally, I want to suggest some political lessons we can draw from this view of history.

What, then, are the relationships between the free labor system of capitalism and homosexuality? First, let me review some features of capitalism. Under capitalism, workers are "free" laborers in two ways. We have the freedom to look for a job. We own our ability to work and have the freedom to sell our labor power for wages to anyone willing to buy it. We are also freed from the ownership of anything except our labor power. Most of us do not own the land or the tools that produce what we need, but rather have to work for a living in order to survive. So, if we are free to sell our labor power in the positive sense, we are also freed, in the negative sense, from any other alternative. This dialectic—the constant interplay between exploitation and some measure of autonomy—informs all of the history of those who have lived under capitalism.

As capital—money used to make more money—expands, so does this system of free labor. Capital expands in several ways. Usually it expands in the same place, transforming small firms into larger ones, but it also expands by taking over new areas of production: the weaving of cloth, for instance, or the baking of bread. Finally, capital expands geographically. In the United States, capitalism initially took root in the Northeast, at a time when slavery was the dominant system in the South and when noncapitalist Native American societies occupied the western half of the continent. During the nineteenth century, capital spread from the Atlantic to the Pacific, and in the twentieth, U.S. capital has penetrated almost every part of the world.

The expansion of capital and the spread of wage labor have effected a profound transformation in the structure and functions of the nuclear family, the ideology of family life, and the meaning of heterosexual relations. It is these changes in the family that are most directly linked to the appearance of a collective gay life.

The white colonists in seventeenth-century New England established villages structured around a household economy, composed of family units that were basically self-sufficient, independent, and patriarchal. Men, women, and children farmed land owned by the male head of household. Although there was a division of labor between men and women, the family was truly an interdependent unit of production: the survival of each member depended on the cooperation of all. The home was a workplace where women processed raw farm products into food for daily consumption, where they made clothing, soap, and candles, and where husbands, wives, and children worked together to produce the goods they consumed.

By the nineteenth century, this system of household production was in decline. In the Northeast, as merchant capitalists invested the money accumulated through trade in the production of goods, wage labor became more common. Men and women were drawn out of the largely self-sufficient household economy of the colonial era into a capitalist system of free labor. For women in the nineteenth century, working for wages rarely lasted beyond marriage; for men, it became a permanent condition.

The family was thus no longer an independent unit of production. But although no longer independent, the family was still interdependent. Because capitalism had not expanded very far, because it had not yet taken over—or socialized—the production of consumer goods, women still performed necessary productive labor in the home. Many families no longer produced grain, but wives still baked into bread the flour they bought with their husbands' wages; or, when they purchased yarn or cloth, they still made clothing for their families. By the mid-1800s, capitalism had destroyed the economic self-sufficiency of many families, but not the mutual dependence of the members.

This transition away from the household family-based economy to a fully developed capitalist free labor economy occurred very slowly, over almost two centuries. As late as 1920, 50 percent of the U.S. population lived in communities of fewer than 2,500 people. The vast majority of blacks in the early twentieth century lived outside the free labor economy, in a system of sharecropping and tenancy that rested on the family. Not only did independent farming as a way of life still exist for millions of Americans, but even in towns and small cities women continued to grow and process food, make clothing, and engage in other kinds of domestic production.

But for those people who felt the brunt of these changes, the family took on new significance as an affective unit, an institution that produced not goods but emotional satisfaction and happiness. By the 1920s among the white middle class, the ideology surrounding the family described it as the means through which men and women formed satisfying, mutually enhancing relationships and created an environment that nurtured children. The family became the setting for a "personal life," sharply distinguished and disconnected from the public world of work and production.[2]

The meaning of heterosexual relations also changed. In colonial New England, the birthrate averaged over seven children per woman of childbearing age. Men and women needed the labor of children. Producing offspring was as necessary for survival as producing grain. Sex was harnessed to procreation. The Puritans did not celebrate *hetero*-sexuality but rather marriage; they condemned *all* sexual expression outside the marriage bond and did not differentiate sharply between sodomy and heterosexual fornication.

By the 1970s, however, the birthrate had dropped to under two. With the exception of the post-World War II baby boom, the decline has been continuous for two centuries, paralleling the spread of capitalist relations of production. It occurred even when access to contraceptive devices and abortion was systematically curtailed. The decline has included every segment of the population—urban and rural families, blacks and whites, ethnics and WASPs, the middle class and the working class.

As wage labor spread and production became socialized, then, it became possible to release sexuality from the "imperative" to procreate. Ideologically, heterosexual expression came to be a means of establishing intimacy, promoting happiness, and experiencing pleasure. In divesting the household of its economic independence and fostering the separation of sexuality from procreation, capitalism has created conditions that allow some men and women to organize a personal life around their erotic/emotional attraction to their own sex. It has made possible the formation of urban communities of lesbians and gay men and, more recently, of a politics based on a sexual identity.

Evidence from colonial New England court records and church sermons indicates that male and female homosexual behavior existed in the seventeenth century. Homosexual *behavior*, however, is different from homosexual *identity*. There was, quite simply, no "social space" in the colonial system of production that allowed men and women to be gay. Survival was structured around participation in a nuclear family. There were certain homosexual acts—sodomy among men, "lewdness" among women—in which individuals engaged, but family was so pervasive that colonial society lacked even the category of homosexual or lesbian to describe a person. It is quite possible that some men and women experienced a stronger attraction to their own sex than to the opposite sex—in fact, some colonial court cases refer to men who persisted in their "unnatural" attractions—but one could not fashion out of that preference a way of life. Colonial Massachusetts even had laws prohibiting unmarried adults from living outside family units.[3]

By the second half of the nineteenth century, this situation was noticeably changing as the capitalist system of free labor took hold. Only when *individuals* began to make their living through wage labor, instead of as parts of an interdependent family unit, was it possible for homosexual desire to coalesce into a personal identity—an identity based on the ability to remain outside the heterosexual family and to construct a personal life based on attraction to one's own sex. By the end of the century, a class of men and women existed who recognized their erotic interest in their own sex, saw it as a trait that set them apart from the majority, and sought others like themselves. These early gay lives came from a wide social spectrum: civil servants and business executives, department store clerks and college professors, factory operatives, ministers, lawyers, cooks, domestics, hoboes, and the idle rich: men and women, black and white, immigrant and native born.

In this period, gay men and lesbians began to invent ways of meeting each other and sustaining a group life. Already, in the early twentieth century, large cities contained male homosexual bars. Gay men staked out cruising areas, such as Riverside Drive in New York City and Lafayette Park in Washington. In St. Louis and the nation's capital, annual drag balls brought together large numbers of black gay men. Public bathhouses and YMCAs became gathering spots for male homosexuals. Lesbians formed literary societies and private social clubs. Some working-class women "passed" as men to obtain better paying jobs and lived with other women—lesbian couples who appeared to the world as husband and wife. Among the faculties of women's colleges, in the settlement houses, and in the professional associations and clubs that women formed one could find lifelong intimate relationships supported by a web of lesbian friends. By the 1920s and 1930s, large cities such as New York and Chicago contained lesbian bars. These patterns of living could evolve because capitalism allowed individuals to survive beyond the confines of the family.[4]

Simultaneously, ideological definitions of homosexual behavior changed. Doctors developed theories about homosexuality, describing it as a condition, something that was inherent in a person, a part of his or her "nature." These theories did not represent scientific breakthroughs, elucidations of previously undiscovered areas of knowledge; rather, they were an ideological response to a new way of organizing one's personal life. The popularization of the medical model, in turn, affected the consciousness of the women and men who experienced homosexual desire, so that they came to define themselves through their erotic life.[5]

These new forms of gay identity and patterns of group life also reflected the differentiation of people according to gender, race, and class that is so pervasive in capitalist societies. Among whites, for instance, gay men have traditionally been more visible than lesbians. This partly stems from the division between the public male sphere and the private female sphere. Streets, parks, and bars, especially at night, were "male space." Yet the greater visibility of white gay men also reflected their larger numbers. The Kinsey studies of the 1940s and 1950s found significantly more men than women with predominantly homosexual histories, a situation caused, I would argue, by the fact that captialism had drawn far more men than women into the labor force, and at higher wages. Men could more easily construct a personal life independent of attachments to the opposite sex, whereas women were more likely to remain economically dependent on men. Kinsey also found a strong positive correlation between years of schooling and lesbian activity. College-educated white women, far more able than their working-class sisters to support themselves, could survive more easily without intimate relationships with men.[6]

Among working-class immigrants in the early twentieth century, closely knit kin networks and an ethic of family solidarity placed constraints on individual autonomy that made gayness a difficult option to pursue. In contrast, for reasons not altogether clear, urban black communities appeared relatively tolerant of homosexuality. The popularity in the 1920s and 1930s of songs with lesbian and gay male themes— "B. D. Woman," "Prove It on Me," "Sissy Man," "Fairey Blues"— suggests an openness about homosexual expression at odds with the mores of whites. Among men in the rural West in the 1940s, Kinsey found extensive incidence of homosexual behavior, but, in contrast with the men in large cities, little consciousness of gay identity. Thus even as capitalism exerted a homogenizing influence by gradually transforming more individuals into wage laborers and separating them from traditional communities, different groups of people were also affected in different ways.[7]

The decisions of particular men and women to act on their erotic/emotional preference for the same sex, along with the new consciousness that this preference made them different, led to the formation of an urban subculture of gay men and lesbians. Yet at least through the 1930s this subculture remained rudimentary, unstable, and difficult to find. How, then, did the complex, well-developed gay community emerge that existed by the time the gay liberation movement exploded? The answer is to be found during World War II, a time when the cumulative changes of several decades coalesced into a qualitatively new shape.

The war severely disrupted traditional patterns of gender relations and sexuality, and temporarily created a new erotic situation conducive to homosexual expression. It plucked millions of young men and women, whose sexual identities were just forming, out of their homes, out of towns and small cities, out of the heterosexual environment of the family, and dropped them into sex-segregated situations—as GIs, as WACs and WAVEs, in same-sex rooming houses for women workers who relocated to seek employment. The war freed millions of men and women from the settings where heterosexuality was normally imposed. For men and women already gay, it provided an opportunity to meet people like themselves. Others could become gay because of the temporary freedom to explore sexuality that the war provided.[8]

Lisa Ben, for instance, came out during the war. She left the small California town where she was raised, came to Los Angeles to find work, and lived in a women's boarding house. There she met for the first time lesbians who took her to gay bars and introduced her to other gay women. Donald Vining was a young man with lots of homosexual desire and few gay experiences. He moved to New York City during the war and worked at a large YMCA. His diary reveals numerous erotic adventures with soldiers, sailors, marines, and civilians at the Y where he worked, as well as at the men's residence club where he lived, and in parks, bars, and movie theaters. Many GIs stayed in port cities like New York, at YMCAs like the one where Vining worked. In his oral histories of gay men in San Francisco, focusing on the 1940s, Allan Bérubé has found that the war years were critical in the formation of a gay male *community* in the city. Places as different as San Jose, Denver, and Kansas City had their first gay bars in the 1940s. Even severe repression could have positive side effects. Pat Bond, a lesbian from Davenport, Iowa, joined the WACs during the 1940s. Caught in a purge of hundreds of lesbians from the WACs in the Pacific, she did not return to Iowa. She stayed in San Francisco and became part of a community of lesbians. How many other women and men had comparable experiences? How many other cities saw a rapid growth of lesbian and gay male communities?[9]

The gay men and women of the 1940s were pioneers. Their decisions to act on their desires formed the underpinnings of an urban subculture of gay men and lesbians. Throughout the 1950s and 1960s, the gay subculture grew and stabilized so that people coming out then could more easily find other gay women and men than in the past. Newspapers and magazines published articles describing gay male life. Literally hundreds of novels with lesbian themes were published.[10] Psychoanalysts complained about the new ease with which their gay male patients found sexual partners. And the gay subculture was not just to be found in the largest cities. Lesbian and gay male bars existed in places like Worcester, Massachusetts, and Buffalo, New York; in Columbia, South Carolina, and Des Moines, Iowa. Gay life in the 1950s and 1960s became a nationwide phenomenon. By the time of the Stonewall Riots in New York City in 1969—the event that ignited the gay liberation movement—our situation was hardly one of silence, invisibility, and isolation. A massive, grass-roots liberation movement could form almost overnight precisely because communities of lesbians and gay men existed.

Although gay community was a precondition for a mass movement, the oppression of lesbians and gay men was the force that propelled the movement into existence. As the subculture expanded and grew more visible in the post-World War II era, oppression by the state intensified, becoming more systematic and inclusive. The Right scapegoated "sexual perverts" during the McCarthy era. Eisenhower imposed a total ban on the employment of gay women and men by the federal government and government contractors. Purges of lesbians and homosexuals from the military rose sharply. The FBI instituted widespread surveillance of gay meeting places and of lesbian and gay organizations, such as the Daughters of Bilitis and the Mattachine Society. The Post Office placed tracers on the correspondence of gay men and passed evidence of homosexual activity on to employers. Urban vice squads invaded private homes, made sweeps of lesbian and gay male bars, entrapped gay men in public places, and fomented local witch hunts. The danger involved in being gay rose even as the possibilities of being gay were enhanced. Gay liberation was a response to this contradiction.

Although lesbians and gay men won significant victories in the 1970s and opened up some safe social space in which to exist, we can hardly claim to have dealt a fatal blow to heterosexism and homophobia. One could even argue that the enforcement of gay oppression has merely changed locales, shifting somewhat from the state to the arena of extralegal violence in the form of increasingly open physical attacks on lesbians and gay men. And, as our movements have grown, they have generated a backlash that threatens to wipe out our gains. Significantly, this New Right opposition has taken shape as a "pro-family" movement. How is it that capitalism, whose structure made possible the emergence of a gay identity and the creation of urban gay communities, appears unable to accept gay men and lesbians in its midst? Why do heterosexism and homophobia appear so resistant to assault?

The answers, I think, can be found in the contradictory relationship of capitalism to the family. On the one hand, as I argued earlier, capitalism has gradually undermined the material basis of the nuclear family by taking away the economic functions that cemented the ties between family members. As more adults have been drawn into the free labor system, and as capital has expanded its sphere until it produces as commodities most goods and services we need for our survival, the forces that propelled men and women into families and kept them there have weakened. On the other hand, the ideology of capitalist society has enshrined the family as the source of love, affection, and emotional security, the place where our need for stable, intimate human relationships is satisfied.

This elevation of the nuclear family to preeminence in the sphere of personal life is not accidental. Every society needs structures for reproduction and childrearing, but the possibilities are not limited to the nuclear family. Yet the privatized family fits well with capitalist relations of production. Capitalism has socialized production while maintaining that the products of socialized labor belong to the owners of private property. In many ways, childrearing has also been progressively socialized over the last two centuries, with schools, the media, peer groups, and employers taking over functions that once belonged to parents. Nevertheless, capitalist society maintains that reproduction and childrearing are private tasks, that children "belong" to parents, who exercise the rights of ownership. Ideologically, capitalism drives people into heterosexual families: each generation comes of age having internalized a heterosexist model of intimacy and personal relationships. Materially, capitalism weakens the bonds that once kept families together so that their members experience a growing instability in the place they have come to expect happiness and emotional security. Thus, while capitalism has knocked the material foundation away from family life, lesbians, gay men, and heterosexual feminists have become the scapegoats for the social instability of the system.

This analysis, if persuasive, has implications for us today. It can affect our perception of our identity, our formulation of political goals, and our decisions about strategy.

I have argued that lesbian and gay identity and communities are historically created, the result of a process of capitalist development that has spanned many generations. A corollary of this argument is that we are *not* a fixed social minority composed for all time of a certain percentage of the population. *There are more of us* than one hundred years ago, more of us than forty years ago. And there may very well be more gay men and lesbians in the future. Claims made by gays and nongays that sexual orientation is fixed at an early age, that large numbers of visible gay men and lesbians in society, the media, and the schools will have no influence on the sexual identities of the young, are wrong. Capitalism has created the material conditions for homosexual desire to express itself as a central component of some individuals' lives; now, our political movements are changing consciousness, creating the ideological conditions that make it easier for people to make that choice.

To be sure, this argument confirms the worst fears and most rabid rhetoric of our political opponents. But our response must be to challenge the underlying belief that homosexual relations are bad, a poor second choice. We must not slip into the opportunistic defense that society need not worry about tolerating us, since only homosexuals become homosexuals. At best, a minority group analysis and a civil rights strategy pertain to those of us who already are gay. It leaves today's youth—tomorrow's lesbians and gay men—to internalize heterosexist models that it can take a lifetime to expunge.

I have also argued that capitalism has led to the separation of sexuality from procreation. Human sexual desire need no longer be harnessed to reproductive imperatives, to procreation; its expression has increasingly entered the realm of choice. Lesbians and homosexuals most clearly embody the potential of this split, since our gay relationships stand entirely outside a procreative framework. The acceptance of our erotic choices ultimately depends on the degree to which society is willing to affirm sexual expression as a form of play, positive and life-enhancing. Our movement may have begun as the struggle of a "minority," but what we should now be trying to "liberate" is an aspect of the personal lives of all people—sexual expression.[11]

Finally, I have suggested that the relationship between capitalism and the family is fundamentally contradictory. On the one hand, capitalism continually weakens the material foundation of family life, making it possible for individuals to live outside the family, and for a lesbian and gay male identity to develop. On the other, it needs to push men and women into families, at least long enough to reproduce the next generation of workers. The elevation of the family to ideological preeminence guarantees that capitalist society will reproduce not just children, but heterosexism and homophobia. In the most profound sense, capitalism is the problem.[12]

How do we avoid remaining the scapegoats, the political victims of the social instability that capitalism generates? How can we take this contradictory relationship and use it to move toward liberation?

Gay men and lesbians exist on social terrain beyond the boundaries of the heterosexual nuclear family. Our communities have formed in that social space. Our survival and liberation depend on our ability to defend and expand that terrain, not just for ourselves but for everyone. That means, in part, support for issues that broaden the opportunities for living outside traditional heterosexual family units: issues like the availability of abortion and the ratification of the Equal Rights Amendment, affirmative action for people of color and for women, publicly funded daycare and other essential social services, decent welfare payments, full employment, the rights of young people—in other words, programs and issues that provide a material basis for personal autonomy.

The rights of young people are especially critical. The acceptance of children as dependents, as belonging to parents, is so deeply ingrained that we can scarcely imagine what it would mean to treat them as autonomous human beings, particularly in the realm of sexual expression and choice. Yet until that happens, gay liberation will remain out of our reach.

But personal autonomy is only half the story. The instability of families and the sense of impermanence and insecurity that people are now experiencing in their personal relationships are real social problems that need to be addressed. We need political solutions for these difficulties of personal life. These solutions should not come in the form of a radical version of the pro-family position, of some left-wing proposals to strengthen the family. Socialists do not generally respond to the exploitation and economic inequality of industrial capitalism by calling for a return to the family farm and handicraft production. We recognize that the vastly increased productivity that capitalism has made possible by socializing production is one of its progressive features. Similarly, we should not be trying to turn back the clock to some mythic age of the happy family.

We do need, however, structures and programs that will help to dissolve the boundaries that isolate the family, particularly those that privatize childrearing. We need community- or worker-controlled daycare, housing where privacy and community coexist, neighborhood institutions—from medical clinics to performance centers—that enlarge the social unit where each of us has a secure place. As we create structures beyond the nuclear family that provide a sense of belonging, the family will wane in significance. Less and less will it seem to make or break our emotional security.

In this respect gay men and lesbians are well situated to play a special role. Already excluded from families as most of us are, we have had to create, for our survival, networks of support that do not depend on the bonds of blood or the license of the state, but that are freely chosen and nurtured. The building of an "affectional community" must be as much a part of our political movement as are campaigns for civil rights. In this way we may prefigure the shape of personal relationships in a society grounded in equality and justice rather than exploitation and oppression, a society where autonomy and security do not preclude each other but coexist.

Notes

This essay is a revised version of a lecture given before several audiences in 1979 and 1980. I am grateful to the following groups for giving me a forum in which to talk and get feedback: the Baltimore Gay Alliance, the San Francisco Lesbian and Gay History Project, the organizers of Gay Awareness Week 1980 at San Jose State University and the University of California at Irvine, and the coordinators of the Student Affairs Lectures at the University of California at Irvine.

Lisa Duggan, Estelle Freedman, Jonathan Katz, Carole Vance, Paula Webster, Bert Hansen, and the editors of this volume provided helpful criticisms of an earlier draft. I especially want to thank Allan Bérubé and Jonathan Katz for generously sharing with me their own research, and Amber Hollibaugh for many exciting hours of nonstop conversation about Marxism and sexuality.

1. I do not mean to suggest that no one has ever proposed that gay identity is a product of historical change. See, for instance, Mary McIntosh, "The Homosexual Role," *Social Problems* 16 (1968): 182–92; Jeffrey Weeks, *Coming Out: Homosexual Politics in Britain* (New York: Quartet Books, 1977). It is also implied in Michel Foucault, *The History of Sexuality,* vol. 1: *An Introduction,* tr. Robert Hurley (New York: Pantheon, 1978). However, this does represent a minority viewpoint and the works cited above have not specified how it is that capitalism as a system of production has allowed for the emergence of a gay male and lesbian identity. As an example of the "eternal homosexual" thesis, see John Boswell, *Christianity, Social Tolerance, and Homosexuality* (Chicago: University of Chicago Press, 1980), where "gay people" remains an unchanging social category through fifteen centuries of Mediterranean and Western European history.

2. See Eli Zaretsky, *Capitalism, the Family, and Personal Life* (New York: Harper and Row, 1976); and Paula Fass, *The Damned and the Beautiful: American Youth in the 1920s* (New York: Oxford University Press, 1977).

3. Robert F. Oaks, "'Things Fearful to Name': Sodomy and Buggery in Seventeenth-Century New England," *Journal of Social History* 12 (1978): 268–81; J. R. Roberts, "The Case of Sarah Norman and Mary Hammond," *Sinister Wisdom* 24 (1980): 57–62; and Joanthan Katz, *Gay American History* (New York: Crowell, 1976), pp. 16–24, 568–71.

4. For the period from 1870 to 1940 see the documents in Katz, *Gay American History,* and idem, *Gay/Lesbian Almanac* (New York: Crowell, 1983). Other sources include Allan Bérubé, "Lesbians and Gay Men in Early San Francisco: Notes Toward a Social History of Lesbians and Gay Men in America," unpublished paper, 1979;

Vern Bullough and Bonnie Bullough, "Lesbianism in the 1920s and 1930s: A New-found Study," *Signs* 2 (Summer 1977): 895–904.

5. On the medical model see Weeks, *Coming Out*, pp. 23–32. The impact of the medical model on the consciousness of men and women can be seen in Louis Hyde, ed., *Rat and the Devil: The Journal Letters of F. O. Matthiessen and Russell Cheney* (Hamden, Conn.: Archon, 1978), p. 47, and in the story of Lucille Hart in Katz, *Gay American History*, pp. 258–79. Radclyffe Hall's classic novel about lesbianism, *The Well of Loneliness*, published in 1928, was perhaps one of the most important vehicles for the popularization of the medical model.

6. See Alfred Kinsey et al., *Sexual Behavior in the Human Male* (Philadelphia: W. B. Saunders, 1948) and *Sexual Behavior in the Human Female* (Philadelphia: W. B. Saunders, 1953).

7. On black music, see "AC/DC Blues: Gay Jazz Reissues," Stash Records, ST-106 (1977) and Chris Albertson, *Bessie* (New York: Stein and Day, 1974); on the persistence of kin networks in white ethnic communities see Judith Smith, "Our Own Kind: Family and Community Networks in Providence," in *A Heritage of Her Own*, ed. Nancy F. Cott and Elizabeth H. Pleck (New York: Simon and Schuster, 1979), pp. 393–411; on differences between rural and urban male homoeroticism see Kinsey et al., *Sexual Behavior in the Human Male*, pp. 455–57, 630–31.

8. The argument and the information in this and the following paragraphs come from my book *Sexual Politics, Sexual Communities: The Making of a Homosexual Minority in the United States, 1940–1970* (Chicago: University of Chicago Press, 1983). I have also developed it with reference to San Francisco in "Gay Politics, Gay Community: San Francisco's Experience," *Socialist Review* 55 (January–February 1981): 77–104.

9. Donald Vining, *A Gay Diary, 1933–1946* (New York: Pepys Press, 1979); "Pat Bond," in Nancy Adair and Casey Adair, *Word Is Out* (New York: New Glide Publications, 1978), pp. 55–65; and Allan Bérubé, "Marching to a Different Drummer: Coming Out During World War II," a slide/talk presented at the annual meeting of the American Historical Association, December 1981, Los Angeles. A shorter version of Bérubé's presentation can be found in *The Advocate*, October 15, 1981, pp. 20–24, and in this volume.

10. On lesbian novels see *The Ladder*, March 1958, p. 18; February 1960, pp. 14–15; April 1961, pp. 12–13; February 1962, pp. 6–11; January 1963, pp. 6–13; February 1964, pp. 12–19; February 1965, pp. 19–23; March 1966, pp. 22–26; and April 1967, pp. 8–13. *The Ladder* was the magazine published by the Daughters of Bilitis.

11. This especially needs to be emphasized today. The 1980 annual conference of the National Organization for Women, for instance, passed a lesbian rights resolution that defined the issue as one of "discrimination based on affectional/sexual preference/orientation," and explicitly disassociated the issue from other questions of sexuality such as pornography, sadomasochism, public sex, and pederasty.

12. I do not mean to suggest that homophobia is "caused" by capitalism, or is to be found only in capitalist societies. Severe sanctions against homoeroticism can be found in European feudal society and in contemporary socialist countries. But my focus in this essay has been the emergence of a gay identity under capitalism, and the mechanisms specific to capitalism that made this possible and that reproduce homophobia as well.

Section III
Sexual Revolutions

Since the late nineteenth century, sexual rebels, reformers, and malcontents of various stripes have focused on Victorian repression as a primary barrier to sexual freedom and openness. When men and women could overcome the sexual strictures bequeathed them by the unenlightened past, so this line of thinking ran—shame over nudity, hypocrisy about premarital sex, taboos against homosexuality, the double standard—then they would be free to follow their "true" desires. Many of us who came of sexual age in the 1960s can recall the self-conscious taboo-breaking of our own radical milieu.

In some ways, the battle against the Victorian form of prudery was won by the end of the 1960s. Americans can now see frontal nudity everywhere, from the newsstand to the Broadway stage; sex has become a common topic on TV talk shows, and pornographic images stare down from billboards. Obviously, this victory over sexual silence is problematic. The sexual rebels of the 1960s conceived their "revolution" in the heart of a more general revolt against the politics and culture of U.S. bourgeois life. By the mid-1970s, however, the new sexual mores had seemingly done more to bolster than to subvert U.S. society. The sexualization of American culture had proceeded at an astonishing speed; the process seemed to possess the capacity for unlimited expansion, as it absorbed once tabooed erotic forms and practices into the service of the mass media.

On one level, then, the sexual revolution seemed to become a resource of American capitalism, a new kind of bread-and-circuses. In American culture, sexual subversion seems quickly to collapse into cultural appropriation: indeed, the narrowness of the distance between the two has led some political radicals to echo Eric Hobsbawm's opinion, advanced in 1969 in the thick of the sexual revolution, that "sexual 'liberation' has only indirect relations with any other kind of liberation."

As sexual iconoclasm became the lubrication of commerce, so the new freedoms became in themselves sources of constraint. As we noted in the introduction, feminists were the first to raise a cry against the patriarchal imperative disguised by the sexual revolution, the assumption of unlimited male access to women's beds. Gay men and lesbians followed with their own criticisms of its overwhelming heterosexual biases. More generally, for all people—men and women, gay and straight—a new set of proscriptions arose in place of the old. As Ellen Ross and Rayna Rapp note in this volume, nineteenth-century women were taught that they need not bother about passions but should simply submit, while our supposedly more liberated generation has learned that any sex short of orgasm isn't worth the trouble. Likewise, a new set of "experts" has arisen to administer these proscriptions. Gone is the minister struggling with the adulterer over the state of his soul; in his place is the psychotherapist who probes into a wife's "unnatural" lack of interest in sex.

A shared desire to explain the conundrum of sexual revolutions, how affirmations of sexuality turn into its negation, underlies the articles in this section. The period from 1880 to 1930 that the three essays cover is especially rich territory, since it is in these years that sexual assumptions recognizably modern began to appear in the middle class. An acceptance of contraception, a belief in women's erotic potential, a toleration of premarital affairs, and a celebration of the nude body coalesced into a distinctly modern sexual ethos. Taken together, these essays demonstrate the extent to which this much-touted break with Victorianism consisted of a remapping of the erotic terrain rather than, as is usually supposed, the abolition of boundaries altogether. The history these scholars trace helps illuminate for us today the processes by which movements of sexual "freedom" have so often ended by constricting homosexuality, female sexuality, and, one might argue, sexual excitement itself.

Family, Sexual Morality, and Popular Movements in Turn-of-the-Century America

Barbara Epstein

Over the last one hundred years of American history, there have been two periods during which issues of family life and sexual morality have been central concerns of popular movements: the decades around the turn of the century, and those from the 1960s to the present. In the years from roughly 1890 to 1920, the social purity movement attacked prostitution and the double standard of sexual morality for men and women, the social hygiene movement addressed the issue of venereal disease and demanded sex education and the public discussion of sexual issues, and the birth control movement campaigned for free access to contraceptive information and devices. None of these were narrow single-issue movements; and while they represented a variety of quite different social visions, and held different views on questions of family and sexual morality, they all saw the reform of sexual morality as central to social change.

For roughly the next four decades, however, the family and sexual morality ceased to be major concerns of popular movements. By the mid-1920s social purity had lost its force, social hygiene had been professionalized, and the birth control movement was in the process of breaking its ties with radicalism and casting aside its aspirations to become a mass movement. There was no lack of popular political activity in these later years, especially in the 1930s and early 1940s, but these movements were mainly concerned with economic democracy and the threat of fascism. Issues of family and sexuality (and, for that matter, issues of culture and psychology more generally) by and large faded from public attention. It was only from the mid-1960s on that we saw a revival of these concerns, as the New Left and youth culture began a critique of American middle-class life, extended in the late 1960s by the women's movement to the organization of the family and the construction of gender, and later broadened by the gay movement to challenge the equation of heterosexuality with normalcy. More recently, of course, a number of New Right groups have also gained considerable followings by calling for a return to traditional patterns of family life and sexual morality.

What, then, accounts for this ebb and flow of public concern with issues of family and sexual morality? Here I will argue that we can understand this history in the context of major shifts in the structure of family life—in the earlier period, changes in specifically white middle-class family life, and in the later period, shifts that cut across class and ethnic lines. Briefly, I argue that the turn of the century witnessed a crisis in middle-class family life that had to do with the increasing need of couples for birth control, and with the question of how birth control could be introduced without separating heterosexuality from marriage or undermining the authority of men within the family. This crisis was registered by a preoccupation on the part of popular movements with questions of family and sexual morality.

None of the early movements put forth a solution to the family crisis that was adopted in any immediate way: most of these activists called for a return to Victorian morality, while a smaller number called for a dramatic break from it; neither constituted a viable solution. Instead, the crisis was resolved in the 1920s—for a time—by a quiet acceptance of contraception on the part of the middle class, a lessening emphasis on motherhood, and a valorization of heterosexual eroticism, especially women's, as a central ingredient of marriage. The solution was sufficient to remove issues of family and sexual morality from the agendas of popular movements for the next several decades. But what might be called the "New Deal" of family life had its limits. The family reform of the 1920s left women's domesticity untouched, and the family continued to rest on male dominance and female subordination. Thus this solution was not able to withstand the strains created by the massive entry of women into the labor force in the decades after World War II. The current family crisis, which stems from this contradiction, calls for a far more profound reorganization of family life.[1]

As many historians have shown, the nineteenth-century middle-class family was based on a clearly defined division of labor between husband and wife, with the male head of household responsible for the economic support of the family and the wife and mother responsible for housekeeping and caring for the children. Although unmarried, usually young women sometimes worked outside the home, it was very rare for a married woman, especially a woman with children, to do so in the middle class. Even when financial difficulties forced a wife to work for pay—taking in boarders, for instance, or sewing, or doing laundry—this did not threaten the fundamental division of labor between men and women. There were no alternatives to the home for childcare, and the jobs available for women, especially married women, did not pay enough to hold out any real possibility of financial independence. A man's ability to support his wife and children adequately was central to the nineteenth-century middle-class notion of masculinity, and the corresponding notion of femininity revolved around a woman's reliance on her husband's support. The great majority of middle-class families were able to attain this ideal family structure.[2]

This form of family organization represented a shift from the farming family of earlier generations, in which the labor of all adults, and usually children as well, was necessary for the family's survival. In this context childcare had been only one of a large number of tasks to which women attended. Men had often looked after young children as well, helping to keep an eye on infants, for example, during the winter months when they worked inside the house. In the commercial towns that grew up in the early nineteenth century, however, productive work increasingly took place away from the home. This change sharply separated women's work, centering around the care of children and the home, and men's productive work in the world outside the home.[3]

This organization of family life raised new problems. On the farm, a large family was an immediate economic asset, for by the time children were six or seven they began to contribute to the family's support. In the towns, however, children took on a different cast. Children and their prospects for success were the *raison d'être* of the middle-class family, but success required a long period of training, especially for boys, and in any event there was little that middle-class children could do to contribute substantially to their families' finances. Children were no longer an asset, but a drain on family resources.

These circumstances fostered a greater interest in, and need for, birth control. Unmarried middle-class young men, as well as married couples, needed birth control: the fact that men often did not marry until they were well enough established to support a family meant that there were likely to be many years during which they were single and at least tempted to be sexually active (young women may have been similarly tempted, but the social consequences were far more serious, and they were more rigorously trained to avoid sex before marriage). In fact, the birthrate did decline steadily during the nineteenth century: in 1800 the average white American woman gave birth, over her lifetime, to 7.04 children; a century later the average had declined to 3.56. The decline began first among the urban, educated, white Anglo-Saxon Protestant population. The rural birthrate also declined (perhaps due in part to the decline of the self-sufficient family farm and the traditional culture that had surrounded it), but throughout the century there was a difference between the two, reflecting the different imperatives regarding children for the two social groups. A similar differential existed between urban native-born middle-class birthrates and those of immigrant working-class groups: immigrant groups tended to have high birthrates on arrival in the United States, and while these declined over time, throughout the century they were higher than the corresponding rates among the WASP middle class.[4]

The decline in the birthrate, especially among middle-class Protestants, was achieved in part through the use of contraceptives. Throughout the nineteenth century some means of contraception were available, at least to people with enough money to acquire them. In guarded and euphemistic language, newspapers advertised various means of contraception, of which pessaries (a term covering a variety of objects placed in the vagina or uterus) were probably the most effective. More reliable than any of these were abortions, which were routinely practiced and legal for most of the century until "quickening," the point (usually in the third month of pregnancy) when the movement of the fetus became evident.[5]

What were the limits to these contraceptive strategies? Abortions could endanger the health or life of the woman, and a more important means of birth control was abstinence, a practice encouraged by the Protestant view that sex was legitimate only when linked to reproduction, and by the middle-class view that women were asexual creatures who preferred to express their love for their husbands in other ways. Given the unreliability of other means of contraception, the dangers to their health from pregnancy, and the burden of childrearing, married women may often have preferred to abstain from sex.[6] While many men may have also hoped to avoid women's pregnancies, the middle-class notion of masculinity did not include a reticence about sex that paralleled that ascribed to women.

Abstinence, however, was associated with even knottier social and sexual problems. The spread of prostitution in the nineteenth century, especially in the latter part of the century, was directly linked to middle-class family arrangements. Young men who put off marriage until their careers or businesses were established often had sex with prostitutes before they married; married men who abstained from sex with their wives could also turn to prostitutes. Working-class men, of course, also visited prostitutes, but what is striking is that in the middle class, where the idea of women's engaging in sex outside marriage was viewed with horror, men's visits to prostitutes were almost taken for granted. There is of course no way of knowing with any precision the number of prostitutes, but William Sanger, in his 1858 *History of Prostitution*, estimated that there was about one prostitute to every fifty-two adult men in the cities that he had investigated: New York, Buffalo, Louisville, New Haven, Norfolk, and Savannah. More vaguely, he estimated that one-fourth of the total population of adult men in these cities visited prostitutes.[7]

Thus every form of birth control available to the middle class was associated with one problem or another: contraceptive devices were not reliable, abortions were dangerous, abstinence was associated with prostitution, and this was in turn associated with venereal disease. Furthermore, both middle-class men and women had reason to fear the very contraceptive devices their circumstances dictated that they needed. For men, birth control evoked female independence. Free access to birth control would have allowed women to decide what portion of their lives they wanted to devote to motherhood and what portion to other pursuits. Male attitudes were evident, for instance, in the medical campaign against abortion of the 1860s and 1870s. The overwhelmingly white, upper-middle-class, native-born, Protestant physicians who supported this campaign opposed abortion on moral grounds, but they also believed that the increasing numbers of women, especially married women resorting to contraceptives or seeking abortions demonstrated a disturbing trend toward the rejection of woman's "natural" role and reflected the deleterious influence of feminism and that the rise in abortions and the falling birthrate among middle-class women constituted a threat to the preeminence of their own class and culture within American society. Alexander Skene, the author of an influential textbook on the diseases of women, argued that the "fulfillment of the injunction 'to multiply'" remained the "highest earthly function of woman." He warned of the dangers of efforts to avoid childbirth:

> The woman who willingly tries to reverse the order of her physical being in the hope of gratifying some fancy or ambition, is almost sure to suffer sooner or later from disappointment and ill-health. Doctors make fortunes (small ones) by trying to restore health and peace of mind to those who violate the laws of morals and health in their efforts to prevent reproduction. In such cases, the relations [physiological processes] are deranged by perverted mind influences. Disease of the maltreated organ follows, and revenges their [sic] wrong by torturing the brain and nervous system.[8]

A report submitted in 1871 to the Iowa State Medical Society, often quoted in the medical campaign against abortion, asked what would become of the country when "American women . . . for selfish and personal ends, butcher or poison their children."[9] A Michigan physician, writing nearly three decades later, drew the connection more clearly between the reaction to women's resort to abortion and nativist sentiment. "The annual destruction of foetuses," he wrote, had become so "truly appalling" among native American women that "the Puritanic blood of '76 will be but sparingly represented in the approaching centenary. . . . America is fast losing her national characteristics."[10]

At the same time, middle-class Protestant women also had reason to fear any general accessibility of safe and effective contraceptives. Even those who publicly supported a woman's right to limit the number of children she bore did not call for the greater availability or use of contraceptives. Historian Linda Gordon has described the late-nineteenth-century movement for "voluntary motherhood," and the related "free love" movement—both of which called for the right of women to refuse their husbands' sexual demands when they did not wish to have children. Voluntary motherhood and free love, like other strains of nineteenth-century feminism, also regarded motherhood as central to women's status in family and society, and sought to elevate it, not to provide any means of freeing sexuality from reproduction. Supporters of voluntary motherhood and free love thus saw in birth control not a means of enabling women to escape motherhood altogether, but a way to improve women's position. Dora Forster, a free lover, wrote:

> I hope the scarcity of children will go on until motherhood is honored at least as much as the trials and hardships of soldiers campaigning in wartime. It will then be worth while to supply the nation with a sufficiency of children. . . . Every nation, having lost the power to enslave woman as mother, will be compelled to recognize her voluntary exercise of that function as by far the most important service of any class of citizens.[11]

Contraceptives were available to middle-class women throughout the nineteenth century, and were undoubtedly used by many, but any public call for their free availability would have directly contradicted the aims of social purity, which were widely and vehemently supported by middle-class women of the time. Freely available contraceptives would have reduced the risks for men in visiting prostitutes, and would have made it easier for men to put off or entirely avoid marriage. The social purity and related woman's temperance movements, the largest U.S. women's movements up to that point in history, undoubtedly reflected mainstream sentiment among women in their defense of the family and in their view that any separation between sexuality and marriage threatened that institution—and therefore threatened women. These movements regarded a restrictive, even anti-sexual, morality as in the best interest of women.[12]

The views held by members of these movements made a good deal of sense given the situation of middle-class women at the time. With the exclusion of married middle-class women from the labor market and their utter dependence on marriage, motherhood seemed to be the only basis for anything remotely resembling female autonomy. Sexuality was in fact an area in which women were extremely vulnerable to men. Unwed pregnancy could ruin a woman's life; sex within marriage might mean venereal disease; pregnancy had its own dangers; and childbirth reinforced a woman's dependence on her husband. The separation of sex from procreation would have made marriage less compelling for men and infidelity easier. It was reasonable for nineteenth-century women, then, to view sex with suspicion, and for women's movements, including feminist movements, to shy away from support for contraception.

The advocates of social purity were, however, fighting a losing battle: by the turn of the century jobs for women were becoming increasingly available, and the need to reinforce women's security within the family was beginning to be balanced by their need to transcend their traditional restrictions to home and childbearing in order to take advantage of the opportunities now becoming available. Furthermore, the culture that the social purity movement represented—the traditional one of the small-town, Protestant middle class—was losing the unquestioned preeminence that it had once enjoyed, at least in the Northeast. An increasingly urban and culturally diverse population was not a likely audience for the social purists' pleas for sharp restrictions on sexual expression. The increasing numbers of women in the workforce, especially unmarried young women, helped to shift the social life of young people out of the home and into the streets, theaters, and dance halls; control over young people's social lives and courtships began to slip away from the family. This was of course especially true for working-class families, which routinely sent young people to work, but for middle-class young people as well, especially young men, the life of the city offered some freedom from close parental supervision.[13]

While the social purists argued for sexual restraint on religious and moral grounds in the language of traditional American Protestantism, by and large failing to capture the urban audience they hoped to address, the social hygiene movement, which espoused sex education in the name of the same traditional values, found greater success. Like the social purists, the doctors who initiated this movement hoped to bring traditional middle-class values to urban, especially working-class, populations. Their more pragmatic approach linked them to Progressivism and won them more support and sympathy from progressive social reformers. Their view of sexual morality was fundamentally the same as that of the social purists; thus their arguments for restricting sexuality, even when joined to an espousal of sex education and the public discussion of sex, were not likely to win them large numbers of converts in the industrial cities of the early twentieth century. But in calling for such public discussion, the supporters of social hygiene inadvertently took a step toward a freer view of sex.[14]

By the turn of the century, cultural and political radicals in Europe, especially England and France, were discussing new and quite different ideas about sexuality. Havelock Ellis, among others, was exploring improved methods of contraception and arguing that the separation of sex from reproduction would enhance sexuality and perhaps allow sexual relations other than heterosexual monogamy to flourish. In the years before World War I, some radicals, especially Emma Goldman and later Margaret Sanger, worked to disseminate knowledge of contraception in the United States. The Mensinga diaphragm, made of vulcanized rubber, constituted a major advance in contraceptive technology and was introduced to the United States from Europe by Margaret Sanger in her New York birth control clinic. The early-twentieth-century U.S. birth control movement was linked with radicalism, especially anarchism; many American birth control advocates in these years saw contraception as a key to social revolution and believed that lifting sexual repression might hasten a more general rebellion against social repression.[15]

The birth control movement, however, did not gain anything like the earlier support for social purity. Even while public enthusiasm for social purity waned, the birth control movement failed to grow commensurately; associated with both sexual radicalism and political or social radicalism, it was doubly isolated. Socialism was a powerful current at the time, within the middle as well as the working class, and in many parts of the Progressive reform movement it was possible for socialist ideas to at least gain a respectful hearing, especially if they were associated with a moral vision compatible with conventional Protestant values. But the anarchism espoused by many early birth controllers, including Goldman and Sanger, was less acceptable, and the views of Havelock Ellis and his followers on sex had little in common with traditional American views.

Thus for differing reasons neither social purity (and the movements surrounding it) nor the birth control campaign was able to create movements that could lead directly to a solution of the family issues that were of concern to the middle class. Nevertheless, over the first two decades of the century large numbers of middle-class people began to take up new attitudes and adopt new practices in the areas of family and sexual morality. Most important, contraceptives were widely, though quietly, accepted. A 1929 study of middle-class women in their early thirties reported that 734 out of 1,000 believed in using contraceptives and that 730 actually practiced contraception; the same study reported that 89.7 percent of 1,200 slightly younger unmarried women believed that contraceptives should be used in marriage.[16] The majority of women in this sample had discarded the anti-contraceptive attitudes of the late nineteenth century.

Technological improvements undoubtedly contributed to the growing popularity of contraception. The Mensinga diaphragm was considerably more effective, when used with contraceptive jelly, than such earlier devices as intravaginal and intrauterine pessaries, jellies and suppositories, and condoms. More fundamentally, the widespread use of contraceptives reflected the waning of one set of ideas about the family and about women, and the rise of a new set. The Victorian axiom that women were asexual creatures had been discredited, especially by the young, and replaced not just by an acceptance of female sexuality but by a valorization of it—as long as sex took place within marriage or led to it. Young men, for instance, were increasingly likely to have their first sexual experiences with girlfriends rather than with prostitutes. Among men born between 1900 and 1909, sex with prostitutes decreased by over 50 percent, while sex with female friends increased by enough to take up the slack. Two-thirds of these friends were fiancées.[17] This growing use of contraception, especially among business and professional families, made smaller families possible. Before 1890 the majority of such families included four or more children; by 1910 the majority of these families were confining themselves to from one to three children.[18]

In nineteenth-century marriage manuals, discussions of sex were generally limited to warnings against excess, reminders that sex should be for the purpose of procreation, or discussions of disease. In contrast the author of a typical marriage manual (from 1922) wrote, "No doubt women differ greatly, but in every woman who truly loves there lies dormant the capacity to become vibrantly alive in response to her lover, and to meet him as a willing and active participant in the sacrament of marriage."[19] Such notions were popularized throughout the media. Any woman who read the popular woman's magazines or went to the movies in the 1920s had to be aware that sex, romance, and companionship were considered important to a successful marriage.[20]

By the 1920s, American culture held out a solution to the family problems of the middle class, a solution that did not please the social purists and that, while to some degree reflecting the impact of feminism, fell far short of what the early birth control advocates had wanted. The widespread middle-class acceptance of contraception made it possible for married women to put off childbearing, but the women who were under the greatest pressure to work outside the home—working-class women—had little access to contraceptives, which required a doctor's prescription. Sex could now take place safely outside marriage (at least within the middle and upper classes) and the possibility of family planning expanded the options of married women. Heterosexual eroticism, and female heterosexual eroticism in particular, had gained public acceptance, but only as long as sexual expression was contained within or firmly tied to the family. With a declining birthrate (and a considerably higher divorce rate than in most of the nineteenth century) sex became a new kind of cement for marriage.

This redefinition of middle-class marriage and sexual morality gave couples a new degree of control over family size and helped to alleviate the older problems caused by prostitution and venereal disease. The emphasis on sexual intimacy, on the importance of the bond between husband and wife, may also have helped to compensate for loosening ties among extended kin; the early twentieth century was a period of much geographic mobility, especially among the professional and business classes. But this redefinition of marriage did not fundamentally alter family structure. Middle-class women might work before marrying, but once they married, certainly once they had children, they stayed at home and depended on their husbands' support. The valorization of women's sexuality could not by itself bring about equality between men and women within the family; that would require an attack on the sexual division of labor, the presumption of women's primary responsibility for childcare. Thus we can see the 1920s redefinition of marriage, or family, as a sort of New Deal of family politics: it allowed for a temporary resolution of a series of family issues without requiring any basic change in the structure of family life.

The changed definition of marriage and family also led to some new problems. The emphasis on marital intimacy carried with it a new and much higher standard for successful marriage; this must have put added strain on many couples. It probably was a factor in the rising divorce rate of the early decades of the twentieth century. It also meant new pressures on women. Nineteenth-century women had played a large role in defining what constituted adequate mothering and housework, the main ingredients of a Victorian wife's role. Once sexual attractiveness and the ability to maintain an intimate relationship with one's husband were added to the list, both men and the media gained a much more direct influence over the definition of femininity. In spite of these problems, issues of family and sexuality faded from the arena of public discussion over the next several decades. Perhaps these problems were not as severe as had been the problems of the turn of the century; or perhaps it was that they were more women's problems than family problems, and in the absence of a feminist movement, women were not yet able to raise them as public issues.

As most of us know, this solution to family issues has not held. Because the family reform of this period left intact women's domesticity and their subordination within the family, it could not address the problems posed by the massive entry of women (including married women, and women with children) into the labor force in the years following World War II. The entry of women into the labor force makes the traditional division of labor between men and women virtually impossible; it has been associated with much turmoil over the redefinition of gender—inside and outside the family. In combination with a number of other developments (mainly the expansion of education for women and improvements in the technology and availability of birth control) this has made possible a new degree of independence for women. It is possible for women to leave marriages; it is possible (though often difficult) for them to raise children by themselves.

These are among the reasons that family life and sexual morality have again become political issues. The consideration of how family and personal life should be redefined was an important element of the New Left and of the 1960s youth culture, as it was at the center of the women's and gay movements that followed. By the middle of the seventies New Right movements were likewise gaining large audiences around the same issues, addressing them from the opposite perspective, seeking ways of reinforcing traditional morality, of bringing back the family stability that seemed to lie somewhere in the past.

Since at least the late nineteenth century, women have served as a "reserve army" for the economy, drawn into the labor force in periods of war or economic expansion, then sent home when the need for their labor is spent. Now, for the first time, women have become a permanent part of the labor force. Indeed, there are no longer large numbers of women who can afford to stay home. Family life is now likely to require two incomes; moreover, the rising number of divorces has thrown many women on their own resources, and discourages young women from thinking that they can count on male support as a way of life. The expansion of women's education and the spread of feminist consciousness have also led many women to seek some life outside the home.

The breakdown of the sexual division of labor has eroded the old resolutions to family tensions. The difference between this family crisis and that of the turn of the century is that this time the question of the equality of men and women in the family is central. At the turn of the century what was fundamentally at stake was the question of how middle-class couples could limit the size of their families without separating heterosexuality from the family, without endangering male control over (or female security within) the family. Today what is at stake is the question of what form, or forms, personal life will take as women's economic dependence on men diminishes. Today what is thrown into question is not just the form of the heterosexual family, but whether heterosexuality and "family" as we know it will continue to be the dominant institutions governing personal life.

Notes

I would like to thank the following people for their comments: Linda Collins, Ruth Milkman, David Plotke, Deborah Rosenfelt, Judith Stacey, Kay Trimberger, and Eli Zaretsky. I would also like to thank Christine Stansell for her suggestions and editorial help.

1. My analysis of the middle-class family crisis and its resolution in the 1920s is similar to that of Paula Fass in *The Damned and the Beautiful: American Youth in the 1920's* (Oxford: Oxford University Press, 1977), in chap. 2, "The Family Redivivus: 1880–1930." My approach differs from hers mainly in that I relate this family history to the history of popular movements. Other discussions of the changes in family and sexual morality, or sexuality, around the turn of the century and during the Progressive period are more concerned with the question of how significant these changes actually were. William O'Neill, in *Divorce in the Progressive Era* (New York: New Viewpoints, 1973), emphasizes continuity, arguing that the option of divorce strengthened the system of family and marriage. Arno Karlen, in *Sexuality and Homosexuality: A New View* (New York: W. W. Norton, 1971), suggests that the changes that could be seen by the 1920s were more in attitude than in behavior, but that these changed attitudes were quite significant. John C. Burnham, in "The Progressive Era Revolution in American Attitudes Toward Sex" (*Journal of American History* 59 [March 1973]: 885–908), takes a similar approach; Howard I. Kushner, in "Nineteenth-Century Sexuality and the 'Sexual Revolution' of the Progressive Era" (*Canadian Review of American Studies* 9, no. 1 [Spring 1978]: 34–49), takes a more cautious view of the significance of changes in the area of sexuality. Carl Degler, in "What Ought to Be and What Was: Women's Sexuality in the Nineteenth Century" (*American Historical Review* 79 [December 1974]) suggests that the actual sexual experience of women in nineteenth-century America may have been quite different from the image given by public discussion. The importance of Degler's findings should be qualified, though, by pointing out that the women who were interviewed for the study that he cites were highly educated and probably from the upper middle class, and that they were interviewed in the very late part of the century; these women hardly reflect the general experience of middle-class women through the nineteenth century. Finally, Elaine Tyler May, in *Great Expectations: Marriage and Divorce in Post-Victorian America* (Chicago: University of Chicago Press, 1980), discusses the importance of changing attitudes toward family and sexuality. For a succinct and very useful discussion of changing feminist stands on contraception, see Linda Gordon, "Why Nineteenth-Century Feminists Did Not Support 'Birth Control' and Twentieth-Century Feminists Do: Feminism, Reproduction, and the Family," in *Rethinking the Family: Some Feminist Questions*, ed. Barrie Thorne with Marilyn Yalom (New York: Longmans, 1982), pp. 40–53.
2. For discussions of nineteenth-century middle-class life in the United States, see Nancy Cott, *The Bonds of Womanhood: "Woman's Sphere" in New England, 1789–1835* (New Haven: Yale University Press, 1977); and Mary P. Ryan, *Cradle of the Middle Class: The Family in Oneida County, New York, 1790–1865* (Cambridge: Cambridge University Press, 1981). For the ideology surrounding domesticity, see Kathryn Kish Sklar, *Catharine Beecher: A Study in American Domesticity* (New Haven: Yale University Press, 1973).
3. For discussions of family life in early U.S. history, in an agrarian setting, see John Demos, *A Little Commonwealth: Family Life in Plymouth Colony* (Oxford: Oxford University Press, 1970); Bernard Farber, *Guardians of Virtue: Salem Families in 1800* (New York: Basic Books, 1972); and E. S. Morgan, *The Puritan Family: Religion and Domestic Relations in Seventeenth-Century New England* (New York: Harper and Row, 1966). Mary Beth Norton, in *Liberty's Daughters: The Revolutionary Experience of American Women, 1750–1800* (Boston: W. W. Norton, 1980) discusses agrarian family life and the beginnings of its transformation in the Revolutionary period.
4. Ansley J. Coale and Melvin Zelnik, *New Estimates of Fertility and Population in the United States* (Princeton: Princeton University Press, 1963), quoted in Linda Gordon, *Woman's Body, Woman's Right: Birth Control in America* (New York: Penguin, 1977). See also Gordon's discussion of fertility rates, pp. 48ff.

5. For discussions of birth control in nineteenth-century America, see Gordon, *Woman's Body, Woman's Right*, pp. 47–71; and James Reed, *From Private Vice to Public Virtue: The Birth Control Movement and American Society Since 1830* (New York: Basic Books, 1978), pp. 3–18. On the history of abortion, see James C. Mohr, *Abortion in America: The Origins and Evolution of National Policy* (Oxford: Oxford University Press, 1977).

6. See Daniel Scott Smith, "Family Limitation, Sexual Control, and Domestic Feminism in Victorian America," in *Clio's Consciousness Raised: New Perspectives on the History of Women*, ed. Mary Hartman and Lois Banner (New York: Harper and Row, 1977), pp. 119–36.

7. William W. Sanger, *The History of Prostitution: Its Extent, Causes, and Effects Throughout the World* (New York: The Medical Publishing Company, 1858), pp. 607ff. On the history of prostitution in nineteenth- and early twentieth-century America see also Vern L. Bullough, *The History of Prostitution* (New Hyde Park: University Books, 1964); and Ruth Rosen and Sue Davidson, eds., *The Maimie Papers* (Old Westbury, N.Y.: The Feminist Press, 1977).

8. Alexander J. C. Skene, *Education and Culture as Related to the Health and Diseases of Women* (Detroit, 1889), pp. 26ff. Quoted in Reed, *From Private Vice to Public Virtue*, p. 41.

9. J. C. Stone, "Report on the Subject of Criminal Abortion," *Transactions of the Iowa State Medical Society* 1 (1871): 30–31, quoted in Mohr, *Abortion in America*, p. 169.

10. J. J. Mulheron, "Foeticide," *Peninsual Journal of Medicine* 10 (September 1874): 390–91. Quoted in Mohr, *Abortion in America*, p. 167.

11. Dora Forster, *Sex Radicalism as Seen by an Emancipated Woman of the New Time* (Chicago: M. Harman, 1905), pp. 39–40. Quoted in Gordon, *Woman's Body, Woman's Right*, p. 113.

12. On the attitudes of the woman's temperance and social purity movements toward the family, see Barbara Epstein, *The Politics of Domesticity: Women, Evangelism and Temperance in Nineteenth-Century America* (Middletown: Wesleyan University Press, 1981). On the male rebellion against marriage in nineteenth-century America, see Barbara Ehrenreich, *The Hearts of Men* (New York: Doubleday/Anchor, 1983).

13. For a discussion of this youth culture, see Fass, *The Damned and the Beautiful*, especially chap. 3, "The World of Youth: The Peer Society"; also James R. McGovern, "The American Woman's Pre-World War One Freedom in Manners and Morals," *Journal of American History* 55 (September 1968): 315–33.

14. On the social hygiene movement, see Burnham, "The Progressive Era Revolution," pp. 885–908. See also Robert E. Riegel, "Changing American Attitudes Toward Prostitution (1800–1920)," *Journal of the History of Ideas* 29 (July–September 1968): 437–52; Roy Lubove, "The Progressive and the Prostitute," *Historian* 24 (May 1962): 308–30; and James H. Timberlake, *Prohibition and the Progressive Movement, 1900–1920* (Cambridge: Harvard University Press, 1963).

15. On the early birth control movement see Gordon, *Woman's Body, Woman's Right* and Reed, *From Private Vice to Public Virtue*. On the role of Emma Goldman see Richard Drinnon, *Rebel in Paradise: A Biography of Emma Goldman* (Chicago: University of Chicago Press, 1961); and Candace Falk, *Love, Anarchy, and Emma Goldman* (New York: Holt, Rinehart, 1983). On the role of Margaret Sanger, see David M. Kennedy, *Birth Control in America: The Career of Margaret Sanger* (New Haven: Yale University Press, 1970).

16. Katherine B. Davis, *Factors in the Sex Lives of Twenty-Two Hundred Women* (New York, 1929), p. 356. quoted in Fass, *The Damned and the Beautiful*, pp. 76–77.

17. Alfred Kinsey et al., *Sexual Behavior in the Human Female* (Philadelphia: W. B. Saunders Co., 1953), pp. 267–69, 300, 330–32. Quoted in Reed, *From Private Vice to Public Virtue*, p. 61.

18. See Ernest Groves and William F. Ogburn, *American Marriage and Family Relationships* (New York, 1929), pp. 134, 154; and Paul C. Glick, *American Families* (New York, 1957), p. 45. These statistics are quoted and discussed in Fass, *The Damned and the Beautiful*, pp. 66–71, 392–93.

19. A. Herbert Gray, *Men, Women, and God* (New York: Association Press, 1922), p. 63. Quoted in Michael Gordon, "From an Unfortunate Necessity to a Cult of Mutual Orgasm: Sex in American Marital Education Literature 1830–1940," in *Studies in the Sociology of Sex,* ed. James M. Henslin (New York: Meredith, 1971), p. 66.

20. See, for instance, Robert S. Lynd and Helen Merrell Lynd, *Middletown: A Study in Modern American Culture* (New York: Harcourt, Brace, and World, 1929), pp. 241ff.

Feminism, Men, and Modern Love: Greenwich Village, 1900–1925

Ellen Kay Trimberger

Greenwich Village became in the 1910s, 1920s, and again in the 1950s a code word for cultural and personal revolt against the conventionality of the American middle class. Unlike isolated, strictly avant-garde bohemians, the writers, artists, and journalists of Greenwich Village have always been in dialogue with the mass media and those who shape and uphold the dominant morality; this dialogue has sometimes radicalized the norm but has as frequently defused the innovations of dissenters. It is this dialogue that makes Greenwich Village a particularly apt site to explore changing practices of modern sexual love. For the ideal of a personal relationship popularized in Greenwich Village before World War I became, in the 1920s, the basis of a new standard for the American middle class—a norm against which the feminist movement, the New Left, and the sexual revolution of the 1960s and 1970s have reacted in different ways.

Greenwich Village in the early days of the century was neither famous nor commercialized. Its village quality—enhanced by an irregular pattern of streets that cut it off from both the north-south and east-west traffic of Manhattan—attracted a diverse group of reformers, socialists, anarchists, feminists, artists, and writers. These "bohemians," mainly from the middle class and often from small towns, were college educated, talented, and intellectually ambitious. Moreover, they were caught up in an intense period of political struggle centered in mass labor strikes and the electoral campaigns of the Socialist Party. In addition to their political goals, Greenwich Village intellectuals sought personal alternatives to the dominant values and life-styles of a rapidly industrializing America. The Villagers prized handmade dresses, sandals, and furniture, just as they valued excellent but simple and inexpensive food.

Although Greenwich Village was seen popularly as synonymous with premarital sex and non-monogamy, the alteration in sexual relations attempted there was actually far more complex than its hedonistic image. Many commentators have noted that the period between 1890 and 1920 ushered in a "modern" sensibility in sexual matters. In the Village, the growing public discourse about sex was certainly modern,[1] as was the advocacy of the right to sexual pleasure independent from concerns about reproduction. Equally modern was an emphasis on women's sexual needs and capacities,[2] and the public identification of diverse sexual identities (especially homosexuality).[3]

Yet there was an additional dimension of modern sexuality that began to be articulated and practiced in Greenwich Village—the desire to combine mutual sexual fulfillment with interpersonal intimacy. Such intimacy necessitated sharing a wide range of life interests and an ability to share psychologically one's innermost thoughts and feelings. Joseph Freeman, writing about his experience in the Village of the 1920s, notes how it was this belief in the emotional dimension of sexuality—not simply the proliferation of sexual affairs—that distinguished the Village from the rest of America:

> Free conduct in love was not the monopoly of the Village. Babbitts too had more than one woman, and Mrs. Babbitt had her lovers. Nor was gaiety the monopoly of the Village. Young people in their twenties were having a "good time" all over prosperous America. What distinguished the Village was not its actions but its attitude toward those actions. On Main Street love affairs were clandestine, in the Village they were open. . . . Sex itself was not the main object, we thought. You could have that in Brooklyn, Chicago, Bronxville or Davenport. But in the provinces you could not talk to your lovers.[4]

Where did these new notions of sexualized intimacy and intimate sex come from? We know little about the social history of modern sexuality, but the intellectual lineage is clearer. Many intellectuals in the Village, for example, were influenced by two European writers, the English Edward Carpenter and the Swedish Ellen Key. Both advocated sexual fulfillment combined with personal intimacy. In *Love's Coming of Age,* published in New York in 1911, Carpenter proclaimed that "marriage shall mean friendship as well as passion, that a comradelike equality shall be included in the word love."[5] Sex was just as necessary as friendship: "Intimacies founded on intellectual and moral affinities alone are seldom very deep and lasting; if the physical basis in any form is quite absent, the acquaintanceship is liable to die away."[6] Likewise, Ellen Key's *Love and Marriage,* translated and published in the United States in the same year, advocated relationships based on "an increasingly soulful sensuousness and an increasingly sensuous soulfulness . . . in a union in which neither the soul betrayed the senses nor the senses the soul."[7]

This idea—that lovers should achieve mutual sexual satisfaction and an intimacy in social interests and inner thoughts—diverged sharply from the norms of nineteenth-century America.[8] Before the early twentieth century, men often separated sexuality and love, while women found it difficult to disconnect sexuality and reproduction:[9] hence the prevalence of a double standard. Intimacy between the middle-class husband and wife came from sharing family and communal traditions, but women rarely participated in the men's public world, and men were usually excluded from the personal intimacies of female kin and friends.[10] Although romantic love was the basis of middle-class marriage, romance and courtship did not imply friendship or psychological sharing. In fact, sentimental love emphasized the differences between the sexes. When nineteenth-century feminists thought about creating more egalitarian marriages, they did so by deemphasizing the importance of sex and passion. Their goal was to free women from personal life so that they could pursue productive work in the public sphere.[11]

The Village ideal of sex and intimacy was heavily influenced by feminism, but the feminist vision was different from that held in the late nineteenth century. Women's sexual fulfillment would be equal to that of men's, the Village radicals assumed. Moreover, heterosexual intimacy would entirely eliminate separate spheres for men and women. Rather, women would share the public interests of men, and men would share the private domestic life that had previously been defined as predominantly female. A woman lover could no longer be only a sexual object, a wifely caretaker, or a childbearer.

As we shall see, however, this new ideal of heterosexual love embodied a *male* interpretation of feminism, one that women often found wanting or in conflict with other personal and feminist aims. Indeed, the lives and writing of Greenwich Village men tell a great deal about how and why this modern conception of sexual love arose. For Max Eastman (1883–1969), Hutchins Hapgood (1869–1944), and Floyd Dell (1889–1969), the three men examined here,[12] love relationships were central to their autobiographies, essays, and novels.[13] These men also indicate candidly and in anguished detail the difficulties in their practice of the new ideal. Furthermore, the male response to the contradictions embedded in the new conception of sex love would soon undermine the feminist content and transform it in the 1920s into the more inegalitarian, but more culturally generalized, standard of companionate marriage.[14] In this *marriage*—rather than simply a love relationship—women's sexual fulfillment was still regarded as important, but intimacy was redefined to emphasize the husband's ability to confide his feelings and problems to a wife safely returned to her domestic sphere. Often cut off from a network of female confidantes, the woman of the 1920s was to put her energy into empathizing with the experiences of men in a world from which she was once again excluded.

The Search for a Woman You Can "Both Talk to and Kiss"

Eastman, Hapgood, and Dell were journalists and essayists well known for their radical commentary on the social, political, and personal questions of the day. Eastman and Dell, editor and assistant editor of the radical periodical *The Masses*,[15] were at the political center of Village life. They were also important in literary circles. Eastman published several books of poetry and literary criticism, and Dell wrote numerous novels, including the successful *Moon-Calf*. Hutchins Hapgood, noted as much for his warm and social personality as for his sympathetic ethnographies of the underdog, deviant and radical,[16] was an important focus of Village social life. In particular, he was central to the success of Mabel Dodge's salon, attracting people from a wide range of political and intellectual persuasions. All three men were also among those who founded another Village institution, the Provincetown Players.

Hapgood, Eastman, and Dell all grew up in Protestant, small-town America.[17] Hapgood, from an affluent business family, graduated from Harvard; Eastman, whose father was a minister, attended Williams College; the working-class Floyd Dell was self-educated. It was the mothers of all three men who inspired their intellectual development and their moral commitment to a better world.[18] Whether born into the middle class or upwardly mobile, Hapgood, Eastman, and Dell all came to Greenwich Village dissatisfied with respectable careers in university teaching or established journalism and seeking a vaguely defined alternative.[19]

This break with conventional careers and a deepening involvement in an alternative political and intellectual life was accompanied by a public espousal of feminist ideals and an active search for egalitarian love/sex relationships. All three chose as their first wives women who were active feminists and/or were independent, talented, and intellectual.

Eastman was publicly committed to feminism from his earliest New York years. His first political activity as a young college graduate arriving in the city was organizing a men's committee supporting suffrage. From 1908 to 1914 he made several nationwide tours as a popular and effective speaker for suffrage. Eastman saw his motivation for this political work as coming from "my unqualified liking for women with brains, character and independence."[20] He looked for this kind of woman as a lover. His first was Inez Milholland, a Vassar graduate and ardent suffragist. Max admired her (he called her an "Amazon") but found himself unwilling to consummate the relationship sexually. On the other hand, he discovered that his "romantic" interests, despite his intentions, came to rest on women who could not "keep a conversation interesting."[21] Some years later, however, when he was twenty-five or twenty-six, he seemed to resolve his difficulties in a relationship with Ida Rauh, a friend of his sister, Crystal Eastman. Rauh was a socialist, feminist, actress, and artist who had renounced her family of rich uptown Jews to become a Village intellectual. She was a brilliant conversationalist who introduced Max to socialists, taught him Marxism, and led him into his first consummated sexual experience. For Eastman, "the miracle had happened, I really loved to talk with a beautiful woman."[22]

Hutchins Hapgood was not a feminist activist comparable to Max Eastman, but he too advocated an egalitarian notion of heterosexual love: "To the sensitively developed human being a merely sensual relationship is impossible; it is inextricably connected with emotion, thought and imagination, with what we call the spiritual. And neither relation is possible to the full unless the other is at the full, too. A beautiful love relation, therefore, is impossible without a delicate sexual adjustment."[23] In New York, as a thirty-year-old journalist, Hapgood found his ideal in Neith Boyce, a fellow reporter and later novelist and writer. With Neith he thought he could combine sex, love, and intellectual companionship. "Our relationship . . . has helped us to express ourselves, has helped our writing, our understanding, our culture and our human connections."[24] Hapgood and Boyce married, had four children, and both pursued intellectual careers. To the world, they seemed to integrate the modern ideal of love in a stable relationship.

Floyd Dell, too, wanted as a young man a woman he could sleep with and "talk with too."[25] "I want a girl that can be talked to and that can be kissed," says the hero of his autobiographical novel *Moon-Calf*, "and I want it to be the same girl."[26] This ideal was tied to his feminism: a woman who was romantically attractive had to be a companion as well, sharing a man's world. In a 1914 essay entitled "Feminism for Men," Dell wrote: "The home is a little dull. When you have got a woman in a box, and you pay rent on the box, her relationship to you insensibly changes character. . . . It is in the great world that a man finds his sweetheart, and in that narrow little box outside of the world that he loses her. When she has left that box and gone back into the great world, a citizen and a worker, then with surprise and delight he will discover her again and never let her go."[27] Only when men and women shared their lives, then, was sexual excitement possible.

Dell's early romantic life ran a similar course to Eastman's and Hapgood's. At age twenty-two, in 1908, he married the talented Margery Curry, a thirty-three-year-old Chicago teacher, a feminist and intellectual (an agent for Charlotte Perkins Gilman). Curry created a bohemian salon in Chicago for the shy Dell. But their marriage collapsed after four years, prompting Dell's move to Greenwich Village.

"Passionately Unsatisfied"

In their first relationships, Dell, Eastman, and Hapgood all floundered in attempts to combine sexual desire and personal intimacy. Often they were more attracted to women who were not their equals, women whom they often did not respect or love. Yet secret sexual liaisons with such women were unacceptable, not because they violated a belief in monogamy, but because they undermined the intimacy desired with their respective wives.

Even as Max Eastman decided to marry Ida Rauh he recognized his greater sexual attraction to a much younger woman—seventeen-year-old Ruth Pickering (Eastman was twenty-seven). Pickering was a neighbor whom Eastman had watched grow up, but, neither intellectual nor political, she did not meet his criteria for a serious relationship. These contradictions between his ideal relationship and his sexual attractions continued to trouble his six-year marriage to Ida. From an early date he began continuous (at first, unconsummated) flirtations with other women—flirtations he always confessed to Ida and that inevitably provoked her anger. After the birth of a child and in the midst of continuing conflicts, they mutually agreed on a short separation. She left and he agreed to do a self-analysis—one that he wrote in a notebook and shared with her on her return. The gist of his analysis was his recognition of his "other sexual desires."[28] Ida was devastated, but still committed to saving the marriage. They agreed to continue living together, but Max also established separate quarters. "Once it was established that I did not have to be faithful to Ida, and did not have to confide in her whether I was or not, desire was no longer a torment."[29] But this solution did not satisfy Ida, who periodically became upset and angry. After months of struggle, Max left the woman he termed, recounting the scene in his autobiography, "my friend and slender-bodied mother."[30]

In response to this failure, Eastman entered a second serious relationship with a woman who was most unmotherly and more willing to experiment with non-monogamy. Yet this alternative created even greater personal turmoil and ended far more tragically. Soon after leaving Ida, Max fell in love with Florence Deshon, a beautiful and talented young actress. Florence, like Ida, was a radical and a feminist, but she was less intellectually developed. Max became her intellectual mentor, a relationship that accorded him great satisfaction. Not only was he with a beautiful actress, but Florence "worked earnestly at reading and studying the things I thought she ought to know and . . . grew gloriously in the year of our love."[31] Florence, however, was more independent than Ida and even more ready to express anger:

> [Florence] felt no glimmer of the wish to "make a home" for a man, and I liked that. But I was unprepared for the extremes in the opposite direction to which she might go. One day, when I was absorbed in writing, she went into the kitchen to get a lunch for both of us. Coming to a blockage in my thoughts, I got up from my desk and strolled out of the house and up the road a little way, wrestling with an idea. When I came back in about 15 minutes, she had put out the oil stove, leaving the food half-cooked, and was in the doorway in a black rage. "What do you think I am, a servant?" she said. "Do you think I came up here to cook for you while you stroll around the countryside?" I was too filled with astonishment to feel any other emotion—unless it was admiration of her beauty, which in fury excelled that of the fiercest maenad. I managed, after a while, to convince her that no question of status was involved, that we merely happened to be doing different things. But the task was not easy.[32]

This was only one of many fights where Max experienced the "black panther" of her anger. For six years Max and Florence were locked in an intense on-again, off-again relationship. Max had many light affairs while Florence had a serious relationship with Charlie Chaplin. Yet neither could let go. Whenever Florence tried to reject Max, he tried to get her back. When she returned, he backed off. After one particularly grueling approach/avoidance sequence—Florence, responding to Eastman's entreaties, chose him over Chaplin, to which Max responded by fleeing—the latter wrote, "I am in love and yet I cannot love. I am out of love, and yet I cannot cease from loving."[33] The love affair ended in 1921. Her career and personal life in shambles, Florence committed suicide.

Floyd Dell's first marriage in Chicago and his subsequent love life in Greenwich Village were just as unsatisfied, but less passionate and certainly less tragic. Dell's writings document his problems in trying to find a woman he could both talk to and kiss. Felix Fay, the young protagonist of his autobiographical novel *Moon-Calf*, discusses the problem with a friend:

> "You know I get two seats to every play, and I usually take a girl along. Sometimes I take an intellectual young woman, and sometimes a kissable one—and I don't find either type satisfactory."
> "That's a startlingly juvenile statement," said Tom Alden, "Why in the world should you not regard intellectual women as kissable?"

"I don't know," confessed Felix. "But the fact is, I like the others better. Perhaps my tastes are vulgar. I am more at home with them—I feel freer. But when I sit beside them in the theater, and hear them laugh at silly jokes, and feel their lack of appreciation of something a little subtle, I—well, I despise them."[34]

Dell, like Eastman, effected a temporary resolution of this conflict with his marriage to Margery Curry, a mature woman, an intellectual and an emotional companion, but one who did not engage him sexually. Soon after their marriage, Dell began to have affairs.

My private life became a bewildered and inconsistent one. I fell in love, and very seriously; and my wife, however hurt, was kind and generous, and willing to end our marriage. It was I who refused to give up our marriage, and after desperate attempts to eat my cake and have it upon one theory or another, I gave up my love affairs to keep my marriage—only, against my will to fall in love with another girl, and give up that love; and then with a third, giving her up in turn.[35]

The two separated in 1913, and Dell left for New York.

Hutchins Hapgood, unlike Dell and Eastman, sustained his first marriage, but not without a similar degree of conflict. Very early in the marriage, Hapgood began to have affairs. He discussed them with Neith, and urged her to experiment as well. "To have her know other men intimately, was with me a genuine desire. I saw in this one of the conditions of greater social relations between her and me, of a richer material for conversation and for a common life together."[36] Hapgood thus believed that if Boyce's sexuality more equitably paralleled his own, his relationship with her would be more intense and intimate. In practice, however, Hapgood found he could not accept his wife's affairs. On one occasion, she asked Hapgood to leave her alone for an evening with a male acquaintance. When he returned and asked what had happened, she refused to tell him, whereupon he became so enraged that he took her by the throat.[37] This scene represents only one of numerous, usually less dramatic, occasions on which Hapgood denied Boyce sexual and emotional autonomy.

In 1914, Hapgood wrote Story of a Lover to express his conflicted feelings about his intense relationship with Boyce. The book's central theme is Hapgood's unceasing attempt to obtain more emotional responsiveness from Boyce. "I did all I could to disturb, to wound, to arouse, to make her calm soul discontented and unhappy, as well as to interest her vividly and constantly."[38] As with Max Eastman, it was psychological depth and emotional intimacy—not primarily sexual fulfillment—that Hapgood sought from a serious relationship.

Later, in response to the pain and depression she felt over Hutch's continuing affairs, Neith contemplated an affair with one of his old college friends. Hapgood's distress led her to break off the relationship, and she subsequently suffered a nervous breakdown. During her recovery, she began to reveal more of her feelings to Hutch, but in so doing, she also leveled criticisms.[39] In turn, Hapgood had second thoughts about whether he wanted this deep intimacy he had so long demanded: "She talked to me as if to her own soul. Never can I forget the terrible, the utter frankness of it. I had longed so for expression from her—longed all our life together, but when it came under those circumstances, it was painful indeed."[40] In truth, Hapgood had demanded from Boyce an increased interest in him, not the revelation of her own deep feelings, particularly if such feelings were critical.

After Neith recovered, they had another child, and settled down again into a life together—one that Hapgood hinted was no longer very sexual. Hapgood continued to have affairs, which were always disappointing, and in his heart, he blamed Neith for his inability to find sexual satisfaction in these affairs as well as in marriage: "I learned the ability for passion from her, but she thwarted my ability to obtain it. With her I could not satisfy my ultimate longing for she had no ultimate longing to meet mine. Because of her, I could not meet the need of others and thereby satisfy my own."[41] The two went through a final cycle of Hapgood's revelations and Boyce's hurt and anger, which was ended this time by the death of their son. Hapgood stopped seeing other women, but in so doing he lost his zest for life. Neith became more maternal toward him, a quality that had been there from the beginning of their relationship. After a year or so she "tacitly gave me to understand that she would be content to have me go my own way." But Hapgood stayed and remained dissatisfied: "Here I am at middle life living with the one woman I want to live with, hopeful for my fine children, interested in a work I have chosen and which was not forced upon me, rich in friends, in good health . . . and yet, in spite of all, passionately unsatisfied."[42]

The anguish these three men expressed over the contradictions between their sexual desires and their need for intimacy with an intellectual woman reveals how seriously they accepted a new ideal of heterosexuality and how far they had moved in *consciousness* from the Victorian double standard. Their experience may well have mirrored a more general condition of the educated middle class. Freud, in an essay published in 1912, "The Most Prevalent Form of Degradation in Erotic Life,"[43] saw men's inability to be sexually stimulated by a valued love object as a widespread problem and the primary cause of impotence. Freud did not advocate egalitarian relationships, nor did he view independent, intellectual women as the most desired love objects; if he had simply been a nineteenth-century man, however, he would not have seen the separation of sexuality and love as a serious problem.

In their attempts at intimacy with talented women, Hapgood, Dell, and Eastman finally could not overcome a subtle form of inequality. Each wanted his woman to be passionately involved with him—a wife to whom he could confess all his deep emotional and psychological problems and conflicts. There is little evidence, however, that any of the men were willing to reciprocate. Max Eastman fled from Florence Deshon's emotional problems and demands and Hutchins Hapgood withdrew from those of Neith Boyce. Although all three men sought a strong, intellectual woman, they seemed to desire a maternal figure—a woman who would subordinate her needs to their own rather than to insist on being an autonomous individual with interests and needs of equal worth.

"You Have Crushed My Soul"

Ellen Key's ideal of a "soulful sensuousness—where neither the soul betrayed the senses nor the senses the soul" does not seem to be one that the wives and lovers of these Greenwich Village men easily achieved. Perhaps they did not even want it. Reading between the lines of the men's autobiographies, I sense that their women wanted not so much sexualized intimacy as fidelity, autonomy, and emotional support to develop their own intellectual and artistic talents. Although I have been unable to locate autobiographical material on the women involved with Max Eastman and Floyd Dell, I have examined the unpublished autobiography and letters of Neith Boyce.[44] The views of one woman cannot be conclusive, but the differences between her views of her marriage and those of her husband are certainly suggestive.

In *Story of a Lover*, Hapgood presents Neith as a strong, aloof, cold, and unemotional woman. This book, and his personal letters to her, are filled with complaints and criticisms of her that stress her failure to meet his needs. Yet her letters to him, written from 1898 through the 1920s, reveal a woman who cared deeply for him, who was continually afraid of losing his love, who over and over again blamed herself for their problems, who hardly ever criticized him and never made demands on him. If his book demonstrates his overpowering ego, her letters evidence an increasing negation of self. These letters certainly support the complaint she wrote to be voiced by the wife in their joint play *Enemies* (Boyce wrote the wife's lines and Hapgood, the husband's):

> You, on account of your love for me, have tyrannized over me, bothered me, badgered me, nagged me, for fifteen years. You have interfered with me, taken my time and strength, and prevented me from accomplishing great works for the good of humanity. You have crushed my soul, which longs for serenity and peace, with your perpetual complaining. . . . You have wanted to treat our relation, and me, as clay, and model it into the form you saw in your imagination.[45]

And Mary Heaton Vorse, a close friend of the Hapgoods, a journalist and longtime Village leftist, corroborates this evaluation in a 1919 review of Hapgood's autobiography:

> The remote lovely woman of whom he wrote was not passive like that. . . . That is what one feels throughout his account—the ceaseless activity of his love, the restless and loving prying into the spirit, the constant closeness would increase the remoteness of any human soul. Quiet would be the only response to such aggression—quiet and silence.[46]

Neith Boyce's letters to her husband also reveal how she tried to adapt to his view of sexuality—tried and failed, and in the process repressed her own needs. Those letters written during their courtship and in the early years of their marriage express her strong belief in monogamy and her pain at his affairs. In 1907 she wrote to Hutch: "I have an abiding love for you—the deepest thing in me. But in a way I hate your interest in sex, because I suffered from it. I assure you that I can never think of your physical passions for other women without pain—even though my reason doesn't find fault with you. But it's instinct and it hurts. The whole thing is sad and terrible, yet we all joke about it every day."[47] Later she tried to adapt, jauntily and casually referring to his lovers and engaging in extended negotiations over his affair with a married woman friend. In this period she wrote to Mable Dodge: "As to your famous question, 'Why do we want men to be monogamous?' I should respond, 'Do we?' So long as they won't be, why should we want them to be? Why want anybody to be what they are not? Perhaps we like the excitement of catching them in *flagrante delicto*—and then their excuses are so amusing! An absolutely faithful man, but what's the use of discussing him. He's a mythical creature. I don't want any mythical creatures. I like them as they are."[48]

That this attitude was more of a desperate attempt to adapt, rather than an expression of her real feelings, is indicated by a passionate letter Neith wrote to Hutch in 1916, admitting how much he had hurt her. Her aloofness, she told him, had been a response to that pain:

> I have been looking back over our emotional history and I think I see one or two things about myself which may interest you! In the first place, I think it's true that I am "primitive"—that is, very instinctive. This is covered up a good deal by my calm and reasonable nature, sometimes by pride, sometimes by a strong unwillingness to be hurt, or if I am, to show it or admit it even to myself. I *know* that your physical infidelities (beginning very early) hurt that instinctive feeling for you in me—that I wished to be reasonable about it—that I therefore tended to be more aloof in my feeling about you because otherwise it would have hurt more—that I accepted your feeling about such things as reasonable—that I didn't blame you—but shrank from it. That as

time went on I didn't feel it less, but came more and more to feel that you didn't belong completely to me nor I to you—that this gave me a more disengaged feeling to other men—that after the Indianapolis episode I did return to you in my feeling, bore you a child and did not think of any man for seven years—that the discovery of your long-continued secret relations was a blow to me deeper than you could realize—that I did then in my feeling really withdraw from you and by last summer had got so far away that I could live without you, that after our break I felt free of you and could really love another man. This is my side of it. I know your side too—my failings toward you—that's why I've never blamed you—why I really have no resentment. I know I am just as much at fault as you and very likely much more, but it won't help us to feel we've both been wrong—for we have—we have both been ignorant and careless and reckless about our relation.[49]

Other Greenwich Village women were more interested than Neith Boyce in their own sexual fulfillment, and at least some were less committed to monogamy. It is probable, however, that these women still experienced much more conflict about monogamy—conflict within themselves and between them and their men. In addition, future research may reveal if Village women—both the more sexually liberated and the less so—were as committed as men to combining sex with emotional and psychological intimacy. Did they too, like Neith Boyce, experience continuing emotional adherence to the nineteenth-century norm of female chastity and service to men, even as they rationally embraced the new belief in sexual fulfillment and companionship? Whatever conflicts women experienced, they had to work them out in a milieu dominated by men. Even the more independent and successful women in Greenwich Village—women like Susan Glaspell, Mary Heaton Vorse, Mary Austin, Crystal Eastman, Dorothy Day, Edna St. Vincent Millay, and Margaret Anderson—operated in a setting where men articulated cultural and ideological positions. Women might give each other private support, but there was not at this time a women's movement that publicly discussed changes in personal life, marriage, and sex, nor one that helped women articulate what changes were in their interests. Men may have had as much or more difficulty in their personal lives, but they also had more social support to work out satisfactory solutions.

"Passionate Egotism"

Hapgood, Dell, and Eastman did not take lightly their inability to achieve transformed personal relations. Each agonized over the conflict and pain in his relationship with a feminist woman. They all spent considerable time in self-examination, psychoanalysis, and struggle with the women involved, and they were preoccupied with these conflicts in their writing. None of them saw failure as inevitable or immediately blamed the woman. Rather, each recognized his own egotism, the extreme need for praise and admiration, as one source of his inability to achieve a stable and viable relationship that combined sex and love with a woman who was his equal. Max Eastman summed it up, "There is so much egotism usually in men's love that I wonder how women stand it at all."[50]

Hapgood clearly recognized the egotism that led him to make excessive emotional demands of Boyce: "She would amusedly call attention to the vanity and egotism in me that demanded above everything else a sympathetic listener."[51] He also saw that his ego was threatened by a woman who was her own person: "I hated as I loved her perfect and never-failing egotism, the unconscious completeness with which she remained herself."[52] In the end, however, he admitted that his ego needs—his demands, complaints, and affairs—had partially destroyed Boyce: "Neith had been caught, her free flight impeded by my all-embracing, passionate egotism."[53]

Dell frankly acknowledged the negative impact of egotism on his relationship with Curry. On his way to the Village in 1914, he wrote a letter to the rabbi who had married him, explaining the breakup of his marriage:

> I suppose that during those five years I have inflicted upon everyone who has cared for me, every variety of cruelty which an arrogant and ignorant idealism can unconsciously devise. . . . My deepest and sincerest emotions were concerned with myself. I was, generally speaking, rather callous in my relations with men, and rather hypocritical in my relations with women. . . . It is of course obvious that anyone with such a disposition is unsatisfactory as a lover and intolerable as a husband.[54]

In a later (1920) essay, Dell observed that "men are interested in themselves—in their own reactions to women—much more than in the women."[55]

Eastman's complaint with Ida Rauh was that she undermined rather than fed his ego: "Ida gave me, so far as could be detected, no admiration at all. She was as stingy with praise as she was generous with possessions. She treated me, from the beginning to the end of our relationship, as though I were a conceited and overconfident person who needed to be damped down."[56] Even his disappointment in her failure to develop a career rebounded back to his own needs: "I felt sure," he reasoned, "that Ida was entering upon a great career as a sculptor, a life of her own that would at the same time withdraw her a little from me and feed my admiration."[57]

With Florence Deshon, things went better at first—her career as an actress did feed his admiration, as did her beauty and her acceptance of

Max as an intellectual mentor. As her career waned, however, so did his devotion. Even her suicide failed to shake his self-involvement: his account of her death is cold, detached, and self-absorbed (he regrets that he did not have a chance to give her a present he had prepared—a book of his own poems). Afterward, he quickly embarked on a trip to Russia and did not return to New York for five years. On the boat to Europe he concluded, with some self-satisfaction, that "Florence's death had liberated me to myself."[58]

The success of Eastman's third marriage would come, in part, from his abandoning the high expectations that had so troubled his previous two relationships. In Russia, he soon began a love affair with Eliena Krylenko, sister of a Bolshevik general who was Lenin's first Minister of Justice. Eliena was a dancer, painter, poet, and linguist, but she also loved to cook, keep house, and garden. She made no demands and dedicated herself to his welfare. In a letter to her in 1924, Eastman told her how she differed from his past loves: "Those loves were not helpful to my work, to my egotism, which is the real force in me. With you it is just the opposite. You gave my self to me as I never possessed it before."[59] Their marriage lasted thirty years, until Eliena's death.

Eastman's need for a supportive, all-giving "mother" also entered into his relationship with her. The companionship he found with Eliena was partially that of a mother and son: "My love for her, though adequately physical was not sensual enough to make me jealous of her physical relations with other men. It was a more realistic than a romantic love. . . . There was so large an admixture of the all-giving mother in Eliena's love for me—she stood so firmly and without visible effort by our compact of independence—that I felt free to be as adolescently romantic about other girls as I liked."[60]

These stories, especially Eastman's, raise fundamental questions about the manner in and the degree to which sexual desire is shaped by gender and family arrangements. If Eastman was dependent on Eliena's maternal nurturance, his extramarital affairs bestowed on him a sexual autonomy that made that dependency less fearsome. In contrast, the all-embracing nature of his relations with Deshon and Rauh—the totality of emotional intimacy and sexual involvement with a strong woman—may have been more threatening, evoking the threats to the self of early childhood dependency and merging with the mother.[61] In turn, these fears may well have been aggravated by Eastman's lack of intimate relations outside his love affairs—thus the latter became even more encompassing.

Eastman himself discerned that some of his problems with Ida and Florence arose from his lack of other sources of intimacy. When he was in turmoil about these relationships he had no one to whom he could talk; rather, he fooled his friends "into thinking I was serenely happy.

It never occurred to me to do otherwise. Thus, there was no let-up in my absolute intimacy with Ida. She was my counsellor and confessor as well as my lover and destroyer. . . . I think everyone needs an intimate friend who is not a lover. The innermost citadel of selfhood ought not to be surrendered in love, much less in marriage, where few can hold it alone."[62] Thus, this modern ideal of heterosexual love seems to be in tension not only with the feminist ideal of women's autonomy, but with the modern (male) emphasis on individuality and selfhood.

"I Did Not Want to be Married to a Girl Artist"

After 1920, Hapgood, Dell, and Eastman became more conservative in their personal and public lives. Dell and Eastman found happiness in what had become a new societal norm, the companionate marriage, which prescribed psychological intimacy and shared sexual pleasure for a husband and wife returned to their separate and unequal spheres. Indeed, Dell made a major contribution to the ideology of companionate marriage. Moreover, their conservative retreat extended beyond their personal politics: Eastman and Dell would be, in the next decades, active participants in shaping American mainstream and even right-wing ideology.[63]

Hutchins Hapgood was a decade older than Dell or Eastman and thought of himself as a "Victorian in the modern world." Despite his Victorianism, however, he was the only one of the three to sustain a relationship to a woman with an independent creative life. To be sure, his marriage continued to be fraught with conflict, especially over his sexual double standard, and, significantly, Hapgood became publicly more anti-feminist. Strong women, as William O'Neill notes, were among the few people to whom he was hostile in his autobiography or to whom he admitted being cruel in life.[64]

Although Max Eastman never joined the ideological attack on feminism, his descriptions of his thirty-year marriage to Eliena Krylenko reveal the sexism implicit in companionate marriage. Eliena was willing to mold herself to his needs, as he proudly reported. Early in their relationship, she promised him: "I'll be anything you want me to be— sister, sweetheart, secretary, slave—I'll be your mother if that is what you want."[65] After leaving Russia, the two lived in Europe for several years. He had none of the tensions over domestic work he had experienced with Florence Deshon:

Eliena kept house, typed my manuscripts, and washed my shirts in a cold well with a fig tree beside it that stood in Villa Martha's front yard. In my memory of those days, she is usually up in a fig tree eating figs, but somehow the clothes got washed and the manuscripts, although she still did not know what many of the

English words meant, were typed and retyped and typed again with inexhaustible energy and patience.[66]

While Eliena provided these traditional wifely services, she pursued her art, but only as a hobby: "I love to see you play all kinds of work so vividly,"[67] Max wrote to her. She also took on new and modern duties, as a companion in whom he could confide.

> If Eliena did not like a girl I was enamoured of she would offer no obstruction, but I might find it uphill work to maintain my dissenting opinion. If she did like her, or even join me in a feeling of love for her, she might invite her to come and stay with us for a while—an experiment in the ménage-à-trois which had the advantage of temporal limitations.[68]

Floyd Dell went further than either Eastman or Hapgood in explicitly rejecting the Village ideal he had helped articulate earlier. After numerous affairs in Greenwich Village, including serious relationships with a photographer, Marjorie Jones, and the poet Edna St. Vincent Millay, by 1919 Dell had concluded that companionship based on shared intellectual or artistic interests could not be the basis for sexual intimacy or marriage:

> I felt quite sure now that I did not want to be married to a girl artist; I wanted to be married to a girl who would not put her career before children—or even before me, hideously reactionary as the thought would have seemed a few years ago. One artist in the family, I was convinced, was enough.[69]

Ten weeks after meeting her in 1919, Dell married a young midwestern woman, B. Marie Gage, and retired from the city to a suburban family life, giving up his active involvement in left journalism and in the intellectual life of the Village. Gage had been a socialist and feminist at the University of Wisconsin, had marched as a suffragist, and had been arrested, tried, and acquitted for pacifist organizing in California during World War I. After her marriage at age twenty-three, however, she abandoned politics as she settled down with Dell's approval to become a housewife and mother.

In *Love in the Machine Age,* published to great acclaim in 1930, Dell articulated the anti-feminism implicit in companionate marriage. He still stressed the importance of integrating sexuality and some kind of intimacy; he rejected the nineteenth-century patriarchal ideal where "sentiments of loyalty, exclusiveness and permanence were expressed in masculine friendships; elements of sexual passion, of rivalry and of free choice were separately expressed in relationships with prostitutes; and social aspects of domesticity and family life were again separately expressed in legitimate arranged marriages."[70] But sex, love, and intimacy could now be effectively integrated only in monogamous marriage—one centered on a full-time wife and mother. Single women, he argued, should work only as a means to find a mate and develop maturity. Single motherhood, on the other hand, was infantile.[71] Young married women might also need to work temporarily to provide an adequate economic base for the marriage. Married women with children, however, should never work. Dell now maintained that work outside the home lacked "not merely the authority and dignity of home-management but also the emotional excitements which family life normally provides."[72] The home that in his Greenwich Village days seemed "a little dull" and a "narrow little box" now had authority, dignity, and emotional excitement.

This marriage advocated by Dell was sexually repressive and intolerant of any deviation from hetersexual monogamy. Divorce, adultery, and premarital sexual relations were acceptable only if they were part of the search for an emotionally fulfilling marriage. Other forms of sexual expression—especially homosexuality and sex simply for pleasure—were immature or neurotic, "steps down from adult love, taken to avoid psychic pain, to escape the almost unbearable consciousness of defeat in life's prime instructive purpose."[73] "Do we want," Dell demanded, "to train young people for . . . living happily ever after in heterosexual matehood, or for living tormented and frustrated lives of homosexuality, frigidity and purposeless promiscuity?"[74] Extreme hostility to homosexuality, as well as to the sexual experimentation he had earlier advocated, accompanied his reformulation of the modern ideal of sexual intimacy into that of the companionate marriage.

These varied retreats from an egalitarian integration of sexuality and intimacy raise interesting theoretical questions. Dell, Eastman, and Hapgood supported the new notions of love in a period of progressive political upheaval from 1900–1917; their retreat from attempts to change personal life coincided with the politically repressive 1920s. Although I do not believe that the search for a more feminist, egalitarian, and satisfying sexuality is deterministically tied to the broader political climate, the question remains: What kind of social, political, and psychological supports are necessary to sustain individuals and groups trying to achieve personal change?

Without knowing anything of the historical precedents, feminists in the 1960s and 1970s renovated the idea that lovers should achieve mutual sexual fulfillment and reciprocal psychological openness and should share worldly interests. In an attempt to make this ideal more of a reality for women, feminists critiqued the inequalities of the companionate marriage. But they also used these ideas about sex and love to reject major aspects of the male-dominated sexual revolution of the 1950s and 1960s as well as, later, a proliferating gay male culture.

Feminists criticized not just the sexist characteristics of the sexual revolutions, but also their attempts to wholly or partially separate sexual pleasure from relationships of psychological intimacy. Recently, however, some feminists have advanced a revisionist position—raising the possibility that it might be positive and liberating for women to focus on sexual pleasure per se. These critics have also argued that, at least in the case of lesbians, power inequities and role playing may enhance sexual pleasure.[75]

Thus, even in recent debates, we see that the contradictions of sexual love faced by left intellectuals in early twentieth-century Greenwich Village still haunt us. Sexual expression versus repression and inhibition, psychological openness versus personal distance and autonomy, equality versus domination and submission—these are the polarities of the debate about the desirable and possible combinations of sexuality, intimacy, and power in modern love. Does the desire for psychological intimacy, openness, and dependency often inhibit sexual expression? Is there an inherent contradiction between the desire to combine sexuality and psychological intimacy, and the equally modern ideal of individual autonomy and self-development? Are the psychological and social threats to autonomy different for men and women, making heterosexual intimacy and desire especially problematic? It is such questions that tie us to our predecessors in Greenwich Village and bind us together as twentieth-century women and men struggling with peculiarly modern dilemmas.

Notes

Research on this topic began under an National Endowment for the Humanities fellowship for college teachers. The essay owes a great deal to the detailed criticism and meticulous editing of Christine Stansell and her co-editors. Special thanks to Ellen DuBois for encouraging me to persist in meeting their high standards. The following friends and colleagues provided helpful commentary on earlier drafts: Ros Baxandall, Wini Breines, Barbara Epstein, Naomi Katz, Ruth Milkman, Judith Newton, Deborah Rosenfelt, Mary Ryan, Herb Schreier, Judy Stacey, Alice Wexler, and Eli Zaretsky.

1. This is a central thesis of Michel Foucault, *The History of Sexuality* (New York: Pantheon, 1978). However, he sees the modernization of sexuality as beginning in the eighteenth century.

2. Paul Robinson, *The Modernization of Sex* (New York: Harper and Row, 1976).

3. Jeffrey Weeks, *Coming Out: Homosexual Politics in Britain, from the Nineteenth Century to the Present*. (London: Quartet Books, 1977).

4. Joseph Freeman, *An American Testament* (London: Victor Gollancz, 1938), p. 233.

5. Edward Carpenter, *Love's Coming of Age* (New York: Mitchell Kennerley, 1911), p. 122.

6. Ibid., p. 18.

7. Ellen Key, *Love and Marriage* (New York: G. P. Putnam's Sons, 1911), pp. 20, 23.

8. Christopher Lasch, in *The New Radicalism in America: 1889–1963* (New York: Vintage Books, 1965), observed the importance of personal relations and intimacy

among the Greenwich Village radicals. However, he did not see their ideas and practice of sexual intimacy as "new." Rather, he believed that "the very idea of intimacy as a mutual baring of souls, a mutual examination of the psyche, seems to be an invention of the last 200 years" (p. 108). Nor did Lasch consider this emphasis on personal life a positive part of a progressive politics. He evaluated it as a weak compensation for a decline of community and family, and a lack of compelling worldly interests. My analysis obviously disagrees with these interpretations by Lasch, as well as with his conclusion that the revolt of the intellectuals had no echoes in the rest of society (p. 147).

9. Leslie Fiedler, *Love and Death in the American Novel* (New York: Stein and Day, 1960); Linda Gordon, *Woman's Body, Woman's Right: A Social History of Birth Control in America* (New York: Penguin Books, 1977).

10. Carroll Smith-Rosenberg, "The Female World of Love and Ritual: Relations Between Women in Nineteenth Century America," *Signs* 1, no. 1 (Autumn 1975): 1–29; Nancy Cott, "Passionlessness: An Interpretation of Victorian Sexual Ideology, 1790–1850," *Signs,* 4, no. 2 (Winter 1978): 219.

11. William Leach, *True Love and Perfect Union: The Feminist Reform of Sex and Society* (New York: Basic Books, 1980).

12. The historian Gerald Marriner has used these autobiographies and is also interested in the personal lives of these men, but his interpretation differs from mine. See "A Victorian in the Modern World: The Liberated Male's Adjustment to the New Woman and the New Morality," *South Atlantic Quarterly,* 76 (1977): 190–203; and his dissertation, "The Estrangement of the Intellectuals in America: The Search for New Life Styles in the Early Twentieth Century" (Ph.D. dissertation, University of Colorado, 1972).

13. Max Eastman's autobiography is in two volumes, *Enjoyment of Living* (New York: Harper and Row, 1948) and *Love and Revolution* (New York: Random House, 1964). Over half of the first volume is devoted to his personal life and probably one-third of the later volume. Hutchins Hapgood in 1914 wrote *Story of a Lover* (published anonymously in New York by Boni & Liveright in 1919), an autobiographical account of his conflicted relationship with his wife and other women. This book is especially appropriate for an analysis of the Village male consciousness and experience of heterosexual love because it is not a retrospective autobiography, but one written in the throes of personal crisis. As such it is much more personally revealing than Hapgood's later autobiography, *A Victorian in the Modern World* (New York: Harcourt, Brace, 1939). Floyd Dell is different from Eastman and Hapgood in that his autobiography contains much less detail about his personal life. But unlike them he wrote numerous essays, novels, and plays focusing on relationships between women and men—all writings that were openly autobiographical.

14. For a feminist analysis of companionate marriage, see Christina Simmons, "Companionate Marriage and the Lesbian Threat," *Frontiers* 4, no. 3 (Fall 1979): 54–59.

15. *The Masses* was published from 1911–1917, when it was suppressed by the government and the editors brought to trial (twice and acquitted twice). Many see *The Masses* as the best American left magazine for its combination of literary work, art, and cartoons, framed by a broad spectrum of left political commentary united in a creative whole. *The Masses* stood for fun, truth, beauty, realism, freedom, peace, feminism, and revolution, and against militarism, capitalism, organized religion, and stuffiness. As its contribution to the sexual revolution, *The Masses* printed nude drawings and articles on birth control, and accepted ads for sexual manuals. See William O'Neill, *The Last Romantic: A Life of Max Eastman* (New York: Oxford University Press, 1978), p. 40.

16. Hapgood wrote insightful, personal, and dramatic human-interest stories about immigrants, workers, union organizers, socialists, anarchists, prostitutes, and thieves. These essays were collected into books, most prominently *The Spirit of the Ghetto*

(1902), *The Spirit of Labor* (1907), and *An Anarchist Woman* (1909). Hapgood also wrote a sympathetic introduction to Alexander Berkman's *Prison Memoirs of an Anarchist* (1912).

17. Eastman grew up in Elmira, New York, the son of two ministers. Hapgood's father was a college graduate and businessman, forced out of Chicago in a recession into the small city of Alton, Illinois. Dell's father lost his butcher shop in a small midwestern town during the depression of the 1870s and was never able to find steady work.

18. Max Eastman's mother was a strong, dynamic woman who gained recognition as a liberal theologian and charismatic preacher. She studied philosophy and psychology as an adult at Harvard summer school. Toward the end of her life she left the ministry because of growing doubts and was psychoanalyzed by one of the first Freudian analysts in the United States. Hapgood's mother was a loving housewife who read Shakespeare to her sons and instilled in Hutchins both a dislike for small-town life and a sympathy for the down and out. Dell's mother encouraged his intellectual interests and supported her shy child, who loved to spend long hours in the public library. All three of their fathers were failures in one way or another. The elder Eastman was a sickly man who withdrew from active preaching; both Hapgood's and Dell's fathers experienced business failures.

19. Hapgood gave up a teaching job at the University of Chicago and Eastman one at Columbia University. Dell resigned from his job as a young, successful book review editor of the *Chicago Evening Post*. Hapgood also drifted away from his position as a columnist working with Lincoln Steffens and Abraham Cahan on the *Commercial Advertiser*.

20. Eastman, *Enjoyment of Living*, p. 315.

21. Ibid., p. 341.

22. Ibid., p. 343.

23. Hapgood, *Story of a Lover*, p. 65.

24. Ibid., p. 71.

25. Floyd Dell, *Homecoming: An Autobiography* (New York: Farrar and Rinehart, 1933), p. 103.

26. Floyd Dell, *Moon-Calf* (New York: Sagamore Press, 1957), p. 253.

27. Floyd Dell, "Feminism for Men," in *Looking at Life* (New York: Alfred A. Knopf, 1924).

28. Eastman, *Enjoyment of Living*, p. 506.

29. Ibid., p. 520.

30. Ibid., p. 573.

31. Eastman, *Love and Revolution*, p. 43.

32. Ibid., p. 42.

33. Ibid., p. 215.

34. Dell, *Moon-Calf*, p. 253.

35. Dell, *Homecoming*, p. 240.

36. Hapgood, *Story of a Lover*, p. 111.

37. Ibid., p. 28.

38. Ibid., p. 35.

39. Ibid., pp. 41, 48.

40. Ibid., p. 170.

41. Ibid., p. 190.

42. Ibid., p. 197.

43. Sigmund Freud, "The Most Prevalent Form of Degradation in Erotic Life" (1912), *Sexuality and the Psychology of Love*, ed. Philip Rieff (New York: Collier Books, 1963), p. 65.

44. I read the Neith Boyce letters in the Beinecke Library, Yale University.

45. Neith Boyce and Hutchins Hapgood, "Enemies," in *The Provincetown Plays: Second Series* (New York: Frank Shay, 1916).

46. Mary Heaton Vorse, review of Hutchins Hapgood, *Story of a Lover, The Sun,* September 28, 1919.
47. Letters in Yale Collection.
48. A 1915(?) letter to Mable Dodge in Yale Collection.
49. I have obtained permission to quote this letter from Beatrice Faust, daughter of Neith Boyce and Hutchins Hapgood.
50. Eastman, *Enjoyment of Living,* p. 35.
51. Hapgood, *Story of a Lover,* p. 29.
52. Ibid., pp. 91–92.
53. Ibid., p. 176.
54. I obtained a copy of this letter from the Newberry Library, Chicago, Floyd Dell Collection.
55. Dell, *Looking at Life,* p. 255.
56. Eastman, *Enjoyment of Living,* p. 362.
57. Ibid., p. 33.
58. Ibid., p. 306.
59. Ibid., p. 401.
60. Ibid., pp. 407, 456–57.
61. See Dorothy Dinnerstein, *The Mermaid and the Minotaur* (New York: Harper and Row, 1976); and Nancy Chodorow, *The Reproduction of Mothering* (Berkeley: The University of California Press, 1978).
62. Eastman, *Enjoyment of Living,* pp. 486–87.
63. Eastman was one of the first American leftists in the 1930s to speak out against Stalin, but thereafter, he moved increasingly to the right. By the 1950s he wrote for *The Reader's Digest* and other conservative journals and he supported McCarthyism. Dell remained a liberal on economic issues, but he wrote influential articles about family life taking an increasingly conservative and anti-feminist position. Interestingly, Eastman remained more ideologically progressive on issues of personal life, and he publicly criticized Dell.
64. William O'Neill, "Hutchins Hapgood: A Reconsideration," *New Republic,* January 19, 1972, pp. 31–32.
65. Eastman, *Love and Revolution,* p. 406.
66. Ibid., p. 442.
67. Ibid., p. 552.
68. Ibid., pp. 407, 456–57.
69. Dell, *Homecoming,* p. 283.
70. Floyd Dell, *Love in the Machine Age* (New York: Farrar and Rinehart, 1930), p. 33.
71. Ibid., p. 152.
72. Ibid., p. 102.
73. Ibid., p. 155.
74. Ibid., p. 364.
75. See *Heresies #12* 3, no. 4 (1981), "Sex Issue."

The New Woman and the
Rationalization
of Sexuality in Weimar Germany
Atina Grossmann

> Sex Reformers and sensitive observers of
> daily life confirm again and again that fe-
> male frigidity in love and marriage is the
> most fundamental major problem in today's
> erotic and family life.
>
> —Margarete Kaiser (1932)[1]

In the tense and chaotic years between the end of World War I, the establishment of the new Weimar Republic in 1918–1919, and the coming to power of the National Socialists in 1933, issues of sexuality—especially female sexuality, gender identity, and heterosexual relations—moved to the center of political life in Germany. The Weimar Sex Reform movement and the "New Woman" of the 1920s were responses to, and expressions of, the multiple crises—political, social, economic, and demographic—that shook post-World War I Germany.

Sex Reform, claiming up to 150,000 members in its various organizations,[2] brought together doctors, social workers, and lay people, many of them associated with working-class political parties, in the name of a commitment to legalized abortion, contraception, sex education, eugenic health, and women's right to sexual satisfaction. Fascinated by and celebratory of the New Woman, the Sex Reformers at the same time sought to control and channel her. Whether Socialists, Communists, feminists, or sexologists, the reformers shared a vision of the rationalization of dangerous erotic impulses, a rationalization that would shape the heterosexual couple in a way that also disciplined women. Concretely, Sex Reform advocates provided advice and information on medical contraception and sexual technique through birth control and sex counseling centers, run by municipal health departments, health insurance services, Communist and Social Democratic welfare organizations, and Sex Reform leagues themselves. The clinics, operating in the context of a mass working-class movement, were staffed by those sympathetic physicians who departed from the general anti-contraception and anti-abortion stance of the medical profession. Thus men of science dominated the movement, although some remarkable women were also involved who, as we shall see, created an alternative discourse around female sexuality.

In general, these sex reformers, drawn from across the Left political spectrum, sought to ease the economic and sexual misery of the working class and to stabilize family life and heterosexuality in all classes. Their premise was that as long as the postwar changes in sexual behavior and values continued—a declining birthrate, married women and mothers working for wages, sexually active youth—such activity should at least be rationalized and controlled by scientifically informed experts. The counseling centers and the numerous journals and illustrated periodicals associated with them provided birth control information for women, but they also attempted to institutionalize certain standards of "healthy," socially responsible sexual behavior. Indeed, they mounted an all-out attack on male sexual insensitivity and female frigidity, which they posited as widespread and disturbing social phenomena.

The new social service institutions of the Weimar Republic— maternal and infant care centers, school medical programs, and the marriage and sex counseling centers—were intended to alleviate conditions of economic despair, but their very existence, their newly systematized files and records, served to document the existence of a "culture of poverty" that was not only material but also emotional and sexual. Women who came to the counseling centers for birth control devices and information or for pregnancy and child care also told of their lack of pleasure in marriage and sexual relations. Their complaints helped to define frigidity as a major social problem that threatened family stability and required the attention of doctors, therapists, social workers, government officials, and the media.

The Weimar Sex Reform movement thus presents to us a "sexual revolution" in all its complexity and ambiguity: sexual satisfaction for women, but satisfaction proclaimed and defined mainly by men; the right to contraception and abortion, but only when "necessary"; active sexuality justified because it was healthy and potentially procreative; orgasm as a eugenic measure. The Sex Reform leagues recognized and encouraged female sexuality, but on male heterosexual terms—in defense of the family. To be sure, women did seem to benefit from this new recognition of the need for female sexual satisfaction; heterosexual couples' lives did seem to improve with the available sex advice and contraceptives. Nonetheless, women were never given the chance to define, envision, and experience their own sexuality—this, despite the fact that the movement prided itself on its humanity and progressivism.

Many participants genuinely sought to apply the tenets of their socialism—the belief in a society where people could be truly fulfilled—to sexuality. The socialist perspective, however, had the adverse effect of phrasing issues of reproduction and sexuality not in terms of women's individual rights to control their own bodies and lives, but in terms of class, state, and social welfare. Eugenics questions were central to the movement. The necessity and feasibility of establishing "scientific" norms of health and unfitness were commonly accepted as part of a "motherhood-eugenics" consensus that, among Sex Reformers, transcended traditional left/right, socialist/conservative distinctions and emphasized the importance of protected motherhood and healthy offspring. Indeed, Sex Reform is especially interesting because the usual political categories do not apply: progressives and conservatives might join on the issue of birth control or the need to reform marriage. It was precisely the convergence of Sexual Reform and eugenics with concerns about sexuality and procreation that defined a particular politics of reproduction in the Weimar era and made it so explosive. The woman and sex questions, so often banned into political marginality, moved to the center of political and social discourse, especially during the crisis years after World War I and then again during the Great Depression (1929–1933).

The New Woman

A much abused and conflated image of flapper, young stenotypist, and working mother, the New Woman symbolized the social and demographic changes with which the Sex Reform movement was concerned. She was a product of the mobilization of female labor during World War I, accustomed to working for wages and managing a household without a man. She represented both a blurring of traditional gender roles and a polarization of gender experience during the war: men in the trenches and women on the home front. The impetus for the new concern with female sexual satisfaction and medical contraception was the fear that the New Woman, having achieved through the Weimar constitution political equality and the vote and having experienced the possibilities of an independently earned income during the war, would no longer settle for inequality within a heterosexual relationship.

The New Woman was not only the intellectual with a Marlene Dietrich-style suit and short mannish haircut or the young white-collar worker in a flapper outfit. She was also the young married factory worker who cooked only one warm meal a day, cut her hair short into a practical Bubikopf, and tried with all available means to keep her family small.[3] The New Woman presented herself differently. She bobbed her hair, smoked in public, shaved her legs, used makeup; indeed, presented herself in such a manner that it sometimes became difficult to distinguish the "honest women" from the "whores."[4] Annual reports on the state of health of the German Reich regularly referred to the problematic *Verwilderung der Sitten*—degeneration of morals—that had followed the war, revolution, and inflation.[5]

After World War I, for the first time, abortion was perceived to be a mass phenomenon among the working class. Although the birthrate had steadily declined in Germany since the 1870s, the downward trend was not taken seriously until after the war, when it hit the working class. Only then did it begin to arouse public and governmental concern about the survival of the German "Volk" and the labor and military capacities of coming generations. The traditional differential in births between rich and poor—the poor producing the masses of workers and soldiers—was becoming ominously narrow. Although women continued to marry (indeed in greater numbers than ever before), families became distinctly smaller, and more and more married women worked for wages. According to the 1925 census, working-class families averaged only 3.9 persons per household.[6] Worried government officials, journalists, and politicians began to speak of a "birth strike."

All of these trends only intensified during the Depression, with its massive unemployment and drastic cutbacks in public services. The Depression particularly affected women who, like men, fell victim to unemployment, but also endured an intensification of household labor. On a material level, social reproduction such as health care and food production were reprivatized into individual households; on an emotional one, women were called upon to stabilize the family in a turbulent time, to soothe the tensions of unemployment, and to mediate the conflicts supposedly caused by increased competition for jobs between men and women.[7] By 1931, at the height of the Depression, with six million officially counted job seekers, it was estimated that there were one million (illegal) abortions annually with about 10,000 to 12,000 fatalities. This averages out to at least two abortions for every woman in Germany.[8]

All these factors—the decline in the birthrate, the high incidence of criminal abortions, the rise in the marriage age, and the increasing number of married women and mothers in the waged labor force—were perceived not only as a population crisis but as a crisis of political and social legitimacy. Women's loyalty to traditional gender roles, their willingness to procreate and socialize children, were considered symbolic of a society's legitimacy. Women's perceived rejection of traditional motherhood seemed even more threatening in the light of new social-psychological studies[9]—themselves the result of the new professions of psychology and social work—that stressed the critical work of the mother in making ends meet, soothing conflict, and in general holding the family together during times of economic uncertainty. The growth of coeducation and youth groups, a general eroticization of media and culture, and an apparent increase in premarital and teenage sexuality—as well as abortion and birth control—were therefore explosive issues because they were symptoms of a more general instability.

The New Woman threatened a state-encouraged population policy based on dedicated and informed motherhood, directed toward replacing the manpower losses of World War I and healing the ravages to health and morality precipitated by war, revolution, and economic instability. In this light, we can turn to the quotation at the beginning of this essay: the concern with female frigidity as a major problem not only in erotic but in family life. "Frigidity"—the German word was *Gefuehlskaelte* (coldness of feeling) or *Empfindungslosigkeit* (lack of sensitivity)—in a woman! What a frightening specter in a time of crisis when women were needed more than ever as the guardians of feeling and emotional security and replenishers of a decimated population.

It was therefore critical that female sexuality, once freed from frigidity, be directed into the proper heterosexual paths: "Our time needs women who know their own bodies, who are in command of the rules of enlightened erotic life—and who can give life to healthy children following the ancient themes of the beauty of body and soul."[10] But if marriage were to be made more attractive to women through more satisfying sexual relationships, sex itself could not be *so* free and attractive that women would be further discouraged from marriage and motherhood. Sex Reform thus walked a delicate balance: the terms of female sexuality were defined and therefore narrowed just as it became technically and economically possible to live out that sexuality.

Sex Reform's New Woman: Emancipated and Domesticated

The Weimar years in Germany represented the beginning of an all-out attack on female frigidity—an attempt to reconcile the New Woman to marriage and motherhood by improving her sex life. Sex Reformers encouraged sexual technique (proficiency) and women's right to orgasm as a means of stabilizing and harmonizing the heterosexual nuclear family. Mutual orgasm between two loving, healthy partners was posited as the highest expression of a new and pure morality that would produce healthier and better adjusted children. Sexual intercourse was the integration, the coming together (literally) of two fundamentally different natures. The Sex Reform movement quite consciously saw its task as the redomestication of the New

Woman: "We don't want to create unwed suffragettes, but rather understanding couples."[11] Women were reoriented toward a more "emancipated" marriage and motherhood.

Sex manuals, Sex Reform journals, and the clinics presented an image of a new domesticated woman. Instead of the weary proletarian wife, grotesquely old and ill before her time, enduring the brutal thrusts of a drunken husband and endless health-destroying pregnancies and abortions,[12] the movement posited a sexually satisfied mother, lover, comrade, and wage earner, outfitted with time-saving household aids, birth control methods, and a sensitive husband in command of the latest sexual techniques. The pivot of the new rationalized domestic culture was the "modern superwoman"; a health- and nutrition-conscious consumer and socializer of children, gainfully employed, and a willing and active sex partner. Certainly the task was daunting: "The fact that the majority of women do not achieve orgasm with the current state of the art of loving is no excuse for negating orgasms in women."[13]

The nineteenth-century ideology of motherhood and sexual passionlessness was revised by a new ideology of heterosexual companionship stressing emotional and sexual intimacy between equal partners. The "Mother of the Race"[14] was integrated with the new Emancipated Woman. Here was a peculiarly feminine double bind: women represented the degeneration of morality in postwar Germany and at the same time were perceived as desperately needed social guardians to restore morality.

Eroticization Rescues Marriage

Sex Reformers touted the eroticization of marriage as "the most effective means of saving us from the crisis in marriage."[15] But men set the norms for that eroticization; the counseling and literature of the Sex Reform movement never assumed that women could control or determine the forms of their own sexual satisfaction. Although many women doctors worked in counseling centers and there were some prominent women Sex Reformers, men wrote most of the important sex manuals[16] and journal articles (which shaped the advice given in the clinics, even by women to women). Th.H. Van de Velde, whose *Ideal Marriage*, first published in Germany in 1928, was "a sex manual par excellence . . . unquestionably the most detailed and rationalized treatment of sexual behavior to see the light of print,"[17] even went so far as to instruct that "the husband is the sexual educator and guide [note that the German word is *Fuehrer*] through whom the woman is educated to full proficiency in love."[18]

Sex Reformers provided men with a guide to the mysteries of the female body and insisted that the time when men could simply ignore the erotic needs of their wives was past. They mapped out a new geography of female desire through "scientific" orgasm curves diagrammed in their journals.[19] The curves proved "scientifically" that women's patterns of arousal and satisfaction were fundamentally different from men's; a difference that spoke to a basic and unbridgeable natural difference between the sexes. It was thus man's task to be so patient, skilled, and considerate that he channeled the two of them toward that fleeting moment of union, the magical simultaneous coital orgasm. Men retained the responsibility for and knowledge of sexuality: "the coldness of most women results from the fact that their lover simply leaves them cold, that he is incapable of awakening their feelings."[20]

If the eroticization of marriage revised older notions of female passionlessness, however, those nineteenth-century notions still entered into the new interpretations. Women's sexuality was dormant, passive, emotional: more diffuse, hidden, less genitally focused. According to the charts, female arousal was slower and more complex; women were slower to come and slower to come down. Their orgasm curves were *not* straightforwardly steep like those of the male, and there were myriad possibilities for something going wrong along the way: "Male sexuality is more concentrated, robust and vigorous, that of the female, fragmented and more differentiated."[21] Thus even if women were slipping out of their old roles, their biology remained fragile.

The Biological Tragedy of Women

Here was the double bind that constituted woman's biological tragedy. Because of her "natural" connection to childbearing, her body was inevitably dominated by the uterus. Woman was therefore more a *Geschlechtswesen*—physical being—than man. Embedded in the physicality of her body, its regular menstruations and pregnancies, she was less rational and capable of abstract thinking. On the other hand, her very physicality made her more diffusely passive and emotional, a less genital creature, less able to derive sexual pleasure from the body that so dominated her identity.

As a totality, then, women were more defined by their sex than men, but they were also less capable of deriving pleasure from their sexuality. Female sexuality as discussed in Sex Reform literature was associated with loss or pain; defloration, menstruation, and childbirth were all at best highly ambivalent experiences that required great care and expert advice (some doctors even recommended medical defloration to avoid the trauma of the "first night"). Friedrich Wolf, a Communist physician, abortion-rights advocate, and "natural healer," titled his pamphlet on gynecological health *Women's Weak Point* and unequivocally noted, "All emancipation notwithstanding, the woman is dependent in much greater measure than a man on the vicissitudes of her body."[22]

Sex Reformers argued, however, that proper male techniques could compensate for women's biological disadvantage: "This knowledge of women's more difficult natural load should cause men to treat women with sensitive consideration and grant them complete equality."[23] Or as a woman sex reformer put it:

> The female has been assigned a passive role by nature. Therefore her sexual feeling is also much more sensitively organized and of a more spiritual nature. The loving female is a sensitively tuned instrument and it totally depends on the male's skill if he approaches the matter tenderly and quietly or with crude and clumsy gropings.[24]

Woman's sexuality was different, but men could be trained to educate it to better accommodate their genital fixations. If woman's sexuality was more generalized throughout her body and psyche, less genitally localized, then Sex Reform aimed to change all that. Indeed, it was only through male manipulations, which would bring her to orgasm during intercourse, that she could truly become "sexual" in the narrow Sex Reform understanding of the term. Woman's diffuse, emotionally laden sensuous experience was not mature sex. Again, Van de Velde set the tone for countless other sex manuals:

> The newly married woman is generally more or less completely "cold" during sexual intercourse. . . . She must be educated into love. Only gradually does the young wife grow into a sexually mature woman experienced in lovemaking.[25]

He warned husbands that continued "frigidity" was dangerous for the marriage:

> Every substantial sexual stimulation of the woman that is not resolved by orgasm causes damage and the accumulation of such experiences will lead to permanent or in any case difficult to treat disadvantages for body and psyche.[26]

Lest there be any doubt about how to avoid such consequences, Van de Velde provided detailed instructions about the efficient sequence of "gaze and word," kiss, tongue kiss, genital foreplay, and intercourse. Anything less than simultaneous orgasm during intercourse was a failure and "unnatural."

Of course, different types of women and families required different strategies. The bourgeoisie received more how-to information on sexual techniques; literature for the working classes focused on the need for and right to contraception, abortion, and eugenic hygiene: the dangers, for instance, of venereal disease, incest, self-induced abortion, bad nutrition and body care, and ignorance about health in reproduction. Parents who were tubercular, alcoholic, mentally unstable—or simply lethargic, exhausted, and poor—were continually reminded of their social responsibility not to procreate.

This class bias was also reflected in theories of female sexual responsiveness according to type: a differentiation that reflected a scientific concern in the 1920s with "character," be it racial, class, or psychological.[27] Many sexologists saw the "primitive vulgar" proletarian woman as more organic and natural, and thus quicker to arouse and climax, than the neurotic, hysterical, educated modern woman—selfish!—whose emotional and sexual immaturity left her in Freud's childish clitoral stage. The bourgeois woman, whose husband was presumably reading how-to manuals, required more clitoral foreplay; she was more sexually demanding and sensitive to pain, whether in sex or childbirth.

All reformers, however, whether they worked with and wrote for a predominantly bourgeois or a proletarian constituency, were united in the conviction that marriage desperately needed to be reformed. They all agreed on the necessity of rationalization and human economy (Menschenoekonomie) in both production and reproduction: that is, intensified productivity and a streamlined work process at the workplace, and eugenics and the encouragement of responsible motherhood and sexual harmony within marriage. Here were the beginnings of what has been called for a later period in the United States "the work ethic of sexuality."[28]

Sex Between Men and Women Is Very Hard Work

Coming did not come naturally for women, at least not during heterosexual intercourse. Indeed, women's torturous path to full sexual satisfaction was reminiscent of the one mapped out by Freud. Freudian tenets did influence Sex Reform. However, while assimilating Freudian notions of women's sexual passivity and of the importance of sexuality in human life, Sex Reform nevertheless rejected Freud's model for sexual harmony in which women underwent profound psychological changes, relinquishing their immature clitoral sexuality in order to become fully mature heterosexual beings. Rather, the burden for sexual satisfaction rested more squarely on the man; he must change his sexual practices to consider women's peculiarities—especially the existence of the clitoris as woman's primary organ of sexual stimulation. But the male-defined goal of orgasm during penetration remained.

The Sex Reformers understood full well that women were not naturally and inevitably frigid. They knew that it was relatively simple for women to attain orgasm through masturbation and lesbian lovemaking. Women's enviable capacity for multiple orgasm was also an accepted canon. Indeed, Van de Velde cautioned overenthusiastic husbands against too vigorous sexual gymnastics, lest they not be able to keep up with their women once awakened: "Their capacity then usually surpasses that of the man. . . . I urge husbands not to accustom their wives, in ill-considered fashion, to maximum accomplishments, which they will not be able to maintain over the long run."[29] The goal was to win women over to regular heterosexual marital lovemaking, not to unleash female sexuality in "ill-considered fashion."

Heterosexual intercourse had to become competitive with the "solitary pleasures" and lesbian sex. In short, Sex Reform called for a reorganization of women's sexual impulses. The real issue was not sexual pleasure, but heterosexual, marital harmony dependent on the woman's being sexually satisfied in intercourse. To that end, the man was to pay more attention to foreplay; the institutionalization of the streamlined step-by-step lovemaking discipline with which many of us in a later generation of Americans also grew up; caresses and stroking, manual and oral stimulation of the clitoris; then the serious business of penetration and intercourse.

Should intercourse fail to produce the desired result, clitoral stimulation might be employed again to "finish up," but such activity was clearly inferior in the hierarchy of sexual practices. The clitoris remained a means to a predefined end. Those sexual activities still classified as perversions when chosen as pleasures in themselves were acceptable as preliminaries and sexual aids:

> Today when one is so eagerly concerned with supporting and strengthening the shaky institution of marriage, one is also looking for ways to combat the dangers of monotony . . . perhaps the loveliest and finest variations are the ones based on tender deviations.[30]

Sex Reformers, pragmatic as they were, were in fact open to experimentation and variety if it would help refresh "tired and boring" marriages. Some advocated separate bedrooms (a cruel joke for most Germans in view of the housing shortage) as a way to reduce monotony. The popular emphasis on physical fitness and health encouraged attention to beauty and physical attractiveness; women were urged not to "let themselves go" for no man enjoyed making love to a weary and uninterested housewife. A list of alternatives to traditional marriage was debated: childless companionate marriage (*Kameradschaftsehe*),[31] the youthful "try-out marriage," polygamy for the benefit of women left tragically single by the shortage of marriageable men after the war, even lesbian relationships within the context of a primary heterosexual commitment. One Sex Reform magazine, called the *Eheberater* ("The

Marriage Counselor") advised: "Basically one can say that a bisexual woman does not endanger a marriage. One must of course be vigilant that the inclination does not go too far towards the female side."[32]

We should note that here too, just as in the focus on female orgasm, such experiments in apparent liberalization also represented a certain narrowing and disciplining of sexual options, involving more state and therapeutic regulation and surveillance. The try-out or companionate marriage was after all suggested as a means of registering and disciplining "wild marriages" or premarital sex.

The Extension of the Assembly Line into the Bedroom

If sex between men and women was such hard work, the work process needed to be improved and streamlined. The changes in the mode of production in Germany during the 1920s—rationalization, mechanization, applied science and technology, all embodied in the assembly line and scientific management—were to be reflected and imitated in the sphere of reproduction. The rationalization of everyday life meant the extension of assembly line techniques into housework and the bedroom. Sex Reform treated the body as a machine that could be trained to perform more efficiently and pleasurably. The goal was to produce a better product, be it a healthy child or a mutual orgasm. Finally, of course, the two goals were related, since satisfying sex produced a better quality of offspring. Sexuality served to help reproduce workers fit for work, but also to inculcate the rhythms of work in their daily lives. If coming did not come naturally and therefore required discipline and concentration, these same skills were necessary to working in a factory. The Sex Reformers were fascinated by the possibilities of science and technology for creating better and happier lives. They amended the nineteenth-century assumption that family life and sexuality should compensate for the toil and stress of wage labor. The home was no longer a "haven in a heartless world," but rather a place where the tempo and hand motions of rationalized labor could be applied to everyday living. Sexuality and work should reinforce each other.

The rationalization of the work process transformed German industries after the mid-1920s.[33] With the application of the principles of Taylorism and human engineering, the discipline of the individual worker—"Production Factor Human Being" (*Produktionsfactor Mensch*)[34]—became more critical than ever. As one of the proponents of the new Taylorized "scientific management" wrote in 1926, "the more the work process has been refined, the more vulnerable it has become."[35] Workers themselves lost control over the work process, but the worker's character became more important as industry required a more sophisticated and individual control. Because the assembly line was so uniquely vulnerable to any break in tempo, the labor discipline of each and every worker took on new importance.

Scientific management mandated not only labor discipline at the workplace but personnel management of the whole of a worker's existence. Ideologues of rationalization seemingly rejected the theory, widely accepted today, that capitalism produced an ever greater split between home and workplace, labor and leisure. Rather, the new technology seemed to blur the lines between work and private behavior. Weimar sex manuals unabashedly recognized the connection.

> Most important is the expression of life rhythms in the rhythms of the erotic . . . people whose lives take place unrhythmically, who can show no regularity in their work process, their time distribution, their production, their leisure and their sleep, also tend to practice unrhythmic, inconsistent, jerky coital motions.[36]

Just as most Sex Reformers did not question the necessity of controlling population quantity and quality, or of a certain sexual division of labor within the family, they did not question this rationalization of the work process or the demands of increased productivity. Reformers rather directed their energies to correcting abuses in the family rather than to challenging the fundamental institutions of the family or the factory. Finally, the goal was to reform people so that institutions could function more smoothly and even humanely. As a popular Sex Reform magazine pointedly put it: "Marriage itself really doesn't need much reform; the people who get married, on the other hand, need a lot of reforming."[37] Standardization and rationalization occurred simultaneously with increasing individualization. The process of sexual relating became more standardized by means of a much more individualized and specialized control: the direct intervention of "experts" into the body through medical birth control and prescribed sexual technique. In turn, expert professionals gained more insight into people's private lives through social welfare and counseling centers. Sex Reform journals, advice books, and pamphlets carried their interventions straight into the home and bedroom.

Thus the same criteria set up for effective rationalization in industry were applied to sexuality: uniformity, standardization, reliability, reproducibility, and predictability.[38] If the "rationality of science defied the irrationality of the marketplace,"[39] as David Noble puts it in his study of the rationalization of American industry, then it could also defy the irrationality of female sexuality. The human body was geared to norms, just like a finely tuned machine, to meet certain scientific standards that had been set up, not by those performing the activity, but by experts seeking control not only over the product but also the process of sexual relating.

The three principles of Taylorized scientific management outlined by Harry Braverman also describe the principles of the Sex Reform movement: the dissociation of the labor process from the skills of the workers, the separation of conception from execution, and the use of this monopoly over knowledge to control each step of the labor process and the manner of its performance.[40] The mystifying veil of the "natural" was stripped away from human sexuality, but sexuality only became newly mystified and reified by the intervention of experts, who far away from the "scene of the action" appeared in the form of guidebooks or white-coated professionals prescribing "standardized motion patterns."[41] Women's particular sexual "skills"—such as the ability to have multiple orgasms—that did not necessarily coincide with the required simultaneous orgasm were ignored in favor of establishing a sexual norm based on the male pattern of sexual satisfaction— the steep plunge to one orgasm.

A Neue Sachlichkeit *in Sexuality*

Thus the frustrating paradox of Sex Reform was that even as it "liberated" female sexuality by recognizing women's desires for pleasure, it subjected it to new taboos and restrictions. All this was done under the flag of "progress," with a breathtakingly innocent faith in the ability of science and technology to regulate and solve human problems. If corollaries to Sex Reform can be found in the rationalization of industry, they can also be found in the new language of art and architecture. The fascination with streamlining and functionalism can also be found in the constructions of the Bauhaus and the New Objectivity *(Neue Sachlichkeit)* in visual expression.

The justification for sexual freedom was its unsentimental rationality; its ability not to release creative and explosive energy, but rather to check and channel that energy. The slogan carved onto the entrance of Magnus Hirschfeld's famous Institute for Sexual Science in Berlin was "Per scientam ad justitiam," to justice through science. Indeed, one could argue that the peculiar character of Sexual Reform was its Enlightenment optimism. The reformers believed that sexuality properly expressed could be tamed and made functional for the good society; that only when it was repressed was sexuality explosive and dangerous. Even Wilhelm Reich, the great apostle of sexual radicalism, contended that a liberated orgasmic (genital, heterosexual) sexuality would create a better socialized (disciplined) human being.[42] The sexually satisfied comrade will be a better comrade, said the radical sex reformer; the sexually satisfied worker will be a better worker, said the bourgeois sex reformer. Both sought to rescue sexuality by taming, domesticating, and rationalizing. Right-wing sexual conservatives, who opposed birth control and the legalization of abortion and homosexuality, were more convinced of the explosiveness of sexuality, sensing within it the terror of the uncontrollable streaming forth, breaking through and invading boundaries.[43] Highly respectful of its potency, they opted for repression, which meant, as always, first the repression of women.

The progressive Sex Reformers, many of them Communist and Social Democratic professionals, were steeped in the tradition of the Enlightenment. They assumed that knowledge could heal and that it was possible to achieve a mastery over nature, over their own instincts. They differed sharply from Freudian analysts in their refusal to accept a necessary contradiction between sexual expression and civilization. Sex was understood in a *sachliche* manner as a natural objective function that simply needed to be perfected and regulated. They sought to domesticate, by defining and categorizing, what might be wild and untameable. In this context of the need for control, their focus on female sexuality becomes more comprehensible.

With this faith in a "normal" sexuality, the boundaries defining deviant groups and behavior sharpened. Even though there were those on the Left who criticized Van de Velde, for instance, for trapping satisfying sexuality within the outmoded and oppressive institution of bourgeois marriage,[44] hardly anyone questioned his "scientific" contributions in terms of the "physiology and technique" of sex. His curves set the standard. Those who did not conform were potentially dangerous.

The new deviants were, most markedly, women who were simply unfit for marriage *(eheuntauglich)*. Interestingly, Sex Reform literature usually portrayed them in a manner suspiciously close to the malicious stereotype of the New Woman: short, dark hair; dressed in a unisex shift, distinctly unmaternal—the image not only of the prostitute but also of the Jewess and the lesbian. Indeed, men were warned that "the homoerotic or bisexual female type plays a relatively large role among the women unfit for marriage, perhaps a larger role than is commonly thought, because many forms of homosexuality are hidden under the mask of frigidity.[45]

Male scientists, writing in serious sexological journals, identified the categories of women to which men should be alert: the "manic, excitable, argumentative, depressive, sad, sensitive, egotistical, and neurotics with an inferiority complex."[46] Some doctors even went so far as to report in the *Journal for Sexual Science* experiments with hormonal treatment of female sexual dysfunction. Interestingly, they discovered that it was easier to medically subdue an "oversexed" woman than to stimulate the "undersexed." In the perplexing case of a husband who was dissatisfied with a wife who oscillated between general coldness and "nymphomania" during her period, it was easier for him to cope with the former. The doctors recommended that the woman should be permanently medicated into coolness—that way, at least the husband would have a peaceful life; if he desired passion, he could always go elsewhere![47] Such an obsession with categorization and a fascination with the power to control "deviance," well-intentioned in the service of liberalization, helped to open the way and provide scientific legitimacy for Nazi racial hygiene programs.

Women's Protest

Only a very few women Sex Reformers protested against this manipulation of female sexuality. Women like Helene Stoecker, Margarete Kaiser, Sofie Lazarsfeld, and Alice Ruehle-Gerstel,[48] while identifying themselves as part of the Sex Reform movement and applauding the newly acknowledged necessity for female orgasm, recognized with remarkable sharpness the trap inherent in trying to liberate female sexuality through sexual norms set by men of science. Caught in the traditional double bind of female professionals, they sought to expropriate and utilize the techniques of male-dominated science while at the same time fighting for recognition of a unique female sensibility in sexuality.

These women offered a truly materialist analysis of frigidity as a symptom of and protest against female subordination and oppression in general. Women's "neurotic inferiority complex" and their frigidity, they argued, had a material base in the social conditions of sexism. They were quite unlike more politically conservative reformers, who worried that modern civilization with its incorporation of women into public life and wage labor had alienated them from their bodies, making them more resistant to both childbearing and orgasm; many of the Sex Reform women understood themselves as modernists and asserted that only a new emancipated woman, self-confident and equal, was truly capable of orgasm. A truly liberated sexuality, they believed, had to await the birth of a female-defined sexuality:[49]

> Frigidity is also a fear of powerlessness. . . . To give in to libido means to subordinate oneself to a man, means to enter a territory where the man sets the tone. This protest-like frigidity is most widespread among women who reject their female role. Frigidity always reveals a "sexual complex" (*Geschlechtskomplex*), a contradiction between sex role and life plan.[50]

Women Sex Reformers wanted the movement to be an expression and affirmation of the New Woman but they recognized that much of the Sex Reform literature read rather more like a response to a threat. Ruehle-Gerstel pointed out the very real dangers facing women who accepted the new Sex Reform: the double bind in which women were rejected as being backward and prudish if not sexually open, and rejected as whores and dangerous women if they really let go. Women's inferiority complex as postulated by male doctors, she argued, was not only a reflection of women's very real inferior social position, but a projection of men's fear of and anxiety about the truly sexually expressive woman. Frigidity could not simply be cured, like a dislocated shoulder, by well-trained hand motions. It required, finally, a social revolution in relations between the sexes, not only a political revolution as called for by the sexual radicals, that would guarantee freedom of abortion, birth control, and sex education.

Women like Ruehle-Gerstel identified the great and fearful silences in the discourse of Sex Reform; today we would say that they were attacking sexism, raising the questions as we have today, of what a feminist vision of sexuality could be. Reading their work over fifty years later, one is struck by the degree to which their critique became invisible. In Germany their books and those of their male colleagues were burnt, their organizations smashed by the Nazis even as some of their eugenic ideas were expropriated into ultimately genocidal race hygiene programs.

On this side of the Atlantic, we have been caught for almost half a century in the combined discourse of Freudianism and Sex Reform. The necessity of continuing to fight for the basic sexual and reproductive rights that leftist Sex Reformers of the 1920s and early 1930s demanded has left us with little energy and time to engage in the necessary critique of that struggle. We remain the products of their sexual revolution. We are only now beginning to pick up where they, our grandmothers, left off. We are confronting the multiple ways in which their sexual revolution (like ours of the 1960s?) freed women only to please men or reject them, liberated women in terms women themselves did not determine, and finally subordinated women's freedom to the interests of family and state. They provided us with no solutions. They did, I think—if we find and listen to them—identify the terms of the argument and raise the essential questions.

Notes

I am grateful to Eva Renate Busse, Frank Mecklenburg, Harold Poor, Chris Stansell, Sally Stein, and the members of my German Women's History Study Group, especially Renate Bridenthal, for their help and criticism in preparing this piece.

1. Margarete Kaiser, *Die Liebe als Kunst* (Berlin: Ibis Verlag, 1932), p. 211.
2. See Atina Grossmann, "Satisfaction Is Domestic Happiness: Mass Working-Class Sex Reform Organizations in the Weimar Republic," in *Towards the Holocaust: The*

Social and Economic Collapse of the Weimar Republic, ed. Michael Dobkowski and Isidor Wallimann (Westport, Conn.: Greenwood Press, 1983) for a more detailed discussion of Sex Reform organizations.

3. Suggestive and detailed descriptions of the working-class woman as New Woman are provided in, for example, Deutscher Textilarbeiter Verband, *Mein Arbeitstag— Mein Wochenende* (1930) and Lisbeth Franzen-Hellersberg, *Die jugendliche Arbeiterin, ihre Arbeitsweise und Lebensform* (Tuebingen: Mohr, 1932).

4. Elizabeth Wilson makes similar observations for England after World War II in her *Only Halfway to Paradise: Women in Postwar Britain: 1945–1968* (London and New York: Tavistock Publications, 1980), especially in chap. 5, "The Boundaries of Sexuality."

5. Bundesarchiv Koblenz R86 (Reichsgesundheitsamt/Ministry of Health), file R86/931.

6. *Statistik des Deutschen Reichs*, vol. 406/1, Volks, Berufs und Betriebszaehlung vom 16 Juni 1925, p. 28.

7. Ruth Milkman makes similar observations about the Great Depression in the United States in "Women's Work and the Economic Crisis: Some Lessons from the Great Depression," in *A Heritage of Her Own: Toward a New Social History of American Women*, ed. Nancy F. Cott and Elizabeth H. Pleck (New York: Simon & Schuster, 1979), pp. 507–41.

8. For a more thorough discussion of abortion as a social phenomenon and political issue during the Weimar Republic, see Atina Grossmann, "Abortion and Economic Crisis: The 1931 Campaign Against Paragraph 218 in Germany," *New German Critique* (Spring 1978), pp. 119–37. For statistics, see especially pp. 121–22 and 125.

9. Mathilde Kelchner, *Kummer und Trost jugendlicher Arbeiterinnen, Eine soziologische Untersuchung an Aufsaetzen von Schuelerinnen der Berufsschule* (Leipzig: Verlag von C. L. Hirschfeld, 1929) and the volumes of the Deutsche Akademie fuer soziale und paedagogische Frauenarbeit's series *Forschungen ueber Bestand und Erschuetterung der Familie in der Gegenwart* (a massive study on the state of and destruction of the contemporary family in Germany published between 1926 and 1932) are only some of many books that could be cited as examples.

10. *Sexual-Hygiene, Zeitschrift des Reichsverbandes fuer Geburtenregelung und Sexualhygiene* (Berlin: Verlag Wilhelm Schoeffer), Jg. 2, nr. 12 (September 1930): 90.

11. Kaiser, *Die Liebe als Kunst*, p. 121.

12. For graphic descriptions of "proletarian sexuality" see, for example, the reports on questionnaires distributed by Otto Ruehle and Alice Ruehle-Gerstel in Alice Ruehle-Gerstel, *Die Frau und der Kapitalismus, Das Frauenproblem der Gegenwart, Eine psychologische Bilanz* (Leipzig: Verlag von S. Hirzel, 1932), pp. 147–235 (reprint ed., Frankfurt: Verlag Neue Kritik); Otto Ruehle, *Illustrierte Kultur-und Sittengeschichte des Proletariats* (reprint ed., Giessen: Focus Verlag, 1977), pp. 40–64; and Wilhelm Reich, "Sexual Misery of the Working Class", in *Sexualnot und Sexualreform, IV Kongress, Wien 1930*, ed. Herbert Steiner (Vienna: Elbemuehle Verlag, 1931).

13. J. R. Spinner, "Die Bedeutung der Lustkurven fuer das Eheglueck" in *Liebe und Ehe, Monatsschrift fuer Liebe und Ehe Wissenschaft* (Berlin: Kultur Verlag), Jg. 1, nr. 2 (July 1928): 53.

14. See Anna Davin, "Imperialism and Motherhood" in *History Workshop* 5 (Spring 1978): 9–65.

15. *Zeitschrift fuer Sexualwissenschaft*, Bd. V, H. 5 (October 1928): 359.

16. The best-known sex manual was certainly Th. H. Van de Velde, *Die Vollkomene Ehe, Eine Studie ueber ihre Physiologie und Technik* (Leipzig, Stuttgart: Benno Konegen Medizinischer Verlag, 1928). Max Hodann, a communist physician, popularized his

work for the working class in *Geschlecht und Liebe in biologischer und gesellschaft-licher Beziehung* (Berlin: Buechergilde Gutenberg, 1932), as did Wilhelm Reich for youth in *Sexueller Kampf der Jugend* (1932; reprint ed., Verlag O, n.d.). The Weimar years produced a plethora of Sex Reform journals, some avowedly scientific, some semipornographic, many published by working-class lay organizations.

17. Michael Gordon, "From an Unfortunate Necessity to a Cult of Mutual Orgasm: Sex in American Marital Education Literature, 1830–1940," in *The Sociology of Sex, An Introductory Reader*, ed. James M. Henslin and Edward Sagarin (New York: Schocken, 1978), p. 77 (a good source of comparative data with the United States).

18. Van de Velde, *Die Vollkomene Ehe*, pp. 167, 165.

19. See, for example, the graphs and curves in ibid., pp. 161–80; Hodann, *Geschlecht und Liebe*, pp. 16–20; Reich, *Sexueller Kampf*, pp. 27–36; and also in *Lexikon der Sexualwissenschaft, ein Nachschlagewerk fuer alle Gebiete medizinsicher, juristischer und soziologischer Sexualforschung* (Wien and Leipzig: Verlag fuer Kulturforschung, 1930).

20. *Der Eheberater, Monatsschrift fuer Hygiene und Volksbelehrung* 3 (1929): 66.

21. Julius Wolf, *Die neue Sexualmoral und das Geburtenproblem unserer Tage* (Jena: Verlag von Gustav Fischer, 1928), p. 14.

22. Friedrich Wolf, *Der Schwache Punkt der Frau, Gesunde Maedchen, Glueckliche Frauen* (Stuttgart: Suddeutsches Verlagshaus, 1930), p. 3.

23. *Sexual-Hygiene* 4, nr. 2 (February 1932).

24. Emilie Fried and Paul Fried, *Liebes-und Ehe-Leben, Ein praktischer Berater fuer die gesunde und harmonische Ehe sowie fuer sexuelle Not-fragen* (Wolfenbuettel: Verlag der Freunde, 1929), p. 35.

25. Van de Velde, *Die Volkommene Ehe*, p. 249.

26. Ibid., p. 177.

27. See Annemarie Troeger, "Die Frau im wesensgemaessen Einsatz," in *Mutterkreuz und Arbeitsbuch*, ed. Frauengruppe Faschismus Forschung (Frankfurt: Fischer, 1981), pp. 246–72 for discussion of "Typenlehre."

28. Lionel S. Lewis and Dennis Brissett, "Sex as Work: A Study of Avocational Counseling," *Social Problems* 15 (1967): 8–18. The authors make the error of identifying the problem as peculiarly American. See also Gordon, "An Unfortunate Necessity."

29. Van de Velde, *Die Volkommene Ehe*, pp. 249–50.

30. Georg Klatt, "Variation," *Neue Generation* (publication of the Deutschen Bundes wie des Internationalen Vereinigung fuer Mutterschutz und Sexualreform in Berlin 27, nr. 7/8/9, (July/August/September 1931): 136.

31. See Ben B. Lindsey and Wainwright Evans, *Die Kameradschaftsehe* (Berlin and Leipzig: Deutsche Verlags Anstalt, n.d.), and Ben B. Lindsey, *Die Revolution der modernen Jugend* (Berlin and Leipzig: Deutsche Verlags Anstalt, n.d.). Both books were translated from the American. U.S. sex reformers like Judge Lindsey and Margaret Sanger were widely read in Germany.

32. *Der Eheberater*, p. 230.

33. For further information on the rationalization of German industry see especially Robert A. Brady, *The Rationalization Movement in German Industry* (1933; reprint ed. New York: Howard Fertig, 1974).

34. Ludwig Preller, *Sozialpolitik in der Weimarer Republik* (Stuttgart; Franz Mittelbach Verlag, 1949), p. 125.

35. Richard Woldt, *Die Lebenswelt des Industriearbeiters* (Leipzig: Verlag von Quelle und Meyer, 1926), p. 25.

36. Kaiser *Die Liebe als Kunst*, p. 237.

37. *Ideal Lebensbund, Monatsschrift fuer Geistes und Koerpererziehung zur Ehe* 3, nr. 2 (February 1929): 47.

38. David Noble's criteria in *America by Design: Technology and the Rise of Corporate Capitalism* (New York: Alfred A. Knopf, 1977), p. 70.

39. Ibid.

40. Harry Braverman, *Labor and Monopoly Capital: The Degradation of Work in the Twentieth Century* (New York: Monthly Review Press, 1974), pp. 113–19.

41. Ibid., p. 182.

42. See, for example, Wilhelm Reich, *Der Sexuelle Kampf der Jugend* (1932: reprint ed., Graz: Verlag O, n.d.), and *Sexualerregung und Sexualbefriedigung, Beantwortung sexueller Fragen* (Graz: Verlag O, 1976), as well as Ernst Bornemann's memoirs of Reich's Berlin clinic in *Die Ur-Szene, Eine Selbstanalyse* (Frankfurt: Fischer, 1977) pp. 22–25.

43. See Klaus Theweleit, *Maennerphantasien* (Frankfurt: Verlag Roter Stern, Vol. 1, 1977; Vol. 2, 1978), a study of Freikorps literature, for a brilliant and original discussion of Right Wing perceptions of sexuality.

44. See Hodann, *Geschlecht und Liebe,* and Reich, *Sexueller Kampf,* as well as the pages of various working-class Sex Reform magazines like *Sexual-Hygiene* and *Volksgesundheit* for the "socialist" and "proletarianized" versions of Van de Velde.

45. Otto Herschan, "Typologie der eheuntauglichen Frau," *Zeitschrift fuer Sexualwissenschaft,* Bd. XVI, H. 5 (October 1929): 325.

46. Ibid., p. 323.

47. *Zeitschrift fuer Sexualwissenschaft,* Bd. XIV, H. 9 (1927): 323–32.

48. See Alice Ruehle-Gerstel, *Die Frau;* Margarete Kaiser, *Die Liebe als Kunst;* Sofie Lazarsfeld, *Erziehung zur Ehe* (Vienna and Leipzig: Verlag von Moritz Perles, 1928); and the pages of *Neue Generation*.

49. See the current debate in Europe and the United States: for example, in Elaine Marks and Isabelle de Courtivon, eds., *New French Feminisms* (Amherst: The University of Massachusetts Press, 1980), especially Luce Irigaray, "This Sex Which Is Not One," pp. 99–106; *Heresies #12* 3, no. 4 (1981), "Sex Issue"; Ethel Spector Person, "Sexuality as the Mainstay of Identity: Psychoanalytic Perspectives," *Signs* 5, no. 4 (Summer 1980): 605–30; the recent "The Scholar and the Feminist Conference" at Barnard College on sexuality (April 24, 1982); and the articles in this volume.

50. Alice Ruehle-Gerstel, *Die Frau,* p. 175.

Section IV
The Institution of Heterosexuality

In a piece surveying the recent burgeoning of historical studies of sexuality, Martha Vicinus observes that this new and important wave of scholarship has necessarily concentrated on categorizing sexualities, particularly those of sexual minorities.[1] Although historians are increasingly critical of this "boundary keeping"—the tendency in the last two hundred years to define more and more separable sexual kinds—they inevitably are caught up in chronicling the historical development of sexual communities as each became self-conscious and isolated. In other words, the historians' critique of sexual boundary keeping seems to be inseparable from their enterprise of describing sexual ghettoes.

The decision whether or not to participate in the breaking down of prescriptive sexual identities represents a separate analytical step: many sexual communities are understandably ambivalent about losing a definition that has meant new freedom to find each other. Indeed, some argue that all sexual tension depends on boundaries.

Collectively, the pieces in this volume make us self-conscious about taxonomy. How has the definition of sexual behavior and sexual community served people? What has it cost them? What contradictions arise inside communities defined by sexual practice? What happens beyond the pale? How are the lines of demarcation drawn and how frequently can we redraw them?

The pieces in this section reflect this new self-consciousness about boundaries by recognizing that heterosexuality—so long considered "natural"—develops within bounds people have set and maintained. Adrienne Rich observes what is indeed remarkable, how completely the assumption of female heterosexuality has "glided so silently into the foundations of our thought"—including feminist thought. She argues that behind the male definition of heterosexual normalcy it is women for whom both men and women long; hence men must enforce their access to women who would otherwise care most ardently for each other. Since women remind us all of the first and profound sensual ties with the mother, women lead a "double life": ostensibly linked to men, they are in truth engaged in a deeper way in what Rich calls the "lesbian continuum," that joins them in mutual support, sensual contact, and sometimes sexual love with other women.

In recent scholarship, other feminists have implicitly disagreed with the notion of "compulsory heterosexuality" by arguing that whatever its ultimate cultural sources and attendant suffering, women *do* choose heterosexuality, a choice that can be embedded in the deepest layers of identity. Ann Snitow's study of Harlequin romances tends to the conclusion that heterosexual romance is deeply libidinized for women; however limiting its pleasures, they are pleasures indeed. Romances try to make the best of the bad bargain women get in marriage, straining to reconcile women's different needs—for home, for safety, for children, for sex—by proposing a psychological deal: courtship will be exquisitely titillating; then women must resign themselves to the hard actualities of marriage. Rich's and Snitow's essays delineate aspects of an ongoing debate in the women's movement: what forces hold the institution of heterosexuality in place and how deep and enduring are women's ties to it?

It might be useful to supercede this debate with another that questions more directly the process and structures behind libidinization itself. How, when, and why have people channeled sexual excitement into the maintenance of social structures? Have women been duped or beaten into complicity with oppressive heterosexual norms or have they in some sense judged that protective ties with men were the best choice they could make under certain circumstances? In other words, while we must recognize heterosexuality as an institution and not women's biological destiny, we may still find women's own reasons for electing sexual and social ties with men. On a grander theoretical scale elsewhere in this volume, Alice Echols argues that feminists ultimately lose more than we gain by insisting on sharp, unchanging distinctions between male and female sexual nature.

Like Rich, poet Irena Klepfisz questions the tyranny of normalcy that dictates that people outside couples (straight or gay) are only "half." The speaker in "they're always curious" doesn't really believe her single life need be impoverished, but she finds the ground is thick with thoughtlessly coupling, complacent people. These, the "curious," still have the power to make her feel lonely by seeing her as one of a "strange breed still unclassified," a woman who lives for herself "even when in love."

The institution of heterosexuality failed to give anything at all to the black women, under slavery and after, whom Rennie Simson describes. These women suffered the relentless coercion from men discussed by Rich. They chose celibacy, a hard-pressed self-reliance, and even self-imposed confinement rather than submit to ties with white men who were brutal masters, or with black men, more subtly dismissive or unkind. In the absence of sources about black women's sexual ties to each other, the world Simson describes is one in which women have sacrificed sex to gain freedom and bodily integrity.

Felicita Garcia tells a related tale of conflict between a woman's self-actualization and male-female partnership. Single motherhood and forming ties with other helping women are preferable to life with her "daughter's father," but she has no regrets about having had sex or a baby. These she accounts among life's riches.

Myra Goldberg's "Issues and Answers" takes a similar look at marriage: Alice loves Richard, even though people looking in at the marriage from the outside see Richard as infantile, dismissive, pompous, and think Alice "could do better." The fact is, people love each other anyway, in the face of each other's limitations, even cruelties. Does the wife in Goldberg's story suffer from "false consciousness" in her affection for a fatuous, dependent, yet peremptory husband? In a sense yes, but are only the worthy to be loved?

Sharon Thompson's story "Garden Paths, Descents" laces the two themes of this section together: to an extraterrestrial outsider, the wife here seems a goddess, enshrined in her own suburban house: indeed, the wife herself had such grandiose hopes during her courtship, for her husband appeared to her from the water like a god. Marriage itself, though, is a chimera: it binds the wife, but the husband still lives unfettered in a world of work that shimmers with sex. Seen from an extraplanetary distance, marriage is a very odd institution indeed. Its asymmetries are tragic or grotesque; nonetheless it is as common, and as sought after by both sexes, as water.

Note

1. "Sexuality and Power: A Review of Current Work in the History of Sexuality," *Feminist Studies* 8, no. 1 (Spring 1982): 133–56.

Compulsory Heterosexuality and Lesbian Existence

Adrienne Rich

I

Biologically men have only one innate orientation—a sexual one that draws them to women—while women have two innate orientations, sexual toward men and reproductive toward their young.[1]

I was a woman terribly vulnerable, critical, using femaleness as a sort of standard or yardstick to measure and discard men. Yes—something like that. I was an Anna who invited defeat from men without ever being conscious of it. (But I am conscious of it. And being conscious of it means I shall leave it all behind me and become—but what?) I was stuck fast in an emotion common to women of our time, that can turn them bitter, or Lesbian, or solitary. Yes, that Anna during that time was . . .

[Another blank line across the page:][2]

The bias of compulsory heterosexuality, through which lesbian experience is perceived on a scale ranging from deviant to abhorrent, or simply rendered invisible, could be illustrated from many other texts than the two just preceding. The assumption made by Rossi, that women are "innately sexually oriented" toward men, or by Lessing, that the lesbian choice is simply an acting-out of bitterness toward men, are by no means theirs alone; they are widely current in literature and in the social sciences.

I am concerned here with two other matters as well: first, how and why women's choice of women as passionate comrades, life partners, co-workers, lovers, tribe, has been crushed, invalidated, forced into hiding and disguise; and second, the virtual or total neglect of lesbian existence in a wide range of writings, including feminist scholarship. Obviously there is a connection here. I believe that much feminist theory and criticism is stranded on this shoal.

My organizing impulse is the belief that it is not enough for feminist thought that specifically lesbian texts exist. Any theory or cultural/ political creation that treats lesbian existence as a marginal or less "natural" phenomenon, as mere "sexual preference," or as the mirror image of either heterosexual or male homosexual relations is profoundly weakened thereby, whatever its other contributions. Feminist theory can no longer afford merely to voice a toleration of "lesbianism" as an "alternative life-style," or make token allusion to lesbians. A feminist critique of compulsory heterosexual orientation for women is long overdue. In this exploratory paper, I shall try to show why.

I will begin by way of examples, briefly discussing four books that have appeared in the last few years, written from different viewpoints and political orientations, but all presenting themselves, and favorably reviewed, as feminist.[3] All take as a basic assumption that the social relations of the sexes are disordered and extremely problematic, if not disabling, for women; all seek paths toward change. I have learned more from some of these books than from others; but on this I am clear: each one might have been more accurate, more powerful, more truly a force for change, had the author felt impelled to deal with lesbian existence as a reality, and as a source of knowledge and power available to women; or with the institution of heterosexuality itself as a beach-head of male dominance.[4] In none of them is the question ever raised, whether in a different context, or other things being equal, women would *choose* heterosexual coupling and marriage; heterosexuality is presumed as a "sexual preference" of "most women," either implicitly or explicitly. In none of these books, which concern themselves with mothering, sex roles, relationships, and societal prescriptions for women, is compulsory heterosexuality ever examined as an institution powerfully affecting all these; or the idea of "preference" or "innate orientation" even indirectly questioned.

In *For Her Own Good: 150 Years of the Experts' Advice to Women* by Barbara Ehrenreich and Deirdre English, the authors' superb pamphlets, *Witches, Midwives and Nurses: A History of Women Healers,* and *Complaints and Disorders: The Sexual Politics of Sickness,* are developed into a provocative and complex study. Their thesis in this book is that the advice given American women by male health professionals, particularly in the areas of marital sex, maternity, and child care, has echoed the dictates of the economic marketplace and the role capitalism has needed women to play in production and/ or reproduction. Women have become the consumer victims of various cures, therapies, and normative judgments in different periods (including the prescription to middle-class women to embody and preserve the sacredness of the home—the "scientific" romanticization of the home itself). None of the "experts'" advice has been either particularly scientific or women-oriented; it has reflected male needs, male fantasies about women, and male interest in controlling women—particularly in the realms of sexuality and motherhood—fused with the requirements of industrial capitalism. So much of this book is so devastatingly informative and is written with such lucid feminist wit that I kept waiting as I read for the basic prescription against lesbianism to be examined. It never was.

This can hardly be for lack of information. Jonathan Katz's *Gay American History*[5] tells us that as early as 1656 the New Haven Colony prescribed the death penalty for lesbians. Katz provides many suggestive and informative documents on the "treatment" (or torture) of lesbians by the medical profession in the nineteenth and twentieth centuries. Recent work by the historian Nancy Sahli documents the crackdown on intense female friendships among college women at the turn of the present century.[6] The ironic title *For Her Own Good* might have referred first and foremost to the economic imperative to heterosexuality and marriage and to the sanctions imposed against single women and widows—both of whom have been and still are viewed as deviant. Yet, in this often enlightening Marxist-feminist overview of male prescriptions for female sanity and health, the economics of prescriptive heterosexuality go unexamined.[7]

Of the three psychoanalytically based books, one, Jean Baker Miller's *Toward a New Psychology of Women*, is written as if lesbians simply do not exist, even as marginal beings. Given Miller's title I find this astonishing. However, the favorable reviews the book has received in feminist journals, including *Signs* and *Spokeswoman*, suggest that Miller's heterocentric assumptions are widely shared. In *The Mermaid and the Minotaur: Sexual Arrangements and the Human Malaise*, Dorothy Dinnerstein makes an impassioned argument for the sharing of parenting between women and men and for an end to what she perceives as the male/female symbiosis of "gender arrangements," which she feels are leading the species further and further into violence and self-extinction. Apart from other problems that I have with this book (including her silence on the institutional and random terrorism men have practiced on women—and children—throughout history, amply documented by Barry, Daly, Griffin, Russell and van de Ven, and Brownmiller,[8] and her obsession with psychology to the neglect of economic and other material realities that help to create psychological reality), I find utterly ahistorical Dinnerstein's view of the relations between women and men as "a collaboration to keep history mad." She means by this, to perpetuate social relations that are hostile, exploitative, and destructive to life itself. She sees women and men as equal partners in the making of "sexual arrangements," seemingly unaware of the repeated struggles of women to resist oppression (our own and that of others) and to change our condition. She ignores, specifically, the history of women who—as witches, *femmes seules*, marriage resisters, spinsters, autonomous widows, and/or lesbians—have managed on varying levels *not* to collaborate. It is this history, precisely, from which feminists have so much to learn and on which there is overall such blanketing silence. Dinnerstein acknowledges at the end of her book that "female separatism," though "not on a large scale and in the long run wildly impractical," has something to teach us: "Separate, women could in principle set out to learn from scratch—undeflected by the opportunities to evade this task that men's presence has so far offered—what intact self-creative humanness is."[9] Phrases like "intact self-creative humanness" obscure the question of what the many forms of female separatism have actually been addressing. The fact is that women in every culture and throughout history *have* undertaken the task of independent, nonheterosexual, woman-connected existence, to the extent made possible by their context, often in the belief that they were the "only ones" ever to have done so. They have undertaken it even though few women have been in an economic position to resist marriage altogether; and even though attacks against unmarried women have ranged from aspersion and mockery to deliberate gynocide, including the burning and torturing of millions of widows and spinsters during the witch persecutions of the fifteenth, sixteenth, and seventeenth centuries in Europe, and the practice of suttee on widows in India.[10]

Nancy Chodorow does come close to the edge of an acknowledgment of lesbian existence. Like Dinnerstein, Chodorow believes that the fact that women, and women only, are responsible for child care in the sexual division of labor has led to an entire social organization of gender inequality, and that men as well as women must become primary carers for children if that inequality is to change. In the process of examining, from a psychoanalytic perspective, how mothering-by-women affects the psychological development of girl and boy children, she offers documentation that men are "emotionally secondary" in women's lives; that "women have a richer, ongoing inner world to fall back on. . . . men do not become as emotionally important to women as women do to men."[11] This would carry into the late twentieth century Smith-Rosenberg's findings about eighteenth- and nineteenth-century women's emotional focus on women. "Emotionally important" can of course refer to anger as well as to love, or to that intense mixture of the two often found in women's relationships with women: one aspect of what I have come to call the "double-life of women" (see below).

Chodorow concludes that because women have women as mothers, "The mother remains a primary internal object [*sic*] to the girl, so that heterosexual relationships are on the model of a nonexclusive, second relationship for her, whereas for the boy they recreate an exclusive, primary relationship." According to Chodorow, women "have learned to deny the limitations of masculine lovers for both psychological and practical reasons."[12]

But the practical reasons (like witch burnings; male control of law, theology, and science; or economic nonviability within the sexual division of labor) are glossed over. Chodorow's account barely glances at the constraints and sanctions that, historically, have enforced or ensured the coupling of women with men and obstructed or penalized our coupling or allying in independent groups with other women. She dismisses lesbian existence with the comment that "lesbian relationships do tend to re-create mother-daughter emotions and connections, but most women are heterosexual" (implied: more mature, having developed beyond the mother-daughter connection). She then adds: "This heterosexual preference and taboos on homosexuality, in addition to objective economic dependence on men, make the option of primary sexual bonds with other women unlikely—though more prevalent in recent years."[13] The significance of that qualification seems irresistible—but Chodorow does not explore it further. Is she saying that lesbian existence has become more visible in recent years (in certain groups?), that economic and other pressures have changed (under capitalism, socialism, or both?), and that consequently more women are rejecting the heterosexual "choice"? She argues that women want children because their heterosexual relationships lack richness and intensity, that in having a child a woman seeks to re-create her own intense relationship with her mother. It seems to be that on the basis of her own findings, Chodorow leads us implicitly to conclude that heterosexuality is *not* a "preference" for women; that, for one thing, it fragments the erotic from the emotional in a way that women find impoverishing and painful. Yet her book participates in mandating it. Neglecting the covert socializations and the overt forces that have channeled women into marriage and heterosexual romance, pressures ranging from the selling of daughters to postindustrial economics to the silences of literature to the images of the television screen, she, like Dinnerstein, is stuck with trying to reform a man-made institution—compulsory heterosexuality—as if, despite profound emotional impulses and complementarities drawing women toward women, there is a mystical/biological heterosexual inclination, a "preference" or "choice" that draws women toward men.

Moreover, it is understood that this "preference" does not need to be explained, unless through the tortuous theory of the female

Oedipus complex or the necessity for species reproduction. It is lesbian sexuality that (usually, and, incorrectly, "included" under male homosexuality) is seen as requiring explanation. This assumption of female heterosexuality seems to me in itself remarkable: it is an enormous assumption to have glided so silently into the foundations of our thought.

The extension of this assumption is the frequently heard assertion that in a world of genuine equality, where men were nonoppressive and nurturing, everyone would be bisexual. Such a notion blurs and sentimentalizes the actualities within which women have experienced sexuality; it is the old liberal leap across the tasks and struggles of here and now, the continuing process of sexual definition that will generate its own possibilities and choices. (It also assumes that women who have chosen women have done so simply because men are oppressive and emotionally unavailable: which still fails to account for women who continue to pursue relationships with oppressive and/or emotionally unsatisfying men.) I am suggesting that heterosexuality, like motherhood, needs to be recognized and studied as a *political institution*—even, or especially, by those individuals who feel they are, in their personal experience, the precursors of a new social relation between the sexes.

II

If women are the earliest sources of emotional caring and physical nurture for both female and male children, it would seem logical, from a feminist perspective at least, to pose the following questions: whether the search for love and tenderness in both sexes does not originally lead toward women; *why in fact women would ever redirect that search;* why species-survival, the means of impregnation, and emotional/erotic relationships should ever have become so rigidly identified with each other; and why such violent strictures should be found necessary to enforce women's total emotional, erotic loyalty and subservience to men. I doubt that enough feminist scholars and theorists have taken the pains to acknowledge the societal forces that wrench women's emotional and erotic energies away from themselves and other women and from woman-identified values. These forces, as I shall try to show, range from literal physical enslavement to the disguising and distorting of possible options.

I do not, myself, assume that mothering-by-women is a "sufficient cause" of lesbian existence. But the issue of mothering-by-women has been much in the air of late, usually accompanied by the view that increased parenting by men would minimize antagonism between the sexes and equalize the sexual imbalance of power of males over females. These discussions are carried on without reference to compulsory heterosexuality as a phenomenon let alone as an ideology. I do not wish to psychologize here, but rather to identify sources of male power. I believe large numbers of men could, in fact, undertake child care on a large scale without radically altering the balance of male power in a male-identified society.

In her essay "The Origin of the Family," Kathleen Gough lists eight characteristics of male power in archaic and contemporary societies that I would like to use as a framework: "men's ability to deny women sexuality or to force it upon them; to command or exploit their labor to control their produce; to control or rob them of their children; to confine them physically and prevent their movement; to use them as objects in male transactions; to cramp their creativeness; or to withhold from them large areas of the society's knowledge and cultural attainments."[14] (Gough does not perceive these power-characteristics as specifically enforcing heterosexuality; only as producing sexual inequality.) Below, Gough's words appear in italics; the elaboration of each of her categories, in brackets, is my own.

Characteristics of male power include the power of men:

1. *to deny women* [our own] *sexuality*
   [by means of clitoridectomy and infibulation; chastity belts; punishment, including death, for female adultery; punishment, including death, for lesbian sexuality; psychoanalytic denial of the clitoris; strictures against masturbation; denial of maternal and postmenopausal sensuality; unnecessary hysterectomy; pseudo-lesbian images in media and literature; closing of archives and destruction of documents relating to lesbian existence];

2. *or to force it* [male sexuality] *upon them*
   [by means of rape (including marital rape) and wife beating; father-daughter, brother-sister incest; the socialization of women to feel that male sexual "drive" amounts to a right;[15] idealization of heterosexual romance in art, literature, media, advertising, and so forth; child marriage; arranged marriage; prostitution; the harem; psychoanalytic doctrines of frigidity and vaginal orgasm; pornographic depictions of women responding pleasurably to sexual violence and humiliation (a subliminal message being that sadistic heterosexuality is more "normal" than sensuality between women)];

3. *to command or exploit their labor to control their produce*
   [by means of the institutions of marriage and motherhood as unpaid production; the horizontal segregation of women in paid employment; the decoy of the upwardly mobile token woman; male control of abortion, contraception, and childbirth; enforced

sterilization; pimping, female infanticide, which robs mothers of daughters and contributes to generalized devaluation of women];

4. *to control or rob them of their children*
[by means of father-right and "legal kidnapping";[16] enforced sterilization; systematized infanticide; seizure of children from lesbian mothers by the courts; the malpractice of male obstetrics; use of the mother as "token torturer"[17] in genital mutilation or in binding the daughter's feet (or mind) to fit her for marriage];

5. *to confine them physically and prevent their movement*
[by means of rape as terrorism, keeping women off the streets; purdah; foot-binding; atrophying of women's athletic capabilities; haute couture, "feminine" dress codes; the veil; sexual harassment on the streets; horizontal segregation of women in employment; prescriptions for "full-time" mothering; enforced economic dependence of wives];

6. *to use them as objects in male transactions*
[use of women as "gifts," bride-price; pimping; arranged marriage; use of women as entertainers to facilitate male deals, for example, wife-hostess, cocktail waitress required to dress for male sexual titillation, call girls, "bunnies," geisha, *kisaeng* prostitutes, secretaries];

7. *to cramp their creativeness*
[witch persecutions as campaigns against midwives and female healers and as pogrom against independent, "unassimilated" women;[18] definition of male pursuits as more valuable than female within any culture, so that cultural values become embodiment of male subjectivity; restriction of female self-fulfillment to marriage and motherhood; sexual exploitation of women by male artists and teachers; the social and economic disruption of women's creative aspirations;[19] erasure of female tradition];[20] and

8. *to withhold from them large areas of the society's knowledge and cultural attainments*
[by means of noneducation of females (60 percent of the world's illiterates are women); the "Great Silence" regarding women and particularly lesbian existence in history and culture;[21] sex-role stereotyping that deflects women from science, technology, and other "masculine" pursuits; male social/professional bonding that excludes women; discrimination against women in the professions].

These are some of the methods by which male power is manifested and maintained. Looking at the schema, what surely impresses itself is the fact that we are confronting not a simple maintenance of inequality and property possession, but a pervasive cluster of forces, ranging from physical brutality to control of consciousness, that suggests that an enormous potential counterforce is having to be restrained.

Some of the forms by which male power manifests itself are more easily recognizable as enforcing heterosexuality on women than are others. Yet each one I have listed adds to the cluster of forces within which women have been convinced that marriage and sexual orientation toward men are inevitable, even if unsatisfying or oppressive components of their lives. The chastity belt; child marriage; erasure of lesbian existence (except as exotic and perverse) in art, literature, film; idealization of heterosexual romance and marriage—these are some fairly obvious forms of compulsion, the first two exemplifying physical force, the second two control of consciousness. While clitoridectomy has been assailed by feminists as a form of woman-torture,[22] Kathleen Barry first pointed out that it is not simply a way of turning the young girl into a "marriageable" woman through brutal surgery; it intends that women in the intimate proximity of polygynous marriage will not form sexual relationships with each other; that—from a male, genital-fetishist perspective—female erotic connections, even in a sex-segregated situation, will be literally excised.[23]

The function of pornography as an influence on consciousness is a major public issue of our time, when a multibillion-dollar industry has the power to disseminate increasingly sadistic, women-degrading visual images. But even so-called soft-core pornography and advertising depict women as objects of sexual appetite devoid of emotional context, without individual meaning or personality: essentially as a sexual commodity to be consumed by males. (So-called lesbian pornography, created for the male voyeuristic eye, is equally devoid of emotional context or individual personality.) The most pernicious message relayed by pornography is that women are natural sexual prey to men and love it; that sexuality and violence are congruent; and that for women sex is essentially masochistic, humiliation pleasurable, physical abuse erotic. But along with this message comes another, not always recognized: that enforced submission and the use of cruelty, if played out in heterosexual pairing, is sexually "normal," while sensuality between women, including erotic mutuality and respect, is "queer," "sick," and either pornographic in itself or not very exciting compared with the sexuality of whips and bondage.[24] Pornography does not simply create a climate in which sex and violence are interchangeable; *it widens the range of behavior considered acceptable from men in heterosexual intercourse*—behavior that reiteratively strips women of their autonomy, dignity, and sexual potential, including the potential of loving and being loved by women in mutuality and integrity.

In her brilliant study *Sexual Harassment of Working Women: A Case of Sex Discrimination*, Catharine A. MacKinnon delineates the intersection of compulsory heterosexuality and economics. Under capitalism, women are horizontally segregated by gender and occupy a structurally inferior position in the workplace; this is hardly news, but MacKinnon raises the question why, even if capitalism "requires some collection of individuals to occupy low-status, low-paying positions . . . such persons must be biologically female," and goes on to point out that "the fact that male employers often do not hire qualified women, *even when they could pay them less than men* suggests that more than the profit motive is implicated" (emphasis added).[25] She cites a wealth of material documenting the fact that women are not only segregated in low-paying service jobs (as secretaries, domestics, nurses, typists, telephone operators, child-care workers, waitresses) but that "sexualization of the woman" is part of the job. Central and intrinsic to the economic realities of women's lives is the requirement that women will "market sexual attractiveness to men, who tend to hold the economic power and position to enforce their predilections." And MacKinnon exhaustively documents that "sexual harassment perpetuates the interlocked structure by which women have been kept sexually in thrall to men at the bottom of the labor market. Two forces of American society converge: men's control over women's sexuality and capital's control over employees' work lives."[26] Thus, women in the workplace are at the mercy of sex-as-power in a vicious circle. Economically disadvantaged, women—whether waitresses or professors—endure sexual harassment to keep their jobs and learn to behave in a complaisantly and ingratiatingly heterosexual manner because they discover this is their true qualification for employment, whatever the job description. And, MacKinnon notes, the woman who too decisively resists sexual overtures in the workplace is accused of being "dried-up" and sexless, or lesbian. This raises a specific difference between the experiences of lesbians and homosexual men. A lesbian, closeted on her job because of heterosexist prejudice, is not simply forced into denying the truth of her outside relationships or private life; her job depends on her pretending to be not merely heterosexual but a heterosexual *woman*, in terms of dressing and playing the feminine, deferential role required of "real" women.

MacKinnon raises radical questions as to the qualitative differences between sexual harassment, rape, and ordinary heterosexual intercourse. ("As one accused rapist put it, he hadn't used 'any more force than is usual for males during the preliminaries.'") She criticizes Susan Brownmiller[27] for separating rape from the mainstream of daily life and for her unexamined premise that "rape is violence, intercourse is sexuality," removing rape from the sexual sphere altogether. Most crucially she argues that "taking rape from the realm of 'the sexual,' placing it in the realm of 'the violent,' allows one to be against it without raising any questions about the extent to which the institution of heterosexuality has defined force as a normal part of 'the preliminaries.' "[28] Never is it asked whether, under conditions of male supremacy, the notion of 'consent' has any meaning."[29]

The fact is that the workplace, among other social institutions, is a place where women have learned to accept male violation of our psychic and physical boundaries as the price of survival; where women have been educated—no less than by romantic literature or by pornography—to perceive ourselves as sexual prey. A woman seeking to escape such casual violations along with economic disadvantage may well turn to marriage as a form of hoped-for protection, while bringing into marriage neither social nor economic power, thus entering that institution also from a disadvantaged position. MacKinnon finally asks:

> What if inequality is built into the social conceptions of male and female sexuality, of masculinity and femininity, of sexiness and heterosexual attractiveness? Incidents of sexual harassment suggest that male sexual desire itself may be aroused by female vulnerability. . . . Men feel they can take advantage, so they want to, so they do. Examination of sexual harassment, precisely because the episodes appear commonplace, forces one to confront the fact that sexual intercourse normally occurs between economic (as well as physical) unequals . . . the apparent legal requirement that violations of women's sexuality appear out of the ordinary before they will be punished helps prevent women from defining the ordinary conditions of their own consent.[30]

Given the nature and extent of heterosexual pressures, the daily "eroticization of women's subordination" as MacKinnon phrases it,[31] I question the more or less psychoanalytic perspective (suggested by such writers as Karen Horney, H. R. Hayes, Wolfgang Lederer, and most recently, Dorothy Dinnerstein) that the male need to control women sexually results from some primal male "fear of women" and of women's sexual insatiability. It seems more probable that men really fear, not that they will have women's sexual appetites forced on them, or that women want to smother and devour them, but that women could be indifferent to them altogether, that men could be allowed sexual and emotional—therefore economic—access to women *only* on women's terms, otherwise being left on the periphery of the matrix.

The means of assuring male sexual access to women have recently received a searching investigation by Kathleen Barry.[32] She documents extensive and appalling evidence for the existence, on a very large scale, of international female slavery, the institution once known as "white slavery" but that in fact has involved, and at this very moment involves, women of every race and class. In the theoretical analysis derived from her research, Barry makes the connection between all enforced conditions under which women live subject to men: prostitution, marital rape, father-daughter and brother-sister incest, wife-beating, pornography, bride-price, the selling of daughters, purdah, and genital mutilation. She sees the rape paradigm—where the victim of sexual assault is held responsible for her own victimization—as leading to the rationalization and acceptance of other forms of enslavement, where the woman is presumed to have "chosen" her fate, to embrace it passively, or to have courted it perversely through rash or unchaste behavior. On the contrary, Barry maintains, "female sexual slavery is present in ALL situations where women or girls cannot change the conditions of their existence; where regardless of how they got into those conditions, e.g., social pressure, economic hardship, misplaced trust or the longing for affection, they cannot get out; and where they are subject to sexual violence and exploitation."[33] She provides a spectrum of concrete examples, not only as to the existence of a widespread international traffic in women, but also as to how this operates—whether in the form of a "Minnesota pipeline" funneling blonde, blue-eyed midwestern runaways to Times Square, or the purchasing of young women out of rural poverty in Latin America or Southeast Asia, or the providing of *maisons d'abattage* for migrant workers in the eighteenth arrondissement of Paris. Instead of "blaming the victim" or trying to diagnose her presumed pathology, Barry turns her floodlight on the pathology of sex colonization itself, the ideology of "cultural sadism" represented by the vast industry of pornography and by the overall identification of women primarily as "sexual beings whose responsibility is the sexual service of men."[34]

Barry delineates what she names a "sexual domination perspective" through whose lens, purporting objectivity, sexual abuse and terrorism of women by men has been rendered almost invisible by treating it as natural and inevitable. From its point of view, women are expendable as long as the sexual and emotional needs of the male can be satisfied. To replace this perspective of domination with a universal standard of basic freedom for women from gender-specific violence, from constraints on movement, and from male right of sexual and emotional access is the political purpose of her book. Like Mary Daly in *Gyn/Ecology*, Barry rejects structuralist and other cultural-relativist rationalizations for sexual torture and anti-woman violence. In her opening chapter, she asks of her readers that they refuse all handy escapes into ignorance and denial. "The only way we can come out of hiding, break through our paralyzing defenses, is to know it all—the full extent of sexual violence and domination of women. . . . In *knowing*, in facing directly, we can learn to chart our course out of this oppression, by envisioning and creating a world which will preclude female sexual slavery."[35]

"Until we name the practice, give conceptual definition and form to it, illustrate its life over time and in space, those who are its most obvious victims will also not be able to name it or define their experience."[36]

But women are all, in different ways and to different degrees, its victims; and part of the problem with naming and conceptualizing female sexual slavery is, as Barry clearly sees, compulsory heterosexuality. Compulsory heterosexuality simplifies the task of the procurer and pimp in worldwide prostitution rings and "eros centers," while, in the privacy of the home, it leads the daughter to "accept" incest/rape by her father, the mother to deny that it is happening, the battered wife to stay on with an abusive husband. "Befriending or love" is a major tactic of the procurer whose job it is to turn the runaway or the confused young girl over to the pimp for seasoning. The ideology of heterosexual romance, beamed at her from childhood out of fairy tales, television, films, advertising, popular songs, wedding pageantry, is a tool ready to the procurer's hand and one he does not hesitate to use, as Barry amply documents. Early female indoctrination in "love" as an emotion may be largely a Western concept; but a more universal ideology concerns the primacy and uncontrollability of the male sexual drive. This is one of many insights offered by Barry's work:

> As sexual power is learned by adolescent boys through the social experience of their sex drive, so do girls learn that the locus of sexual power is male. Given the importance placed on the male sex drive in the socialization of girls as well as boys, early adolescence is probably the first significant phase of male identification in a girl's life and development. . . . As a young girl becomes aware of her own increasing sexual feelings . . . she turns away from her heretofore primary relationships with girlfriends. As they become secondary to her, recede in importance in her life, her own identity also assumes a secondary role and she grows into male identification.[37]

We still need to ask why some women never, even temporarily, "turn away from heretofore primary relationships" with other females. And why does male-identification—the casting of one's social, political, and intellectual allegiances with men—exist among lifelong sexual lesbians? Barry's hypothesis throws us among new questions, but it clarifies the diversity of forms in which compulsory heterosexuality presents itself. In the mystique of the overpowering, all-conquering male sex drive, the penis-with-a-life-of-its-own, is rooted the law of male sex-right to women, which justifies prostitution as a universal cultural assumption on the one hand, while defending sexual slavery within the family on the basis of "family privacy and cultural uniqueness" on the other.[38] The adolescent male sex drive, which, as both young women and men are taught, once triggered cannot take responsibility for itself or take no for an answer, becomes, according to Barry, the norm and rationale for adult male sexual behavior: a condition of *arrested sexual development*. Women learn to accept as natural the inevitability of this "drive" because we receive it as dogma. Hence marital rape, hence the Japanese wife resignedly packing her husband's suitcase for his weekend in the *kisaeng* brothels of Taiwan, hence the psychological as well as economic imbalance of power between husband and wife, male employer and female worker, father and daughter, male professor and female student.

The effect of male-identification means

> internalizing the values of the colonizer and actively participating in carrying out the colonization of one's self and one's sex. . . . Male identification is the act whereby women place men above women, including themselves, in credibility, status, and importance in most situations, regardless of the comparative quality the women may bring to the situation. . . . Interaction with women is seen as a lesser form of relating on every level.[39]

What deserves further exploration is the double-think many women engage in and from which no woman is permanently and utterly free: however woman-to-woman relationships, female support networks, a female and feminist value system, are relied on and cherished, indoctrination in male credibility and status can still create synapses in thought, denials of feeling, wishful thinking, a profound sexual and intellectual confusion.[40] I quote here from a letter I received the day I was writing this passage: "I have had very bad relationships with men—I am now in the midst of a very painful separation. I am trying to find my strength through women—without my friends, I could not survive." How many times a day do women speak words like these, or think them, or write them, and how often does the synapse reassert itself?

Barry summarizes her findings:

> Considering the arrested sexual development that is understood to be normal in the male population, and considering the numbers of men who are pimps, procurers, members of slavery gangs, corrupt officials participating in this traffic, owners, operators, employees of brothels and lodging and entertainment facilities, pornography purveyors, associated with prostitution, wife beaters, child molesters, incest perpetrators, johns (tricks) and rapists, one cannot but be momentarily stunned by the enormous male population engaging in female sexual slavery. The huge number of men engaged in these practices should be cause for

declaration of an international emergency, a crisis in sexual violence. But what should be cause for alarm is instead accepted as normal sexual intercourse.[41]

Susan Cavin, in her rich and provocative, if highly speculative, dissertation, suggests that patriarchy becomes possible when the original female band, which includes children but ejects adolescent males, becomes invaded and outnumbered by males; that not patriarchal marriage, but the rape of the mother by the son, becomes the first act of male domination. The entering wedge, or leverage, that allows this to happen is not just a simple change in sex ratios; it is also the mother-child bond, manipulated by adolescent males in order to remain within the matrix past the age of exclusion. Maternal affection is used to establish male right of sexual access, which, however, must ever after be held by force (or through control of consciousness) since the original deep adult bonding is that of woman for woman.[42] I find this hypothesis extremely suggestive, since one form of false consciousness that serves compulsory heterosexuality is the maintenance of a mother-son relationship between women and men, including the demand that women provide maternal solace, nonjudgmental nurturing, and compassion for their harassers, rapists, and batterers (as well as for men who passively vampirize them). How many strong and assertive women accept male posturing from no one but their sons?

But whatever its origins, when we look hard and clearly at the extent and elaboration of measures designed to keep women within a male sexual purlieu, it becomes an inescapable question whether the issue we have to address as feminists is not simple "gender inequality," nor the domination of culture by males, nor mere "taboos against homosexuality," but the enforcement of heterosexuality for women as a means of assuring male right of physical, economical, and emotional access.[43] One of many means of enforcement is, of course, the rendering invisible of the lesbian possibility, an engulfed continent that rises fragmentedly to view from time to time only to become submerged again. Feminist research and theory that contributes to lesbian invisibility or marginality is actually working against the liberation and empowerment of woman as a group.[44]

The assumption that "most women are innately heterosexual" stands as a theoretical and political stumbling block for many women. It remains a tenable assumption, partly because lesbian existence has been written out of history or catalogued under disease; partly because it has been treated as exceptional rather than intrinsic; partly because to acknowledge that for women heterosexuality may not be a "preference" at all but something that has had to be imposed, managed, organized, propagandized, and maintained by force is an immense step to take if you consider yourself freely and "innately" heterosexual. Yet the failure to examine heterosexuality as an institution is like failing to admit that the economic system called capitalism or the caste system of racism is maintained by a variety of forces, including both physical violence and false consciousness. To take the step of questioning heterosexuality as a "preference" or "choice" for women—and to do the intellectual and emotional work that follows—will call for a special quality of courage in heterosexually identified feminists but I think the rewards will be great: a freeing-up of thinking, the exploring of new paths, the shattering of another great silence, new clarity in personal relationships.

III

I have chosen to use the terms *lesbian existence* and *lesbian continuum* because the word *lesbianism* has a clinical and limiting ring. *Lesbian existence* suggests both the fact of the historical presence of lesbians and our continuing creation of the meaning of that existence. I mean the term *lesbian continuum* to include a range—through each woman's life and throughout history—of woman-identified experience; not simply the fact that a woman has had or consciously desired genital sexual experience with another woman. If we expand it to embrace many more forms of primary intensity between and among women, including the sharing of a rich inner life, the bonding against male tyranny, the giving and receiving of practical and political support; if we can also hear in it such associations as *marriage resistance* and the "haggard" behavior identified by Mary Daly (obsolete meanings: "intractable," "willful," "wanton," and "unchaste" . . . "a woman reluctant to yield to wooing")[45]—we begin to grasp breadths of female history and psychology that have lain out of reach as a consequence of limited, mostly clinical, definitions of "lesbianism."

Lesbian existence comprises both the breaking of a taboo and the rejection of a compulsory way of life. It is also a direct or indirect attack on male right of access to women. But it is more than these, although we may first begin to perceive it as a form of nay-saying to patriarchy, an act of resistance. It has of course included role playing, self-hatred, breakdown, alcoholism, suicide, and intrawoman violence; we romanticize at our peril what it means to love and act against the grain, and under heavy penalties; and lesbian existence has been lived (unlike, say, Jewish or Catholic existence) without access to any knowledge of a tradition, a continuity, a social underpinning. The destruction of records and memorabilia and letters documenting the realities of lesbian existence must be taken very seriously as a means of keeping heterosexuality compulsory for women, since what has been kept from our knowledge is joy, sensuality, courage, and community, as well as guilt, self-betrayal, and pain.[46]

Lesbians have historically been deprived of a political existence through "inclusion" as female versions of male homosexuality. To equate lesbian existence with male homosexuality because each is stigmatized is to deny and erase female reality once again. To separate those women stigmatized as "homosexual" or "gay" from the complex continuum of female resistance to enslavement, and attach them to a male pattern, is to falsify our history. Part of the history of lesbian existence is, obviously, to be found where lesbians, lacking a coherent female community, have shared a kind of social life and common cause with homosexual men. But this has to be seen against the differences: women's lack of economic and cultural privilege relative to men; qualitative differences in female and male relationships, for example, the prevalence of anonymous sex and the justification of pederasty among male homosexuals, the pronounced ageism in male homosexual standards of sexual attractiveness, and so forth. In defining and describing lesbian existence I would hope to move toward a dissociation of lesbian from male homosexual values and allegiances. I perceive the lesbian experience as being, like motherhood, a profoundly *female* experience, with particular oppressions, meanings, and potentialities we cannot comprehend as long as we simply bracket it with other sexually stigmatized existences. Just as the term *parenting* serves to conceal the particular and significant reality of being a parent who is actually a mother, the term *gay* serves the purpose of blurring the very outlines we need to discern, which are of crucial value for feminism and for the freedom of women as a group.

As the term lesbian has been held to limiting, clinical associations in its patriarchal definition, female friendship and comradeship have been set apart from the erotic, thus limiting the erotic itself. But as we deepen and broaden the range of what we define as lesbian existence, as we delineate a lesbian continuum, we begin to discover the erotic in female terms: as that which is unconfined to any single part of the body or solely to the body itself, as an energy not only diffuse but, as Audre Lorde has described it, omnipresent in "the sharing of joy, whether physical, emotional, psychic," and in the sharing of work; as the empowering joy which "makes us less willing to accept powerlessness, or those other supplied states of being which are not native to me, such as resignation, despair, self-effacement, depression, self-denial."[47] In another context, writing of women and work, I quoted the autobiographical passage in which the poet H.D. described how her friend Bryher supported her in persisting with the visionary experience that was to shape her mature work:

I knew that this experience, this writing-on-the-wall before me, could not be shared with anyone except the girl who stood so bravely there beside me. This girl had said without hesitation, "Go on." It was she really who had the detachment and integrity of the Pythoness of Delphi. But it was I, battered and dissociated . . . who was seeing the pictures, and who was reading the writing or granted the inner vision. Or perhaps, in some sense, we were "seeing" it together, for without her, admittedly, I could not have gone on.[48]

If we consider the possibility that all women—from the infant suckling her mother's breast, to the grown woman experiencing orgasmic sensations while suckling her own child, perhaps recalling her mother's milk-smell in her own; to two women, like Virginia Woolf's Chloe and Olivia, who share a laboratory;[49] to the woman dying at ninety, touched and handled by women—exist on a lesbian continuum, we can see ourselves as moving in and out of this continuum, whether we identify ourselves as lesbian or not. It allows us to connect aspects of woman-identification as diverse as the impudent, intimate girl-friendships of eight- or nine-year-olds and the banding together of those women of the twelfth and fifteenth centuries known as Beguines who "shared houses, rented to one another, bequeathed houses to their room-mates . . . in cheap subdivided houses in the artisans' area of town," who "practiced Christian virtue on their own, dressing and living simply and not associating with men," who earned their livings as spinners, bakers, nurses, or ran schools for young girls, and who managed—until the Church forced them to disperse—to live independent both of marriage and of conventual restrictions.[50] It allows us to connect these women with the more celebrated "Lesbians" of the women's school around Sappho of the seventh century B.C.; with the secret sororities and economic networks reported among African women; and with the Chinese marriage resistance sisterhoods—communities of women who refused marriage, or who if married often refused to consummate their marriages and soon left their husbands—the only women in China who were not footbound and who, Agnes Smedley tells us, welcomed the births of daughters and organized successful women's strikes in the silk mills.[51] It allows us to connect and compare disparate individual instances of marriage resistance: for example, the type of autonomy claimed by Emily Dickinson, a nineteenth-century white woman genius, with the strategies available to Zora Neale Hurston, a twentieth-century black woman genius. Dickinson never married, had tenuous intellectual friendships with men, lived self-convented in her genteel father's house, and wrote a lifetime of passionate letters to her sister-in-law Sue Gilbert and a smaller group of such letters to her friend Kate Scott Anthon. Hurston married twice but soon left each husband, scrambled her way from Florida to Harlem to Columbia University to Haiti and finally back to Florida, moved in and out of white patronage and poverty, professional success and failure; her survival relationships were all with women, beginning with her mother. Both of these women in their vastly different circumstances were marriage resisters, committed to their own work and selfhood, and were later characterized as "apolitical." Both were drawn to men of intellectual quality; for both of them women provided the ongoing fascination and sustenance of life.

If we think of heterosexuality as the "natural" emotional and sensual inclination for women, lives such as these are seen as deviant, as pathological, or as emotionally and sensually deprived. Or, in more recent and permissive jargon, they are banalized as "life-styles." And the work of such women—whether merely the daily work of individual or collective survival and resistance, or the work of the writer, the activist, the reformer, the anthropologist, or the artist—the work of self-creation—is undervalued, or seen as the bitter fruit of "penis envy," or the sublimation of repressed eroticism, or the meaningless rant of a "manhater." But when we turn the lens of vision and consider the degree to which, and the methods whereby, heterosexual "preference" has actually been imposed on women, not only can we understand differently the meaning of individual lives and work, but we can begin to recognize a central fact of women's history: that women have always resisted male tyranny. A feminism of action, often, though not always, without a theory, has constantly reemerged in every culture and in every period. We can then begin to study women's struggle against powerlessness, women's radical rebellion, not just in male-defined "concrete revolutionary situations"[52] but in all the situations male ideologies have not perceived as revolutionary: for example, the refusal of some women to produce children, aided at great risk by other women; the refusal to produce a higher standard of living and leisure for men (Leghorn and Parker show how both are part of women's unacknowledged, unpaid, and ununionized economic contribution); that female antiphallic sexuality which, as Andrea Dworkin notes, has been "legendary," which, defined as "frigidity" and "puritanism," has actually been a form of subversion of male power—"an ineffectual rebellion, but . . . rebellion nonetheless."[53] We can no longer have patience with Dinnerstein's view that women have simply collaborated with men in the "sexual arrangements" of history; we begin to observe behavior, both in history and in individual biography, that has hitherto been invisible or misnamed; behavior that often constitutes, given the limits of the counterforce exerted in a given time and place, radical rebellion. And we can connect these rebellions and the necessity for them with the physical passion of woman for woman that is central to lesbian existence: the erotic sensuality that has been, precisely, the most violently erased fact of female experience.

Heterosexuality has been both forcibly and subliminally imposed on women, yet everywhere women have resisted it, often at the cost of physical torture, imprisonment, psychosurgery, social ostracism, and extreme poverty. "Compulsory heterosexuality" was named as one of the "crimes against women" by the Brussels Tribunal on Crimes against Women in 1976. Two pieces of testimony, from women from two very different cultures, suggest the degree to which persecution of lesbians is a global practice here and now. A report from Norway relates:

> A lesbian in Oslo was in a heterosexual marriage that didn't work, so she started taking tranquillizers and ended up at the health sanatorium for treatment and rehabilitation. . . . The moment she said in family group therapy that she believed she was a lesbian, the doctor told her she was not. He knew from "looking into her eyes," he said. She had the eyes of a woman who wanted sexual intercourse with her husband. So she was subjected to so-called "couch therapy." She was put into a comfortably heated room, naked, on a bed, and for an hour her husband was to . . . try to excite her sexually. . . . The idea was that the touching was always to end with sexual intercourse. She felt stronger and stronger aversion. She threw up and sometimes ran out of the room to avoid this "treatment." The more strongly she asserted that she was a lesbian, the more violent the forced heterosexual intercourse became. This treatment went on for about six months. She escaped from the hospital, but she was brought back. Again she escaped. She has not been there since. In the end she realized that she had been subjected to forcible rape for six months.

(This, surely, is an example of female sexual slavery according to Barry's definition.) And from Mozambique:

> I am condemned to a life of exile because I will not deny that I am a lesbian, that my primary commitments are, and will always be to other women. In the new Mozambique, lesbianism is considered a left-over from colonialism and decadent Western civilization. Lesbians are sent to rehabilitation camps to learn through self-criticism the correct line about themselves. . . . If I am forced to denounce my own love for women, if I therefore denounce myself, I could go back to Mozambique and join forces in the exciting and hard struggles of rebuilding a nation, including the struggle for the emancipation of Mozambiquan women. As it is, I either risk the rehabilitation camps, or remain in exile.[54]

Nor can it be assumed that women like those in Carroll Smith-Rosenberg's study, who married, stayed married, yet dwelt in a profoundly female emotional and passional world, "preferred" or "chose" heterosexuality. Women have married because it was necessary, in order to survive economically, in order to have children who would not suffer economic deprivation or social ostracism, in order to remain respectable, in order to do what was expected of women because coming out of "abnormal" childhoods they wanted to feel "normal," and because heterosexual romance has been represented as the great female adventure, duty, and fulfillment. We may faithfully or ambivalently have obeyed the institution, but our feelings—and our sensuality—have not been tamed or contained within it. There is no statistical documentation of the numbers of lesbians who have remained in heterosexual marriages for most of their lives. But in a letter to the early lesbian publication *Ladder,* the playwright Lorraine Hansberry had this to say:

> I suspect that the problem of the married woman who would prefer emotional-physical relationships with other women is proportionally much higher than a similar statistic for men. (A statistic surely no one will ever really have.) This because the estate of woman being what it is, how could we ever begin to guess the numbers of women who are not prepared to risk a life alien to what they have been taught all their lives to believe was their "natural" destiny—AND—their only expectation for ECONOMIC security. It seems to be that this is why the question has an immensity that it does not have for male homosexuals. . . . A woman of strength and honesty may, if she chooses, sever her marriage and marry a new male mate and society will be upset that the divorce rate is rising so—but there are few places in the United States, in any event, where she will be anything remotely akin to an "outcast." Obviously this is not true for a woman who would end her marriage to take up life with another woman.[55]

This *double-life*—this apparent acquiescence to an institution founded on male interest and prerogative—has been characteristic of female experience: in motherhood, and in many kinds of heterosexual behavior, including the rituals of courtship; the pretense of asexuality by the nineteenth-century wife; the simulation of orgasm by the prostitute, the courtesan, the twentieth-century "sexually liberated" woman.

Meridel LeSueur's documentary novel of the Depression, *The Girl,* is arresting as a study of female double-life. The protagonist, a waitress in a Saint Paul working-class speakeasy, feels herself passionately attracted to the young man Butch, but her survival relationships are with Clara, an older waitress and prostitute, with Belle, whose husband owns the bar, and with Amelia, a union activist. For Clara and Belle and the unnamed protagonist, sex with men is in one sense an escape from the bedrock misery of daily life; a flare of intensity in the grey, relentless, often brutal web of day-to-day existence:

It was like he was a magnet pulling me. It was exciting and powerful and frightening. He was after me too and when he found me I
would run, or be petrified, just standing in front of him like a
zany. And he told me not to be wandering with Clara to the
Marigold where we danced with strangers. He said he would
knock the shit out of me. Which made me shake and tremble, but
it was better than being a husk full of suffering and not knowing
why.[56]

Throughout the novel the theme of double-life emerges; Belle remi-
nisces of her marriage to the bootlegger Hoinck:

You know, when I had that black eye and said I hit it on the
cupboard, well he did it the bastard, and then he says don't tell
anybody. . . . He's nuts, that's what he is, nuts, and I don't see
why I live with him, why I put up with him a minute on this earth.
But listen kid, she said, I'm telling you something. She looked at
me and her face was wonderful. She said, Jesus Christ, Goddam
him I love him that's why I'm hooked like this all my life, Goddam
him I love him.[57]

After the protagonist has her first sex with Butch, her women friends
care for her bleeding, give her whiskey, and compare notes.

My luck, the first time and I got into trouble. He gave me a little
money and I come to St. Paul where for ten bucks they'd stick a
huge vet's needle into you and you start it and then you were on
your own. . . . I never had no child. I've just had Hoinck to
mother, and a hell of a child he is.[58]

Later they made me go back to Clara's room to lie down. . . . Clara
lay down beside me and put her arms around me and wanted me
to tell her about it but she wanted to tell about herself. She said
she started it when she was twelve with a bunch of boys in an old
shed. She said nobody had paid any attention to her before and
she became very popular. . . . They like it so much, she said, why
shouldn't you give it to them and get presents and attention? I
never cared anything for it and neither did my mama. But it's the
only thing you got that's valuable.[59]

Sex is thus equated with attention from the male, who is charismatic
though brutal, infantile, or unreliable. Yet it is the women who make
life endurable for each other, give physical affection without causing
pain, share, advise, and stick by each other. (*I am trying to find my
strength through women—without my friends, I could not survive.*)
LeSueur's *The Girl* parallels Toni Morrison's remarkable *Sula*, another
revelation of female double-life:

Nel was the one person who had wanted nothing from her, who
had accepted all aspects of her. . . . Nel was one of the reasons
[Sula] had drifted back to Medallion. . . . The men . . . had

merged into one large personality: the same language of love, the same entertainments of love, the same cooling of love. Whenever she introduced her private thoughts into their rubbings and go-ings, they hooded their eyes. They taught her nothing but love tricks, shared nothing but worry, gave nothing but money. She had been looking all along for a friend, and it took her a while to discover that a lover was not a comrade and could never be—for a woman.

But Sula's last thought at the second of her death is, "Wait'll I tell Nel." And after Sula's death, Nel looks back on her own life:

"All that time, all that time, I thought I was missing Jude." And the loss pressed down on her chest and came up into her throat. "We was girls together," she said as though explaining something. "O Lord, Sula," she cried, "Girl, girl, girlgirlgirl!" It was a fine cry—loud and long—but it had no bottom and it had no top, just circles and circles of sorrow.[60]

The Girl and *Sula* are both novels that reveal the lesbian continuum in contrast to the shallow or sensational "lesbian scenes" in recent commercial fiction.[61] Each shows us woman-identification untarnished (till the end of LeSueur's novel) by romanticism; each depicts the competition of heterosexual compulsion for women's attention, the diffusion and frustration of female bonding that might, in a more con-scious form, reintegrate love with power.

IV

Woman-identification is a source of energy, a potential springhead of female power, violently curtailed and wasted under the institution of heterosexuality. The denial of reality and visibility to women's passion for women, women's choice of women as allies, life companions, and community; the forcing of such relationships into dissimulation and their disintegration under intense pressure, have meant an incalcula-ble loss to the power of all women *to change the social relations of the sexes, to liberate ourselves and each other*. The lie of compulsory female heterosexuality today afflicts not just feminist scholarship, but every profession, every reference work, every curriculum, every or-ganizing attempt, every relationship or conversation over which it hov-ers. It creates, specifically, a profound falseness, hypocrisy, and hysteria in the heterosexual dialogue, for every heterosexual relation-ship is lived in the queasy strobelight of that lie. However we choose to identify ourselves, however we find ourselves labeled, it flickers across and distorts our lives.[62]

The lie keeps numberless women psychologically trapped, trying to fit mind, spirit, and sexuality into a prescribed script because they cannot look beyond the parameters of the acceptable. It pulls on the energy of such women even as it drains the energy of "closeted" lesbians—the energy exhausted in the double-life. The lesbian trapped in the "closet," the woman imprisoned in prescriptive ideas of the "normal," share the pain of blocked options, broken connections, lost access to self-definition freely and powerfully assumed.

The lie is many-layered. In Western tradition, one layer—the romantic—asserts that women are inevitably, even if rashly and tragically, drawn to men; that even when that attraction is suicidal (e.g., *Tristan und Isolde, Kate Chopin's *The Awakening*) it is still an organic imperative. In the tradition of the social sciences it asserts that primary love between the sexes is "normal," that women *need* men as social and economic protectors, for adult sexuality, and for psychological completion; that the heterosexually constituted family is the basic social unit; that women who do not attach their primary intensity to men must be, in functional terms, condemned to an even more devastating outsiderhood than their outsiderhood as women. Small wonder that lesbians are reported to be a more hidden population than male homosexuals. The black lesbian/feminist critic, Lorraine Bethel, writing on Zora Neale Hurston, remarks that for a black woman—already twice an outsider—to choose to assume still another "hated identity" is problematic indeed. Yet the lesbian continuum has been a lifeline for black women both in Africa and the United States.

> Black women have a long tradition of bonding together . . . in a Black/women's community that has been a source of vital survival information, psychic and emotional support for us. We have a distinct Black woman-identified folk culture based on our experiences as Black women in this society; symbols, language and modes of expression that are specific to the realities of our lives. . . . Because Black women were rarely among those Blacks and females who gained access to literary and other acknowledged forms of artistic expression, this Black female bonding and Black woman-identification has often been hidden and unrecorded except in the individual lives of Black women through our own memories of our particular Black female tradition.[63]

Another layer of the lie is the frequently encountered implication that women turn to women out of hatred for men. Profound skepticism, caution, and righteous paranoia about men may indeed be part of any healthy woman's response to the woman-hatred embedded in male-dominated culture, to the forms assumed by "normal" male sexuality, and to *the failure even of "sensitive" or "political" men to perceive or find these troubling*. Yet woman-hatred is so embedded in culture, so "normal" does it seem, so profoundly is it neglected as a social phenomenon, that many women, even feminists and lesbians, fail to identify it until it takes, in their own lives, some permanently unmistakable and shattering form. Lesbian existence is also represented as mere refuge from male abuses, rather than as an electric and empowering charge between women. I find it interesting that one of the most frequently quoted literary passages on lesbian relationship is that in which Colette's Renée, in *The Vagabond*, describes "the melancholy and touching image of two weak creatures who have perhaps found shelter in each other's arms, there to sleep and weep, safe from man who is often cruel, and there to taste *better than any pleasure, the bitter happiness of feeling themselves akin, frail and forgotten* [emphasis added]."[64] Colette is often considered a lesbian writer; her popular reputation has, I think, much to do with the fact that she writes about lesbian existence as if for a male audience; her earliest "lesbian" novels, the Claudine series, were written under compulsion for her husband and published under both their names. At all events, except for her writings on her mother, Colette is a far less reliable source on lesbian existence than, I would think, Charlotte Brontë, who understood that while women may, indeed must, be one another's allies, mentors, and comforters in the female struggle for survival, there is quite extraneous delight in each other's company and attraction to each others' minds and character, which proceeds from a recognition of each others' strengths.

By the same token, we can say that there is a *nascent* feminist political content in the act of choosing a woman lover or life partner in the face of institutionalized heterosexuality.[65] But for lesbian existence to realize this political content in an ultimately liberating form, the erotic choice must deepen and expand into conscious woman-identification—into lesbian/feminism.

The work that lies ahead, of unearthing and describing what I call here lesbian existence, is potentially liberating for all women. It is work that must assuredly move beyond the limits of white and middle-class Western women's studies to examine women's lives, work, and groupings within every racial, ethnic, and political structure. There are differences, moreover, between lesbian existence and the lesbian continuum—differences we can discern even in the movement of our own lives. The lesbian continuum, I suggest, needs delineation in light of the double-life of women, not only women self-described as heterosexual but also of self-described lesbians. We need a far more exhaustive account of the forms the double-life has assumed. Historians need to ask at every point how heterosexuality as institution has been organized and maintained through the female wage scale, the enforcement of middle-class women's "leisure," the glamorization of so-called sexual liberation, the withholding of education from women, the imagery of "high art" and popular culture, the mystification of the "personal" sphere, and much else. We need an economics that comprehends the institution of heterosexuality, with its doubled workload for women and its sexual divisions of labor, as the most idealized of economic relations.

The question inevitably will arise: Are we then to condemn all heterosexual relationships, including those that are least oppressive? I believe this question, though often heartfelt, is the wrong question here. We have been stalled in a maze of false dichotomies that prevents our apprehending the institution as a whole: "good" versus "bad" marriages; "marriage for love" versus arranged marriage; "liberated" sex versus prostitution; heterosexual intercourse versus rape; Liebeschmerz versus humiliation and dependency. Within the institution exist, of course, qualitative differences of experience; but the absence of choice remains the great unacknowledged reality, and in the absence of choice, women will remain dependent on the chance or luck of particular relationships and will have no collective power to determine the meaning and place of sexuality in their lives. As we address the institution itself, moreover, we begin to perceive a history of female resistance that has never fully understood itself because it has been so fragmented, miscalled, erased. It will require a courageous grasp of the politics and economics, as well as the cultural propaganda, of heterosexuality to carry us beyond individual cases or diversified group situations into the complex kind of overview needed to undo the power men everywhere wield over women, power that has become a model for every other form of exploitation and illegitimate control.

Notes

This piece first appeared in the United Kingdom as a pamphlet published by Onlywomen Press.

1. Alice Rossi, "Children and Work in the Lives of Women," paper delivered at the University of Arizona, Tucson, February 1976.
2. Doris Lessing, *The Golden Notebook* (1962; New York: Bantam Books, 1977), p. 480.
3. Nancy Chodorow, *The Reproduction of Mothering* (Berkeley: University of California Press, 1978); Dorothy Dinnerstein, *The Mermaid and the Minotaur: Sexual Arrangements and the Human Malaise* (New York: Harper and Row, 1976); Barbara Ehrenreich and Deirdre English, *For Her Own Good: 150 Years of the Experts' Advice to Women* (Garden City, N.Y.: Doubleday/& Anchor, 1978); Jean Baker Miller, *Toward a New Psychology of Women* (Boston: Beacon Press, 1976).
4. I could have chosen many other serious and influential recent books, including anthologies, that would illustrate the same point: e.g., *Our Bodies, Ourselves*, the Boston Women's Health Collective's bestseller (New York: Simon and Schuster, 1976), which devotes a separate (and inadequate) chapter to lesbians, but whose message is that heterosexuality is most women's life preference; Berenice Carroll, ed., *Liberating Women's History: Theoretical and Critical Essays* (Urbana: University of Illinois Press, 1976), which does not include even a token essay on the lesbian

presence in history, though an essay by Linda Gordon, Persis Hunt, et al. notes the use by male historians of "sexual deviance" as a category to discredit and dismiss Anna Howard Shaw, Jane Addams, and other feminists ("Historical Phallacies: Sexism in American Historical Writing"); and Renate Bridenthal and Claudia Koontz, eds., *Becoming Visible: Women in European History* (Boston: Houghton Mifflin, 1977), which contains three mentions of male homosexuality but no materials that I have been able to locate on lesbians. Gerda Lerner, ed., *The Female Experience: An American Documentary* (Indianapolis: Bobbs-Merrill, 1977), contains an abridgment of two lesbian/feminist position papers from the contemporary movement but no other documentation of lesbian existence. Lerner does note in her preface, however, how the charge of deviance has been used to fragment women and discourage women's resistance. Linda Gordon, in *Woman's Body, Woman's Right: A Social History of Birth Control in America* (New York: Viking Press, 1976), notes accurately that "it is not that feminism has produced more lesbians. There have always been many lesbians, despite high levels of repression; and most lesbians experience their sexual preference as innate" (p. 410).

5. Jonathan Katz, *Gay American History* (New York: Thomas Y. Crowell, 1976).
6. Nancy Sahli, "Smashing: Women's Relationships Before the Fall," *Chrysalis: A Magazine of Women's Culture* 8 (1979): 17–27. A version of the article was presented at the Third Berkshire Conference on the History of Women, June 11, 1976.
7. This is a book I have publicly endorsed. I would still do so, though with the above caveat. It is only since beginning to write this article that I fully appreciated how enormous is the unasked question in Ehrenreich and English's book.
8. Kathleen Barry, *Female Sexual Slavery* (Englewood Cliffs, N.J.: Prentice-Hall, 1979); Susan Brownmiller, *Against Our Will: Men, Women, and Rape* (New York: Simon and Schuster, 1975); Mary Daly, *Gyn/Ecology: The Meta-Ethics of Radical Feminism* (Boston: Beacon Press, 1978); Susan Griffin, *Woman and Nature: The Roaring Inside Her* (New York: Harper and Row, 1978); Diana Russell and Nicole van de Vens, eds., *Proceedings of the International Tribunal on Crimes Against Women* (Millbrae, Calif.: Less Femmes, 1976).
9. Dinnerstein, *Mermaid*, p. 272.
10. Daly, *Gyn/Ecology*, pp. 184–85; 114–33.
11. Chodorow, *Reproduction of Mothering*, pp. 197–98.
12. Ibid., pp. 198–99.
13. Ibid., p. 200.
14. Kathleen Gough, "The Origin of the Family," in *Toward an Anthropology of Women*, ed. Rayna Reiter (New York: Monthly Review Press, 1975), pp. 69–70.
15. Barry, *Female Sexual Slavery*, pp. 216–19.
16. Anna Demeter, *Legal Kidnapping* (Boston: Beacon Press, 1977), pp. xx, 126–28.
17. Daly, *Gyn/Ecology*, pp. 132, 139–41, 163–65.
18. Barbara Ehrenreich and Deirdre English, *Witches, Midwives, and Nurses: A History of Women Healers* (Old Westbury, N.Y.: Feminist Press, 1973); Andrea Dworkin, *Woman Hating* (New York: E. P. Dutton, 1974), pp. 118–54; Daly, *Gyn/Ecology*, pp. 178–222.
19. See Virginia Woolf, *A Room of One's Own* (London: Hogarth Press, 1929), and idem, *Three Guineas* (1938; New York: Harcourt Brace, 1966); Tillie Olsen, *Silences* (Boston: Delacorte Press, 1978); Michelle Cliff, "The Resonance of Interruption," *Chrysalis: A Magazine of Women's Culture* 8 (1979): 29–37.
20. Mary Daly, *Beyond God the Father* (Boston: Beacon Press, 1973), pp. 347–51; Olsen, *Silences*, pp. 22–46.
21. Daly, *Beyond God the Father*, p. 93.
22. Fran P. Hosken, "The Violence of Power: Genital Mutilation of Females," *Heresies* 6 (1979): 28–35; Russell and van de Ven, *Proceedings*, pp. 194–95.
23. Barry, *Female Sexual Slavery*, pp. 163–64.

24. The issue of "lesbian sadomasochism" needs to be examined in terms of the dominant cultures' teachings about the relation of sex and violence, and also of the acceptance by some lesbians of male homosexual mores. I believe this to be another example of the double-life of women.

25. Catherine A. MacKinnon, *Sexual Harassment of Working Women: A Case of Sex Discrimination* (New Haven, Conn.: Yale University Press, 1979), pp. 15–16.

26. Ibid., p. 174.

27. Brownmiller, *Against Our Will*.

28. MacKinnon, *Sexual Harassment*, p. 219. Susan Schecter writes: "The push for heterosexual union at whatever cost is so intense that . . . it has become a cultural force of its own that creates battering. The ideology of romantic love and its jealous possession of the partner as property provide the masquerade for what can become severe abuse" (*Aegis: Magazine on Ending Violence Against Women* [July–August 1979]: 50–51).

29. MacKinnon, *Sexual Harassment*, p. 298.

30. Ibid., p. 220.

31. Ibid., p. 221.

32. Barry, *Female Sexual Slavery*.

33. Ibid., p. 33.

34. Ibid., p. 103.

35. Ibid., p. 5.

36. Ibid., p. 100.

37. Ibid., p. 218.

38. Ibid., p. 140.

39. Ibid., p. 172.

40. Elsewhere I have suggested that male-identification has been a powerful source of white women's racism, and that it has been women who were seen as "disloyal" to male codes and systems who have actively battled against it (Adrienne Rich, "Disloyal to Civilization: Feminism, Racism, Gynephobia," in *On Lies, Secrets, and Silence: Selected Prose, 1966–1978* [New York: W. W. Norton, 1979]).

41. Barry, *Female Sexual Slavery*, p. 220.

42. Susan Cavin, "Lesbian Origins," Ph. D. diss., Department of Sociology, Rutgers, The State University of New Jersey, 1978, chap. 6.

43. For my perception of heterosexuality as an economic institution, I am indebted to Lisa Leghorn and Katherine Parker, who allowed me to read the unpublished manuscript of their book, *Woman's Worth: Sexual Economics and the World of Women* (London and Boston: Routledge and Kegan Paul, 1981).

44. I would suggest that lesbian existence has been most recognized and tolerated where it has resembled a "deviant" version of heterosexuality; e.g., where lesbians have, like Stein and Toklas, played heterosexual roles (or seemed to in public) and have been chiefly identified with male culture. See also Claude E. Schaeffer, "The Kuterai Female Berdache: Courier, Guide, Prophetess and Warrior," *Ethnohistory* 2, no. 3 (Summer 1965): 193–236. (Berdache: "an individual of a definite physiological sex [m. or f.] who assumes the role and status of the opposite sex and who is viewed by the community as being of one sex physiologically but as having assumed the role and status of the opposite sex" [Schaeffer, p. 231].) Lesbian existence has also been relegated to an upper-class phenomenon, an elite decadence (as in the fascination with Paris salon lesbians such as Renée Vivien and Natalie Clifford Barney), to the obscuring of such "common women" as Judy Grahn depicts in her *The Work of a Common Woman* (New York: St. Martin's Press, 1980) and *True to Life Adventure Stories* (Oakland, Calif.: Diana Press, 1978).

45. Daly, *Gyn/Ecology*, p. 15.

46. "In a hostile world in which women are not supposed to survive except in relation with and in service to men, entire communities of women were simply erased.

History tends to bury what it seeks to reject" (Blanche W. Cook, "'Women Alone Stir My Imagination': Lesbianism and the Cultural Tradition," *Signs* 4, no. 4 [Summer 1979]: 719–20). The Lesbian Herstory Archives in New York City is one attempt to preserve contemporary documents on lesbian existence—a project of enormous value and meaning, still pitted against the continuing censorship and obliteration of relationships, networks, communities, in other archives and elsewhere in the culture.

47. Audre Lorde, *Uses of the Erotic: The Erotic as Power,* Out & Out Books Pamphlet No. 3 (New York: Out & Out Books [476 2d Street, Brooklyn, New York 11215], 1979).

48. Adrienne Rich, "Conditions for Work: The Common World of Women," in *On Lies, Secrets, and Silence,* p. 209; H.D., *Tribute to Freud* (Oxford: Carcanet Press, 1971), pp. 50–54.

49. Woolf, *A Room of One's Own,* p. 126.

50. Gracia Clark, "The Beguines: A Mediaeval Women's Community," *Quest: A Feminist Quarterly* 1, no. 4 (1975): 73–80.

51. See Denise Paulmé, ed., *Women of Tropical Africa* (Berkeley: University of California Press, 1963), pp. 7, 266–67. Some of these sororities are described as "a kind of defensive syndicate against the male element"—their aims being "to offer concerted resistance to an oppressive patriarchate," "independence in relation to one's husband and with regard to motherhood, mutual aid, satisfaction of personal revenge." See also Audre Lorde, "Scratching the Surface: Some Notes on Barriers to Women and Loving," *Black Scholar* 9, no. 7 (1978): 31–35; Marjorie Topley, "Marriage Resistance in Rural Kwangtung," in *Women in Chinese Society,* ed. M. Wolf and R. Witke (Stanford, Calif.: Stanford University Press, 1978), pp. 67–89; Agnes Smedley, *Portraits of Chinese Women in Revolution,* ed. J. MacKinnon and S. MacKinnon (Old Westbury, N.Y.: Feminist Press, 1976), pp. 103–10.

52. See Rosalind Petchesky, "Dissolving the Hyphen: A Report on Marxist-Feminist Groups 1–5," in *Capitalist Patriarchy and the Case for Socialist Feminism,* ed. Zillah Eisenstein (New York: Monthly Review Press, 1979), p. 387.

53. Andrea Dworkin, *Pornography: Men Possessing Women* (New York: G. P. Putnam Sons, 1981).

54. Russell and van de Ven, *Proceedings,* pp. 42–43, 56–57.

55. I am indebted to Jonathan Katz's *Gay American History* for bringing to my attention Hansberry's letters to *Ladder* and to Barbara Grier for supplying me with copies of relevant pages from *Ladder,* quoted here by permission of Barbara Grier. See also the reprinted series of *Ladder,* ed. Jonathan Katz et al. (New York: Arno Press); and Deirdre Carmody, "Letters by Eleanor Roosevelt Detail Friendship with Lorena Hickok," *New York Times,* 21 October 1979.

56. Meridel LeSueur, *The Girl* (Cambridge, Mass.: West End Press, 1978), pp. 10–11. LeSueur describes, in an afterword, how this book was drawn from the writings and oral narrations of women in the Workers Alliance who met as a writers' group during the Depression.

57. Ibid., p. 20.

58. Ibid., pp. 53–54.

59. Ibid., p. 55.

60. Toni Morrison, *Sula* (New York: Bantam Books, 1973), pp. 103–4, 149. I am indebted to Lorraine Bethel's essay, "'This Infinity of Conscious Pain': Zora Neale Hurston and the Black Female Literary Tradition," in *All the Women Are White, All the Blacks Are Men, But Some of Us Are Brave: Black Women's Studies,* ed. Gloria T. Hull, Patricia Bell Scott, and Barbara Smith (Old Westbury, N.Y.: The Feminist Press, 1982.)

61. See Maureen Brady and Judith McDaniel, "Lesbians in the Mainstream: The Image of Lesbians in Recent Commercial Fiction," *Conditions* 6 (1979).

62. See Russell and van de Ven, *Proceedings* p. 40: ". . . few heterosexual women realize their lack of free choice about their sexuality, and few realize how and why compulsory heterosexuality is also a crime against them."

63. Bethel, "This Infinity of Conscious Pain."

64. Dinnerstein, the most recent writer to quote this passage, adds ominously: "But what has to be added to her account is that these 'women enlaced' are sheltering each other not just from what men want to do to them, but also from what they want to do to each other" (*The Mermaid*, p. 103). The fact is, however, that woman-to-woman violence is a minute grain in the universe of male-against-female violence perpetrated and rationalized in every social institution.

65. Conversation with Blanche W. Cook, New York City, March 1979.

they're always curious
Irena Klepfisz

they're always curious about what you eat as if you were
some strange breed still unclassified by darwin & whether
you cook every night & wouldn't it be easier for you to
buy frozen dinners but i am quick to point out that my intra-
venous tubing has been taken out and they back up saying *i*
could never just cook for one person but i tell them it's
the same exactly the same as for two except half

but more they're curious about what you do when the urge
is on & if you use a coke bottle or some psychedelic dildo
or electric vibrator or just the good old finger or whole
hand & do you mannippppulllaaatttte yourself into a clit
orgasm or just kind of keep digging away at yourself & if
you mind it & when you have affairs doesn't it hurt when it's
over & it certainly must be lonely to go back to the old finger

& they always cluck over the amount of space you require
& certainly the extra bedroom seems unnecessary & i try to
explain that i like to move around & that i get antsy when
i have the urge so that it's nice to have an extra place
to go when you're lonely & after all it seems small compensation for using the good old finger & they're surprised because they never thought of it that way & it does seem reasonable come to think of it

& they kind of probe about your future & if you have a will or
why you bother to accumulate all that stuff or what you plan
to do with your old age & aren't you scared about being put
away somewhere or found on your bathroom floor dead after
your downstairs neighbor has smelled you out but then of course
you don't have the worry of who goes first though of course
you know couples live longer for they have something to live
for & i try to explain i live for myself even when in love but
it's a hard concept to explain when you feel lonely

The Afro-American Female: The Historical Context of the Construction of Sexual Identity

Rennie Simson

A number of contemporary psychologists and sociologists see the relationship between the black male and the black female as one beset by sexual conflict. They suggest that black women have been conditioned by society to view black men as the white society views them, namely as nonproductive, unreliable, weak. Thus black women have come to think of black men as poor providers, and as a result they have developed a high degree of self-reliance. According to census figures released in December 1980, 41 percent of all black households are headed by women. This self-reliance, in turn, has caused the black male to view the black female as aggressive, domineering, pushy, and so forth. Obviously these views are greatly oversimplified and contain a high degree of stereotyping, but they have, nevertheless, played an important role in formulating relationships between black males and black females, and they have also played a significant role in the construction of the sexual self by the black woman.

In order to fully understand the construction of this sexual self, we must go back and view the black woman within the context of her early experience in American life. Past attempts to do this have failed to focus on the one constituency in American life best qualified to give us the appropriate insights needed to form an adequate understanding of the black woman's experience in America: namely, the black woman herself. Past efforts to delineate the experience of black women relied very heavily on the pens of empathetic black males and sympathetic whites. As Bert Lowenberg and Ruth Bogin commented in their recent work, *Black Women in Nineteenth-Century American Life*, "If the black male's words, before the most recent period of ferment, were recorded only spasmodically, those of the Black female were still less frequently set down on paper."[1] This neglect was recognized by the nineteenth-century Afro-American novelist Pauline Hopkins in one of her articles in the series Famous Women of the Negro Race: "In writing of the attainments of a people it is important that the position of its women be clearly defined."[2]

The construction of the sexual self of the Afro-American woman has its roots in the days of slavery. During those days the black woman was thought of, at best, as a worker and, at worst, as an object for sexual gratification and as a breeder of more slaves. That she was a fellow human being endowed with certain needs, desires, and rights was a matter to which little thought was given by her owner.

Before the nineteenth century, black Americans produced little in the way of a written record of their experiences. This is not astonishing since it was illegal in most states for slaves to read and write, and slavery was not banned in any state until Pennsylvania declared slavery illegal in 1780. As soon as black people learned to write they began to present their experiences in literary form and we see Afro-American poetry, drama, fiction, and autobiography all developing and expanding during the nineteenth century.

In pre-Civil War United States the first literary form in which black people exercised their talents to any great extent was the autobiography. Approximately eighty autobiographies, known as "slave narratives," were published before the Civil War and the striking consistency of their themes presents a coherent picture of slave life. Although autobiography is not sociology, the works of nineteenth-century black writers can tell us a great deal about the style of life among early black Americans.

Harriet Jacobs and Elizabeth Keckley were two of the very few Afro-American women to publish slave narratives. Their autobiographies, Jacobs's *Incidents in the Life of a Slave Girl* (1861) and Keckley's *Behind the Scenes* (1868), are of great significance in helping us to understand how black women during slavery formed an image of the sexual self.

Jacobs was owned by a Mr. Flint, whose only interest in her was to use her as a way of satisfying his sexual lust. To this end he used every means of forcing her compliance to his desires short of rape. That her position was not unique was stated by Jacobs in her introduction: "I do earnestly desire to arouse the women of the North to a realizing sense of the condition of two millions of women in the South, still in bondage, suffering what I suffered, and most of them far worse."[3] When Jacobs was but fifteen years old her master "began to whisper foul words"[4] in her ear. He was doggedly persistent in his efforts to seduce her and finally, to avoid becoming the mistress of Flint, Jacobs became the mistress of another influential white man whom she hoped would help her. She became pregnant and rationalized her situation by stating, "It seems less demeaning to give one's self, than to submit to compulsion."[5] Flint, however, was not to be discouraged and for seven years Jacobs hid in a little cubbyhole in her grandmother's attic to avoid any further contact with him. Of this experience she wrote: "I hardly expect that the reader will credit me when I affirm that I lived in that dismal little hole, almost deprived of light and air, and with no space to move my limbs, for nearly seven years."[6] She concluded that "slavery is terrible for men; but it is far more terrible for women."[7]

Keckley, too, suffered the torment of sexual abuse at an early age. When she was eighteen, she was whipped by a male friend of her mistress for no discernible reason. When she asked the man why this beating was about to be administered, he simply replied, "No matter, I am going to whip you, so take your dress down this instant."[8] She refused to cooperate, so the man tied her, ripped off her dress, and beat her bare flesh as he had proclaimed he would do. A few years later she became the object of the sexual lust of another white man and he pursued her for four years. Of this experience she wrote, "I do not care to dwell upon this subject for it is one that is fraught with pain. Suffice it to say, that he persecuted me for four years, and I—I became a mother."[9] Obviously, such experiences as Jacobs and Keckley endured played a major role in the development of their definition of the sexual self. Although Keckley and Jacobs did not mention witnessing during childhood the sexual abuses imposed on other slave women, they were, no doubt, subject to viewing, if indirectly and from a distance, experiences similar to those they themselves endured.

Female sexual chastity was the heritage of both the Christian culture of the South and the African civilizations from which the slaves had come. Sexual "purity" was considered the noblest virtue of the white woman of the South. The white woman who gave up her chastity, especially for a black male, was regarded as a fallen woman. Although the white woman was in a position of having some (if not much) choice about her sexual life, such was obviously not the case with the black woman. She was alone and helpless. The white woman often hated her as a rival and Jacobs in her autobiography clearly showed that Flint's wife detested and feared her.

The black male was as powerless as the black female. Jacobs fell in love with a young black man, but Flint refused to give his permission for their marriage and the young man, sensing his powerlessness, became frustrated and took off for the North. Black women were equally powerless to help one another. Jacobs's grandmother did what she could, but there was no way she could save her granddaughter from the sexual assaults of her master. The white man who fathered Jacobs's two children had very little interest in her or her children's personal welfare. Thus, early in life, Jacobs came to view herself as sexually helpless. She was an object, a toy to be used by the white male as he saw fit. However, after the first sense of helplessness passed, she made a strong effort to control the controllable—hence, her determination to hide in her grandmother's attic for several years.

Jacobs's attempt to maintain control over her life is also shown in her pattern of living after her escape to freedom in the North. She mentioned no sexual attachments and relied on herself for financial support. Keckley too learned self-reliance. A brief marriage with a Mr. Keckley ended in divorce as she found him "a burden instead of a helpmate."[10] No children issued from this marriage as Keckley did not wish to bring any more slaves into the world and thus fulfill her function as a breeder. When her marriage was terminated she said of her husband, "Let charity draw around him the mantle of silence."[11] Keckley never mentioned another sexual relationship and, like Jacobs, she remained self-supporting for the rest of her life.

The sexual experiences of these two early Afro-American women writers were so painful that they tended to negate their identity as sexual beings in their later life. Though unusual among nineteenth-century black women in that they were published authors, their sexual vulnerabilty, their precarious struggle for autonomy, were typical. Their early encounters with men were of such a nature as to dissuade and discourage them from future contact with the opposite sex. Their white sisters often showed them the hostility displayed by one sexual rival toward another. This early lack of sisterly confidence and affection between white and black women may well lie at the core of the distrust that is frequently displayed today between women of these two races in matters pertaining not only to physical and sexual attractiveness, but to political and intellectual issues as well. Thus black women identified themselves as strong survivors who had only themselves to rely on to struggle through life.

A sense of helplessness followed by a strengthened sense of self is also a central pattern in the works of contemporary Afro-American women writers. In her novel *The Bluest Eye*, Toni Morrison commented on the position of the Afro-American female:

> Everybody in the world was in a position to give them orders. White women said "Do this." White children said, "Give me that." White men said, "Come here." Black men said, "Lay down." The only people they need not take orders from were black children and each other.[12]

Black women and black children could comfort one another but they, singly or in combination, were unable to alter the existing social structure, which assigned them their position in society. Nevertheless, they learned to cope with an environment that they could not change but that they redefined to fit their needs. Morrison expressed this view in *The Bluest Eye*:

But they [black women] took all of that [their treatment by society] and re-created it in their own image. They ran the houses of white people and knew it. When white men beat their men, they cleaned up the blood and went home to receive abuse from the victim. . . . the hands that felled trees also cut umbilical cords; the hands that wrung the necks of chickens and butchered hogs also nudged African violets into bloom.[13]

Clearly Morrison, as well as Jacobs and Keckley, has presented us a portrait of women who have survived with their sense of identity intact. It was on this basic foundation of self-reliance that the sexual self of the black female was constructed.

This early foundation is reflected in the works of other Afro-American women writers of the nineteenth century. The black female in the post-Civil War period saw that marriage to a black male offered her the same kinds of abuses to which the white woman was exposed within marriage. In addition, she was often faced with a husband who was unable to support her so that she had to rely on herself for survival just as her sisters had done in the days of slavery. The black male was much less employable than the black female, who could always find some type of work as a domestic in a white household. Since the traditional family image held up to all Americans portrayed the man as the provider, this frequent role reversal in the black family played havoc with the construction of a sexual self.

Two nineteenth-century Afro-American women evangelists wrote of their negative experiences in their marital relations. Julia Foote, in her autobiography, *A Brand Plucked from the Fire* (1886), described her husband as an uncaring man who constantly shipped out to sea and had little regard for his wife's welfare. She turned to her career as a preacher and became entirely self-supporting, as did Amanda Smith, another evangelical preacher, who detailed her experiences in a book entitled simply *An Autobiography* (1893). She wrote of her husband: "I am nearly heartbroken; James is so unkind, and I began to tell all my good works; how I did this and how I did that and all I could to make things pleasant and yet he was unkind."[14]

Black women of the nineteenth century were keenly aware that for all women a double standard existed when it came to matters of sex. Journalist and anti-lynching crusader Ida Wells Barnett wrote in her autobiography, *Crusade for Justice*, of the double standard established by the white southern male, a standard that was a significant factor in the lynching of many innocent black men.

I also found that what the white man of the South practiced as all right for himself, he assumed to be unthinkable in white women. They could and did fall in love with the pretty mulatto and quadroon girls as well as black ones, but they professed an inability to imagine white women doing the same thing with Negro and mulatto men. Whenever they did so and were found out, the cry of rape was raised, and the lowest element of the white South was turned loose to wreak its fiendish cruelty on those too weak to help themselves.[15]

Frances Harper, no doubt the best known Afro-American woman writer of the second half of the nineteenth century, also rejected the double standard, which "excuses all in the male and accuses all in the female."[16] She expressed her views in a poem entitled simply "The Double Standard."

> Crime has no sex and yet today
> I wear the brand of shame
> Whilst he amid the gay and proud
> Still bears an honored name.
>
> Can you blame if I've learned to think
> Your hate of vice a sham,
> When you so coldly crushed me down
> And then excused the man.[17]

Perhaps the strongest nineteenth-century documents identifying the black female as an independent, self-reliant being were written by the Afro-American writers Julia Cooper and Alice Dunbar Nelson. In *A Voice from the South*, Cooper admonished women to stop thwarting their own desires in order to make themselves attractive to man. With obvious sarcasm she suggested the question for women no longer should be, "How shall I so cramp, stunt, simplify and nullify myself as to make me eligible for the honor of being swallowed up into some little man?"[18] Alice Dunbar Nelson, wife of the famous poet Paul Lawrence Dunbar, also had some harsh words for the institution of marriage; in her essay "The Woman" she asked:

Why should she hasten to give this liberty up in exchange for a serfdom, sweet sometimes it is true, but which too often becomes galling and unendurable. . . . What housewife dares call a moment her own?[19]

Black women were militant by necessity: self-reliance was survival.

The black female has held a unique position in American society. She has been forced to construct a sexual self based on a set of criteria quite different from those set for her white sister. For centuries of her American experience there was seldom, if ever, in her environment any positive male figure who had either the power or the inclination to administer to the needs of her well-being. The black male was too helpless and the white male too powerful and self-centered to aid her in developing positive relations with men. Her white sister was often too remote and unconcerned to be of much assistance. In such a situation the black female was forced to turn inward and seek what strength she could from within herself. Though this was particularly true before the twentieth century, the results of such a long-standing experience are still in evidence today. We must examine the words of Afro-American women writers so that we can understand their own analysis of the factors leading to their construction of a sexual life.

Notes

The research for this article was made possible in part by a grant from the American Philosophical Society.

1. Bert Lowenberg and Ruth Bogin, *Black Women in Nineteenth-Century American Life* (University Park, Penn.: Pennsylvania State University Press, 1976), p. 5.
2. Pauline Hopkins, "Famous Women of the Negro Race," *The Colored American Magazine* 4 (November 1901): 46.
3. Harriet Jacobs, *Incidents in the Life of a Slave Girl* (Boston: Negro History Press, 1861), p. 6.
4. Ibid, p. 44.
5. Ibid, p. 85.
6. Ibid, p. 224.
7. Ibid, p. 119.
8. Elizabeth Keckley, *Behind the Scenes* (New York: G. W. Carleton and Co., 1868), p. 33.
9. Ibid, p. 39.
10. Ibid, p. 50.
11. Ibid., p. 50.
12. Toni Morrison, *The Bluest Eye* (New York: Pocket Books, 1972), p. 109.
13. Ibid, p. 109–10.
14. Amanda Smith, *An Autobiography* (Chicago: Meyer and Brothers, 1893), p. 62.
15. Ida Wells Barnett, *Crusade for Justice* (Chicago: University of Chicago Press, 1970), p. 70.
16. Frances Harper, *The Sparrows Fall and Other Poems* (n.p., n.d.), p. 13.
17. Ibid, p. 13.
18. Julia Cooper, *A Voice from the South* (Boston: Negro University Press, 1851), p. 85.
19. Alice Dunbar Nelson, *Violets and Other Tales* (n.p., 1895), p. 25.

I Just Came Out Pregnant
Felicita Garcia

I was only sixteen when I came out pregnant. I had to leave school and everything. The school didn't want me. They wanted to send me away, and it was like, "No, I don't want to go away. I don't want to lose my family. This is all I am."

I went through changes with her father. He hurt me a lot. I was fifteen when I met him and I was a virgin. He'll be twenty-six now. He's five years older than me. He claimed I wasn't a virgin and maybe that kid is not his. He hurt me, I guess, because I was his first virgin and I was young. I was his only girlfriend that was a virgin. They were always womens that he had. He was just scared. He told my girlfriend he was just scared I was going to leave him. He said I was so pretty and there were a lot of guys that would look at me. That's why he was the way he was to me—because he was afraid he was going to lose me. I told him it was wrong of him because if he would have trusted me and given me a little space to breathe, then I would have been with him. It would have been different and gotten me what I wanted. But I like my freedom.

I hadn't expected to come out pregnant. I was so naive. I didn't figure I would come out pregnant in a couple of months, and when I found out, I broke down. "Oh my God, my mother's going to kill me." That's what I kept saying. "My mother's going to kill me." Father was the one who was the strict one in the house. Father always said, "If your mother wouldn't have broke up, this wouldn't have happened to none of you. You know, it wouldn't have been like that." 'Cause we were straight A's in school. We all had 95's always in school, and we were straight because of my father. We knew how strict he was, and we were always goody-goody in school. We were with my father until my brother was about two years old. I was about twelve or thirteen. I cried because I was so close to my father. I was daddy's little girl, and my father spoiled me in his own way, and I was so hurt because I didn't have my father, and I didn't want to live down here in Manhattan. We used to live in Brooklyn in the projects, and there were nights down here I couldn't sleep because I would hear the mice, and there were roaches crawling onto the walls, and I wasn't used to all that. It blew my mind because down here I found everything strange. So strange. I was used to living with mainly black people. There were a few Puerto Rican but the majority were black people. When I came down here, it freaked me out because there was so much dope out on the street, all the shooting out here. I couldn't understand.

Before I moved here, all I knew about sex was where the baby came from—in the stomach. I was very naive when I first moved down here, and then I started learning about sex. My girlfriend? Her brother had little porno films and I was watching and it was like, "Oh my God!" You know, you'd be watching. You'd always find somebody touching somebody out in the street or somewhere. Somebody would take off their clothes. You always would catch somebody doing something. It was like, "Oh my God, look what they doing!" In the hall, behind the stairs, on the roof, you'd catch somebody going to bed with each other. Anywhere. They're going to bed with anybody anywhere. It was like, "Oh my God, I didn't know they do that."

You had to be fast to live out here. To catch up on life out here, and that's how it is. That's how come so many girls come out pregnant, 'cause they're so grown. You grow up fast over here. When I was fourteen, I thought I was a woman. I came over here when I was thirteen. When I hit fourteen, I thought I was about eighteen years old. I was going out dancing and partying, coming home at three and four o'clock in the morning. Sometimes I'd come home at ten o'clock in the morning. My mother would slap me down, but there were places that let you in. I had a fake ID. I went in. I partied all night. I came home like nothing.

But you had to be grown to live out here. You had to catch up on everything. The guys just wanted to get something out of you and that's it. I didn't let nobody touch me until I met my daughter's father, and my girlfriend said, "It's all right. Nothing will happen." I said, "I don't want to come out pregnant." She said, "It doesn't matter if you come out pregnant. You'll have your baby. It'll be all right." Everything was the positive side. She never told me, "Well, you're going to go through changes and get stuck up." Everything was the positive side.

In my mother's house, I had so much freedom. I used to have guy friends, and they used to come to my room, and it was all right. But then my mother was living with this man in my house, and it blew all our minds. She was living with somebody else, and he was fresh. I guess that's what made me want to leave out of my house more. Because I told my mother, "Before he abuses me, I'd rather let somebody else do it, a man that I would really want for him to do it." She didn't say nothing back. It blew her mind. She didn't know what to do. I was always going out. I would just tell her, "Mommy, I'll be back in a couple hours," and disappear. He was following me, too. I didn't know it, but there were times that he would follow me, and his daughter told me that he tried to abuse her. I was scared, and I didn't know what to do. Then my father found out, and he wanted to take my mother to court, and I told him, "Don't do that to her." He said, "I'm going to take her to court and put her away." I said, "No, no, please. Leave her alone. Don't bother her." Because wherever my mother went, we went behind her. She always took us everywhere. She never left us behind with nobody at all. So it was always, "Mommy, mommy, mommy, mommy," everything.

Then when I first had sex, I felt dirty. I felt real dirty. I said, "Oh my God, my mother's going to know that I'm dirty and that I let him touch me." I didn't talk to him for a while. I had sex at his mother's house the first time. It was in his mother's house.

I was four months when I told my sister I come out pregnant. I didn't tell nobody till four months. To this day, I never told my mother I was pregnant. She knew. The mothers know, I guess.

I was scared. I didn't know what was going to happen. Where was I going to live? I had my own room in my mother's house and my mother gave me everything I wanted. I didn't know what was going to happen with the baby's father. Are we going to last? What about the baby? I thought ahead to her future. How was it going to be for her? I said, "When I have my baby, I want the best for my baby. No matter how I am going to do it, I am going to give her the best."

My sister said, "Well, think about it. It's hard. It's really hard to have a baby." I would tell her, "I know," but it was like, I don't know it yet because I haven't gone through it. But I was telling her, "I know." So I said, "Don't worry, don't worry. Her father is going to get us an apartment." And I would tell her, "Don't tell me what to do. You have your own life, so live your own life." We weren't close. We were never close until we came out pregnant and our bellies were real big. Now we are like best of friends. I'm close with my mother now, too. Very close. And there are times when I tell her I'm sorry.

When I was about six months pregnant, I moved out of my mother's house, and I went to live with my daughter's father. I used to wash his clothes in the washing machine around two blocks away, and I had to carry a big basket full of clothes down the stairs with my belly. I had nobody to help me. Or I was always kneeling and washing his clothes by hand. I was doing like oldtime rough work, and I couldn't believe it. My mother used to tell me, "Felicita, if you want, stay with me. You don't have to go to that." And I told her, "No, mommy. That's my baby's father. I have to do it." I was always cooking and cleaning and mopping, and I used to get pains in my stomach because I was constantly moving dressers and everything. I was moving the clothes up and down from off the floor.

I went to the hospital one day for my appointment, and the doctor told me he'd leave me in because I was carrying my baby so low, and I was swollen. I used to eat a lot, and I was gaining a lot of weight. I went up to 179 pounds from 100, and the doctor told me my ankles were swollen, I had toxemia, and he told me he was going to leave me in. I said, "I'm not supposed to give birth yet. I've still got two more weeks." He said, "No, we've got to leave you in." They took me downstairs. They said, "We're going to check you in, Felicita." I called up my mommy. I said, "Mommy, mommy, they're going to leave me in the hospital." My daughter's father came and he brought my pajamas and clothes, and then they took me down, and they induced labor. I was having convulsions when I was in labor, and my blood pressure went up, and I had fever, too.

When I was in labor, I kept telling my mother to forgive me for everything I've done to her. That's what I kept telling her. "Mommy, mommy, I'm sorry. I'm sorry for all the pain I gave you." I said, "Now I know what it is for you to have a child." She started crying and crying, and I told her, "I'm sorry, mommy. I'm sorry. I didn't mean for it to end this way." I told her I was sorry because I hurt her. I yelled at her. All the things that a kid does when they yell at their mother and talk back and because I just came out pregnant and never told her and I hurt her a lot because I was the baby of the girls. Because it was just me and my sister were the only girls, and I got four brothers. When I was pregnant, she'd ask me what was wrong and I'd tell her, "Nothing, mommy, nothing nothing." There was nothing wrong. And I just told her, "Mommy, forgive me. I didn't mean for it to end this way." She had wanted me to finish school. She would tell me, "Felicita, do you want the baby? You could keep it. It's up to you. If you want to have an abortion, it's up to you." She said, "You're not a little girl anymore. It's up to you. Just remember it's a big responsibility," and I told her, "Mommy, this is my first child. If I'm woman enough to do something like this, then I'm woman enough to keep this child. If other girls want to give up their babies, that's them. But I feel that if I'm woman enough to make a mistake like this, then this is my responsibility to keep this child."

As the baby came out, that's when they put me to sleep. I didn't get to see her. I didn't see her for two days because my fever was up and my blood pressure was up high. Everybody saw my baby except me. And then I had her. I just remember her head was smashed a little on one side, and I said, "Oh my God, my baby's going to come out with a busted head," and I thought it was all the struggling I did. That I hurt her. But the lady said, "It'll grow back to normal," and that's what happened. In a couple of days, her head went round. She was real hairy. All over her face, she had hair. I got scared. I said, "Wow, I got a hairy baby."

After a while, I couldn't believe that she was mine. I was tripped on it. I took off all her clothes. I said, "This is mine. Really mine." I cried nights with her because I couldn't sleep. I wouldn't take naps during the day while she was asleep. I was always cleaning. You know, washing her clothes. Taking care of the house. Cooking for my mother. I stayed for a while with my mother. Not too long. About a week. Then I moved out. Then I was doing everything on my own. Then I was living with her father. Then I had to deal with him. We lived together for almost four years and then I decided to leave him.

He always wanted me to be a housewife, and I wanted to be somebody. I wanted to go to school, to do something. He wouldn't let me go to school or do something. He stopped me from school and everything. He always had me home. Home, home, home, home. I would go out with my daughter to my girlfriend's house in Brooklyn and that's it. Home. He would go out, go to the movies with his friends and everything. He only took me to the movies twice in three years and that's it. I never got to go anywhere. After we broke up, I went crazy. I went dancing. I went to places I hadn't been—to museums that I haven't been to since I was young, and I got to see New York. And it's been fun. I've been enjoying every minute of it. I've been dressing up better. I've lost weight. I make myself look good. Before, I didn't care what I looked like. I was getting fat, and he was helping me get fat. He was no help. He didn't care if I blew up like an elephant.

About a year after we were living together, he hit me. He slapped me when we were arguing, and I went to hit him back, and he slapped me, and I said, "I can't hit him because he's going to beat me." Then I ran away from home for a week. He said, "I'm sorry. I'll never do it again." I said, "No, I don't want to live with you anymore, because if I keep living with you, you're going to keep hitting me. No," I said, "I'm not a ragdoll for you to be hitting on me." He said, "Okay." He apologized. He said, "I won't hit you anymore." I said, "Okay." I went back to him and three years later I left him. He gave me two black eyes after we left each other and everything because I answered him back, you know. He started to talk to me dirty. He never talked to me dirty and I told him, "I am not no cheap little tramp for you to talk to me like that. You know." But he hit me and I just went in back of him and he just whacked me one, you know. And I said, "No, I don't need to deal with that. I don't need it. I don't need no mens to touch me." I said, "The next man that touched me, I'll pick up a stick or something. I am going to crack his head to show him that I'm no little piece of doll that he should beat me. Or his child." I used to tell my daughter's father, "I'm not your child. I might be young, but I am not your child for you to scold me and demand me to do something. If I want to do it, I'll do it of my own will—not because you say so or because you're the boss." I tell him, "I could be my own boss. It's not always what you say."

Finally, I decided, I'll wait until my baby goes to the bathroom and when she stops her bottle and her Pampers, I'll wait till she's three, and she's learned how to talk well, and then I'll leave him and go to work, and I'll leave her with my mother to babysit. Because I'll know then if something happens, she talks to me. She tells me everything. Because I said in case mama is not around, and I need to leave her with a babysitter, if anything happened, my daughter could tell me. So I said, "I'd rather wait until she is big enough before I go to work." I wanted to go to school, but I needed money, so I said I'd have to get a job.

I want the best for my little girl. I want to give her everything. I don't take money from him for myself. I tell him, "You want to see your daughter? You buy her things, because I don't want you to say that I used up her money. So you buy her what she needs and that'll be good enough for me."

In the beginning, he threatened to cut my face when I left him. It took almost a year for him to leave me alone. He was always pushing and pulling me and telling me and trying to put me down. I went into a depression. I was getting sick, and I almost had a nervous breakdown. I was afraid to leave my house. He was always threatening me. Finally I told him how sick I was getting, and, well, then he stopped. He said, "Okay. I'm sorry. I didn't mean to get you like that, but I couldn't believe that you left me." I said, "But I told you I was leaving a month before." And then he understood.

Now everything is his daughter, and he always says, "Take care of yourself." He's always asking if I need anything. I tell him, "No, I don't need nothing." I never asked him for anything, not even when we lived together. I always supported myself because I didn't want to ask him for anything. If I would ask him for anything, he would tell me, "For what?" I would tell him, "What do you do with your money?" He would tell me, "It's none of your business." So I said, "Okay. You keep your money. I'll take care of myself. I don't need you. Put it that way: I don't need you or any other man."

I like it better this way.

I don't want no more kids because I don't want to have a child from another father and go through the changes that my daughter has a stepfather. That father will treat my daughter a little different than the second child I have, and I don't want her to go through that because I seen what my sister went through with my father. My father raised her since she was two but my father was always hard on her, and I said, "But that's not her father, for him to be hitting her." I say now, "I don't want no man to touch my child." I guess I'm selfish with her. I say, "If I want, I'll remarry when she's big and on her own." I don't want no more children unless me and her father decide, well, okay, we'll have another one. But I wouldn't want to have competition with two kids. It could be different. Maybe he'll treat my daughter good, but I don't want to take a chance with that. I don't want nobody to hurt my child. I've been hurt too much in my life. My sister's been hurt and I guess the pain that she's hurt I feel, and I don't want my daughter to go through that. I'm so afraid for somebody to push or hit her. You know, I have this boyfriend, and he hit her one time, and I practically jumped him. He hit her on the hand, and I told him, "If you ever touch my child again, I will kill you. Don't touch my child.' Nobody touches my child but my mother while she's with her. That's it. Nobody. Not even her father hits her.

This organization I work for, it works with youth, and there are a lot of young girls come around here. I tell them, "If you're not a virgin, take pills and think about the future. Go to school." I tell them, "Look where I'm at now. Without a diploma, it's hard to find a job. I've got a lot of experience because I volunteered and everything. But you can't volunteer for the rest of your life. You have to get somewhere in this world." I tell them, "Keep going to school and if you're a virgin, don't make the mistake." I tell them, it's a big responsibility to have a child. I say, "You know what you do? Babysit somebody's child and you'll know what it is to have that child all day with you." They don't know what it is. "Babysit," I tell them. "You babysit a small baby, a couple months old? Ask if you can stay with that baby for overnight. Stay in their house and let the baby sit in your room, and you'll see how it feels to be a mother in one night." I say, "Think about your life, your future." I say, "Be free and enjoy life as much as you could and don't get no man that can't give you anything." I say, "Because none of these mens out here ain't going to give you anything." I say, "Suppose you get a boyfriend that gets $125 a week, and the rent is $200. How do you expect to support each other with $125 a week? You can't do nothing," I tell them. "You can't." I say, "I could barely make it, me and my child, and I live with my mother, and you're going to go living with somebody else?" They say, "It's true, what you're saying." I say, "I'm not saying that don't have a child. Don't get a boyfriend. But look for your happiness first. What you want in life. What you want to be in life. And try to *be* somebody, and not just fall back. Keep going up ahead." I remind them all the time. I ask them everyday, "Did you go to school?" They tell me, "Yes." I say, "Good. How did you do in school?" And they tell me like, "I did okay." If they're not in school, I ask them why. I tell them, "I don't want to find out that you're out of school, because I'm going to squeal on you. I'm going to call up the school and say you played hooky. I'm only playing, but it's for your own good. It's not for me," I tell them. "It's for you." I say, "Be somebody. That's all. Just be somebody." And I say, "Once you're somebody, you don't have to worry about nothing else. As long as you got a good-paying job, then if you feel like you want to have a child, then you have a child. But go to school and enjoy yourselves. That's all. Don't get hooked up. Enjoy life." I tell them, "Don't let no man beat you. Don't let no man hit on you." I tell them, "He'll make you stay home and be a housewife."

I still mean to make something of myself. I want to be like a social worker or a counselor. I always like to work with young people or kids. Since I was little, I was always babysitting. Now I see the kids I babysat for and they are taller than I am, and I say, "I used to babysit him! I used to change his Pampers!" And that's still what I want to be.

I like my life now. I do what I want. I don't need to do anything for nobody but for my child. I try my best for her. I want a future for myself to show her that she could do it too. I don't want her to have the teenage life I had. I want her to see the world. I want her to go places. I want her to go out and enjoy herself and not to get caught up as young as I did for nobody. I want for her to be free. I don't want her to go through changes. I went through changes my whole teenage life. I can't say I enjoyed my teenage life. Now is when I'm enjoying myself.

Mass Market Romance:
Pornography for Women Is Different
Ann Barr Snitow

I

Last year 109 million romantic novels were sold under an imprint you will not see in the *New York Times* best-seller lists or advertised in its *Book Review*. The publisher is Harlequin Enterprises, Ltd., a Canadian company, and its success, a growth of 400 percent since 1976, is typical of the boom in romantic fiction marketed for women.[1]

At a bookstore or drugstore a Harlequin Romance costs 95¢, but the company does a large percentage of its business through the mail, sending 8 titles a month to 12 million subscribers in North America. Since a Harlequin is almost always 188 pages long (55,000–58,000 words), subscribers could be reading about three hundred and seventy-five pages a week. Reading is more private and more absorbing than television. A book requires stopping the housework, waiting for that lunch or coffee break at the office. "Your passport to a dream," say the television ads for Harlequins, which picture a weary secretary sinking gratefully into solitary reading on her lunch hour.

If one includes the large number of novels published by other companies but essentially keeping to the Harlequin formula—"clean, easy to read love stories about contemporary people, set in exciting foreign places"[2]—the number of books of this specific genre being sold has risen to several hundred million a year. This is a figure in another statistical universe from the sales of books we usually call "best-sellers." This article offers a series of hypotheses about the appeal Harlequin romances have for the women reading them.

II

To analyze Harlequin romances is not to make any literary claims for them. Nevertheless, it would be at best grossly incurious, and at worst sadly limited, for literary critics to ignore a genre that millions and millions of women read voraciously. Though I propose to do a literary

258

analysis of Harlequin romances as a way to get at the nature and power of their appeal, they are not art but rather what Lillian Robinson has called "leisure activities that *take the place* of art."[3] This is to say that they fill a place left empty for most people. How do they fill it, and with what?

After a recent talk I gave about Harlequin romances, a member of the audience asked, "Would a reader of Harlequin romances be insulted by your lecture?" This is a disturbing question because the terms I use here to describe the Harlequin formula and its appeal *are* insulting, but to whom? In describing the sensibility of the Harlequin type of romance, I am not presuming to describe the sensibility of its readers. In matters of popular culture, we are not what we eat.

The old line about commercial popular culture, that it is soma for the masses produced by a cynical elite, has been replaced, and properly so, by a more complex idea of the relation between the consumers and sellers of mass culture: in this newer view, popularity is by definition considered a species of vitality. In other words, consumers are not seen merely as passive repositories, empty vessels into which debilitating ideologies are poured. This recognition of the force of popular forms, of their appeal to the depth structures in all our minds, is an important development in our critical thinking.[4]

Certainly the romantic novels for women I will discuss here reflect a complex relationship between readers and publishers. Who is manipulating whom? Each publisher is the prisoner of past successes, trying to find again the somewhat mysterious combination of elements that made a particular book hit the taste of the street. The way in which people experience mass cultural products in a heterogeneous society is erratic, subject to many forces. Harlequins, for example, are only one strain in the mass paperback market aimed primarily at women readers. There are also Gothics (now rather passé), spectaculars, historical romances, family sagas, fotonovelas, and true confessions.[5] Each one of these has its own species of appeal. Does each also have its own specific audience? The mass audience may be manipulated in some ways and may be controlling the market in others but it is also and always omnivorous, capable of digesting contradictory cultural impulses and at the same time resisting suggestion altogether.

In this essay I try to steer a careful course between critical extremes, neither assuming that romance novels are dope for catatonic secretaries, nor claiming for them a rebellious core of psychological vitality. I observe in these books neither an effective top-down propaganda effort against women's liberation, nor a covert flowering of female sexuality. Instead, I see them as accurate descriptions of certain *selected* elements of female consciousness. These novels are too pallid to shape consciousness but they feed certain regressive elements in the female experience. To observe that they express primal structures in our social relations is not to claim either a cathartic usefulness for them or a dangerous power to keep women in their place.

The books are interesting because they define a set of relations, feelings, and assumptions that do indeed permeate our minds. They are *mass* paperbacks not only because they are easy to read pablum but also because they reflect—sometimes more, sometimes less consciously, sometimes amazingly naively—commonly experienced psychological and social elements in the daily lives of women. That the books are unrealistic, distorted, and flat are all facts beside the point. (I am not concerned here with developing an admiration for their buried poetics.) Their particular sort of unreality points to what elements in social life women are encouraged to ignore; their distortions point to larger distortions culture-wide; their lack of richness merely bares what is hidden in more inclusive, more personally controlled works of art, the particular nature of the satisfactions we are all led to seek by the conditions of our culture.

III

What is the Harlequin romance formula? The novels have no plot in the usual sense. All tension and problems arise from the fact that the Harlequin world is inhabited by two species incapable of communicating with each other, male and female. In this sense these Pollyanna books have their own dream-like truth: our culture produces a pathological experience of sex difference. The sexes have different needs and interests, certainly different experiences. They find each other utterly mystifying.

Since all action in the novels is described from the female point of view, the reader identifies with the heroine's efforts to decode the erratic gestures of "dark, tall and gravely handsome"[6] men, all mysterious strangers or powerful bosses. In a sense the usual relationship is reversed: woman is subject, man, object. There are more descriptions of his body than of hers ("Dark trousers fitted closely to lean hips and long muscular legs . . .") though her clothes are always minutely observed. He is the unknowable other, a sexual icon whose magic is maleness. The books are permeated by phallic worship. Male is good, male is exciting, without further points of reference. Cruelty, callousness, coldness, menace, are all equated with maleness and treated as a necessary part of the package: "It was an arrogant remark, but Sara had long since admitted his arrogance as part of his attraction."[7] She, on the other hand, is the subject, the one whose thoughts the reader knows, whose constant reevaluation of male moods and actions make up the story line.

The heroine is not involved in any overt adventure beyond trying to respond appropriately to male energy without losing her virginity. Virginity is a given here; sex means marriage and marriage, promised at the end, means, finally, there can be sex.

While the heroine waits for the hero's next move, her time is filled by tourism and by descriptions of consumer items: furniture, clothes, and gourmet foods. In *Writers Market* (1977) Harlequin Enterprises stipulates: "Emphasis on travel." (The exception is the occasional hospital novel. Like foreign places, hospitals offer removal from the household, heightened emotional states, and a supply of strangers.) Several of the books have passages that probably come straight out of guide books, but the *particular* setting is not the point, only that it is exotic, a place elsewhere.[8]

More space is filled by the question of what to wear. "She rummaged in her cases, discarding item after item, and eventually brought out a pair of purple cotton jeans and a matching shift. They were not new. She had bought them a couple of years ago. But fortunately her figure had changed little, and apart from a slight shrinkage in the pants which made them rather tighter than she would have liked, they looked serviceable."[9] Several things are going on here: the effort to find the right clothes for the occasion, the problem of staying thin, the problem of piecing together outfits from things that are not new. Finally, there is that shrinkage, a signal to the experienced Harlequin reader that the heroine, innocent as her intent may be in putting on jeans that are a little too tight, is wearing something revealing and will certainly be seen and noted by the hero in this vulnerable, passive act of self-exposure. (More about the pornographic aspects later. In any other titillating novel one would suspect a pun when tight pants are "serviceable" but in the context of the absolutely flat Harlequin style one might well be wrong. More, too, about this style later on.)

Though clothes are the number one filler in Harlequins, food and furniture are also important and usually described in the language of women's magazines:[10] croissants are served hot and crispy and are "crusty brown,"[11] while snapper is "filleted, crumbed and fried in butter" and tomato soup is "topped with grated cheese and parsley"[12] (this last a useful, practical suggestion anyone could try).

Harlequins revitalize daily routines by insisting that a woman combing her hair, a woman reaching up to put a plate on a high shelf (so that her knees show beneath the hem, if only there were a viewer), a woman doing what women do all day, is in a constant state of potential sexuality. You never can tell when you may be seen and being seen is a precious opportunity. Harlequin romances alternate between scenes of the hero and heroine together in which she does a lot of social lying to save face, pretending to be unaffected by the hero's presence while her body melts or shivers, and scenes in which the heroine is essentially alone, living in a cloud of absorption, preparing mentally and physically for the next contact.

The heroine is alone. Sometimes there is another woman, a competitor who is often more overtly aware of her sexuality than the heroine, but she is a shadow on the horizon. Sometimes there are potentially friendly females living in the next bungalow or working with the patient in the next bed, but they, too, are shadowy, not important to the real story, which consists entirely of an emotionally isolated woman trying to keep her virginity and her head when the only person she ever really talks to is the hero, whose motives and feelings are unclear: "She saw his words as a warning and would have liked to know whether he meant [them] to be."[13]

The heroine gets her man at the end, first, because she is an old-fashioned girl (this is a code for no premarital sex) and, second, because the hero gets ample opportunity to see her perform well in a number of female helping roles. In the course of a Harlequin romance, most heroines demonstrate passionate motherliness, good cooking, patience in adversity, efficient planning, and a good clothes sense, though these are skills and emotional capacities produced in emergencies, and are not, as in real life, a part of an invisible, glamorless work routine.

Though the heroines are pliable (they are rarely given particularized character traits; they are all Everywoman and can fit in comfortably with the life-style of the strong-willed heroes be they doctors, lawyers, or marine biologists doing experiments on tropical islands), it is still amazing that these novels end in marriage. After one hundred and fifty pages of mystification, unreadable looks, "hints of cruelty"[14] and wordless coldness, the thirty-page denouement is powerless to dispell the earlier impression of menace. Why should this heroine marry this man? And, one can ask with equal reason, why should this hero marry this woman? These endings do not ring true, but no doubt this is precisely their strength. A taste for psychological or social realism is unlikely to provide a Harlequin reader with a sustaining fantasy of rescue, of glamour, or of change. The Harlequin ending offers the impossible. It is pleasing to think that appearances are deceptive, that male coldness, absence, boredom, are not what they seem. The hero *seems* to be a horrible roué; he *seems* to be a hopeless, moody cripple; he *seems* to be cruel and unkind; or he *seems* to be indifferent to the heroine and interested only in his work; but always, at the end a rational explanation of all this appears. In spite of his coldness or preoccupation, the hero really loves the heroine and wants to marry her.

In fact, the Harlequin formula glorifies the distance between the sexes. Distance becomes titillating. The heroine's sexual inexperience adds to this excitement. What is this thing that awaits her on the other side of distance and mystery? Not knowing may be more sexy than finding out. Or perhaps the heroes are really fathers—obscure, forbidden objects of desire. Whatever they are, it is more exciting to wonder about them than to know them. In romanticized sexuality the pleasure lies in the distance itself. Waiting, anticipation, anxiety—these represent the high point of sexual experience.

Perhaps there is pleasure, too, in returning again and again to that breathless, ambivalent, nervous state *before* certainty or satiety. Insofar as women's great adventure, the one they are socially sanctioned to seek, is romance, adventurousness takes women always back to the first phase in love. Unlike work, which holds out the possible pleasures of development, of the exercise of faculties, sometimes even of advancement, the Harlequin form of romance depends on the heroine's being in a state of passivity, of not knowing. Once the heroine knows the hero loves her, the story is over. Nothing interesting remains. Harlequin statements in *Writers Market* stress "upbeat ending essential here" (1977). Here at least is a reliable product that reproduces for women the most interesting phase in the love/marriage cycle and knows just when to stop.

IV

What is the world view implied by the Harlequin romance formula? What are its implicit values? The novels present no overt moral superstructure. Female virginity is certainly an ideal, but an ideal without a history, without parental figures to support it or religious convictions to give it a context. Nor can one say money is a value; rather it is a given, rarely mentioned. Travel and work, though glamorous, are not really goals for the heroine either. They are holding patterns while she awaits love.

Of course, the highest good is the couple. All outside events are subordinated to the psychodrama of its formation. But the heroine must struggle to form the couple without appearing to do so. Her most marketable virtue is her blandness. And she is always proud when she manages to keep a calm façade. She lies constantly to hide her desires, to protect her reputation. She tries to cover up all signs of sexual feeling, upset, any extreme of emotion. She values being an ordinary woman and acting like one. (Indeed, for women, being ordinary and being attractive are equated in these novels. Heroes are of course expected to have a little more dash and sometimes sport scars.) Finally, the heroine's value system includes the given that men are all right, that they will turn into husbands, despite appearances to the contrary.

The world of Harlequin novels has no past. (At most, occasionally the plot requires a flashback.) Old people hardly appear except as benevolent peripheral presences. Young women have no visible parents, no ties to a before. Everyone is young though the hero is always quite a bit older than the heroine. Is this why there are no parents, because the lover is really *in loco parentis?*

Harlequins make no reference to a specific ethnic group or religion. (In this they differ from a new popular mass form, the family saga, which is dense with ethnic detail, national identity, *roots.*) Harlequins are aggressively secular: Christmas is always the tinsel not the religious Christmas. One might expect to find romance linked, if only sentimentally, to nature, to universal categories, to first and last things. Harlequins assiduously avoid this particular shortcut to emotion (while of course exploiting others). They reduce awe of the unknown to a speculation on the intentions of the cold, mean stranger and generally strip romance of its spiritual, transcendent aspect.

At the other extreme from the transcendent, Harlequins also avoid all mention of local peculiarities beyond the merely scenic. They reduce the allure of difference, of travel, to a mere travelogue. The couple is alone. There is no society, no context, only surroundings. Is this what the nuclear family feels like to many women? Or is this, once again, a fantasy of safety and seclusion, while in actuality the family is being invaded continually and is under pressures it cannot control?

The denatured quality of Harlequins is convenient for building an audience: anyone can identify. Or, rather, anyone can identify with the fantasy that places all the characters in an upper-class, polite environment familiar not in experience but in the ladies' magazines and on television. The realities of class—workers in dull jobs, poverty, real productive relations, social divisions of labor—are all, of course, entirely foreign to the world of the Harlequin. There are servants in the novels lest the heroine, like the reader, be left to do all the housework, but they are always loyal and glad to help. Heroines have familiar service jobs—they are teachers, nurses, nursery-maids—but the formula finds a way around depicting the limitations of these jobs. The heroine can do the work ordinary women do while still seeming glamorous to the reader either because of *where* the heroine does her work or how she is rescued from doing it.

All fiction is a closed system in many respects, its language mainlining into areas of our conscious and subconscious selves by routes that by-pass many of the things we know or believe about the real world of our daily experience. This by-passing is a form of pleasure, one of art's pleasing tricks. As Fred Kerner, Harlequin's director of publishing, said when describing the formula to prospective authors in *The Writer:* "The fantasy must have the same appeal that all of us discovered when we were first exposed to fairy tales as children."[15] I do not wish to imply that I would like to remove a Harlequin romance from the hands of its readers to replace it with an improving novel that includes a realistically written catalogue of woman's griefs under capitalism and in the family. My purpose here is diagnostic. A description of the pared-down Harlequin formula raises the question: What is it about this *particular* formula that makes it so suggestive, so popular, with such a large female readership, all living under capitalism, most living—or yearning to live—in some form of the family?

Harlequins fill a vacuum created by social conditions. When women try to picture excitement, the society offers them one vision, romance. When women try to imagine companionship, the society offers them one vision, male, sexual companionship. When women try to fantasize about success, mastery, the society offers them one vision, the power to attract a man. When women try to fantasize about sex, the society offers them taboos on most of its imaginable expressions except those that deal directly with arousing and satisfying men. When women try to project a unique self, the society offers them very few attractive images. True completion for women is nearly always presented as social, domestic, sexual.

One of our culture's most intense myths, the ideal of an individual who is brave and complete in isolation, is for men only. Women are grounded, enmeshed in civilization, in social connection, in family, and in love (a condition a feminist culture might well define as desirable) while all our culture's rich myths of individualism are essentially closed to them. Their one socially acceptable moment of transcendence is romance. This involves a constant return in imagination to those short moments in the female life cycle, courtship. With the exception of the occasional gourmet meal, which the heroine is often too nervous to eat, all other potential sources of pleasure are rigidly excluded from Harlequin romances. They reinforce the prevailing cultural code: pleasure for women is men. The ideal of romance presented in these books is a hungry monster that has gobbled up and digested all sorts of human pleasures.

There is another way in which Harlequin romances gloss over and obscure complex social relations: they are a static representation of a quickly changing situation—women's role in late capitalism. They offer a comfortably fixed image of the exchange between men and women at the very moment when the social actuality is confusing, shifting, frightening. The average American marriage now lasts about five years. A rape takes place every twelve minutes. While the social ferment of the sixties gave rise to the Gothic form in cheap fiction—family dramas that were claustrophic and anti-erotic compensations for an explosion of mobility and sexuality—in the seventies we have the blander Harlequins, novels that are picaresque and titillating, written for people who have so entirely suffered and absorbed the disappearance of the ideal of home that they don't want to hear about it any more. They want instead to read about premarital hopefulness.

Harlequin romances make bridges between contradictions; they soothe ambivalence. A brutal male sexuality is magically converted to romance; the war between men and women who cannot communicate ends in truce. Stereotyped female roles are charged with an unlikely glamour, and women's daily routines are revitalized by the pretense that they hide an ongoing sexual drama.

In a fine piece about modern Gothic romances, Joanna Russ points out that in these novels, "'Occupation: Housewife' is simultaneously avoided, glamorized, and vindicated."[16] Female skills are exalted: it is good to nurture, good to observe every change in expression of the people around you, important to worry about how you look. As Russ says, the feminine mystique is defended and women are promised all sorts of psychological rewards for remaining loyal to it. Though in other respects, Gothics are very different from Harlequins, they are the same in this: both pretend that nothing has happened to unsettle the old, conventional bargain between the sexes. Small surface concessions are made to a new female independence (several researchers, misreading I believe, claim that the new heroines are brave and more interested in jobs than families[17]) but the novels mention the new female feistiness only to finally reassure readers that *plus ça change, plus c'est la même chose*. Independence is always presented as a mere counter in the sexual game, like a hairdo or any other flirtatious gesture; sexual feeling utterly defeats its early stirrings.

In fact, in Harlequin romances, sexual feeling is probably the main point. Like sex itself, the novels are set in an eternal present in which the actual present, a time of disturbing disruptions between the sexes, is dissolved and only a comfortably timeless, universal battle remains. The hero wants sex; the heroine wants it, too, but can only enjoy it after the love promise has finally been made and the ring is on her finger.

V

Are Harlequin romances pornography?

She had never felt so helpless or so completely at the mercy of another human being . . . a being who could snap the slender column of her body with one squeeze of a steel-clad arm.

No trace of tenderness softened the harsh pressure of his mouth on hers . . . there was only a savagely punishing intentness of purpose that cut off her breath until her senses reeled and her body sagged against the granite hardness of his. He released her wrists, seeming to know that they would hang helplessly at her sides, and his hand moved to the small of her back to exert a pressure that crushed her soft outlines to the unyielding dominance of his and left her in no doubt as to the force of his masculinity.[18]

In an unpublished talk,[19] critic Peter Parisi has hypothesized that Harlequin romances are essentially pornography for people ashamed to read pornography. In his view, sex is these novels' real *raison d'être*, while the romance and the promised marriage are primarily salves to the conscience of readers brought up to believe that sex without love and marriage is wrong. Like me, Parisi sees the books as having some active allure. They are not just escape; they also offer release, as he sees it, specifically sexual release.

This is part of the reason why Harlequins, so utterly denatured in most respects, can powerfully command such a large audience. I want to elaborate here on Parisi's definition of *how* the books are pornography and, finally, to modify his definition of what women are looking for in a sex book.

Parisi sees Harlequins as a sort of poor woman's D. H. Lawrence. The body of the heroine is alive and singing in every fiber; she is overrun by a sexuality that wells up inside her and that she cannot control. ("The warmth of his body close to hers was like a charge of electricity, a stunning masculine assault on her senses that she was powerless to do anything about."[20]) The issue of control arises because, in Parisi's view, the reader's qualms are allayed when the novels invoke morals, then affirm a force, sexual feeling, strong enough to override those morals. He argues further that morals in a Harlequin are secular; what the heroine risks is a loss of social face, of reputation. The books uphold the values of their readers, who share this fear of breaking social codes, but behind these reassuringly familiar restraints they celebrate a wild, eager sexuality that flourishes and is finally affirmed in "marriage," which Parisi sees as mainly a code word for "fuck."

Parisi is right: *every* contact in a Harlequin romance is sexualized:

> Sara feared he was going to refuse the invitation and simply walk off. It seemed like an eternity before he inclined his head in a brief, abrupt acknowledgement of acceptance, then drew out her chair for her, his hard fingers brushing her arm for a second, and bringing an urgent flutter of reaction from her pulse.[21]

Those "hard fingers" are the penis; a glance is penetration; a voice can slide along the heroine's spine "like a sliver of ice." The heroine keeps struggling for control but is constantly swept away on a tide of feeling. Always, though, some intruder or some "nagging reminder" of the need to maintain appearances stops her. "His mouth parted her lips with bruising urgency and for a few delirious moments she yielded to her own wanton instincts." But the heroine insists on seeing these moments as out of character: She "had never thought herself capable of wantonness, but in Carlo's arms she seemed to have no inhibitions."[22] Parisi argues that the books' sexual formula allows both heroine and reader to feel wanton again and again while maintaining their sense of themselves as not that sort of women,

I agree with Parisi that the sexually charged atmosphere that bathes the Harlequin heroine is essentially pornographic (I use the word pornographic as neutrally as possible here, not as an automatic pejorative). But do Harlequins actually contain an affirmation of female sexuality? The heroine's condition of passive receptivity to male ego and male sexuality is exciting to readers, but this is not necessarily a free or deep expression of the female potential for sexual feeling. Parisi says the heroine is always trying to humanize the contact between herself and the apparently under-socialized hero, "trying to convert rape into love making." If this is so, then she is engaged on a social as well as a sexual odyssey. Indeed, in women, these two are often joined. Is the project of humanizing and domesticating male sexual feeling an erotic one? What is it about this situation that arouses the excitement of the anxiously vigilant heroine and of the readers who identify with her?

In the misogynistic culture in which we live, where violence toward women is a common motif, it is hard to say a neutral word about pornography either as a legitimate literary form or as a legitimate source of pleasure. Women are naturally overwhelmed by the woman-hating theme so that the more universal human expression sometimes contained by pornography tends to be obscured for them.

In recent debates, sex books that emphasize both male and female sexual feeling as a sensuality that can exist without violence are being called "erotica" to distinguish them from "pornography."[23] This distinction blurs more than it clarifies the complex mixture of elements that make up sexuality. Erotica is soft core, soft focus; it is gentler and tenderer sex than that depicted in pornography. Does this mean true sexuality is diffuse while only perverse sexuality is driven, power hungry, intense, and selfish? I cannot accept this particular dichotomy. It leaves out too much of what is infantile in sex—the reenactment of early feelings, the boundlessness and omnipotence of infant desire and its furious gusto. In pornography all things tend in one direction, a total immersion in one's own sense experience, for which one paradigm must certainly be infancy. For adults this totality, the total sexualization of everything, can only be a fantasy. But does the fact that it cannot be actually lived mean this fantasy must be discarded? It is a memory, a legitimate element in the human lexicon of feelings.

In pornography, the joys of passivity, of helpless abandon, of response without responsibility are all endlessly repeated, savored, minutely described. Again this is a fantasy often dismissed with the pejorative "masochistic" as if passivity were in no way a pleasant or a natural condition.

Yet another criticism of pornography is that it presents no recognizable, delineated characters. In a culture where women are routinely objectified it is natural and progressive to see as threatening any literary form that calls dehumanization sexual. Once again, however, there is another way to analyze this aspect of pornography. Like a lot of far more respectable twentieth-century art, pornography is not about personality but about the explosion of the boundaries of the self. It is a fantasy of an extreme state in which all social constraints are overwhelmed by a flood of sexual energy. Think, for example, of all the pornography about servants fucking mistresses, old men fucking young girls, guardians fucking wards. Class, age, custom—all are deliciously sacrificed, dissolved by sex.

Though pornography's critics are right—pornography *is* exploitation—it is exploitation of *everything*. Promiscuity by definition is a breakdown of barriers. Pornography is not only a reflector of social power imbalances and sexual pathologies; it is also all those imbalances run riot, run to excess, sometimes explored *ad absurdum*, exploded. Misogyny is one content of pornography; another content is the universal infant desire for complete, immediate gratification, to rule the world out of the very core of passive helplessness.

In a less sexist society, there might be a pornography that is exciting, expressive, interesting, even, perhaps, significant as a form of social rebellion, all traits that, in a sexist society, are obscured by pornography's present role as escape valve for hostility toward women, or as metaphor for fiercely guarded power hierarchies. Instead, in a sexist society, we have two pornographies, one for men, one for women. They both have, hiding within them, those basic human expressions of abandon I have described. The pornography for men enacts this abandon on women as objects. How different is the pornography for women, in which sex is bathed in romance, diffused, always implied rather than enacted at all. This pornography is the Harlequin romance.

I described above the oddly narrowed down, denatured world presented in Harlequins. Looking at them as pornography obviously offers a number of alternative explanations for these same traits: the heroine's passivity becomes sexual receptivity and, though I complained earlier about her vapidity, in pornography no one need have a personality. Joanna Russ observed about the heroines of Gothic romances something true of Harlequin heroines as well: they are loved as babies are loved, simply because they exist.[24] They have no particular qualities, but pornography by-passes this limitation and reaches straight down to the infant layer where we all imagine ourselves the center of everything by birthright and are sexual beings without shame or need for excuse.

Seeing Harlequins as pornography modifies one's criticism of their selectivity, their know-nothing narrowness. Insofar as they are essentially pornographic in intent, their characters have no past, no context; they live only in the eternal present of sexual feeling, the absorbing interest in the erotic sex object. Insofar as the books are written to elicit sexual excitation, they can be completely closed, repetitive circuits always returning to the moment of arousal when the hero's voice sends "a velvet finger"[25] along the spine of the heroine. In pornography, sex is the whole content; there need be no serious other.

Read this way, Harlequins are benign if banal sex books, but sex books for women have several special characteristics not included in the usual definitions of the genre pornography. In fact, a suggestive, sexual atmosphere is not so easy to establish for women as it is for men. A number of conditions must be right.

In *The Mermaid and the Minotaur*, an extraordinary study of the asymmetry of male and female relationships in all societies where children are primarily raised by women, Dorothy Dinnerstein discusses the reasons why women are so much more dependent than men on deep personal feeling as an ingredient, sometimes a precondition, for sex. Beyond the obvious reasons, the seriousness of sex for the partner who can get pregnant, the seriousness of sex for the partner who is economically and socially dependent on her lover, Dinnerstein adds another, psychological reason for women's tendency to emotionalize sex. She argues that the double standard (male sexual freedom, female loyalty to one sexual tie) comes from the asymmetry in the way the sexes are raised from infancy. Her argument is too complex to be entirely recapitulated here but her conclusion seems crucial to our understanding of the mixture of sexual excitement and anti-erotic restraint that characterizes sexual feeling in Harlequin romances:

> Anatomically, coitus offers a far less reliable guarantee of orgasm—or indeed of any intense direct local genital pleasure—to woman than to man. The first-hand coital pleasure of which she is capable more often requires conditions that must be purposefully sought out. Yet it is woman who has less liberty to conduct this kind of search . . . societal and psychological constraints . . . leave her less free than man to explore the erotic resources of a variety of partners, or even to affirm erotic impulse with any one partner. These constraints also make her less able to give way to simple physical delight without a sense of total self-surrender—a disability that further narrows her choice of partners, and makes her still more afraid of disrupting her rapport with any one partner by

acting to intensify the delight, that is, by asserting her own sexual wishes. . . .

What the double standard hurts in women (to the extent that they genuinely, inwardly, bow to it) is the animal center of self-respect: the brute sense of bodily prerogative, of having a right to one's bodily feelings. . . . Fromm made this point very clearly when he argued, in *Man for Himself,* that socially imposed shame about the body serves the function of keeping people submissive to societal authority by weakening in them some inner core of individual authority. . . . On the whole . . . the female burden of genital deprivation is carried meekly, invisibly. Sometimes it cripples real interest in sexual interaction, but often it does not: indeed, it can deepen a woman's need for the emotional rewards of carnal contact. What it most reliably cripples is human pride.[26]

This passage gives us the theoretical skeleton on which the titillations of the Harlequin formula are built. In fact, the Harlequin heroine cannot afford to be only a mass of responsive nerve endings. In order for her sexuality, and the sexuality of the novels' readers, to be released, a number of things must happen that have little to do directly with sex at all. Since she cannot seek out or instruct the man she wants, she must be in a state of constant passive readiness. Since only one man will do, she has the anxiety of deciding, "Is this *the* one?" Since an enormous amount of psychic energy is going to be mobilized in the direction of the man she loves, the man she sleeps with, she must feel sure of him. A one-night stand won't work; she is only just beginning to get her emotional generators going when he is already gone. And orgasm? It probably hasn't happened. She couldn't tell him she wanted it and couldn't tell him *how* she wanted it. If he is already gone, there is no way for her erotic feeling for him to take form, no way for her training of him as a satisfying lover to take place.

Hence the Harlequin herione has a lot of things to worry about if she wants sexual satisfaction. Parisi has said that these worries are restraints there merely to be deliciously overridden, but they are so constant an accompaniment to the heroine's erotic feelings as to be, under present conditions, inseparable from them. She feels an urge toward deep emotion; she feels anxiety about the serious intentions of the hero; she role-plays constantly, presenting herself as a nurturant, passive, receptive figure; and all of this is part of sex to her. Certain social configurations feel safe and right and are real sexual cues for women. The romantic intensity of Harlequins—the waiting, fearing, speculating—are as much a part of their functioning as pornography for women as are the more overtly sexual scenes.

Nor is this just a neutral difference between men and women. In fact, as Dinnerstein suggests, the muting of spontaneous sexual feeling, the necessity that is socially forced on women of channeling their sexual desire, is in fact a great deprivation. In *The Mermaid and the Minotaur* Dinnerstein argues that men have a number of reasons, social and psychological, for discomfort when confronted by the romantic feeling and the demand for security that so often accompany female sexuality. For them growing up and being male both mean cutting off the passionate attachment and dependence on woman, on mother. Women, potential mother figures themselves, have less need to make this absolute break. Men also need to pull away from that inferior category, Woman. Women are stuck in it and naturally romanticize the powerful creatures they can only come close to through emotional and physical ties.

The Harlequin formula perfectly reproduces these differences, these tensions, between the sexes. It depicts a heroine struggling, against the hero's resistance, to get the right combination of elements together so that, for her, orgasmic sex can at last take place. The shape of the Harlequin sexual fantasy is designed to deal women the winning hand they cannot hold in life: a man who is romantically interesting—hence, distant, even frightening—while at the same time he is willing to capitulate to her needs just enough so that she can sleep with him not once but often. His intractability is exciting to her, a proof of his membership in a superior class of beings but, finally, he must relent to some extent if her breathless anticipation, the foreplay of romance, is to lead to orgasm.

Clearly, getting romantic tension, domestic security, and sexual excitement together in the same fantasy in the right proportions is a delicate balancing act. Harlequins lack excellence by any other measure, but they are masterly in this one respect. In fact, the Harlequin heroine is in a constant fever of anti-erotic anxiety, trying to control the flow of sexual passion between herself and the hero until her surrender can be on her own terms. If the heroine's task is "converting rape into love making," she must somehow teach the hero to take time, to pay attention, to feel, while herself remaining passive, undemanding, unthreatening. This is yet another delicate miracle of balance that Harlequin romances manage quite well. How do they do it?

The underlying structure of the sexual story goes something like this:

1. The man is hard (a walking phallus).
2. The woman likes this hardness.
3. But, at the outset, this hardness is *too hard*. The man has an ideology that is anti-romantic, anti-marriage. In other words, he will not stay around long enough for her to come, too.
4. Her final release of sexual feeling depends on his changing his mind, but *not too much*. He must become softer (safer, less likely

to leave altogether) but not too soft. For good sex, he must be hard, but this hardness must be *at the service of the woman*.

The following passage from Anne Mather's *Born Out of Love* is an example:

> His skin was smooth, more roughly textured than hers, but sleek and flexible beneath her palms, his warmth and maleness enveloping her and making her overwhelmingly aware that only the thin material of the culotte suit separated them. He held her face between his hands, and his hardening mouth was echoed throughout the length and breadth of his body. She felt herself yielding weakly beneath him, and his hand slid from her shoulder, across her throat to find the zipper at the front of her suit, impelling it steadily downward.
>
> "No, Logan," she breathed, but he pulled the hands with which she might have resisted him around him, arching her body so that he could observe her reaction to the thrusting aggression of his with sensual satisfaction.
>
> "No?" he probed with gentle mockery, his mouth seeking the pointed fullness of her breasts now exposed to his gaze. "Why not? It's what we both want, don't deny it.". . .
>
> Somehow Charlotte struggled up from the depth of a sexually-induced lethargy. It wasn't easy, when her whole body threatened to betray her, but his words were too similar to the words he had used to her once before, and she remembered only too well what had happened next. . . .
>
> She sat up quickly, her fingers fumbling with the zipper, conscious all the while of Logan lying beside her, and the potent attraction of his lean body. God, she thought unsteadily, what am I doing here? And then, more wildly: Why am I leaving him? *I want him!* But not on his terms, the still small voice of sanity reminded her, and she struggled to her feet.[27]

In these romantic love stories, sex on a woman's terms is romanticized sex. Romantic sexual fantasies are contradictory. They include both the desire to be blindly ravished, to melt, and the desire to be spiritually adored, saved from the humiliation of dependence and sexual passivity through the agency of a protective male who will somehow make reparation to the woman he loves for her powerlessness.

Harlequins reveal and pander to this impossible fantasy life. Female sexuality, a rare subject in all but the most recent writing, is not doomed to be what the Harlequins describe. Nevertheless, some of the barriers that hold back female sexual feeling are acknowledged and finally circumvented quite sympathetically in these novels. They are sex books for people who have plenty of good reasons for worrying about sex.

While there is something wonderful in the heroine's insistence that sex is more exciting and more momentous when it includes deep feeling, she is fighting a losing battle as long as she can define deep feeling only as a mystified romantic longing on the one hand, and as marriage on the other. In Harlequins the price for needing emotional intimacy is that she must passively wait, must anxiously calculate. Without spontaneity and aggression, a whole set of sexual possibilities is lost to her just as, without emotional depth, a whole set of sexual possibilities is lost to men.

Though one may dislike the circuitous form of sexual expression in Harlequin heroines, a strength of the books is that they insist that good sex for women requires an emotional and social context that can free them from constraint. If one dislikes the kind of social norms the heroine seeks as her sexual preconditions, it is still interesting to see sex treated not primarily as a physical event at all but as a social drama, as a carefully modulated set of psychological possibilities between people. This is a mirror image of much writing more commonly labeled pornography. In fact one cannot resist speculating that equality between the sexes as child rearers and workers might well bring personal feeling and abandoned physicality together in wonderful combinations undreamed of in either male or female pornography as we know it.

The ubiquity of the books indicates a central truth: romance is a primary category of the female imagination. The women's movement has left this fact of female consciousness largely untouched. While most serious women *novelists* treat romance with irony and cynicism, most women do not. Harlequins may well be closer to describing women's hopes for love than the work of fine women novelists. Harlequins eschew irony; they take love straight. Harlequins eschew realism; they are serious about fantasy and escape. In spite of all the audience manipulations inherent in the Harlequin formula, the connection between writer and reader is tonally seamless; Harlequins are respectful, tactful, friendly toward their audience. The letters that pour in to their publishers speak above all of involvement, warmth, human values. The world that can make Harlequin romances appear warm is indeed a cold, cold place.

Notes

This piece first appeared in *Radical History Review* 20 (Spring/Summer 1979).

1. Harlequin is 50 percent owned by the conglomerate controlling the *Toronto Star*. If you add to the Harlequin sales figures (variously reported from between 60 million to 109 million for 1978) the figures for similar novels by Barbara Cartland and those contemporary romances published by Popular Library, Fawcett, Ballantine, Avon, Pinnacle, Dell, Jove, Bantam, Pocket Books, and Warner, it is clear that hundreds of thousands of women are reading books of the Harlequin type.

2. Blurb in Harlequin Romance. Elizabeth Graham, *Mason's Ridge* (Toronto: Harlequin Books, 1978), and others. (Quotation cited from *Best Sellers*.)

3. Lillian S. Robinson, *Sex, Class, and Culture* (Bloomington: Indiana University Press, 1978), p. 77.

4. In her article "Integrating Marxist and Psychoanalytic Approaches to Feminist Film Criticism" (*Jump Cut*, Fall 1979), Ann Kaplan gives a useful survey of this shift in Left critical thinking about mass culture. See also Robinson, *Sex, Class, and Culture*, and Stuart Ewen, *Captains of Consciousness* (New York: McGraw-Hill, 1976.)

5. Kate Ellis has explored the nature and history of Gothic romances: "Paradise Lost: The Limits of Domesticity in the Nineteenth-Century Novel," *Feminist Studies* 2, no. 2/3 (1975): 55–63; "Charlotte Smith's Subversive Gothic," *Feminist Studies* 3, no. 3/4 (Spring-Summer 1976): 51–55; and "Feminism, Fantasy, and Women's Popular Fiction," forthcoming. In "Women Read Romances that Fit Changing Times," *In These Times,* 7–13 February 1979, she gives a more general survey of the different kinds of mass market paperbacks available to women, each with its own particular appeal.

6. Rachel Lindsay, *Prescription for Love* (Toronto: Harlequin Books, 1977), p. 10.

7. Rebecca Stratton, *The Sign of the Ram* (Toronto: Harlequin Books, 1977), pp. 56, 147.

8. Here is an example of this sort of travelogue prose: "There was something to appeal to all age groups in the thousand-acre park in the heart of the city—golf for the energetic, lawn bowling for the more sedate, a zoo for the children's pleasure, and even secluded walks through giant cedars for lovers—but Cori thought of none of these things as Greg drove to a parking place bordering the Inlet." Graham, *Mason's Ridge,* p. 25.

9. Anne Mather, *Born Out of Love* (Toronto: Harlequin Books, 1977), p. 42

10. See Joanna Russ, "Somebody's Trying to Kill Me and I Think It's My Husband: The Modern Gothic," *Journal of Popular Culture* 6, no. 4 (Spring 1973) 1: 666–91.

11. Mather, *Born Out of Love,* p. 42.

12. Daphne Clair, *A Streak of Gold* (Toronto: Harlequin Books, 1978), p. 118.

13. Lindsay, *Prescription for Love,* p. 13.

14. Stratton, *The Sign of the Ram,* p. 66. The adjectives "cruel" and "satanic" are commonly used for heroes.

15. May 1977, p. 18.

16. Russ, "Somebody's Trying to Kill Me," p. 675.

17. See for example, Josephine A. Ruggiero and Louise C. Weston, "Sex Role Characterizations of Women in Modern Gothic Novels," *Pacific Sociological Review* 20, no. 2 (April 1977): 279–300.

18. Graham, *Mason's Ridge,* p. 63.

19. Delivered April 6, 1978, Livingston College, Rutgers University.

20. Stratton, *The Sign of the Ram,* p. 132.

21. Ibid., p. 112.

22. Ibid., pp. 99, 102, and 139.

23. Gloria Steinem, "Erotica and Pornography: A Clear and Present Difference," *MS.* (November 1978), and other articles in this issue. An unpublished piece by Brigitte Frase, "From Pornography to Mind-Blowing" (MLA talk, 1978), strongly presents my own view that this debate is specious. See also Susan Sontag's "The Pornographic Imagination," in *Styles of Radical Will* (New York: Delta, 1978), and the Jean Paulhan preface to *Story of O*, "Happiness in Slavery" (New York: Grove Press, 1965).

24. Russ, "Somebody's Trying to Kill Me," p. 679.

25. Stratton, *The Sign of the Ram,* p. 115.

26. Dorothy Dinnerstein, *The Mermaid and the Minotaur: Sexual Arrangements and Human Malaise* (New York: Harper and Row, 1976), pp. 73–75.

27. Mather, *Born Out of Love,* pp. 70–72.

Issues and Answers
Myra Goldberg

After the Grubers have left the party, the balding man waves his cigar and opens the discussion.

"Why does Alice stay with Richard?" he says.

"She could do better," says the woman across the table.

Everyone agrees that Alice could do better.

Alice is limited, but likable, the hostess observes.

"Alice is no idiot," says the host. "Richard read her master's thesis last week. He says she writes well."

"My husband is attached to Richard," says the hostess.

The host denies his attachment to Richard. He and Richard went to graduate school together. Now Richard appears on educational television shows. He represents libertarian socialism to the public.

The balding man leans over to me and whispers that the host wants his views taken into account when Richard pontificates.

Everyone hears the whisper. Everyone turns to me. I'm new to the group. I'm cautious. I review the evening with the issue in mind: (why does Alice stay with Richard?):

Dinner began with the hostess's announcement that we could sit wherever we pleased. Alice sat beside me. Richard started for the chair beside Alice, but it was taken, so he reached out and tapped the chair on my right, then sat down and looked back over at Alice. He frowned. He shrugged. He opened his hands and trapped a space between them. He peered into the space.

I offered to exchange places with him.

Alice shook her head. "It's good for him."

Three chairs were adjusted, so we wouldn't touch, beneath the table. Three plates of cold noodles and sesame paste were set before us. Alice and I praised the hostess for the noodles. Richard poked his fork among the coils.

"Richard, you ate them on Ninety-sixth Street, at that restaurant," said Alice. "You loved them."

Richard reexamined the noodles. "These are different," he said. Then he turned to me.

I inquired about his presence at this gathering, what the connection was. The connection, he said brightening, was the host, an old friend from graduate school, they put out *PARTICIPANTS* together, a theoretical organ, I must have seen it.

I'd never seen it.

The balding man on Richard's right captured his attention by having seen it.

I turned to Alice.

Short, plump Alice with the gray streak in her hair. Alice was pleased to meet me, really pleased, even the corners of her eyes were pleased, even her pocketbook was pleased, she opened it, to take my phone number, and I expected a gift, a key chain or a miniature book of verse, merely for being so interesting to Alice.

Alice inquired about my summer vacation.

I told her about my bungalow in the Adirondacks. A screened-in sleeping porch. A washing machine with a wringer outside. A real clothesline strung between two pine trees for towels and bathing suits. A pile of women's magazines for when it rains. It rains a lot.

"We were thinking of going to Italy next year," said Alice. "But maybe something in the Adirondacks would be cheaper."

"I don't go there because it's cheaper," I said.

"Of course not," said Alice. "How stupid of me."

I shook my head.

The hostess took the noodle plates away. Set the shrimp out. I overheard Richard telling the balding man that 40 percent of Richard's students shouldn't be in college. "They're wasting their time," he said. "They don't read. They're completely nonverbal."

Alice began wondering if Richard would like it in the Adirondacks. "He needs people around," she said.

"There are people in the Adirondacks," I said.

Alice looked thoughtful. I became fearful that she'd tap Richard on the shoulder and ask him to consider my description of the women's magazines, the rain, the wringer. "There's no reason for Richard to like it," I said. "It touches me. That's all."

Alice nodded.

Richard told the balding man that his students (the 40 percent) would be better off working.

The balding man began listing all the job possibilities for nonverbal people. "Taxi driver. All-purpose kitchen utensil demonstrator in front of Woolworths."

"Just give me one minute of your time, ladies and gentlemen," I said, leaning over, "Sixty seconds . . ."

"And I will demonstrate to each and every one of you," said the man.

"An extraordinary machine. It chops. It mops. It shops. It picks your socks up off the floor."

Alice smiled. Then she covered up her mouth with her hand.

Richard leaned over to her.

"Alice," he said. "Are you really going to eat all those shrimp?"

Alice looked down at her shrimp.

Black beans clung to pink-and-white flesh on the right side of her plate. I looked away and caught a glimpse of the balding man looking puzzled. Then we both watched Alice pass her plate to Richard, who picked the shrimp off with his fork, one at a time, and handed the plate back to Alice.

I began to eat my own shrimp in a rush, for fear that Richard would ask for them, or Alice, for Richard's sake.

"Richard loves shrimp," said Alice.

"So do I."

Chocolate mousse arrived. The balding man grinned and lifted the mousse cup, examined it from angles. "Pretty," he said, holding the cup out to Alice. "For you."

"Oh, no, I couldn't," she said flushing.

"I could," I said, too softly for the man to hear me.

The balding man ate his own mousse, slowly, considering each mouthful.

Coffee was served. Cream and sugar passed around. Richard delivered some observations on the rising cost of raw materials. Quoted himself on the question of underdevelopment. "It's a state of mind," he said.

"Rickets is not a state of mind," said the woman across the table, who'd just had a baby.

Richard stared at her.

"What she means—" said Alice.

"I know what she means," said Richard.

But before he could begin to clarify his own position, the balding man began a story about driving through Georgia.

Everyone waited for the tenant farmer and his rickety children to appear. Instead, the man pulled into the parking lot of a Dunkin' Donuts Shoppe. "I like the waitresses," he explained. "I like their little waists and big thighs. And their beehives. Especially their beehives." He stuck both hands out at the side of his head to indicate a hairdo. "They're the same all over the country," he said. "And I'm the same too. I mean, I always have the same thought."

He paused and leaned forward.

"You have to understand," he said.

Then he hunched over, wrapped his arms around himself and began rocking back and forth. "That's my mother," he announced, straightening up. "She's about as tall as this table and she wears a wig, a *sheital*."

"A beehive wig?" asked the woman across the table.

The man laughed. "So every time I go into one of those places, I get transfixed. 'That woman is a mother,' I think. It always gets to me."

"Alice," whispered Richard. "I'm tired. I want to go home."

"Shh," said Alice.

Everyone heard the shh. Everyone turned to the balding man. The man turned to Alice and assured her that he'd lost the gist of his anecdote already.

"Rickets," said Alice softly. "It had something to do with rickets. States of mind."

"You've got a good memory," said the man.

"Alice," said Richard.

Alice shook her head. "Go on," she said. Then she waited for the man to walk into the doughnut shop and discover that this particular waitress was someone he'd known in high school. Gloria Fishel, as a matter of fact.

"I knew Gloria," said the hostess.

"Then you'd know why I stopped going to Dunkin' Donuts after that. Still, I miss the thought. I feel years older without it."

Alice stood up. "I'm terribly sorry," she said. "Richard has to get up early tomorrow morning."

Everyone understood. Everyone had to get up early on Sunday morning sometimes. Everyone said good-bye as the Grubers moved into the hallway to get their coats on. The front door opened, closed again. The balding man moved into Richard's empty seat beside me. Then, when he was sure that the Grubers were outside, on Broadway, by the newstand, checking the *Times* to see that the book review was there, he lit up again, waved his cigar, and opened the discussion.

"Why does Alice stay with Richard?" he says.

"She could do better," says the woman across the table.

Everyone agrees that Alice could do better. The host's attachment to Richard is dismissed. The balding man leans over to me and whispers. Everyone hears the whisper. Everyone turns to me. I'm cautious. I miss my turn to comment, reviewing the evening. I hear the woman across the table say that after she had a baby, Alice called her up to find out what it felt like, being a mother. The woman across the table said she didn't know what it would feel like to Alice. Now Alice is getting books out of the library to help her make a decision. "Can you imagine?"

"Still," says the man beside me, "Richard."

He shakes his head. I go back to the woman-across-the-table's question: Can I imagine? Can I follow Alice and Richard up Broadway, past the drunks, past the men who cry out "mama" (they smack their lips at Alice, they make wet sounds), past the sleeping doorman, into the elevator cage. A right, a left, a right again, in the corridor upstairs. A key jiggles, a police lock falls open, a light gets switched on inside an entryway.

Light falls on the entryway, on the bookshelves, on Richard's publications and the publications of his friends. Light falls on Alice, checking the mirror, trying to see what she looked like to us tonight.

Alice and Richard enter the bedroom together. Richard tells Alice about the errors he's been noticing in the publications of the man with the cigar. The source of the errors became clear to him tonight, he says. Alice rubs her ankles as Richard decides to denounce the man in his next article. She stares at Richard's guitar in the corner. Then she thinks with satisfaction that Richard never denounces his old friends (bending to pick his socks off the floor, as she leaves for the bathroom.)

Wet sounds. Alice returns, large breasts encased in a blue woolen bathrobe with a monogram on the pocket. She's been wearing the bathrobe since Barnard. She likes it, just as Richard likes his guitar, his old friends from graduate school. Richard is in bed already, propped up against the pillows, running his fingers down a column of figures in the *Times*.

Alice studies Richard's absorption as Richard studies the price of coffee, replays his part in the underdevelopment discussion. Alice thinks that she has never been as absorbed in anything as Richard is in the financial page. Richard looks up at her. "Aren't you coming to bed?" he says.

Alice takes her bathrobe off and comes to bed. Richard finishes examining the figures, pulls the chain on the lamp, slides down, down, in the bed where Alice is waiting for him, arms wide, nylon and lace in a V between her breasts. Richard rests his head against the V as if he's listening for something. Then he looks up, questioning. Alice nods.

A beer bottle crashes against a lamp post outside.

Alice lifts her breast out of its nylon jacket.

Richard presses his forehead against it, his lips.

He's eager, avid.

Alice is grave, focused. She guides him to her other breast. She rocks him, hands locked around his back.

Richard comes up for air. "Oh, Alice," he says.

"Why shouldn't Alice stay with Richard?" I say out loud. "She loves him."

Everyone looks startled.

Everyone looks like they have doubts about me now, although they liked me well enough at the beginning of the evening.

The balding man lights another cigar, a big one, it takes a long time to begin to smoke. "That's a good point," he says finally.

Nobody else says anything.

The hostess suggests a move into the living room.

Everyone stands, except the balding man. Then he stands too. His arm is rising. His fingers form themselves into a fist. He turns to me. He punches me gently, just below the shoulderblade. We grin at each other.

"Hey," says the host. "What's going on over there?"

Garden Paths, Descents
Sharon Thompson

Henry. Quiet ministerial Henry. Henry who is always after something. Henry of the eight-track mind, of a thousand-and-one scenarios. Henry who appears reserved not because he is aloof from this world but because he is keeping tabs on every prick, every cunt, every bishop, pawn, domino, die, thrill, stock, mutual fund, commodity, joker, Ouija board, prediction, and piece of ass in every game that has been or is or might be going on within or in distant proximity to his territory, which is every square foot, brain cell, and energy quantum in the universe, more if there is more. Henry who kills, among other things, ladies. Henry who slices women up like sushi and leaves them lying on their rice-white beds, dying for more. Henry. Quiet ministerial Henry.

Like most predatory animals, Henry is low profile. He moves quickly, stays close to walls, wears a beige suit, a white shirt faintly striped with sand, an understated tie that reminds Glinda, his secretary, of scrub brush on dunes.[1]

Camouflage. Against the light coffee walls, beside the scraggly man-sized dracaenae, he casts no shadow. He is white on white. If he is perceived at all, it is as a mild imperfection in the paint.

Walking down the corridor, scanning his mail, he frowns over a memo. His pace slows. He is taking a much stronger interest in his work than he did when he first hired Glinda—for example, he now picks up his mail on the way into the office as if it is extremely important to get a head start, and he has been demanding finished correspondence before lunch as well as at four o'clock. There is more correspondence too. Glinda is very rushed. She does not resent this. She knows Henry must be under heavy pressure to run her so hard.

Except for occasional remarks to colleagues about pieces of silver and ass, Henry keeps his sexual and economic goals and objectives to himself. Now and then someone gets an inkling that there might be more to him than meets the eye but only Henry's wife Betty knows for sure, and who would listen to the opinions of a blond burb babe wearing pink and yellow plaid bermudas and driving a powder blue station wagon trimmed with metal photographs of wood?

Betty gets out of the wagon to buy her Henry a Pathmark pork roast. Henry loves pork in all its varieties but they hardly ever have it since it is too expensive to fit into Betty's lean budget. Today this Pathmark is having a sale. Betty has driven twenty miles to take advantage of it. After locking the wagon door, Betty pulls down the pantlegs of her bermudas. Oh, how has she let time so pass her by? Faded, tight, they are the same bermudas she wore bicycling around campus the spring afternoon she met Henry, and they cut into her thighs the way her wedding ring cuts into her fourth finger left hand. Sometimes it hurts so much she wants to cut her finger off.

Henry passes a door market "fire exit." Were he to go through that door, he would reach his office on the north side of the building in thirty seconds but he chooses the long way around instead, past the gleaming square spaces occupied by the corporation's highest executives. These spaces look south and east to the sea and river in order to encourage their occupants to "think expansion."[2] Outside the executive offices sit a dozen secretaries, whom Henry greets with chivalrous intimacy, calling them his long-legged roses, and for whom he has laid more best plans than one.

Henry goes back to his office, pulls a draft memo out of his files, looks it over, emits a low whistle, and takes it out to Glinda for retyping. The memo is entitled, "The Economic and Sociological Advantages of Word Processing." He returns to his office, closes his door and draperies, and muses over his future as the director of word processing. Henry is in charge of office services and such an enterprise would naturally fall under his sovereignty. Let others give men orders, a calling that seems to Henry an inexplicable perversion, nor is he one to go after dreams that cannot be realized. He makes those moves on the board that are open to the mediocre but canny, and as other men are moved by ambition, he is moved by desire and sensuality. In relation to the exercise of authority, all he has ever wanted is to command women. Unlike those who aspire toward offices that look out on the sea and the river, Henry would rest content with a view of a hundred women whose fingers moved over their keyboards like tiny enameled butterflies lighting on dahlias.

Riding down the garden path on her white bicycle, Betty sees Henry dive into the pond. Straddling her bicycle, pink cardigan knotted around her neck, moth wispy hair tied back with a pink satin ribbon that has a yellow stripe down its middle and alternating pink and yellow hoops along its edges, she waits for him to come up. As she waits she thinks of herself as strawberry ice cream and lemon sherbert, pink and blond, sweet and tangy, glazing as the sun shines lime upon her through the trees. Lime, and mint. She wonders about Henry and if he will think her good enough to eat.

Pleased with the impression he made on the president, Henry comes up behind Glinda carrying his memo and blows in her ear; the tip of his tongue darts to her lobe. She makes believe nothing is happening. She giggles.

Betty gets home from the supermarket at eleven. She lies down to take a nap. Betty has a headache. She has a headache all the time but only really notices when she gets tired. Ordinarily it runs in the back of her mind like the sound of electric typewriters in an office. It is her habit. She has it instead of cigarettes, ice cream, bowling, golf, bridge, community theater, other wives, or the worker who is filling the potholes on her leafy home street, which is so quiet and peaceful that the Venusian explorer, Cartimandua, takes it as a temple complex sacred to the goddess Elizabeth. "Like the sanctuary of Aphaea,"[3] she writes, "Elizabethtown, New Jersey, provides individual houses for its priestesses, who come together only for ceremonial purposes—at the bath, for example, in the season of the sacred heat of transformation, or at the temple, a long, wide, arched structure with parallel netted altars, symbolizing the insubstantial but ensnaring nature of everyday linear reality as it is perceived by the enlightened human mind. In daily ritual at this temple, priestesses propel white balls back and forth by means of instruments resembling the holy form of Isis, an action that suggests both the reactive character of daily human life and also the inspirational potential of soaring over the mundane, the net—samsara. Like temple complexes throughout this place called by the invocational form of the objective third person plural, Elizabethtown provides shelter and sustenance for priestesses who serve a multiplicity of goddesses, such as Janet, Sally, Dot, Cathy, Cindy, Alice, Gloria, Laura, Nancy, Kay, Lisa, and many others, but it is dedicated primarily to Elizabeth and its chief priestess is known as 'Betty,' a diminutive form of Elizabeth indicating the priestesses' inferior mortal status."[4]

The explorer peered in the window at Henry's sleeping wife, chief priestess of Elizabethtown, New Jersey. "The duties of a high priestess," she wrote, "are extremely arduous. To generate strength, many priestesses practice one of two forms of meditation. The first involves contemplating a glass screen encased, usually, in wood, a material cut from a tall plant said to contain and/or symbolize all human knowledge; over the screen pass gray and white and/or brightly colored lines at an extremely high speed, transmitting energy. A higher form of meditation involves lying in daylight hours on a raised platform. In good weather, many lie directly in the rays of the sun, uncovering their entire bodies except for the highest and lowest points, which are considered sacred. Significantly, like higher and developing beings throughout the universe, these priestesses spend many hours alone, strengthening their powers; whereas their night-worshippers and young have extremely low tolerances for solitude."[5]

At 10:30 Henry comes out of his office and asks Glinda to get him some coffee. He puts seventy cents in her palm, his fingers touching for an instant below the line of her heart. The coins are warm. "Get yourself some too," he says. She rises from her desk, straightens her tawny blazer, and goes to the cafeteria where she orders two coffees—one black, one with milk and sugar. "Milk and sugar," he says, watching her stir an extra packet of white crystals into her coffee. "Everything about you is so womanly." She say she eats too much sugar. He says he likes sweet women.

Women feel, but do not think Henry is conscious of, the moist pearly web of translucent desire that he exudes as continuously as he breathes. They think he is shy and easily startled like an undomes-ticated animal, and they stay very still when he is by. This is partly why Glinda does not react when he tongues her ear. She feels flattered, as if a deer has come up and eaten out of her hand. Another reason that she does not become angry is that she believes she is irresistible and that he is therefore blameless. But like mist settling in a valley, Henry's desire moistens every woman he meets—the file clerk with her faint gray features like letters smudged on a carbon copy; the woman he calls my "blacklacquer dragonlady," who sells tickets at the porno-graphic movie; the woman he calls "waterlily," who serves his sushi; Glinda in her tawny blazer; even the cleaning woman who comes into his office when he works late.

He falls on her. Her huge white nylon undies, her supphose and garter belt, tissues, dustrags, and Red Cross shoes are vacuumed up as he pumps into her.

He wakes up. It is five o'clock. Time to meet the file clerk in an out-of-the-way coffee shop he chose because it looks like a brothel. She has gotten there before him. She is dipping a powdered sugar doughnut into a light coffee. Above the counter, against the red-flocked wallpaper, under the street lantern, her body appears small, her shoulders rounded like those of a twelve-year-old child waiting for her mama to get off work. He knows, however, that under the counter, she has the goods: her hips are wide, rich. It is as if all her nourishment, all her powdered sugar and light coffee, flows to that part of her body, which is silent, full, dark, like a southern marsh. He wants to enter her there in long hip boots. Birds rush from the vines when he steps forward: cardinals, orioles, blue jays, scarlet tanagers. They screech around the coupling pair. "You are one of the most exciting women I have ever known," he says, tipping his head, kissing her sallow lips, removing her glasses. She blinks, the coffee shop gone fuzzy, romantic, a blur of red and gold. "What a place," he says, "for love to bloom." With a stained index finger (she has changed a typewriter ribbon today, she has touched many carbons), she smooths her hair and curls it behind her small ears; she runs her finger down the narrow gray hollow of her cheek. She cannot see anything clearly. Tossing her head, she feels her long Castilian waves. She scans the room with pecan eyes. All the men in the coffee shop gaze at her passionately but she is his. His. Fixing her intense eyes on him, she takes a final bite of her powdered sugar doughnut, licks the powder from her fingertips, and slides off the stool as if the floor is a pool of warm spring water. He watches and his eyes gleam like specula.

Water rolling off him in translucent pearls, he comes up on the other side of the pond and sees her. His eyes catch light. She feels golden. She smiles. A rainbow between them. He leaps and shakes his body in the air, joyous to see her. She feels her body rising up too. Stops herself. Angry. Embarrassed. What is happening to her. She doesn't even know him. She looks down. Propped against a tree, his worn copy of *The Portable Aristotle,*[6] neatly folded on a bed of moss, his wire rims. She crosses a synapse. She does know him. He is in her philosophy class. Without his egghead paraphernalia, he does not look like himself at all. This is a man I can trust—she thinks what they all think—only I will know he is wonderful. Gladdened, she waves. He paddles across the pond to her with round-muscled arms. She toes down her kickstand, she walks to the edge of the water. He reaches shallow water, he starts to stand up. She covers her eyes. He says it is all right, he is "decent," a suggestiveness in this voice that tosses all possibilities into the air. She takes her hand away from her eyes as he rises up, his jockey shorts voluminous around him like wet diapers. She laughs happily. He enfolds her like dumpling dough over warm sweet apples and holds her until they are both moist through and they lie down on the moss to dry out, on the sunny moss where he takes her in the 1950s college manner, coming not in her honeysuckle grotto, which he does not even see, although his hand reaches down into her pink lollipops, feeling like a gardener into her, breaking earth, learning that she is silky, guessing that she is blond there, He removes his hand. He strokes her hair and cheek with it, turning her on with her own musksmell, and comes against her pink and yellow plaid zipper plaque, comes lime, mint, strawberries, and lemon. Yes, he found her good enough to eat in pink and yellow plaid bermudas and pink satin ribbon that has a yellow stripe down its middle and alternating pink and yellow hoops along its edges and pink cotton lollipop panties yes he said yes he did Yes.

Now she waits for him, her nightworshipper, in a house that smells of burning pig. Oh, how has she let time so pass her by?

Notes

1. Fire Island, June 1973.
2. Excerpt from the opening speech delivered by Edward H. Lederer, president of Atomic Enterprises, Inc., at the corporation's annual sales conference held at Muirfield, Scotland, May 1973.
3. "Aphaea, a temple located on Aegina, 'a Greek island, in the Saronic gulf. . . . Tradition derives the name from Aegina, the mother of Aecus, who was born in and ruled the island. . . . Inscriptions found by the recent excavations seem to prove that the shrine belonged not to Zeus of Athena as formerly supposed, but to the local goddess, Aphaea, identified by Pausanias with Britomartis and Dictynna.'" *Encyclopaedia Britannica*, 11th ed., I, "A to Annoy," From "Report from Usa," Cartimandua, July 9, 1974, f. 23.
4. Ibid., f. 24.
5. Ibid.
6. "ARISTOTLE, philosopher, psychologist, logician, moralist, political thinker, biologist, the founder of literary criticism . . . worked for 20 years by the side of Plato . . . the inventor of the syllogism . . . a pervading conception of growth . . . distinguishes his thought from that of Plato . . . [whose] universe was . . . static. . . . The universe of Aristotle is dynamic; his world is engaged in becoming; the 'nature' of each thing is a potentiality which moves through development (a process which is also 'nature') to an actuality which is true and final and perfect 'nature'—for 'nature is the end,' as he writes in *Politics*, 'and what each thing is when fully developed we call its nature.'" Encyclopaedia Britannica, II, "Annual Register to Baltic Sea," p. 353, s.v. "Aristotle." From "Report from Usa," Cartimandua, May 1, 1959, f. 3.

Section V
Domination, Submission,
and the Unconscious

For feminists in the 1960s and 1970s, sex was the sum of the civil relationships that surrounded it: power dynamics in bed reflected power relations outside the bedroom door. In particular, the denial of female erotic pleasure—which members of consciousness-raising groups discovered to be so widespread in women's lives—was a quintessential expression of the sexism that oppressed women elsewhere. The lack of attention men paid the clitoris was not simply a regrettable oversight, but a keystone in the edifice of male domination, a domination reproduced and perpetuated in heterosexual lovemaking.

The new frankness of sexual discussions encouraged a generation of young women to assert themselves in bed and to discard proscriptions that did not serve their erotic needs. But as old norms gave way, new injunctions, often unspoken and only half-understood, took their place. Certain kinds of sexual behavior, it seemed, perpetuated social injustice; others transcended it. The trick, as feminists adjured each other and their lovers, was to purge the bedroom of inequality, something that could be accomplished only by discriminating between proper and improper erotic technique.

Recently, some feminists have begun to clarify and reject these assumptions about the erotic expression of power. Lesbian practitioners of sadomasochism—deemed by many feminists to be the epitome of patriarchal "roles"—have argued that the play of domination and submission in their rituals is harmless, entirely distinct from the exploitation of the world outside the bedroom. Lesbians involved in butch/femme relationships, roundly denounced in the women's movement for their replication of oppressive gender roles, have defended their activities as the creation of a specifically female tension of erotic opposites. Elsewhere in this volume, Amber Hollibaugh and Cherríe Moraga meditate on the aggressive and passive roles in lovemaking and wonder if the business of roles and power isn't a "much richer territory" than we had thought. Indeed, the theme of erotic roles and their relation to gender has been central to this new discussion. In this section, for instance, Sharon Olds gives poetic reconsideration to male sexuality and replaces our older image of the monolithically insensitive man with a far more complex view of men's sexual histories.

Underlying these new approaches to women's sexuality is a view of sex as a human realm with its own historical dynamics, distinct—if not autonomous from—civil society. Of course, this insight is hardly new: long ago Freud discovered that sexual desire and behavior might follow a trajectory quite different from the rest of a person's life. As we have noted in our introduction, however, feminists have only recently surmounted their early mistrust of psychoanalysis. In turning to the work of theorists like Jessica Benjamin, we can begin to integrate Freud's great insights—the centrality of fantasy and unconscious desire to sexuality—into a feminist understanding of erotic life. Ann Kaplan explores a specific instance of this general theme when she analyzes movies as if they were dreams, decoding the unconscious workings of common sexual imagery.

Of course, we still express our sexual impulses within a broad social context—one that is permeated with relations of domination on which our unconscious draws. Jacquelyn Hall's essay on lynching and rape in the postbellum South shows how easily sexual excitement lends itself to social violence; Barbara Omolade's evocation of the experience of black women reminds us of how racial exploitation feeds upon the eroticization of race.

As Benjamin notes, however, we can illuminate not only individual but social expressions of domination and violence through examining the early childhood experiences from which our desires and unconscious motivations spring. If each person's sexuality has its own history, then that history is rooted in the experience of domination and submission: of being small and ruled—a child—in a world of large and dominating adults. As we mature, we seek in various socially accessible ways—racial domination, for one—to resolve the mysterious, vague yearnings that stem from this power relation, to consummate the unrealized sexual relations we set up—and were set up for—as children. The child's curious eroticization of the world, the subtle, powerful, and fearful sexuality depicted in Nancy Harrison's "Movie," lives on with us, mostly forgotten in our conscious lives, replayed only in dreams like those of which Sharon Thompson writes, where the rooms of our parents' houses open onto the streets of our adulthood.

Finally, a willingness to examine rather than to condemn power dynamics and their unconscious sources allows us to consider a subject rarely treated by feminists—sexual excitement. Benjamin speaks of the paradoxical desires for independence and dependence that enter into sadomasochistic excitement. As psychoanalyst Robert Stoller has argued, hostility, stemming from early experiences of power and powerlessness, may well be a central element in most sexual excitement. If some sexual conduct can be sanitized—at least superficially—of un-equal "roles," a heightened, all-encompassing sexual passion cannot.

The erotic paradox, then, is the meeting point of dependence and independence, self-affirmation and self-obliteration, domination and submission, childhood and adulthood. The pieces that follow show that to ignore this paradox, with all its entanglements, in favor of some norm of politically desired behavior, is to cut ourselves off from a crucial area of human experience.

Master and Slave:
The Fantasy of Erotic Domination

Jessica Benjamin

This essay is concerned with the violence of erotic domination. It is about the strange union of rationality and violence that is made in the secret heart of our culture and sometimes enacted in the body. This union has inspired some of the holiest imagery of religious transcendence and now comes to light at the porno newsstands, where women are regularly depicted in the bonds of love. But the slave of love is not always a woman, nor always a heterosexual; the fantasy of erotic domination permeates all sexual imagery in our culture. This rational violence mingles love with issues of control and submission. It is a controlled, ritualized form of violence that is expressed in sexual fantasy and in some carefully institutionalized, voluntary sexual practices. This fantasy also flows beneath the surface of "normal" adult love. But its origins lie in the experience of early infancy, and they are charged with the yearning for mutual recognition; its psychology has implications for political as well as for erotic life.

The fantasy of erotic domination embodies the desire for both independence and recognition. However alienated from the original desires, however disturbing or perverse their form, the impulses to erotic violence and submission express deep yearnings for selfhood and transcendence. In identifying these deeper roots of erotic domination, we hope to understand the eroticism of religious and political movements as well. Putting aside moral judgment, let us take this fantasy as fantasy. Let us see what it tells us about the longings that are denied fulfillment in our culture except in outbursts of collective or individual deviance or madness.

Examined closely, sexual eroticism appears as the heir to religious eroticism; that is, in sexuality we have a new religion or a substitute for one. The original erotic component, the desire for recognition, seems to emerge in sadomasochism, as it once did in the lives and confessions of saints. The common psychological root of these erotic experiences can be found in the earliest issues of intimacy and separation in infancy.

In order to become human beings, we have to receive recognition from the first people who care for us. In our society it is usually the mother who bestows recognition. She responds to our communications, our acts, and our gestures so that we feel they are meaningful. Her recognition makes us feel that vital connection to another being as necessary to human survival as food. In most Western families the individual acquires a self, or sense of identity, against the background of such an individual maternal presence. This process of acquiring a self is referred to as *differentiation*. Differentiation means developing the ability to see ourselves and others as independent and distinct beings;[1] It means that we have learned that our acts and intentions can have an impact on others, and theirs on us. Perhaps the most difficult part of this process is, as Simone de Beauvoir put it, coming to terms with the existence of an Other—recognizing her without effacing ourselves, asserting ourselves without effacing her. This difficulty is crystallized in the most familiar conflict of differentiation—that between the need to establish autonomous identity and the need to be recognized by the other. The child's independent acts require a recognizing audience and so reaffirm its dependency on others.

In light of this early conflict in differentiation, I will explore the fantasy of erotic domination and its place in our culture: first, how the issues of autonomy and recognition that arise in the course of early differentiation reappear in relationships of domination, especially erotic domination; second, how the denial of recognition derives from the male experience of differentiation and the repudiation of maternal nurturance;[2] and third, how this repudiation gives rise to a form of individuality and rationality that permeates our culture and intensifies the conflict between our needs for self-assertion and transcendence. This conflict is the core of the fantasy of erotic domination.

I will argue that the individualistic emphasis on strict boundaries between self and others promotes a sense of isolation and unreality. Paradoxically, the individualism of our culture seems to make it more difficult to accept an other's independence and to experience the other person as real. In turn, it is difficult to connect with others as living erotic beings, to feel erotically alive oneself. Violence acquires its importance in erotic fantasy as an expression of the desire to break out of this numbing encasement. The importance currently assumed by violent fantasy can in part be attributed to the increasingly rational, individualistic character of our culture, to the increasing deprivation of nurturance and recognition in ordinary human intercourse.

In presenting this analysis I am aware of its limitations. I am not attempting here to explain all forms of violence nor all male violence against women. I am confining my discussion to rational violence—a controlled, ritualized form of violence. I use "rational" to refer not to the motive of violence but to its calculated form of expression. A great many other forms of violence in our culture do not fall into this category, chief among them assaults on women. The danger has always been that women and other victims of violence will be blamed or will blame themselves[3] for "provoking" it. This has led to an attitude of counter-blame: the discussion of erotic domination or rational violence in which participation is voluntary or fantasized seems to some an apology for male violence in general. This analysis of the psychological and cultural roots of violence in fantasy life is an attempt to lift the discussion out of the bog of blame and apology into something more like understanding.

My analysis is not based on the study of sadomasochistic practices but on a single, powerful study of the erotic imagination, Pauline Réage's *The Story of O*.[4] Réage's tale weaves a net in which the issues of dependency and domination are inextricably intertwined, in which the conflict between the need for autonomy and that for recognition can be resolved only by total renunciation of self. It is a masterful illustration of the idea that the root of the problem of domination is a failure to achieve true differentiation. We shall unravel Réage's story with the help of Hegel's analysis of domination, and Georges Bataille's interpretation of Hegel in his study of eroticism.

The problem of domination begins with the denial of dependency. No one can really extricate herself or himself from dependency on others, from the need for recognition. In the first relationship of dependency between child and parent this is an especially painful and paradoxical fact. A child wants not only to achieve independence, but to be recognized as independent—recognized by the very people on whom he has been most dependent. This paradox constantly confounds our struggle for autonomy; it is the paradox of recognition. To escape from this conflict it is all too tempting to imagine that one can become independent without recognizing the other person as an equally autonomous agent in her or his own right. One need only imagine that the other person is not separate—she belongs to me, I control and possess her.

Psychological domination is ultimately a failure to recognize the other person as like, although separate from oneself. The self that is strong enough to define itself not only through separateness but also through commonality with other subjects is able to recognize other subjects. This self is able to differentiate and need not objectify the other in order to separate. It is able to feel it exists when it is with the other and when alone.

How does such a self develop? Perhaps the best formulation of the relationship between the struggle for selfhood and domination was presented by Hegel in his discussion of the master-slave relationship.[5] Hegel's formulation reflected an implicit awareness of an idea that psychologists have only recently articulated: that autonomous selfhood develops through being able to affect others by one's acts. Hegel explained that in order to exist for oneself, one had to exist for an other, and that in desiring an other, one wants to be recognized. We try to realize this desire in an act, but if this act completely destroys the other, the other cannot recognize us. If it consumes the other, leaving her or him with no consciousness, then we come to incorporate or embody this dead, not-conscious being. As a person who is utterly destroyed can give no recognition, the alternative is to subjugate, to enslave him or her. But to be alive in relation to another person we must act in such a way as not to negate fully the other, and the desire in our act must be recognized by the other.

Let us say that the first other we encounter is our mother: then it is through our ability to have an impact on her that we experience ourselves as existing and our intentions as meaningful and potent. If our acts have no impact on her, we feel powerless. But if we overpower her, there is no one to recognize us. When we affect her it is necessary that she does not simply dissolve under the impact of our actions, that she both maintain her integrity and respond to us as effective persons.[6] If, for example, the mother sets no limits for the child, if she obliterates herself and her own interests (as women often have been encouraged to do), she ceases to perform the role of other person. It is this self-obliteration on the part of the "permissive" parent that makes the child who "gets everything it wants" so unhappy. When the parent provides no limit for the child, the child feels abandoned. If the mother does not at some point remove herself from the child's control she becomes simply an object, which no longer exists outside the self. What I am describing here is a dialectic of control: if I completely control the other, then the other ceases to exist, and if the other completely controls me, then I cease to exist. True differentiation means maintaining the essential tension of the contradictory impulses to assert the self and respect the other.

If we are unable to recognize an other without effacing ourselves or to assert ourselves without effacing the other, this tension breaks down. The two impulses that should contribute to differentiation are split. In Hegel as in Freud, and indeed in most theories of differentiation in our culture, this splitting is considered inevitable. According to Freud the earliest self wants to be omnipotent, or rather it has the fantasy that it is so. Subsequent omnipotence fantasies are seen as regressions to this necessary first stage.[7] Hegel says that self-consciousness wants to be absolute. It wants to be recognized by the other in order to place itself in the world and make itself the world. The I wants to prove this at the expense of the other; it wants to think itself the only one; it abjures dependency.

For Hegel and Freud, then, the self gives up omnipotence only when it realizes its dependency—in Freud, through animal desire or physiological need; in Hegel, through the desire for recognition. The subject discovers that if it completely devours or controls the other, it can no longer get what it originally wanted. So the subject learns better. But although the subject may relinquish the wish to control or devour the other completely, it does so unwillingly, with a persistent if unconscious wish to fulfill the old omnipotence fantasy.[8] This is a far cry from a real appreciation of the other's existence as a person. The truth in this view of the self seems to be that acknowledging dependency is painful, and that denying recognition to others because of this pain leads to domination. Similarly, violence is predicated on the denial of the other person's independent subjectivity and autonomy. Violence is a way of expressing or asserting control over an other, of establishing one's own autonomy and negating the other person's. It is a way of repudiating dependency while attempting to avoid the consequent feeling of aloneness. It makes the other an object but retains possession of her or him.

In erotic fantasy, the struggle to the death for recognition is captured metaphorically by violating the other's will or submitting to the other's will—by risking the psychological, if not the physical self. Georges Bataille first used the Hegelian analysis of the master-slave relationship to understand that eroticism centers around maintaining the tension between life and death of self.[9] The significance of eroticism, he says, is that it allows transgression of the most fundamental taboo, that separating life from death. Life means discontinuity, the confinement of each individual to a separate, isolated existence. Death means continuity; in death, not life, each individual is united with the rest, sunk back into the sea of nondifferentiation. We might also call this merging a throwback to the original oneness with the mother. Such merging or boundary loss is experienced as psychic death once we have differentiated— the proverbial return to the womb. Hence the loss of differentiation is feared as psychic death.

The body stands for discontinuity, individuality, and life. Consequently the violation of the body in erotic violation breaks the taboo between life and death and breaks through our discontinuity from the other. While this break is the hidden secret of all eroticism, it is most clearly expressed in erotic violation. The breakdown of the tension within the individual between life and death, between assertion and loss of self, occurs in the form of violator and violated. One person maintains his or her boundary, and one allows her or his boundary to be broken.

Not surprisingly, Bataille explains that in the ritualized form of transgression known as sacrifice, the man is the actor and the woman is the victim. Still, he argues, the woman performs the function of breaking her discontinuity, of risking death, for both of them. And, I would add, the man upholds the boundaries of reason and control for both, by subjecting his violence to ritual limits. Together the partners form the whole—the tension in which the assertion and loss of self are united. Together they achieve the transcendence of which neither, alone, is capable. The notion that each partner represents one pole in a split unity suggests a paradoxical and intimate relationship between violence and control. The continual problem in relations of domination, Bataille suggests, is "that the slave by accepting defeat . . . has lost the quality without which he is unable to *recognize* the conqueror so as to satisfy him. The slave is unable to give the master the *satisfaction* without which the master can no longer rest."[10] The exhaustion of satisfaction that occurs when all resistance is vanquished, all tension is lost, means that the relationship has come full circle, returned to the emptiness from which it was an effort to escape. Total loss of tension, de-differentiation, means death of the self. Perhaps the most important way in which human beings experiment with the loss of differentiation is through sex—death by other means. Recently this connection between sex and death has emerged explicitly in the imagery of erotic domination provided for mass consumption. But of course this awareness is much older.

It may not be wholly surprising that the description of erotic submission in *The Story of O* closely parallels the struggle to the death for recognition that Hegel and then Bataille described. In this text, as in many other descriptions of masochism or voluntary submission, one is struck by the fact that masochism seems to require an other who remains in control. The replay of the infant's struggle to differentiate in the adult erotic relationship is clear in *The Story of O*, which suggests how the original failure of differentiation occurs, and how an individual strives to transcend and finally repeats that failure in the relation of domination.

Perhaps the greatest objection to this work has been directed against its depiction of O's voluntary submission. The story of O's masochism is not seen as an allegory of the desire for recognition but simply as the story of a woman victimized—too weak or brainwashed or hopeless to resist her degradation.[11] Such a viewpoint cannot, of course, explain what satisfaction is sought and found in submission, what psychological motivations lead to oppression, humiliation, or subservience. Instead it seeks to deny the unpleasant fact that people really do consent to relationships of domination, and that fantasies of domination play a vigorous part in the mental lives of those who do not actually do so.

The Story of O confronts us rather boldly with this unpleasant idea, told as it is most scrupulously from the point of view of the woman who submits (and, to judge from a recent interview, representing as it does the fantasy life of its woman author).[12] The novel makes clear that behind the physical humiliation and abuse that O suffers is a search for an ultimately unattainable spiritual or psychological satisfaction. De Beauvoir has pointed out that masochism is essentially a desire for subordination to another person, rather than for the experience of pain as such.[13] Masochism is a search for recognition of the self by an other who alone is powerful enough to bestow this recognition. But it is a search for recognition that is alienated or distorted because the element of freedom is replaced by the element of force. De Beauvoir then distinguishes this submissive impulse from the impulse to transcend the self by freely giving oneself to another person. The masochist is unable to give herself freely and must or wishes to be forced to do so. But the desire for transcendence, the hope of being recognized, is discernible behind the masochist's submission. It is these hopes and desires that O's story reveals to us.

At the beginning of *The Story of O*, our heroine, whose name is evidently given by the letter's designation of the word Open or opening *(Ouvert)* or of the orifice itself, is brought to Roissy castle, established by men for the ritual violation and subjugation of women. We know nothing else about it, the men, or her lover, René, and we learn little more throughout the book. The first night she is there the men deliver this speech to O:

> You are here to serve your masters. . . . you will drop whatever you are doing and ready yourself for what is really your one and only duty: to lend yourself. Your hands are not your own, nor are your breasts, nor most especially, any of your orifices, which we may explore or penetrate at will. . . . you have lost all right to privacy or concealment. . . . you must never look any of us in the face. If the costume we wear . . . leaves our sex exposed, it is not for the sake of convenience . . . but for the sake of insolence, so that your eyes will be directed there upon it and nowhere else so that you may learn that there resides your master. . . . it is perfectly all right for you to grow accustomed to being whipped— since you are going to be every day throughout your stay—this is less for our pleasure than for your enlightenment. . . . both this flogging and the chain . . . attached to the ring of your collar . . . are intended less to make you suffer, scream, or shed tears than to make you feel, through this suffering, that you are not free but fettered, and to teach you that you are totally dedicated to something outside yourself.[14]

A great deal is contained in this short text. First, O is to lose all subjectivity, all possibility of using her body for action; she is to be merely a thing. Second, she is to be continually violated, even when she is not actually being used—the main transgression of her self's boundary occurs through her having to be always available and open. Third, what strikes me as very important, is that her masters are to be recognized by her in a particular indirect form. The penis represents or symbolizes their desire.[15] By interposing it between them they can maintain a self, a subjectivity independent of her recognition. And this subjectivity is expressed through the masters' power over her in a more general way, in their ability totally to organize, calculate, and control the effect they are having on her. Indeed, what they do is "more for her enlightenment than their pleasure"—even in using her they do not need her. Rather, their acts express a rational control, a rational violation through which they objectify their rational intentions. Each act has such a goal that asserts their mastery. They enjoy not so much their pleasure, as the fact that they can take it. They enjoy not so much her pain, as the fact that they have a visible effect upon her: they leave their marks.

Why must they find enjoyment more in their command than in her service, and why must it be mediated through calculation, or symbolized by the penis? Because they must always maintain their separate subjectivity, they must never become dependent. Otherwise, they would suffer the fate of Hegel's master, who in becoming dependent on his slave gradually loses subjectivity to him. A further danger for the master is that the subject always becomes the object he consumes. ("You are what you eat.") Thus they must be careful never to wholly consume her as will-less object, but rather to command and consume her *will*. They always ask her, "O, do you consent?" Of course, in consuming her will, they are negating hers and being recognized in theirs; they are inevitably depreciating her will and turning her into an object. When her objectification is complete, when she has no more will, they cannot engage with her without becoming filled with her thing-like nature. They must perform their violation rationally and ritually both in order to maintain their boundaries and to make her will the object of their will.

Finally, the symbolization of male mastery through the penis emphasizes the difference between them and her. It signifies the male pronouncement of difference over sameness. Each act the master takes against the slave, O, is one that establishes his separateness, his difference from her—through his power to negate her. In the tension between recognition of like humanity and negation of Otherness, the male represents the one-sided extreme. He is continually placing himself outside her by saying "I am not you." He is using her to establish his objective reality by imposing it on her. The rational function, the calculation, objectivity, and control, is linked to this one-sided differencing, this "I am not you," in the manner that Bataille saw as inherently linked with discontinuity. Violence, in the service of reason, has the same intention of asserting the self-boundary of control. The penis symbolizes the fact that, however interdependent the master and slave become, the master will always maintain the boundary—the rigidity, antagonism, and polarization of their respective parts.

Through the movement of the dialectic of control, the narrative reveals the consequences of such separation through negating the other. The story is really driven forward by the problematic nature of control as a means of differentiation. Because the slave who is completely dominated loses the quality of being able to recognize, because she who is once possessed no longer exists outside, the struggle must be prolonged. O must be enslaved piece by piece. New levels of resistance must be found, so that she can be vanquished anew. She must acquiesce in ever deeper humiliation, pain, and bondage, and she must will her submission ever anew. The narrative moves through these ever deeper levels of submission, tracing the impact of each fresh negation of her will, the defeat of her resistance, unto her death.

The narrative problem, the culmination of the dialectic, occurs at the point when O has submitted and can no longer recognize René, and he has exhausted the possibilities of violating her boundaries. The problem is solved by the introduction of Sir Stephen, the older stepbrother to whom René gives O. O then realizes that she is an object in René's effort to win prestige from Sir Stephen, who is more important to René than she can ever be. Sir Stephen does not "love" or recognize O (at least, not at first), and so her submission to him is a submission to a pure power who requires no recognition from her in return. She is, he tells her, to be humiliated by one who does not love her in the presence of one who does. Sir Stephen is thoroughly rational, calculating, and self-controlled in his desire.

Equally suggestive is the fact that René looks up to Sir Stephen as to a father. There is more than a hint of the Oedipal relationship here. Sir Stephen is the authority not only for O, but also for René. He is the person in whose eyes René wants to be recognized. The entrance of Sir Stephen suggests a reinterpretation of the story up to that point. We now see that René is weak and has always been under the influence of the more powerful older man. This development in the story reminds us that male domination is rooted in a struggle for recognition between men in which women are mere objects or tokens: the prize. In terms of psychological development, the relationship of domination is not only based on the pre-Oedipal drama of mother-child separation, but is also perpetuated in the Oedipal triad. In the Oedipal conflict, the father enforces the separation of the boy from his mother, demanding not merely that he relinquish her as a love object, but also as a subject with whom to identify. The father's aggression or interference, which the boy internalizes or identifies with, is reenacted in the repudiation and objectification of the mother. In other words, the boy's posture of repudiating the mother and asserting his own boundaries is inspired by the powerful and different father. Seeking recognition from this father, the boy is aspiring not to be nurtured but to gain prestige. He gains it by repudiating the mother as visibly, as violently, as possible.

The realization that René is willing to relinquish her for Sir Stephen plunges O into despair, for she can exist only if René recognizes her. Without his love, which signifies his dependency on her, life is absolutely void. She thinks, paraphrasing a Protestant text she saw as a child, "It is a fearful thing to be cast out of the hands of the living God." We see that her experience has a religious character. This is elaborated not only in the ritual violation of her body as the barrier to continuity, infinity; she herself also experiences her lover as a god whom she adores and cannot stand to be parted from. While God represents the ultimate oneness, the ability to stand alone, O represents the lost soul who is elevated by union with the ideal omnipotent other.

The author tells us that abandonment by God is experienced as punishment and an indication of guilt. Typically, one asks what one has done to deserve this and looks for the cause in oneself. Abandoned by René, punished by Sir Stephen, O finds the guilt in her wantonness. O is actually willing to risk death in order to continue to be the object of her lover's desire, to be recognized. Her great longing is to be known, and in this respect she is like any lover, for the secret of love is to be known as oneself. But O's desire to be known is rather like that of the sinner who wants to be known by God. Sir Stephen thrills her, in part, because he knows her, from the moment he meets her, to be bad, wanton, "easy," reveling in her abasement.

O's deepest guilt stems not, however, from her desire to be recognized by René or Sir Stephen, but from the possibility that she will be tempted to *act* on her desire. To act is to be a subject. O refuses to masturbate in front of Sir Stephen because her deepest shame is connected to this flagrant act of autonomy, one that says "I can satisfy myself." We also find out that O has always desired to possess women, to have them give themselves to her, but she has never given herself prior to meeting René. So O is being punished for two aspects of her subjectivity, the desire to be known, and the desire to act, to be separate. In particular I suspect that the latter, perhaps because it is the prerogative of the male, is her real sin: the assertion of autonomy, of the self as agent.

It is equally true that O's fate is the result of her inability both to give herself and to assert herself. She is not able to give herself as a whole and separate person. Rather she must be forced to open herself. Underlying O's fear of yielding and asserting herself is her fear of abandonment and loss of the other.[16] It is not difficult to see O's continual consent to her own enslavement as a flight from the aloneness of the free agent. Yet I do not merely mean to say that O is in flight from freedom. She is searching for another kind of freedom. The freedom she seeks is devotion to her god. True freedom may consist of freely giving oneself in a reciprocal relationship. O finds a kind of substitute transcendence in losing herself to enslavement. This loss of self is the opposite of losing the other. Her search for the boundless, for true union, turns into submission because she is not separate and cannot bear aloneness. At the same time the pain to which she submits is a continual substitute and transposition of the psychic pain of loss and abandonment she fears.

There is another way in which pain is connected to the search for transcendence. Pain is the violent rupture of the self-organization. O welcomes this loss of self-organization, under certain conditions at any rate. Conversely, pleasure always involves a certain amount of control or mastery of stimuli. Hence it is the master who can know pleasure, and the slave who must experience pain. In her violation and loss of self through pain, O's body is "moving" to her masters (as another captive woman is moving to O). This "emotion," however, is always checked and finally diminished as she becomes more a dehumanized object, as it is only the spectacle of her that moves them. O finally attains independence by being willing to go all the way, to risk her life in order to gain recognition. This risk is an effort to win recognition from her idealized lovers. In performing the tasks they set her, she is seeking affirmation of herself, seeking to find the heroic self she had never been able to express.

Seemingly contradictory, but perhaps complementary, is the use of pain to symbolize birth, selfhood, and separation. The psychic pain of separation is captured in the physical pain inflicted on the violated. The closeness of birth and death, self-loss, and self-affirmation in pain remind us that the most intense sense of selfhood involves contradictory feelings. True differentiation. I have argued, is a whole, in tension between negation and recognition, affirming singularity and connectedness, continuity and discontinuity at once. O's hope—that in complete submission and acceptance of pain she will find her elusive self—may be seen as an attempt to experience self by risking death.

If we accept that O's consent to pain and enslavement is a search for transcendence, we still want to know why she chooses this form, rather than the possibility of reciprocal giving of self. We want to know this in the same way that we want to know why for Hegel the struggle for recognition ends in the power relationship instead of in reciprocal, equal self-sovereignty. Bataille suggests an answer with his idea of the transgression that both breaks and upholds the law. It allows one partner to remain rational and in control, while the other loses her boundaries. In fact, it is the master's rational, calculating, even instrumentalizing, attitude that excites submission, the image of his exquisite control that makes for his thrilling machismo. The pleasure, fo both partners, is in his mastery. Were both partners to give up self and control, the disorganization of self would be total. The masochistic ego would not be able to identify with the part in control. O could not then experience her loss of control as a controlled loss. She could not "safely" give in to her urge to lose control. When the boundary is freely dissolved, rather than broken by one who maintains his boundary, one is left unprotected before the infinite, the terrifying unknown. It may be, then, that the primary motivation for maintaining inequality in the erotic relationship, and ultimately for establishing the master-slave constellation, is the fear of ego loss—the boundless. And perhaps the boundless infinity of plenitude is as fearful as the infinity of emptiness.

The master-slave relationship actually perpetuates the problem it is designed to resolve. The rigid division into master and slave, sadist and masochist, ultimately exhausts its potential for transcendence. Neither partner can be both recognized and active-negating. Like the couple in the cuckoo clock, one must always be out when the other is in; they never meet. If the tension dissolves, death or abandonment is the inevitable end of the story, and *The Story of O* is deliberately left open to both conclusions. This ambiguity is appropriate because for the masochist the end or intolerable fate is abandonment, while for the sadist it is the death/murder of the other, whom he destroys. The mastery he achieves over the other is unsatisfactory, because when the other is drained of resistance she can only be vanquished by death. Metaphorically, the sadomasochistic relationship tends toward deadness, numbness, the exhaustion of sensation. This is ironic because the relationship is first introduced in order to escape this numbness by pain, this encasement by violation. The sadist, at least, is caught in the dialectic of objectification where the subject becomes increasingly like the objectified other he consumes.[17] In one form or another, controlling the other person out of existence is the inevitable end. The relation of domination is built simultaneously on the effort to push the other outside the self and the denial of the other's separate reality. Eventually the other's unreality becomes more powerful than the sadist's effort to separate himself. The frustration of feeling that there is no other person there, no one to recognize me, is repeated. And indeed the masochist's dilemma is feeling that she does not exist, that she is without will or desire, numb and purposeless. Violence and submission have provided only a temporary escape.

Violence, we may generalize, is an attempt at differentiation, at bringing the self or the other or both to life. The fantasy of erotic domination, the play with violence, is an attempt to relive an original effort at differentiation that failed. Just as the masochist is seeking not so much pain as servitude, the sadist is seeking not to injure the other but to combat the other's will. And it may well be that the response sought by the sadist is the opposite of what it appears. On the surface the sadist wants the other's submission. But in addition, less obviously, the sadist may be hoping for a response he never got, the response of an intact person who assures him that his assertion of self is in fact not so destructive[18] If the relationship remains limited to the level of play, if the masochist gets up and walks away a free person, this deeper satisfaction is partially achieved. We might speculate that the expression of violence is a replay of the original thwarted impulse to discover the other person as an intact being who could respond and set limits at the same time.

Yet the original need for a relationship of differentiation with another person is not really solved in erotic domination. What finally leads the partners back to frustration is that each continues to deny one side of the self. In adult erotic domination the sadist does not have the satisfaction of the other providing a limit, but has to control her or his own impulses. The masochist does get this satisfaction, but not for her own differentiating activity, only vicariously for the sadist's. Both partners are involved in controlling the other to conform to a fantasy, and to that extent the sense of relating to a real other is diminished. The aliveness and spontaneity that come from an unscripted relationship is missing.

Having referred repeatedly to a failure of differentiation as the core experience underlying erotic domination, let me now give this failure a context in the development of gender identity and gender domination in our culture. The peculiar pattern we see in this kind of ritualized violence is that of polarity or splitting: controller and controlled, violator and violated, assertive and yielding. The male experience of differentiation in our culture seems to point to an explanation of this tendency to polarize, to emphasize difference, to assert control, and to introduce rational calculation into eroticism. Making the other an object and instrument of one's own will seems to characterize a specific form of domination for which our culture provides a context.

The objectification of women in our culture seems to be rooted in the intense repudiation of the mother and maternal nurturance. As Nancy Chodorow has argued, this repudiation seems also to stamp the formation of male gender identity. Male children achieve their distinct identity by denying their identification or oneness with their mothers.[19] Initially all infants not only love their mothers but also identify with them and wish to emulate them. But boys discover that they cannot be, or become, her. Their experience of gender is that of a radical discontinuity and difference from the person to whom they are most attached, a disruption that girls are spared in gender development. The repudiation of the mother by men has meant that she is not recognized by the child in the normal course of differentiation. She is not seen as an independent person, another subject, but as something other: as nature, as an instrument or object, as less-than-human. An objectifying attitude comes to replace the earlier interactions of infancy, which contained the germ of mutual recognition. A male child's independence is bought at the price of saying: I am nothing like she who serves and cares for me. Thus male identity emphasizes difference from the nurturer over sameness, separation over connectedness, boundaries over continuity.[20]

The male experience of differentiation has stamped the image of individuality in our culture, for until recently the idea of "man" and "individual" were synonymous. In turn, women's own denial of their subjectivity corresponds to the male perception of the mother. She has become the one who is undifferentiated, the one who is object. She serves men as their other, their counterpart, the side of themselves they repress.[21] It follows from this gender division that the masochistic position is associated with the female, the sadistic with the male. That actual men and women often play the opposite role does not contradict this association. It affirms rather that erotic transgression is an opportunity to express what is ordinarily denied. Regardless of who plays which role, each gender represents only one part of a polarized whole, one aspect of the self-other relationship. This division prohibits the experience of true independence, of experiencing self and other as equally intact persons. One person is not allowed to play the subject, as women so long could not, and so cannot be an other who resists and recognizes her partner. One person is unable to perceive the other as subject, defines himself always in relation to an object. The groundwork for this division is laid in the mother's lack of subjectivity for her children, particularly in the male child's repudiation of his commonality with her.

Differentiation that occurs without appreciation of the mother's subjectivity is perfectly consonant with the development of rational faculties. The individual is able cognitively to distinguish self from other, knows that he is physically and mentally distinct, is able to perform socially as if other persons were subjects. But at the deepest level of feeling there is not that vibrant aliveness of knowing that I am I and you are you. The ability to experience self as real and other as real is greatly diminished, the ability to feel desire in response to another is also diminished. This makes the fantasy of erotic domination appealing as a way to break violently out of numbness. This kind of differentiation I call "false differentiation." It is actually the norm in our culture, coinciding with the male experience of the mother as different, Other, object.

To an increasing extent this form of individuality is becoming de-gendered: that is, male and female roles are no longer as binding as they once were. However, the insistence on boundaries and the conflict between our needs for autonomy and recognition remain entrenched in our norm of individuality.[22] The "false" resolution to this conflict of differentiation, in which the need for the other and the other's subjectivity are denied, persists. The traditionally female side of selfhood—stressing dependency, connectedness, yielding over separateness, difference, assertiveness, and above all stressing nurturance over control—is derogated whether or not it is associated with women directly.

For some time I have considered how dualistic individuality and false differentiation are linked to male hegemony in the culture. I have looked for the link between rationality as a masculine mental attitude and rationality as a pervasive tendency in the culture. It would seem that the male way of establishing and protecting individuality dovetails with what Western culture has defined as rationality. The Western rational world view emphasizes difference over sameness, boundaries over continuity, polarity and opposition over mutuality and interdependence. It does not tolerate the simultaneous experience of contradictory impulses, ambivalence. The tension that is true differentiation is seen in this view as an irreconcilable opposition, for example, between independence and dependence. The other, the whole world outside the thinking subject, is always "the Object." Evelyn Keller has pointed out the relationship between the way boys differentiate and their development of a scientific or objective approach to the world.[23] The basic tendencies of Western rationality correspond to the male repudiation of the mother, in which the other is objectified and instrumentalized. In other words, that attitude toward maternal nurturance and recognition which infuses early male identity formation also infuses the rationality that is dominant in our culture. It might be called "male rationality." Male hegemony in the culture is expressed by the generalization of rationality and the exclusion of nurturance, the triumph of individualistic, instrumental values in all forms of social interaction.

The increasing rationalization of our society has long been noted, as well as the dangerous and destructive way in which human power—for example, over nature—can now be exercised. Male rationality and violence are linked within institutions that appear to be genderless, so impersonal do they seem. Yet they exhibit the same tendency to control and objectify every living thing that we find in erotic domination. Rationalization and depersonalization in all public areas of life have by now virtually banished nurturance to the private household, the dwindling maternal world. The repudiation of recognition between persons and its displacement by impersonal forms of social intercourse is the social homologue of the male repudiation of the mother. The domestic confinement of nurturance literally sets the stage for the inability to appreciate the mother's subjectivity by depriving the maternal role of social recognition. The intensification of the parent-child relationship that results from privatized nurturance puts a weight on parents that was once borne by kin, community, and neighborhood. As a result the instrumental tendency to see children as products, touchstones of one's self-esteem, reflections of success or failure, is also intensified. Mothers are both more vulnerable to their children's conflicts and to the idealized, phony images of motherhood broadcast by the media. In a variety of ways, rationalization at the societal level reproduces the conditions for false differentiation and male rationality at the individual level.[24]

The tendency toward rationality in our culture has a number of important consequences. Ironically, domestic privatization seems to encourage strange new collective forms of violation. The secularization of society has eroded many of the previously existing forms of communal life that allowed for ritual transcendence. The experience of losing the self, of continuity, is increasingly difficult to obtain except in the erotic relationship. Consequently, sexual eroticism has become the heir to religious eroticism. Erotic masochism or submission expresses the same need for transcendence of self—the same flight from separation and discontinuity—formerly satisfied and expressed by religion. Love is the new religion, and the psychological components of erotic domination are repeated in the eroticized cult politics of our era.

I believe that we are facing unbearably intensified privatization and discontinuity, unrelieved by expressions of continuity. Given that social structure and culture enforce individual isolation so rigidly, the transgression that attempts to break it may necessarily be more violent. The increase of aestheticized and eroticized violence in our media (return of the repressed) suggests the fallacy in our ordinary understanding of control and self-control. The more rigid and tenacious the boundary between individuals, and the more responsible each individual for maintaining it, the greater the danger it will collapse. If the sense of boundary is established by physical, bodily separation, then sexual and phsyical violence (if not in reality, then in fantasy) are experienced as ways of breaking the boundary. The fantasy, as well as the playing out of rational violence, does offer a controlled form of transcendence, the promise of the real thing. Sadomasochistic imagery may be popular because it embodies this promise of transcendence without its fearful reality. Similarly, if masochists far outnumber sadists, it may be because people are in flight from discontinuity and rationality—especially men who have been charged with upholding it. The rejection of male rationality and control by men has become at least thinkable, because it represents an intolerable strain.

Beneath the sensationalism of power and powerlessness, the yearning to know and be known lies numbed. Real transcendence, I have argued, implies that persons are able to achieve a wholeness in which the opposing impulses for recognition and differentiation are combined. The psychological origins of erotic domination can be traced to one-sided differentiation, that is, to the splitting of these impulses and their assignment to women and men, respectively. In fact, all forms of gender distinction and domination in our culture bear the mark of this split. I would conclude not that the issues of differentiation and recognition are the explanation for gender domination, but that they help to reveal some of its inner workings.

A number of political implications can be drawn from this analysis of domination. I believe we are facing a crisis of male rationality and the resurgence of erotic fantasy. A politics that denies these issues, that tries to sanitize or rationalize the erotic, fantastic components of human life, will not defeat domination, but only vacate the field. Most of the feminist response to the increase in overt expressions of erotic domination has been at the level of moral condemnation rather than of understanding.[25] But no political movement can give expression to our real hopes and longing if it condemns without understanding the alienated forms in which these longings have appeared.

Unfortunately, this same tendency to assert that we need not understand sexuality often characterizes the opposition to moralism.[26] The defenders of sadomasochism have argued, rightly, that fantasy and play cannot and should not be legislated, and that such fantasy does not mean the advocacy of violence and domination in politics or "real life." However, this defense does not extend to asking what such fantasies mean and why they hold such power over our imagination. On the manifest level it may be true that the forbidden is exciting because it is forbidden. But as Freud pointed out, things are taboo precisely because they are exciting—otherwise they need not be prohibited. The question of what makes erotic domination exciting cannot be begged by defending or condemning it, by referring to either "different flavors" or to "male rage." The power of a fantasy, the fantasy of rational violence, must be attributed to the interplay of great social forces and deep human needs. A politics that dares to address these forces and appeal to these needs is no easy achievement. Even to envision dissolving that fantasy, so as to tolerate the tension of true differentiation and mutual recognition, will be difficult indeed.

Notes

This article is a condensation of a paper that originally appeared in *Feminist Studies* 6, no. 1 (Spring 1980) and in H. Eisenstein and A. Jardine, eds., *The Future of Difference*, (Boston: G. K. Hall, 1980).

1. There is a wide literature, psychoanalytic and developmental, on early differentiation. Perhaps the most influential recent work on what they call "separation-individuation" is Margaret Mahler, Fred Pine, and Anni Bergman, *The Psychological Birth of the Human Infant* (New York: Basic Books, 1975).

2. I refer here to the matrix of thought that has addressed the issue of women's mothering, including, above all, the work of Nancy Chodorow, *The Reproduction of Mothering: Psychoanalysis and the Sociology of Gender* (Berkeley: University of California Press, 1978); Dorothy Dinnerstein, *The Mermaid and the Minotaur: Sexual Arrangements and Human Malaise* (New York: Harper and Row, 1976); and Adrienne Rich, *Of Woman Born: Motherhood as Experience and Institution* (New York: W. W. Norton, 1976).

3. This point was originally well developed by Susan Brownmiller in reference to rape in *Against Our Will: Men, Women, and Rape* (New York: Simon and Schuster, 1975). Her view, like much of what has since been written on violence against women, often tends toward counter-blame, the condemnation of the male gender as inherently destructive.

4. Pauline Réage, *The Story of O*, transl. S. d'Estree (New York: Grove Press, 1965). As to the broader relevance of this study for the pornographic imagination or sadomaschostic fantasy, the best testimony is probably the power of the text and the exceedingly wide recognition it received. In fact, feminist critics have sometimes mistaken *The Story of O* for an affirmation of female degradation; see, for example, Andrea Dworkin, "Woman as Victim; Story of O," *Feminist Studies* 2, no. 1 (1974): 107–11. In addition, *Nine and a Half Weeks* by Elizabeth McNeill (New York: Dutton, 1978), an ostensibly authentic account of a sadomasochistic affair written by the woman participant, describes a kind of slavish psychological dependence uncannily similar to that of *O*.

5. G. W. F. Hegel, "The Independence and Dependence of Self-Consciousness: Master and Slave," chap. 4, of *The Phenomenology of Spirit* (Hamburg: Felix Meiner, 1952), pp. 141–50.

6. A variety of psychologists and psychoanalysts embrace this view of how selfhood develops. For example, developmentalists refer to a sense of effectance or of efficacy. See R. Schaffer, *Mothering* (Cambridge: Harvard University Press, 1977); and M. D. S. Ainsworth and S. M. Bell, "Mother-Infant Interaction and the Development of Competence," in *The Growth of Competence*, ed. K. Connelly and Jerome Bruner (New York: Academic Press, 1974), pp. 97–118. The psychoanalyst D. W. Winnicott writes of parental recognition of the baby's "spontaneous gestures" in "Ego Distortion in Terms of True and False Self," in *Maturational Processes and the Facilitating Environment* (New York: International University Press, 1965), pp. 140–52.

7. This idea is developed by Freud in several ways before reaching the point of coherence usually attributed to it today. In "Instincts and Their Vicissitudes" (1915), he reflects on primary narcissism, the state in which the ego attributes all that is pleasurable to itself and is essentially hostile to all that is outside. Later in 1930 he writes more specifically in *Civilization and Its Discontents* (New York: W. W. Norton, 1961) of the "narcissistic enjoyment" of destructiveness owing to its presenting the ego with a fulfillment of the latter's old wishes for omnipotence.

8. It is interesting that the argument that male fear of and rage at women explain pornography, made by Susan Lurie in *Take Back the Night*, relies on this Freudian model that omnipotence, the mother's total accommodation, is only given up unwillingly and is compensated for by the fantasy of a powerful penis. I find this argument somewhat one-sided; it ignores the child's own passionate wish to do things himself. It also makes the existence of the phallus, rather than the parental interaction with the child (e.g. how much they respect its burgeoning autonomy), decisive. See

Susan Lurie, "Pornography and the Dread of Woman: The Dilemma of Male Sexuality," in *Take Back the Night*, ed. L. Lederer (New York: Morrow, 1980). It must be said that despite the biologistic tendency of Lurie's argument, her article represents the only rational, serious attempt to explain the appeal of pornography in the entire section labeled, with characteristic simplemindedness, "Who Benefits"—as if violent or derogatory attitudes toward women made men happy, healthy, and wise.

9. Georges Bataille, *Death and Sensuality* (New York: Walker, 1962).

10. Georges Bataille, "Hemingway in the Light of Hegel," *Semiotexte* 2, no. 2 (1976): 1.

11. See Dworkin, "Woman as Victim."

12. Regine Deforges, *Confessions of O: Conversations with Pauline Réage*, Sabine d'Estree trans. (New York: Viking, 1979).

13. See Simone de Beauvoir, *The Second Sex*, (New York: Vintage, 1974), pp. 444–46. In her discussion of the Woman in Love, de Beauvoir describes the religious enthusiasm of "abolishing the self boundaries which separate her from her lover"—an enthusiasm that inspires the woman in love with man and the woman in love with God—but she distinguishes this "ecstatic union" from masochism, even though it may degenerate into self-debasement and destruction for the woman.

14. Réage. *Story of O*, pp. 15–17.

15. Gayle Rubin provides a more general theory of the phallus as symbol and mediation of male desire, in "The Traffic in Women: Notes on the 'Political Economy' of Sex," in *Toward an Anthropology of Women*, ed. Rayna R. Reiter (New York: Monthly Review Press, 1975), pp. 157–210. See also Nancy Chodorow. "Difference, Relation and Gender in Psychoanalytic Perspective." *Socialist Review* 9, no. 4 (July–August 1979): 51–70.

16. The theme of abandonment and loss is probably central to the development of masochistic fantasies, in which physical pain comes to stand for the psychic pain that can no longer be experienced. This idea has been developed in reference to particular clinical cases by Robert Stoller *Sexual Excitement* (New York: Simon and Schuster, 1980) and Mosad Khan, *Alienation in Perversions* (New York: International University Press, 1979).

17. Gender pronouns are used here for clarity, but in no way express an inevitable set of roles.

18. I have here condensed my argument about the underlying intent of certain kinds of violence. The idea that destructiveness is really an effort to place the other outside of the self by seeing that she or he survives is developed in D. W. Winnicott, "The Use of an Object and Relation Through Identifications," in *Playing and Reality* (Middlesex: Penguin, 1974), pp. 101–11.

19. Chodorow, *The Reproduction of Mothering*.

20. Ibid. See also Chodorow, "Difference, Relation, and Gender."

21. De Beauvoir, *The Second Sex*, first formulating the idea of women as Other has provided a beginning point for this analysis of the self-other relationship as applied to men and women, and more generally for an understanding of how the domination of women and the domination of nature/the world are connected. See also Dinnerstein, *The Mermaid and the Minotaur*.

22. I have developed the relationship between the polarity of gender and the formation of individuality in our culture at greater length in "The Oedipal Riddle: Authority, Autonomy and the New Narcissism," in *The Problem of Authority in America*, ed. J. Diggins and M. Kann (Philadelphia: Temple University Press, 1982).

23. Evelyn Fox Keller, "Gender and Science," *Psychoanalysis and Contemporary Thought* 1, no. 3 (1978): 409–53.

24. For a discussion of the relationship between rationality, patriarchy, and particular forms of socialization see my discussion in "Authority and the Family Revisited: A World without Fathers," *New German Critique* 4, no. 3 (Winter 1978): 35–57.

25. Typical of this sort of moral condemnation is *Take Back the Night,* and especially the Robin Morgan slogan "Pornography is the theory, rape is the practice." A refreshing and critical relief from this tendency to collapse fantasy and reality, thought and action is the *Heresies # 12* 3, no. 4 (1981), "Sex Issue."

26. Outspoken in representing this position has been Pat Califia. See "Feminism and Sadomasochism," in ibid.

Outside the Operating Room
of the Sex-Change Doctor
Sharon Olds

Outside the operating room of the sex-change doctor, a tray of penises.

There is no blood. This is not Vietnam, Chile, Buchenwald. They were surgically removed, under anesthetic. They lie there neatly, each with a small space around it.

The anesthetic is wearing off now. The chopped-off sexes lie on the silver tray.

One says *I am a weapon thrown down. Let there be no more killing.*

Another says *I am a thumb lost in the threshing machine. Gold straw fills the air. I will never have to work again.*

The third says *I am a caul removed from his eyes. Now he can see.*

The fourth says *I want to be painted by Géricault, a still life with a bust of Apollo, a drape of purple velvet, and a vine of ivy leaves.*

The fifth says *I was a dirty little dog, I knew he'd have me put to sleep.*

The sixth says *I am safe. Now no one can hurt me.*

Only one is unhappy. He lies there weeping in terrible grief, crying out *Father, Father!*

Movie
Nancy Harrison

It is 1951 and there are four of you in the car. It is a black Buick with heavy chrome which makes the black look dull. But it shines in the light from the poles overhead at the drive-in movie. You try to see past your mother's head. Your father's arm is white in the light through the window. He is bracing it against the edge of the window where the speaker is hung. Your little brother's head looks bald in the light. It is blond, shaved close for the summer. He looks innocent and unhappy as he sits on the seat next to you, his legs out in front of him, his head resting against the back of the seat as if he were an old man. The way he is looking he couldn't see anything but the sky through the top of the window at the front of the car. He is too little to be at the movies with you and your parents.

You are eating a picnic supper that your mother has brought. You reach your hand into the front seat and she hands you a tomato cut up into quarters with salt and pepper already on it. She has already put two paper napkins underneath so it won't drip. You catch the seeds and the juice where they fall onto your hand and suck them into your mouth, your lips curled like a fleshy straw. Your tongue works like an animal's. Your mouth feels good, hot on the tomato which is soft and cool. You pretend it is flesh and you are a carnivore. Something like a vampire, but furious, worse than bloodsucking.

"Cut it out," your father says.

"What?" you say, complaining.

"That noise. Cut it out."

You suck silently, viciously. The tomato is worn out, flaccid, but still yielding. You devour it.

The napkins are limp in your hand, wet. You can see flecks of pepper sticking to the damp surface. You take up one on the tip of your finger. It is black, like a tiny hole in the darkness at the tip of your white finger. You apply it to your tongue. It burns so minutely it brings a sneer to your lips.

"Here," you say peremptorily. You thrust the wet ball of paper at your mother. Your father turns his head toward you but his eyes remain on the screen. Your mother takes the napkin and thrusts it between her legs where the large sack is, where the rest of the supper and all the trash have gone. The movie hasn't started yet. Just the previews and some advertisements.

The movie is *Pandora and the Flying Dutchman* with Ava Gardner and James Mason. You are not sure about Ava Gardner but you like James Mason, his voice, which sounds cruel to you. The sounds in the film are the important thing. Outside, at a drive-in, the picture can get lost against the sky. It is the sound which brings you back to it. You can see the pictures sometimes from the road while you are driving by and they make no sense at all. They aren't even interesting. It is because there is no sound.

The sounds in *Pandora and the Flying Dutchman* are real. Water, for instance. Many of the pictures are green; there are trees moving to the sound of the wind blowing through them. You are only eleven but there is something about the picture which is sexy. You know it is sexy because you can feel it. As the picture goes along Ava Gardner's face begins to feel very good with the trees and the water, and her eyes listening to James Mason's voice. At the end she is dead as you knew she would be. Because of the sounds. And the way her mouth and eyes moved when she listened to his voice.

Your mother seems interested in the picture. She is very pretty. Her hair is brown and curly and her mouth is red and full.

Your father is bored. You don't know why he agrees to come to the movies at the drive-in, but the four of you have been doing it for the last several months. You think this is a movie they shouldn't bring children to but you are glad they did.

The part about the murder. It is more exciting than the kissing. There is something you don't understand but you find it thrilling when it happens and when you know it is going to happen again. It is a sound. It is at night and the green tropical trees are blowing in the wind. The walls of the bungalow are white. There are footsteps. A pair of men's shoes with the bottom of the trouser legs flapping against ankles. The shoes move quickly and without much noise against the cement walk. Black, brown, white, and green. Black, brown, white, green. Like a picture of the earth. The man's shoes move in the center of the screen. They move around a corner and stop at a door to the bungalow. All the sounds on the screen are hushed. There is only the rushing and breathing. The man whose shoes you see on the screen is breathing hard. Then it stops. He opens the door. It is dark inside. He walks forward. The picture moves up from his shoes. You feel a movement, but you do not see it. That is when you hear the sound. It is a knife. It goes into the man's back and you hear the sound. You do not even hear the outrush of his breath, or his surprise. It is the sound of the knife against bone, through his flesh and clothes, men's heavy clothes. It is the only sound on the screen and when the man's body crumples and falls to the floor in the darkness, so that only a little of it can be seen in the moonlight, the sound is still echoing in the stillness which is your own breath held and not let out yet. You are waiting for another blow, another sound.

At the end of the movie Ava Gardner is found dead on a beach, her body wrapped around and around with a fishing net, like a mermaid in seaweed. She is very beautiful and you knew it had to end that way. It is quiet at the end of the movie. Her skin is wet with water and her hair and the lines of the net wet the same color, one a little darker, a little fresher. Her mouth is very red, very beautiful as if she were cold but still warm from the blood inside. The real sound is the knife going into the man's body, which was the only real sound during the entire movie and which cut the movie right in half, down the middle, so that the sound was one which you knew was coming. After you heard it, it was the only one which lasted up to and past the sound of the stillness, which was the woman's body on the beach.

You look at your father to see if he hears the sound. He could not help but hear it, but as he lifts the speaker up and out the window to hang it back in its place outside the car he acts as if nothing had happened. The body of Ava Gardner is still lying on the screen. The colors are black and brown and white, only her lips are red and the warmth of her flesh to show what had happened.

I was thinking of the knife in my father's back.

As I stood up in the back seat I could hear the sound. I stood up with my stomach pressed against the seat in front of me. The air coming through the window was cool on my face after the sticky wetness of the heat at the movie. He could not hear the sound as he drove the car forward through the dark toward our house. He was pretending. He drove the car forward with a quiet look on his face. My mother was quiet too, looking toward the road in front of us. My brother was the only one who made any noise. A low-pitched humming yell restrained and held low so that it was like the baaing of a sheep. I looked at his bald-shaved head, his summer hair. He was the innocent one in the car.

The driveway was white; it was the concrete in the moonlight. My father parked the car in the driveway. My mother gathered the large paper bag from between her legs, my brother baaed and banged his head softly against the edge of the window to keep time. My father sighed as the sleeves of his white shirt moved to open the door and roll up the windows. I looked for the blood on his shirt but the shadows were so deep I could not make out the one splash from the other. In my disappointment I lingered in the car sitting on the edge of the scratchy back seat. The windows were rolled up and the silence in the car was loud. I did not hear my father's voice when he called to me to get out, to come inside. But I did hear the noise of the knife in his back. And I looked at him very cruelly as he raised his voice to me. My mother was asleep on the porch, no longer waiting for either of us although she was standing near the door. I waited for the moonlight to show the knife in my father's back. I could hear the noise. Does he remember Ava Gardner on the beach? No. Does he hear the noise? I think so. Yes.

They have gone inside and left me, for a punishment. My father walks to the front door, which is inside the screen porch, and my mother follows with the sack in one hand and my little brother's hand in the other. My mother comes back to the front door and turns the light on so I won't feel scared. She leaves the door open a crack so she can hear me if I yell. I make no noise at all.

It is dark in the car but lighter where the moon is. It is almost as bright as if it were morning. It will only stop being bright if the moon goes behind a bank of clouds. It would look like the sky in the movie. The moon moved like a ship against the clouds and through them. I cannot restrain my curiosity and I move toward the window and look up at the sky. The moon is full and lights up the sky even when it goes in and out of clouds. My mouth is open so that I can look better. I know it is open because I can feel it. My eyes and my mouth open wider and wider. I like it very much.

My father cannot stand the silence. He is afraid of the noise and of the silence, the one will come only after the other. He bangs the door and comes after me through the porch.

"All right, all right," I say, "I'm coming." I do not want him to walk outside again after he has already gone in the house. He has to stay in the house.

He will not stay in the house without me. I must get out of the car in order to keep him inside the front porch; he is rattling the screen door right now. I'M COMING. He shoves the door all the way open and waits for me to prove it. I look at his large white arm pressed against the wooden frame and the screen. I hear my mother and my little brother even without seeing them. I hear the water running from where I am walking inside the porch under the outstretched arm of my father. He looks down at me, at the top of my head. I can see the movement but I do not look up at him. I wait for him to pass me, after I hear the door slam shut. It is amazing how loud a weak screen door can slam. It is the extra shaking, the wire screening, which is either old and rusted or new and vibrating.

It makes then a rattle or a hum, one or the other; in any case it is a loud noise for a thin and flimsy door. Does he hear the other sound?

He will not walk in front of me; he waits for me to walk in front of him out of the porch and into the living room.

There is no light in the living room, only in the bedroom where I hear my mother putting my brother to bed. It is surprising how in a quiet house the noise of sheets and mattresses bumping, of legs and skin scraping against sheets, can make a noise you can hear from one room to the other. That is the noise I hear and my mother's footsteps as she walks across the part of the floor that gives, making a creak when your foot is lifted from it. My father knows I do not like to walk into darkened rooms. He waits until I have walked into the dark living room before he moves past me and toward the light in the other part of the house. Their bedroom.

My mother comes into the darkened living room. I am walking toward the bedroom which I share with my brother. My father is leaving the living room and disappearing into the other part of the house. We are like three people walking in the street. Everybody going a different direction. Is she going to speak to me? I can still see my father's back disappearing. It's your bedtime she says. She looks tired and beautiful in the light from the other part of the house. I can see her hair and the part of her face which is not in shadow. Her feet are very small on the living room rug. Here, she says, and cups my cheek in her hand, I left the light on next to the bed. I look through the bedroom door. It is true. There is a light which reflects dimly against the shiny paint of the open door. *Thank you* I say to my mother, but I do not say it out loud.

I have almost forgotten the sound, but I remember it again when I lie down in the bed and cover my body with a sheet. Only a sheet, I don't like heavy things on my body. I can feel the air through the sheet. I didn't really forget the noise. I had to forget it while I walked through the darkened living room. I have turned off the lamp next to my bed and in my own darkness it is almost light. The sheets are gray in the light from the moon outside and the walls, almost, are white. It *is* like a kind of light in the room.

Before I go to sleep I see again my mother in the shadow waves of the living room, her small feet on the living room rug. His white back in a t-shirt has almost left the room. She is looking toward me and we both know. I think she knows. My feet are almost as large, as small, as hers. I hear the footsteps of the man's shoes on the sidewalk, the flap of his trouser legs, which reveals the sound. In another part of the house my father is sleeping or reading lying flat on his back. He will turn over soon. My mother is in the kitchen, rattling paper bags and shutting cupboards. Wiping a cloth over a surface before she turns the light out and goes to bed. I hear water running. I like to hear the sound of water running. It is a soothing, a curling sound. After it has stopped I listen for the other. As I lie under my sheet the air presses the sheet against my legs, my toes, my stomach. I put my hands across my stomach. It is a nice, round, flat stomach. I listen to the flapping of the trousers which is the sound. It is in my mind, I have to listen hard to hear it on the sidewalk outside. It is outside my father's window, where he has now turned over. His back is to the window and to the door which leads outside. He doesn't hear the sound, and after my mother has gone to bed he will not hear it until he thinks, yes, he is hearing it, and by then, when he will have stood up with his back to the door and to the window, it will have been too late.

The footsteps are near the window. I hear the sound as I see my father sleeping. Does he hear the sound? I don't think so. He must hear the sound because it cannot happen without it. I remember: the man in the suit is the one who walks into the darkness and the sound is made by the knife going into his back. My father is in a white t-shirt and boxer shorts. He is in the room where the man walks in. *Who* is hearing the sound besides me? It is a nagging question. I get up very quietly. Even the floor is quiet. I tiptoe to their bedroom and look at my father. I am looking through the window where the man is. I must hear the sound if it is going to happen. My father is still sleeping. The only sound in the room is his breathing. My mother seems not to breathe in her sleep. I wait. I can hear the sound outside the window. I cannot stand in their bedroom all night. I walk over to my father's bed and look at his back. I hear the sound. He is still breathing.

I go to sleep sure of some things and uncertain of others. Some things cannot be planned, those you make a list of and like or dislike according to the completeness of your list. If it is a good list that is good enough and is contenting. I go to sleep content, listening to the sound which I can hear in my father's back.

In the morning I wake up early. I am very excited. My brother is still sleeping, the soft bristles of his bald blond hair float his head on the pillow, but he pushes his face into it. His hand is on the pillow near his face. It still looks like a baby's or a doll's. He wakes up when I do, no matter how quiet I am. In fact, I can simply lie in the bed across from him and think and he will wake up in a few minutes as if my brain has been rustling or my thoughts have been whispering aloud. It's okay, Willy, go back to sleep. Sometimes that works. It does this morning. He smiles at me against the pillow. You can talk him into almost anything, he is that sweet and my younger brother. It makes me feel sentimental, even though I am only eleven years old. I smile at my brother with his eyes closed.

No one is in the kitchen. There are no noises in the house. I am going to look at my father sleeping. I no longer hear the sound. I am looking for a knife.

I go to their bedroom and my father is lying on his side, his back turned away from me. I go back to the den and through the side door to go around the corner of the house and look in the window. His back is huge and white with the t-shirt spread over it. His bare feet show on top of the covers, one bare leg is drawn up at the knee and covers his stomach. His shorts are high up his thigh in wrinkles so his leg can pull his knee up that way. There is no knife. Maybe he heard the sound in time. Maybe he had heard the sound and waited for it, or had gotten rid of it in some way. I cannot believe it. I sit down under the window, under the chinaberry tree where the lavender blossoms have fallen down, and scrape in the dirt with my toes. I get up again and look hard at the white back. Right there is where the sound would be. I can hear it. I sit down again and listen to it. It is still there. Nothing happens in a day. Even in the movies: days pass. Centuries. Sometimes it has to be done over and over again. The sound is still there. If he can hear it. I will make him listen to it.

At breakfast there are fried eggs and bacon and toast with cinnamon and sugar. My father eats with his newspaper across from me. My mother's egg is last. My little brother will eat only toast and bacon. My father drinks milk at breakfast like a child. This morning I take his milk away from him and he doesn't notice. I do not look at my father, only at the empty milk glass. It affects me strangely to look at his milk glass. I cannot hear anything as I drink my own milk. It covers my hearing as it rushes down my throat.

Street Dream #1
Sharon Thompson

I dreamed that I was in a house with my lover. We had separate bedrooms and it was her parents' house. The halls were streets. My lover wanted to stop sleeping with me. She said she had another lover. She said this had nothing to do with her mother. I went into her bedroom, crossing the street against the light. It was her parents' bedroom but they were gone. Please, I said. I began. She stopped me. She said that when we made love it was less interesting than being alone. Yes, I said. It's like that. I went away. The streets were dark. I slept for a while, woke up very early. I wanted to ask her why it was like that. Parked cars in the road, nothing moving. I opened the door to her parents' room. Her brother was there. He was huge. He looked as if he had slept in his clothes. I asked if he knew where his sister was sleeping. He said in her sister's bedroom. I went in. A window of her mother's room looked through to this room. My lover was lying on a park bench. This room was Union Square. My lover had on all her clothes and her purse was by her side, the strap clutched in her hands as if she thought I was going to rape and rob her. I said her name. She sat up stiffly. I sat down on the bench in front of her and put my hands on her shoulders. I said, Can't you even look at me? She said, I'm afraid. I thought, that's not it. I got up to leave. It was morning. Cars honking. Gasoline fumes. Her mother paced in the window.

Is the Gaze Male?
E. Ann Kaplan

Since the beginning of the recent women's liberation movement, American feminists have been exploring the representation of female sexuality in the arts—literature, painting, film, and television.[1] The first wave of feminist critics adopted a broadly sociological approach, looking at sex roles women were seen to occupy in all kinds of imaginative works, from high art to mass entertainment. Roles were assessed as "positive" or "negative" according to some externally constructed criteria for the fully autonomous, independent woman.

Feminist film critics were the first to object to this prevailing critical approach, largely because of the general developments taking place in film theory at the beginning of the 1970s.[2] They noted the lack of awareness about the way images are constructed through the mechanism of whatever artistic practice is involved; representations, they pointed out, are mediations, embedded through the art form in the dominant ideology. Influenced by the work of Claude Lévi-Strauss, Roland Barthes, Jacques Lacan, Christian Metz, Julia Krîsteva, and others, women began to apply the tools of psychoanalysis, semiology, and structuralism in analyzing the representation of women in film.[3] I will not duplicate the history of these theoretical developments here; let it suffice to note, by way of introduction, that increasing attention has been given first, to cinema as a signifying practice, to *how meaning is produced* in film rather than to something that used to be called its "content"; and second, to the links between the processes of psychoanalysis and those of cinema.[4] Feminists have been particularly concerned with how sexual difference is constructed psychoanalytically through the Oedipal process, especially as this is read by Lacan. For Lacan, woman cannot enter the world of the symbolic, of language, because at the very moment of the acquisition of language, she learns that she lacks the phallus, the symbol that sets language going through a recognition of difference; her relation to language is a negative one, a lack. In patriarchal structures, thus, woman is located as other (enigma, mystery), and is thereby viewed as outside of (male) language.

The implications of this for cinema are severe: dominant (Hollywood) cinema is seen as constructed according to the unconscious of patriarchy, which means that film narratives are constituted through a phallocentric language and discourse that parallels the language of the unconscious. Women in film, thus, do not function as signifiers for a signified (a real woman) as sociological critics have assumed, but signifier and signified have been elided into a sign that represents something in the male unconscious.[6]

Two basic Freudian concepts—voyeurism and fetishism—have been used to explain what exactly woman represents and the mechanisms that come into play for the male spectator watching a female screen image. (Or, to put it rather differently, voyeurism and fetishism are mechanisms the dominant cinema uses to *construct* the male spectator in accordance with the needs of his unconscious.) The first, voyeurism, is linked to the scopophilic instinct (i.e., the male pleasure in his own sexual organ transferred to pleasure in watching other people having sex). Critics argue that the cinema relies on this instinct, making the spectator essentially a voyeur. The drive that causes little boys to peek through keyholes of parental bedrooms to learn about their sexual activities (or to get sexual gratification by thinking about these activities) comes into play when the male adult watches films, sitting in a dark room. The original eye of the camera, controlling and limiting what can be seen, is reproduced by the projector aperture that lights up one frame at a time; and both processes (camera and projector) duplicate the eye at the keyhole, whose gaze is confined by the keyhole "frame." The spectator is obviously in the voyeur position when there are sex scenes on the screen, but screen images of women are sexualized no matter what the women are doing literally, or what kind of plot may be involved.

According to Laura Mulvey (the British filmmaker and critic whose theories are central to new developments), this eroticization of women on the screen comes about through the way the cinema is structured around three explicitly male looks or gazes: there is the look of the camera in the situation where events are being filmed (called the profilmic event)—while technically neutral, this look, as we have seen, is inherently voyeuristic and usually "male" in the sense of a man doing the filming; there is the look of the men within the narrative, which is structured so as to make women objects of their gaze; and finally there is the look of the male spectator that imitates (or is necessarily in the same position as) the first two looks.[7]

But if women were simply eroticized and objectified, things might not be too bad, since objectification may be an inherent component of both male and female eroticism. (As I will show later on, however, things in this area are not symmetrical.) But two further elements enter in: to begin with, men do not simply look; their gaze carries with it the power of action and of possession that is lacking in the female gaze. Women receive and return a gaze, but cannot act on it. Second, the sexualization and objectification of women is not simply for the purposes of eroticism; from a psychoanalytic point of view, it is designed to annihilate the threat that woman (as castrated, and possessing a sinister genital organ) poses. In her 1932 article "The Dread of Woman," Karen Horney goes to literature to show that "men have never tired of fashioning expressions for the violent force by which man feels himself drawn to the woman, and side by side with his longing, the dread that through her he might die and be undone."[8] Later on, Horney conjectures that even man's glorification of women "has its source not only in his cravings for love, but also in his desire to conceal his dread. A similar relief, however, is also sought and found in the disparagement of women that men often display ostentatiously in their attitudes."[9] Horney goes on to explore the basis of the dread of women not only in castration (more related to the father), but in fear of the vagina.

But psychoanalysts agree that, for whatever reason—the fear of castration (Freud), or the attempt to deny the existence of the sinister female genital (Horney)—men endeavor to find the penis in women.[10] Feminist film critics have seen this phenomenon (clinically known as fetishism) operating in the cinema; the camera (unconsciously) fetishizes the female form, rendering it phallus-like so as to mitigate woman's threat. Men, that is, turn "the represented figure itself into a fetish so that it becomes reassuring rather than dangerous" (hence overvaluation, the cult of the female star).[11]

The apparently contradictory attitudes of glorification and disparagement pointed out by Horney thus turn out to be a reflection of the same ultimate need to annihilate the dread that woman inspires. In the cinema, the twin mechanisms of fetishism and voyeurism represent two different ways of handling this dread. As Mulvey points out, fetishism "builds up the physical beauty of the object, turning it into something satisfying in itself," while voyeurism, linked to disparagement, has a sadistic side, and is involved with pleasure through control or domination, and with punishing the woman (guilty for being castrated).[12] For Claire Johnston, both mechanisms result in woman's not being presented qua *woman* at all. Extending the *Cahiers du Cinéma* analysis of *Morocco,* Johnston argues that Sternberg represses "the idea of woman as a social and sexual being," thus replacing the opposition man/woman with male/nonmale.[13]

With this brief look at feminist film theories as background, we can turn to the question of the gaze: as it stands, current work using psychoanalysis and semiology has demonstrated that the dominant cinematic apparatus is constructed by men for a male spectator.

Women as women are absent from the screen *and* from the audience. Several questions now arise: first, is the gaze *necessarily* male (i.e., for reasons inherent in the structure of language, the unconscious, all symbolic systems, and thereby all social structures)? Or would it be possible to structure things so that women own the gaze? Second, would women want to own the gaze, if it were possible? Third, in either case, what does it mean to be a female spectator? Women are in fact present in audiences: what is happening to them as they watch a cinematic apparatus that constructs a male viewer? Does a woman spectator of female images have any choice other than either identifying as female object of desire, or if subject of desire, then appropriating the male position? Can there be such a thing as the female subject of desire? Finally, if a female subject is watching images of lesbians, what can this mean to her? How do such images inform women's actual, physical relations with other women?[14]

It is extremely important for feminist film critics to begin to address these questions. First, behind these questions, posed largely in structural terms, lie the larger questions concerning female desire and female subjectivity: Is it possible for there to be a female voice, a female discourse? What can a feminine specificity mean? Second, those of us working within the psychoanalytic system need to find a way out of an apparently overwhelming theoretical problem that has dramatic consequences for the way we are constituted, and constitute ourselves, not just in representation but also in our daily lives. Is there any escape from the overdetermined, phallocentric sign? The whole focus on the materialization of the signifier has again brought daily experience and art close together. Now critics read daily life as structured according to signifying practices (like art, "constructed," not naively experienced), rather than the earlier oversimplification of seeing art as a mere reflection/imitation of lived experience (mirroring it, or, better, presenting it as through a transparent pane of glass).

Finally, the growing interest in psychoanalytic and semiological approaches has begun to polarize the feminist film community,[15] and I want to begin by addressing some objections to current theoretical work, since they will lead us back to the larger questions of the female gaze and female desire. In a roundtable discussion in 1979, some women voiced their displeasure with theories that were themselves originally devised by men, and with women's preoccupation with how we have been seen/placed/positioned by the dominant male order. Julia LeSage, for instance, argues that the use of Lacanian criticism has been destructive in reifying women "in a childlike position that patriarchy has wanted to see them in"; for LeSage, the Lacanian framework establishes "a discourse which is totally male."[16] And Ruby Rich objects to theories that rest with the apparent elimination of women from both screen and audience. She asks how we can move beyond our placing, rather than just analyzing it. [17]

As if in response to Rich's request, some feminist film critics have begun to take up the challenge of moving beyond the preoccupation with how women have been constructed in patriarchal cinema. In a recent paper on *Gentlemen Prefer Blondes*, Lucie Arbuthnot and Gail Seneca attempt to appropriate for themselves some of the images hitherto defined as repressive. They begin by expressing their dissatisfaction not only with current feminist film theory as outlined above, but also with the new theoretical feminist films, which, they say, "focus more on denying men their cathexis with women as erotic objects than in connecting women with each other." In addition, these films, by "destroying the narrative and the possibility for viewer identification with the characters, destroy both the male viewer's pleasure and our pleasure."[18] Asserting their need for identification with strong female screen images, they argue that Hollywood films offer many examples of pleasurable identification; in a clever analysis, the relationship between Marilyn Monroe and Jane Russell in *Gentlemen Prefer Blondes* is offered as an example of strong women, who care for one another, providing a model we need.

However, looking at the construction of the film as a whole, rather than simply isolating certain shots, it is clear that Monroe and Russell are positioned, and position themselves, as objects for a specifically male gaze. The men's weakness does not mitigate their diegetic power, leaving to the women merely the limited control they can wield through their sexuality. The film constructs them as "to-be-looked-at," and their manipulations end up merely comic, since "capturing" the men involves their "being captured." The images of Monroe show her fetishized placement, aimed at reducing her sexual threat, while Russell's stance is a parody of the male position.[19] The result is that the two women repeat, in exaggerated form, dominant gender stereotypes.

Yet Arbuthnot and Seneca begin from important points: first, the need for films that construct *women* as the spectator and yet do not offer *repressive* identifications (as, for example, Hollywood women's films do);[20] and second, the need for feminist films that satisfy our craving for *pleasure*. In introducing the notion of pleasure, Arbuthnot and Seneca pinpoint a central and little-discussed issue. Mulvey was aware of the way feminist films as counter-cinema would deny pleasure, but she argued that this denial was a necessary prerequisite for freedom, and did not go into the problems involved.[21] Arbuthnot and Seneca locate the paradox in which feminist film critics have been caught without realizing it: namely, that we have been analyzing Hollywood (rather than, say, avant-garde) films, largely because they bring us pleasure; but we have (rightly) been wary of admitting the degree to which the pleasure comes from identifying with our own objectification. Our positioning as "to-be-looked-at," as object of the gaze, has, through our positioning, come to be sexually pleasurable.

However, it will not do to simply enjoy our oppression unproblematically; to appropriate Hollywood images to ourselves, taking them out of the context of the total structure in which they appear, will not get us very far. In order to fully understand *how it is* that women take pleasure in the objectification of women, one has to have recourse to psychoanalysis. Since criticisms like those voiced by LeSage, Rich, and Arbuthnot and Seneca are important, and reflect the deepening rift in the feminist film community, it is worth dwelling for a moment on why psychoanalysis is necessary as a feminist tool at this point in our history.

As Christian Metz, Stephen Heath, and others have shown, the processes of cinema mimic in many ways those of the unconscious. The mechanisms Freud distinguishes in relation to dream and the unconscious have been likened to the mechanisms of film.[22] In this analysis, film narratives, like dreams, symbolize a latent, repressed content, only now the "content" refers not to an individual unconscious but to that of patriarchy in general. If psychoanalysis is a tool that will unlock the meaning of dreams, it should also unlock that of films.

But of course the question still remains as to the ideology of psychoanalysis: is it true, as Talking Lips argues at the start of the film *Sigmund Freud's Dora,* that psychoanalysis is a discourse shot through with bourgeois ideology, functioning "almost as an Ideological State Apparatus," with its focus the individual, "outside of real history and real struggle?"[23] Or is psychoanalysis, although developed at a time when bourgeois capitalism was the dominant form, a theory that applies *across* history rather than being *embedded in* history?

Of these two possibilities, the first seems to me to be true. Psychoanalysis and cinema are inextricably linked both to each other and to capitalism, because both are products of a particular stage of capitalist society. The psychic patterns created by capitalist social and interpersonal structures (especially the nuclear family) required at once a machine for their unconscious release and an analytic tool for understanding and adjusting disturbances caused by the structures confining people. To this extent, both mechanisms support the status quo; but they are not eternal and unchanging, being rather inserted in history and linked to the particular social formation that produced them.

For this very reason, we have to begin by using psychoanalysis if we want to understand how we have been constituted, and the kind of linguistic and cultural universe we live in. Psychoanalysis may indeed have been used to oppress women, in the sense of forcing us to accept a positioning that is inherently antithetical to subjectivity and autonomy; but if that is the case, we need to know exactly *how* this has functioned to repress what we could potentially become. Given our positioning as women raised in a historical period dominated by Oedipal structuring and discourse, we must start by examining the psychoanalytic processes as they have worked to position us as other (enigma, mystery), and as eternal and unchanging, however paradoxical this may appear. For it is only in this way that we can begin to find the gaps and fissures through which we can reinsert woman in history, and begin to change ourselves as a first step toward changing society.

Let us now return to the question of women's pleasure in being objectified and see what we can learn about it through psychoanalysis. We saw earlier that the entry of the father as the third term disrupts the mother/child dyad, causing the child to understand the mother's castration and possession by the father. In the symbolic world the girl now enters she learns not only subject/object positions but the sexed pronouns "he" and "she." Assigned the place of object (since she lacks the phallus, the symbol of the signifier), she is the recipient of male desire, the passive recipient of his gaze. If she is to have sexual pleasure, it can only be constructed around her objectification; it cannot be a pleasure that comes from desire for the other (a subject position)— that is, her desire is to be desired.

Given the male structuring around sadism that I have already discussed, the girl may adopt a corresponding masochism.[24] In practice, this masochism is rarely reflected in more than a tendency for women to be passive in sexual relations; but in the realm of fantasy, masochism is often quite prominent. In an interesting paper, "The 'Woman's Film': Possession and Address," Mary Ann Doane has shown that in the one film genre that constructs a female spectator, that spectator is made to participate in what is essentially a masochistic fantasy. Doane notes that in the major classical genres, the female body *is* sexuality, providing the erotic object for the male spectator. In the woman's film, the gaze must be de-eroticized (since the spectator is now assumed to be female), but in doing this the films effectively disembody their spectator. The repeated masochistic scenarios are designed to immobilize the female viewer, refuse her the imaginary identification that, in uniting body and identity, gives back to the male spectator his idealized (mirror) self, together with a sense of mastery and control.[25]

Later on in her paper, Doane shows that Freud's "A Child Is Being Beaten" is important in distinguishing the way a common masochistic fantasy works out for boys and for girls. In the male fantasy, "sexuality remains on the surface" and the man "retains his own role and his own gratification in the context of the scenario. The 'I' of identity remains." But the female fantasy is, first, desexualized, and, second, "necessitates the woman's assumption of the position of spectator, outside of the event." In this way, the girl manages, as Freud says, "to escape from the demands of the erotic side of her life altogether."[26]

Perhaps we can phrase this a little differently and say that in locating herself in fantasy in the erotic, the woman places herself as either passive recipient of male desire, or, at one remove, positions herself as *watching* a woman who is passive recipient of male desires and sexual actions. Although the evidence we have to go on is slim, it does seem that women's sexual fantasies would confirm the predominance of these positionings. Nancy Friday's volumes, for instance, provide discourses on the level of dream and, however questionable as scientific evidence, show narratives in which the woman speaker largely arranges the scenario for her sexual pleasure so that things are done to her, or in which she is the object of men's lascivious gaze.[27] Often, there is pleasure in anonymity, or in a strange man approaching her when she is with her husband. Rarely does the dreamer initiate the sexual activity, and the man's large, erect penis usually is central in the fantasy. Nearly all the fantasies have the dominance-submission pattern, with the woman in the latter place.

It is significant that in the lesbian fantasies that Friday has collected women occupy *both* positions, the dreamer excited either by dominating another woman, forcing her to have sex, or enjoying being so dominated. These fantasies suggest either that the female positioning is not as monolithic as critics often imply, or that women occupy the "male" position when they become dominant. Whichever the case may be, the prevalence of the dominance-submission pattern as a sexual turn-on is clear. At a discussion about pornography organized by Julia LeSage at the Northwestern Conference on Feminist Film Criticism, gay and straight women admitted their pleasure (in both fantasy and actuality) in being "forced" or "forcing" someone else. Some women claimed that this was a result of growing up in Victorian-style households where all sexuality was repressed, but others denied that it had anything to do with patriarchy. Women wanted, rightly, to accept themselves sexually, whatever the turn-on mechanism.[28] But to simply celebrate whatever gives us sexual pleasure seems to me both problematic and too easy: we need to analyze how it is that certain things turn us on, how sexuality has been constructed in patriarchy to produce pleasure in the dominance-submission forms, before we advocate these modes.

It was predictable that many of the male fantasies in Friday's book *Men in Love* would show the speaker constructing events so that he is in control: again, the "I" of identity remains central, as it was not in the female narrations.[29] Many male fantasies focus on the man's excitement arranging for his woman to expose herself (or even give herself) to

other men, while he watches. The difference between this male voyeurism and the previous female form is striking: the women do not own
the desire, even when they watch; their watching is to place responsibility for sexuality at yet one more remove, to distance themselves
from sex; the man, on the other hand, owns the desire and the woman,
and gets pleasure from exchanging the woman, as in Lévi-Strauss'
kinship system.

Yet some of the fantasies in Friday's book show men's wish to be
taken over by an aggressive woman who would force them to become
helpless, like the little boy in his mother's hands. The Women Against
Pornography guided trip around Times Square corroborated this; after
a slide show that focused totally on male sadism and violent sexual
exploitation of women, we were taken on a tour that showed literature
and film loops expressing as many fantasies of male as of female submission. The situations were the predictable ones, showing young boys
(but sometimes men) seduced by women in a form of authority—
governesses, nursemaids, nurses, schoolteachers, stepmothers. (Of
course, it is significant that the corresponding dominance-submission
female fantasies have men in authority positions that carry much more
status—professors, doctors, policemen, executives: these men seduce
the innocent girls, or young wives, who cross their paths.)

Two interesting things emerge from all this: one is that dominance-
submission patterns are apparently a crucial part of both male and
female sexuality as constructed in western capitalism. The other is that
men have a far wider range of positions available: more readily both
dominant and submissive, they vacillate between supreme control and
supreme abandonment. Women, meanwhile, are more consistently
submissive, but not excessively abandoned. In their own fantasies,
women do not position themselves as exchanging men, although a man
might find being exchanged an exciting fantasy.

But the important question remains: when women are in the dominant position, are they in the *masculine* position? Can we envisage a
female dominant position that would differ qualitatively from the male
form of dominance? Or is there merely the possibility for both sex
genders to occupy the positions we now know as masculine and
feminine?

The experience of recent films of the 1970s and 1980s would support
the latter possibility, and explain why many feminists have not been
excited by the so-called liberated woman on the screen, or by the fact
that some male stars have recently been made to seem the object of the
female gaze. Traditionally male stars did not necessarily (or even
primarily) derive their glamour from their looks or their sexuality, but
from the power they were able to wield within the filmic world in
which they functioned (i.e., John Wayne); these men, as Laura Mulvey

has shown, became ego ideals for the men in the audience, corresponding to the image in the mirror, who was more in control of motor coordination than the young child looking in. "The male figure," Mulvey notes, "is free to command the stage . . . of spatial illusion in which he articulates the look and creates the action."[30]

Recent films have begun to change this pattern: a star like John Travolta (*Saturday Night Fever*, *Urban Cowboy*, *Moment by Moment*) has been rendered the object of woman's gaze and in some of the films (i.e., *Moment by Moment*) placed explicitly as a sexual object to a woman who controlled the film's action. Robert Redford likewise has begun to be used as the object of female desire (i.e., in *Electric Horseman*). But it is significant that in all these films, when the man steps out of his traditional role as the one who controls the whole action, and when he is set up as a sex object, the woman then takes on the masculine role as bearer of the gaze and initiator of the action. She nearly always loses her traditionally feminine characteristics in so doing—not those of attractiveness, but rather of kindness, humaneness, motherliness. She is now often cold, driving, ambitious, manipulating, just like the men whose position she has usurped.

Even in a supposedly feminist film like *My Brilliant Career* the same processes are at work. The film is interesting because it places in the foreground the independent minded heroine's dilemma in a clearly patriarchal culture: in love with a wealthy neighbor, the heroine makes him the object of her gaze, but the problem is that, as female, her desire has no power. Men's desire naturally carries power with it, so when the hero finally concedes his love for her, he comes to get her. However, being able to conceive of "love" only as "submission," an end to autonomy and to her life as a creative writer, the heroine now refuses. The film thus plays with established positions, but is unable to work through them to something else.

What we can conclude from the discussion so far is that our culture is deeply committed to clearly demarcated sex differences, called masculine and feminine, that revolve on, first, a complex gaze-apparatus; and, second, dominance-submission patterns. This positioning of the two sex genders clearly privileges the male through the mechanisms of voyeurism and fetishism, which are male operations, and because his desire carries power/action, where woman's usually does not. But as a result of the recent women's movement, women have been permitted in representation to assume (step into) the position defined as masculine, as long as the man then steps into *her* position, so as to keep the whole structure intact.

It is significant, of course, that while this substitution is made to happen relatively easily in the cinema, in real life any such "swapping" is fraught with the immense psychological difficulties that only psychoanalysis can unravel. In any case, such "exchanges" do not do much for either sex, since nothing has essentially changed: the roles remain locked into their static boundaries. Showing images of mere reversal may in fact provide a safety valve for the social tensions that the women's movement has created by demanding a more dominant role for women.

We have thus arrived at the point where we must question the necessity for the dominance-submission structure. The gaze is not necessarily male (literally), but to own and activate the gaze, given our language and the structure of the unconscious, is to be in the masculine position. It is for this reason that Julia Kristeva and others have said that it is impossible to know what the feminine might be; while we must reserve the category "women" for social demands and publicity, Kristeva says that by "woman" she means "that which is not represented, that which is unspoken, that which is left out of meanings and ideologies."[31] For similar reasons, Sandy Flitterman and Judith Barry have argued that feminist artists must avoid claiming a specific female power residing in the body of women that represents "an inherent feminine artistic essence which could find expression if allowed to be explored freely." The impulse toward this kind of art is understandable in a culture that denies satisfaction in being a woman, but it results in motherhood's being redefined as the seat of female creativity, while women "are proposed as the bearers of culture, albeit an alternative one."[32]

Barry and Flitterman argue that this form of feminist art, along with some others that they outline, is dangerous in not taking into account "the social contradictions involved in 'femininity.'" They suggest that "a radical feminist art would include an understanding of how women are constituted through social practices in culture," and argue for "an aesthetics designed to subvert the production of 'woman' as commodity," much as Claire Johnston and Laura Mulvey had earlier stated that to be feminist, a cinema had to be a counter-cinema.[33]

The problem with all these arguments is that they leave women trapped in the position of negativity—subverting rather than positing. Although the feminists asserting this point of view are clearly right in placing in the foreground women's repression in representation and culture (and in seeing this work as a necessary first step), it is hard to see how women can move forward from these awarenesses. If certain feminist groups (i.e., Women Against Pornography) err on the side of eliding reality with fantasy (i.e., in treating an image's violating of women on the same level as a literal act of violation on the street), feminist critics err on the side of seeing a world constructed only of signifiers, of losing contact with the "referred" world of the social formation.

The first error was in positing an unproblematic relationship between art and life in the sense that (1) art was seen as able simply to imitate life, as if through a transparent pane of glass; and (2) that representation was thought to affect social behaviour directly; but the second error is to see art and life as both equally "constructed" by the signifying practices that define and limit each sphere. The signifier is here made material, in the sense that it is all there is to know. Discussing semiology in relation to Marxism, Terry Eagleton points out the dangers of this way of seeing for a Marxist view of history. History evaporates in the new scheme; since the signified can never be grasped, we cannot talk about our reality as human subjects. But, as he goes on to show, more than the signified (which in Saussure's scheme obediently followed the signifier, despite its being arbitrary) is at stake: "It is also," he says, "a question of the referent, which we all long ago bracketed out of being. In re-materializing the sign, we are in imminent danger of de-materializing its referent; a linguistic materialism gradually reverts itself into a linguistic idealism."[34]

Eagleton no doubt overstates the case when he talks about "sliding away from the referent," since neither Saussure nor Althusser denied that there *was* a referent. But it is true that while semiologists talk about the eruption of "the real" (i.e., accidents, death, revolution), on a daily basis they tend to be preoccupied with life as dominated by the prevailing signifying practices of a culture. It may be true that all lived experience is mediated through signifying practices, but we should not therefore pay exclusive attention to this level of things. In attempting to get rid of an unwelcome dualism, inherent in western thought at least since Plato, and rearticulated by Kant on the brink of the modern period, some semiologists run the danger of collapsing levels of things that need to remain distinct if we are to work effectively in the political arena to bring about change.

Thus while it is essential for feminist film critics to examine signifying processes carefully in order to fully understand the way women have been constructed in language and the non-verbal arts, it is equally important not to lose sight of the need to find strategies for changing discourse, since these changes would, in turn, affect the structuring of the social formation.

Some feminist film critics have begun to face this challenge. The directors of *Sigmund Freud's Dora*, for example, suggest that raising questions is the first step toward establishing a female discourse, or, perhaps, that asking questions is the only discourse available to women as a resistance to patriarchal domination. Since questions lead to more questions, a kind of movement is in fact taking place, although it is in a nontraditional mode. Sally Potter structured her film *Thriller* around this very notion, and allowed her heroine's investigation of herself as heroine to lead to some (tentative) conclusions. And Laura Mulvey has suggested that even if one accepts the psychoanalytic positioning of women, all is not lost, since the Oedipus complex is not completed in women; she notes that "there's some way in which women aren't colonized," having been "so specifically excluded from culture and language."[35]

From this position, psychoanalytic theory allows us to see that there is more possibility for women to change themselves (and perhaps to bring about social change) just because they have not been processed, as have little boys, through a clearly defined, and ultimately simple, set of psychic stages. The girl's relationship to her mother remains forever unresolved, incomplete; in heterosexuality, she is forced to turn away from her primary love object, destined never to return to it, while the boy, through marrying someone like his mother, can regain his original plenitude in another form. The girl must transfer her need for love to the father, who, as Nancy Chodorow has shown, never completely satisfies.[36]

Mulvey thus suggests that patriarchal culture is not monolithic, not cleanly sealed. There are gaps, fissures through which women can begin to ask questions and introduce change. The directors of *Sigmund Freud's Dora* end their film with a series of letters from a daughter (who is sometimes called Dora) read out by her mother, some of which deal with the place of the mother in psychoanalysis. The daughter's comments illuminate the fact that Freud dismisses Dora's mother (in his famous account of the case history), instead of talking about her "as the site of the intersection of many representations" (of which the historical mother is just one). She suggests that Freud's omission was not merely an oversight, but, given his system, a necessity.

Mulvey and Wollen's earlier film, *Riddles of the Sphinx*, confronted the repression of mothering in patriarchal culture directly; the film argued that women "live in a society ruled by the father, in which the place of the mother is repressed. Motherhood, and how to live it or not to live it, lies at the root of the dilemma."[37] In an interview, Mulvey noted the influence of psychoanalysis on her conception of the mother-child exchange ("the identification between the two, and the implications that has for narcissism and recognition of the self in the 'other'"), but she went on to say that this is an area rarely read from the mother's point of view.[38]

Motherhood thus becomes one place from which to begin to reformulate our position as women, just because men have not dealt with it theoretically or in the social realm (i.e., by providing free child care, free abortions, maternal leave, after-school child programs, etc.). Motherhood has been repressed on all levels except that of hypostatization, romanticization, and idealization.[39] Yet women have been struggling with lives as mothers—silently, quietly, often in agony, often in bliss, but always on the periphery of a society that tries to make us all, men and women, forget our mothers.

But motherhood, and the fact that we were all mothered, will not be repressed; or, if the attempt is made, there will be effects signaling "the return of the repressed." The entire construction of woman in patriarchy as a lack could be viewed as emerging from the need to repress mothering and the painful memory traces it has left in the man. The phallus as signified can be set in motion only given the other with a lack, and this has resulted in the male focus on castration. But is it possible that this focus was designed to mask an even greater threat that mothering poses? And if we look from the position of women, need this lack in reality have the dire implications men would have us believe? The focus on women as (simply) sex object, or (more complexly) as fetishized (narcissistic male desire) that we have been tracing through Hollywood films, may be part of the apparatus that represses mothering. The insistence on rigidly defined sex roles, and the dominance-submission, voyeurism-fetishism mechanisms may be constructed to this end.

In placing the problem of mothering in the foreground in this way, one is not necessarily falling into the trap of essentialism. First, I am not denying that motherhood has been constructed in patriarchy by its very place as repressed; nor, second, am I saying that women are inherently mothers; nor, third, that the only ideal relationship that can express female specificity is mothering. I am saying rather, that motherhood is one of the areas that has been left vague, allowing us to reformulate the position as given, rather than discovering a specificity outside the system we are in.[40] It is a place to start rethinking sex-difference, not an end.

Let me review briefly some of the main ways in which motherhood can be thought of within psychoanalysis. First, and most conservatively, motherhood has been analyzed as an essentially narcissistic relationship, and as involved with the problem of castration. In this way, it parallels male fetishism; just as men fetishize women in order to reduce their threat (finding themselves thus in the other), so women fetishize the child, looking in the child for the phallus to "make up" for castration; second, motherhood can be seen as narcissistic, not in the sense of finding the phallus in the child, but of finding *the self* in the child (this parallels male fetishizing of women in another way); women here do not relate to the child as other, but as an extension of their own egos; third, and most radically (but this is also the position that can lead to essentialism), one could argue that since the law represses mothering, a gap is left through which it may be possible to subvert patriarchy.

The problem with this latter (and most hopeful) position, however, is that of how to express motherhood after the period of the imaginary. One could argue that women are faced with an impossible dilemma: to remain in blissful unity with the child in the imaginary (or to try to hold onto this realm as long as possible), or to enter the symbolic in which mothering is repressed, cannot be "spoken," cannot represent a position of power. Here the only resistance is silence.[41]

But is this not one of those places where a rigid adherence to the theoretical formulation of imaginary and symbolic betrays the inadequacy of the theory? Is not mothering, in fact, now being "spoken," even through patriarchal discourse? Both Dorothy Dinnerstein and Nancy Chodorow "speak" a discourse about mothering that, while remaining within psychoanalysis, breaks new ground.[42] And the feminist films about mothering now appearing begin to investigate and move beyond patriarchal representations.[43]

On the social/historical level, in addition, we are living in a period in which mothers are increasingly living alone with their children, offering the possibility for new psychic patterns to emerge; fathers are increasingly becoming involved with childrearing, and also living alone with their children. Freud's own kind of science (which involved studying the people brought up in strict Victorian, bourgeois households) applied rigorously to people today results in very different conclusions. Single mothers are forced to make themselves subject in relation to their children; they are forced to invent new symbolic roles, which combine positions previously assigned to fathers with traditional female ones. The child cannot position the mother as object to the father's law, since in single-parent households *her* desire sets things in motion.

A methodology is often not per se either revolutionary or reactionary, but open to appropriation for a variety of usages. At this point, feminists may have to use psychoanalysis, but in a manner opposite to the traditional one. Other kinds of psychic processes obviously can exist and may stand as models for when we have worked our way through the morass that confronts us as people having grown up in western capitalist culture. Julia Kristeva, for example, suggests that desire functions in a very different manner in China, and urges us to explore Chinese culture, from a very careful psychoanalytic point of view, to see what is possible.[44]

Many of the mechanisms we have found in Hollywood films which echo deeply embedded myths in western capitalist culture are thus not inviolable, eternal, unchanging, or inherently necessary. They rather reflect the unconscious of patriarchy, including a fear of the pre-Oedipal plenitude with the mother. The domination of women by the male gaze is part of men's strategy to contain the threat that the mother embodies, and to control the positive and negative impulses that memory traces of being mothered have left in the male unconscious. Women, in turn, have learned to associate their sexuality with domination by the male gaze, a position involving a degree of masochism in finding their objectification erotic. We have participated in and perpetuated our domination by following the pleasure principle, which leaves us no options, given our positioning.

Everything, thus, revolves around the issue of pleasure, and it is here that patriarchal repression has been most negative. For things have been structured to make us forget the mutual, pleasurable bonding that we all, male and female, enjoyed with our mothers. Some recent experimental (as against psychoanalytic) studies have shown that the gaze is first set in motion in the mother-child relationship. [45] But this is a *mutual* gazing, rather than the subject-object kind that reduces one of the parties to the place of submission. Patriarchy has worked hard to prevent the eruption of a (mythically) feared return of the matriarchy that might take place were the close mother-child bonding returned to dominance, or allowed to stand in place of the law of the father.

This is by no means to argue that a return to matriarchy would be either possible or desirable. What rather has to happen is that we move beyond long-held cultural and linguistic patterns of oppositions: male/female (as these terms currently signify); dominant/submissive; active/passive; nature/civilization; order/chaos; matriarchal/patriarchal. If rigidly defined sex differences have been constructed around fear of the other, we need to think about ways of transcending a polarity that has only brought us all pain. [46]

Notes

The material in this essay appears in another form in E. Ann Kaplan, *Women in Film: Both Sides of the Camera* (London and New York: Methuen, 1983).

1. See works by Kate Millett, Linda Nochlin, Molly Haskell, articles in the few issues of *Women in Film* (1972–1975), and articles in *Screen* and *Screen Education* throughout the 1970s. For a summary of early developments across the arts, see Lucy Arbuthnot's Ph.D diss., New York University, 1982.
2. See especially work by Christian Metz, Jean-Louis Comolli, Raymond Bellour, Roland Barthes, and essays in *Cahiers du Cinema* in France; in England, the work by Stephen Heath, Colin McCabe, Paul Willémen, and others in *Screen* and elsewhere.
3. See especially the work of Claire Johnston, Pam Cook, and Laura Mulvey from England, and subsequent work by the *Camera Obscura* group.
4. Christine Gledhill, "Recent Developments in Feminist Film Criticism," *Quarterly Review of Film Studies* 3, no. 4 (1978): 458–93; E. Ann Kaplan, "Aspects of British Feminist Film Criticism, *Jump Cut*, nos. 12–13 (December 1976); 52–56; and Kaplan, "Integrating Marxist and Psychoanalytic Concepts in Feminist Film Criticism," *Millenium Film Journal* (April 1980): 8–17.

5. Jacques Lacan, "The Mirror Phase as Formative of the Function of the 'I'" (1949), in *New Left Review* 51 (September–October 1968): 71–77. See also essays on Lacan in Anthony Wilden, *System and Structure: Essays in Communication and Exchange* (London: Tavistock Publications, 1972).

6. For a background to semiological concepts, see work by Roland Barthes, Julia Kristeva, and Umberto Eco among others. Terence Hawkes, *Structualism and Semiology* (London: Methuen, 1977), and Rosalind Coward and John Ellis, *Language and Materialism* (London: Routledge and Kegan Paul, 1977) provide useful summaries of relevant material.

7. Laura Mulvey, "Visual Pleasure and Narrative Cinema," *Screen* 16, no. 3 (Autumn 1975): 6–18.

8. Karen Horney, "The Dread of Woman" (1932), in *Feminine Psychology* (New York: W. W. Norton, 1967), p. 134.

9. Ibid., p. 136.

10. For a useful discussion of fetishism, see Otto Fenichel, *The Psychoanalytic Theory of Neurosis* (New York: W. W. Norton, 1945), pp. 341–345.

11. Mulvey, "Visual Pleasure," p. 14.

12. Ibid.

13. Claire Johnston, "Woman's Cinema as Counter-Cinema," in *Notes on Women's Cinema* ed. Claire Johnston (London: Screen Pamphlet, 1973), p. 26.

14. Some of these questions are raised in the letters read by a mother toward the end of the film *Sigmund Freud's Dora*, made by Anthony McCall, Andrew Tyndall, Claire Pajaczkowska, and Jane Weinstock.

15. This has been evident in feminist film sessions at various conferences, but was particularly clear at the Lolita Rodgers Memorial Conference on Feminist Film Criticism, held at Northwestern University, November 14–16, 1980. For a report of some differences, see Barbara Klinger, "Conference Report," *Camera Obscura* 7 (Spring 1981): 137–43.

16. "Women and Film: A Discussion of Feminist Aesthetics," *New German Critique* 13 (Winter 1978): 93.

17. Ibid., p. 87.

18. Lucy Arbuthnot and Gail Seneca, "Pre-Text and Text in *Gentlemen Prefer Blondes*," paper delivered at the Conference on Feminist Film Criticism, Northwestern University, November 1980.

19. See Maureen Turim, "Gentlemen Consume Blondes," in *Wideangle* 1, no. 1 (1979): 52–59. Carol Rowe also (if somewhat mockingly) shows Monroe's phallicism in her film *Grand Delusion*.

20. See Mary-Anne Doane, "The Woman's Film: Possession and Address," paper delivered at the Conference on Cinema History, Asilomar, Monterey, May 1981.

21. Mulvey, "Visual Pleasure," pp. 7–8, 18.

22. See the essays in *Edinburgh Magazine* 1 (1977) by Coward, Metz, Heath, and Johnston. Also the issue of *Screen* 16, no. 2 (Summer 1975), on "Psychoanalysis and Cinema," especially the piece by Metz.

23. See E. Ann Kaplan, "Feminist Approaches to History, Psychoanalysis, and Cinema in *Sigmund Freud's Dora*," *Millenium Film Journal* 7/8/9 (Fall/Winter 1979): 173–85.

24. Charles Brenner offers perhaps the most accessible account of Freud's notion of the Oedipus complex in his *An Elementary Textbook of Psychoanalysis* (New York: Anchor Books, 1957), pp. 108–141.

25. Freud's work is central to any discussion of sadism and masochism. Since I wrote this paper, these issues have been discussed by Kaja Silverman in "Masochism and Subjectivity," *Framework* 12 (1981): 2–9, and by Joel Kovel, *The Age of Desire* (New York: Pantheon, 1981).

26. Doane, "The Woman's Film," pp. 3–8.

27. Nancy Friday, *My Secret Garden: Women's Sexual Fantasies* (New York: Pocket Books, 1981).

28. Unpublished transcript of a discussion, organized by Julia LeSage, at the Conference on Feminist Criticism, Northwestern University, November 1980. See also for discussion of dominance-submission patterns, Pat Califa, "Feminism and Sadomasochism," *Heresies 12*, pp. 32ff.

29. Nancy Friday, *Men in Love* (New York: Dell, 1980).

30. Mulvey, "Visual Pleasure," pp. 12–13.

31. Julia Kristeva, "La femme, ce n'est jamais ça," trans. Marilyn A. August, in *New French Feminisms*, ed. E. Marks and I. de Courtivron (Amherst: University of Massachusetts Press, 1980), p. 37.

32. Sandy Flitterman and Judith Barry, "Textual Strategies: The Politics of Art-Making," *Screen* 2, no. 3 (Summer 1980): 37.

33. Ibid., p. 36.

34. Terry Eagleton, "Aesthetics and Politics," *New Left Review* (1978).

35. "Women and Representation: A Discussion with Laura Mulvey" (collective project by Jane Clarke, Sue Clayton, Joanna Clelland, Rosie Elliott, and Mandy Merck), *Wedge* (London) 2 (Spring 1979): 49.

36. Nancy Chodorow, "Psychodynamics of the Family," in *The Reproduction of Mothering* (Berkeley: University of California Press, 1978), pp. 191–209.

37. "*Riddles of the Sphinx:* A Film by Laura Mulvey and Peter Wollen; Script," *Screen* 18, no. 2 (Summer 1977): 62.

38. Jacquelyn Suter and Sandy Flitterman, "Textual Riddles: Woman as Enigma or Site of Social Meanings? An Interview with Laura Mulvey," *Discourse* 1, no. 1 (Fall 1979): 107.

39. Ibid., pp. 109–120.

40. Ibid., pp. 116–19.

41. Mulvey, "Women and Representation," p. 49.

42. Dinnerstein, *The Mermaid and the Minotaur* (New York: Harper and Row, 1976) and Chodorow, *The Reproduction of Mothering*.

43. See, for example, films by Laura Mulvey and Peter Wollen, Michelle Citron, Marjorie Keller, and Helke Sander.

44. Kristeva, "Les Chinoises à 'contre-courant,'" *New French Feminisms*, p. 240.

45. Eleanor Maccoby and John Martin, "Parent-Child Interaction," in *Handbook of Child Psychology*, ed. E. M. Hetherington (New York: John Wiley & Sons: in press). One has obviously to be careful here about introducing discourses that work on an entirely different level than the theoretical, psychoanalytic discourse that I have mainly been considering. It may be, however, that the confronting of the psychoanalytic discourse with more empirically based kinds of discourse could lead to an opening up of the theory, to suggestions for a way out of the theoretical impasse in which psychoanalytic frameworks place women.

46. See the important essay by Jessica Benjamin, "Master and Slave: The Fantasy of Erotic Domination," in this volume.

"The Mind That Burns in Each Body": Women, Rape, and Racial Violence

Jacquelyn Dowd Hall

I
Hostility Focused on Human Flesh

> FLORIDA TO BURN NEGRO AT STAKE:
> SEX CRIMINAL SEIZED FROM JAIL,
> WILL BE MUTILATED, SET AFIRE IN
> EXTRA-LEGAL VENGEANCE FOR
> DEED
>
> —Dothan (Alabama)
> *Eagle,* October 26, 1934

> After taking the nigger to the woods . . .
> they cut off his penis. He was made to eat it.
> Then they cut off his testicles and made him
> eat them and say he liked it.
>
> —Member of a lynch mob, 1934[1]

Lynching, like rape, has not yet been given its history. Perhaps it has been too easily relegated to the shadows where "poor white" stereotypes dwell. Perhaps the image of absolute victimization it evokes has been too difficult to reconcile with what we know about black resilience and resistance. Yet the impact of lynching, both as practice and as symbol, can hardly be underestimated. Between 1882 and 1946 almost 5,000 people died by lynching. The lynching of Emmett Till in 1955 for whistling at a white woman, the killing of three civil rights workers in Mississippi in the 1960s, and the hanging of a black youth in Alabama in 1981 all illustrate the persistence of this tradition of ritual violence in the service of racial control, a tradition intimately bound up with the politics of sexuality.

Vigilantism originated on the eighteenth-century frontier where it filled a vacuum in law enforcement. Rather than passing with the frontier, however, lynching was incorporated into the distinctive legal system of southern slave society.[2] In the nineteenth century, the industrializing North moved toward a modern criminal justice system in which police, courts, and prisons administered an impersonal, bureaucratic rule of law designed to uphold property rights and discipline unruly workers. The South, in contrast, maintained order through a system of deference and customary authority in which all whites had informal police power over all blacks, slave owners meted out plantation justice undisturbed by any generalized rule of law, and the state encouraged vigilantism as part of its overall reluctance to maintain a strong system of formal authority that would have undermined the planter's prerogatives. The purpose of one system was class control, of the other, control over a slave population. And each tradition continued into the period after the Civil War. In the North, factory-like penitentiaries warehoused displaced members of the industrial proletariat. The South maintained higher rates of personal violence than any other region in the country and lynching crossed over the line from informal law enforcement into outright political terrorism.

White supremacy, of course, did not rest on force alone. Routine institutional arrangements denied to the freedmen and women the opportunity to own land, the right to vote, access to education, and participation in the administration of the law. Lynching reached its height during the battles of Reconstruction and the Populist revolt; once a new system of disfranchisement, debt peonage, and segregation was firmly in place, mob violence gradually declined. Yet until World War I, the average number of lynchings never fell below two or three a week. Through the twenties and thirties, mob violence reinforced white dominance by providing planters with a quasi-official way of enforcing labor contracts and crop lien laws and local officials with a means of extracting deference, regardless of the letter of the law. Individuals may have lynched for their own twisted reasons, but the practice continued only with tacit official consent.[3]

Most importantly, lynching served as a tool of psychological intimidation aimed at blacks as a group. Unlike official authority, the lynch mob was unlimited in its capriciousness. With care and vigilance, an individual might avoid situations that landed him in the hands of the law. But a lynch mob could strike anywhere, any time. Once the brush fire of rumor began, a manhunt was organized, and the local paper began putting out special editions announcing a lynching in progress, there could be few effective reprieves. If the intended victim could not be found, an innocent bystander might serve as well.

It was not simply the threat of death that gave lynching its repressive power. Even as outbreaks of mob violence declined in frequency, they were increasingly accompanied by torture and sexual mutilation. Descriptions of the first phase of Hitler's death sweep are chillingly applicable to lynching: "Killing was ad hoc, inventive, and in its dependence on imagination, peculiarly expressive . . . this was murder uncanny in its anonymous intimacy, a hostility so personally focused on human flesh that the abstract fact of death was not enough."[4]

At the same time, the expansion of communications and the development of photography in the late nineteenth and early twentieth centuries gave reporting a vividness it had never had before. The lurid evocation of human suffering implicated white readers in each act of aggression and drove home to blacks the consequences of powerlessness. Like whipping under slavery, lynching was an instrument of coercion intended to impress not only the immediate victim but all who saw or heard about the event. And the mass media spread the imagery of rope and faggot far beyond the community in which each lynching took place. Writing about his youth in the rural South in the 1920s, Richard Wright describes the terrible climate of fear:

> The things that influenced my conduct as a Negro did not have to happen to me directly; I needed but to hear of them to feel their full effects in the deepest layers of my consciousness. Indeed, the white brutality that I had not seen was a more effective control of my behavior than that which I knew. The actual experience would have let me see the realistic outlines of what was really happening, but as long as it remained something terrible and yet remote, something whose horror and blood might descend upon me at any moment, I was compelled to give my entire imagination over to it.[5]

A penis cut off and stuffed in a victim's mouth. A crowd of thousands watching a black man scream in pain. Such incidents did not have to occur very often, or be witnessed directly, to be burned indelibly into the mind.

II
Never Against Her Will

> White men have said over and over—and we have believed it because it was repeated so often—that not only was there no such thing as a chaste Negro woman—but that a Negro woman could not be assaulted, that it was never against her will.
> —Jessie Daniel Ames (1936)

Schooled in the struggle against sexual rather than racial violence, contemporary feminists may nevertheless find familiar this account of lynching's political function, for analogies between rape and lynching have often surfaced in the literature of the anti-rape movement. To carry such analogies too far would be to fall into the error of radical feminist writing that misconstrues the realities of racism in the effort to illuminate sexual subordination.[6] It is the suggestion of this essay, however, that there is a significant resonance between these two forms of violence. We are only beginning to understand the web of connections among racism, attitudes toward women, and sexual ideologies. The purpose of looking more closely at the dynamics of repressive violence is not to reduce sexual assault and mob murder to static equivalents but to illuminate some of the strands of that tangled web.

The association between lynching and rape emerges most clearly in their parallel use in racial subordination. As Diane K. Lewis has pointed out, in a patriarchal society, black men, as men, constituted a potential challenge to the established order.[7] Laws were formulated primarily to exclude black men from adult male prerogatives in the public sphere, and lynching meshed with these legal mechanisms of exclusion. Black women represented a more ambiguous threat. They too were denied access to the politico-jural domain, but since they shared this exclusion with women in general, its maintenance engendered less anxiety and required less force. Lynching served primarily to dramatize hierarchies among men. In contrast, the violence directed at black women illustrates the double jeopardy of race and sex. The records of the Freedmen's Bureau and the oral histories collected by the Federal Writers' Project testify to the sexual atrocities endured by black women as whites sought to reassert their command over the newly freed slaves. Black women were sometimes executed by lynch mobs, but more routinely they served as targets of sexual assault.

Like vigilantism, the sexual exploitation of black women had been institutionalized under slavery. Whether seized through outright force or voluntarily granted within the master-slave relation, the sexual access of white men to black women was a cornerstone of patriarchal power in the South. It was used as a punishment or demanded in exchange for leniency. Like other forms of deference and conspicuous consumption, it buttressed planter hegemony. And it served the practical economic purpose of replenishing the slave labor supply.

After the Civil War, the informal sexual arrangements of slavery shaded into the use of rape as a political weapon, and the special vulnerability of black women helped shape the ex-slaves' struggle for the prerequisites of freedom. Strong family bonds had survived the adversities of slavery; after freedom, the black family served as a bulwark against a racist society. Indeed, the sharecropping system that replaced slavery as the South's chief mode of production grew in part from the desire of blacks to withdraw from gang labor and gain control over their own work, family lives, and bodily integrity. The sharecropping family enabled women to escape white male supervision, devote their productive and reproductive powers to their own families, and protect themselves from sexual assault.[8]

Most studies of racial violence have paid little attention to the particular suffering of women.[9] Even rape has been seen less as an aspect of sexual oppression than as a transaction between white and black men. Certainly Claude Lévi-Strauss's insight that men use women as verbs with which to communicate with one another (rape being a means of communicating defeat to the men of a conquered tribe) helps explain the extreme viciousness of sexual violence in the post-emancipation era.[10] Rape *was* in part a reaction to the effort of the freedmen to assume the role of patriarch, able to provide for and protect his family. Nevertheless, as writers like Susan Griffin and Susan Brownmiller and others have made clear, rape is first and foremost a crime against women.[11] Rape sent a message to black men, but more centrally, it expressed male sexual attitudes in a culture both racist and patriarchal.

Recent historians of Victorian sexuality have traced the process by which a belief in female "passionlessness" replaced an older notion of women's dangerous sexual power.[12] Even at the height of the "cult of true womanhood" in the nineteenth century, however, views of women's sexuality remained ambivalent and double-edged. The association between women and nature, the dread of women's treacherous carnality, persisted, rooted, as Dorothy Dinnerstein persuasively argues, in the earliest experiences of infancy.

In the United States, the fear and fascination of female sexuality was projected onto black women; the passionless lady arose in symbiosis with the primitively sexual slave. House slaves often served as substitute mothers; at a black woman's breast white men experienced absolute dependence on a being who was both a source of wish-fulfilling joy and of grief-producing disappointment. In adulthood, such men could find in this black woman a ready object for the mixture of rage and desire that so often underlies male heterosexuality. The black woman, already in chains, was sexually available, unable to make claims for support or concern; by dominating her, men could replay the infant's dream of unlimited access to the mother.[13] The economic and political challenge posed by the black patriarch might be met with death by lynching, but when the black woman seized the opportunity to turn her maternal and sexual resources to the benefit of her own family, sexual violence met her assertion of will. Thus rape reasserted white dominance and control in the private arena as lynching reasserted hierarchical arrangements in the public transactions of men.

III
Lynching's Double Message

> The crowds from here that went over to see
> [Lola Cannidy, the alleged rape victim in
> the Claude Neal lynching of 1934] said he
> was so large he could not assault her until he
> took his knife and cut her, and also had
> either cut or bit one of her breast [sic] off.
> —Letter to Mrs. W. P. Cornell,
>   October 29, 1934, Association of
>   Southern Women for the Prevention
>   of Lynching Papers

> . . . more than rape itself, the fear of rape
> permeates our lives. . . . and the best de-
> fense against this is not to be, to deny being
> in the body, as a self, to . . . avert your gaze,
> make yourself, as a presence in the world,
> less felt.
> —Susan Griffin, *Rape: The Power of
>   Consciousness* (1979)

In the 1920s and 1930s, the industrial revolution spread through the South, bringing a demand for more orderly forms of law enforcement. Men in authority, anxious to create a favorable business climate, began to withdraw their tacit approval of extralegal violence. Yet lynching continued, particularly in rural areas, and even as white moderates criticized lynching in the abstract, they continued to justify outbreaks of mob violence for the one special crime of sexual assault. For most white Americans, the association between lynching and rape called to mind not twin forms of white violence against black men and women, but a very different image: the black rapist, "a monstrous beast, crazed with lust";[14] the white victim—young, blond, virginal; her manly Anglo-Saxon avengers. Despite the pull of modernity, the emotional logic of lynching remained: only swift, sure violence, unhampered by legalities, could protect white women from sexual assault.

The "protection of white womanhood" was a pervasive fixture of racist ideology. In 1839, for example, a well-known historian offered this commonly accepted rationale for lynching: black men find "something strangely alluring and seductive . . . in the appearance of the white woman; they are aroused and stimulated by its foreignness to their experience of sexual pleasures, and it moves them to gratify their lust at any cost and in spite of every obstacle." In 1937, echoing an attitude that characterized most local newspapers, the Jackson, Mississippi, *Daily News* published what it felt was the *coup de grace* to anti-lynching critics: "What would you do if your wife, daughter, or one of your loved ones was ravished? You'd probably be right there with the mob." Two years later, 65 percent of the white respondents in an anthropological survey believed that lynching was justified in cases of sexual assault.[15] Despite its tenacity, however, the myth of the black rapist was never founded on objective reality. Less than a quarter of lynch victims were even accused of rape or attempted rape. Down to the present, almost every study has underlined the fact that rape is overwhelmingly an intraracial crime, and the victims are more often black than white.[16]

A major strategy of anti-lynching reformers, beginning with Ida B. Wells in the 1880s and continuing with Walter White of the NAACP and Jessie Daniel Ames of the Association of Southern Women for the Prevention of Lynching, was to use such facts to undermine the rationalizations for mob violence. But the emotional circuit between interracial rape and lynching lay beyond the reach of factual refutation. A black man did not literally have to attempt sexual assault for whites to perceive some transgression of caste mores as a sexual threat. White women were the forbidden fruit, the untouchable property, the ultimate symbol of white male power. To break the racial rules was to conjure up an image of black over white, of a world turned upside down.

Again, women were a means of communication and, on one level, the rhetoric of protection, like the rape of black women, reflected a power struggle among men. But impulses toward women as well as toward blacks were played out in the drama of racial violence. The fear of rape was more than a hypocritical excuse for lynching; rather, the two phenomena were intimately intertwined. The "southern rape complex" functioned as a means of both sexual and racial suppression.[17]

For whites, the archetypal lynching for rape can be seen as a dramatization of cultural themes, a story they told themselves about the social arrangements and psychological strivings that lay beneath the surface of everyday life. The story such rituals told about the place of white women in southern society was subtle, contradictory, and demeaning. The frail victim, leaning on the arms of her male relatives, might be brought to the scene of the crime, there to identify her assailant and witness his execution. This was a moment of humiliation. A woman who had just been raped, or who had been apprehended in a clandestine interracial affair, or whose male relatives were pretending that she had been raped, stood on display before the whole community. Here was the quintessential Woman as Victim: polluted, "ruined for life," the object of fantasy and secret contempt. Humiliation, however, mingled with heightened worth as she played for a moment the role of the Fair Maiden violated and avenged. For this privilege—if the alleged assault had in fact taken place—she might pay with suffering in the extreme. In any case, she would pay with a lifetime of subjugation to the men gathered in her behalf.

Only a small percentage of lynchings, then, revolved around charges of sexual assault; but those that did received by far the most attention and publicity—indeed, they gripped the white imagination far out of proportion to their statistical significance. Rape and rumors of rape became the folk pornography of the Bible Belt. As stories spread the rapist became not just a black man but a ravenous brute, the victim a beautiful young virgin. The experience of the woman was described in minute and progressively embellished detail, a public fantasy that implied a group participation in the rape as cathartic as the subsequent lynching. White men might see in "lynch law" their ideal selves: patriarchs, avengers, righteous protectors. But, being men themselves, and sometimes even rapists, they must also have seen themselves in the lynch mob's prey.

The lynch mob in pursuit of the black rapist represented the trade-off implicit in the code of chivalry: for the right of the southern lady to protection presupposed her obligation to obey. The connotations of wealth and family background attached to the position of the lady in the antebellum South faded in the twentieth century, but the power of "ladyhood" as a value construct remained. The term denoted chastity, frailty, graciousness. "A lady," noted one social-psychologist, "is always in a state of becoming: one acts like a lady, one attempts to be a lady, but one never *is* a lady." Internalized by the individual, this ideal regulated behavior and restricted interaction with the world.[18] If a woman passed the tests of ladyhood, she could tap into the reservoir of protectiveness and shelter known as southern chivalry. Women who abandoned secure, if circumscribed, social roles forfeited the claim to personal security. Together the practice of ladyhood and the etiquette of chivalry controlled white women's behavior even as they guarded caste lines.

Proslavery theorist Thomas R. Dew spelled out this dialectic. The "essence of manhood," he wrote, is "predation." The essence of womanhood is "allure." Only the rise of gallantry and the patriarchal family offered a haven from male aggression. Stripped to its bare essentials, then, the difference between the sexes was the opposition between the potential rapist and the potential victim of sexual assault, and the family metaphor that justified slavery offered the exchange of dependence for protection to the mistress as well as to the slaves. Dew's notion of female sexuality, however, did not deny her passions of her own. On the contrary, because her role was not to seek, "but to be sought . . . not to woo, but to be wooed," she was forced to suppress her "most violent feelings . . . her most ardent desires."[19] In general, the law of rape expressed profound distrust of women, demanding evidence of "utmost resistance," corroboration by other witnesses in addition to the victim's word, and proof of the victim's chastity—all contrary to the rules of evidence in other forms of violent crime. In sharp contrast, however, when a black man and a white woman were concerned intercourse was prima facie evidence of rape. The presiding judge in the 1931 Scottsboro trial, in which nine black youths were accused of rape, had this to say:

> Where the woman charged to have been raped, as in this case is a white woman, there is a very strong presumption under the law that she would not and did not yield voluntarily to intercourse with the defendant, a Negro; and this is true, whatever the station in life the prosecutrix may occupy, whether she be the most despised, ignorant and abandoned woman of the community, or the spotless virgin and daughter of a prominent home of luxury and learning.[20]

Lynching, then, like laws against intermarriage, masked uneasiness over the nature of white women's desires. It aimed not only to engender fear of sexual assault but also to prevent voluntary unions. It upheld the comforting fiction that at least in relation to black men, white women were always objects and never agents of sexual desire.

Although the nineteenth-century women's movement for the most part advocated higher moral standards for men, not sexual liberation for women, opponents insisted that it threatened the family and painted feminists as spinsters or libertines, sexual deviants in either case. It may be no accident, then, that the vision of the black man as a threatening beast flourished during the first phase of the southern women's rights movement, a fantasy of aggression against boundary-transgressing women as well as a weapon of terror against blacks. Certainly the rebelliousness of that feminist generation was circumscribed by the feeling that women were hedged about by a "nameless horror." The South, wrote one turn-of-the-century woman, had become "a smoldering volcano, the dark of its quivering night . . . pierced through by the cry of some outraged woman."[21]

When women in the 1920s and 1930s did begin to assert their right to sexual expression and to challenge the double standard Thomas Dew's injunctions implied, inheritors of the plantation legend responded with explicit attacks that revealed the sanctions at the heart of the chivalric ideal. William Faulkner's *The Sanctuary*, published in 1931, typified a common literary reaction to the fall of the lady. The corncob rape of Temple Drake—a "new woman" of the 1920s—was the ultimate revenge against the abdicating white virgin. Her fate represented the "desecration of a cult object," the implicit counterpoint to the idealization of women in a patriarchal society.[22]

IV
Lady Insurrectionists

> The lady insurrectionists gathered together
> in one of our southern cities. . . . They said
> calmly that they were not afraid of being
> raped; as for their sacredness, they would
> take care of it themselves; they did not need
> the chivalry of lynching to protect them and
> did not want it.
> —Lillian Smith, *Killers of the Dream* (1949)

On November 1, 1930, twenty-six white women from six southern states met in Atlanta to form the Association of Southern Women for the Prevention of Lynching. Organized by Texas suffragist Jessie Daniel Ames, the association had a central, ideological goal: to break the circuit between the tradition of chivalry and the practice of mob murder. The association was part of a broader interracial movement; its contribution to the decline of lynching must be put in the perspective of the leadership role played by blacks in the national anti-lynching campaign. But it would be a mistake to view the association simply as a white women's auxiliary to black-led struggles. Rather, it represented an acceptance of accountability for a racist mythology that white women had not created but that they nevertheless served, a point hammered home by black women's admonitions that "when Southern white women get ready to stop lynching, it will be stopped and not before."[23]

Jessie Ames, the association's leader, stood on the brink between two worlds. Born in 1883 in a small town in East Texas, a regional hotbed of mob violence, she directed the anti-lynching campaign from Atlanta, capital of the New South. She drew eclectically on the nineteenth-century female reform tradition and advocated an implicitly feminist anti-racism that looked backward to the abolitionist movement as well as forward to feminists of our own times.

Ames had come to maturity in a transitional phase of the women's movement, when female reformers used the group consciousness and Victorian sense of themselves as especially moral beings to justify a great wave of female institution building. When Jessie Ames turned from suffrage to the reform of race relations, she looked naturally to this heritage for her constituency and tactics. The association drew its members from among small-town church women, schooled for decades in running their own affairs within YWCAs, women's clubs, and missionary societies and sensitized by the temperance and suffrage movements to a politics that simultaneously stressed domestic order and women's rights.[24] Ames's strategy for change called for enfranchised women to exercise moral influence over the would-be lynchers in their own homes, political influence over the public officials who collaborated with them, and cultural influence over the editors and politicians who created an atmosphere where mob violence flourished. Like Frances Willard and the temperance campaign, she sought to extend women's moral guardianship into the most quintessentially masculine affairs.

Ames's tenacity and the emotional energy of her campaign derived from her perception that lynching was a women's issue: not only an obstacle to regional development and an injustice to blacks, but also an insult to white women. Along with black women leaders before her, who had perceived that the same sexual stereotyping that allowed black women to be exploited caused black men to be feared, she challenged both racist and patriarchal ideas.[25] Disputing the notion that blacks provoked mob action by raping white women, association members traced lynching to its roots in white supremacy.[26] More central to their campaign was an effort to dissociate the image of the lady from its connotations of sexual vulnerability and retaliatory violence. If lynching held a covert message for white women as well as an overt one for blacks, then the anti-lynching association represented a woman-centered reply. Lynching, it proclaimed, far from offering a shield against sexual assault, served as a weapon of both racial and sexual terror, planting fear in women's minds and dependency in their hearts. It thrust them in the role of personal property or sexual objects, ever threatened by black men's lust, ever in need of white men's protection. Asserting their identity as autonomous citizens, requiring not the paternalism of chivalry but the equal protection of the law, association members resisted the part assigned to them.

If, as Susan Brownmiller claims, the larger anti-lynching movement paid little attention to lynching's counterpart, the rape of black women, the women's association could not ignore the issue. For one thing, black women in the interracial movement continually brought it to their attention, prodding them to take responsibility for stopping both lynching and sexual exploitation. For another, from slavery on, interracial sex had been a chronic source of white women's discontent.[27] In 1920, for example, a white interracialist and women's rights leader, who had come to her understanding of racial issues through pioneering meetings with black women, warned a white male audience:

> The race problem can never be solved as long as the white man goes unpunished [for interracial sex], while the Negro is burned at the stake. I shall say no more, for I am sure you need not have

anything more said. When the white men of the South have come to that position, a single standard for both men and women, then you will accomplish something in this great problem.[28]

In the winter of 1931, Jessie Daniel Ames called a meeting of black and white women for an explicit discussion of the split female image and the sexual double standard. The women, she thought, should gather in closed session with no men present "because there are some vices of Southern life which contribute subtly to [lynching] that we want to face by ourselves." The black leader Nannie Burroughs agreed: "All meetings with white and colored women on this question should be held behind closed doors and men should not be admitted." White male attitudes, the group concluded, originated in a slave system where black women "did not belong to themselves but were in effect the property of white men." They went on to explore the myths of black women's promiscuity and white women's purity, and noted how this split image created a society that "considers an assault by a white man as a moral lapse upon his part, better ignored and forgotten, while an assault by a Negro against a white woman is a hideous crime punishable with death by law or lynching." Relationships among women interracialists were far from egalitarian, nor could they always overcome the impediments to what Ames called "free and frank" discussion.[29] Yet on occasions like this one the shared experience of gender opened the way for consciousness-raising communication across the color line.

If such discussions of male behavior had to be held behind closed doors, even more treacherous was the question of sex between black men and white women. In 1892, Memphis anti-lynching reformer and black women's club leader Ida B. Wells was threatened with death and run out of town for proclaiming that behind many lynchings lay consensual interracial affairs. Over sixty years later, in the wake of the famous Scottsboro case, Jessie Daniel Ames began delving beneath the surface of lynchings in which white women were involved. Like Barnett, she found that black men were sometimes executed not for rape but for interracial sex. And she used that information to disabuse association members of one of the white South's central fictions: that, as a Mississippi editor put it, there had never been a southern white woman so depraved as to "bestow her favors on a black man."[30]

But what of lynching cases in which rape actually had occurred? Here association leaders could only fall back on a call for law and order, for they knew from their own experience that the fear engendered in their constituency by what some could bring themselves to call only "the unspeakable crime" was all too real. "Whether their own minds perceive danger where none exists, or whether the fears have been put in their minds by men's fears," Ames commented, women could not but see themselves as potential victims of black assault.[31] It would be left to a future generation to point out that the chief danger to white women came from white men and to see rape in general as a feminist concern. Association leaders could only exorcise their own fears of male aggression by transferring the means of violence from mobs to the state and debunking the myth of the black rapist.

In the civil rights movement of the 1960s, white women would confront the sexual dimension of racism and racial violence by asserting their right to sleep with black men. Anti-lynching reformers of the 1930s obviously took a very different approach. They abhorred male violence and lynching's eroticism of death, and asserted against them a feminine standard of personal and public morality. They portrayed themselves as moral beings and independent citizens rather than vulnerable sexual objects. And the core of their message lay more in what they were than in what they said: southern ladies who needed only their own rectitude to protect them from interracial sex and the law to guard them from sexual assault. When Jessie Ames referred to "the crown of chivalry that has been pressed like a crown of thorns on our heads," she issued a cry of protest that belongs to the struggle for both racial and sexual emancipation.[32]

V

The Decline of Chivalry

> As male supremacy becomes ideologically untenable, incapable of justifying itself as protection, men assert their domination more directly, in fantasies and occasionally in acts of raw violence.
>
> —Christopher Lasch,
> *Marxist Perspectives* (1978)

In the 1970s, for the second time in the nation's history, rape again attracted widespread public attention. The obsession with interracial rape, which peaked at the turn of the nineteenth century but lingered from the close of the Civil War into the 1930s, became a magnet for racial and sexual oppression. Today the issue of rape has crystallized important feminist concerns.

Rape emerged as a feminist issue as women developed an independent politics that made sexuality and personal life a central arena of struggle. First in consciousness-raising groups, where autobiography became a politicizing technique, then in public "speakouts," women broke what in retrospect seems a remarkable silence about a pervasive aspect of female experience. From that beginning flowed both an analysis that held rape to be a political act by which men affirm their power over women and strategies for change that ranged from the feminist self-help methods of rape crisis centers to institutional reform of the criminal justice and medical care systems. After 1976, the movement broadened to include wife-battering, sexual harassment, and, following the lead of Robin Morgan's claim that "pornography is the theory, rape the practice," media images of women.[33]

By the time Susan Brownmiller's *Against Our Will: Men, Women and Rape* gained national attention in 1975, she could speak to and for a feminist constituency already sensitized to the issue by years of practical, action-oriented work. Her book can be faulted for supporting a notion of universal patriarchy and timeless sexual victimization; it leaves no room for understanding the reasons for women's collaboration, their own sources of power (both self-generated and derived), the class and racial differences in their experience of discrimination and sexual danger. But it was an important milestone, pointing the way for research into a subject that has consistently been trivialized and ignored. Many grass-roots activists would demur from Brownmiller's assertion that all men are potential rapists, but they share her understanding of the continuum between sexism and sexual assault.[34]

The demand for control over one's own body—control over whether, when, and with whom one has children, control over how one's sexuality is expressed—is central to the feminist project because, as Rosalind Petchesky persuasively argues, it is essential to "a sense of being a person, with personal and bodily integrity," able to engage in conscious activity and to participate in social life.[35] It is this right to bodily integrity and self-determination that rape, and the fear of rape, so thoroughly undermines. Rape's devastating effect on individuals derives not so much from the sexual nature of the crime (and anti-rape activists have been concerned to revise the idea that rape is a "fate worse than death" whose victims, if no longer "ruined for life," are at least so traumatized that they must rely for recovery on therapeutic help rather than on their own resources) as from the experience of helplessness and loss of control, the sense of one's self as an object of rage. And women who may never be raped share, by chronic attrition, in the same helplessness, "otherness," lack of control. The struggle against rape, like the anti-lynching movement, addresses not only external dangers but also internal consequences: the bodily muting, the self-censorship that limits one's capacity to "walk freely in the world."[36]

The focus on rape, then, emerged from the internal dynamics of feminist thought and practice. But it was also a response to an objective increase in the crime. From 1969 to 1974, the number of rapes rose 49 percent, a greater increase than for any other violent crime. Undoubtedly rape statistics reflect general demographic and criminal trends, as well as a greater willingness of victims to report sexual attacks (although observers agree that rape is still the most underreported of crimes).[37] But there can be no doubt that rape is a serious threat and that it plays a prominent role in women's subordination. Using recent high-quality survey data, Allan Griswold Johnson has estimated that, at a minimum, 20 to 30 percent of girls now twelve years old will suffer a violent attack sometime in their lives. A woman is as likely to be raped as she is to experience a divorce or to be diagnosed as having cancer.[38]

In a recent anthology on women and pornography, Tracey A. Gardner has drawn a parallel between the wave of lynching that followed Reconstruction and the increase in rapes in an era of anti-feminist backlash.[39] Certainly, as women enter the workforce, postpone marriage, live alone or as single heads of households, they become easier targets for sexual assault. But observations like Gardner's go further, linking the intensification of sexual violence directly to the feminist challenge. Such arguments come dangerously close to blaming the victim for the crime. But they may also contain a core of truth. Sociological research on rape has only recently begun, and we do not have studies explaining the function and frequency of the crime under various historical conditions; until that work is done we cannot with certainty assess the current situation. Yet it seems clear that just as lynching ebbed and flowed with new modes of racial control, rape—both as act and idea—cannot be divorced from changes in the sexual terrain.

In 1940, Jessie Ames released to the press a statement that, for the first time in her career, the South could claim a "lynchless year," and in 1942, convinced that lynching was no longer widely condoned in the name of white womanhood, she allowed the Association of Southern Women for the Prevention of Lynching to pass quietly from the scene. The women's efforts, the larger, black-led anti-lynching campaign, black migration from the rural South, the spread of industry—these and other developments contributed to the decline of vigilante justice. Blacks continued to be victimized by covert violence and routinized court procedures that amounted to "legal lynchings." But after World War II, public lynchings, announced in the papers, openly accomplished, and tacitly condoned, no longer haunted the land, and the black rapist ceased to be a fixture of political campaigns and newspaper prose.

This change in the rhetoric and form of racial violence reflected new attitudes toward women as well as toward blacks. By the 1940s few southern leaders were willing, as Jessie Ames put it, to "lay themselves open to ridicule" by defending lynching on the grounds of gallantry, in part because gallantry itself had lost conviction.[40] The same process of economic development and national integration that encouraged the South to adopt northern norms of authority and control undermined the chivalric ideal. Industrial capitalism on the one hand and women's assertion of independence on the other weakened paternalism and with it the conventions of protective deference.[41] This is not to say that the link between racism and sexism was broken; relations between white women and black men continued to be severely sanctioned, and black men, to the present, have drawn disproportionate punishment for sexual assault. The figures speak for themselves: of the 455 men executed for rape since 1930, 405 were black, and almost all the complainants were white.[42] Nevertheless, "the protection of white womanhood" rang more hollow in the postwar New South and the fear of interracial rape became a subdued theme in the nation at large rather than an openly articulated regional obsession.

The social feminist mainstream, of which Jessie Ames and the anti-lynching association were a part, thus chipped away at a politics of gallantry that locked white ladies in the home under the guise of protecting them from the world. But because such reformers held to the genteel trappings of their role even as they asserted their autonomous citizenship, they offered reassurance that women's influence could be expanded without mortal danger to male prerogatives and power. Contemporary feminists have eschewed some of the comforting assumptions of their nineteenth-century predecessors: women's passionlessness, their limitation to social housekeeping, their exclusive responsibility for childrearing and housekeeping. They have couched their revolt in explicit ideology and unladylike behavior. Meanwhile, as Barbara Ehrenreich has argued, Madison Avenue has perverted the feminist message into the threatening image of the sexually and economically liberated woman. The result is a shift toward the rapaciousness that has always mixed unstably with sentimental exaltation and concern. Rape has emerged more clearly into the sexual domain, a crime against women most often committed by men of their own race rather than a right of the powerful over women of a subordinate group or a blow by black men against white women's possessors.[43]

It should be emphasized, however, that the connection between feminism and the upsurge of rape lies not so much in women's gains but in their assertion of rights within a context of economic vulnerability and relative powerlessness. In a perceptive article published in 1901, Jane Addams traced lynching in part to "the feeling of the former slave owner to his former slave, whom he is now bidden to regard as his fellow citizen."[44] Blacks in the post-Reconstruction era were able to express will and individuality, to wrest from their former masters certain concessions and build for themselves supporting institutions. Yet they lacked the resources to protect themselves from economic exploitation and mob violence. Similarly, contemporary feminist efforts have not yet succeeded in overcoming women's isolation, their economic and emotional dependence on men, their cultural training toward sub-mission. There are few restraints against sexual aggression, since up to 90 percent of rapes go unreported, 50 percent of assailants who are reported are never caught, and seven out of ten prosecutions end in acquittal.[45] Provoked by the commercialization of sex, cut loose from traditional community restraints, and "bidden to regard as his fellow citizen" a female being whose subordination has deep roots in the psyches of both sexes, men turn with impunity to the use of sexuality as a means of asserting dominance and control. Such fear and rage are condoned when channeled into right-wing attacks on women's claim to a share in public power and control over their bodies. Inevitably they also find expression in less acceptable behavior. Rape, like lynching, flourishes in an atmosphere in which official policies toward members of a subordinate group give individuals tacit permission to hurt and maim.

In 1972 Anne Braden, a southern white woman and long-time activist in civil rights struggles, expressed her fear that the new anti-rape movement might find itself "objectively on the side of the most reactionary social forces" unless it heeded a lesson from history. In a pamphlet entitled *Open Letter to Southern White Women*—much circulated in regional women's liberation circles at the time—she urged anti-rape activists to remember the long pattern of racist manipulation of rape fears. She called on white women, "for their own liberation, to refuse any longer to be used, to act in the tradition of Jessie Daniel Ames and the white women who fought in an earlier period to end lynching," and she went on to discuss her own politicization through left-led protests against the prosecution of black men on false rape charges. Four years later, she joined the chorus of black feminist criticism of *Against Our Will*, seeing Brownmiller's book as a realization of her worst fears.[46]

Since this confrontation between the Old Left and the New, between a white woman who placed herself in a southern tradition of feminist anti-racism and a radical feminist from the North, a black women's movement has emerged, bringing its own perspectives to bear. White activists at the earliest "speakouts" had acknowledged "the racist image of black men as rapists," pointed out the large number of black women among assault victims, and debated the contradictions involved in looking for solutions to a race and class-biased court system. But not until black women had developed their own autonomous organizations and strategies were true alliances possible across racial lines.

A striking example of this development is the Washington, D.C., Rape Crisis Center. One of the first and largest such groups in the country, the center has evolved from a primarily white self-help project to an aggressive interracial organization with a multifaceted program of support services, advocacy, and community education. In a city with an 80 percent black population and more than four times as many women as men, the center has recruited black leadership by channeling its resources into staff salaries and steering clear of the pitfalls of middle-class voluntarism on the one hand and professionalism on the other. It has challenged the perception of the anti-rape movement as a "white woman's thing" by stressing not only rape's devastating effect on women but also its impact on social relations in the black community. Just as racism undermined working-class unity and lynching sometimes pitted poor whites against blacks, sexual aggression now divides the black community against itself. In a society that defines manhood in terms of power and possessions, black men are denied the resources to fulfill their expected roles. Inevitably, they turn to domination of women, the one means of manhood within their control. From consciousness-raising groups for convicted rapists to an intensive educational campaign funded by the city's public school system and aimed at both boys and girls from elementary through high school, the center has tried to alter the cultural plan for both sexes that makes men potential rapists and women potential victims.[47]

As the anti-rape movement broadens to include Third World women, analogies between lynching and rape and the models of women like Ida B. Wells and Jessie Daniel Ames may become increasingly useful. Neither lynching nor rape is the "aberrant behavior of a lunatic fringe."[48] Rather, both grow out of everyday modes of interaction. The view of women as objects to be possessed, conquered, or defiled fueled racial hostility; conversely, racism has continued to distort and confuse the struggle against sexual violence. Black men receive harsher punishment for raping white women, black rape victims are especially demeaned and ignored, and, until recently, the different historical experience of black and white women has hindered them from making common cause. Taking a cue from the women's antilynching campaign of the 1930s as well as from the innovative tactics of black feminists, the anti-rape movement must not limit itself to training women to avoid rape or depending on imprisonment as a deterrent, but must aim its attention at changing the behavior and attitudes of men. Mindful of the historical connection between rape and lynching, it must make clear its stand against *all* uses of violence in oppression.

Notes

My title comes From Adrienne Rich, "Disloyal to Civilization: Feminism, Racism, Gynephobia," in Rich, *On Lies, Secrets and Silences: Selected Prose, 1966–1978* (New York: W. W. Norton, 1979), p. 299. Parts of this essay are taken from Jacquelyn Dowd Hall, *Revolt Against Chivalry: Jessie Daniel Ames and the Women's Campaign Against Chivalry* (New York: Columbia University Press, 1979), and full documentation can be found in that work. See also Hall, "'A Truly Subversive Affair': Women Against Lynching in the Twentieth-Century South," in *Women of America: A History*, ed. Carol Berkin and Mary Beth Norton (Boston: Houghton Mifflin, 1979). Thanks to Rosemarie Hester, Walter Dellinger, Loretta Ross, Nkenge Toure, Janet Colm, Kathleen Dowdy, and Nell Painter for their help and encouragement.

1. Quoted in Howard Kester, *The Lynching of Claude Neal* (New York: National Association for the Advancement of Colored People, 1934).
2. Michael Stephen Hindus, *Prison and Plantation: Crime, Justice, and Authority in Massachusetts and South Carolina, 1767–1878* (Chapel Hill: University of North Carolina Press, 1980), pp. xix, 31, 124, 253.
3. For recent overviews of lynching, see Robert L. Zangrando, *The NAACP Crusade Against Lynching, 1909–1950* (Philadelphia: Temple University Press, 1980); McGovern, *Anatomy of a Lynching;* and Hall, *Revolt Against Chivalry*.
4. Terrence Des Pres, "The Struggle of Memory," *The Nation*, 10 April 1982, p. 433.
5. Quoted in William H. Chafe, *Women and Equality: Changing Patterns in American Culture* (New York: Oxford University Press, 1977), p. 60.
6. Margaret A. Simons, "Racism and Feminism: A Schism in the Sisterhood," *Feminist Studies* 5 (Summer 1979): 384–401.
7. Diane K. Lewis, "A Response to Inequality: Black Women, Racism, and Sexism," *Signs* 3 (Winter 1977): 341–42.
8. Jacqueline Jones, *Freed Women?: Black Women, Work, and the Family During the Civil War and Reconstruction*, Working Paper No. 61, Wellesley College, 1980; Roger L. Ransom and Richard Sutch, *One Kind of Freedom: The Economic Consequences of Emancipation* (New York: Cambridge University Press, 1977), pp. 87–103.
9. Gerda Lerner, *Black Women in White America: A Documentary History* (New York: Random House, 1972), is an early and important exception.
10. Robin Morgan, "Theory and Practice: Pornography and Rape," *Take Back the Night: Women on Pornography*, ed. Laura Lederer (New York: William Morrow, 1980), p. 140.
11. Susan Griffin, "Rape: The All-American Crime," *Ramparts* (September 1971): 26–35; Susan Brownmiller, *Against Our Will: Men, Women, and Rape* (New York: Simon and Schuster, 1975). See also Kate Millet, *Sexual Politics* (Garden City, N.Y.: Doubleday & Co., 1970).
12. Nancy F. Cott, "Passionlessness: An Interpretation of Victorian Sexual Ideology, 1790–1850," *Signs* 4 (Winter 1978): 219–36.
13. Dorothy Dinnerstein, *The Mermaid and the Minotaur: Sexual Arrangements and Human Malaise* (New York: Harper and Row, 1977). See also Phyllis Marynick Palmer, "White Women/Black Women: The Dualism of Female Identity and Experience," unpublished paper presented at the American Studies Association, September 1979, pp. 15–17. Similarly, British Victorian eroticism was structured by class relations in which upper-class men were nursed by lower-class country women. See Ellen Ross and Rayna Rapp in this volume.
14. A statement made in 1901 by George T. Winston, president of the University of North Carolina, typifies these persistent images: "The southern woman with her helpless little children in a solitary farm house no longer sleeps secure. . . . The black brute is lurking in the dark, a monstrous beast, crazed with lust. His ferocity is

almost demoniacal. A mad bull or a tiger could scarcely be more brutal" (quoted in Charles Herbert Stember, *Sexual Racism: The Emotional Barrier to an Integrated Society* [New York: Elsevier, 1976], p. 23).

15. Philip Alexander Bruce, *The Plantation Negro as a Freeman* (New York: Putnam's, 1889), pp. 83–84; Jackson *Daily News*, 27 May 1937; Hortense Powdermaker, *After Freedom: A Cultural Study in the Deep South* (1939; New York: Atheneum, 1969), pp. 54–55, 389.

16. For a contradictory view, see, for example, S. Nelson and M. Amir, "The Hitchhike Victim of Rape: A Research Report," in *Victimology: A New Focus. Vol. 5: Exploiters and Exploited*, ed. M. Agopian, D. Chappell, and G. Geis, and I. Drapkin and E. Viano (1975), p. 47; and "Black Offender and White Victim: A Study of Forcible Rape in Oakland, California," in *Forcible Rape: The Crime, The Victim, and the Offender* (New York: Columbia University Press, 1977).

17. Winthrop Jordan, *White over Black: American Attitudes Toward the Negro, 1550–1812* (Baltimore: Penguin Books, 1969); W. J. Cash, *The Mind of the South* (New York: Knopf, 1941), p. 117.

18. This reading of lynching as a "cultural text" is modeled on Clifford Geertz, "Deep Play: Notes on the Balinese Cockfight," in *The Interpretation of Cultures: Selected Essays by Clifford Geertz* (New York: Basic Books, 1973), pp. 412–53. For "lady-hood," see Greer Litton Fox, " 'Nice Girl': Social Control of Women Through a Value Construct," *Signs* 2 (Summer 1977): 805–17.

19. Quoted in William R. Taylor, *Cavalier and Yankee: The Old South and American National Character* (Garden City, N.Y.: Doubleday/Anchor, 1963), pp. 148–51.

20. Dan T. Carter, *Scottsboro: An American Tragedy* (Baton Rouge: Louisiana State University Press, 1969), p. 36.

21. Belle Kearney, *A Slaveholder's Daughter* (New York: Abbey Press, 1900), p. 96; Myrta Lockett Avary, *Dixie after the War* (1906; New York: Negro Universities Press, 1969), pp. 377–90. See also John E. Talmadge, *Rebecca Latimer Felton: Nine Stormy Decades* (Athens: University of Georgia Press, 1960), pp. 98–124.

22. Leslie Fiedler, *Love and Death in the American Novel* (New York: Delta, 1966), pp. 320–24.

23. Rich, "Disloyal to Civilization"; Jessie Daniel Ames to Mary McLeod Bethune, 9 March 1938, Association of Southern Women for the Prevention of Lynching (ASWPL) Papers, Atlanta University, Atlanta, Georgia. (henceforth cited as ASWPL Papers). For black women's prior activities, see Ida B. Wells, *Crusade for Justice: The Autobiography of Ida B. Wells* (Chicago: University of Chicago Press, 1970); Lerner, *Black Women*, pp. 194–215; Bettina Aptheker, *Lynching and Rape: An Exchange of Views*, Occasional Paper No. 25, American Institute of Marxist Studies (1977); and Angela Y. Davis, *Women, Race, and Class* (New York: Random House, 1982), pp. 169–98.

24. For this reform tradition, see Estelle Freedman, "Separatism as Strategy: Female Institution Building and American Feminism, 1870–1930," *Feminist Studies* 5 (Fall 1979): 512–29; Mari Jo Buhle, *Women and American Socialism, 1780–1920* (Urbana: University of Illinois Press, 1981); and Barbara Leslie Epstein, *The Politics of Domesticity: Women, Evangelism, and Temperance in Nineteenth-Century America* (Middletown, Conn.: Wesleyan University Press, 1981).

25. Deb Friedman, "Rape, Racism—and Reality," *Aegis* (July/August, 1978): 17–26.

26. Jessie Daniel Ames to Miss Doris Loraine, 5 March 1935, ASWPL Papers.

27. Anne Firor Scott, "Women's Perspective on the Patriarchy in the 1850's," *Journal of American History* 6 (June 1974): 52–64.

28. Carrie Parks Johnson Address, Commission on Interracial Cooperation (CIC), CIC Papers, Atlanta University, Atlanta, Georgia.

29. Jessie Daniel Ames to Nannie Burroughs, 24 October 1931; Burroughs to Ames, 30

October 1931, ASWPL Papers; "Appendix F, Digest of Discussion," n.d. [November 20, 1931], Jessie Daniel Ames Papers, University of North Carolina at Chapel Hill.

30. Jackson (Mississippi) *Daily News*, February 1931, ASWPL Papers.

31. Jessie Daniel Ames, "Lynchers' View on Lynching," ASWPL Papers.

32. Quoted in Wilma Dykeman and James Stokely, *Seeds of Southern Change: The Life of Will Alexander* (Chicago: University of Chicago Press, 1962), p. 143.

33. Noreen Connell and Cassandra Wilsen, eds., *Rape: The First Sourcebook for Women* (New York: New American Library, 1974); Morgan, "Theory and Practice."

34. Interview with Janet Colm, director of the Chapel Hill-Carrboro (North Carolina) Rape Crisis Center, April 1981. Two of the best recent analyses of rape are Ann Wolbert Burgess and Lynda Lytle Holmstrom, *Rape: Crisis and Recovery* (Bowie, Md.: Robert J. Brady Co., 1979) and Lorenne M. G. Clark and Debra J. Lewis, *Rape: The Price of Coercive Sexuality* (Toronto: Canadian Women's Educational Press, 1977).

35. Rosalind Pollack Petchesky, "Reproductive Freedom: Beyond 'A Woman's Right to Choose,'" *Signs* 5 (Summer 1980): 661–85.

36. Adrienne Rich, "Taking Women Students Seriously," in *Lies, Secrets and Silences*, p. 242.

37. Vivian Berger, "Man's Trial, Women's Tribulation: Rape Cases in the Courtroom," *Columbia Law Review* 1 (1977): 3–12. Thanks to Walter Dellinger for this reference.

38. Allan Griswold Johnson, "On the Prevalence of Rape in the United States," *Signs* 6 (Fall 1980): 136–46.

39. Tracey A. Gardner, "Racism in Pornography and the Women's Movement," in *Take Back the Night*, p. 111.

40. Jessie Daniel Ames, "Editorial Treatment of Lynching," *Public Opinion Quarterly* 2 (January 1938): 77–84.

41. For a statement of this theme, see Christopher Lasch, "The Flight from Feeling: Sociopsychology of Sexual Conflict," *Marxist Perspectives* 1 (Spring 1978): 74–95.

42. Berger, "Man's Trial, Woman's Tribulation," p. 4. For a recent study indicating that the harsher treatment accorded black men convicted of raping white women is not limited to the South and has persisted to the present, see Gary D. LaFree, "The Effect of Sexual Stratification by Race on Official Reactions to Rape," *American Sociological Review* 45 (October 1980): 842–54. Thanks to Darnell Hawkins for this reference.

43. Barbara Ehrenreich, "The Women's Movement: Feminist and Antifeminist," *Radical America* 15 (Spring 1981): 93–101; Lasch, "Flight from Feeling." Because violence against women is so inadequately documented, it is impossible to make accurate racial comparisons in the incidence of the crime. Studies conducted by Menachen Amir in the late 1950s indicated that rape was primarily intraracial, with 77 percent of rapes involving black victims and black defendants and 18 percent involving whites. More recent investigations claim a somewhat higher percentage of interracial assaults. Statistics on reported rapes show that black women are more vulnerable to assault than white women. However, since black women are more likely than white women to report assaults, and since acquaintance rape, most likely to involve higher status white men, is the most underreported of crimes, the vulnerability of white women is undoubtedly much greater than statistics indicate (Berger, "Man's Trial, Woman's Tribulation," p. 3, n. 16; LaFree, "Effect of Sexual Stratification," p. 845, n. 3; Johnson, "On the Prevalence of Rape," p. 145).

44. Quoted in Aptheker, *Lynching and Rape*, pp. 10–11.

45. Berger, "Woman's Trial, Man's Tribulation," p. 6; Johnson, "On the Prevalence of Rape," p. 138.

46. Anne Braden, "A Second Open Letter to Southern White Women," *Generations:*

Women in the South, a special issue of *Southern Exposure* 4 (Winter 1977), edited by Susan Angell, Jacquelyn Dowd Hall, and Candace Waid.

47. Interview with Loretta Ross and Nkenge Toure, Washington, D.C., May 12, 1981. See also Rape Crisis Center of Washington, D.C., *How to Start a Rape Crisis Center* (1972, 1977).

48. Johnson, "On the Prevalence of Rape," p. 137.

Hearts of Darkness
Barbara Omolade

The sexual history of the United States began at the historical moment when European men met African women in the "heart of darkness"[1]—Mother Africa. They faced each other as conqueror and conquered: African women captives were considered the sexual property of the European conquerors.[2]

The African sexuality confronted by European men was an integral part of a sensuality that permeated music, dance, and religion. West African women often performed dances such as the "crotch dance, an improvised folk drama enacted by women at the height of the birth celebration, in which women strike their crotches firmly with both their hands."[3] However tactile, pleasurable, and comfortable these daily creative art forms, they were not necessarily indicative of sexual promiscuity. Rather, African cultures taught men and women to use their bodies in fluid, rhythmic ways, within a sexual code of behavior that frequently countenanced murdering women who committed adultery and often practiced female clitoridectomy.[4] The African woman who faced the European man was a wife, a mother, a daughter, a sister, nestled in tribal societies and protected by fathers, husbands, and brothers who upheld the sanctity and primacy of marriage and motherhood for women.

Nevertheless, in the hip-shaking, bare-breasted women with sweating bodies who danced to drums played by intense black men, in the market women and nursing mothers wrapped in African cloth, in the scantily clad farming women, the European man saw a being who embodied all that was evil and profane to his sensibilities. He perceived the African's sensual ways according to his own cultural definitions of sex, nudity, and blackness as base, foul, and bestial. He did not attempt to understand how Africans defined their own behavior.[5] He made assumptions and invented knowledge about their behavior as he created the conditions for this "knowledge" to become the reality. He viewed the African expression of sensuality through public rites, rituals, and dances as evidence of the absence of any sexual codes of behavior, an idea that both fascinated and repelled him and also provided him with a needed rationale for the economic exploitation of African men and women.

As historian Richard Hofstadter explains:

> Naked and libidinous: for the white man's preoccupation with Negro sexuality was there at the very beginning, an outcome not only of his own guilt at sexual exploitation—his easy access to the black woman was immediately blamed on *her* lasciviousness—but also of his envious suspicion that some extraordinary potency and ecstatic experience were associated with primitive lust.[6]

Within the strange "commingling of desire and hate,"[7] white men would continue to penetrate and plunder Mother Africa for five centuries while creating a world view centered around the myth of race and racism that upheld white supremacy and the total domination of black people.

The sexual history of the United States became fused with contradiction and duality, with myth and distortion, with the white man's hate and desire for the black woman, with competition and jealousy between white and black women for white men, with love and struggle between black men and black women. American sexual history reflects the development of patriarchal control stretched to its maximum extent by European men operating within a racial caste system supported by state power in which white maleness becomes the only definition of being. Simultaneously, the extremes of American patriarchy, particularly under slavery, pushed black women outside traditional patriarchal protection, thereby transforming all previous definitions of womanhood, particularly the idea that woman requires male protection because of her innate weakness and inferiority.[8] Black women were oppressed and exploited labor and as such were forced to redefine themselves as women outside of and antagonistic to the racial patriarch who denied their being. Most black women refused to accept the traditional notions of subordination of woman to man. The black woman resisted racial patriarchy by escaping, stealing, killing, outsmarting, and bargaining with her white master while she had sex with him, had babies by him, ministered to his needs growing "to know all there was to know about him."[9] At the same time, most black women accepted traditional notions of patriarchy from black men because they viewed the Afro-Christian tradition of woman as mother and wife as personally desirable and politically necessary for black people's survival.

The racial patriarchy of the white man enabled him to enact his culture's separation between the goodness, purity, innocence, and fraility of woman with the sinful, evil strength, and carnal knowledge of woman by having sex with white women who came to embody the former and black women who came to embody the latter.[10] The white man's division of the sexual attributes of women based on race meant that he alone could claim to be sexually free: he was free to be sexually active within a society that upheld the chastity and modesty of white women as the "repositories of white civilization."[11] He was free to be irresponsible about the consequences of his sexual behavior with black women within a culture that placed a great value on the family as a sacred institution protecting women, their progeny and his property. He was free to use violence to eliminate his competition with black men for black or white women, thus breaking the customary allegiance among all patriarchs. He was also free to maintain his public hatred of racial mixing while privately expressing his desire for black women's bodies. Ultimately, white men were politically empowered to dominate all women and all black men and women; this was their sexual freedom.

From the beginning, the founding fathers assumed the patriarchal right to regulate and define the sexual behavior of their servants and slaves according to a fusion of Protestantism, English Common Law, and personal whim. During the early colonial period the distinctions between indentured servant and slave were blurred and relative: most workers, black and white, male and female, worked without direct payment or without control over their labor. These laborers shared enough common experiences to jointly attack their masters and to have sex with each other.[12] The master's racial attitudes of antipathy toward black people and his fears of a unified antagonistic force of all workers, including Indian women and men, demanded that the category "white" be expanded to give political power and freedom to all white men (theoretically and potentially, if not at that actual historical time) and patriarchal protection and white privilege to all white women. Thus, during the later colonial period, black men and white women who had sex, married, and/or had children were punished and persecuted as American society denied them the right to choose each other as mates.[13] The category "white" would also mean that the people designated "black" could be held in perpetual slavery.[14] Therefore, laws were passed and practices instituted to regulate the sexual and social behavior of white and black, servants and slaves. The legal and actual distinction between slave and servant was widened with "slavery reflecting life-long power relationships, while servitude became a more temporary relationship of service."[15] In other words, in spite of the common experiences of black and white workers in colonial America, indentured servants were whitened as slaves became black.

Though black people were less than 5 percent of the population in the later part of the seventeenth century, a 1662 Virginia statute stipulated that "all offspring follow the condition of the mother in the event of a white man getting a Negro with child."[16] A 1664 statute prohibited all unions between the races.[17] In 1665, the first English slave code in New York provided that slavery was for life.[18] Colonial law and custom reflected the parameters that would continue to govern American sexual behavior: regardless of who impregnated black women, any offspring would be slave. As Hofstadter puts it, this "guaranteed in a society where interracial sex usually involved the access of white men to black women, that without other provisions to the contrary, the mulatto population would be slave."[19] Well before the institution of slavery was firmly established in the antebellum South during the nineteenth century, these laws and others prohibiting black political participation, ownership of land, and the right to carry arms[20] were aimed at creating a black population in perpetual servitude.

Slavery and slaveholders dominated American political and economic life for about two hundred years. As Carl Degler describes it:

> The labor of slaves provided the wherewithal to maintain lawyers and actors, cotton factors and publishers, musicians in Charleston, senators in Washington, and gamblers on the Mississippi river boats. Slave holders were agricultural entrepreneurs in a capitalistic society: their central importance as a class resided not in their numbers, which were admittedly small, but in their ability to accumulate surplus for investment.[21]

Degler's phrase "ability to accumulate surplus for investment" tends to obscure all traces of the inhumanity of slavery: black women's bodies were a primary means of accumulating the surplus: "My mother was young—just 15 or 16 years old. She had 14 chillen and you know that meant a lots of wealth."[22] New slave owners with one or two slaves attempting to "construct an initial labor force" and establish an economic base in order to realize profits broke up slave communities or African clans by obtaining individual slaves through purchase, gift, or marriage. The fecundity of black women was key to the slave owner's goal. Gutman documents that as one planter said, "An owner's labor force doubled through natural increase every 15 years."[23] A slave, looking back, agrees:

> They would buy a fine girl and a fine man and just put them together like cattle; they would not stop to marry them. If she was a good breeder, they was proud of her. I was stout and they were saving me for a breeding woman, but by the time I was big enough I was free. I had an aunt in Mississippi and she had about 20 children by her marster.[24]

"Natural increase" meant that the black woman was encouraged and sometimes forced to have sex frequently in order to have babies, whether by black men or white men, in stable or unstable relationships.

But as early as 1639, black women resisted forced sex:

> [O]ne source . . . tells of a Negro woman being held as a slave on Noddles Island in Boston harbor. Her master sought to mate her with another Negro, but, the chronicler reported, she kicked her prospective lover out of bed, saying that such behavior was "beyond her slavery."[25]

But though it was beyond *her* concept of enslavement, it was not beyond her master's, for every part of the black woman was used by him. To him she was a fragmented commodity whose feelings and choices were rarely considered: her head and her heart were separated from her back and her hands and divided from her womb and vagina. Her back and muscle were pressed into field labor where she was forced to work with men and work like men. Her hands were demanded to nurse and nurture the white man and his family as domestic servant whether she was technically enslaved or legally free. Her vagina, used for his sexual pleasure, was the gateway to the womb, which was his place of capital investment—the capital investment being the sex act and the resulting child the accumulated surplus, worth money on the slave market.

The totalitarian system of slavery extended itself into the very place that was inviolable and sacred to both African and European societies—the sanctity of the woman's body and motherhood within the institution of marriage. Although all women were slaves under patriarchy, the particular enslavement of black women was also an attack on all black people. All sexual intercourse between a white man and a black woman irrespective of her conscious consent became rape, because the social arrangement assumed the black woman to be without any human right to control her own body.[26] And the body could not be separated from its color.

Racial oppression tends to flow from the external to the internal: from political institutions, social structures, the economic system and military conquest, into the psyche and consciousness and culture of the oppressed and the oppressor. In contrast, sexual oppression tends to direct itself directly to the internal, the feeling and emotional center, the private and intimate self, existing within the external context of power and social control. Black women fused both racial and sexual oppression in their beings and movements in both black and white worlds.

Black women moved through the white man's world: through his space, his land, his fields, his streets, and his woodpiles.

> The Negro woman carried herself like a queen, tall and stately in spite of her position as a slave. The overseer, the plantation owner's son sent her to the house on some errand. It was necessary to pass through a wooded pasture to reach the house and the

overseer intercepted her in the woods and forced her to put her head between the rails in an old stake and rider fence, and there in that position, my great, great grandfather was conceived.[27]

In the white man's world, black women would have a place: "I know at least 50 places in my small town where white men are positively raising two families—a white family in the 'Big House' in front, and a colored family in a 'Little House' in the backyard."[28] In the white man's world, black women were separated from black men: "When I left the camp my wife had had two children by some one of the white bosses, and she was living in fairly good shape in a little house off to herself."[29] They became the teachers of sex to white boys: "Testimony seems to be quite widespread to the fact that many if not most southern boys begin their sexual experiences with Negro girls."[30]

White men tortured and punished black women who refused them: For fending off the advances of an overseer on a Virginia plantation, Minnie Falkes' mother was suspended from a barn rafter and beaten with a horsewhip "nekkid" til blood run down her back to her heels.[31] Madison Jefferson adds:

> Women who refused to submit themselves to the brutal desires of their owners, are repeatedly whipt to subdue their virtuous repugnance, and in most instances this hellish practice is but too successful—when it fails, the women are frequently sold off to the south.[32]

The black woman worked in the white man's home, both before and after formal emancipation. She knew her master/lover as a man; she was intimate with his humanity; she fed him and she slept with him; she ministered to his needs.[33] One slave remarked, "Now mind you all of the colored women didn't have to have white men, some did it because they wanted to and some were forced. They had a horror of going to Mississippi and they would do anything to keep from it."[34]

Black women and white women were sisters under the oppression of white men in whose houses they both lived as servants. In the antebellum South, Mary Chesnut wrote, "There is no slave after all like a wife."[35] A white woman married to the planter/patriarch endured, suffered, and submitted to him in all things. White women, though viewed as pure and delicate ladies by southern myth, had to serve their husband/masters as did the female servants and slaves; managing the household, entertaining the guests, overseeing the feeding and clothing of both slaves and relatives.[36]

Both white and black women were physically weakened and often died from birthing too many of the master's children. White men often had several wives in succession because many died in childbirth. While white wives visited relatives for long periods of time to have space between pregnancies,[37] exercising a much-needed control over childbearing, black women all too often filled the gap for both recreational and procreational sex. Ann Firor Scott writes of one South Carolinian who thought, "The availability of slave women for sex avoided the horrors of prostitution. He pointed out that men could satisfy their sexual needs while increasing their slave property."[38] To be a white woman in the antebellum South meant accepting the double standard; brothers, fathers, and mates could enjoy sex with her sisters in bondage, black women. White women however, were prevented from enjoying sex because they were viewed as "pure women incapable of erotic feeling."[39]

Many southern white women privately disliked the double standard and the horrors of the sexual life it implied: "Under slavery we lived surrounded by prostitutes like patriarchs of old, our men live in one house with their wives and concubines."[40] An ex-slave woman agreed:

Just the other day we were talking about white people when they had slaves. You know when a man would marry, his father would give him a woman for a cook and she would have children right in the house by him and his wife would have children too. Sometimes the cook's children favored him so much that the wife would be mean to them and make him sell them.[41]

Yet for all the private outrage of white women at the "injustice and shame" to all womanhood of the sexual activities of white men, black women stood alone without the support of their sisters. Most white women sadistically and viciously punished the black woman and her children for the transgressions of their white men. One study states:

To punish black women for minor offenses, mistresses were likely to attack with any weapon available—a fork, butcher knife, knitting needle, pan of boiling water. Some of the most barbaric forms of punishment resulting in the mutilation and permanent scaring of female servants were devised by white mistresses in the heat of passion.[42]

White women used the social relationship of supervisor of black women's domestic labor to act out their racial superiority, their emotional frustrations, and their sexual jealousies. Black women slaves and domestic servants were useful buffers between white men and white women, pulling them together, resolving their conflicts, maintaining continuity and structure for the white family whose physical and emotional needs they fulfilled.[43]

When the daughter and son of the white man and the black woman faced the father, they reflected the fruits of his passion as well as the duplicity of his life. Their light skin or light eyes, their straight hair or nose reflected himself to himself and yet he still refused to acknowledge paternity. The exceptional white father/master/lover who cared would often free his black children and wife, hustle them out of town, educating and supporting them from afar, helping them rise within black society while hoping for silence and anonymity. But in spite of traditional patriarchal concerns for fatherhood, most white fathers did nothing for their colored children. Most colored children shared the experience of this ex-slave: "My grandfather was an Irishman and he was a foreman, but he had to whip his children and grandchildren just like the others."[44] Those few slaveholders who loved and respected their slave wives were limited by societal criticism and the law from formally marrying them.[45]

Though she had no privacy, away from the view of all, could the black woman have ever desired and loved her master/lover? Could she have separated the hands that whipped her body from the hands that gripped her body in lovemaking? After all, the master/lover was only a man, who desired the slave woman and had the power to take her as a woman. Patriarchal society would define the perfect man as the perfect master, and it was the submissiveness of the slave woman that made her the perfect slave and the perfect woman. After all, a man's power over a woman was like the master's power over a slave. It came from "innate superiority."[46] But the intimate place of desire and fulfillment of the submissive and perfected woman was in violent conflict with the rage and humiliation and forced labor of being a slave woman forced to lie in the arms of the enslaver, the enemy ultimately responsible for her humiliation and her suffering. Yet the woman could not be separated from the color. One black woman remembers:

> One mark in particular stands out in my memory, one she bore just above her right eye. As well as she liked to regale me with stories of her scars, this one she never discussed with me. Whenever I would ask a question concerning it, she would simply shake her head and say "White men are as low as dogs, child. Stay from them." It was only after her death, and since I became a woman that I was told by my own mother that she received that scar at the hands of her master's youngest son, a boy of about 18 years, at the time she conceived their child, my grandmother, Ellen.[47]

Though mulattoes were "common as blackberries,"[48] most black women resisted white men's sexual advances and resented being a convenient scapegoat for the white women's sexual supression. Black women were often unwilling participants in the sexual lives of white men and women. In spite of close contact, many did not necessarily admire or identify with white families. They often longed to go home to the black world to care for their own men and children.

As she crossed the tracks to the black world she could breathe a little easier, soften and slow up her steps. She could smile at her neighbors and kin along the road or warn them away with her stern and tired face. They understood that her day had been rough. The care of her children, her men, and her sisters would occupy her time now. She would find private space in cleaning her house, tending her garden, fixing her room with doilies and trinkets. She would sew sister's dress, braid her baby girl's hair, and fix that hat for Sunday's church meeting. In this world there was space for her to pull herself together. The space was contained and narrow but it did give her easement from the white man's world and his desire for her body.

Against the white man's animal panting and arbitrary carnal desires that stalked their daughters, the old ones' harsh words and demands of modesty emphasized with a slap or a hard look forced the girls to hide and conserve the precious darkness between their legs. The old ones would frequently frustrate and confuse their daughters' sexual desires, for though their rage originated from the sexual abuses of white men, they extended taboos against all sexual expression.

African cultural values taught deference and respect to the elderly, who set parameters for sexual, romantic, and marital relationships within tribal rituals and rites. Within slave and rural black communities away from the interferences of white men, the deference continued.[49] Young black men courted and romanced young women with African-like ritual and respect, always under the watchful eyes of the old ones.

> When this courting process proceeded naturally and freely, the couple might eventually have a child, or if the girl had already had her first baby (often by a different man) they might marry and settle into a long-lasting monogamous union.[50]

The old ones in the new world were consulted for their approval and consent to marital plans or pregnancies by their daughters and sons. Sometimes, mothers and grandmothers (fathers and grandfathers also) were unmoved by romance or youthful passion and clamped down on their daughters' sexual desires for any but the most stable mates with the firmness of an iron chastity belt.

Though black women were mothers, midwives, and farmers, with daughters growing up close to them, frequently in crowded homes with many siblings and relatives, most young black women learned little explicit information about sex.[51] Thus, in spite of and because of the historical sexual abuse of black women, both black men and black women lived sexually conservative lives characterized by modesty and discretion. In fact, most black women were reluctant to openly discuss specific sexual abuses against their person by white men, even within their own families.[52]

The black man moved toward the black woman, clothing her raped and abused body with the mantle of respectable womanhood, giving protection and sometimes claiming ownership of her. Many black men agreed with white men that "wives should submit themselves to their husbands in all things."[53] As the dominant institution within the black community, the black church reinforced and supported the traditional patriarchal views of men claiming wardship over women.

Protecting black women was the most significant measure of black manhood and the central aspect of black male patriarchy. Black men felt outrage and shame at their frequent inability to protect black women, not merely from the whippings and hard work, but also from the master/lover's touch. During and after slavery, black men spoke out angrily against the harsh treatment of black women, many vowing never to allow black women to be sexually abused and economically exploited again.[54] Their methods often became rigidly patriarchal; however, they did in many instances keep black women from becoming the open prey of the white man. W. E. B. Du Bois summed up the feelings of many black men:

> . . . but one thing I shall never forgive, neither in this world nor in the world to come: it's [the white South's] wanton and continued and persistent insulting of the black womanhood which it sought and seeks to prostitute to its lust.[55]

After the Civil War, black men and black women married each other in droves, giving their unions legitimacy and validating their right to choose and love each other.[56] Many felt that the slave master could no longer come between black men and black women for the law connected them. Yet in their successful attempts to recapture political and economic power, white men claimed a glorified past of total domination over black people, continuing to enter the "heart of darkness" as their right.

Although during Reconstruction terror and hunger forced black men and black women into peonage and sharecropping, the black community resisted the new chains of white male domination. Women vowed to stand by their men, never to return to the fields, to the kitchens, or to the beds of white men. As the white community attacked and extended its dominion, black women carved out new ways to survive as well as uphold their marriages and the implied sanctity of their bodies.

Black men struggled to farm their own land in order to provide for their families, keeping wives and daughters away from white men's farms and arms. Many asserted as one ex-slave did to his white father/master who doubted his ability to provide for his family, "I am going to feed and clothe them and I can do it on bare rock."[57] Black women withdrew from farm labor for the white man, and when they had to work, they insisted on day work rather than sleep-in domestic work.[58]

Black women also sewed, dressed hair, washed clothes, and cooked meals in their own homes for wages in order to keep out of the white men's homes.

In the context of the black community of resistance, "heterosexual privilege usually became the only privilege black women had. For without racial or sexual privilege, marriage and motherhood becomes the last resort."[59] The very traditional experiences of motherhood and sex within marriage were not necessarily viewed as oppressive to black women, for they were the literal and symbolic weapons she could utilize to assure the biological and social reproduction of black people. Marriage and motherhood were humanizing experiences that gave her life meaning, purpose, and choice. These experiences were denied within the racist milieu where her humanity was questioned and her human rights and privileges to love and be loved were denied.

The African values retained within the black community in combination with its learned Christian values reinforced sexual loyalty and monogamy for black women. Although white society described her as an insatiable animal with no feelings of love and commitment, in one way or another, and with a variety of consequences, black women have been monogamous, serially monogamous, and sexually loyal partners to black men (and sometimes white men also).

Black men held a wide range of views about black women from those that reinforced female subordination to those that reinforced equal social relations between the sexes. Many black men, moving away from traditional patriarchal views, supported and encouraged independence in their wives, and more often in their daughters.[60] Black women were supported by black men in building black elementary schools and community institutions and in encouraging their daughters to become educated as teachers to escape the "abominations" of the white man. As teachers, black women could be kept within the black community away from the sexual advances of white men and under the watchful protecting eyes of male principals and ministers as well. Teaching required of black women an even more rigorous adherence to a sex code enjoining chastity and model womanhood than that guiding other black women.[61]

Sex codes upholding the values of monogamy and sexual loyalty were part of the extended kinship networks that provided valuable emotional, physical, and economic support for black women. Kin accepted children sired by white men into the family. There was no such thing as "illegitimacy," for each child was considered part of the community, where its mother might be stigmatized, but rarely ostracized. Women abandoned by their husbands were viewed with sympathy. To a great extent, black women forced into sexual relations with white men were still considered suitable mates by black men. There was the widespread practice of black men parenting children not sired by them, even when a child's father was white. Nearly every black family had a white absentee father or grandfather and a wide range of skin colors. Only those women who continued to live outside the sexual code, which condemned adultery and promiscuity with white or black men, were viewed as sinful.[62] Both during and after slavery, black women and men have had a complex history of struggling together to maintain stable, monogamous families, transmuting the destructive forces from without, cooperating and supporting each other from within.

The historical oppression of black women and men should have created social equality between them, but even after the end of slavery when the white patriarch receded, maleness and femaleness continued to be defined by patriarchal structures, with black men declaring wardship over black women. In the black community, the norm of manhood was patriarchal power; the norm of womanhood was adherence to it, though both black men and women selected which aspects of these norms they would emphasize.

Many black women became enraged at the thought of being owned and taken by any man, even if he had black skin. The whippings, the work, the penetration by the whipper and the white master/lover left them with rage and rebellion against the traditional roles of wife and mother. They would resist as Rose Williams resisted when

> forced to live with a man named Rufus because the master wanted them "to bring forth portly chillen" warned the slave to stay away from her "fore I busts yous brains out and stomp on dem." She finally relented when threatened with a whipping, but she never married explaining, "after what I done for de massa I's never wants no truck with any man—de lawd forgive dis cullud woman, but he have to 'scuse me and look for some others for to 'plenish de earth."[63]

Black women within the rural black community often defied the restrictions on their womanhood and sexuality by living alone (near family and kin) and working their own farms, running their own lives without men as mates and protectors, frequently sojourning for truth and God. Many of these women learned these independent ways from their fathers and brothers. Women often lived with women as both emotional and sexual companions. Women in urban black communities had several male lovers and companions but did not submit to them in traditional ways because they maintained an independent life as community workers, political and social activists, and workers within the paid labor force.

At the beginning of the twentieth century both rural and urban black women followed the role models of black female artists, singers, dancers, and actresses who expressed and reinforced the sensuality of African traditions by shaking and shimmying on stages and in clubs and roadhouses. Black women leaving the restrictions of the rural south agreed with Bessie Smith:

> I'm a young woman and ain't done runnin' roun' . . .
> Some people call me a hobo, some call me a bum.
> Nobody knows my name, nobody knows what I've done.
> See that long, lonesome road? Lord you know it's gotta end.
> And I'm a good woman and I can get plenty men.[64]

These black women lived lives of explicit sexuality and erotic excitement with both men and women. As they broke away from the traditional paternal restraints within the black community, they were castigated for seeming to reflect the truth of the white man's views of black women as whorish and loose. But these "wild women"[65] did not care, modeling for southern rural black women a city life full of flashy clothes, fast cars, and access to sophisticated men.

However, most black women did not have access to the mobility of a freer sexual life even within marriage until the 1960s, when large-scale urbanization, a shift from domestic to clerical jobs, and the break-up of the traditional kinship networks of the rural South took place. Even then, black women's sexuality was still contained within a white male patriarchy that continued to view her as already sexually liberated.

Black woman could not be completely controlled and defined by her own men, for she had already learned to manage and resist the advances of white men, earning and internalizing a reputation for toughness and strength, for resiliency and resolve, that enhanced the myth of her as both matriarch and wild woman. Her political resistance increased her potential to become a woman of power, capable of defining herself and rising to protect herself and her children, frequently throwing the mantle of protection over black men as well.

Slavery and womanhood remained interconnected long after the formal bondage of black people was over. Being a black woman with a black man could still mean slavery. And the woman could not be separated from the color. Being a black woman without a black man could also still mean slavery. And the color could not be separated from the woman.

These contradictions have been fully explored by only a few black women, for black women and black men continue to be engaged in a community of struggle to create a space in which to live and to survive:

> Black women speaking with many voices and expressing many individual opinions, have been nearly unanimous in their insistence that their own emancipation cannot be separated from the emancipation of their men. Their liberation depends on the liber-

ation of the race and the improvement of life in the black community.[66]

Sex between black women and black men, between black men and black men, between black women and black women, is meshed within complex cultural, political, and economic circumstances. All black sexuality is underlined by a basic theme: where, when, and under what circumstances could/would black men and black women connect with each other intimately and privately when all aspects of their lives were considered the dominion of the public, white master/lover's power?

If the sexual act between white men and black women was a ritual reenactment of domination, the oppression failed to completely dampen the sexual expression of black women within the black community, which often became a ritual enactment of affirmation of her freedom and happiness within intense emotional connections with her men, her sisters, her children, her gods, and more often with herself. In spite of centuries of personal and political rape, black women could still say, "i found god in myself/and i loved her/i loved her fiercely."[67]

History, traditionally written as a record of public events, has obscured and omitted the relationship between public events and private acts. Therefore, sex has always been in the closet of American history hidden away from and kept outside the public realm of political and economic events. White men used their power in the public sphere to construct a private sphere that would meet their needs and their desire for black women, which if publically admitted would have undermined the false construct of race they needed to maintain public power. Therefore, the history of black women in America reflects the juncture where the private and public spheres and personal and political oppression meet.

The master/lover ruled over the world; he divided it up and called everyone out of their name. During the day, he would call her "wench," "negress," "Sable Venus," "dusky Sal," and "Auntie." He described and wrote about her endurance, ate her biscuits, and suckled her breasts. At night he would chant false endearments and would feel engulfed within her darkness. He would accuse her of raping herself, naming his lesser brothers as the fathers of his and her children. He would record every battle, keep every letter, document each law, building monuments to himself, but he would never tell the true story, the complete story of how he used to rape to make the profit, of how he used the bodies of women to satisfy his needs. He would never tell how he built a society with the aid of dark-skinned women, while telling the world he did it alone.

He would cover the tracks between his house and hers, he would deny the semen-stained sheets she was forced to wash. History would become all that men did during the day, but nothing of what they did during the night. He would forget her children. He would deny his love or lust for her. He would deny his failure to obey his own laws. He refused to listen to the logical extension of his argument for the massacres, the slave raids, the genocide, the lynch mobs, the Ku Klux Klan. He could not live up to his own fears and arguments against mongrelization of the race, the separation of black from white. He built an exterior world that reflected his fragmented insides.

But the woman learned to face him, the rapist who hated and loved her with such passion. She learned to use her darkness to create light. She would make the divided, white and black, external and internal world into wholeness. She would "lean on Jesus," reaching out to help and for help, and would gather around her children and kin to help them make the world whole and livable. She would mother all the children—black and white—and serve both men—conqueror and conquered—knowing "all there was to know," for she could not separate the color from the woman.

Only a few daring men, mostly black ones, would recognize that only she understood what it had taken for white men to dominate the world and what it would mean, finally, to be free. But some black women who voiced what they knew did not survive:

> A slave woman ain't allowed to respect herself, if she would. I had a pretty sister, she was whiter than I am, for she took more after her father. When she was 16 years old, her master sent for her. When he sent for her again, she cried and didn't want to go. She told mother her troubles, and she tried to encourage her to be decent and hold up her head above such things if she could. Her master was so mad, to think she had complained to her mother, that he sold her right off to Louisiana, and we heard afterward that she died there of hard usage.[68]

But others sold down river survived and remembered their mothers and fathers, remembered the white master/lover, the black master/lover, and the black brother/lover. They, in their turn, gave their daughters and sons the gifts of determination and freedom, the will to love and the strength to have faith. Some would accept these gifts, some would reject them. History, however, would obliterate the entire story, occasionally giving it only a false footnote. But deep within the daughters' hearts and minds it would be remembered and this memory would become the historical record everything had to be measured by.

Notes

1. Joseph Conrad, *Heart of Darkness* (New York: Dell Publishing, 1960).
2. See Susan Brownmiller, *Against Our Will* (New York: Simon and Schuster, 1975).
3. T. Obinkaram Echewa, "African Sexual Attitudes," *Essence* 2, no. 9 (January 1981): 56.
4. Sarah La Forey, "Female Circumcision," unpublished ms.
5. Winthrop Jordan, *White over Black* (Chapel Hill: University of North Carolina Press, 1968), pp. 3–43.
6. Richard G. Hofstadter, *America at 1750: A Social Portrait* (New York: Vintage Books, 1973), p. 108.
7. Conrad, *Heart of Darkness*, p. 116.
8. Angela Davis, "Reflections on the Black Woman's Role in the Community of Slaves," *Black Scholar* 3, no. 4 (December 1971): 7.
9. Barbara Chase-Riboud, *Sally Hemings* (New York: Viking Press, 1979), p. 284.
10. Jordan, *White over Black*, pp. 3–43.
11. Ibid., p. 148.
12. Gary Nash, *Red, White, and Black: The Peoples of Early America*, 2d ed. (Englewood Cliffs, N.J.: Prentice-Hall, 1982), pp. 115–126.
13. A. Leon Higgenbotham, Jr., *In the Matter of Color: Race and the American Legal Process—The Colonial Period* (Oxford: Oxford University Press, 1978), pp. 43–47.
14. Jordan, *White over Black*, pp. 138–39.
15. Ibid.
16. Cited in Carl Degler, *Out of Our Past: Forces That Shaped Modern America* (New York: Harper and Row, 1959), p. 32.
17. Ibid., p. 83.
18. Hofstadter, *America at 1750*, p. 111.
19. Ibid., p. 115.
20. Ibid., p. 116.
21. Degler, *Out of Our Past*, p. 163.
22. ————, *Autobiographical Accounts of Negro Ex-Slaves* (Nashville: Fisk University Press, 1968), p. 2.
23. Herbert Gutman, *The Black Family in Slavery and Freedom, 1750–1925* (New York: Pantheon Books, 1976), pp. 138, 76.
24. *Autobiographical Accounts*, p. 1.
25. Degler, *Out of Our Past*, p. 34.
26. Davis, "Black Woman's Role," passim.
27. E. Franklin Frazier, *The Negro Family in the United States* (Rev. ed., Chicago: University of Chicago Press, 1948), p. 53.
28. Gerda Lerner, ed., *Black Women in White America* (New York: Vintage Books, 1973), p. 156.
29. Ibid., p. 154.
30. John Dollard, *Caste and Class in a Southern Town*, rev. ed. (Garden City, N.Y.: Doubleday/Anchor, 1949), p. 139.
31. Jacqueline Jones, "My Mother Was Much of a Woman: Black Women, Work, and the Family Under Slavery," unpublished ms., 1980.
32. Quoted in John Blassingame, ed., *Slave Testimony: Two Centuries of Letters, Speeches, Interviews, and Autobiographies* (Baton Rouge: Louisiana State University Press, 1977), p. 221.
33. Chase-Riboud, *Sally Hemings*, p. 284.
34. *Autobiographical Accounts*, pp. 1–2.
35. Quoted in Anne Firor Scott, *Southern Lady: From Pedestal to Politics, 1830–1930* (Chicago: University of Chicago Press, 1970), p. 50.
36. Ibid., pp. 34–36.

37. Ibid., p. 37.
38. Ibid., p. 52.
39. Jordan, *White over Black*, p. 148.
40. Scott, *Southern Lady*, p. 52.
41. *Autobiographical Accounts*, p. 1.
42. Jones, "My Mother Was Much of a Woman," pp. 41–42.
43. David Katzman, "Domestic Service: Women's Work," in *Women Working: Theories and Facts in Perspective*, ed. Ann Stromberg and Shirley Harkness (Calif.: Mayfield Publishing Company, 1978), pp. 381–83.
44. *Autobiographical Accounts*, p. 1.
45. Frazier, *Negro Family*, p. 67.
46. Chase-Riboud, *Sally Hemings*, p. 40.
47. Frazier, *Negro Family*, p. 47.
48. Scott, *Southern Lady*, p. 53.
49. Barbara Omolade, "African and Slave Motherhood," Masters Thesis, Goddard College, 1979.
50. Jones, "My Mother Was Much of a Woman," p. 36.
51. Results of Oral History Class Projects—Black Women's History Courses 1978–1982—comp. and ed. Barbara Omolade.
52. Frazier, *Negro Family*, pp. 73–124.
53. Joanne Grant, *Black Protest: History Documents and Analysis from 1619 to the Present* (New York: Fawcett World Library, 1968), p. 33.
54. Blassingame, *Slave Testimony*, passim.
55. W. E. B. Du Bois, *Darkwater* (New York: Schocken Books, 1925), p. 172.
56. Gutman, *Black Family*, p. 17.
57. Lerner, *Black Women in White America*, p. 291.
58. David Katzman, *Seven Days a Week: Women and Domestic Service in Industrializing America* (New York: Oxford University Press, 1978), pp. 85–90.
59. Barbara Smith, "Toward a Black Feminist Criticism," *Conditions: Two* 1, no. 2 (October 1977): 25–52.
60. Lerner, *Black Women in White America*, pp. 79, 220.
61. See, for example, Franklin Frazier, *Black Bourgeoisie* (Glencoe, Ill.: Free Press, 1957), pp. 71–78.
62. Frazier, *Negro Family*, passim; oral history survey, cited in n. 51.
63. Gutman, *Black Family*, p. 85.
64. Lawrence Levine, *Black Culture and Black Consciousness* (Oxford: Oxford University Press, 1977), p. 275.
65. Ida Cox, "Wild Women Don't Have the Blues" (Northern Music Co., 1924).
66. Lerner, *Black Women in White America*, p. xxv.
67. Ntozake Shange, quoted in Carol P. Christ, *Diving Deep and Surfacing: Women Writers on Spiritual Quest* (Boston: Beacon Press, 1980), p. 117.
68. Blassingame, *Slave Testimony*, p. 256.

Section VI
On Sexual Openness

Sex radicals have traditionally postulated a hidden core of sexual being—call it eros or libido or instinct—that needs to be discovered, revealed, opened. But there has also been disagreement about this "drive" theory. Is sex a necessity like eating, a biological force that, when dammed up, causes a loss of human vitality? The question of whether or not there is a repressed entity—"sex"—that can be set free remains controversial.

If, as the pieces in this book argue, sexuality is a biological potential that is always expressed through socially constructed means, "openness" and "freedom" can only be relative terms. The concept "social construction" implies social control, sexual communities each with its own particular kind of openness and taboo. Ironically, then, openness, like other ideals of sexual practice, may well be constructed at the expense of other possibilities, such as an arousing erotic secrecy, or periodic celibacy, or the exclusive preference for one sexual practice over another. In other words, the ideal of sexual openness requires social definition and redefinition; it is a historically shifting quest for change and improvement in sexual mores.

Without such critical scrutiny, the ideal of sexual openness is merely bland. As Carole Vance points out in this section, the "openness" of many sexologists seeks to banish the social dimensions of sex. By narrowly defining sex as "what is done in bed," Vance's liberal sexologists ultimately belittle the experience; by silently legislating that issues of gender inequality or sexual preference are irrelevant to the pure science of sex, they trivialize the political struggle for a genuine, materially based sexual solidarity and mutuality.

Amber Hollibaugh and Cherríe Moraga are seeking a different sort of openness in their willingness to reveal themselves in conversation. They argue that one can't change a sexuality one hasn't been able to explore in all its aspects. By discussing race, class, lesbianism, and role playing, they seek to illuminate the complexity of their sexual impulses. Through openness, they discover not the universal sexuality of Vance's sexologists but, rather, thorny and challenging sexual differences.

As Carole Rosenthal shows in "The Teacher," openness is also a philosophical impossibility. Not only is it often inappropriate to tell all, but of course we cannot do so, no matter how much we might want to. Since there is no total disclosure, our attention must be upon the nature of our selectivity. How conscious is the speaker of his or her own choices to reveal or suppress thoughts, images, impulses? For many of these feelings, there are no words at all. Hollibaugh and Moraga discuss how limited and limiting they found the feminist language of sex, how grossly inadequate to the task of describing a wide variety of sexual experiences and feelings. Rosenthal extends this insight to include all language. The people in her story communicate their contradictory sexual desires indirectly and inadequately. Openness is bald and threatening; secrets are painful and misleading: there is no simple formula for sexual expressiveness.

Jayne Cortez's "In the Morning" is the most ambivalent of aubades, a poem that expresses the wild mixture of feelings inevitable in an open, inclusive expression of sexual passion. In contrast, the little boy in Sharon Olds' "Bestiary" rejects Cortez's inclusiveness of love, hate, pain, and passion; he is at the stage of "hydraulics" when sex is "entrances, exits," a narrow excitement that seeks a literal opening in the world. Finally, the little girl in Alix Kates Shulman's story is "uncorrupted" in her sexual pleasures by virtue of sweet ignorance. Is not ignorance, too, a form of openness? It would seem that openness can include or exclude: it is an empty set until we establish meaning.

Gender Systems, Ideology, and Sex Research
Carole S. Vance

Current sex research and therapy rest on initial assumptions, largely implicit, concerning the social order and the relationship of women to men, and individuals to society. Whether these assumptions are valid and useful remains to be decided. A necessary first step, however, is the articulation of these premises and their hidden meanings, an articulation that sex researchers, with few exceptions, have not done but in fact have strenuously avoided.[1]

Amid the diversity of meanings attached to the terms "gender," "gender role," and "gender system" in describing relations between women and men, this analysis uses "gender" and "gender system" following the theoretical formulation presented in Gayle Rubin's "The Traffic in Women: Notes on the 'Political Economy' of Sex."[2] Gender is seen as the product of culture, not biology, even though biological and anatomical markers are used to assign individuals to gender groups.

> Gender is a socially imposed division of the sexes. It is a product of the social relations of sexuality. Kinship systems rest upon marriage. They therefore transform males and females into "men" and "women," each an incomplete half which can only find wholeness when united with the other. Men and women are, of course, different. But they are not as different as day and night, earth and sky, yin and yang, life and death. In fact, from the standpoint of nature, men and women are closer to each other than either is to anything else—for instance, mountains, kangaroos, or coconut palms. The idea that men and women are more different from one another than either is from anything else must come from somewhere other than nature. . . . But the idea that men and women are two mutually exclusive categories must arise out of something other than a nonexistent "natural" opposition. Far from being an expression of natural differences, exclusive gender identity is the suppression of natural similarities.[3]

Rubin defines the "sex-gender system" as "the set of arrangements by which a society transforms biological sexuality into products of human activity."[4] Within this framework she describes the transformation

381

of the penis, an organ with no inherent social character, into the phallus, an organ that symbolizes and indicates male authority, dominance, and social power. Biology does not cause this transformation, but rather is the "raw material" transformed by cultural operations. The sex-gender system is "the part of social life which is the locus of the oppression of women, of sexual minorities, and of certain aspects of human personality within individuals."[5] Its organization thus includes relations of production, reproduction, and the family, as well as the enculturation of gender in childhood and adult life. Anthropological examination suggests that among human groups, the existence of gender systems is universal, although the configurations of systems vary widely. Every gender system, regardless of its unique content, exhibits an ideology or cognitive system that presents gender categories as unalterable. Thus, whatever the cultural cosmology as to the origin of such divisions, the categories male and female are seen as natural in the sense of a structure given in the nature of the world.

Many researchers in sexual behavior theoretically acknowledge cross-cultural variation, the flexibility of human behavior, and the power of enculturation; however, they rarely analyze the powerful ways in which the gender system and gender ideologies of their own society inform their work. The study of sexual behavior, valuable in its own right, is a powerful tool for raising innovative questions about social relations and social structure, yet much of this research avoids these questions. I suggest that a critical social and historical analysis of the implicit premises in sex research will not only improve the quality of the work in a narrow sense, but will also illuminate the relationship among scientific investigation, the social context in which it occurs, and for what purposes and for whose benefit it is conducted.[6]

In this essay, I will examine the gender assumptions and gender ideologies implicit in the "Program in Human Sexuality," held during July 1977 at the Center for Sex Research, located at a major university in the United States.[7] This program is a significant one for a number of reasons:

1. The Center for Sex Research, a major center of broadly based sex research in America, is highly influential and respected. Far from subscribing to an ivory-tower model of research, the center collects and disseminates data with the expectation of influencing personal action, conduct in the helping professions, and social policy.

> The primary purpose of the Center is to conduct research on human sexual behavior by gathering data, analyzing them, and making the resultant information available to those who need it. The underlying philosophy is that any satisfactory social policy or personal decision about sex must be made on the basis of factual information rather than on ignorance, and it is the function of the Center to provide such information.

Through publications, lectures, consultations, and voluminous correspondence, this needed information has been provided to psychiatrists, legislators, physicians, psychologists, attorneys, medical researchers, social workers, and other professionals concerned with human behavior.[8]

2. The center has been a model for the development of other sex research centers and training programs.

3. The center's program has received funding from the National Institute of Mental Health (NIMH); indeed, almost one-half of the participants in the 1977 program, primarily those working in clinical and social service positions, were sponsored by NIMH. The importance of the center in applied research programs is clear:

The change in public attitudes toward sexual matters has increased the expectation that health, mental health, social work, and other professionals will provide accurate answers to sex questions and adequate services to help solve sexual problems. The goal of the ten-day program is to provide an opportunity for professionals to acquire the factual information and special skills necessary to help meet this public need.[9]

4. Speakers were among the most prominent investigators in the field of sex research.[10]

The program included the following topics:

mammalian sexual behavior, anthropological perspectives on human sexuality, human sexual behaviors, sexual development, and sexually transmitted diseases. In addition, current sociosexual issues such as professional ethics, censorship, rights of minority groups, and various clinical techniques will be discussed. Other sessions will focus on the sexual problems of the physically and mentally handicapped, institutionalized populations, and other special groups.[11]

Approximately eighty participants attended the training program; the majority, fifty, were women. The participants were professionals: educators, clinicians, some doctors, social workers; most held higher degrees. By contrast, the speakers were predominantly male, fourteen men and seven women. Female speakers typically worked in applied-health settings and discussed sexual issues of adolescence, the retarded, and those with special medical problems. This division of labor left the larger, more intellectual and theoretical work to the men. As for the center, the research staff was largely male; the supporting staff largely female. The director lamented the relative lack of women in sex research.

Ethnographic analysis of the programs's content and structure reveals an adherence to sexist and heterosexist paradigms, which were rarely analyzed or related to social structure. Basic questions about femininity and masculinity, the social construction of gender, and the relations between subordinates and superordinates were not addressed. Film presentations illustrated these paradigms in heterosexual relations, particularly a short cartoon, *Deep Donut* (1976), intended as a comic counterpart to the movie *Deep Throat*. The plot is brief: a donut sits inside her house. A pickle drives up in a car, exits, and enters the house carrying a bouquet of flowers. The pickle first sits on a rocking chair, then moves to the couch to be closer to the donut. The donut edges away. The pickle pursues the donut, chasing her around the room, around the sofa and onto the floor at a frantic pace. The donut manages to evade the pickle, even as he races after her in furious pursuit. Finally the donut hops into bed in the adjacent bedroom, and the pickle follows. The pickle rubs in and out of the donut's hole and finally ejaculates. They snuggle. The pickle exits the house.

A second cartoon, *Genesis*, ostensibly about sexual repression, depicts the creation of the first humans. God creates man and gives him a penis, but warns him not to use it. Man is unhappy. God creates woman and gives her sexual organs: breasts. It is remarkable that the clitoris, the obvious homologue, is omitted. (This analogy between nonhomologous organs such as penis and breast is based, perhaps, on the fact that both are pleasurable organs for men.)

The third cartoon, *Kama Sutra,* depicts the adventures of a couple. The male partner announces that they prefer variety in their sex life, although the female partner, Evelyn, never speaks. The cartoon follows their copulations in various settings and countries. Evelyn, depicted as a ridiculous figure, is tied up, beaten, thrown down the stairs, and turned into a typewriter upon which he pounds; in short, she is a passive subject who is fucked with great delight and vigor by her partner. At the conclusion, Evelyn, thoroughly injured by these energetic copulations, lies in a hospital bed, enclosed from head to foot in a body cast; her partner leaps upon her and penetrates her once again.

These cartoons were presented as lighthearted, benign commentaries on sexual relations, which most of the audience found quite comic. When questioned about the significance of these films, the staff replied that they were amusing and reflected audiovisual materials currently available for teaching and counseling. Audiovisual materials used in the program were selected almost at random, subject to no discussion and analysis, merely viewed. The cartoons were presented as having no meaning of a problematic or questionable character requiring evaluation, much less critique. In reality, however, they uncritically reflected malignant themes in heterosexual relations, namely: forced penetration, male violence, female compliance and passivity, definition of female sexuality to serve the goals of male sexuality, and the equation of vaginal penetration with sex. Participants who pointed out these themes in the cartoons were called "critical" and "intellectualizing"; they were "campaigning" or "carrying a cross."

Persistent themes in the program, reflecting the operation of the gender system and ideology in the larger society, included the pronounced interest in heterosexual sex, usually called "sex," a term that ordinarily did not include homosexual sex or the paraphilias,[12] which required special linguistic markers. Description and depiction of heterosexual sex consistently showed men unclothing and cajoling women, while initiating new and escalated sexual activities; men set the pace and timing of activities. Women cooperated with unflagging enthusiasm, most vigorously performing fellatio, although in no film did a male perform cunnilingus. The missionary position, though not uniformly employed, was the favored position for orgasm. All heterosexual contact culminated in vaginal penetration, indicating a progression through hierarchies of sexual activity, from the now acceptable normal "foreplay" to "real sex." Heterosexual sex, then, requires genital contact, male erection, and penetration.

Homosexual sex showed more variety, although ideological definitions of female and male sexual styles were evident in contrasts between lesbian and gay sexual interaction depicted on film. Men's interaction was continuously filmed and highly genital, proceeding straight to orgasm. Interestingly, visual material did not depict anal intercourse, a behavior omitted in an appeal to straight sensibility. Anal intercourse was treated in lectures as a strictly homosexual activity. In contrast with films on gay men's sex, lesbian sex occurred in a field of daisies, chronicled by discontinuous jump cuts. Sexual activity, never genital, consisted of running in slow motion through sun-dappled fields, hand-holding, and mutual hair-combing. Note that the films shown were recent, liberal, and widely distributed for sex education and counseling.

Gender ideologies were most evident in Richard Green's lecture on transsexualism, which proceeded from the assumption that effeminate behaviors, feelings, and attitudes are best housed in female bodies, where they become merely "feminine." Social intolerance for incongruous combinations of physical form and gender identity, and personal intolerance for these incongruities displayed by individual transsexuals, were not analyzed; rather, the research discussed concentrated on locating the cause of transsexualism in family pathology or prenatal hormones. The alteration or mutilation of the body to be socially consistent with personality, fantasy, and desire is the ultimate sign of the objective and subjective power of gender assumptions—assumptions that went entirely unquestioned.

Gender ideologies were evident in the importance of the couple, the ideal unit of sexual and affectional life. Courtship was described as a lifelong search, interrupted by marriage, for the partner; social life was organized by the principle of Noah's ark, two by two. The primacy of the couple and the isolation of the couple from social life and social forces render sexual behavior an essentially private act. The unit of therapy was the couple "in distress"; monogamy, order, and stability were prime goals. Alan Bell reported preliminary results from the San Francisco study of homosexuals, which detailed diverse living patterns in the homosexual community. Five types of living arrangements were discerned by the researchers, one of which, the closed couple, was described in glowing terms. This couple, whether lesbian or gay male, had a home tastefully furnished with photographs of the Bay, radiated warmth, and provided the interviewer with freshly baked chocolate chip cookies. In short, they were married.

Though sex research is inevitably based on theoretical and conceptual models, researchers and therapists alike maintain that they have no theory, no basic assumptions, no axe to grind. They are just collecting the facts. In their written work, this atheoretical posture manifests itself as an isolation from contemporary intellectual issues and debates. Although many sex researchers were initially trained in medicine or in one of the social sciences, they are rapidly transformed into that peculiar creature, the "sexologist." Responsibility for this transformation must in part be assigned to professional disciplines that have systematically discouraged the study of sexuality and penalized scholars who pursued such studies.[13] The resulting intellectual isolation and theoretical impoverishment can be seen in most sex research journals. Thus, as sex is isolated and privatized within the couple, the study of sexuality is encapsulated within "sexology."

The theoretical position of most sex researchers, evident (though implicit) in their work, is functional and ahistorical. Cross-cultural examples are plucked from "primitive" societies that exist in homogeneous and consistent splendor, without name or date. Normative patterns of sexual behavior are simply described—evidently white, middle-class norms—and general statements about sexual behavior are not modified by class, race, or ethnicity, apparently insignificant features. Society is analyzed as an integrated, homeostatic, cooperative organism, in which power differences and conflict are not addressed. So too within the family, power relations are ignored, as are the material bases for female subordination and male authority.

Such an analysis is illustrated by a lecture on negotiation within the family, now that women are becoming "equal":

Clearly, therefore, one of the prime tasks of educators, clinicians, therapists, and clergy is to make most single and married persons aware of the importance of negotiation and also to teach them how to do it. . . . A phrase used in the literature that I like very much is MJP, maximum joint profit. . . . What we want to stimulate in men and women is the desire and capability to negotiate for the maximum benefit of all parties concerned. . . . We want to stress especially to women that this bargaining posture should begin prior to any formal marriage. And if they cannot establish the MJP, that is, the maximum joint profit negotiating patterns in advance, they are far better off remaining unattached.

In doing so, the men give up the right to pontificate. That same right, the refusal to negotiate, was once held by political leaders and business executives, but they have long since lost that right. But I think most people are agreed that both societies and individuals are better off because political and economic leaders lost the right to pontificate and were forced to negotiate. They justify that what they want is good for us all.[14]

Despite the speaker's use of an economic metaphor in which male-female interactions are conceptualized in terms of capitalist labor relations, he avoids recognizing inequality and coercion in male-female relations by maintaining that they are absent from relationships between capital and labor as well. Both gender relations and economic relations are characterized by cooperative negotiation for mutual benefit. Husbands will give up power, it is suggested, if wives learn to negotiate properly; inequality is just a matter of bad communication. Cooperation and harmony are emphasized: conflict is minimized.

Thus, sexual behavior is seen as an isolated and private event, not connected to the distribution of resources and power, the gender system, the organization of production, or race and class. Participants at this program who attempted to link sexual behavior with social structure were greeted with incomprehension. A psychiatrist doing sex therapy reported on therapeutic interventions with couples: frequently, the presenting complaint was the female's inability to experience orgasm during vaginal penetration, although many of these women were orgasmic during masturbation or other forms of clitoral stimulation. When asked about the possible reasons leading individuals to seek sex therapy, that is, to perceive a sexual experience as a "dysfunction" and seek professional help for it, the therapist replied "that it was healthy to want to come with your husband inside you." Furthermore, women never came to her clinic complaining that they could reach orgasm during penetration, but not during masturbation. Such a condition was not a problem. Practitioners of sex therapy operate on an implicit principle of resolving mechanical and hydraulic difficulties, products of individual, not cultural, origin.

The diversity of sexual behavior, both human and nonhuman, was surveyed in detailed lectures about mammalian and human cross-cultural behavior and depicted in a dizzying filmic display of mice, rabbits, skunks, elephants, and Australian aborigines—to little avail, in that the possible causes of such diversity were never suggested. For anthropologists, cross-cultural diversity requires an explanation of human similarities and differences. The ecological and structural causes of cross-cultural diversity were never pursued, leaving the viewer with a profound insight: "Gee whiz, aren't people funny." This welter of data is not unlike Alfred Kinsey's favored arguments from cultural relativism or animal behavior, with which he attempted to normalize "perverse" behavior by noting that it was done somewhere, at some time, by some group. "Innocence by association," as Paul Robinson calls it, may serve political ends of sexual minorities, but the inability or unwillingness to connect sexual behavior with social structure suggests that sexual behavior is essentially unexplainable, and investigation in this topic is futile.

Little attention was given in the program to methodological problems, despite the fact that sex research involves difficult questions about adequacy and interpretation of data and choices of research strategies. A related issue was a division between the intellectual and the experiential: experiencing something for yourself was often referred to as a superior form of knowledge. The same researchers who investigated large samples with elaborate methodologies derogated this information as "just statistics" and turned instead to highly idiosyncratic and individual examples of behavior. Perhaps the medical preference, whether in physical or psychiatric medicine, for the case history and clinical anecdote accounts for some of this behavior, yet even participants trained in more objective methods of data collection put forth formulations and hypotheses that were to be believed on the strength of experience, not experiment.

Researchers in sexual behavior were encouraged to obtain special subjective experiences in the program, thought essential to their work; experiences involved introspection and awareness of one's own attitudes and values. These experiences were institutionalized in the Sexual Attitudes Reassessment (SAR); no longer a California specialty, such SAR groups are persistent features of sex conferences and training programs for researchers, therapists, and doctors. Thought and feeling were not so much seen as different though integrated ways to experience the world as they were seen as mutually exclusive categories. Intellectual process and operations were seen as a defense, or escape, from the real thing, emotional experience. Participants were exhorted to be "open" to others, and to be "vulnerable." The valuation of experience was correlated with the use of a special vocabulary: "vulnerable," "comfort index," "negotiate," "to resonate with," "to touch base with," "to bounce off of," "to trust," and "to share." Thus, few presenters gave papers and requested comments and criticisms; rather, they "shared their thoughts" and "hoped for mutual trust and vulnerability."

To use Robinson's term, most of the speakers and participants were "sexual enthusiasts" or "modernists."[15] Sexuality was good, normal, and healthy, not dangerous and polluting. Sexual behavior was unnecessarily limited by foolish and irrational beliefs and taboos, which would fall before the onslaught of science, much in keeping with Kinsey's view. Many were not just enthusiasts, but missionaries and proselytizers. The clerical background of some sex researchers and more sex therapists deserves further attention. The blurring of traditional boundaries between research and applied work, seen in the increasing overlap between sex research and sex therapy, enlarges the field of proselytizing considerably. As for personal stance, the researchers were unabashed liberals: they were tolerant. They wished everyone to do their own thing. They were proud of being liberals. Careful scrutiny of this liberality, resting as it does on the isolation of the couple and the narrow definition of sex as what is done in bed—unrelated to social and political institutions—reveals it to be a small thing indeed. All permutations of bodies and organs were tolerable, given that they were private. The conventionalized lesbian or gay, acceptable to straight sensibility, was the favored deviant on film. The audience's initial acceptance of lesbian sex (the delightful running through the daisies) was called into question by the disapproval of and wholesale exodus from the film *In the Best Interests of the Children* (1977), which portrayed lesbian mothers and their children coping with straight reactions to the political and social implications of lesbianism. The paraphilias were neatly segregated in one session and given short shrift because they do not lead to the couple, stability, or cookie baking.

Although this analysis has concentrated on intellectual matters and style, anthropologists are also properly concerned with the meaning of interpersonal interactions, presentation of self, and ritual. Repeatedly, the anti-intellectualism previously described was used as a controlling device. The opposition between feeling and thought and the elevation of feeling to a superior position were used consistently to deflect criticism, both of specific research and the program in general. Analytic comments, based on feminist and gay analysis, that questioned heterosexist assumptions or conclusions were labeled "intellectual," "critical," "intellectualizing," "spectatoring," "distancing," terms clearly pejorative and designed to silence the critics. In a very sharp reversal, a professional meeting ostensibly designed to disseminate information and skills became instead a communion of feelings and experience.

Those who did not share in that particular communion were isolated and silenced. This maneuver began the first day of the program when results from a "study" of twenty participants in a previous program were presented. "We found eight types: the voyeur, the executive, the 'into' therapy person, the verifier, the patient, the sexologist, the experimenter, the cautious experimenter." Each type was ridiculed in turn. The speaker added:

> I would also like to suggest that you remember you are the program. . . . In my clinic we have a one-liner: that good relationships between the couples we treat depends more on being the right person than finding the right person. And I really mean to you seriously, personally and professionally, that the success of this program rests highly to the degree you'll be vulnerable.[16]

Group solidarity and jointness of experience and reaction were emphasized. On the first day, comparisons were made between the program, college, and summer camp. Advice was given on conducting interpersonal relations, productive conduct, and the possibility of meeting a new "significant other" during the program. Staff members took a somewhat unexpected interest in participants' emotional state: one hoped that participants "would not decompensate" as they had last year, while another staff member noted that "if you were in pain," he would be available for consultation.

Criticism was deflected through a second device, control of time and consequent limited public discussions of controversial issues. When objections were raised, discussion was cut short; there was not enough time to continue. Participants were assured they could continue this most valuable discussion in the coffee hour, or cocktail hour, that is, among four or five people rather than eighty. Controlling public speech and limiting communication was an important device of social control utilized by the program's staff.

The Sexual Attitudes Reassessment workshop deserves further analysis as ritual. The printed prospectus of the program noted:

> There will be a two-day workshop on sexual attitudes, utilizing small groups and experienced facilitators, when participants will have the opportunity to examine their sexual values in a setting which emphasizes the implications for professional roles.[17]

The SAR alternated small-group discussion with viewing of movies and presentations to the entire group. Topics of discussion included sexual attitudes and values, sexual vocabulary, courtship, masturbation, homosexuality, and sex roles. Participation was presented as a challenge:

> Another one is you can take a look at your personal value system for ten days. I think that is very, very important. You will only be able to do that if you are vulnerable and open. . . . If you haven't

signed up, I think it is a mistake. It's part of the gestalt that forms here.[18]

Such personal reassessment is increasingly part of the training given to sex researchers, therapists, and doctors. It is a routine feature of sexuality conferences and has been exported to Europe and South America. Participants frequently attend again and again; they comment that they always gain something from this reassessment.

Within the small group, people are to discuss personal and intimate topics, usually involving sexuality. One is supposed to be "trusting," that is, tell intimate details to relative strangers one will not see again. They in turn are expected to be accepting, supporting, reassuring, and understanding. Criticism and hostility (or at least their overt expression) are discouraged. The SAR group, in which the participant spends the bulk of two very long days, functions as an intense peer pressure group that requires the suppression of conflict and difference and the façade of agreement and acceptance. Political analysis, feminist, gay, or any other, is seen as irrelevant to these inner confessions and so treated by group members, who warn against "intellectualizing" and "distancing." Fundamental gender ideologies are accepted and rarely questioned. Thus, within the SAR, "affirmation of one's own sexuality is crucial. If you define sexuality as the totality of our maleness and femaleness . . . I think our goal is an affirmation, a celebration of who we are."[19]

The equation of sexuality with gender and the exhortation to celebrate who we *are*, more critically viewed as who we have been forced to be, leads not to insight and reevaluation but to obfuscation and confusion. The superficiality of such uncritical examination became clear in the sexual vocabulary session, in which participants were to overcome their inhibitions by uttering aloud words for the anus, breasts, and male and female genitals. This exercise would suggest that the shame, humiliation, and degradation associated with such words as "pussy," "cunt," and "twat" comes simply from the magical power of a word, which can be exorcised by uttering it once in public, instead of from men's structural power to define women's sexuality (and women themselves) at either extreme: the good, withholding cockteaser to the bad, too-sexual slut.

The participants in the SAR had largely favorable responses. They had an opportunity to talk about taboo subjects, which they had never discussed before. They were reluctant to return home, called "reentry," where they did not talk of these things. Although the relief and release resulting from more free and honest speech is not to be dismissed, the structural reasons for this normally inhibited discourse and alienation were never discussed. Alternate social arrangements were not considered. SAR participants did not expect to communicate with their "significant others" in this new way.[20] Instead, they hoped to attend other SARs, for renewed opportunities for initimacy and self-revelation with strangers. Clearly, it is easier to fuck than talk sex with one's significant other.

The operation of a SAR group combines overt warmth, vulnerability, and support while masking covert gender antagonism, power struggle, and manipulation within intense, claustrophobic relations detached from other social groups and structures. In its double messages and social isolation, the SAR group resembles the heterosexual and heterosexist family.

Analysis of social events concerns what was absent as well as what was evident. Absent from the program were discussions of repression, sex and politics, eroticism, desire, social meaning, and social construction. Absent were analyses and theoretical questions raised by the women's movement and the gay movement. Absent was discussion of alternative social structures. Absent was an analysis of the gender system, gender ideology, and their influence on sexual behavior.

The themes I have discussed here, based on ethnographic analysis of a research and training seminar at a major center for sex research, are themes also present in a careful reading of the recent sex research and therapy literature. During the program, these trends were exemplified in language, interpersonal behavior, and organization.

The increasing amount of sex research currently being conducted requires a critical social and historical analysis of the ideological foundations of such research and its relationship to prevailing gender systems. Those who wish to study the relationship between gender systems, sexuality, and power must study those of the present as well as the past. Although recent work has suggested possible directions for the study of sexuality,[21] in my view what is required is a rethinking of sexuality and gender, and their articulation to a degree that we can barely imagine now. It is a task that could easily occupy feminist scholars for the next ten years and will be possible only for those prepared to question and possibly reject a number of cherished beliefs (be they Marxist, feminist, or commonsensical), to the extent that all these have been deeply influenced by gender ideologies we no longer find useful or true. These questions might begin with: What is our paradigm of sexuality? What are our assumptions about "natural" sexuality? What is the relationship between fantasy and action, the individual and society? It is premature to list the directions this work will take because it will be collaborative and interdisciplinary. However, I believe it must begin with a reexamination of major sex theorists, a social history of institutions that have sponsored recent sex research, an analysis of formulations concerning sex "drive" and energy, empirical research on sexual fringe groups, and a delineation of the social construction of heterosexuality.[22] Critical analysis is needed not only for a scientifically accurate account of human sexuality, but at the very least as a necessary step in the direction of autonomy and choice in sexual matters and sexual life.

Notes

My thanks to John D'Emilio, Muriel Dimen, Frances M. Doughty, Lisa Duggan, Peter Fry, Jonathan Katz, David Schwartz, and the editors of *Feminist Studies* for their criticisms and suggestions. Special thanks to Paula Webster for her insight and encouragement, not to mention *maritúna*. This text is a revised version of the paper that appeared in *Feminist Studies* 6, no. 1 (Spring 1980): 129–43.

1. This paper was presented at the conference "Constructing a History of Power and Sexuality," New York University, April 1, 1978.
2. Gayle Rubin, "The Traffic in Women: Notes on the 'Political Economy' of Sex," in *Toward an Anthropology of Women*, ed. Rayna R. Reiter (New York: Monthly Review Press, 1975), pp. 157–210.
3. Ibid., pp. 179–80.
4. Ibid., p. 159.
5. Ibid.
6. An analysis of significant sex researchers, Ellis, Kinsey, and Masters and Johnson, appears in Paul Robinson, *The Modernization of Sex* (New York: Harper and Row, 1976).
7. As an anthropologist interested in sexuality and gender, I attended the "Program in Human Sexuality" to get an overview of contemporary research in sexual behavior. A review of the anthropological literature disabused me of the myth that anthropology as a discipline has been more receptive to the study of sexuality than other social sciences, or has accumulated a wealth of data. I began the program with great interest. Although I did not initially intend to study the ideology of sex research, it became apparent after the first day that unexamined assumptions about gender and gender relations figured prominently both in the "scientific" research on sexuality and in the structure of the program. A critical analysis of the implicit premises of sex research seemed in order.

   Data were collected through standard anthropological techniques of participant observation. I attended morning, afternoon, and evening sessions and took notes throughout. Direct quotes are transcribed from tape recordings of speakers' formal presentations and from the question and answer periods that followed.

   Following anthropological custom, the Center for Sex Research is a pseudonym, in this case less to protect the privacy of the center and more to suggest that the uncritical acceptance of gender ideology is not characteristic of a particular center, but is widespread in the field. Nor is the influence of this ideology restricted to mainstream or conservative sex research and theory, because it is evident, I would contend, in leftist and feminist thought on sexuality as well. This point was developed by Ellen DuBois, Gayle Rubin, and myself at the panel "Sexuality, Feminism, and Culture," presented at *The Second Sex* conference, New York Institute for the Humanities, New York University, September 28, 1979. A more detailed analysis of the role of gender ideology in the feminist involvement in the current antipornography movement is forthcoming.
8. Unpaged descriptive brochure sent to program participants, 1977.
9. Informational letter sent to program participants, 1977.
10. They included Richard Green, Alan Bell, Anke Ehrhardt, and Paul Gebhard.

11. Informational letter, 1977.
12. The paraphilias include exhibitionism, voyeurism, age-inappropriate sex, cross-dressing, fetishism, and sadomasochism.
13. See the comments made in response to the rejection of a symposium on sexual behavior at the annual meeting of the American Anthropological Association in Carole Vance and Paula Webster, "Rejection of Symposium Protested," *Anthropology Newsletter* 19 (January 1978): 13.
14. Dr. John Scanzoni, lecture, "Gender Roles, Negotiation, and Marital Change," "Program in Human Sexuality," July 22, 1977.
15. Robinson, *The Modernization of Sex*, pp. 1–3.
16. Dr. F. Paul Pearsall, lecture, "Sexual Attitudes and Values," "Program in Human Sexuality," July 22, 1977.
17. Informational letter, 1977.
18. Pearsall, lecture.
19. Ibid.
20. Although a fuller description of participants' reactions to the program would be interesting, especially because the majority were women, the sudden nature of the ethnography precluded a detailed investigation. Judging from their public comments and a sample of private conversations, however, female participants, like their male counterparts, were not critical of the program and its assumptions.
21. Robinson, *The Modernization of Sex*; Jeffrey Weeks, *Coming Out: Homosexual Politics in Britain from the Nineteenth Century to the Present* (London: Quartet Books, 1977); Michel Foucault, *The History of Sexuality*, vol. 1 (New York: Pantheon Books, 1978); Robert A. Padgug, "On Conceptualizing Sexuality in History," *Radical History Review* 20 (Spring/Summer 1979): 3–23; Lillian Faderman, *Surpassing the Love of Men* (New York: William Morrow, 1981); *Heresies #12* 3 (1981), "Sex Issue"; Hannah Alderfer, Beth Jaker, and Marybeth Nelson, *Diary of a Conference on Sexuality* (New York: Faculty Press, 1982).
22. Paula Webster, "The Politics of Rape in Primitive Society," *Heresies #6* (Summer 1978): 16–22; and Lucy Gilbert and Paula Webster, *Bound by Love* (Boston: Beacon Press, 1982).

The Teacher
Carole Rosenthal

Although I'd had several of these students, all graduate art students, many of them as old as me, the previous semester, the class threatened insurrection. Nothing obvious, but constant challenges to my authority. A very smart and sadistic bearded man in the back row raised his hand every time I talked. When I called on him, the first words out of his mouth were, "I don't agree with what you're saying." Then he would cite research sources, often common, sometimes obscure—but much worse for me if they were common than obscure, because I'm supposed to be an expert on the course I'm teaching. I'm supposed to know everything. How else can I explain my qualifications, which should be obvious? A photographer, recently returned to school, working on his M.F.A., this student, whose name is Paul, knows my subject better than I do in ways. Yet his views are too narrow, glinting when you turn them sideways, but invisible and dangerous. He lacks insight. He identifies with the critics. "Look into yourself," I invite him passionately. He's terribly good-looking, but an unremarkable type. And just at the point where he reaches for moral superiority over me, flipping up his neat fingers to say that the mistreated prostitute in *Notes from the Underground* is "the sole character in the whole book to take any positive action, the only *worthwhile* character"—*he's* not so infatuated with the Underground Man's curse of consciousness as I am, he accuses me—I suddenly realize that he is only flirting with me. His attacks are seductions. He wishes to gain my power. During the class break when I pass him on the stairs as I'm going down for coffee and he's coming up, he looks at his gold watch and goes, "Tsk, tsk, tsk. Late again," shaking his head. Sadism, not scholarship, but for what purpose?

Maybe I'll fall in love with him. I imagine his photographs, which I've never seen, as fine-grained, detailed, sharp edges—all landscapes in black and white, overexposed views from afar. His eyes are light and wide, his hair sandy and curling. But he still looks ordinary to me, disappointingly even-featured. His beard, shaved at the sides, is a goatee, old-fashioned and pretentious in my mind; and he looks like someone who ought to be wearing a monocle, too. Instead he wears gold chains around his neck, one skinny, one thick and braided. Perhaps it's his predictability, the hand that raises that I'm admiring: "I don't agree. . . ."

At the beginning of the term, another handsome man in class, and certainly flashier, a silver-haired Australian with leather wristlets and embroidered boots, argued with me a lot too—"Not necessarily," he grinned after every interpretation. "Of course not necessarily!" I snapped back—but his points were silly and poorly researched, and he grew sheepish when I retaliated, a baby with a need to be looked at who now sleeps through lectures with his head lolling on his arm in the front row: a painter.

But most of the students in this class are photographers because of a woman photography major named Tasha—a girl, really, she seems to me—who took a graduate course with me last fall and fell in love with it. She recommended my classes to everyone. She's very sweet, tall and thin. Her eyes bulge. Her hair is sandy-colored, like Paul's. Six months ago she wore her hair long and swaying loose to her buttocks. But this year she cut it all off, cropped above her ears. I asked her about that haircut during a coffee break. She said, "Yeah, I broke up with my boyfriend."

"I thought it was a gesture," I told her. "I've done the same thing. I think that when women cut off their long hair, they're often making statements about their identities."

She's intrigued. I'm right. She's thought about it. I've hit the nail on the head. Naturally she wants to hear more. Like, who *am* I? The teacher. But what is the teacher really like? Here's a story about the teacher: The teacher cut off all her long hair into a short burr, a style called "the pixie" back in those days when she turned thirteen years old because, although this wasn't in her mind then, the teacher's sister had long dark glamorous wavy hair. I shared a room with my sister. Her hair spread about her on the pillow, rippled over the covers. I pulled my own covers up around me, showing the chopped top of my head, making a lump out of my body. Nobody could tell if I was a boy or a girl. If a rapist came into the room I shared with my sister, right away he'd be attracted to her, never to me. I could disguise myself as a crunch of covers, a pillow, a disarray of comforters, not even a person, I thought then. But I was too large. My sister ground her teeth down at night in her sleep and made tension noises: *uhh, uhhhh, uhh*. Unattractive. But not too often, not every night. I thought my chances against an intruder were good if I cut my hair. Yet this is just what I didn't want to tell Tasha. Too personal. A teacher must measure out what to show a student about her own life. One must be personal, but also self-protective. I'm more revealing, more personal than most teachers, too personal, sometimes, because I'm dying to get through to them, I want the students to care about my subject matter, intensely. In front of the classroom, everybody's looking at you. Or they should be looking. You're too exposed. I'm careful about it. As we stand in line together in the cafeteria, holding our styrofoam cups, I say, "Yes, Tasha. I know. I once cut off my hair too when I broke up with one of my boyfriends." But that's not the time I'm thinking of, as it happens.

Usually, when a class is difficult, especially graduate students, I rise to meet them. One challenger, one real challenger swinging his gold necklaces like Paul, can wind up a whole class. What makes you think you know more than I do? they're wondering. Okay. Disagree! Everyone gets a kick out of it. Especially when they're adults. It works well. Competing for insights, inciting each other, playfully, trying to hold on. They have a chance of besting me. Not a good one. But if at first it only seems about as rewarding as a dry fuck, more frustration than pleasure and too much worry about what everyone else is thinking about you, soon the urgency, the curiosity, takes over, and the questions build. I oversimplify. Of course, the answers are temporary.

From the front of the classroom, one can only speculate about one's students. Who are they? Two very smart photographers are lesbian lovers; I see them walking together on campus, hips bumping, or lounging under a tree. They share a studio together and write "uterine" poetry. I'm making this up, all except the poetry description. I heard it after class. Another student, Betty Ann Manitou, gathering her notes, heard it too and she giggled, peeking up at me through the bars of her fingers. But I neither have, nor want, any way of knowing them better.

The problem comes after Paul's complaint about me to the Administration. I don't know why he's complaining about me. But word slips to me from a junior faculty member at a planning committee. Is it my teaching? Does he mistake enthusiasm for weakness, my involvement for slipshod lecturing? But the class gets wind of it and it excites them. It excites me too, but with a kind of fear. I haven't done anything. I'm innocent. Besides, I have tenure, the Administration can't get rid of me. (Although I've had to sue to get it, sex-discrimination charges.) Now for them to hurt me I'd really have to act bad, to commit "moral turpitude," I believe the term is. But I confess: I don't like to be noticed this way. I'm already called a troublemaker. When I take Paul aside, tugging him surreptitiously from the doorway, the mere act of laying my hand on him seems challenging, an assertion of dominance on my part. "What are you really asking me?" he shrugs. Whatever has passed between Paul and the Dean—a new Dean, a woman my own age, incidentally—remains a secret from me.

The news spreads like flames. The students are like stalled horses, snorting nervously, jostling each other once they hear. And the class becomes uncontrollable. And too sudden. At any minute any statement can become volatile, more than its surfaces. "I don't agree with you." "I don't agree with you either." "D. H. Lawrence is a Nazi!" "So's your mother!" Hands wave in disagreement. I laugh it off. Betty Ann Manitou smiles shyly—or is it slyly?—over bitten fingernails. From the front of the room, standing while everyone else sits, it's hard to tell. But Tasha is the most excited. Or the most disappointed in me. She asks for my phone number to get together for lunch. "As friends, not as teacher and student." But I make excuses to her. Too busy. "Too busy for friendship?" She's scandalized. What is life all about, anyway? She takes Paul aside in the hallway, but I'm listening to her. "Did you really report her? But why? What did she do that you could officially complain about?" Out of loyalty, I imagine she's defending me. I can't hear the answer. Only a single word: "Responsibility." Certainly I've prepared hard for this class—and partially in fear of Paul's judgments. Perhaps harder than for any other. Doesn't he realize what I'm trying to give? How much he's gotten from me? And doesn't Tasha? But Tasha's words, her voice, clear, slender and so penetrating that it's almost childish, carries on the dark air down the long hall where I'm bent over pretending to drink at the water fountain. "I don't think it's fair to blame one person for everything. Sure, I had a hard time last year," she's explaining. "But I didn't take it personally. It never occurred to me until this moment that she could be creating problems in my own life."

Paul grumbles an answer, shutting his eyes authoritatively, as if bored. Again I strain to hear while pretending to look elsewhere. But I could tell nothing. His face is clear, decorous, his brow unfurrowed.

There's no reason for me to be troubled. I lie awake at night, looking up at my cracked ceiling, reminding myself that I did nothing wrong. The opposite. I tried too hard. ("Don't like him more than he likes you," my mother warned me when I started dating. *Never too much zeal,* Samuel Butler advises. The same counsel. It applies everywhere.) I feel sorry for poor Tasha, but outraged also. Didn't she recommend my course to everyone? Why did she sign up for two semesters with me if she didn't like it, if she changes her mind so easily? Besides, students love to talk about teachers, to feel oppressed by them. Human nature. Uncontrollable. I picture groups of students in the Dean's office, huddled in deep chairs, dark leather on the far side of a glossy desk, seated too low to be quite comfortable. "That's your opinion," freshmen are always answering. But what's provable? "At least I put up a good fight," I've heard them assuring each other. There's no reason to be frightened, to prepare my defenses early, a series of myclonic jerks, while I'm supposed to be sleeping.

There are only three of us in the back of the cafeteria on the last day before finals. Me, Tasha, and Paul, all drinking coffee and sitting in the faculty section, in deep armchairs, and they're here because I invited them. They've responded to my overtures. I'm wondering, is it my imagination? Is the trouble in that class some tiny thing I've exaggerated? Paul glances at Tasha questioningly. As if: *Should* we join her? It occurs to me then that he's shy, he's not aware of his good looks and his real intellectual authority, he still feels vulnerable. He needs his self-confidence built up, I've been taking him at face value. Why else would he be surprised that I'm asking him, thinking, *Is it all right? Is it all right?*

I smile gently, trying to confer warmth. Tasha and Paul carried their tall cups clumsily, almost furtively, past a fourth person I didn't notice at first, near the wall, a research assistant to the Dean whom I barely know socially. I hope she doesn't mind that I've brought students back here; I ask her, tentatively. Not at all. When I go to get free refills of coffee, a faculty privilege, Paul volunteers to go with me. But he doesn't speak about anything serious except books until we're alone on line, a steel tray rail on one side and a guard rail on the other, up against the cash register where the cashier, a mean redhead who always miscounts your change, has disappeared to another part of the cafeteria where she's wiping down a steam table.

He turns abruptly. "Don't take it to heart. I enjoy the class. It makes me think, and it's a kind of discipline that's very good for me. But I don't like being bossed and being told what I'm supposed to think, or what an author intended or what I ought to be experiencing. This is my way of remedying that, of taking charge and responsibility for my actions." At no point does he say that I'm a good teacher, that he recognizes how hard I'm trying, only that he's stimulated himself. But I hear beneath the arrogance, an apology, a plea that passes as an explanation, too humbling to be spoken publicly, and I'm moved by it enough to reach out and touch the golden hair on his bare forearm lightly, an arm of muscular complexity, roped by veins, not pressing him further, an understanding. He knows I understand him, which is the problem exactly, which is why he's undertaken to challenge me. The fact that he's in love with me—if love is what you can call this desperate dissembling and these disguises—has caused him to report me. More than fear, it's a purification ritual. Necessary beyond both our desiring. He strokes my throat, narrow bones, curved hollows, and my breastbone, stopping short at the closed button. There's no one else in line, no one waiting in this cul-de-sac in the cafeteria, but anyone could come in and see us. We stare at each other deeply. I'm swooning, clutching at the guard rail secretly, but we stand no closer in acknowledgment. We know each other well enough to be parts of each other, we both understand, but words for expressing it, for speaking and justifying these feelings, aren't available. I don't know what to say to him. I don't want to limit him, I must make sure to give him enough space. To be disrespectful, to disrupt the fragility of his selfhood, that would be devastating. Finally, I can think only of these words: "I wish you wouldn't," and I sway backward, fumble for loose change, and go away from him because I need to sit down.

He follows me, but he avoids my eyes, balancing his coffee on the plush arm of the stuffed chair. Tasha leans back in her chair with her legs stretched straight, unyielding, in front of her, but slumped, almost to convey that she's too comfortable, looking stuck and surrounded by her chair, as if it has been rising up on her. She rolls her eyes at Paul.

"Did you tell her?"

"Not yet."

"I haven't said anything to her either."

"What?" I grip my cup too tightly and my nail sinks into it so that it springs a leak. Muddy liquid drips onto me. "Tell me what?"

They squint sympathetically at each other. Paul's lips furl forward confidentially. "Even Tasha doesn't know the full extent. We're concerned about the discomfort in the classroom."

I glance over at the woman I don't know, the Dean's research assistant, embarrassed because I regard this as family business, private, an ongoing relationship, too personal for an outsider to know about. But she pretends not to be listening. Or maybe she isn't, genuinely. A book of poems, bound in red, rests on her knee.

"What discomfort? I'm certainly not uncomfortable," I lie for her benefit.

"I'm not either, but everyone else is," Paul says, apparently truthfully, and concerned.

Tasha takes a deep breath. She's arrogated unto herself a new role: Courageous Truth-Teller. She claims I trained her that way. "Well, I am. I'm really not happy or comfortable. Something's wrong. And this has happened to me for two semesters now, both times when I took a course with you, but I've never been able to get hold of it." She turns to Paul for approval, rising now with her unmanicured hands on her slim hips, light reflecting in her bulgy sincere eyes and shimmering, irridescing on the burr of her chopped hair. She makes a demand of him. "Did you really report her to the Administration? If you did, I think I might too."

This stuns me. But instead of saying so, of blocking Tasha, I throw a peek at the woman near the wall who politely ignores us, then sees me glowering, looks up alarmed, and turns a page, then another page of her poetry.

"I think the more individual reports that are made, the more weight the words carry, usually. But I'd like to know what you said. You see, I didn't realize that the class was having such a profound influence on me. When I had a class with her last semester I thought that I was enjoying it, the constant pounding at myself, the back-and-forth, the constant questioning and shaking up ideas I thought I was sure about already. When my life went wrong, naturally I thought it was my fault. So many things I believed turned out to be different from what they appeared to be. But the truth is, I'm terribly paranoid sometimes, and your idea never occurred to me. I tend toward omnipotence, I tend to take too much responsibility, and frankly I've been having problems all my life. Because I know myself well, because I'm trying to know myself better, I overcompensate. I take too much blame. I'm careful not to blame anyone unfairly. Particularly when I like them personally. But if you reported the class to the Administration it might be my duty to do so also. For the record, not for anything specific. But I really wish you could convince me so that I don't feel guilty about it."

"I wish you wouldn't," I murmur. It seems unfair to push this neurotic, easily influenced girl any further. My role is to reveal, not interfere. To help her come to her own decisions. But how honestly and how very much I mean the few words I say to her. How can this help you? I want to say. Tasha, Tasha. Why did you sign up for my course a second time? Bringing Paul and the other photography students with you, your responsibility, your fault, actually. But I can't defend myself in front of the research assistant. If Tasha has changed her mind, that's her right, my encouragement. I take defection in stride. At least I want it to appear that way, what can you do about human nature?

But Paul refuses to accept Tasha. He springs from the deep chair furiously. "You can't report her! She did nothing to you, you can't report her just because somebody else did! Look, you're making a big mistake. This is the way I do things. Look, I don't let anyone, no matter how much I respect them, have authority over me. I go to a higher authority. That's my way, my reasoning." Obviously, he's possessive about it. "My right. But you're sick. You are paranoid, like you said, and you're trying to push off the responsibility for your whole life onto another person. Trust your instincts like I do, but question your reasons for trusting them. Your reasons have nothing to do with my reasons!"

The woman reading poetry looks up from where the book balances on her knee, startled, and stares. So do I. But I, like Paul and like Tasha, am also on my feet now. Paul's defense of me is too strong. He doesn't need to defend me so strenuously against unhappy, sexless Tasha. Then I collapse damply with the realization that he is defending me, that he is attacking the poor girl who has revealed herself to him in defense of me. No, don't do it! I want to yell at him. But there is more, there are many more accusations spewing, too many of them. And my weepy sexuality convulses, below any surfaces that would be visible to anybody, thank goodness, deep inside me, unconscionable, and I fall backward into the faculty armchair, listening, watching, spread-legged. But not before Tasha, unable to defend herself against Paul's vigor and eloquence, starts wailing loudly, at first trying not to cry, then surrendering, hurling herself the length of her stringy arms and body at Paul's knees in a flying wrestling tackle—a leap of faith, I think afterward, wryly—trying to attack him directly and pull him down instead of crying, but falling at his expensively shod soft leather feet, she falls short instead, with her hands clasping him by the ankles, as if she is grateful to him.

He gazes down at her, interested. "Very gutsy of you," he says, admiringly. But he's not going to stop telling her what he thinks of her, how wrong she is to try to catch up to him. "They're nothing alike, your reasons and my reasons. The two have no similarities to speak of. Yours aren't even legitimate or thought through." By this time he's repeating himself, however, his voice grows louder, then louder still and he's making it impossible for anybody to continue reading poetry. The research assistant sets her shoulders straight and leaves, huffily.

"Stop it, Paul," I say to him. Only once. I can't help him and I'm afraid of sounding beggarish. I shouldn't commit myself by talking to him commandingly out loud, though. He wouldn't want anyone to know that I have that power over him. He denies my power. He calls it a killing power, and I'm afraid that's because it might make him kill me in order to deny it. Nor do I want anyone else to know I have that power over him. But what about Tasha, lying there on the floor? So I give him signals, what he ought to be doing, in sign language.

"You are paranoid and you are weak! Don't go blaming it on anyone besides yourself," he's saying to Tasha.

CUT! CUT! CUT! CUT! I'm giving him signals from show business, as if he's on the air. I slash my index finger across my throat to show him that he ought to stop it.

He doesn't stop though, despite my frantic, monotonous, unending signals to do so. He continues to degrade Tasha, who sprawls, limp, powerless, and despairing, flat on her back now, staring wide-eyed at the ceiling, covered by square white sound-absorbent tiles.

But why doesn't he stop it? I catch his eye. A brief headshake. He laughs at my intensity. But at the same time, his eyetooth flashes ambivalently and he seems to grow uneasy. When I look down at myself, at the front of my blouse which he hasn't even dared to unbutton, I realize why. Little drops of blood are splashing on me. My slashing—the long nail on my index finger, my silent signaling—has grown too sharp, too frenzied. I've been sawing at my own throat, a narrow scratch actually, but I have an irrational fear of gurgling blood when I try to speak about it, and I find it humiliating, as embarrassing as when I was in junior high school science class and started menstruating unexpectedly, my first time, blood leaking uncontrollably into the desk seat and onto the floor, until the teacher sent someone to the art supply room for a huge fold of newsprint to wrap around me.

I rush off to the bathroom to clean up, and worry about how serious it is, have I wounded myself badly? From inside the closed stalls for the toilets, someone flushes. I run water hard to drown out the snuffling noises I'm making. Outside, though the enormous open windows, pigeons are nesting in cornices or strutting on the sill, little eyes glittering rustily, watching from one side of their tiny tilted heads, then the other, incurious. No depth, no dimension, no convergence of points of view with these birds. Their vision is strictly monocular, reality all the way. They're fascinated by movement, and that's all these shimmering gray birds can see of me. A student washes her hands and leaves, oblivious to the pink water. Outside the window, the day is warm. Summer is starting. Finals tomorrow. If only I can clean up, it will soon be over. What then? Will Paul and I run away together, or will his hard pride get the better of us?

What We're Rollin Around in Bed With:
Sexual Silences in Feminism
Amber Hollibaugh and Cherríe Moraga

The Critique

Ironically, the whole notion of "the personal is political," which surfaced in the early part of the women's liberation movement (and which many of us have used to an extreme), is suddenly dismissed when we begin to discuss sexuality. We have become a relatively sophisticated movement, so many women think they now have to have the theory before they expose the experience. It seems we simply did not take our feminism to heart enough. This most privatized aspect of ourselves, our sex lives, has dead-ended into silence within the feminist movement.

For a brief moment in its early stages, the feminist movement did address women's sexual pleasure, but this discussion was quickly swamped by recognition of how much pain women had suffered around sex in relation to men (e.g., marriage, the nuclear family, wife-battering, rape, etc.). In these early discussions, lesbianism was ignored and heterosexuality was not understood as both an actual sexual interaction *and* a system. No matter how we play ourselves out sexually, we are all affected by the system inasmuch as our sexual values are filtered through a society where heterosexuality is considered the norm. It is difficult to believe that there is anyone in the world who hasn't spent some time in great pain over the choices and limitations that characterize the system.

By analyzing the institution of heterosexuality, feminists learned what's oppressive about it and why people cooperate with it or don't, but we didn't learn what is *sexual*. We don't really know, for instance, why men and women are still attracted to each other, even through all that oppression. There is something genuine that happens between heterosexuals, but gets perverted in a thousand different ways. There *is* heterosexuality outside of heterosexism.

What grew out of this kind of "nonsexual" theory was a "transcendent" definition of sexuality where lesbianism (since it exists outside the institution of heterosexuality) came to be seen as the practice of feminism. It set up a "perfect" vision of egalitarian sexuality, where we could magically leap over our heterosexist conditioning into mutually orgasmic, struggle-free, trouble-free sex. We feel this vision has become both misleading and damaging to many feminists, and in particular to lesbians. Who created this sexual model as a goal in the first place? Who can really live up to such an ideal? There is little language, little literature that reflects the actual sexual struggles of most lesbians, feminist or not.

The failure of feminism to answer all the questions about women, in particular about women's sexuality, is the same failure the homosexual movement suffers from around gender. It's a confusing of those two things—that some of us are both female and homosexual—that may be the source of some of the tension between the two movements and of the inadequacies of each. When we walk down the street, we are both female and lesbian. We are working-class white and working-class Chicana. We are all these things rolled into one and there is no way to eliminate even one aspect of ourselves.

The Conversation

CM: *In trying to develop sexual theory, I think we should start by talking about what we're rollin around in bed with. We both agree that the way feminism has dealt with sexuality has been entirely inadequate.*

AH: Right. Sexual theory has traditionally been used to say *people have been forced to be this thing; people could be that thing.* And you're left standing in the middle going, "Well, I am here; and I don't know how to get there." It hasn't been able to talk realistically about what people *are* sexually.

I think by focusing on roles in lesbian relationships, we can begin to unravel who we really are in bed. Hiding how profoundly roles shape your sexuality can be seen as an example of how other things about sex get hidden. There's a lot of different things that shape the way that people respond—some not so easy to see, some more forbidden, as I perceive sadomasochism to be. Like with sadomasochism—when I think of it I'm frightened. Why? Is it because I might be sexually fascinated with it and I don't know how to accept that? Who am I there? The point is that when you deny that roles, sadomasochism, fantasy, or any sexual differences exist in the first place, you can only come up with neutered sexuality, where everybody's got to be basically the same because anything different puts the element of power and deviation in there and threatens the whole picture.

CM: *Exactly. Remember how I told you that growing up what*

turned me on sexually, at a very early age, had to do with the fantasy of capture, taking a woman, and my identification was with the man, taking? Well, something like that would be so frightening to bring up in a feminist context—fearing people would put it in some sicko sexual box. And yet, the truth is, I do have some real gut-level misgivings about my sexual connection with capture. It might feel very sexy to imagine "taking" a woman, but it has sometimes occurred at the expense of my feeling, sexually, like I can surrender myself to a woman; that is, always needing to be the one in control, calling the shots. It's a very butch trip and I feel like this can keep me private and protected and can prevent me from fully being able to express myself.

AH: But it's not wrong, in and of itself, to have a capture fantasy. the real question is: Does it *actually* limit you? For instance, does it allow you to eroticize someone else, but never see yourself as erotic? Does it keep you always in control? Does the fantasy force you into a dimension of sexuality that feels very narrow to you? If it causes you to look at your lover in only one light, then you may want to check it out. But if you can't even dream about wanting a woman in this way in the first place, then you can't figure out what is narrow and heterosexist in it and what's just play. After all, it's only *one* fantasy.

CM: *Well, what I think is very dangerous about keeping down such fantasies is that they are forced to stay unconscious. Then, next thing you know, in the actual sexual relationship, you become the capturer, that is, you try to have power over your lover, psychologically or whatever. If the desire for power is so hidden and unacknowledged, it will inevitably surface through manipulation or what-have-you. If you couldn't play capturer, you'd be it.*

AH: Part of the problem in talking about sexuality is *it's so enormous* in our culture that people don't have any genuine sense of dimension. So that when you say "capture," every fantasy you've ever heard of from Robin Hood to colonialism comes racing into your mind and all you really maybe wanted to do was have your girlfriend lay you down.

But in feminism, we can't even explore these questions because what they say is, in gender, there is a masculine oppressor and a female oppressee. So whether you might fantasize yourself in a role a man might perform or a woman in reaction to a man, this makes you sick, fucked-up, and you had better go and change it.

If you don't speak of fantasies, they become a kind of amorphous thing that envelops you and hangs over your relationship and you get terrified of the silence. If you have no way to describe what your desire is and what your fear is, you have no way to negotiate with your lover. And I guarantee you, six months or six years later, the relationship has paid. Things that are kept private and hidden become painful and deformed.

When you say that part of your sexuality has been hooked up with capture, I want to say that absolutely there's a heterosexist part of that, but what part of that is just plain dealing with power, sexually? I don't want to live outside of power in my sexuality, but I don't want to be trapped into a heterosexist concept of power either. But what I feel feminism asks of me is to throw the baby out with the bathwater.

For example, *I think the reason butch/femme stuff got hidden within lesbian-feminism is because people are profoundly afraid of questions of power in bed*. And though everybody doesn't play out power the way I do, the question of power affects who and how you eroticize you sexual need. And it is absolutely at the bottom of all sexual inquiry. Given the present state of the movement, it's impossible to say I'm a femme and I like it—no apologies—without facing the probability of a heavy fight.

CM: *But what is femme to you? I told you once that what I thought of as femme was passive, unassertive, and so forth, and you didn't fit that image. And you said to me, "Well, change your definition of femme."*

AH: My fantasy life is deeply involved in a butch/femme exchange. I never come together with a woman, sexually, outside of those roles. It's saying to my partner, "Love me enough to let me go where I need to go and take me there. Don't make me think it through. Give me a way to be so in my body that I don't have to think; that you can fantasize for the both of us. You map it out. You are in control."

It's hard to talk about things like giving up power without it sounding passive. I am willing to give myself over to a woman equal to her amount of wanting. I expose myself for her to see what's possible for her to love in me that's female. I want her to respond to it. I may not be doing something active with my body, but more eroticizing her need that I feel in her hands as she touches me.

In the same way, as a butch, you want and conceive of a woman in a certain way. You dress a certain way to attract her and you put your sexual need within these certain boundaries to communicate that desire. . . . And yet, there's a part of me that feels maybe all this is not even a question of roles. Maybe it's much richer territory than that.

CM: *Yes, I feel the way I want a woman can be a very profound experience. Remember I told you how when I looked up at my lover's face when I was making love to her (I was actually just kissing her breast at the moment), but when I looked up at her face, I could feel and see how deeply every part of her was present? That every pore in her body was entrusting me to handle her, to take care of her sexual desire. This look on her face is like nothing else. It fills me up. She entrusts me to determine where she'll go sexually. And I honestly feel a power inside me strong enough to heal the deepest wound.*

AH: Well, I can't actually see what I look like, but I can feel it in my lover's hands when I look the way you described. When I open myself up more and more to her sensation of wanting a woman, when I eroticize that in her, I feel a kind of ache in my body, but it's not an ache to *do* something. I can feel a hurt spot and a need and it's there and it's just the tip of it, the tip of that desire and that is what first gets played with, made erotic. It's light and playful. It doesn't commit you to exposing a deeper part of yourself sexually. Then I begin to pick up passion. And the passion isn't butch or femme. It's just passion.

But from this place, if it's working, I begin to imagine myself being the *woman that a woman always wanted*. That's what I begin to eroticize. That's what I begin to feel from my lover's hands. I begin to fantasize myself becoming more and more female in order to comprehend and meet what I feel happening in her body. I don't want her not to be female to me. Her need is female, but it's butch because I am asking her to expose her desire through the movement of her hands on my body and I'll respond. I want to give up power in response to her need. This can feel profoundly powerful and very unpassive.

A lot of times how I feel it in my body is I feel like I have this fantasy of pulling a woman's hips into my cunt. I can feel the need painfully in another woman's body. I can feel the impact and I begin to play and respond to that hunger and desire. And I begin to eroticize the fantasy that *she can't get enuf of me*. It makes me want to enflame my body. What it feels like is that I'm in my own veins and I'm sending heat up into my thighs. It's very hot.

CM: *Oh honey, she feels the heat,* too.

AH: Yes, and I am making every part of my body accessible to that woman. I completely trust her. There's no place she cannot touch me. My body is literally open to any way she interprets her sexual need. My power is that I know how to read her inside of her own passion. I can hear her. It's like a sexual language; it's a rhythmic language that she uses her hands for. My body is completely in sync with a lover, but I'm not deciding where she's gonna touch me.

CM: *But don't you ever fantasize yourself being on the opposite end of that experience?*

AH: Well, not exactly in the same way, because with butches you can't insist on them giving up their sexual identity. You have to go through that identity to that other place. But you don't have to throw out the role to explore the sexuality. There are femme ways to orchestrate sexuality. I'm not asking a woman not to be a butch. I am asking her to let me express the other part of my own character, where I am actively orchestrating what's happening. I never give up my right to say that I can insist on what happens sexually. . . . quite often what will happen is I'll simply seduce her. Now, that's very active. The seduction can be very profound, but it's a seduction as a femme.

CM: *What comes to my mind is something as simple as you comin over and sittin on her lap. Where a butch, well, she might just go for your throat if she wants you.*

AH: Oh yes, different areas for different roles! What's essential is that your attitude doesn't threaten the other person's sexual identity, but plays with it. That's what good seduction is all about. I play a lot in that. It's not that I have to have spike heels on in order to fantasize who I am. Now that's just a lot of classist shit, conceiving of a femme in such a narrow way.

CM: *Well, I would venture to say that some of these dynamics that you're describing happen between most lesbians, only they may both be in the same drag of flannel shirts and jeans. My feeling, however, is—and this is very hard for me—what I described earlier about seeing my lover's face entrusting me like she did, well, I want her to take me to that place, too.*

AH: Yes, but you don't want to have to deny your butchness to get there. Right?

CM: *Well, that's what's hard. To be butch, to me, is not to be a woman. The classic extreme-butch stereotype is the woman who sexually refuses another woman to touch her. It goes something like this: She doesn't want to feel her femaleness because she thinks of you as the "real" woman and if she makes love to you, she doesn't have to feel her own body as the object of desire. She can be a kind of "bodiless lover." So when you turn over and want to make love to her and make her feel physically like a woman, then what she is up against is QUEER. You are a woman making love to her. She feels queerer than anything in that. Get it?*

AH: Got it. Whew!

CM: *I believe that probably from a very early age the way you conceived of yourself as female has been very different from me. We both have pain, but I think that there is a particular pain attached if you identified yourself as a butch queer from an early age as I did. I didn't really think of myself as female, or male. I thought of myself as this hybrid or somethin. I just kinda thought of myself as this free agent until I got tits. Then I thought, oh oh, some problem has occurred here. . . . For me, the way you conceive of yourself as a woman and the way I am attracted to women sexually reflect that butch/femme exchange—where a woman believes herself so woman that it really makes me want her.*

But for me, I feel a lot of pain around the fact that it has been difficult for me to conceive of myself as thoroughly female in that sexual way. So retaining my "butchness" is not exactly my desired goal. Now that, in itself, is probably all heterosexist bullshit—about what a woman is supposed to be in the first place—but we are talkin about the differences between the way you and I conceive of ourselves as sexual beings.

AH: I think it does make a difference. I would argue that a good femme does not play to the part of you that hates yourself for feelin like a man, but to the part of you that knows you're a woman. Because it's absolutely critical to understand that femmes are women to women and dykes to men in the straight world. *You and I are talkin girl to girl.* We're not talkin what I was in straight life.

I was ruthless with men, sexually, around what I felt. *It was only with women I couldn't avoid opening up my need to have something more than an orgasm.* With a woman, I can't refuse to know that the possibility is just there that she'll reach me some place very deeply each time we make love. That's part of my fear of being a lesbian. I can't refuse that possibility with a woman.

You see, I want you as a woman, not as a man; but, I want you in the way *you* need to be, which may not be traditionally female, but which is the area that you express as *butch*. Here is where in the other world you have suffered the most damage. Part of the reason I love to be with butches is because I feel I repair that damage. I make it right to want me that hard. Butches have not been allowed to feel their own desire because that part of butch can be perceived by the straight world as male. I feel that as a femme I get back my femaleness and give a different definition of femaleness to a butch. That's what I mean about one of those unexplored territories that goes beyond roles, but goes through roles to get there.

CM: *How I fantasize sex roles has been really different for me with different women. I do usually enter into an erotic encounter with a woman from the kind of butch place you described, but I have also felt very ripped off there, finding myself taking all the sexual responsibility. I am seriously attracted to butches sometimes. It's a different dynamic, where the sexuality may not seem as fluid or comprehensible, but I know there's a huge part of me that wants to be handled in the way I described I can handle another woman.. I am very compelled toward that "lover" posture. I have never totally reckoned with being the "beloved" and, frankly, I don't know if it takes a butch or a femme or what to get me there. I know that it's a struggle within me and it scares the shit out of me to look at it so directly. I've done this kind of searching emotionally, but to combine sex with it seems like very dangerous stuff.*

AH: Well, I think everybody has aspects of roles in their relationships, but I feel pretty out there on the extreme end. . . . I think what feminism did, in its fear of heterosexual control of fantasy, was to say that there was almost no fantasy safe to have, where you weren't going to have to give up power or take it. There's no sexual fantasy I can think of that doesn't include some aspect of that. But I feel like I have been forced to give up some of my richest potential sexually in the way feminism has defined what is, and what's not, "politically correct" in the sexual sphere.

CM: *Oh, of course when most feminists talk about sexuality, including lesbianism, they're not talkin about Desire. It is significant to me that I came out only when I met a good feminist, although I knew I was queer since eight or nine. That's only when I'd risk it because I wouldn't have to say it's because I want her. I didn't have to say that when she travels by me, my whole body starts throbbing.*

AH: Yes, it's just *correct*.

CM: *It was okay to be with her because we all knew men were really fuckers and there were a lot of "okay" women acknowledging that. Read: white and educated. . . . But that's not why I "came out." How could I say that I wanted women so bad I was gonna die if I didn't get me one, soon! You know, I just felt the pull in the hips, right?*

AH: Yes, really— . . . well, the first discussion I ever heard of lesbianism among feminists was: "We've been sex objects to men and where did it get us? And here when we're just learning how to be friends with other women, you got to go and sexualize it." That's what they said! "Fuck you. Now I have to worry about you looking down my blouse." That's exactly what they meant. It horrified me. "No no no," I wanted to say, "that's not me. I promise I'll only look at the sky. *Please* let me come to a meeting. I'm really okay. I just go to the bars and fuck like a rabbit with women who want me. You know?"

Now from the onset, how come feminism was so invested in that? They would not examine sexual need with each other except as oppressor/oppressee. Whatever your experience was you were always the victim. So how do dykes fit into that? Dykes who wanted tits, you know?

Now a lot of women have been sexually terrorized and this makes sense, their needing not to have to deal with explicit sexuality, but they made men out of every sexual dyke. "Oh my god, *she* wants me, too!"

So it became this really repressive movement, where you didn't talk dirty and you didn't want dirty. It really became a bore. So after meetings, we *ran* to the bars. You couldn't talk about wanting a woman, except very loftily. You couldn't say it hurt at night wanting a woman to touch you. . . . I remember at one meeting breaking down after everybody was talking about being a lesbian very delicately. I began crying. I remember saying, "I can't help it. I just . . . want her. I want to feel her." And everybody forgiving me. It was this atmosphere of me exorcising this *crude* sexual need for women.

CM: *Shit, Amber . . . I remember being fourteen years old and there was this girl, a few years older than me, who I had this crush on. And on the last day of school, I knew I wasn't going to see her for months! We had hugged good-bye and I went straight home. Going into my bedroom, I got into my unmade bed and I remember getting the sheets, winding them into a kind of rope, and pulling them up between my legs and just holding them there under my chin. I just sobbed and sobbed because I knew I couldn't have her, maybe never have a woman to touch. It's just pure need and it's whole. It's like using sexuality to describe how deeply you need/want intimacy, passion, love.*

Most women are not immune from experiencing pain in relation to their sexuality, but certainly lesbians experience a particular pain and oppression. Let us not forget, although feminism would sometimes like us to, that lesbians are oppressed in this world. Possibly, there are some of us who came out through the movement who feel immune to "queer attack," but not the majority of us (no matter when we came out), particularly if you have no economic buffer in this society. If you have enough money and privilege, you can separate yourself from heterosexist oppression. You can be sapphic *or somethin, but you don't have to be* queer.

The point I am trying to make is that I believe most of us harbor plenty of demons and old hurts inside ourselves around sexuality. I know, for me, that each time I choose to touch another woman, to make love with her, I feel I risk opening up that secret, harbored, vulnerable place . . . I think why feminism has been particularly attractive to many "queer" lesbians is that it kept us in a place where we wouldn't have to look at our pain around sexuality anymore. Our sisters would just sweep us up into a movement. . . .

AH: Yes, it's not just because of feminism we were silent. Our own participation in that silence has stemmed from our absolute terror of facing that profound sexual need. Period.

There is no doubt in my mind that the feminist movement has radically changed, in an important way, everybody's concept of lesbianism, straight or gay. There's not a dyke in the world today (in or out of the bars) who can have the same conversation that she could have had ten years ago. It seeps through the water system or somethin, you know? Still, while lesbianism is certainly accepted in feminism, it's more as a political or intellectual concept. It seems feminism is the last rock of conservatism. It will not be sexualized. It's *prudish* in that way. . . .

Well, I won't give my sexuality up and I won't *not* be a feminist. So I'll build a different movement, but I won't live without either one.

Sometimes, I don't know how to handle how angry I feel about feminism. We may disagree on this. We have been treated in some similar ways, but our relationship to feminism has been different. Mine is a lot longer. I really have taken a lot more shit than you have, specifically around being femme. I have a personal fury. The more I got in touch with how I felt about women, what made me desire and desirable, the more I felt outside the feminist community and that was just terrifying because, on the one hand, it had given me so much. I loved it. And then, I couldn't be who I was. I felt that about class, too. I could describe my feelings about being a woman, but if I described it from my own class, using that language, my experience wasn't valid. I don't know what to do with my anger, particularly around sexuality.

CM: *Well, you've gotta be angry. . . . I mean what you were gonna do is turn off the tape, so we'd have no record of your being mad. What comes out of anger . . . if you, one woman, can say* I have been a sister all these years and you have not helped me *. . . that speaks more to the failure of all that theory and rhetoric than more theory and rhetoric.*

AH: Yeah. . . . Remember that night you and me and M. was at the bar and we were talkin about roles? She told you later that the reason she had checked out of the conversation was because she knew how much it was hurting me to talk about it. You know, I can't tell you what it meant to me for her to know that. The desperation we all felt at that table talking about sexuality was so great, wanting people to understand why we are the way we are.

CM: *I know. . . . I remember how at that forum on sadomasochism that happened last spring, how that Samois* [a lesbian-feminist S/M group in the San Francisco Bay Area] *woman came to the front of the room and spoke very plainly and clearly about feeling that through sadomasochism she was really coping with power struggles in a tangible way with her lover. That this time, for once, she wasn't leaving the relationship. I can't write her off. I believed her. I believed she was a woman in struggle. And as feminists, Amber, you and I are interested in struggle.*

The Challenge

We would like to suggest that, for dealing with sexual issues both personally and politically, women go back to consciousness-raising (CR) groups. We believe that women must create sexual theory in the same way we created feminist theory. We simply need to get together in places where people agree to suspend their sexual values, so that all of us can feel free to say what we do sexually or want to do or have done to us. We do have fear of using feelings as theory. We do not mean to imply that feelings are everything. But they are the place to start if we want to build a broad-based, cross-cultural movement that recognizes the political implications of sexual differences.

We believe our racial and class backgrounds have a huge effect in determining how we perceive ourselves sexually. Since we are not a movement that is working-class-dominated or a movement that is Third World, we both hold serious reservations as to how this new CR will be conceived. In our involvement in a movement largely controlled by white middle-class women, we feel that the values of their cultures (which may be more closely tied to an American-assimilated puritanism) have been pushed down our throats. The questions arise then: *Whose* feelings and *whose* values will be considered normative in these CR groups? If there is no room for criticism in sexual discussion around race and class issues, we foresee ourselves being gut-checked from the beginning.

We also believe our class and racial backgrounds have a huge effect in determining how we involve ourselves politically. For instance, why is it that it is largely white middle-class women who form the visible leadership in the anti-porn movement? This is particularly true in the Bay Area, where the focus is less on actual violence against women and more on sexist ideology and imagery in the media. Why are women of color not particularly visible in this sex-related single-issue movement? It's certainly not because we are not victims of pornography.

More working-class and Third World women can be seen actively engaged in sex-related issues that *directly* affect the life-and-death concerns of women (abortion, sterilization abuse, health care, welfare, etc.). It's not like we choose this kind of activism because it's an "ideologically correct" position, but because we are the ones pregnant at sixteen (straight *and* lesbian), whose daughters get pregnant at sixteen, who get left by men without child care, who are self-supporting lesbian mothers with no child care, and who sign forms to have our tubes tied because we can't read English. But these kinds of distinctions between classes and colors of women are seldom absorbed by the feminist movement as it stands to date.

Essentially, we are challenging other women and ourselves to look where we haven't, to arrive at a synthesis of sexual thought that originates and develops from our varied cultural backgrounds and experiences. We refuse to be debilitated one more time around sexuality, race, or class.

In the Morning
Jayne Cortez

Disguised in my mouth as a swampland
nailed to my teeth like a rising sun
you come out in the middle of fish-scales
you bleed into gourds wrapped with red ants
you syncopate the air with lungs like screams from yazoo
like X rated tongues
and nickel plated fingers of a raw ghost man
you touch brown nipples into knives
and somewhere stripped like a whirlwind
stripped for the shrine room
you sing to me through the side face of a black rooster

In the morning in the morning in the morning
all over my door like a rooster
in the morning in the morning in the morning

And studded in my kidneys like perforated hiccups
inflamed in my ribs like three hoops of thunder through a screw
a star-bent-bolt of quivering colons
you breathe into veiled rays and scented ice holes
you fire the space like a flair of embalmed pigeons
and palpitate with the worms and venom and wailing flanks
and somewhere inside this fever
inside my patinaed pubic and camouflaged slit
stooped forward on fangs
in rear of your face
you shake to me in the full crown of a black rooster

In the morning in the morning in the morning

Masquerading in my horn like a river
eclipsed to these infantries of dentures of diving spears
you enter broken mirrors through fragmented pipe spit
you pull into a shadow ring of magic jelly

415

you wear the sacrificial blood of nightfall
you lift the ceiling with my tropical slush dance
you slide and tremble with the reputation of an earthquake
and when i kick through walls
to shine like silver
when i shine like brass through crust in a compound
when i shine shine shine
you wail to me in the drum call of a black rooster

In the morning in the morning in the morning
gonna kill me a rooster
in the morning
early in the morning
way down in the morning
before the sun passes by
in the morning in the morning in the morning

In the morning
when the deep sea goes through a dogs bite
and you spit on top of your long knife

In the morning in the morning
when peroxide falls on a bed of broken glass
and the sun rises like a polyester ball of menses
in the morning
gonna firedance in the petro
in the morning
turn loose the blues in the funky jungle
in the morning
I said when you see the morning coming like
a two-headed twister
let it blow let it blow
in the morning in the morning
all swollen up like an ocean in the morning
early in the morning
before the cream dries in the bushes
in the morning
when you hear the rooster cry
cry rooster cry
in the morning in the morning in my evilness of this morning

I said
disguised in my mouth as a swampland
nailed to my teeth like a rising sun

you come out in the middle of fish-scales
you bleed into gourds wrapped with red ants
you syncopate the air with lungs like screams from yazoo
like X rated tongues
and nickel plated fingers of a raw ghost man
you touch brown nipples into knives
and somewhere stripped like a whirlwind
stripped for the shrine room
you sing to me through the side face of a black rooster

In the morning in the morning in the morning

Bestiary
Sharon Olds

Nostrils flared, ears pricked,
Gabriel asks me if people can mate with
animals. I say it hardly
ever happens. He frowns, fur and
skin and hooves and slits and pricks and
teeth and tails whirling in his brain.
You *could* do it, he says, not wanting the
world to be closed to him in any
form. We talk about elephants
and parakeets, until we are rolling on the
floor, laughing like hyenas. Too late,
I remember love—I backtrack
and try to slip it in, but that is
not what he means. Seven years old,
he is into hydraulics, pulleys, doors which
fly open in the side of the body,
entrances, exits. Flushed, panting,
hot for physics, he thinks about lynxes,
eagles, pythons, mosquitoes, girls,
casting a glittering eye of use
over creation, wanting to know
exactly how the world was made to receive him.

A Story of a Girl and Her Dog
Alix Kates Shulman

1

Lucky Larrabee was an only child, and unpredictable. At eight, she was still trying to sail down from the garage roof with an umbrella. She never ate ice cream without a pickle. She was afraid of nothing in the world except three boys in her class and her uncle Len who patted her funny. She brought home every stray dog in the neighborhood. She upset the assistant principal by participating in the Jewish Affair.

Naturally her parents worried; but they adored her nevertheless and all the more.

There is little Lucky, wearing red anklets with stripes down the sides and poorly tied brown oxfords while everyone else has on loafers, her hair hanging down in strings, her chin thrust out, absolutely refusing to sing the words Jesus or Christ. Why? Two Jewish girls in her class will not sing, and though she has never been Jewish before, Lucky has joined them. She says it is a free country and you can be anything you like. I'm a Jew, she says and will not sing Jesus.

Everyone knows she's no more Jewish than their teacher. It is ridiculous! But she insists and what can they do? She is ruining the Christmas Pageant. They'll get her at recess, they'll get her after school, they'll plant bad pictures in her desk, they'll think of something. But it won't work. Incorrigible little fanatic!

Okay. She doesn't have to sing. But will she just mouth the words silently during the program please? No one will have to know.

No, she won't. If they try to make her, she swears she'll hold her breath until she faints instead. Perhaps she'll do it anyway! Perhaps she'll hold it till she's dead! That'll show them who's a Jew and who isn't.

Is something wrong at home, Mrs. Larrabee? Does Lucky eat a good enough breakfast? Get enough sleep? She is very thin. Has she grown thinner? Not meaning to alarm you, but Lucky has been unusually

419

sullen in class lately—doesn't participate in the class discussions as she used to, doesn't volunteer her answers, no longer seems interested in current events, spends too much time daydreaming, picking at scabs, being negative. She doesn't seem to be trying. Her fingernails. Is there any known source of tension at home? The school likes to be kept informed about these matters as we try to keep parents informed about progress at school. Don't you agree, parents and teachers ought to be working closely together in harmony, for the benefit of the child. The only concrete suggestion the school can make at this time is some companionship and diversion for Lucky. Another child perhaps, or a dog. Meanwhile, we'll just keep an eye on her. Thank you so much for coming in. These conferences are always helpful in any case, even if they do no more than clear the air.

As the Larrabees had been half considering buying a dog for Christmas anyway, they decided it would do no harm to seem accommodating and took the step. They waited until a month had elapsed after the Christmas Pageant so Lucky would not suspect a connection, and then, piling into the new family Nash, backing out of the cinder drive, they drove straight out Main Street beyond the city limits and continued on into the country to buy a dog.

2

Naturally, Lucky was permitted by the concerned Larrabees to pick out the pup herself, with only one restriction. It had to be a boy dog, they said, because if they took home a girl dog, sooner or later they would have to have her spayed, which would be cruel and unnatural and would make her into a fat, lazy, unhappy bitch, or they'd have to let her have babies. For keeping her locked up during heat (also cruel and unnatural) couldn't be expected to work forever; creatures have a way of eluding their jailors in quest of forbidden knowledge—witness the fate of Sleeping Beauty, Bluebeard's wives, etc., and the unwanted litters of the neighborhood bitches. And if they let her go ahead and have her babies, well, either they'd have to keep the puppies (a certain portion of which could be expected to be females too), generating an unmanageable amount of work, anxiety, and expense, even supposing they had the facilities, which of course they did not. Or they'd have to wrench the pups away from their mother (equally cruel and unnatural as well as a bad example for a child) and worry about finding a decent home for each of them besides. No, no, it could be any pup she chose as long as it was male.

The seven mongrel puppies from which she was permitted to choose one were to her untutored eyes and arms indistinguishable as to sex unless she deliberately looked. So she was perfectly happy to restrict her choice to the four males, though she did feel sorry for the females who, it seemed, were condemned to suffer a cruel and unnatural life or else bring on like Eve more trouble than they were worth—particularly since cuddling them in the hollow between her neck and shoulder felt quite as wonderful as cuddling the males. But such, she accepted, was family life.

She chose neither the runt she was temperamentally drawn to but upon whom her father frowned, nor the jumper of the litter over whom her mother voiced certain reasonable reservations, but instead picked from the two remaining males the long-eared, thoughtful-eyed charmer who endeared himself to her by stepping across three of his siblings as though they were stepping stones in order to reach her eager fingers wiggling in the corner of the box and investigate them with his adorable wet nose. Curiosity: the quality her parents most admired in Lucky herself. He sniffed and then licked her fingers in a sensual gesture she took for friendship, and although she continued to examine all the pups for a considerable time, picking them up and cuddling them individually, deliberating at length before rendering her final decision, she knew very early the one she would take home. It pained her to reject the others, particularly the runt and a certain female who tickled her neck lovingly when she held her up and was pure when she peeked underneath. But by eight Lucky had already learned through experience that one could not have everything one wanted, that every choice entailed the rejection of its alternatives, and that if she didn't hurry up and announce her selection, much as she enjoyed playing with all the puppies, she'd provoke her father's pique and lose the opportunity to decide herself.

She named the dog Skippy because of the funny way he bounced when he walked. An unimaginative name perhaps, but direct (a quality she instinctively valued) and to her inexperienced mind which did not know that the dog would stop bouncing once it got a few months older, appropriate. Her parents thought she might have selected a name with more flair, but naturally they said nothing.

3

The day of Lucky's brightening (her word, for no one ever taught her another) seemed like an ordinary late-summer Saturday. Unsuspectingly, she was just finishing a treasured bath, where she had spent a long time sending the water back and forth between the sides of the tub to simulate ocean waves. She was studying the movement of the water, its turbulence, its cresting at the edges and doubling back, trying to imagine how the process could possibly illuminate, as her father declared, the mysteries of the ocean's waves and tides; and afterward when her brain had grown weary of encompassing the continental coasts, which she had never seen, the earth and the moon, she filled her washcloth with puffs of air which she could pop out in little explosions into the water sending big bubbles rippling through the bath like porpoises.

Up through the open bathroom window drifted the familiar sounds of her father setting up the barbecue in the backyard and her mother bringing out the fixings on a tray. Next door Bertie Jones was still mowing the lawn while from the Jones's screened-in porch the ballgame droned on. Summer days; dog days.

Lucky climbed reluctantly from the tub, now cold, and examined herself in the mirror. Whistle gap between her front teeth, a splash of freckles, short protruding ears, alert: Lucky herself. If she had known what delights awaited her in the next room, she would not have lingered to peel a strip of burnt skin from her shoulder or scratch open a mosquito bite. But she was a nervous child who had never, from the day she learned to drop things over the edge of her high chair for her mother to retrieve, been able to let well enough alone. Three full minutes elapsed before she finally wrapped herself in a towel and padded into her bedroom where Skip, banished from the backyard during dinner preparations, awaited her with wagging tail.

"Skippy Dip!" she cried, dropping to her knees and throwing her arms around him. She hugged his neck and he licked her face in a display of mutual affection.

She tossed her towel at the door, sat down on the maple vanity bench, made a moue at her freckle face in the mirror, and in a most characteristic pursuit, lifted her left foot to the bench to examine an interesting blister on her big toe, soaked clean and plump in her long bath.

Suddenly Skip's wet little nose, as curious as on the day they had met, delved between her legs with several exploratory sniffs.

"Skip!" Lucky giggled in mock dismay, "Get out of there," pushing his nose aside and quickly lowering her foot, for she did know a little. Skip retreated playfully but only until Lucky returned (inevitably) to the blister. For like any pup who has not yet completed his training, he could hardly anticipate every consequence or generalize from a single instance. You know how a dog longs to sniff at things. When Lucky's knee popped up again, exposing that interesting smell, Skip's nose returned as though invited.

Suddenly Lucky felt a new, intriguing sensation. *"What's this?"*

She had once, several years earlier, felt another strange sensation in the groin, one that had been anything but pleasant. She and Judy

Jones, the girl next door, had been playing mother and baby in a game of House. As Lucky lay on the floor of that very room having her "diaper" changed by a maternal Judy, the missing detail to lend a desired extra touch of verisimilitude to the game struck Lucky. "Baby powder!" she cried. "Sprinkle on some baby powder!"

"Baby powder?" blinked Judy.

"Get the tooth powder from the bathroom shelf. The Dr. Lyons."

In the first contact with Skip's wet nose, Lucky remembered her words as if they still hung in the room. She didn't stop to remember the intervening events: how Judy obediently went to the bathroom but couldn't find the Dr. Lyons; how after finally finding it she could barely manage to get the tin open. Lucky's memory flashed ahead to the horrible instant when the astringent powder fell through the air from a great (but not sufficiently great) height onto the delicate tissue of her inner labia and stung her piercingly, provoking a scream that brought her poor mother running anxiously from a distant room.

But the sensation produced by her pal Skippy was in every respect different. It was cool not hot; insinuating not shocking; cozy, provocative, delicious. It drew her open and out, not closed in retreat. No scream ensued; only the arresting thought, *What's this?* Like the dawning of a new idea or the grip of that engaging question, What makes it tick? If she had had the movable ears of her friend's species, they would have perked right up. *What's this?* The fascination of beginnings, the joy of the new. Something more intriguing than a blister.

She touched Skip's familiar silky head tentatively, but this time did not quite push it away. And he, enjoying the newness too (he was hardly more than a pup), sniffed and then, bless him, sniffed again. And following the natural progression for a normally intelligent dog whose interest has been engaged—as natural and logical as the human investigator's progress from observed phenomenon to initial hypothesis to empirical test—the doggie's pink tongue followed his nose's probe with a quizzical exploratory lick.

4

What would her poor parents have thought if they had peeked in? They would have known better than to see or speak evil, for clearly these two young creatures, these trusting pups (of approximately the same ages when you adjust for species), were happy innocents. They would probably have blamed themselves for having insisted on a male pup. They might even have taken the poor animal to the gas chambers of the ASPCA and themselves to some wildly expensive expert who would only confuse and torment them with impossibly equivocal advice until they made some terrible compromise. At the very least, there would have been furious efforts at distraction and that night much wringing of hands.

Fortunately our Adam and Eve remain alone to pursue their pragmatic investigations. The whole world is before them.

5

The charcoal is now ready to take on the weenies. Mrs. Larrabee kisses her husband affectionately on the neck as she crosses the yard toward the house. She opens the screen door, leans inside, and yells up the stairs, "Dinner."

"Just a minute," says Lucky, squeezing her eyes closed. One more stroke of that inquisitive tongue—only one more!—and Lucky too will possess as her own one of nature's most treasured recipes.

Waves and oceans, suns and moons, barbecues, bubbles, blisters, tongues and tides—what a rich banquet awaits the uncorrupted.

Notes on Contributors

Jessica Benjamin has written numerous articles on feminism, psychoanalysis, and social theory. Originally a sociologist, she has also done postdoctoral research on the mother-infant relationship and trained as a psychoanalytic psychotherapist. She practices psychotherapy in New York City and is at work on a book on erotic domination.

Jayne Cortez is the recipient of a National Endowment for the Arts Fellowship, a Creative Artists Service Program Grant (CAPS), and an American Book Award. Her poetry has been published in many journals, magazines, and anthologies, including *New Black Voices*, *Black Sister*, *Mundus Artium*, and *Présence Africaine*. She is the author of five books of poetry, and has made three recordings. Her latest book is *Firespitter*, and her record *There It Is* was released in 1982.

John D'Emilio is the author of *Sexual Politics, Sexual Communities: The Making of a Homosexual Minority in the United States, 1940–1970*. His writing on sexual history and politics has appeared in the *Body Politic*, *Socialist Review*, *Gay Community News*, and *Christopher Street*. He teaches history at the University of Carolina at Greensboro.

Alice Echols is a doctoral candidate in history at the University of Michigan, where she supports herself by teaching in the women's studies program and by djing in clubs. She has been active in the lesbian-feminist community since 1973.

Deirdre English is the executive editor of *Mother Jones* and co-author, with Barbara Ehrenreich, of *For Her Own Good: 150 Years of the Experts' Advice to Women*. She has written articles on a wide range of subjects and co-directed two award-winning antiwar films, *D.C. III* (1971) and *The Year of the Tiger* (1974).

Barbara Epstein teaches U.S. history at the University of California at Santa Cruz and is the author of *The Politics of Domesticity: Women, Evangelism, and Temperance in Nineteenth-Century America* (1981).

Felicita Garcia has worked with VISTA, Charas, and Advocates for Children. She is currently attending the College of Staten Island, and hopes to become a social worker.

Myra Goldberg, who has been a draft counselor and an English teacher, writes and lives in New York City and Berkeley, California. Her stories have appeared in *Transatlantic Review, Feminist Studies, Ploughshares, New England Review,* and other places. "Issues and Answers" is part of a collection of stories entitled *Goosedown*.

Atina Grossmann, a long-time activist in the reproductive rights movement, wrote a dissertation on population policy and sexual politics in Weimar Germany for Rutgers University. She is an assistant professor of history at Mount Holyoke College, and the co-editor of a forthcoming collection on women in Weimar and Nazi Germany to be published by Monthly Review Press as part of the New Feminist Library.

Jacquelyn Dowd Hall teaches history at the University of North Carolina at Chapel Hill and is the author of *Revolt Against Chivalry: Jessie Daniel Ames and the Women's Campaign Against Lynching,* which won the Frances B. Simkins Award of the Southern Historical Association and the Lillian Smith Award. She is director of the Southern Oral History Program and is now working on a book about industrial workers in the South.

Nancy Harrison was born in Biloxi, Mississippi, spent the greater part of her childhood in El Paso, Texas, and lives at present in Austin, Texas, where she has just completed her dissertation on Jean Rhys. "Movie" is part of a novel in progress. Other pieces have appeared in *Sinister Wisdom* and *Feminary*. Her essay, "Women's Voices," is a section of the chapter, "Contemporary Rhetoric," in *The Present State of Scholarship in Historical and Contemporary Rhetoric*.

Amber Hollibaugh is a freelance writer now living in New York and is associate editor of *Socialist Review*. She was co-founder of the San Francisco Lesbian and Gay History Project and a northern California organizer for the campaign against the Briggs initiative, which would have barred homosexuals and their supporters from advocating or engaging in public or private homosexual activity or activism.

E. Ann Kaplan is an associate professor in film and English at Rutgers University. She has written extensively about women in journals such as *Jump Cut, Wide Angle, Quarterly Review of Film Studies, Millenium Film Journal,* and published an anthology, *Women in Film Noir*. She is the author of *Fritz Lang: A Guide to References and Resources* and *Women and Film: Both Sides of the Camera*. She has also edited an anthology of essays on television.

Irena Klepfisz is the author of two books of poetry, *periods of stress* and *Keeper of Accounts*. Her poetry, fiction, and essays have appeared in numerous feminist and lesbian/feminist journals and anthologies, and her writings on anti-Semitism and Jewish identity were recently included in *Nice Jewish Girls: A Lesbian Anthology*. She is a member of *Di Vilde Chayes*, a Jewish lesbian/feminist collective.

Cherríe Moraga is a chicana poet and activist. Her publications include *This Bridge Called My Back: Writings by Radical Women of Color, Cuentos: Stories by Latinas*, and *Loving in the War Years: Lo Que Nunca Pasó Por Sus Labios*. She is a founding member of Kitchen Table: Women of Color Press, New York City.

Joan Nestle is co-founder of the Lesbian Herstory Archives and a teacher in the SEEK Program at Queens College, CUNY. She has been active in her community for over twenty years.

Sharon Olds's first book of poems, *Satan Says*, received the San Francisco Poetry Center Award for 1981. She was a Guggenheim Fellow in 1981–82 and an NEA grant recipient for 1982–83.

Barbara Omolade, writer and historian, teaches adult working students in college. For nearly twenty years she has participated in the Civil Rights movement and other political struggles concerned with liberation and freedom. She is the mother of three school-age children.

Kathy Peiss recently completed her dissertation on gender relations between American working-class women and men in the years 1880 to 1920. She currently teaches in the American Studies Department at the University of Maryland Baltimore County, where she has developed a women's studies minor.

Rayna Rapp is an editor of *Feminist Studies* and is active in the reproductive rights movement. She is a member of the Anthropology Department at the New School for Social Research and the editor of *Toward an Anthropology of Women*.

Adrienne Rich has been publishing poetry, nonfiction, and essays for over thirty years. Her most recent book of prose is *On Lies, Secrets, and Silence;* her tenth and latest book of poems is *A Wild Patience Has Taken Me This Far*. She is a lesbian and a feminist and has been co-editor, with Michelle Cliff, of the lesbian/feminist journal SINISTER WISDOM.

Carole Rosenthal's work has appeared in a wide variety of magazines and anthologies, including *Transatlantic Review, Viva, Mother Jones, Ellery Queen's Magazine*, and *13th Moon*, in scholarly publications, in *Love Stories by New Women, Masterpieces of Mystery*, and more. These days she is working on a novel.

Ellen Ross teaches history and women's studies at Ramapo College, where she is coordinator of women's studies. She is working on a book,

"In Time of Trouble": Motherhood and Survival in Working-Class London, 1870–1918.

As an essayist and novelist, Alix Kates Shulman has written extensively on sexual themes. Her novels include *Memoirs of an Ex-Prom Queen*, *Burning Questions*, and *On the Stroll*. She has taught fiction writing at the New School for Social Research, Yale, and New York University, and has been an active feminist since 1967.

Rennie Simson is professor of English at the State University of New York Morrisville and also teaches in the Afro-American Studies Department, Syracuse University. Her articles have appeared in numerous publications, including the *Review of Afro-American Issues and Culture*, *Obsidian*, and *Educational Dimensions*. She has been the recipient of a National Endowment for the Humanities Grant and an American Philosophical Society Grant and is an associate editor of the *Review of Afro-American Issues and Culture*.

Ann Barr Snitow teaches English and women's studies at Rutgers University. A founding member of New York Radical Feminists in 1970, she was a regular reviewer on WBAI-FM radio in New York for many years. Her articles and reviews have appeared in *Aphra*, *Signs*, *Feminist Studies*, *Radical History Review*, *Socialist Review*, and *The Nation*, and she is presently at work on a study of sex, love, and romance in recent novels by American women.

Christine Stansell, an activist in the women's movement since 1970, teaches American history at Princeton University. Her writing on women has appeared in *Ms.*, *Monthly Review*, and *Feminist Studies*. Her book, *City of Women: The Female Laboring Poor in New York, 1784–1860*, will appear soon.

Sharon Thompson has been an activist in the reproductive rights movement. Her stories and articles have appeared in a number of feminist and women's publications, including *Feminist Studies* and *Heresies*, and she is currently gathering life histories about teenage sexuality and romance.

Ellen Kay Trimberger is the coordinator of women's studies at Sonoma State University in California. Her articles include "Women in the Old and New Left: The Evolution of a Politics of Personal Life," in *Feminist Studies*, "E. P. Thompson: Understanding the Process of History," in *Visions and Method in Historical Sociology*, and she is the author of *Revolution from Above: Military Bureaucrats and Development*.

Carole S. Vance is an anthropologist at Columbia University and a director of the Institute for the Study of Sex and History in New York

City. Her recent work concerns female genital operations in the Middle East and Africa. She was the Academic Coordinator of the Scholar and the Feminist IX Conference, "Towards a Politics of Sexuality," held at Barnard College on April 24, 1982. She is currently editing the conference proceedings. While young and naive, she was a founding member of the Committee on the Status of Women in Anthropology, American Anthropological Association.

Judith Walkowitz teaches history at Rutgers University and is an editor of *Feminist Studies*. She is the author of *Prostitution and Victorian Society: Women, Class and the State* and is working on a new book on the social and cultural responses to the Jack the Ripper murders.

Ellen Willis is a staff writer at the *Village Voice* and the author of *Beginning to See the Light*, a collection of essays on culture and politics. She has been a feminist activist since 1968 and was a co-founder of the original Redstockings.